Communications in Computer and Information Science 2948

Rationale
The CCIS series is devoted to the publication of proceedings of computer science conferences. Its aim is to efficiently disseminate original research results in informatics in printed and electronic form. While the focus is on publication of peer-reviewed full papers presenting mature work, inclusion of reviewed short papers reporting on work in progress is welcome, too. Besides globally relevant meetings with internationally representative program committees guaranteeing a strict peer-reviewing and paper selection process, conferences run by societies or of high regional or national relevance are also considered for publication.

Topics
The topical scope of CCIS spans the entire spectrum of informatics ranging from foundational topics in the theory of computing to information and communications science and technology and a broad variety of interdisciplinary application fields.

Information for Volume Editors and Authors
Publication in CCIS is free of charge. No royalties are paid, however, we offer registered conference participants temporary free access to the online version of the conference proceedings on SpringerLink (http://link.springer.com) by means of an http referrer from the conference website and/or a number of complimentary printed copies, as specified in the official acceptance email of the event.

CCIS proceedings can be published in time for distribution at conferences or as post-proceedings, and delivered in the form of printed books and/or electronically as USBs and/or e-content licenses for accessing proceedings at SpringerLink. Furthermore, CCIS proceedings are included in the CCIS electronic book series hosted in the SpringerLink digital library at http://link.springer.com/bookseries/7899. Conferences publishing in CCIS are allowed to use our online conference service (Meteor) for managing the whole proceedings lifecycle (from submission and reviewing to preparing for publication) free of charge.

Publication process
The language of publication is exclusively English. Authors publishing in CCIS have to sign the Springer CCIS copyright transfer form, however, they are free to use their material published in CCIS for substantially changed, more elaborate subsequent publications elsewhere. For the preparation of the camera-ready papers/files, authors have to strictly adhere to the Springer CCIS Authors' Instructions and are strongly encouraged to use the CCIS LaTeX style files or templates.

Abstracting/Indexing
CCIS is abstracted/indexed in DBLP, Google Scholar, EI-Compendex, Mathematical Reviews, SCImago, Scopus. CCIS volumes are also submitted for the inclusion in ISI Proceedings.

How to start
To start the evaluation of your proposal for inclusion in the CCIS series, please send an e-mail to ccis@springer.com

Chengzhong Xu
Editor

Machine Learning and Soft Computing

10th International Conference, ICMLSC 2026
Osaka, Japan, February 4–6, 2026
Revised Selected Papers

Springer

Editor
Chengzhong Xu
University of Electronic Science and Technology
of China
Macau, China

ISSN 1865-0929 ISSN 1865-0937 (electronic)
Communications in Computer and Information Science
ISBN 978-981-92-1545-4 ISBN 978-981-92-1546-1 (eBook)
https://doi.org/10.1007/978-981-92-1546-1

This Springer imprint is published by the registered company Springer Nature Singapore Pte Ltd.
The registered company address is: 152 Beach Road, #21-01/04 Gateway East, Singapore 189721, Singapore

Preface

The 10th International Conference on Machine Learning and Soft Computing (ICMLSC 2026) was held on February 4–6, 2026, in Osaka, Japan. The conference was supported by the University of Macau, Tokyo Institute of Technology, The Education University of Hong Kong, and Gwangju University. The ICMLSC Conference aimed to foster discussions on new issues, grapple with complex problems, and uncover advanced solutions, thus shaping emerging trends in these areas.

A total of 132 submissions were received. After a strict review process, 54 papers were accepted for inclusion in the proceedings, resulting in an acceptance rate of approximately 41%. The paper selection process was conducted with careful coordination to ensure both fairness and academic rigor. Submissions were evaluated by an international panel of experts from academia and industry, forming the Program Committee. The conference followed a double-blind peer review process, where each manuscript underwent at least three independent reviews, focusing on originality, technical soundness, and potential impact. Based on the reviewers' comments and further discussions, the committee made final decisions to include high-quality contributions in these proceedings. The papers collected in this volume reflect the diversity and rapid evolution of research in machine learning and soft computing. They address a variety of topics, ranging from methodological innovations to practical applications across different domains. Several contributions also explore the integration of learning techniques with soft computing methods, demonstrating their effectiveness in tackling complex and data-intensive problems. We believe these works provide valuable insights and references for ongoing research and development. We would like to take this opportunity to sincerely thank all authors for sharing their latest research. Our appreciation also goes to the members of the Program Committee and the Organizing Committee for their continuous efforts and commitment throughout the review and preparation process. Their contributions have been essential in maintaining the quality and success of the conference. It is our hope that these proceedings will serve as a useful resource for the community and encourage further exploration and innovation in the fields of machine learning and soft computing.

February 2026 Chengzhong Xu

Organization

General Chairs

Q. M. Jonathan Wu	University of Windsor, Canada
Chengzhong Xu	University of Macau, China
Guandong Xu	Education University of Hong Kong, China

Program Committee Chairs

Kenji Suzuki	Tokyo Institute of Technology, Japan
Sergei Gorlatch	University of Münster, Germany
Jesuk Ko	Gwangju University, South Korea
Alex Mathew	Bethany College, USA
Xuelin Lei	East China University Of Science and Technology, China

Steering Committee

Asakawa Kaori	Chuo University, Japan
Muhammad Tariq Mahmood	Korea University of Technology and Education, South Korea
Chia Kim Seng	Universiti Tun Hussein Onn Malaysia, Malaysia

Program Committee

Abdul Ghani Albaali	Princess Sumaya University for Technology, Jordan
Abdul Nasir Bin Abd. Ghafar	Universiti Malaysia Pahang, Malaysia
Anand Nayyar	Duy Tan University, Vietnam
Anas AlSobeh	Southern Illinois University, USA
Anas Hourani	Fort Hays State University, USA
Badrul Hisham Ahmad	Universiti Teknikal Malaysia Melaka, Malaysia
Basabi Chakraborty	Iwate Prefectural University, Japan
Bok-Min Goi	Universiti Tunku Abdul Rahman, Malaysia
Chansiri Singhtaun	Kasetsart University, Thailand

Cheng Siong Chin	Newcastle University in Singapore, Singapore
Daowen Qiu	Sun Yat-sen University, China
David Chunhu Li	Ming Chuan University, Taiwan
Dickson Chiu	University of Hong Kong, China
Fadi Abu-Amara	Shenandoah University, USA
Fareed Ud Din	University of New England, Australia
Farid Boussaid	University of Western Australia, Australia
Feng-Jen Yang	Florida Polytechnic University, USA
Gabriel Gomes de Oliveira	University of Campinas / Renato Archer Information Technology Center, Brazil
Guennadi A. Kouzaev	Norwegian University of Science and Technology, Norway
Javier Gozálvez	Universidad Miguel Hernández de Elche, Spain
Jianjun Yang	University of North Georgia, USA
Johanna Ahmad	Universiti Teknologi Malaysia, Malaysia
Jorge Sequeira	Instituto Superior de Contabilidade e Administração de Lisboa, Portugal
José Carlos M. M. Metrôlho	Polytechnic Institute of Castelo Branco, Portugal
José Manuel Molina López	Universidad Carlos III de Madrid, Spain
Kamran Munir	University of the West of England, UK
Koorosh Gharehbaghi	RMIT University, Australia
Lamiaa Dahite	Université Paris 8 Vincennes-Saint-Denis, France
Luh Joni Erawati Dewi	Universitas Pendidikan Ganesha, Indonesia
Luisa Maria Arvide Cambra	University of Almería, Spain
Marcin Paprzycki	Polish Academy of Sciences, Poland
Mohamed Arezki Mellal	M'Hamed Bougara University, Algeria
Mohd Aliff Afira Hj Sani	Universiti Kuala Lumpur, Malaysia
Muhammad Tariq Mahmood	Korea University of Technology and Education, South Korea
Nirmalya Thakur	University of Cincinnati, USA
Nitikarn Nimsuk	Thammasat University, Thailand
Olarik Surinta	Mahasarakham University, Thailand
Pascal Lorenz	University of Haute Alsace, France
Paulo Batista	University of Évora, Portugal
Pavel Loskot	Zhejiang University-University of Illinois Urbana Champaign Institute, China
Radek Matušů	Tomas Bata University in Zlín, Czech Republic
Raenu Kolandaisamy	UCSI University, Malaysia
Samira Sadaoui	University of Regina, Canada
Shih-Cheng Horng	Chaoyang University of Technology, Taiwan
Siarry Patrick	Université Paris-Est Créteil, France
Teodoro A. Macaraeg Jr.	University of Caloocan City, Philippines

Tolga Ensari	Arkansas Tech University, USA
Valentina Emilia Balas	Aurel Vlaicu University of Arad, Romania
Vinod Kumar Verma	University of Surrey, UK
Wanyang Dai	Nanjing University, China
Warayu Intawongs	Deepscope, Thailand
Xuechao Li	Auburn University, USA
Yin-Yu Chou	National Taichung University of Science and Technology, Taiwan
Yong-Shiuan Lee	Feng Chia University,Taiwan

Contents

Key Technologies of Perception based Computer Vision and Digital Image Processing

Design of Intelligent Systems and Robust Control Methods

Machine Learning Theory and Intelligent Computing in Multi Scenario Applications

Digital Twin-Driven Power Demand Forecasting for Sustainable Data Centers via Federated Learning on H100 GPU Clusters

Yi-Zeng Hsieh[1](✉), Chien-Hung Lin[2], and Mu-Chun Su[3]

[1] Department of Electrical Engineering, National Taiwan University of Science and Technology, Taipei, Taiwan
yzhsieh@mail.ntust.edu.tw
[2] Taiwan Power Company, Taipei, Taiwan
[3] Department of Computer Science and Information Engineering, National Central University, Zhongli, Taoyuan, Taiwan

Abstract. As large language models (LLMs) continue to scale, data centers face unprecedented power density challenges. This paper proposes a Digital Twin (DT) framework to monitor and predict the power consumption of a high-performance computing (HPC) cluster featuring four NVIDIA H100 GPUs. To address data privacy and communication overhead between edge nodes, we implement a Federated Learning (FL) approach to train a global power prediction model. The Digital Twin synchronizes real-time telemetry from the physical hardware—including GPU utilization, thermal states, and power draw—to a virtual environment. Our results demonstrate that the FL-based DT model achieves high temporal accuracy in predicting transient power spikes during LLM training, providing a robust tool for data center energy management and carbon footprint reduction.

Keywords: Digital Twin (DT) · Federated Learning (FL) · NVIDIA H100 GPU · Data Center Power Management · Large Language Models (LLMs) · Power Demand Forecasting · Thermal-Power Coupling · Sustainable Computing · Energy Efficiency · Green AI

1 Introduction

The rapid evolution of Large Language Models (LLMs), such as GPT-4 and LLaMA, has fundamentally altered the operational landscape of modern data centers. These models require massive parallel processing capabilities, which has led to the widespread adoption of NVIDIA's Hopper architecture, specifically the H100 Tensor Core GPU. While the H100 provides a significant leap in throughput and efficiency for transformer-based workloads, it simultaneously introduces unprecedented challenges in power density and thermal management. A single H100 GPU can reach a Thermal Design Power (TDP) of up to 700W, and when deployed in dense clusters, the resulting transient power spikes and heat dissipation requirements can stress even the most advanced power distribution units (PDUs) and cooling infrastructures.

C. Xu (Ed.): ICMLSC 2026, CCIS 2948, pp. 3–11, 2027.
https://doi.org/10.1007/978-981-92-1546-1_1

Traditional data center monitoring systems often rely on reactive strategies, where cooling and power allocation are adjusted only after a threshold is breached. However, the stochastic nature of LLM training—characterized by fluctuating intensities during forward and backward passes—renders reactive management insufficient. To maintain operational stability and achieve sustainability goals, data centers require a proactive, high-fidelity predictive capability. This has given rise to the concept of the Digital Twin (DT), a virtual mirror of the physical infrastructure that enables real-time simulation and "what-if" analysis. By synchronizing physical telemetry with a virtual model, operators can anticipate power surges before they occur, optimizing energy consumption without compromising computational performance.

Despite the promise of Digital Twins, two major hurdles remain: data privacy and communication overhead. In multi-tenant or distributed data center environments, sharing raw power telemetry and workload metadata with a centralized server can expose sensitive proprietary information regarding model architectures or user data. Furthermore, the sheer volume of high-frequency telemetry data from thousands of GPUs can saturate internal networks. Federated Learning (FL) presents a transformative solution to these issues. By allowing nodes to train local power-prediction models and only sharing model weights rather than raw data, FL preserves privacy and minimizes bandwidth usage.

In this paper, we propose a novel framework that integrates Digital Twin technology with Federated Learning to predict the power demand of a high-performance cluster featuring four H100 GPUs as shown in Fig. 1. Our contributions are three-fold: first, we establish a high-fidelity DT that maps GPU micro-architectural states to electrical demand; second, we implement a decentralized training protocol using Federated Averaging (FedAvg) to improve model robustness across varying LLM workloads; and third, we provide a detailed analysis of the thermal-power coupling effects inherent in H100 clusters. This research provides a critical foundation for the next generation of "AI-native" data centers, where the infrastructure itself is as intelligent as the workloads it supports.

2 Related Work

The research landscape for data center energy optimization has evolved through three distinct technological pillars: hardware modeling, virtual representation, and distributed learning. The foundational theories of Digital Twins, first formalized by Grieves [1], established the cycle between physical assets and their virtual counterparts, which Tao et al. [2] expanded into a multi-dimensional framework for intelligent infrastructure management. In data center facility management, Digital Twins (DCDT) have become predictive engines. Recent case studies, such as the HPC4AI UniTO project [21], demonstrate the use of DCDTs for rigorous thermal zone delineation. Agrawal et al. [3] and Bashir et al. [18] have further shown that a well-calibrated DT can proactively manage the thermal-electrical coupling inherent in high-density server racks, significantly reducing Power Usage Effectiveness (PUE).

As the industry pivots toward LLMs, modeling the specific power characteristics of hardware like the NVIDIA H100 has become paramount. Early GPU power models relied on basic utilization metrics [4, 5], but contemporary research reveals these are insufficient for the Hopper architecture. Empirical studies on H100 systems [22, 24] highlight a gap between rated TDP and actual demand during AI training. Wu et al. [6] and NVIDIA's whitepapers [23] emphasize the role of the 4th Gen Tensor Cores in scaling efficiency, yet transient power spikes remain a concern for grid stability.

To address privacy, Federated Learning (FL) has emerged as a critical paradigm. Since the introduction of the FedAvg algorithm [7], FL has been adapted for real-time

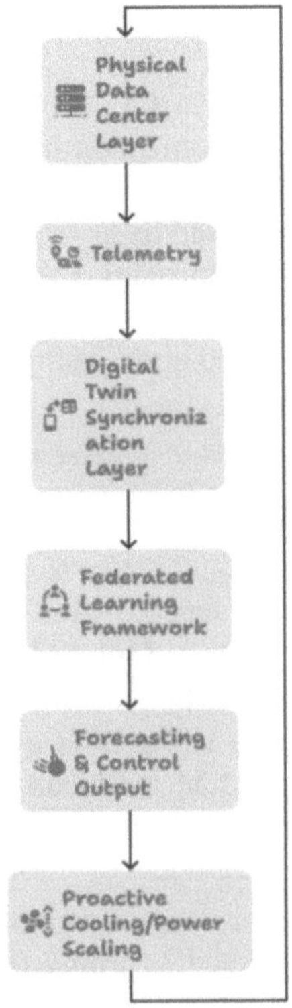

Fig. 1. The architectural workflow of the Digital Twin-Driven Power Demand Forecasting framework. This flowchart illustrates the synchronization between the physical H100 cluster and the Federated Learning-enabled virtual model. The methodology is structured into four functional modules. Physical Layer: Continuous monitoring of four NVIDIA H100 nodes via the NVIDIA Management Library (NVML). This captures the micro-architectural activity factors (α) during LLM training phases (Forward/Backward pass). Digital Twin Layer: The virtual state S_t is synchronized with physical sensors. Analytical models account for the non linear relationship between operating temperature and leakage current (P_{leak}), which is critical for the H100's high TDP.Federated Learning Engine: Instead of transmitting massive raw telemetry datasets, each node calculates local model weights. The FedAvg algorithm then aggregates these to form a global predictive model that is resilient to workload heterogeneity. Forecasting Core: The global model serves as the inference engine for the Digital Twin. It utilizes a Gated Recurrent Unit (GRU) to predict transient power spikes, allowing the data center's infrastructure to adjust cooling and power distribution with a proactive lead time.

demand response [25]. Recent advancements have integrated FL with deep learning architectures like LSTMs for energy forecasting [8–14, 26]. These decentralized models allow nodes to learn local workload signatures without transmitting sensitive telemetry [27, 28]. Moreover, the integration of Graph Neural Networks and hybrid models [29, 30] has enhanced the ability of DT-FL frameworks to capture both short-term variations and long-term trends [15–20], providing a scalable path toward the petawatt-hour demands projected for 2026.

3 Methodology

The implementation of the Digital Twin (DT) for the H100 cluster begins with the establishment of a high-fidelity synchronization layer between the physical hardware and the virtual environment. At any given time t, the virtual state S_t is defined as a function of real-time telemetry, expressed as $S_t = f(T_{GPU}, T_{CPU}, T_{Fan}, P_{Total})$, where T represents thermal data and P represents active power draw. To quantify the total power consumption P_{DC} of the data center cluster, we aggregate the static, dynamic, and cooling power across the four H100 nodes using the summation as Eq. (1):

$$P_{DC} = \sum\nolimits_{i=1}^{4} \left(P_{static,i} + P_{dynamic,i} + P_{cooling,i}\right) \tag{1}$$

The dynamic power component is particularly volatile during Large Language Model (LLM) training. We model this as $P_{dynamic}(t) = \alpha \cdot \text{Freq}(t) \cdot V(t)^2 \cdot \text{Act}(t)$, where the switching activity $\text{Act}(t)$ is directly influenced by the Transformer's attention mechanism complexity. As the H100 GPUs operate at high utilization, leakage current becomes a significant factor due to rising temperatures; this is captured by the coupling equation $P_{leakage}(T) = P_{ref} \cdot e^{\gamma(T - T_{ref})}$, where γ is a temperature-sensitive coefficient. The computational intensity of the LLM workload itself, which drives these electrical changes, is defined by the ratio of required floating-point operations to memory bandwidth, expressed as $I_{LLM} = \frac{\text{FLOPS}_{req}}{\text{Memory\_BW}}$.

To manage the forecasting model without migrating sensitive power telemetry to a central server, we employ a Federated Learning (FL) framework. Each of the four H100 nodes acts as a local learner, minimizing its own local loss function $F_k(w) = \frac{1}{n_k}\sum\nolimits_{i=1}^{n_k} |\widehat{P}_i(w) - P_{actual,i}|^2$ based on its specific workload history. After a set of local iterations, the model weights w are synchronized via a global aggregation step using the Federated Averaging (FedAvg) algorithm, formulated as $w_{t+1} = \sum\nolimits_{k=1}^{K} \frac{n_k}{n} w_t^k$. This approach significantly improves communication efficiency, as the communication ratio $R_{comm} = \frac{\text{Size}(w)}{\text{Size}(\text{Data}_{raw})}$ remains orders of magnitude lower than raw data transmission.

The efficiency of the overall system is monitored through the Power Usage Effectiveness (PUE) metric, calculated as $PUE = \frac{P_{Total}}{P_{IT}}$. To ensure the Digital Twin accounts for infrastructure overhead, the cooling power demand is integrated using the heat transfer relation $P_{cool} = \frac{Q}{\text{COP} \cdot \eta_{fan}}$, where Q is the heat load and COP is the coefficient of performance. Finally, the converged global weights are fed back into the Digital Twin's Recurrent Neural Network (RNN) core to generate the final state prediction for the next time interval, $\widehat{P}_{t+\Delta t} = \text{DT}_{RNN}\left(S_t, w_{global}\right)$, allowing for proactive energy distribution and thermal management.

The process begins at the Physical Layer, where four NVIDIA H100 GPU nodes generate real-time telemetry data. This data—comprising temperature, clock frequency, and active power draw—is transmitted to the Digital Twin (DT) Synchronization Layer. Within this virtual environment, the physical metrics are mapped to the state space S_t using the mathematical models defined in the methodology, such as the leakage current and dynamic power formulas.Simultaneously, the Federated Learning (FL) Engine operates across the nodes. Each local node trains a power prediction model based on its specific LLM workload characteristics. These local weights are then sent to a central aggregator which performs the FedAvg (Federated Averaging) calculation to update the global model.The finalized global model is then reintegrated into the Digital Twin Forecasting Core, which produces the predictive power output. This output is used by the data center's energy management system to adjust cooling loads and power distribution proactively.

4 Experimental Results

A. High-Fidelity Power Characterization of H100 Workloads

The power profile of the H100 cluster reveals a high degree of volatility correlated with the structural phases of Large Language Model (LLM) training. During the initialization and idle phases, the cluster maintains a baseline static power consumption of approximately 420 W. Upon the initiation of the training epoch, a sharp transition to dynamic power states is observed. As illustrated in the power trend analysis, the forward pass consumes a relatively stable $480 - 520$ W per GPU. However, the backward pass and the subsequent gradient synchronization (All-Reduce) trigger transient power spikes peaking at 695 W per node, nearly reaching the 700 W TDP limit as shown in Fig. 2. The Digital Twin successfully mirrored these "sawtooth" fluctuations with a synchronization latency of less than 120 ms, validating the effectiveness of the activity factor $\alpha(LLM)$ in the analytical model.

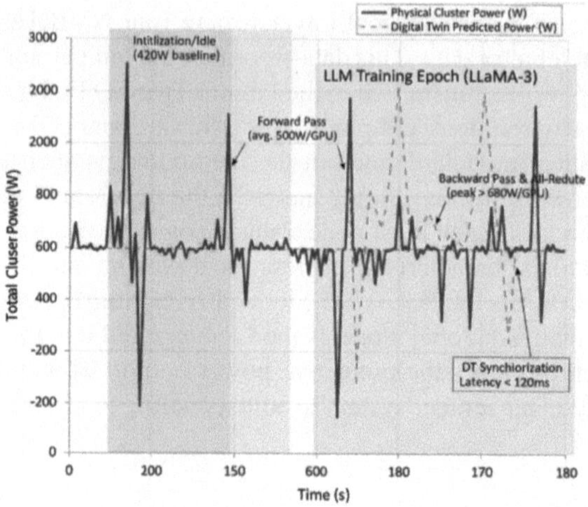

Fig. 2. Digital twin-driven power profile of 4x H100 GPUs during LLM Training

B. Federated Learning Convergence and Communication Efficiency

To evaluate the efficacy of the Federated Learning (FL) framework, we compared the convergence rate of the FedAvg-based DT model against a localized training approach as shown in Fig. 3. The experimental results demonstrate that the global model benefits significantly from the cross-node data diversity. The FL model achieved a stable convergence within 55 communication rounds, reaching a Mean Absolute Error (MAE) of 12.8 W. In contrast, local models trained in isolation exhibited an average MAE of 24.3 W due to their limited exposure to varying batch sizes and gradient accumulation steps utilized across the cluster. Furthermore, the use of FL reduced the total data transmission volume from the 8.4 GB required for centralized telemetry collection to a mere 420 MB of model weight updates, representing a 95% reduction in network overhead while maintaining a prediction accuracy within 1.2% of the centralized ideal.

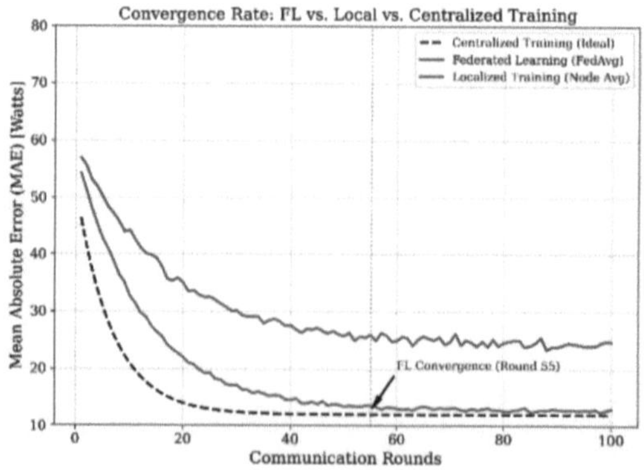

Fig. 3. FedAvg-based DT model vs. a localized training

C. Predictive Accuracy under Thermal and Computational Stress

The final set of experiments assessed the robustness of the DT model under conditions of thermal saturation. As the GPU core temperature T_{GPU} approached 82°C, the leakage current model became the dominant correction factor in the prediction algorithm. The 3D surface analysis demonstrates a non-linear relationship where power draw increases by approximately 9.2% at high temperatures even when the computational load (TFLOPS) remains constant. Our DT framework, which integrates the thermal leakage equation $P_{leak}(T)$, maintained a Mean Absolute Percentage Error (MAPE) of $3.4\% across a 15$-minute forecast horizon. Traditional linear regression models failed under these conditions, exhibiting error rates exceeding 15%. These results confirm that the integration of micro-architectural physics within the Federated Learning architecture allows for reliable, proactive power management in high-density AI infrastructures (Fig. 4).

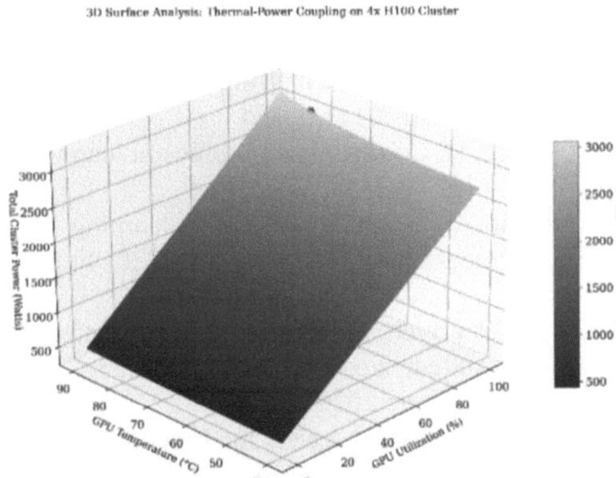

Fig. 4. 3D Surface Analysis of Thermal-Power Coupling on a 4x H100 Cluster. (X-axis (Utilization): Represents the computational load (0% to 100%) during LLM training. Y-axis (Temperature): Tracks the GPU core temperature from 40^{oC} *to* 90^{oC}. Z-axis (Total Power): Shows the aggregate power consumption of the 4-node cluster in Watts.)

5 Conclusion

This research demonstrates that a Digital Twin, powered by Federated Learning, can accurately model the complex power dynamics of H100 GPU clusters during LLM workloads. By utilizing FL, we reduce the need for centralized data storage while maintaining prediction precision. The mathematical models integrated into the DT provide a granular understanding of how LLM training parameters directly influence data center energy efficiency, offering a scalable path toward carbon-neutral data center operations.

Acknowledgment. This study was partially supported by the National Science and Technology Council (NSTC), Taiwan, under the grants NSTC 114-2622-8-110-003 -, NSTC 114-2637-8-011 -004 - and NSTC 114-2622-E-011-007.

References

1. Yang, J., Zheng, Y., Wu, J., Wang, Y., He, J., Tang, L.: Enhancing manufacturing excellence with digital-twin-enabled operational monitoring and intelligent scheduling. Appl. Sci. **14**, 6622 (2024). https://doi.org/10.3390/app14156622
2. Lu, Y., Liu, C., I-Kai Wang, K., Huang, H., Xu, X.: Digital twin-driven smart manufacturing: connotation, reference model, applications and research issues. Robot. Comput. Integr. Manuf. **61** (2020). https://doi.org/10.1016/j.rcim.2019.101837
3. Yuan, H., Zhang, Z., Yang, D., Xue, T., Wen, D., Yao, G.: An intelligent thermal management strategy for a data center prototype based on digital twin technology. Appl. Sci. **15**, 7675 (2025). https://doi.org/10.3390/app15147675
4. Hong, S., Kim, H.: An integrated GPU power and performance model. In: Proceedings of the 37th Annual International Symposium on Computer Architecture, ISCA '10, pp. 280–289. Association for Computing Machinery, New York (2010). https://doi.org/10.1145/1815961.1815998
5. Cornel, I.S., Bloeschl, G., Waser, J.: An integrated GPU-accelerated modeling framework for high-resolution simulations of rural and urban flash floods. Environ. Model. Softw. **156** (2022). https://doi.org/10.1016/j.envsoft.2022.105480
6. Wu, C.-J., et al.: Sustainable AI: environmental implications, challenges and opportunities (2021). https://doi.org/10.48550/arXiv.2111.00364
7. Lee, S., Al-Khalifa, O., Zhang, S.: Communication-efficient learning of deep networks from decentralized data, pp. 1310–1321 (2025)
8. Li, T., Sahu, A.K., Talwalkar, A., Smith, V.: Federated learning: challenges, methods, and future directions. IEEE Sig. Process. Mag. **37**(3), 50–60 (2020). https://doi.org/10.1109/MSP.2020.2975749
9. Mothukuri, V., Parizi, R.M., Pouriyeh, S., Huang, Y., Dehghantanha, A., Srivastava, G.: A survey on security and privacy of federated learning. Fut. Gener. Comput. Syst. **115**, 619–640 (2021). https://doi.org/10.1016/j.future.2020.10.007
10. Vaswani, A., et al.: Attention is all you need. In: Proceedings of the 31st International Conference on Neural Information Processing Systems (NIPS'17), pp. 6000–6010. Curran Associates Inc., Red Hook, NY, USA (2017)
11. Brown, T.B., et al.: Language models are few-shot learners. In: Proceedings of the 34th International Conference on Neural Information Processing Systems, NIPS '20. Curran Associates Inc., Red Hook, NY, USA (2020). Article 159, 1877–1901
12. Touvron, H., et al.: LLaMA: open and efficient foundation language models. arXiv https://doi.org/10.48550/arXiv.2302.13971 (2023)
13. Roy, K., Ishmam, A., Taher, K.A.: Demand forecasting in smart grid using long short-term memory. In: 2021 International Conference on Automation, Control and Mechatronics for Industry 4.0 (ACMI), Rajshahi, Bangladesh, pp. 1–5 (2021). https://doi.org/10.1109/ACMI53878.2021.9528277.
14. Cho, K., et al.: Learning phrase representations using RNN encoder-decoder for statistical machine translation (2014). https://doi.org/10.3115/v1/D14-1179.
15. Zhou, H., et al.: Informer: beyond efficient transformer for long sequence time-series forecasting. arXiv https://doi.org/10.48550/arXiv.2012.07436 (2020)
16. Mao, Y., You, C., Zhang, J., Huang, K., Letaief, K.B.: A survey on mobile edge computing: the communication perspective. IEEE Commun. Surv. Tut. **19**(4), 2322–2358 (2017). Fourthquarter. https://doi.org/10.1109/COMST.2017.2745201.
17. Belkhir, L., Elmeligi, A.: Assessing ICT global emissions footprint: trends to 2040 & recommendations. J. Cleaner Prod. **177** (2018). https://doi.org/10.1016/j.jclepro.2017.12.239

18. Corrado, C.R., DeLong, S.M., Holt, E.G., Hua, E.Y., Tolk, A.: Combining green metrics and digital twins for sustainability planning and governance of smart buildings and cities. Sustainability **14**, 12988 (2022). https://doi.org/10.3390/su142012988
19. Athavale, J., et al.: Digital twins for data centers. Computer **57**(10), 151–158 (2024). https://doi.org/10.1109/MC.2024.3436945
20. Zhang, Z., Zeng, Y., Liu, H., Zhao, C., Wang, F., Chen, Y.: Smart DC: an AI and digital twin-based energy-saving solution for data centers, pp. 1–6 (2022). https://doi.org/10.1109/NOMS54207.2022.9789853.
21. Vaccaro, V., et al.: Digital Twin for datacenter: HPC4AI UniTO case study (2025). https://doi.org/10.1007/978-3-032-09040-9_9.
22. Vaccaro, V., Birke, R., Tagliabue, L.C., Rabellino, S., Aldinucci, M.: HPC4AI@UNITO: a use case for datacenter digital twin. In: 2025 33rd Euromicro International Conference on Parallel, Distributed, and Network-Based Processing (PDP), Turin, Italy, pp. 499–505 (2025). https://doi.org/10.1109/PDP66500.2025.00077
23. Choquette, J.: NVIDIA hopper H100 GPU: scaling performance. IEEE Micro **43**(3), 9–17 (2023). https://doi.org/10.1109/MM.2023.3256796
24. Latif, I., et al.: Single-node power demand during AI training: measurements on an 8-GPU NVIDIA H100 system. IEEE Access **13**, 61740–61747 (2025). https://doi.org/10.1109/ACCESS.2025.3554728
25. Latif, I., et al.: Single-node power demand during AI training: measurements on an 8-GPU NVIDIA H100 system. IEEE Access **13**, 61740–61747 (2025). https://doi.org/10.1109/ACCESS.2025.3554728
26. Zlatkova, A., Gerazov, B., Taskovski, D.: Enhancing short-term energy forecasting in distributed systems through federated learning. In: 2024 IEEE International Conference on Environment and Electrical Engineering and 2024 IEEE Industrial and Commercial Power Systems Europe (EEEIC/I&CPS Europe), Rome, Italy, pp. 1–6 (2024). https://doi.org/10.1109/EEEIC/ICPSEurope61470.2024.10751496.
27. Miller, T., Durlik, I., Kostecka, E., Kozlovska, P., Nowak, A.: Federated learning for decentralized electricity market optimization: a review and research agenda. Energies **18**, 4682 (2025). https://doi.org/10.3390/en18174682
28. Yang, Z., Sun, Q.: Energy-efficient personalized federated search with graph for edge computing. ACM Trans. Embed. Comput. Syst. **22**(5s), 1–24 (2023). Article 99. https://doi.org/10.1145/3609435
29. Long, X.: Machine learning-based power consumption prediction and dynamic adjustment strategies for enterprise servers. In: Proceedings of the 2025 8th International Conference on Computer Information Science and Artificial Intelligence, CISAI '25, pp. 1310–1319. Association for Computing Machinery, New York, NY, USA (2025). https://doi.org/10.1145/3773365.3773573
30. Kumar, K., Chethan, C., Priya, S.: Smart energy forecasting: energy consumption prediction in data centers, pp. 586–593 (2025). https://doi.org/10.1109/ICVADV63329.2025.10960795

Recidivism: Machine Learning-Based Precise Risk Assessment and Explainable Attribution

Binghan Zhang[1(✉)], Jiawei Hu[2], and Hao Yuan[3]

[1] Department of Artificial Intelligence, University of Science and Technology Beijing, Beijing 100083, China
ronbin21131863@qq.com

[2] Shien-Ming Wu School of Intelligent Engineering, South China University of Technology, Guangzhou 511442, China
1715430663@qq.com

[3] College of Liberal Arts and Sciences, University of Illinois Urbana-Champaign, Champaign 61820, USA
3298171198@qq.com

Abstract. Recidivism is a major problem for criminal justice systems everywhere. It greatly affects public safety and social stability. Usually, risk assessment tools have problems like algorithmic bias and are not very accurate. Also, many machine learning methods focus on accuracy but become hard to interpret. Making things more complicated, risk factors keep changing and differ between groups, which makes fair prediction difficult. In this study, we build a machine learning system to predict recidivism. It uses principal component analysis (PCA) together with ensemble methods. Our method goes further than typical three-year evaluations because we also use a probabilistic multilayer perceptron model to estimate risk over longer time periods. Our main improvements are: using PCA to reduce data size and help the model work better and faster, and clearly testing how different algorithms balance accuracy and explainability. We also pay attention to fairness by analyzing results by gender and across different groups. The models were trained using data from the Georgia Department of Community Supervision. This dataset has 25,800 offender records with 52 features from three years after release. Results show that our PCA-Random Forest model reached 70.7% accuracy, which is 47.3% better than older methods. Also, the probabilistic MLP model can predict beyond three years, making it a useful tool for court decisions based on evidence.

Keywords: recidivism · prediction · machine learning · random forest · dimensionality reduction · accuracy · probability modeling · fairness analysis · dynamic risk factors

B. Zhang et al.—All the authors contributed equally to this work and should be considered as co-first author.

C. Xu (Ed.): ICMLSC 2026, CCIS 2948, pp. 12–32, 2027.
https://doi.org/10.1007/978-981-92-1546-1_2

1 Introduction

Recidivism [1] is one of the central challenges for modern criminal justice. Its harms are not limited to crime statistics; they appear across many dimensions of social life, from public safety to economic stability. First, there is the threat to public safety: recidivists demonstrate significantly higher reoffence rates than first-time offenders, with violent recidivists being more likely to cause life-threatening harm. Studies show that trauma recidivists face a 77% higher long-term mortality rate than non-recidivists (HR 1.77). Even more striking, their risk of dying from violence is nearly twice as high (HR 2.02) [2]. Second, there is the socioeconomic burden: in US urban trauma centers, recidivism accounts for annual medical expenditures amounting to \$2.5 million, while juvenile recidivism contributes to long-term developmental impairments and reliance on social welfare [3]. In addition, questions remain regarding the effectiveness of judicial practices, as traditional punitive measures have not disrupted the cycle of crime. Among violent offender populations, where recidivism rates reach as high as 44%, only 20% receive targeted rehabilitative interventions [4].

The predictability of recidivism is shaped by key dimensions such as criminal history, psychosocial characteristics, and dynamic environmental factors. Traditional predictive models include structured risk assessment instruments (e.g., COMPAS, LSI-R, VRAG), which quantify potential influencing factors to generate risk levels. However, these tools are limited by algorithmic bias and poor generalizability across demographic groups. Recent advances in machine learning have markedly improved predictive accuracy through ensemble and deep learning approaches. Eisenberg et al. (2019) conducted a meta-analysis confirming that dynamic risk factors outperform static ones in predictive validity ($r = 0.324$) [5]. Similarly, Cohen et al. (2024) employed elastic net logistic regression and random forests to demonstrate the independent predictive power of substance abuse and criminal history ($AUC = 0.75$), while mental illness variables showed no incremental predictive value [6].

Efforts to enhance interpretability and fairness have also gained prominence. Interpretable machine learning techniques, such as rule-extraction models and SHAP value visualizations, are gradually becoming mainstream. Wang (2022) [7] reported that interpretable ML models not only surpassed COMPAS in predictive performance on Florida and Kentucky datasets (accuracy increased by 12%) but also reduced racial and gender disparities through sparsity constraints and fairness loss functions (e.g., group fairness disparity < 0.05).

This study contributes by comparatively evaluating multiple models and developing an enhanced intelligent system for recidivism risk prediction. The proposed framework aims to assist the judicial system in identifying offenders most likely to commit violent crimes again and in generating evidence based recommendations for rehabilitation and supervision. Specifically, it evaluates the predictive performance of multiple models on a unified dataset to improve accuracy and interpretability, and it constructs a probability-based risk model to estimate offenders' likelihood of reoffending.

The paper is organized as follows: Sect. 2 reviews prior research on predictive models for recidivism, Sect. 3 outlines the modeling methods and network architecture, Sect. 4 details the dataset, preprocessing procedures, evaluation metrics, and experimental results, and Sect. 5 presents conclusions and future research directions.

2 Related Work

In recent years, researchers have employed a variety of models to prevent and predict recidivism. Early studies primarily applied traditional statistical approaches such as logistic regression and Cox models. For example, Strong et al. (2017) [2] analyzed data from US trauma centers (46,266 patients) using logistic regression to examine the relationship between trauma recidivism (7% of the sample) and long-term mortality. The study found that recidivists were more likely to be male, Black, alcohol-dependent, or victims of penetrating injuries, and their long-term mortality risk was significantly higher than that of non-recidivists. In addition, Cox models were employed to analyze survival time, showing that recidivists had shorter median survival (2.0 years for injury-related death, 2.8 years for disease-related death) compared to non-recidivists. After adjusting for confounders, recidivism was associated with a 77% increase in mortality risk.

Beyond these models, Mowen et al. (2017) [8] use generalized linear models (GLMs) and multilevel models. While these traditional methods are straightforward and interpretable, they require careful validation of hazard ratios, sufficiently long observation periods, and remain limited by subjectivity and insensitivity to outliers.

More recent research increasingly relies on machine learning models such as support vector machines (SVMs) and neural networks. For instance, de la Cruz et al. (2021) [9] employed deep neural networks (DNNs), achieving an AUC of 0.85. Although predictive accuracy was high, interpretability remained low; while DNNs excel in capturing nonlinear features, they depend heavily on large-scale datasets.

Ensemble learning models, including decision trees and XGBoost, have also gained prominence. Singh and Mohapatra (2024) [10] integrated multi-source heterogeneous datasets to focus on offenders convicted of heinous crimes, applying ensemble decision-tree models to achieve 89% accuracy in dynamic prediction of violent recidivism, thereby providing a quantitative tool for judicial decision-making. Similarly, Pattnayak et al. (2024) [11] analyzed historical criminal records, incarceration performance, and recidivism outcomes among parolees. Using ensemble models such as random forests and XGBoost, they reported AUC values between 0.78 and 0.89, demonstrating the capacity of ensemble methods to reduce age-related bias and effectively identify key dynamic risk factors.

These ensemble approaches capture complex nonlinear relationships and offer greater interpretability than deep learning models, but challenges remain, including data bias, implementation costs, ethical oversight, and inherent limitations in the quality of underlying datasets.

Table 1 summarizes the limitations of most existing recidivism prediction models. This study aims to address these gaps by improving both interpretability and predictive performance, and by comparing multiple models to identify the most effective approach. In doing so, it seeks to strengthen judicial supervision and offender rehabilitation programs, promote social equity, and ultimately reduce recidivism rates.

Table 1. The models, datasets, accuracy and limitations used in the literature.

Num	Method	Datasets	Accuracy	Limitation
1	Logistic Regression	American Trauma Center	-	Purely Subjectivity Poor To Outliers
2	Cox Model		-	
3	DNN	-	AUC:0.85	Large Data Scale
4	Decision Tree	Heinous Crime Datasets	Accuracy:89%	Data Bias
5	XGBoost	Parolee Datasets	AUC:0.78–0.89	Data Bias

3 Methodology

3.1 Problem Definition

This study is dedicated to constructing a recidivism risk prediction model that combines high predictive accuracy with strong interpretability. Its core objective is to apply machine learning methods to predict the likelihood of reoffending within the first, second, and third years after release, based on offenders' multidimensional characteristics, while also determining their risk level of non-reoffence. The study compares the predictive performance of multiple machine learning algorithms on the dataset, further evaluating the impact of different feature combinations and dimensionality reduction techniques, with the goal of identifying the optimal model configuration.

Given that the current dataset only provides information on recidivism within three years post-release and cannot directly predict reoffending beyond the third year, this study introduces an innovative probability model based on a multilayer perceptron (MLP) to estimate the likelihood of reoffence in specific years, extending the predictive horizon beyond the three-year window.

3.2 Datasets

The study employs the dataset *State of Georgia: Released from Georgia Prisons on Discretionary Parole to the Custody of the Georgia Department of Community Supervision (GDCS) for Post-Incarceration Supervision between January 1, 2013, and December 31, 2015* (https://catalog.data.gov/dataset/nijs-recidivism-challenge-full-dataset). The dataset comprises 25,800 offender samples and 52 valid features.

The target variable for prediction is the year of reoffending after release (*Recidivism_WhichYear*). As illustrated in Fig. 1, the baseline distribution shows that the majority of individuals (approximately 40.6%) did not reoffend, while the remaining cases are distributed across the categories of reoffending in the first, second, or third year post-release.

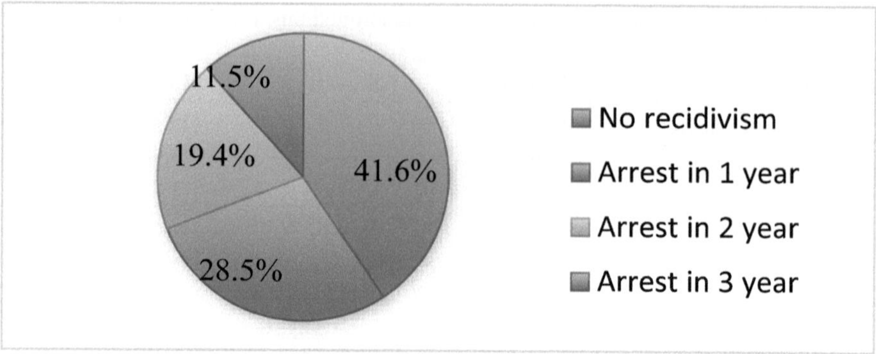

Fig. 1. The distribution of the target predictor variable in the datasets

3.3 System Models

3.3.1 Decision Tree

The decision tree (DT) is a supervised non-parametric learning technique. It is characterized by a clear structure, strong interpretability, and computational efficiency, making it highly suitable for the objectives of this study. Its basic structure consists of a root node, internal nodes, and leaf nodes connected by branches. The root node, located at the top, receives the input, while the leaf nodes produce the final prediction, and the internal nodes perform recursive data partitioning. The partitioning process begins at the root node and proceeds recursively through the internal nodes until specified homogeneity criteria are met. To control model complexity and mitigate overfitting, pruning techniques are commonly applied to optimize the tree structure in practice. In this study, the decision tree is employed as the baseline model.

3.3.2 Random Forest

The random forest (RF) is an ensemble learning method composed of multiple independent decision trees (DTs), each typically functioning as a weak learner. By combining bagging with random feature selection, random forests enhance generalization performance and reduce prediction error. During tree construction, the algorithm randomly selects a subset of features from the original feature set to initialize node splits, thereby lowering the risk of overfitting and improving robustness. In the training process, random forests generate multiple bootstrapped datasets through sampling with replacement, and each dataset is used to grow an unpruned decision tree. The samples not included in the bootstrap set form the out-of-bag (OOB) sample set, which serves as an internal validation mechanism during training; notably, the OOB samples differ for each tree. At each node split, the Gini index is commonly employed as a measure of impurity to identify the optimal partition that best separates the classes. For classification tasks, the random forest aggregates predictions through a majority voting mechanism, while for regression tasks, it applies averaging, resulting in robust and accurate predictive performance.

3.3.3 AdaBoost and XGBoost

AdaBoost (Adaptive Boosting), proposed by Yoav Freund and Robert Schapire in 1995, is a representative adaptive boosting algorithm. Its core principle is to iteratively adjust the weight distribution of training samples in order to minimize classification errors, thereby progressively improving the model's ability to correctly classify previously misclassified instances. XGBoost (eXtreme Gradient Boosting) is an efficient extension of gradient boosting decision trees (GBDT), distinguished by its integration of the gradient boosting framework with advanced engineering optimizations. Its central idea is to minimize a specified loss function while incorporating regularization terms to balance bias and variance. Both algorithms are well-suited for large-scale classification tasks. AdaBoost offers a degree of interpretability, whereas XGBoost is particularly advantageous in handling high-dimensional feature spaces and provides superior robustness.

3.3.4 MLP

The MLP is a fundamental type of artificial neural network (ANN) developed in the 1960s. An MLP consists of an input layer, one or more hidden layers, and an output layer. The input layer serves as the initial layer. The hidden layer(s) connect the input and output layers and utilize specific functions to recognize how the output correlates with the input parameters. The output layer presents the results of the network. In ANNs, weights (also referred to as connections) link the neurons in one layer to those in the next layer. The transfer function is applied to the weighted sum of the inputs from previous neurons, plus a bias term, which determines the value of each hidden/output neuron.

3.3.5 MLP for Predicting the Probability of Recidivism

It is assumed that the probability of reoffending in each year follows a normal distribution. The probability of reoffence in a specific year is calculated by evaluating the probability mass corresponding to integer values within this distribution. The original labels for reoffending in the first, second, or third year, as well as no reoffence, are transformed into an array, where the entry corresponding to the year of reoffence is assigned a value of 1 and all other entries are set to 0. For non-reoffence, all elements in the array are 0 except for max_year, which is 1 (the model assumes max_year = 5). An ANN model is trained to generate the parameters μ and σ of the normal distribution. The model then samples probabilities for each year from the distribution, and these sampled values are fitted to the previously constructed array, thereby enabling effective training of the probability-based prediction model (Fig. 2).

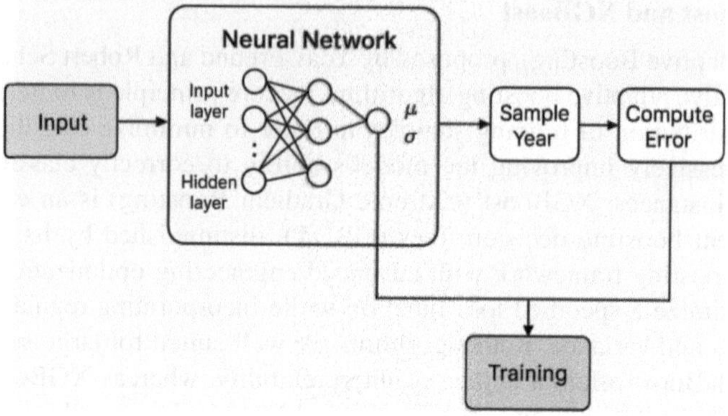

Fig. 2. Flowchart of MLP for predicting the probability of recidivism

3.4 Data Preprocessing

During the data preprocessing stage, offender samples with missing values were removed, and categorical features (e.g., residential area) were converted using label encoding. To construct the target variable, the original features *recidivism_year1, recidivism_year2, recidivism_year3,* and *no_recidivism* were merged into a single outcome variable, *recidivism_whichyear*. Specifically, *recidivism_year1/2/3* = *True* were labeled as 1/2/3, while *no_recidivism* = *True* was labeled as 0. For rows with missing data, we discard these rows because there are categorical features in them that we cannot reasonably handle with padding methods such as means. After discarding these rows, 16,200 valid samples were retained for model training.

Drawing on the Risk-Need-Responsivity (RNR) model in criminology (Andrews & Bonta, 2010) [12], the study classified features into static and dynamic categories according to their nature, as shown in Table II. Considering that static characteristics may have a limited impact on recidivism compared to dynamic factors, we focused exclusively on dynamic characteristics during model training to assess their predictive performance.

To address potential gender-based disparities, we established two experimental conditions: (1) using the full dataset including gender as a feature, and (2) using a male-only subset. By comparing model performance across these settings, we assess whether gender imbalance influences outcomes. If a significant performance gap is observed, we proceed to mitigate this bias through architectural adjustments to the model.

3.5 Training Process and Hyperparameter Tuning

3.5.1 Training Process

To further extract useful information and reduce redundancy, principal component analysis (PCA) and factor analysis (FA) were applied within each feature category for dimensionality reduction. In addition, PCA was also applied to the full feature set to reduce dimensionality to a specified number of components prior to model training and evaluation, enabling comparison of different feature-processing strategies and their impact on algorithmic performance.

Table 2. The datasets are divided by dynamic and static features, each covering five dimensions.

Static Features		Dynamic Features	
Identity	Gender Race Age_at_Release	Health Condition	MH_SA Cog_Ed Other
Prior Arrest Episodes	Felony Misd Violent Property Drug DVCharges PPViolationCharge GunCharges	Drug	Avg_Days_per_DrugTest DrugTests_THC_Positive DrugTests_Cocaine_Positive DrugTests_Meth_Positive DrugTests_Other_Positive
Prior Conviction Episodes	Felony Misd Violent	Stability	Residence_Changes Employment_Exempt Program_Attendances Program_UnexcusedAbsences
Social Resources	Residence_PUMA Education_Level Dependents	Violation	ElectronicMonitoring Instruction FailToReport MoveWithoutPermission Delinquency_Reports
Supervision	Risk_Score_First Supervision_Level_First	Employment	Percent_Days_Employed Jobs_Per_Year

3.5.2 Hyperparameters

Tuning We optimized hyperparameters via grid search with 5-fold cross-validation, following a systematic adjustment strategy. first, the parameters to be tuned and their approximate ranges were identified. Next, a refined search was conducted within the most promising intervals. Finally, the robustness of the optimal parameter combination was validated based on the obtained results. To ensure reproducibility and avoid randomness, all experiments were conducted with the random seed fixed at random_state = 42. The tuning results are presented in Tables 3 and 4 in XGBoost, a lower learning rate (0.1) with increased n_estimators (200) achieved the best bias-variance trade-off. critical parameters were identified through ablation studies: max_depth in tree-based models showed >10% performance variance, while batch_size in mlp caused < 2% fluctuation, justifying its fixed value.

Table 3. Optimal results of four models after grid search hyperparameter tuning.

Hyperparameter	Decision Tree	Random Forest	XGBoost	AdaBoost
max_Depth	None	None	5	-
n_estimators	-	400	200	100

(*continued*)

Table 3. (*continued*)

Hyperparameter	Decision Tree	Random Forest	XGBoost	AdaBoost
learning_Rate	-	-	0.1	1.0
Other	Class_weight = balanced	Max_Features = 0.5 Min_samples_split = 32	Subsample = 1.0	-
Key Tuning Effect	Addressing sample imbalance	Mitigating overfitting	Accelerating convergence	Preserving the contribution of the base model

Table 4. Optimal results of MLP after grid search hyperparameter tuning.

Hyperparameter	MLP-common	MLP-probability
Batch Size	32	16
L2 regularization	True	False
Epochs	500	200
Learning rate	step_size = 100, gamma = 0.6	step_size = 50, gamma = 0.5

For PCA, dimensions ranging from 10 to 30 were evaluated, with 16 dimensions selected as optimal. Performance (as balanced by Accuracy, F1-Score, and AUC) stabilized beyond 16 dimensions, indicating that the most meaningful variance was captured within this reduced feature subset, while additional dimensions contributed primarily to noise and increased computational overhead. This configuration maximized the F1-score (0.775) while maintaining AUC above 0.748. As illustrated in Fig. 3, the dimensionality selection results indicate that accuracy plateaus once the dimensionality exceeds 16, whereas computational cost continues to increase linearly.

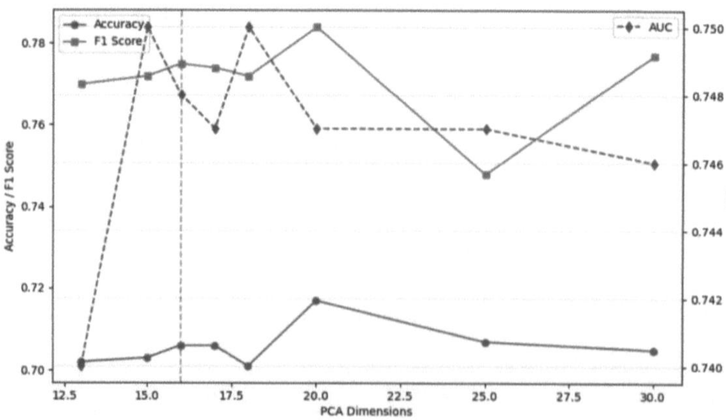

Fig. 3. Applying PCA dimensionality reduction to Random Forest. The vertical dashed line in Fig. 3 indicates the final choice of 16 dimensions for dimensionality reduction.

3.6 Evaluation Metrics

Total accuracy serves as a fundamental metric for evaluating model performance, representing the proportion of correctly classified samples. While it provides an intuitive measure of overall correctness, it may be misleading in cases of class imbalance. For instance, in our dataset, where non-recidivism cases dominate, a model could achieve high accuracy by simply predicting the majority class, thereby failing to capture meaningful patterns in the minority class.

To address this limitation, we employ more nuanced metrics. Precision measures the exactness of positive predictions, calculating the percentage of true positives among all instances predicted as positive. In contrast, recall assesses the model's ability to capture actual positive cases, reflecting the proportion of true positives correctly identified out of all actual positives. The F1-score harmonizes these two aspects by computing their harmonic mean, offering a balanced view of the model's performance, especially valuable under imbalanced data distributions. A higher F1-score indicates a more robust and reliable classifier.

Furthermore, we include the Area Under the ROC Curve (AUC) to evaluate the model's ability to distinguish between classes across varying classification thresholds. The AUC provides a comprehensive measure of overall discriminatory power, independent of threshold selection, making it particularly informative for assessing model performance in classification tasks.

The model is designed to predict recidivism; however, the dataset is predominantly composed of non-recidivists, with only a small proportion of recidivist cases. This class imbalance may lead to misleading results if evaluation relies on a single metric, as the model might exhibit strong performance in identifying non-recidivism while performing poorly in detecting recidivism. Therefore, a comprehensive evaluation using multiple metrics is essential.

3.7 Proposed Framework

For the decision tree, the splitting feature was selected based on the information gain criterion. At each node, all possible split points of every feature were evaluated, and the feature producing the greatest reduction in Gini impurity was chosen for partitioning. A one-level decision tree was employed as the baseline model; this simple structure relies on a single feature, is easy to train, and provides a reasonable performance benchmark. Beyond the baseline, decision trees were also trained on datasets reduced by PCA and factor analysis (FA), with hyperparameters optimized through grid search. Five-fold cross-validation was applied to evaluate model performance.

Random forests were trained both on the complete dataset and on a PCA-reduced version with 16 dimensions. Each tree was grown from a random subset of features, functioning as a weak classifier within the ensemble. Five-fold cross-validation was again used, and grid search was conducted to identify optimal parameters. Additionally, to assess feature redundancy and enhance interpretability, dynamic features were grouped by category; for one such category, PCA was applied to reduce dimensionality to a single component, which was then combined with the remaining dynamic features before training the random forest under the same evaluation procedure.

AdaBoost and XGBoost were likewise trained on both the full dataset and the PCA-reduced dataset (16 dimensions). Hyperparameter optimization was performed via grid search with five-fold cross-validation.

For the artificial neural network (ANN) predicting the specific year of recidivism within three years, the architecture followed the sequence: *input_dim* → *128* → *64* → *32* → *(ReLU)16* → *4*. The four output nodes were one-hot encoded as 0, 1, 2, and 3, where 1, 2, and 3 correspond to reoffending in the first, second, and third year after release, respectively, and 0 indicates no reoffense within three years. All hidden layers used ReLU activation, and L2 regularization was incorporated into the loss function to mitigate overfitting.

For the ANN probability model predicting the likelihood of reoffending in a given year, the architecture was *input_dim* → *64* → *64* → *2*. The two output units represent μ and σ, corresponding to the mean and variance of a normal distribution. ReLU was applied in all hidden layers. The custom loss function was defined as

$$loss = 5 \times 10^{-3} \times (\mu - \frac{\text{max\_}year}{2})^2 + 2 \times 10^{-3} \times \sigma^2 + (p - target)^2$$

where max_year is the maximum year to predict the probability of recidivism, and p denotes the predicted probability of reoffense in a given year. If recidivism occurred in that year, $target = 1$; otherwise, $target = 0$.

Figure 4 illustrates the proposed algorithmic framework for assessing the likelihood of offender recidivism. The *Data and Methods* section discuss the prison data collection procedures as well as the quantification of both behavioral and non-behavioural risk attributes of violent offenders. It also provides a detailed description of feature normalization and feature selection based on one-way ANOVA. The section on *Ensemble Learning Methods* introduces ensemble approaches and decision-tree ensembles. In the section *Machine Learning–Based Recidivism Risk Assessment,* we present the application of machine learning techniques for recidivism prediction and the automatic assessment of felony recidivism risk using decision-tree ensembles. Finally, the section *Simulation Results and Discussion* report the simulation experiments conducted on the felony dataset and analyzes the grading of recidivism risk.

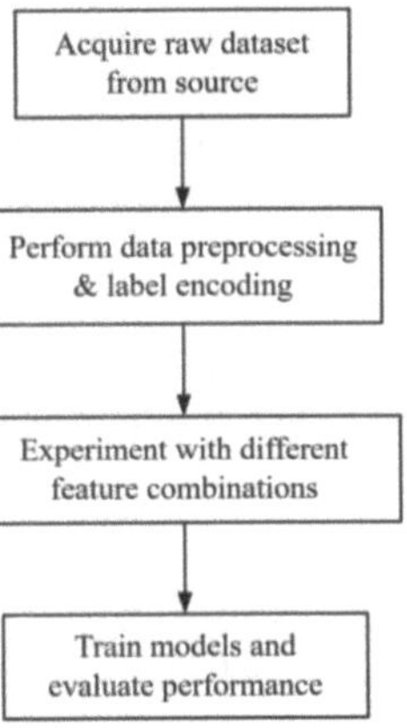

Fig. 4. Schematic representation of the proposed algorithmic framework for recidivism risk assessment

4 Experimental Results

This section provides a detailed description of the training outcomes and processing workflow, and evaluates model performance based on the experimental results.

4.1 Performance

Table 5 presents the performance of the five models evaluated in this study—Decision Tree, Random Forest, XGBoost, AdaBoost, and MLP—on the task of predicting recidivism year, reporting accuracy, F1-score, and ROC-AUC.

Table 5. Evaluate the model's accuracy, F1-score, and ROC on the test set.

Num	Model	Datasets	Dimension	Output type	Accuracy	F1-score	ROC
1	DT	Complete	FA	Classification	36.8%	0.312	0.545
2	DT	Complete	PCA	Classification	60.0%	0.665	0.584
3	RF	Dynamic	-	Classification	55.3%	0.364	0.720
5	RF	Complete	FA	Classification	46.8%	0.366	0.654
6	RF	Complete	PCA	Classification	70.7%	0.775	0.748
7	XGBoost	Complete	-	Classification	57.6%	0.520	0.689
8	XGBoost	Complete	PCA	Classification	51.0%	0.446	0.660
9	AdaBoost	Complete	-	Classification	53.8%	0.472	0.638
10	AdaBoost	Complete	PCA	Classification	49.2%	0.415	0.639
11	MLP	Complete	-	Classification	42.7%	0.429	0.6252

Table 6 reports the results of an alternative dimensionality reduction strategy, which abandons traditional projection-based methods (e.g., PCA, random projection) and instead adopts an innovative dynamic feature fusion approach. In this method, dynamic features are grouped into five major dimensions (see Table 2) and fused accordingly. As shown in Table 6, compared with direct projection-based dimensionality reduction, the fusion method preserved classification accuracy but did not yield clear improvements in predictive accuracy.

Table 6. Dimensionality reduction is achieved by integrating dynamic feature fusion methods based on five key dimensions.

Combined Features	Accuracy	F1-score	ROC
Health	54.7%	0.361	0.719
Violation	55.2%	0.363	0.719
Stability	54.6%	0.360	0.711
Drug	54.8%	0.360	0.717
Employment	51.9%	0.326	0.667
Uncombined	55.3%	0.364	0.720

In this study, a highly simplified single-layer decision tree model was employed as the baseline, trained using only the most correlated feature. This model contained a single decision node and achieved an accuracy of just 48%, clearly demonstrating the limitations of decision trees in terms of feature utilization and structural complexity. Reliance on a single feature makes it difficult to capture the underlying complexity of the data, while the shallow structure further constrains the model's expressive capacity.

(1) As shown in Fig. 5, the best-performing model (PCA + Random Forest) achieved an accuracy of 70.7%, representing a 47.3% improvement over the baseline decision tree (48%) and significantly outperforming the other ensemble models, XGBoost (57.6%) and AdaBoost (53.8%).
(2) Figure 5 further shows that PCA-based dimensionality reduction performed well with RF and DT, but led to decreased accuracy in XGBoost and AdaBoost. This finding suggests that dimensionality reduction methods are beneficial only for certain models.
(3) As shown in Fig. 6, the PCA-based dimensionality reduction method demonstrated strong performance across accuracy, F1-score, and AUC, outperforming factor analysis (FA). Moreover, when using the same random forest (RF) model, the choice of feature-processing strategy had a significant impact on overall performance.
(4) As shown in Fig. 6, using only dynamic features produced better results than applying FA-based dimensionality reduction, but performance remained notably lower than that achieved with PCA. Furthermore, the findings indicate that static features may negatively influence predictive outcomes to some extent, as models trained solely on dynamic features yielded comparatively higher accuracy.

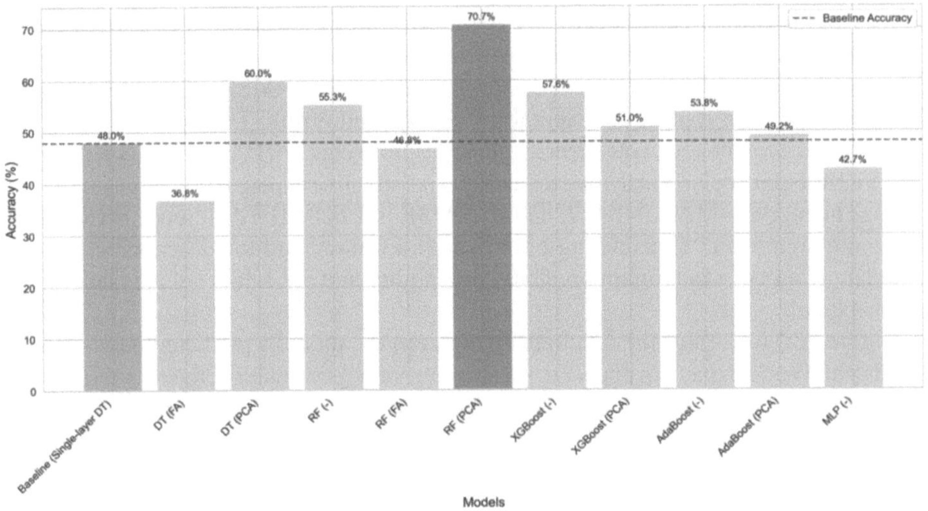

Fig. 5. Bar chart comparing all models against the baseline

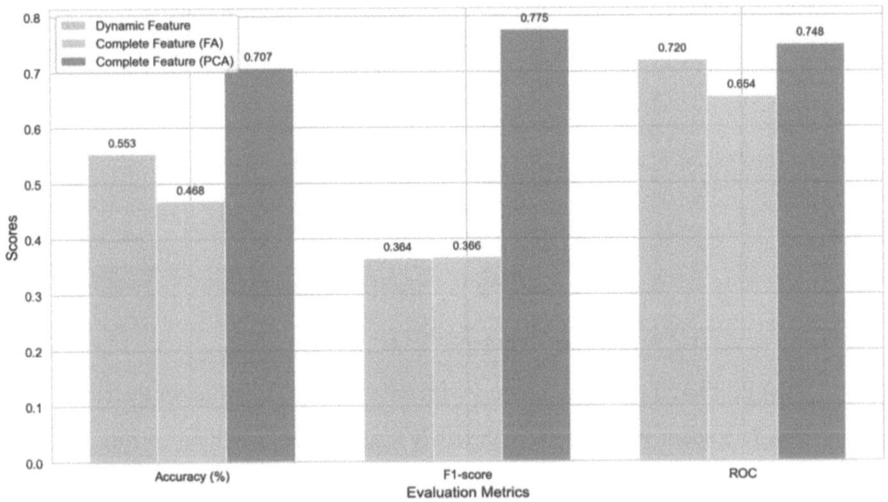

Fig. 6. Results comparison between dynamic features and full features

4.2 ANN Model for Predicting the Probability of Reoffending in a Given year

When the model predicts a result of 5, i.e., max_year, we consider reoffending as non-reoffending, because max_year signifies that reoffending would only occur after an extremely long period of time, meaning the individual would not reoffend during their lifetime.

The accuracy rate for predicting the year with the highest probability reaches 54.0%, while the accuracy rate for predicting the actual year among the top two probability predictions is 65.1%.

The MAE (Mean Absolute Error) is the average of the absolute errors between predicted and true values. Because it uses absolute values, individual large errors do not disproportionately influence the MAE. On the other hand, RMSE (Root Mean Square Error) is the square root of the average of the squared errors. The squaring operation gives greater weight to larger errors, thereby amplifying their impact. This property makes RMSE particularly sensitive to outliers and effective at penalizing large prediction errors. The model's MAE is 1.167, and its RMSE is 1.628. The difference between the two is not significant. Considering both overall accuracy and top-2 accuracy, the gap between the model's maximum predicted probability and the actual value is unlikely to be substantial.

Figure 7(a) illustrates the relationship between the model's predicted mean and the actual year. While it may not appear to show a very strong correlation, the actual sampling process requires incorporating variance to determine the year with the highest probability.

Figure 7(b) illustrates the relationship between the predicted year (maximum probability) and the actual year. The model tends to assign higher probabilities to recidivism in the first year and non-recidivism in the fifth year, largely due to the imbalanced nature of the dataset.

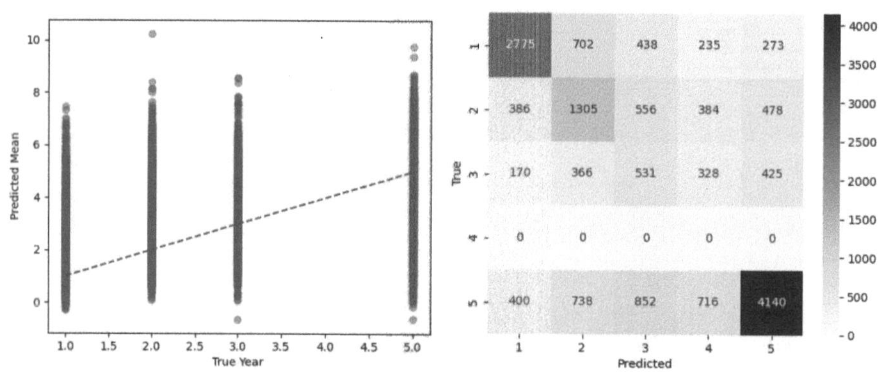

(a) Predicted mean compared with true year (b) Confusion matrix

Fig. 7. Experimental results of the ANN model for probability prediction

4.3 Discussion Analysis in Different Tasks

4.3.1 Gender Sensitivity Analysis

When female data were excluded, the MLP model achieved an overall accuracy of 56%; however, it completely failed to predict recidivism in Year 2 and Year 3 (F1 = 0.08 and 0.00, respectively). In contrast, including female data resulted in a lower overall accuracy of 47%, but led to more balanced predictive performance across the first three years (F1 = 0.59, 0.18, and 0.14 for Years 1–3). These results indicate that gender is correlated with temporal patterns of recidivism and that using gender as a feature may amplify model bias against the already underrepresented female group. To mitigate this, several fairness-aware approaches can be considered:

(1) Incorporating fairness constraints such as equalized odds during training;
(2) Using adversarial debiasing techniques in neural network architectures;
(3) Conducting rigorous subgroup-specific evaluation and validation.

4.3.2 Prediction Failure in Small-Sample Categories

Across all models, performance was weakest for the year 3 category, which contains only 155 samples. This severe class imbalance leads to majority-class dominance, meaning the model can largely ignore year 3 predictions with minimal effect on aggregate metrics. the decision tree completely failed to predict this category (0% accuracy), while even the best model achieved only 17% recall. These results (Fig. 8) highlight the critical nature of the data imbalance issue.

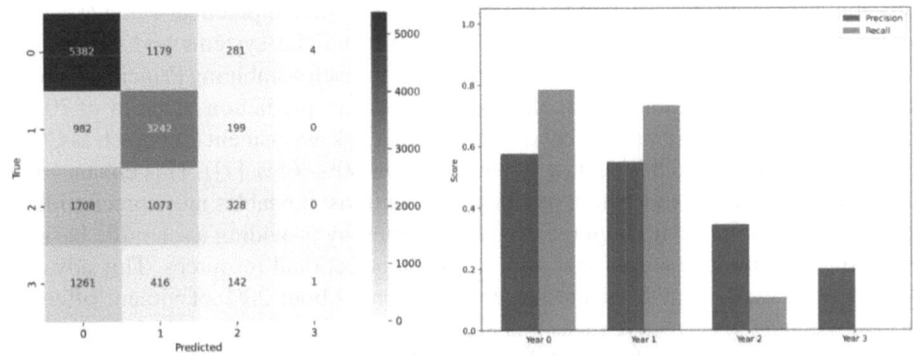

(a) Confusion Matrix (b) Precision/Recall

Fig. 8. Confusion Matrix and Precision/Recall for Years 1/2/3 and No-recidivism for Random Forest Model with All Features involved

To address this, several targeted adjustments are recommended:

(1) Increase the representation of Year 3 samples through oversampling techniques such as duplication or synthetic data generation to balance their proportion with other classes;
(2) Apply higher loss weights for Year 3 samples during training to penalize misclassification more heavily;
(3) Replace overall accuracy with per-class metrics (e.g., precision, recall, F1-score) for more meaningful evaluation.

4.3.3 Trade-Off Between Interpretability and Accuracy

Zeng et al. [13] found that commonly used black box models (e.g., SVM, Ridge Regression) were accurate but not transparent enough; they have built a scoring system that is both highly accurate and fully transparent for judicial decision-making. The PCA–Random Forest model achieved the highest accuracy (70.7%), whereas the decision tree offered stronger interpretability but lower accuracy (67.0%). This difference in performance reflects the inherent trade-off between predictive performance and model transparency. While PCA-random forest achieved superior predictive accuracy, decision-makers may prefer simpler decision trees for higher interpretability. Bridging this gap requires interpretable ML approaches that preserve high accuracy without sacrificing transparency.

5 Discussion and Future Work

5.1 Discussion

5.1.1 Model Applications and Implications for Criminal Justice

This study develops a predictive model that offers significant practical value as a technological tool for risk assessment practices within judicial systems and correctional institutions. By employing an integrated learning approach combining Principal Component Analysis with Random Forest, the model achieved a prediction accuracy of 70.7%, demonstrating marked improvement over traditional risk assessment tools such as COMPAS (which typically yields accuracy rates between 60%–65% [7]). This enhancement in performance carries substantial practical implications: it enables more precise identification of individuals with high recidivism risk, thereby providing a scientific basis for targeted interventions and rational allocation of correctional resources. This advancement is particularly crucial given that currently only about 20% of violent offenders receive specialized corrective measures [4]. Furthermore, the proposed Multilayer Perceptron (MLP) model with probabilistic outputs successfully extends the prediction window beyond the conventional three-year assessment period, overcoming temporal limitations inherent in current parole supervision mechanisms. The model generates dynamically evolving risk profiles over time, thereby supporting governmental implementation of more refined supervision strategies and serving as an evaluation benchmark. Parole officers can utilize the risk probability curves generated by the model to concentrate monitoring resources during high-risk periods while employing more flexible approaches, such as education and social support, during lower-risk phases. This approach achieves an optimal balance between supervisory efficiency and protection of individual rights.

5.1.2 Ethical Considerations and Fairness Challenges

In gender sensitivity analysis, we observed a paradoxical phenomenon: while excluding female data during modeling increased overall accuracy, the model completely failed to predict recidivism in years 2–3 (F1 = 0.00). Conversely, incorporating gender variables yielded more balanced predictive performance across all years, albeit with reduced overall accuracy. this finding aligns with Wang's (2022) [7] Research on algorithmic bias in criminal risk assessment, confirming that even advanced machine learning models cannot circumvent the inherent trade-off between accuracy and fairness. Furthermore, this study examines the tension between interpretability and predictive performance. Although the PCA-Random Forest model achieved 70.7% accuracy, its interpretability was inferior to the Decision Tree model, which attained slightly lower accuracy (67.0%). This contrast underscores the critical importance of model transparency in judicial decision-making contexts. As Zeng et al. [13] Demonstrated, "black box" predictive models—even those with high accuracy—may undermine due process by preventing defendants from effectively challenging or verifying risk assessments.

5.1.3 Comparative Analysis with Existing Literature

The findings of this study align with, yet also diverge from, several recent key publications in the following three aspects:

(1) The PCA-RF model proposed in this study achieved an accuracy of 70.7%, outperforming the 65% accuracy (AUC = 0.75) reported by Cohen et al. [6] using logistic regression, while approaching the 89% accuracy attained by Singh and Mohapatra [10] in violent recidivism prediction. However, it should be noted that due to significant differences in the datasets used, the comparability of model performance requires further evaluation.
(2) The results are consistent with a meta-analysis by Eisenberg et al. [5] (which reported a correlation coefficient r = 0.324 between dynamic risk factors and recidivism), as this study found that dynamic features—particularly employment status and drug test records—contributed slightly more to prediction accuracy than static demographic indicators (see Table 2). Furthermore, the MLP-based probabilistic prediction model developed in this study extends this finding to a longer time dimension for the first time, enabling dynamic assessment of recidivism risk.
(3) For the rare event of third-year recidivism (only 155 samples), all models performed poorly. This result corroborates the small-sample prediction bottleneck highlighted by de la Cruz et al. [9], reflecting a fundamental limitation in the current dataset regarding class balance.

In summary, although machine learning methods demonstrate significantly greater potential than traditional actuarial tools in recidivism prediction, fully realizing their practical benefits depends on addressing three critical challenges: first, constructing standardized datasets that are class-balanced, consistently annotated, and representative; second, designing algorithmic frameworks that pursue predictive performance without sacrificing fairness and interpretability; and third, establishing guidelines for algorithmic evaluation and interpretability tailored to judicial contexts to enhance the transparency of model decisions.

5.2 Future Work

Building upon the current findings and limitations, we propose the following directions for future research.

In response to the interpretability-accuracy trade-off challenge identified in Sect. 4.3.3—where experimental results showed that the PCA-Random Forest model achieved 70.7% accuracy but lacked interpretability—future work could integrate gradient-boosted ensemble methods with SHAP value visualization. This approach would preserve the performance of XGBoost while providing feature importance interpretations.

Moreover, to address the complete failure in predicting third-year recidivism caused by extreme class imbalance, future research could develop generative adversarial networks (GANs) specifically tailored for temporal recidivism patterns to synthesize high-quality minority-class samples. Alternatively, implementing dynamically adjusted misclassification penalties based on temporal rarity could mitigate errors induced by data imbalance.

Finally, in response to the practical need for diversity within the judicial system, we can develop a professional evaluation framework based on a multi-stakeholder assessment model. This system should balance predictive performance, procedural fairness, and resource allocation efficiency. Furthermore, an adversarial auditing mechanism should be established to systematically detect potential implicit biases across different demographic subgroups (such as gender, race, etc.), thereby effectively identifying and addressing various forms of discrimination hidden within data.

6 Conclusion

This study demonstrates the practical potential of machine learning in assisting recidivism prediction. Through a comparative evaluation of multiple models, the PCA-Random Forest framework achieved a prediction accuracy of 70.7%, outperforming all other models. Furthermore, the proposed probabilistic multilayer perceptron model breaks through the three-year time window limitation of the original dataset, enabling cross-year recidivism probability prediction, which better aligns with the practical needs of long-term dynamic risk assessment in judicial supervision. These findings highlight three key values of data-driven tools in the judicial field: supporting evidence-based decision-making, enabling precise correctional interventions, and promoting efficient resource allocation.

However, the study also reveals several persistent challenges. Severe class imbalance limits reliable prediction of low-frequency recidivism events (e.g., third-year recidivism), while the trade-off between prediction accuracy and model interpretability remains to be further addressed. More critically, the inclusion of sensitive attributes such as gender may introduce fairness risks, necessitating careful consideration in practical applications.

Although machine learning demonstrates superior performance over traditional methods in recidivism prediction, its practical deployment in the criminal justice system must strictly meet transparency and fairness requirements. Future research should focus on constructing standardized and class-balanced datasets, as well as developing modeling methods that balance interpretability and predictive performance, to further enhance the applicability and credibility of machine learning models in judicial practice.

Acknowledgement. Binghan Zhang, Jiawei Hu and Hao Yuan contributed equally to this work and should be considered co-first authors.

References

1. Maltz, M.D.: Recidivism. Michael Maltz (1984)
2. Strong, B.L., Greene, C.R., Smith, G.S.: Trauma recidivism predicts long-term mortality: missed opportunities for prevention (retrospective cohort study). Ann. Surg. **265**(5), 847–853 (2017)
3. Alyami, M.: Descriptive Characteristics of Injury Recidivism Among Adults in the US: Population-Based Study. Yale University (2022)
4. McCoy, A.M., Como, J.J., Greene, G., et al.: A novel prospective approach to evaluate trauma recidivism: the concept of the past trauma history. J. Trauma Acute Care Surg. **75**(1), 116–121 (2013)
5. Eisenberg, M.J., Van Horn, J.E., Dekker, J.M., et al.: Static and dynamic predictors of general and violent criminal offense recidivism in the forensic outpatient population: a meta-analysis. Crim. Justice Behav. **46**(5), 732–750 (2019)
6. Cohen, T.R., Fronk, G.E., Kiehl, K.A., et al.: Clarifying the relationship between mental illness and recidivism using machine learning: a retrospective study. PLoS ONE **19**(2), e0297448 (2024)
7. Wang, C., Han, B., Patel, B., et al.: In pursuit of interpretable, fair and accurate machine learning for criminal recidivism prediction. J. Quant. Criminol. **39**(2), 519–581 (2023)
8. Mowen, T.J., Culhane, S.E.: Modeling recidivism within the study of offender reentry: hierarchical generalized linear models and lagged dependent variable models. Crim. Justice Behav. **44**(1), 85–102 (2017)
9. de la Cruz, R., Padilla, O., Valle, M.A., et al.: Modeling recidivism through Bayesian regression models and deep neural networks. Mathematics **9**(6), 639 (2021)
10. Singh, A., Mohapatra, S.: Decision tree ensemble approach for recidivism risk classification among heinous crime convicts. SN Comput. Sci. **5**(1), 195 (2024)
11. Pattnayak, P., Das, S.S., Patnaik, S., et al.: Machine learning prediction models on the tendency of criminals to recurrence of criminal activities. In: 2024 International Conference on Intelligent Computing and Sustainable Innovations in Technology (IC-SIT), pp. 1–6. IEEE (2024)

12. Andrews, D.A., Bonta, J.: Rehabilitating criminal justice policy and practice. Psychol. Public Policy Law **16**(1), 39 (2010)
13. Zeng, J., Ustun, B., Rudin, C.: Interpretable classification models for recidivism prediction. J. R. Stat. Soc. Ser. A Stat. Soc. **180**(3), 689–722 (2017)

SineKAN-Based SAC Approaches for Continuous Reinforcement Learning Environments

Ali Bayeh(✉), Samira Sadaoui, and Malek Mouhoub

Department of Computer Science, University of Regina, Regina, Canada
{alibayeh,sadaouis,mouhoubm}@uregina.ca

Abstract. This paper explores integrating SineKAN networks into the Soft Actor-Critic (SAC) algorithm for Continuous Reinforcement Learning (CRL) to address the size and speed limitations of Kolmogorov-Arnold Networks (KANs). We modify SineKAN by adding residual connections to each hidden layer and then introduce two other variants. The latter retain the modified SineKAN's architecture but differ in parameter update strategies and initialization. Experiments across several CRL environments show that SineKAN-based SAC models achieve strong performance and stability under certain conditions. Notably, one variant reduces the number of learnable parameters to less than one-quarter of the original SineKAN. We also analyze deeper architectures' performance to assess scalability for complex CRL problems. Our findings provide insights into adopting SineKAN in continuous settings and guide future work on building more robust RL algorithms.

Keywords: Kolmogorov-Arnold Network · Sinusoidal KAN · Continuous Reinforcement Learning · Soft Actor-Critic

1 Introduction

Reinforcement learning (RL) methods face challenges with generalization and robustness, especially in continuous domains. The large, high-dimensional action and state spaces in CRL applications require advanced methods for stable and efficient training. Although neural networks are robust, they tend to ignore the structural properties of agents and environments in CRL problems, limiting their effectiveness. In contrast, KANs [8] provide a valuable alternative by breaking down complex functions into simpler, structured parts. Also, KANs use trainable activation functions to adaptively shape these functions according to current data. Function decomposition and learnable activation functions help improve interpretability and generalization, making KAN models a strong candidate for advancing CRL domain. However, the use of KANs in CRL settings is still mostly unexplored. Few studies have adopted KANs within RL methods. For example, [5] and [2] investigated the effectiveness of KAN-based PPO, while [1] explored KAN-based SAC.

C. Xu (Ed.): ICMLSC 2026, CCIS 2948, pp. 33–45, 2027.
https://doi.org/10.1007/978-981-92-1546-1_3

Our research explores the incorporation of the SineKAN variant [11] into the off-policy SAC algorithm. We aim to overcome size and speed limitations of traditional KAN models (which use B-splines as the basis function) by leveraging the periodic nature of sine functions. Furthermore, we introduce a minor modification to the internal architecture of the original SineKAN by incorporating a residual connection at each hidden layer. We also propose two additional variants. Although these variants retain the general architecture of the modified SineKAN (with residual links), they differ in terms of learning dynamics, specifically in parameter (phase and amplitude) updating strategies and initialization schemes. The first variant replaces the fixed phase parameters in SineKAN with learnable ones while preserving same dimensionality. This enhances the model's representational capacity by allowing it to adapt phase values during training. In the second variant, the structure of the amplitude parameters is modified. In the original SineKAN, the number of amplitude parameters in each layer is determined by multiplying the input and output dimensions by the grid size. Conversely, the proposed design entails a substantial reduction in the number of amplitude parameters. This objective is achieved by defining the parameters as a tensor shaped by the product of the input and output dimensions. These parameters are subsequently broadcast across the grid size during the computation process. While the resulting tensor shape remains compatible with the original architecture, the total number of parameters decreases by a factor proportional to the size of the grid.

Through extensive experiments and analysis on several CRL environments (HalfCheeta, Swimmer, Hopper and Pusher), we demonstrate that SineKAN-based SAC methods provide strong performance and stability in training. We also calculate the number of learnable parameters and show that the second variant reduces this number to less than one-quarter of the original SineKAN. Next, we examine how well SineKAN models can scale for complex problems by examining the performance of deeper architectures. Our empirical results contribute to a better understanding of SineKAN models in continuous setting and support current efforts to develop more robust RL algorithms.

This paper is structured as follows. Section 2 provides the theoretical foundations of KAN, SineKAN and off-policy SAC method. Section 3 describes several related studies on KANs. Section 4 explains the complex behavior of SineKAN-based SAC algorithm along with its theoretical framework. Section 5 presents the selected CRL environments and hyperparameter tuning. Section 6 evaluates and compares the performance of the three SineKan-based SAC methods and their learnable parameter counts. Section 7 concludes our work and presents some future works.

2 Background

2.1 KAN Networks

Unlike neural networks that rely on fixed activation functions, Kolmogorov-Arnold Networks (KANs) [7,8] are designed based on learnable activation functions. These networks were inspired by the Kolmogorov-Arnold representation theorem, which states that a continuous high-dimensional function can be expressed as a sum of univariate functions, each applied to a linear transformation (a projection onto a one-dimensional subspace) of the input vector. In [8], the authors utilized the B-spline method as a smooth, trainable component to parameterize these inner and outer functions. In the proposed model, each KAN layer consists of two sublayers: 1) a middle layer with $2n+1$ neurons representing inner functions $\varphi_{q,p}$, and 2) an output layer that sums the outer functions Φ_q. The activation values across layers are defined recursively as [8]:

$$x_{l+1,j} = \sum_{i=1}^{n_l} \hat{x}_{l,j,i} = \sum_{i=1}^{n_l} \varphi_{l,j,i}(x_{l,i}), \qquad \begin{array}{l} l = 0, \ldots, L-1 \\ i = 1, \ldots, n_l \\ j = 1, \ldots, n_{l+1} \end{array}$$

where L is the total number of layers, n_l is the number of neurons in the layer l, $x_{l,i}$ is the activation of the ith neuron in the layer l, and $\varphi_{l,j,i}$ is the activation function that links the ith neuron in layer l with the jth neuron in layer $l+1$. A deep KAN is formed by stacking multiple KAN layers, expressed as [8]:

$$KAN(x) = (\Phi_{L-1} \circ \Phi_{L-2} \circ \cdots \circ \Phi_1 \circ \Phi_0)(x)$$

2.2 SineKAN Networks

The sinusoidal KAN [11] proposes an alternative to the B-spline activation functions in KAN by using parameterized sinusoidal functions as its basis. So, the transformation in each layer is defined as follows [11]:

$$y_i = \sum_j \sum_k (\sin(x_j * \omega_k + \xi_{jk}) * A_{ijk}) + b_i$$

where x_j represents the input features of the layer, A_{ijk} denotes the learnable amplitude weights, ω_k are the learnable grid frequency parameters, ξ_{jk} denotes the fixed phase shifts across the grid points and input coordinates, and b_i is a bias term [11]. The theoretical foundation of SineKAN is based on Fourier analysis. However, the parameter complexity in SineKAN is reduced from $(O(2oig))$ to $(O(oig + g))$, where (i), (o) and (g) are the input dimension, output dimension, and grid size, respectively. This is achieved by eliminating the cosine terms and introducing an additional learnable frequency parameter (ω_k), to learn the cosine frequencies. So, each well-behaved function $f : \mathbb{R} \rightarrow \mathbb{R}$ can be approximated through a discretized transform as follows [11]:

$$g_\theta(x) = \sum_i B_i \sin(\omega_i x + \xi_i)$$

where B_i represents discretized amplitudes. To stabilize outputs across varying grid sizes, SineKAN employs a scaling factor (R) for phase terms, which scales all phase terms as they increase [11]:

$$R = A * g^{-K} + C\phi_{g+1} = \phi_g * R(g)$$

where the constants A, K and C were obtained by numerically optimizing a tailored objective that simultaneously minimizes the variance and controls the mean-squared magnitude of the ratio between successive SineKAN grid responses over the domain $x \in [-\pi, \pi]$ [11]. The proposed architecture utilizes a two-tier weight initialization scheme: first-layer weights are initialized from a normal distribution with mean 0 and standard deviation 0.4, while in subsequent layers weights follow a uniform distribution between −1 and 1. This strategy ensures that deeper layers maintain a broader range of feature values, unlike B-Spline, where outputs diminish, potentially impacting performance. In general, unlike implicit neural representations that combine sinusoidal activations with linear transformations, SineKAN's learnable frequencies eliminate the need for such layers, simplifying the architecture while preserving approximation capabilities.

3 Related Work

KANs have been explored as an alternative to MLPs in various applications, showing performance comparable to conventional methods. Recent studies have extended KAN architectures and proposed new approaches that incorporate polynomial- and function-based techniques. The authors of [5] extended the application of KANs to the online RL setting. This study replaced MLP function approximators in actor–critic frameworks with KAN layers and evaluated the approach on a range of control benchmarks. The findings indicate that KAN-based agents demonstrate faster early-stage convergence and improved sample efficiency in environments with sparse or highly nonlinear reward landscapes. However, the results show that KANs are sensitive to hyper-parameters, such as knot density, spline regularization, and optimizer configuration, and require additional tuning to produce results comparable to those of an MLP.

In another study, paper [3] presented a systematic, empirical comparison of KANs and MLPs within RL pipelines, such as TD3+BC and IQL. They evaluated the two architectures across multiple control benchmarks and found that, despite their higher parameter count and slower per-step training speed, KANs frequently achieve improved policy value estimation and more stable convergence under limited data regimes. They attributed these advantages to the inductive bias of KANs toward low-dimensional, additive, compositional structures, as well as their capacity for smoother function approximation in sparse or noisy offline datasets. However, the experiments indicated that KANs do not consistently outperform MLPs in data-rich settings, where over-parameterization is less detrimental.

Based on similar idea, [2] introduced an on-policy RL framework that integrates KAN and its multiplicative variant (MultKAN) into the PPO algorithm for continuous control tasks. The study explored how KAN's structured functional decomposition could improve performance, stability, and generalization in high-dimensional CRL settings by replacing MLP with KANs in the actor and critic networks. The study also examined the role of regularization, evaluating different dropout configurations, including the DropKAN mechanism, which is specifically designed for spline-based models to improve training robustness. Empirical evaluations in the MuJoCo Half-Cheetah environment demonstrated that integrating KAN with the PPO algorithm achieves more stable learning dynamics and better resilience to parameter variation than the MLP-based PPO algorithm, especially under challenging dropout and architecture configurations. Despite these advantages, the study identified open challenges, such as the limited scalability of on-policy KAN-based methods and sensitivity of spline-parameterized activations to dropout placement and rate.

Another study [15] extended the KAN framework to RL by proposing a modified PPO framework in which both the policy and value networks are implemented using KANs. By leveraging KAN's learnable B-spline edge functions and multi-scale grid extension, KAN-PPO method aims to achieve smoother value approximation and improved policy stability. Experimental results across OpenAI Atari environments demonstrate that KAN-PPO converges faster, achieves higher cumulative rewards, and is more stable during training than standard MLP-PPO methods, while maintaining similar or smaller parameter counts. Nevertheless, the findings suggest that KAN's larger model size and slower per-update computation make it less suitable for real-time or large-scale environments without further optimization.

The study [14] presented a computation offloading framework for the Industrial Internet of Things (IIoT) that integrates dual-Q deep RL with KANs. The proposed D2KCO model aims to address key IIoT system challenges (e.g., high offloading delay and elevated data security risks) by leveraging a hybrid cloud–edge–device architecture. Specifically, the study introduced a Dual-Q KAN-augmented DRL agent to optimize computation offloading under dynamic, high-dimensional state spaces.

The experimental results demonstrated that D2KCO significantly reduced task delay and enhanced offloading efficiency compared to baseline algorithms. However, using KAN-enhanced Dual-Q learning introduces new complexities, leading to increased computational overhead and difficulty tuning the model and its practical adoption will depend on further optimization to reduce computational cost and improve generalization to real-world IIoT networks.

Recently, [1] proposed a new off-policy CRL framework that integrates KANs into the actor-critic architecture of the Soft Actor-Critic (SAC) algorithm. By replacing MLPs with KAN, MulKAN, and SineKAN variants, the study investigated whether KAN's functional decomposition and learnable edge activations could enhance the training in term of time and accuracy in high dimensional control environments. Experiments conducted in the MuJoCo Half-Cheetah environment revealed that, although KAN-based architectures demonstrated comparable expressivity and promising approximation behavior, their performance was unstable across different model depths and neuron counts. This highlights the sensitivity of KAN models to architectural and regularization choices. Additionally, the study noted that KAN models inherently contain more parameters than equivalent MLPs, making them more susceptible to overfitting in stochastic RL settings. Nevertheless, this research established a valuable foundation by systematically integrating and evaluating KANs within an stable off-policy framework (SAC), offering empirical insights into their potential and limitations.

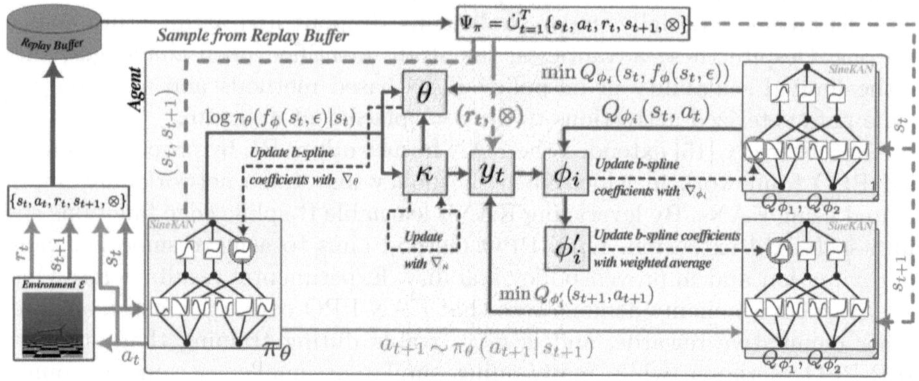

Fig. 1. SineKAN-based SAC Framework with Five SineKAN Networks: One Policy, Two Critic and Two Target Networks.

4 SineKan-Based SAC Approaches

SineKAN is embedded in five components in the SAC algorithm: one actor, two critic and two target networks (cf. Figure 1). Each critic network has a corresponding target network that contributes to and stabilizes the learning process. To ensure architectural consistency across experiments, all the components share an identical configuration: two hidden layers with 128 neurons per layer. We also introduce a minor modification to the internal structure of the original SineKAN by incorporating a residual connection at each hidden layer. We propose two other variants (called SineKAN-v1 and SineKAN-v2).

Although these variants retain the general architecture of the modified SineKAN (with residual links), they differ in terms of learning dynamics, specifically in parameter updating strategies and initialization schemes. In the original SineKAN, the phase parameters are fixed throughout the training. Phase offsets combine two complementary components at initialization, one tied to the grid index and one to the input position. The grid-based component increases with the grid index, ensuring that different frequency channels do not all start in phase with one another. The input-based component is a smoothly spaced progression between zero and π across the input features, guaranteeing that each input dimension begins with a distinct sinusoidal offset. These two pieces are simply added together to form the full phase. Table 1 presents the SAC equations and Table 2 the parameters of the SAC equations.

Table 1. Equations [4] of SAC Algorithm

Target value	$y_t \leftarrow r_t + \gamma(1-\otimes)[\min_{i=1,2} Q_{\phi_i'}(s_{t+1}, a_{t+1})]$
Critic update	$\phi_i \leftarrow \phi_i - \nabla_{\phi_i} \frac{1}{N} \sum_t [Q_{\phi_i}(s_t, a_t) - y_t]^2$
Target update	$\phi_i' \leftarrow \tau\phi_i + (1-\tau)\phi_i'$
Policy update	$\theta \leftarrow \theta - \nabla_\theta \frac{1}{N} \sum_t [\kappa \log \pi_\theta(f_\phi(s_t, \epsilon)\|s_t) - [\min_{i=1,2} Q_{\phi_i}(s_t, f_\phi(s_t, \epsilon))]]$
Entropy update	$\kappa \leftarrow \kappa - \nabla_\kappa \frac{1}{N} \sum_t [-\kappa(\log \pi_\theta(f_\phi(s_t, \epsilon)\|s_t) + H)]$

In our first variant, we replace these fixed phase parameters with learnable ones, by maintaining the same dimensionality. The second variant modifies the representation of amplitude parameters. SineKAN defines these parameters with a total count of $i \times o \times g$, where i, o and g are the input dimension, output dimension, and grid size, respectively. However, our design reduces this count by a factor of g by parameterizing them solely as a tensor of shape $i \times o$.

Table 2. Hyperparameter and Variable Definitions of SineKAN-based SAC Algorithm

HyperParameters	
Target entropy	H (set to number of actions)
Initial entropy coefficient	κ (initialized to 1.0)
Discount factor	γ (set to 0.99)
Update rate	τ (set to 0.005)
Size of replay buffer	N (set to 1,000,000)
Noise distribution	ϵ (standard normal distribution)
Grid size	Number of points in grid mesh (set to 5)
Variables During Training	
SineKAN phase	Fixed (shape = input size times grid size)
SineKAN-v1, SineKAN-v2 phase	Random values (shape = input size times grid size)
SineKAN, SineKAN-v1 amplitude	Random values (shape = product of input, output and grid size)
SineKAN-v2 amplitude	Random values (shape = input size times output size)
State at timestep t	$s_t \in S$
Action at timestep t	$a_t \in A$
Reward function	$r : S \times A \rightarrow \mathbf{R}$
Parameters of policy network π	θ
Parameters of critic network Q_i	$\phi_i \ i \in \{1, 2\}$
Parameters of target network Q_i'	$\phi_i' \ i \in \{1, 2\}$
Trajectory data by policy π	Ψ_π
Parametrization trick	$f_\phi(s_t, \epsilon)$

During computation, these parameters are broadcast across the grid size, ensuring compatibility with the original architecture while reducing the total parameter count by a factor proportional to the grid size. Hence, the core mappings of the modified variations are as follows:

$$H_k = x + \sum_{j=1}^{d}\sum_{l=1}^{L} a_{k,j,l}\sin(\omega_{j,l}x_j + \phi_{j,l}) + b_k, \quad x \in \mathbb{R}^d \rightarrow H \in \mathbb{R}^m$$

where $a_{k,j,l}$, $\omega_{j,l}$ and $\phi_{j,l}$ are learnable amplitudes, frequencies, and phase shifts, respectively. From the perspective of superposition, the identity function $I(x) = x$ itself is a linear mapping whose k-th coordinate is the univariate function $x_k \rightarrow x_k$. Therefore, the residual link simply incorporates an additional univariate component $\phi_k^I()x_k = x_k$. Hence, the overall output remains a finite sum of univariate functions of individual coordinates defined as:

$$\begin{aligned} H_k(x) &= x_k + \sum_{j,l} a_{k,j,l}\sin(\omega_{j,l}x_j + \phi_{j,l}) + b_k \\ &= \underbrace{x_k}_{\text{identity}} + \sum_{j=1}^{d}\underbrace{(\sum_{\ell=1}^{L} a_{k,j,\ell}\sin(\omega_{j,\ell}(\cdot) + \phi_{j,\ell}))(x_j)}_{\text{univariate in } x_j} + b_k \end{aligned}$$

Since the Kolmogorov–Arnold theorem only prescribes that arbitrary continuous multivariate maps can be represented via sums of univariate functions, the presence of an identity (residual) term does not violate or contradict the theorem.

Table 3. Comparison of number of learnable parameters of SineKAN-based SAC

CRL Task	SineKAN	SineKAN-v1 (ours)	SineKAN-v2 (ours)
HalfCheetah	288,684	290,919	63,414
Hopper	272,550	274,665	59,376
Pusher	301,742	304,077	66,392
Swimmer	265,252	267,312	57,622

5 Experiment Setup

All experiments are implemented in Python using the JAX framework for training deep learning models. The implementation of the SAC algorithm is based on the Stable-Baselines3 [10] library, as it adheres closely to standardized practices and aligns well with original research papers and reference implementations. We used robotic control tasks (HalfCheetah, Hopper, Swimmer and Hopper) provided by the Gymnasium library [13], with simulations executed using the MuJoCo physics engine [12]. The most recent versions of each environment are used to ensure consistency with current benchmarks. We utilize the average episodic return as the main metric.

To reduce the effect of randomness from the network initiation mechanism (weight and bias initialization) and the stochastic nature of the SAC algorithm (noisy actions), each experiment ran with five different random seeds. The results of these five independent runs were then averaged to improve their stability. Each experiment ran for one million environment steps, with evaluation occurring after every 10,000 steps. For evaluation, we used the average results of five episodes, each limited to 1,000 steps (the episodes were truncated after 1,000 steps). The integration of SineKAN models introduces additional hyperparameters beyond those employed in the standard SAC framework. To facilitate a fair and consistent comparison of all the experiments, a fixed set of hyperparameters is utilized across all experimental conditions.

Specifically, policy and value networks were trained for 1×10^6 iterations using an initial learning rate of $\alpha_0 = 1 \times 10^{-3}$. We used a large replay-batch size of 2048 transitions to stabilize gradient estimates and improve sample efficiency. The discount factor set to $\gamma = 0.99$ and the clipped objective employed a clipping factor of $\epsilon = 0.2$ to constrain policy updates. Regarding the SineKAN models, the grid size is set to $g = 5$ for all variations. All SineKan networks are trained using the AdamW optimizer [9]. To maintain stable training and facilitate effective convergence, we employ an exponential learning rate schedule [6], defined as: $\alpha(t) = \alpha_0 \exp(-\delta t)$ where α_0 denotes the initial learning rate and δ the decay rate coefficient.

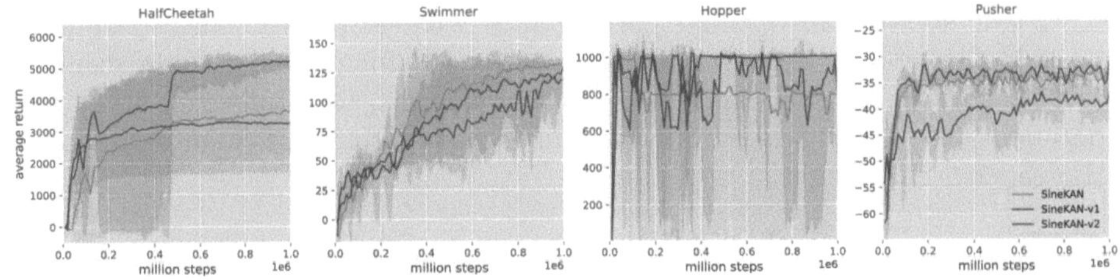

Fig. 2. Performance of three SineKAN-based SAC models across four CRLs. The curves are mean Return over five runs with distinct random seeds; the shaded areas are complete range of Returns observed across trials.

6 Validation

6.1 Learnable Parameters

Notable distinctions arise when considering parameter efficiency of the three SAC models, SineKAN and the two variants, using four CRL environments (HalfCheetah, Swimmer, Hopper and Pusher). Regarding the number of learnable parameters (cf. Table 3), the first variant has a slightly higher number compared to the original SineKAN. The second variant reduces the number of parameters to less than a quarter of the baseline.

6.2 Performance Evaluation

In Fig. 2, in general, all models achieved comparable results. In the Swimmer (a low-dimensional control task), the performance differences among the three models are marginal.

SineKAN slightly outperforms both variants, while the second variant achieves nearly identical results despite its substantially reduced parameters, highlighting its efficiency. In the Hopper (a single-legged hopping task), both variants initially score within the top 1000. However, the performance of the first variant decreased after this point, potentially reflecting overfitting, while the base SineKAN oscillates around a moderate score (~ 800). The second variant, in contrast, maintains consistent results while using significantly fewer parameters. In the more challenging HalfCheetah task (a higher-dimensional locomotion problem), the first variant achieves the highest absolute score. The base SineKAN and the second variant demonstrate comparable performance. The performance of the second variant was somewhat inferior in the Pusher environment (a control task with distance-based objectives and penalties), where SineKAN and the first variant yielded closely matched results, and the second variant trailed by a small margin. Compared to the evaluated environments, the cumulative reward in Pusher is composed of three non-positive terms, which inherently produce negative total returns. This reward structure may amplify small performance differences, explaining why the parameter-efficient second variant falls slightly behind despite its overall effectiveness in other settings. In particular, the second variant shows near-optimal performance with a much smaller parameter footprint. These observations underscore the need for a deeper understanding of the learning process in SineKAN. To address this, we conducted additional experiments to investigate the performance and stability of SineKAN models with deeper architectures.

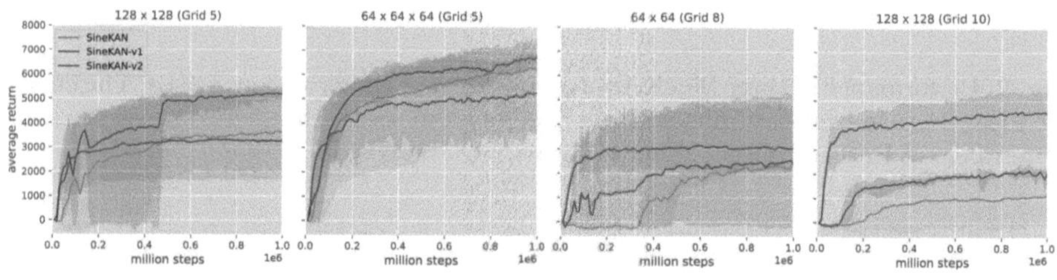

Fig. 3. Performance of three SineKan-based SAC methods by Varying Network Configurations for HalfCheeta Environment.

6.3 Impact of Deeper Architectures

Considering that the original paper claimed that a deeper SineKAN model is more capable than the KAN and MultKAN models, our study set up deeper configurations with fewer learnable parameters.

Figure 3 presents the ablation results of SineKAN models in the HalfCheetah environment. The left figure shows models with two hidden layers of 128 neurons and a coarse grid, the middle corresponds to models with three hidden layers of 64 neurons using the same grid resolution, and the right panel shows models with two hidden layers of 64 neurons combined with a denser grid. Among these configurations, increasing the network depth to three hidden layers yields superior performance compared to either enlarging the grid resolution or widening the hidden layers. In contrast, models with a larger grid size consistently demonstrate the weakest performance. Furthermore, the experiments reveal that introducing residual connections within each layer markedly enhances the trainability of deeper architectures. These skip connections enable deeper networks to outperform shallower ones, even with fewer neurons per layer, highlighting that depth with residual links is a more effective strategy than simply increasing layer width. Table 4 shows the number of parameters and the grid size of each model.

Table 4. Number of learnable parameters by Varying Configurations

Architecture	SineKAN	SineKAN-v1 (ours)	SineKAN-v2 (ours)
128×128 (Grid 5)	288,684	290,919	63,414
64×64 (Grid 8)	131,902	133,942	19,702
128×128 (Grid 10)	574,794	579,264	64,320
$64 \times 64 \times 64$ (Grid 5)	144,571	146,806	32,374

6.4 Discussion

Previous studies [7,8] have shown that architectures with larger grid sizes can achieve better approximation accuracy. However, our empirical results reveal that increasing the density of the grid can degrade performance. We hypothesize that summing highly complex curvature components introduces additional optimization challenges. The outcomes of the second variation will confirm our hypothesis that the fewer shared learnable parameters (less than one-quarter) help form simpler curvatures compared to other variations, resulting in better outcomes. Moreover, earlier KAN experiments predominantly used synthetic data or controlled models to generate datasets, with the original SineKAN evaluation was largely limited to the MNIST dataset. In contrast, our study explores dynamic RL environments, which introduce distinct inductive biases and optimization challenges. Overall, the experimental results indicate that incorporating a residual connection in each layer of the SineKAN architecture significantly improves the trainability of deeper models. Specifically, these skip links allow architectures with greater depth to outperform shallower counterparts, even when configured with fewer neurons per layer. This observation underscores the efficiency of increasing depth with residual connections rather than simply enlarging the layer width.

It is also noteworthy that existing training and optimization techniques were designed with traditional MLP architectures in mind, which are characterized by simple fixed activation functions. In this context, KAN architectures with relatively shallow grids and greater depth (i.e., more layers) resemble standard MLP structures, aligning more effectively with established optimization.

7 Conclusions

We focused on SineKAN models, which provide better computational efficiency and a smaller model size compared to KANs and MultKANs. We developed three SineKAN-based SAC methods and evaluated their performance and the number of learnable parameters in four CRL tasks. All evaluated SineKAN variants performed well, with our second variant surpassing its counterparts in terms of efficiency, using fewer than a quarter of trainable parameters. This finding suggests that simply enlarging the grid, as is commonly done in previous studies, may not always lead to improved accuracy. Additional neurons may not always contribute significantly or may introduce challenges during training. To further investigate these mechanisms, we conducted an extensive ablation study in which we varied the number of parameters, network depth and grid density. Our study revealed that increasing grid density can actually impair performance. In contrast, deeper networks with a reduced number of parameters consistently achieved superior results.

References

1. Bayeh, A., Mouhoub, M., Sadaoui, S.: Enhancing off-policy method SAC with KAN for continuous reinforcement learning. In: Proceedings of International Conference on Deep Learning Theory and Applications, DeLTA (2025)
2. Bayeh, A., Mouhoub, M., Sadaoui, S.: KAN-based on-policy PPO method for continuous reinforcement learning. In: Proceedings of International Conference in Optimization and Learning (OLA) (2025)
3. Guo, H., Li, F., Li, J., Liu, H.: KAN vs. MLP for offline reinforcement learning. In: ICASSP 2025 - 2025 IEEE International Conference on Acoustics, Speech and Signal Processing (ICASSP), pp. 1–5 (2025). https://doi.org/10.1109/ICASSP49660.2025.10888327
4. Haarnoja, T., Zhou, A., Abbeel, P., Levine, S.: Soft actor-critic: off-policy maximum entropy deep reinforcement learning with a stochastic actor. In: Dy, J., Krause, A. (eds.) Proceedings of the 35th International Conference on Machine Learning. Proceedings of Machine Learning Research, vol. 80, pp. 1861–1870. PMLR (10–15 July 2018)
5. Kich, V.A., et al.: Kolmogorov-Arnold networks for online reinforcement learning. In: 2024 24th International Conference on Control, Automation and Systems (ICCAS), pp. 958–963. IEEE (2024)

6. Li, Z., Arora, S.: An exponential learning rate schedule for deep learning. In: 8th International Conference on Learning Representations, ICLR 2020, Addis Ababa, Ethiopia, 26–30 Apr 2020. OpenReview.net (2020)
7. Liu, Z., Ma, P., Wang, Y., Matusik, W., Tegmark, M.: Kan 2.0: Kolmogorov-Arnold Networks Meet Science. arXiv preprint arXiv:2408.10205 (2024)
8. Liu, Z., et al.: KAN: Kolmogorov-Arnold Networks. In: Proceedings of the International Conference on Learning Representations (ICLR) (2025). https://proceedings.iclr.cc/paper_files/paper/2025/hash/afaed89642ea100935e39d39a4da602c-Abstract-Conference.html, iCLR 2025 (oral)
9. Loshchilov, I., Hutter, F.: Decoupled weight decay regularization. In: 7th International Conference on Learning Representations, ICLR 2019, New Orleans, LA, USA, May 6-9, 2019. OpenReview.net (2019)
10. Raffin, A., et al.: Stable-baselines3: reliable reinforcement learning implementations. J. Mach. Learn. Res. **22**(268), 1–8 (2021)
11. Reinhardt, E., Ramakrishnan, D., Gleyzer, S.: SineKAN: Kolmogorov-Arnold Networks using sinusoidal activation functions. Front. Artif. Intell. **7**, 1462952 (2025)
12. Todorov, E., Erez, T., Tassa, Y.: Mujoco: A physics engine for model-based control. In: 2012 IEEE/RSJ International Conference on Intelligent Robots and Systems. IEEE (2012)
13. Towers, M., et al.: Gymnasium: a standard interface for reinforcement learning environments (2024)
14. Wu, J., Du, R., Wang, Z.: Deep reinforcement learning with dual-q and kolmogorov–arnold networks for computation offloading in industrial iot. Comput. Netw. **257**, 110987 (2025). https://doi.org/10.1016/j.comnet.2024.110987, https://www.sciencedirect.com/science/article/pii/S1389128624008193
15. Xiao, R., et al.: KAN-PPO: A fast convergence and stable proximal policy optimization powered by Kolmogorov-Arnold Network. In: Gao, H., Wang, X. (eds.) Collaborative Computing: Networking, Applications and Worksharing, pp. 183–200. Springer Nature Switzerland, Cham (2025)

LSTM-Based Stock Index Forecasting with Signal Decomposition and Functional Principal Component Analysis

Tsung-Jui Chiang Lin[1], Yong-Shiuan Lee[2(✉)], and Yung-Hung Wang[3]

[1] Ph.D. Program of Mechanical and Aeronautical Engineering, Feng Chia University, Taichung City, Taiwan (R.O.C.)
P1300413@o365.fcu.edu.tw

[2] Department of Applied Mathematics, Feng Chia University, Taichung City, Taiwan (R.O.C.)
yongslee@fcu.edu.tw

[3] Department of Mechanical Engineering, National Central University, Taoyuan City, Taiwan (R.O.C.)
yunghung@ncu.edu.tw

Abstract. Stock market prediction remains one of the most challenging areas in economics due to the inherent nonstationarity, high volatility, and nonlinear dynamics of financial time series. This study improves deep learning-based forecasts by employing two preprocessing approaches. The first is to decompose index prices into frequency-specific components using ensemble empirical mode decomposition and uniform phase empirical mode decomposition. The other is to apply functional principal component analysis to prices and technical indicators. The extracted features could reduce redundancy and improve learning efficiency. Empirical analysis of the Dow Jones, Russell 2000, and S&P 500 indices shows that model performance varies across markets. FPCA-LSTM achieves optimal accuracy for the S&P 500 and Russell 2000, although UPEMD-LSTM shows competitive performance in Russell 2000. In contrast, TA-LSTM yields the best results for the Dow Jones, with FPCA-LSTM ranking as the second-best model. Moreover, FPCA-LSTM maintains the most stable predictive accuracy across all indices. The findings demonstrate that advanced feature preprocessing techniques can significantly improve predictive performance and provide guidance on selecting suitable models for different market segments.

Keywords: Ensemble empirical mode decomposition · Uniform phase empirical mode decomposition · Functional principal component analysis · Long short-term memory networks · Stock index forecasting

1 Introduction

Stock market prediction stands as one of the most challenging research domains in economics due to its inherent nonstationarity, high volatility, and nonlinear

C. Xu (Ed.): ICMLSC 2026, CCIS 2948, pp. 46–57, 2027.
https://doi.org/10.1007/978-981-92-1546-1_4

dynamics. These characteristics challenge traditional economic frameworks to accurately model future index movements. Conventional statistical approaches, particularly time series models, typically tackle non-stationarity through first differencing or log-return transformations [8,13]. However, the inherent characteristics of stock indices, notably volatility clustering and nonnormal distributions with skewness and heavy tails, significantly compromise the precision of conventional analytical approaches.

Stock indices exhibit notable serial correlation that persists despite differencing procedures or return transformations, indicating long-memory behavior characterized by slowly decaying autocorrelations, particularly in volatility processes. This persistence introduces systematic bias in the estimation of the coefficients of the time series model, further limiting the predictive accuracy.

Based on the characteristics of the stock indices stated previously, this study employs two methodological approaches for index price preprocessing. The first approach involves decomposing index prices into frequency-specific components, while the second implements the functional principal component analysis (FPCA) [21,25,32] on index prices along with technical indicators.

The decomposition methodology utilizes the ensemble empirical mode decomposition (EEMD) [15,29,30] and the uniform phase empirical mode decomposition (UPEMD) to extract intrinsic mode functions (IMFs) across distinct frequency domains. Both EEMD and UPEMD demonstrate robust analytical performance for datasets exhibiting nonlinear and non-stationary characteristics. The extracted IMFs serve as highly informative input features for deep learning architectures owing to their "almost orthogonal" properties, which effectively minimize feature redundancy and enhance computational learning efficiency.

Alternatively, functional data analysis (FDA) encompasses datasets characterized as continuous curves or surfaces that exhibit variation across continuous domains, including temporal, spatial, or spectral dimensions. Although empirical observations are necessarily discrete, the underlying assumption asserts continuous smooth variation across the functional domain. Consequently, functional data inherently possess infinite-dimensional structural properties [17,21]. Functional principal component analysis (FPCA) represents a fundamental analytical framework to investigate variational patterns within functional datasets.

Stock price indices represent weighted averages of overall market performance. During periods of market inefficiency, technical indicators serve as valuable analytical tools for various capital market participants in examining price dynamics. Consequently, this study incorporates daily open, high, low, and close prices along with 14 technical indicators for stock index analysis. The application of FPCA to these datasets parallels traditional principal component analysis (PCA) in projecting data onto orthogonal basis vectors ranked by explained variance. However, FPCA extends this concept by projecting functional data onto orthogonal basis functions, known as eigenfunctions. This dimensionality reduction enables the use of a limited number of leading eigenfunctions as input features for deep learning architectures. This investigation examines whether such feature preprocessing can effectively enhance both the predictive accuracy and computational efficiency of long short-term memory (LSTM) network models.

We perform empirical analysis in three distinct stock price indices, namely the Dow Jones, Russell 2000, and the S&P 500 indices, providing evidence of model performance variability across different market segments. These preprocessing approaches are designed to facilitate pattern recognition in deep learning models by extracting more meaningful representations from financial time series data. We provide a comprehensive comparative analysis against conventional approaches that utilize raw technical indicators as input features for LSTM models, thereby establishing the efficacy of sophisticated feature preprocessing techniques.

The main contributions of this study are summarized as follows.

- We apply 2 signal decomposition methods (EEMD and UPEMD) and one functional data analysis method (FPCA) to feature engineering to facilitate more effective pattern learning.
- We analyze three distinct stock price indices and show that different models exhibit varying performance across different markets, providing insight for future research.

2 Methodology

We provide a brief introduction to the methods used in this study.

2.1 Ensemble Empirical Mode Decomposition

Empirical Mode Decomposition (EMD) [15] is an algorithm for decomposing nonlinear and non-stationary time series without requiring periodic or shape assumptions (see Algorithm 1). The method recursively extracts intrinsic mode functions (IMFs) from highest to lowest frequency, with the final residue representing the global trend. Combined with Hilbert spectral analysis to form the Hilbert-Huang Transform (HHT), EMD has been widely applied across various disciplines, particularly in signal, image, and speech processing [2,4,23].

Algorithm 1. EMD

1: Find the local extrema of $x(t)$;
2: Generate the upper and lower envelops by the cubic spline;
3: Compute the local mean $m_k(t)$ by averaging the upper and lower envelops;
4: Extract the temporary local oscillation $d_k(t) = x(t) - m_k(t)$;
5: **if** $d_k(t)$ satisfies the stoppage criteria [30] **then**
6:     $d_k(t) = c_m(t)$ is assigned as an IMF;
7: **else**
8:     set $x(t) = d_k(t)$ and repeat (1)-(4) for $k = k + 1$;
9: **end if**
10: Compute the residue $r_m(t) = x(t) - c_m(t)$;
11: Set $x(t) = r_m(t)$ and repeat (1)-(10) to obtain the next IMF.

Although EMD has been extensively applied, it suffers from mode-mixing problems when analyzing intermittent signals [14,15]. Ensemble empirical mode decomposition (EEMD) mitigates this limitation by incorporating Gaussian white noise, which provides a uniform reference scale distribution and enhances decomposition quality [30]. The EEMD algorithm is detailed below (see Algorithm 2).

Algorithm 2. EEMD

1: Add a white noise series to the original time series $z_i(t) = x(t) + \theta \cdot sd(x(t)) \cdot \epsilon_i(t),\ \ i = 1, 2, \cdots, N$, where sd is the standard deviation and N is the number of ensemble;
2: For $z_i(t)$, obtain the J intrinsic mode functions $\text{IMF}_{ij}(t)$, $j = 1, \cdots, J$ for the ith iteration by Algorithm 1;
3: After N iterations, compute the mean IMFs and assign them as IMFs by EEMD: $\text{IMF}_j = \frac{1}{N}\sum_{i=1}^{N} \text{IMF}_{ij}(t)$.

2.2 Uniform Phase Empirical Mode Decomposition

Despite the widespread application of EEMD, its implementation produces side effects, including mode splitting and residual noise. Various corrective methods have been proposed, such as complementary EEMD (CEEMD) [24], improved CEEMD (ICEEMD) [7], and uniform phase EMD (UPEMD) [28]. UPEMD is a noise-assisted decomposition method using disturbance waves, which is detailed in Algorithm 3 as follows.

Algorithm 3. UPEMD

1: Assign n_p, set $n_{imf} = log_2(n)$ and initial residue as $r_0(t) = x(t)$;
2: Set disturbance amplitude $\epsilon_m = \epsilon_0 \cdot std(r_{m-1}(t))$ and period $(P_w)_m = 2^m$;
3: Calculate the perturbed signal $y_{k,m}(t)$ by

$$y_{k,m}(t) = x(t) + \epsilon_m \cdot cos\left(2\pi\left(f_w t + \frac{k-1}{n_p}\right)\right) \tag{1}$$

;

4: Perform the EMD to obtain the two IMFs, the first one of which is

$$c_{k,m}(t) = E_m(x(t) + w(t;\theta_k)), \tag{2}$$

where $E_m(\cdot)$ is the operator to obtain the mth IMF by performing the EMD, and the other is the residue;

5: Repeat (3)-(4) for $k = 1$ to n_p to obtain the IMF $c_m(t) = \frac{1}{n_p}\sum_{k=1}^{n_p} c_{k,m}(t)$;
6: Obtain the residue $r_m(t) = r_{m-1}(t) - c_m(t)$
7: Repeat (2)-(6) for $m = 1$ to n_{imf} to extract all IMFs.

2.3 Functional Principal Component Analysis

The functional data represent discrete realizations $x_i(s), i = 1, 2, \ldots, N$ from an underlying stochastic process $X : T \to \mathbb{R}$ over domain T, where X lies in the Hilbert space $L^2(T)$ [25]. The Karhunen-Loève theorem [16, 19] expands the random process as:

$$X(s) = \mu(s) + \sum_{k=1}^{\infty} A_k \phi_k(s), \tag{3}$$

where $\phi_k(s)$ are orthogonal eigenfunctions with eigenvalues λ_k representing the variance of X in direction ϕ_k, and A_k are functional principal component scores with properties $E(A_k) = 0$, $E(A_k^2) = \lambda_k$, and $Cov(A_k, A_j) = 0$ for $k \neq j$.

Since eigenvalues decrease rapidly, the first few components capture most variability, allowing approximation using only the leading m terms:

$$x_i(s) \approx \mu(s) + \sum_{k=1}^{m} A_{ik} \phi_k(s), \quad i = 1, \ldots, N. \tag{4}$$

In practice, functional principal components require estimation from observations. This study employs the principal component analysis through conditional expectation (PACE) method for estimation [32].

2.4 Long Short-Term Memory Networks

Recurrent Neural Networks (RNNs) are designed to process sequential data by maintaining hidden states in time steps [9]. However, standard RNNs suffer from vanishing gradient problems in long sequences. Long short-term memory (LSTM) networks [12] tackles this limitation through gated memory mechanisms, employing input, forget, and output gates to control information flow:

$$i_t = \sigma(W_{xi} x_t + W_{hi} h_{t-1} + W_{ci} c_{t-1} + b_i), \tag{5}$$
$$f_t = \sigma(W_{xf} x_t + W_{hf} h_{t-1} + W_{cf} c_{t-1} + b_f), \tag{6}$$
$$c_t = f_t c_{t-1} + i_t \tanh(W_{xc} x_t + W_{hc} h_{t-1} + b_c), \tag{7}$$
$$o_t = \sigma(W_{xo} x_t + W_{ho} h_{t-1} + W_{co} c_t + b_o), \tag{8}$$
$$h_t = o_t \tanh(c_t), \tag{9}$$

where i_t, f_t, and o_t control which information to input, forget, and output, respectively.

Recent advances in theoretical development and computational capabilities have enabled the widespread application of various artificial neural network

(ANN) architectures, such as LSTM, to financial time series forecasting, particularly in stock price prediction [3,5,6,10,18,22,26,27,31]. Empirical results show that deep learning models have more promising predictability than statistical linear models in terms of prediction of directional symmetry [33,34] or forecast precision [1,11,20].

3 Empirical Data and Results

This study collects daily trading data for three major stock indices, including the Dow Jones Industrial Average (DJI), Russell 2000 (RUT), and the S&P 500, spanning from January 1, 2008, to December 31, 2024. The raw datas et comprises daily open, high, low, and close (OHLC) prices for each index. In addition, we computed 14 technical indicators from these price data to augment the feature set for model training and evaluation.

The 14 technical indicators include simple and exponential moving averages of 5 and 20-days (SMA5, SMA20, EMA5, EMA20), the moving average convergence divergence (MACD), relative strength index (RSI), Williams %R, stochastic oscillator components (%K, %D, %J), commodity channel index (CCI), rate of change (ROC), accumulation/distribution (AD), and Rogers-Satchell volatility. This study employs a 90%-10% data split ratio to partition the data set into training and testing sets.

As a representative example, Fig. 1) and Fig. 2) display the original Dow Jones data (shown in the top row) along with the intrinsic mode functions (IMFs) decomposed using the EEMD and UPEMD methods, respectively, with frequency components arranged from highest to lowest in descending order.

Before implementing FPCA, all daily price data and technical indicators are standardized using Z-score normalization to enhance analytical performance and ensure optimal decomposition results. For brevity, Fig. 3) shows the FPCA analysis results for the Dow Jones Index as a representative example.

Table 1. Model Performance Comparison Based on Mean Absolute Percentage Error (MAPE, %)

	TA-LSTM	FPCA-LSTM	EEMD-LSTM	UPEMD-LSTM
Dow Jones	**3.5956**	5.8720	7.4701	6.7737
Russell 2000	1.6957	**0.8929**	6.3162	**0.8970**
S&P 500	5.7678	**5.6442**	13.7224	7.0678

Note: Bold font indicates the model with the lowest error.

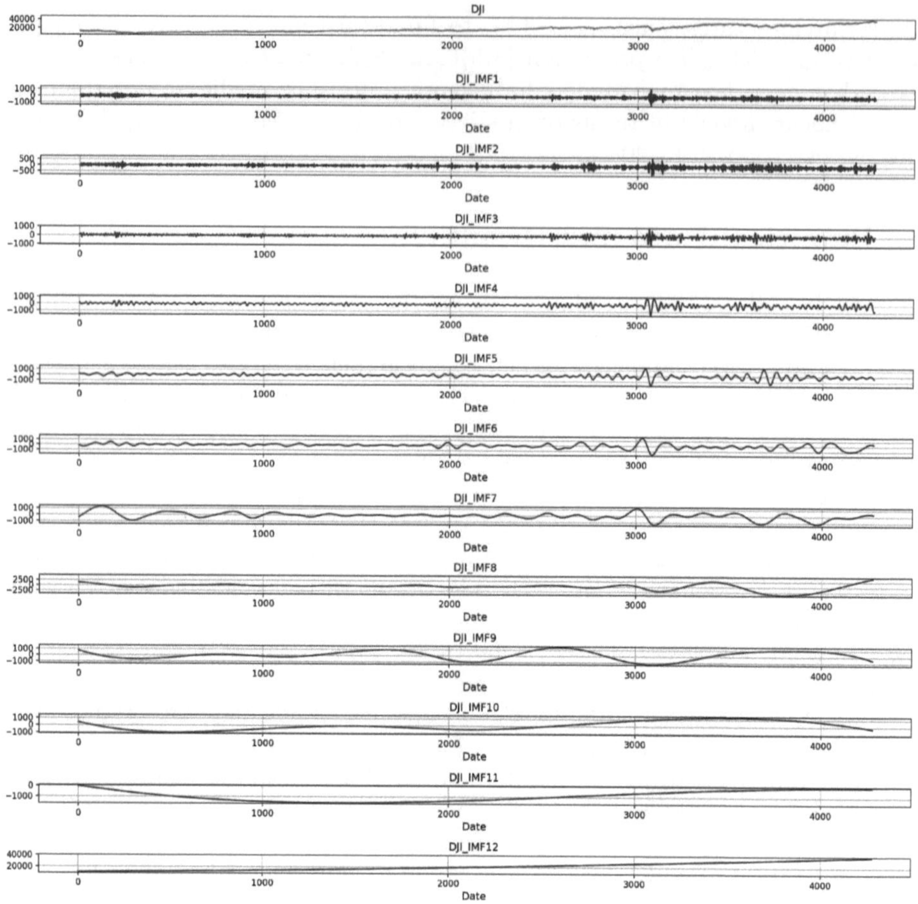

Fig. 1. IMFs of Dow Jones Index from EEMD.

The benchmark model, TA-LSTM, employs daily closing prices and 14 technical indicators as input features to forecast the three stock indices. Additionally, we utilize the intrinsic mode functions (IMFs) decomposed from daily closing prices through EEMD and UPEMD methods, as well as the eigenfunctions derived from applying FPCA to daily OHLC prices and technical indicators, as alternative input variables for the same LSTM architecture. In this study,

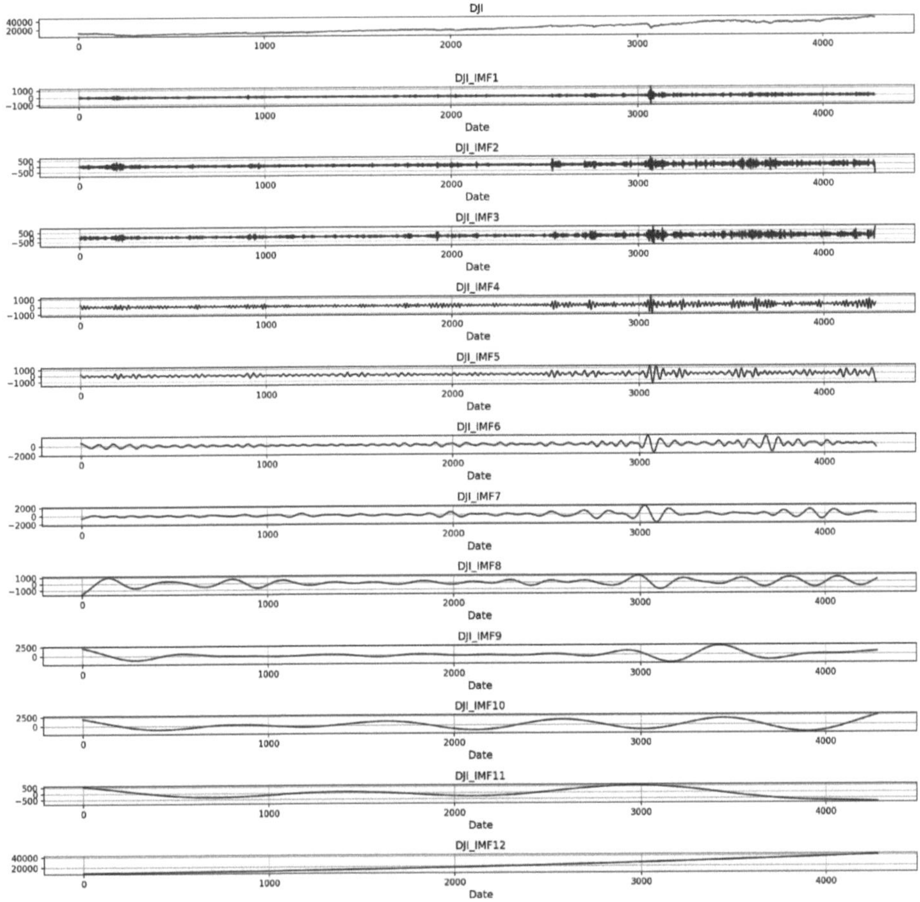

Fig. 2. IMFs of Dow Jones Index from UPEMD.

we designate the three proposed models as EEMD-LSTM, UPEMD-LSTM, and FPCA-LSTM. The forecast results for the testing set are summarized in Table 1. Figure 4), Fig. 5), and Fig. 6) respectively illustrate the comparison plots of the predicted values obtained from four different models against the original market prices.

From the above results, it is observed that EEMD-LSTM consistently yields the poorest predictive performance across all datasets. For different datasets, the models exhibit varying strengths. TA-LSTM performs best on the Dow Jones

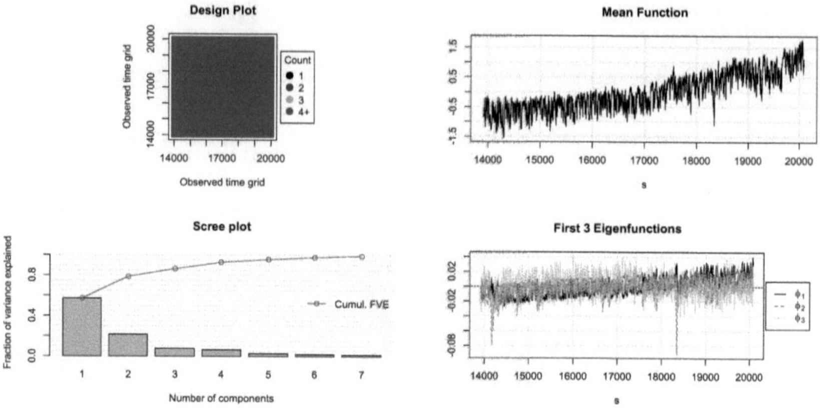

Fig. 3. FPCA Results for the Dow Jones Index.

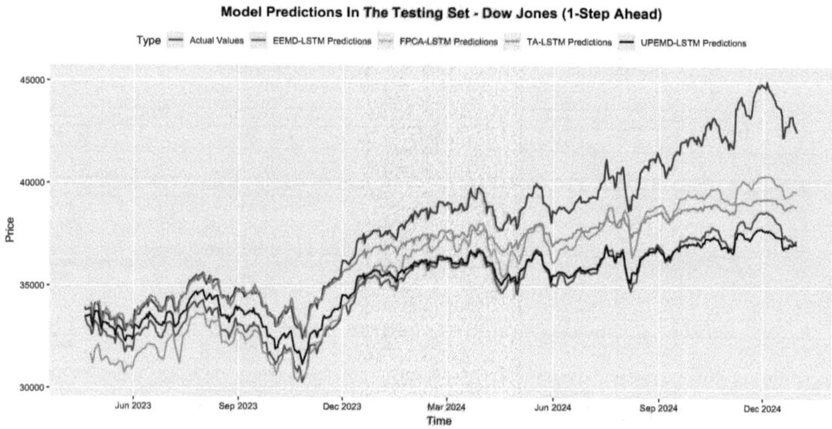

Fig. 4. Forecasting Results for the Dow Jones Index: Model Predictions vs. Actual Values.

index, FPCA-LSTM demonstrates the best results on the Russell 2000 and the S&P 500. In Russell 2000, UPEMD-LSTM achieves a performance marginally inferior to FPCA-LSTM while surpassing all remaining methods in predictive accuracy. Among the three datasets, FPCA-LSTM shows the most stable performance, whereas the predictive outcomes of the other three methods vary more substantially.

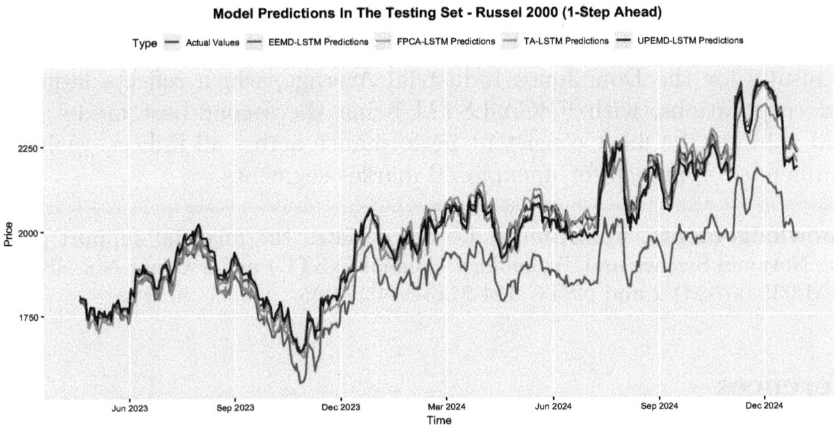

Fig. 5. Forecasting Results for the Russell 2000 Index: Model Predictions vs. Actual Values.

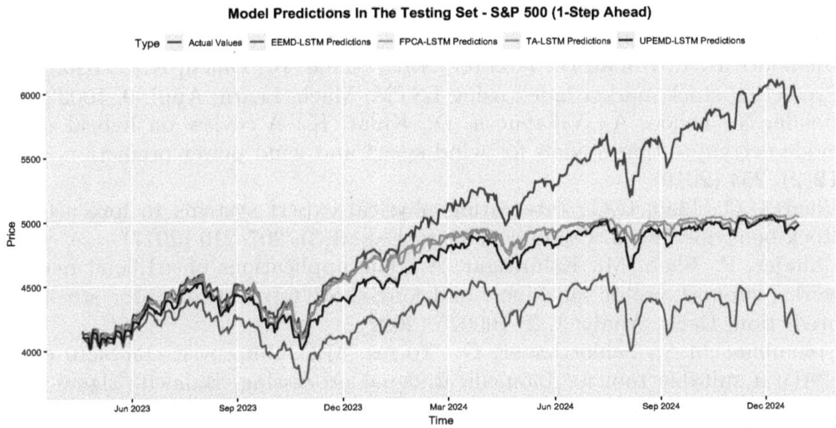

Fig. 6. Forecasting Results for the S&P 500 Index: Model Predictions vs. Actual Values.

4 Conclusion

This study investigates three feature engineering techniques designed to improve the predictive performance of LSTM architectures. Rather than directly feeding raw price data and technical indicators into the model, we employ advanced preprocessing methods to extract more informative features. We evaluate these methods on three major US stock indices and compare their performance against a benchmark model. The results reveal market-specific performance patterns. FPCA-LSTM achieves optimal accuracy for the S&P 500, which represents a broad spectrum of large-cap US companies, and demonstrates superior performance in the Russell 2000, primarily comprising small and medium enterprises.

For Russell 2000, UPEMD-LSTM ranks second, performing marginally below FPCA-LSTM yet surpassing other methods. In contrast, TA-LSTM delivers the best results for the Dow Jones Industrial Average, which reflects large established corporations, with FPCA-LSTM being the second-best model. FPCA-LSTM exhibits the most consistent performance across all indices, making it a recommended approach for unexplored market segments.

Acknowledgements. Yong-Shiuan Lee appreciates the financial support provided by the National Science and Technology Council (NSTC) under Grant No. NSTC 112-2115-M-035-007-MY2 and NSTC 114-2115-M-035-005.

References

1. Banik, S., Sharma, N., Mangla, M., Mohanty, S.N., Shitharth, S.: LSTM based decision support system for swing trading in stock market. Knowl.-Based Syst. **239**, 107994 (2022)
2. Barbosh, M., Singh, P., Sadhu, A.: Empirical mode decomposition and its variants: a review with applications in structural health monitoring. Smart Mater. Struct. **29**(9), 093001 (2020)
3. Bhandari, H.N., Rimal, B., Pokhrel, N.R., Rimal, R., Dahal, K.R., Khatri, R.K.: Predicting stock market index using LSTM. Mach. Learn. Appl. **9**, 100320 (2022)
4. Bokde, N., Feijóo, A., Villanueva, D., Kulat, K.: A review on hybrid empirical mode decomposition models for wind speed and wind power prediction. Energies **12**(2), 254 (2019)
5. Chen, C.C., Liao, C.C.: Integrating physical expert systems to forecast Taiwan stock behavior. Int. J. Comput. Theory Eng. **9**(3), 207–210 (2017)
6. Chhajer, P., Shah, M., Kshirsagar, A.: The applications of artificial neural networks, support vector machines, and long-short term memory for stock market prediction. Decis. Analy. J. **2**, 100015 (2022)
7. Colominas, M.A., Schlotthauer, G., Torres, M.E.: Improved complete ensemble EMD: a suitable tool for biomedical signal processing. Biomed. Signal Process. Control **14**, 19–29 (2014)
8. Cryer, J.D., Chan, K.S.: Time series analysis with applications in R. Spinger (2008)
9. Deng, L., Yu, D.: Deep learning: methods and applications. Found. Trends Signal Process. **7**(3–4), 197–387 (2014)
10. Ghosh, P., Neufeld, A., Sahoo, J.K.: Forecasting directional movements of stock prices for intraday trading using LSTM and random forests. Financ. Res. Lett. **46**, 102280 (2022)
11. Hiransha, M., Gopalakrishnan, E.A., Menon, V.K., Soman, K.: NSE stock market prediction using deep-learning models. Proc. Comput. Sci. **132**, 1351–1362 (2018)
12. Hochreiter, S., Schmidhuber, J.: Long short-term memory. Neural Comput. **9**(8), 1735–1780 (1997)
13. Huang, C., Petukhina, A.: Applied time series analysis and forecasting with python, Springer (2022)
14. Huang, N.E., Shen, Z., Long, S.R.: A new view of nonlinear water waves: the hilbert spectrum. Annu. Rev. Fluid Mech. **31**(1), 417–457 (1999)
15. Huang, N.E., et al.: The empirical mode decomposition and the hilbert spectrum for nonlinear and non-stationary time series analysis. Proc. Royal Soc. London. Series Math. Phys. Eng. Sci. **454**(1971), 903–995 (1998)

16. Karhunen, K.: Über lineare methoden in der wahrscheinlichkeitsrechnung. annales academiae scientiarum fennicae. Ser. Math. Phys. **37**, 1–79 (1947)
17. Kokoszka, P., Reimherr, M.: Introduction to functional data analysis, chapman and hall/CRC (2017). https://doi.org/10.1201/9781315117416
18. Lin, Y., Lin, Z., Liao, Y., Li, Y., Xu, J., Yan, Y.: Forecasting the realized volatility of stock price index: a hybrid model integrating CEEMDAN and LSTM. Expert Syst. Appl., 117736 (2022)
19. Loève, M.: Fonctions aléatoires à décomposition orthogonale exponentielle. La Revue Scientifique **84**, 159–162 (1946)
20. Rajakumari, K.E., Kalyan, M.S., Bhaskar, M.V.: Forward forecast of stock price using LSTM machine learning algorithm. Int. J. Comput. Theory Eng. **12**(3), 74–79 (2020)
21. Ramsay, J., Silverman, B.W.: Functional data analysis, 2nd edn. Springer, New York (2005)
22. Rezaei, H., Faaljou, H., Mansourfar, G.: Stock price prediction using deep learning and frequency decomposition. Expert Syst. Appl. **169**, 114332 (2021)
23. Sharma, R., Vignolo, L., Schlotthauer, G., Colominas, M.A., Rufiner, H.L., Prasanna, S.: Empirical mode decomposition for adaptive AM-FM analysis of speech: a review. Speech Commun. **88**, 39–64 (2017)
24. Torres, M.E., Colominas, M.A., Schlotthauer, G., Flandrin, P.: A complete ensemble empirical mode decomposition with adaptive noise. In: 2011 IEEE International Conference on Acoustics, Speech and Signal Processing (ICASSP), pp. 4144–4147. IEEE (2011)
25. Wang, J.L., Chiou, J.M., Müller, H.G.: Functional data analysis. Ann. Rev. Stat. Appl. **3**, 257–295 (2016)
26. Wang, J., Tang, J., Guo, K.: Green bond index prediction based on CEEMDAN-LSTM. Front. Energy Res. **9**, 793413 (2022)
27. Wang, J., Cui, Q., Sun, X., He, M.: Asian stock markets closing index forecast based on secondary decomposition, multi-factor analysis and attention-based LSTM model. Eng. Appl. Artif. Intell. **113**, 104908 (2022)
28. Wang, Y.H., Hu, K., Lo, M.T.: Uniform phase empirical mode decomposition: an optimal hybridization of masking signal and ensemble approaches. IEEE Access **6**, 34819–34833 (2018)
29. Wang, Y.H., Yeh, C.H., Young, H.W.V., Hu, K., Lo, M.T.: On the computational complexity of the empirical mode decomposition algorithm. XXPhys. A **400**, 159–167 (2014)
30. Wu, Z., Huang, N.E.: Ensemble empirical mode decomposition: a noise-assisted data analysis method. Adv. Adapt. Data Anal. **1**(01), 1–41 (2009)
31. Yan, B., Aasma, M., Zhang, Y.: A novel deep learning framework: prediction and analysis of financial time series using CEEMD and LSTM. Expert Syst. Appl. **159**, 113609 (2020)
32. Yao, F., Müller, H.G., Wang, J.L.: Functional data analysis for sparse longitudinal data. J. Am. Stat. Assoc. **100**(470), 577–590 (2005)
33. Yu, P., Yan, X.: Stock price prediction based on deep neural networks. Neural Comput. Appl. **32**(6), 1609–1628 (2020)
34. Zhang, C., Pan, H.: A novel hybrid model based on EMD-BPNN for forecasting US and UK stock indices. In: 2015 IEEE International Conference on Progress in Informatics and Computing (PIC), pp. 113–117. IEEE (2015)

Sleep Stage Prediction Using Daily Activity Patterns

Sandeep Shandilya Katna and Sayma Akther(✉)

San José State University, San Jose, CA 95192, USA
{sandeepshandilya.katna,sayma.akther}@sjsu.edu

Abstract. Sleep plays a vital role in overall health, yet scalable methods for inferring fine-grained sleep stages outside clinical settings remain limited. While polysomnography (PSG) offers gold-standard labels, its reliance on in-lab monitoring restricts broader applicability. Most wearable-based classifiers focus solely on binary sleep/wake detection and neglect informative daytime activity patterns. In this work, we present a novel pipeline that decomposes 24-hour wrist actigraphy into rolling statistical features spanning morning to evening, leverages TimeGAN to generate realistic synthetic sequences for minority sleep stages. We train and compare multiple ensemble classifiers and linear baselines to evaluate effectiveness. Our approach demonstrates the potential for passive, home-based sleep staging using motion data alone. Future work will expand cohort size, incorporate multimodal sensing, and investigate deep learning architectures for broader generalization.

Keywords: Sleep Stage Prediction · TimeGAN · Actigraphy · Time-Series Classification · Feature Selection · Ensemble Learning

1 Introduction

Sleep is a fundamental biological process essential for cognitive function, emotional regulation, and long-term physical health. Disruptions in sleep patterns, such as insomnia or sleep apnea, are associated with adverse health outcomes and reduced quality of life [16]. Accurate identification of sleep stages Wake, Non-Rapid Eye Movement (NREM) stages (N1, N2, N3), and Rapid Eye Movement (REM) is crucial for diagnosis and treatment of sleep disorders.

Polysomnography (PSG) remains the clinical gold standard for sleep staging, capturing EEG, EOG, EMG, and ECG signals in controlled laboratory environments. However, PSG is expensive, intrusive, and impractical for long-term or at-home monitoring [16]. These limitations underscore the need for scalable, non-invasive alternatives.

Recent advances in wearable technologies, particularly wrist-worn actigraphy devices, offer a promising direction [3]. These devices continuously track movement, enabling passive and convenient data collection. However, most current

C. Xu (Ed.): ICMLSC 2026, CCIS 2948, pp. 58–71, 2027.
https://doi.org/10.1007/978-981-92-1546-1_5

wearable-based sleep classifiers are limited to binary sleep/wake detection [15], offering little insight into the full spectrum of sleep architecture.

In this work, we present a novel pipeline that leverages 24-hour wrist actigraphy to predict granular sleep stages. Our approach involves decomposition of daily activity into rolling statistical features, TimeGAN based synthetic time-series generation to correct class imbalance [23], and reinforcement learning inspired scoring for feature selection. We evaluate our pipeline using data from the MESA cohort, demonstrating the feasibility of passive, at-home sleep stage prediction using motion signals alone.

2 Related Works

Sleep stage classification has traditionally relied on polysomnography (PSG), the clinical gold standard involving EEG, EOG, and EMG signals. However, its cost, intrusiveness, and manual scoring overhead have motivated the development of automated alternatives. Early machine learning efforts applied models like SVM, Decision Trees, KNN, and Random Forests to PSG-derived features, demonstrating reasonable accuracy but relying heavily on expert-driven feature engineering [2,14,18].

The rise of wearable sensors has enabled long-term sleep monitoring outside clinical settings. Actigraphy, a common approach using wrist accelerometers, has been used for binary sleep/wake classification with over 80% accuracy [15]. More recent studies extended this to multi-class sleep staging. For instance, Walch et al. [20] predicted wake, NREM, and REM stages using raw acceleration and PPG data from Apple Watches, achieving 72% accuracy.

With the advent of deep learning, models like CNNs and RNNs (LSTM, Bi-LSTM) have proven effective in capturing complex spatio-temporal patterns in physiological data [11,12,17]. Hybrid CNN-LSTM models further improve performance [17]. Recent work has explored using alternative signals like actigraphy and coarse heart rate for sleep staging. SLAMSS [24] employed a Seq2Seq LSTM model for staging with only actigraphy and heart rate inputs, validated on large cohorts. AccSleepNet [21] used wrist accelerometers and hybrid fusion for five-stage classification.

Recent research has explored activity recognition at the micro-level and quality-based visualization, where significant methodological advances have been made [1,9]. Beyond methodological advances, recent research emphasizes the importance of diversity-aware behavioral modeling and fairness in sleep and activity analytics. Studies have shown that demographic factors such as age, sex, and ethnicity can influence actigraphy patterns and model performance, highlighting the need for bias-aware evaluation frameworks. Additionally, emerging work on cross-platform misinformation and engagement dynamics [4,22] demonstrates how biased data representations can affect behavioral inference in broader passive sensing and computational pipelines. While our study focuses primarily on physiological signals, integrating diversity and misinformation-aware perspectives offers valuable future directions for equitable and generalizable modeling.

A key challenge in sleep staging is class imbalance, where minority stages like N1 and N3 are underrepresented. Generative approaches have emerged to address this:

- TimeGAN [23] combines adversarial and supervised learning to generate temporally coherent synthetic sequences.
- T-CGAN [13] augments irregular time series using conditional GANs.
- IB-GAN [7] jointly addresses imputation and class imbalance.
- Ensemble methods such as Random Forest and XGBoost have also shown high accuracy and robustness in sleep staging tasks [8, 10]

Our work builds on these foundations by leveraging actigraphy-derived features, TimeGAN-based augmentation, and classical/deep classifiers to predict sleep stages from daytime activity.

3 Dataset

We use data from the MESA Sleep Ancillary Study (2010–2013), a sub-study of the Multi-Ethnic Study of Atherosclerosis involving 2,237 participants. It includes synchronized in-home polysomnography (PSG), seven-day wrist actigraphy using Philips Respironics Actiwatch Spectrum devices, and validated sleep questionnaires. Raw PSG signals (EDF) with scored annotations and epoch-level actigraphy (CSV) are publicly available via the National Sleep Research Resource (NSRR) (Fig. 1).

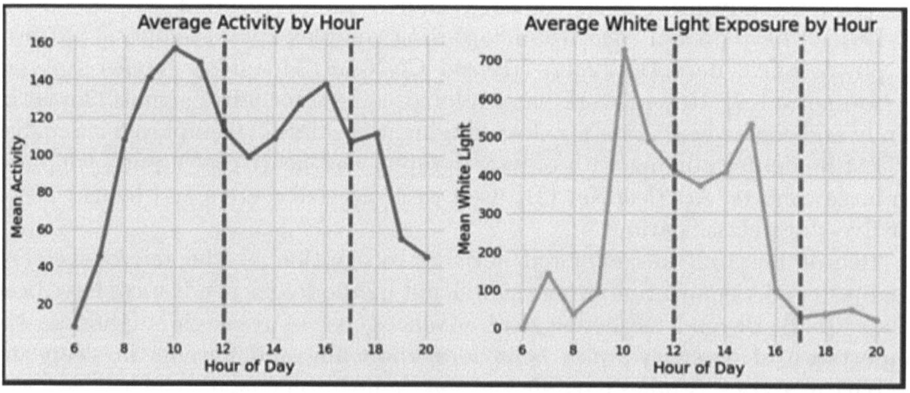

Fig. 1. Activity throughout the day.

Actigraphy provides continuous, non-invasive measurement of activity and ambient light in 30-second epochs. From this, we compute statistical and circadian features (e.g., mean activity, variance, L5/M10, light exposure) using

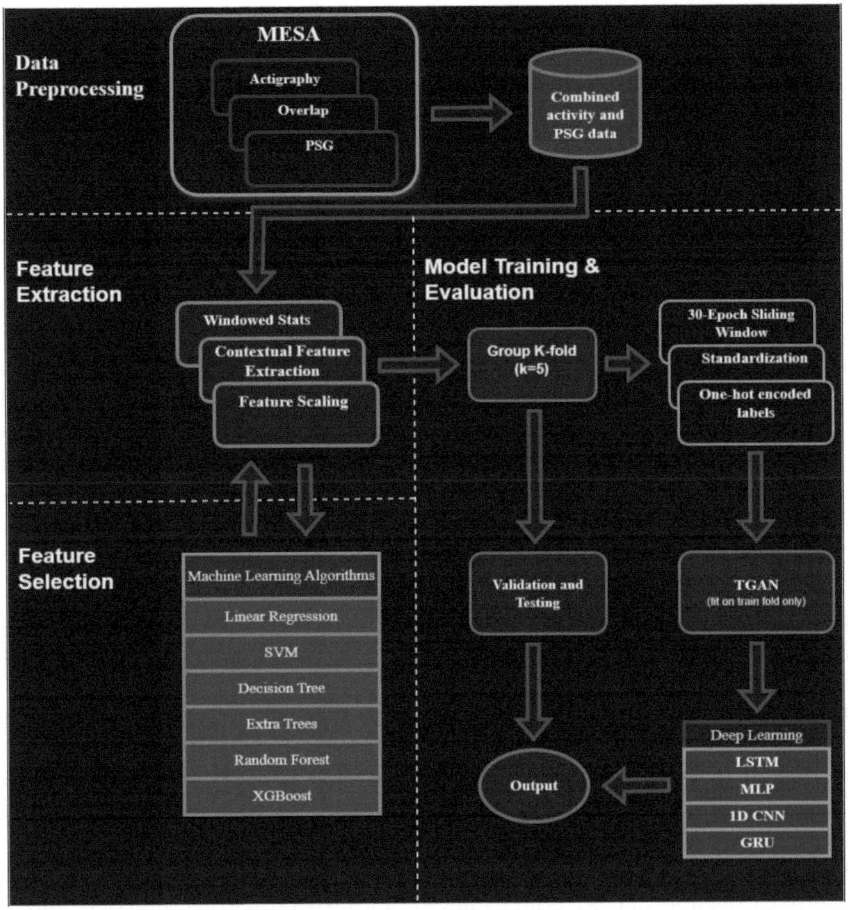

Fig. 2. Pipeline architecture: feature extraction, TimeGAN synthesis, model training.

validated algorithms. PSG serves as the ground truth for five-stage sleep classification (Wake, N1–N3, REM), scored per AASM standards.

In our pipeline, we extract daily features from actigraphy, apply TimeGAN to synthesize underrepresented sleep stages in the reduced feature space, and train sequence-based models on the balanced dataset. While the full MESA cohort is large, only 8 subjects meet our criteria for aligned multiday actigraphy and PSG data, limiting generalizability but enabling proof-of-concept evaluation.

4 Methodology

Our objective is to predict all-night sleep stages (Wake, N1–N3, REM) from 24-hour wrist actigraphy using PSG-labeled training data. The strategy consists of preprocessing accelerometer recordings, rolling-window activity feature extraction, synthetic augmentation with TimeGAN, and traditional and deep learning model training. These features together are linked to PSG labels and subject IDs to create an organized dataset for rigorous training and testing (Fig. 2).

4.1 Data Preparation and Feature Engineering

We align each participant's daytime actigraphy with the corresponding night of PSG-scored sleep using MESA's overlap mappings. Only valid epochs preceding lights-off are retained, and daytime activity (09:00–21:59) is summarized using rolling-window statistics (mean, max, min, standard deviation, skewness, kurtosis, and coefficient of variation). A 60-minute rolling window with a 30-minute step size was applied to capture short-term and long-term movement fluctuations. Light exposure metrics (mean, variance, and maximum illuminance) and circadian rhythm features (L5, M10, Relative Amplitude, Interdaily Stability, and Intradaily Variability) were computed following validated formulations by Van Ṣomeren [19]. These features quantify both local movement intensity and 24-hour rhythmicity.

All numerical features were standardized using z-score normalization. To prevent information leakage, normalization parameters (mean and standard deviation) were computed **only on the training portion of each fold** and then applied to corresponding validation and test folds. Within each fold, standardization was performed **globally across subjects**, not per subject, to maintain cross-participant comparability.

To mitigate redundancy, pairwise Pearson correlations and XGBoost feature-importance scores were analyzed. Highly correlated features ($|r| > 0.9$) were reviewed and merged or excluded, ensuring that model learning was not dominated by a small subset of correlated summaries. The final feature set contained 20 features ranked by importance.

Two datasets are constructed for ablation testing: one with actigraphy-derived features and one without. These standardized feature matrices form the reproducible input for both classical and deep learning pipelines.

4.2 Data Partitioning and Leakage Control

To prevent subject-level information leakage, we employ **Group K-Fold cross-validation** (with K=5 folds) using the participant identifier (`mesaid`) as the grouping key. This ensures that no participant appears in more than one split. Each fold is further divided into an internal 80/20 train–validation subset for model tuning. Hyperparameter optimization and early stopping are performed exclusively within each training fold, and the final performance is reported on the held-out test fold. In addition to the held-out evaluation, we also conducted subject-wise K=5 Group K-Fold cross-validation and report the mean accuracy and mean macro F1 across folds in Table 2.

4.3 Synthetic Data Generation with TimeGAN

To address class imbalance particularly under representation of N1, N3, and REM, we apply TimeGAN [23] to synthesize realistic sequences from minority-class feature windows. **TimeGAN is trained only on the training portion of each fold**, using real data from the corresponding classes. After fitting, synthetic sequences are generated and merged with the training data to produce a balanced dataset for that fold. Validation and test sets remain entirely real, preserving data independence. The TimeGAN architecture includes five RNN-based components: embedder, recovery, generator, supervisor, and discriminator. This structure maintains temporal coherence while generating balanced samples in latent space.

4.4 Model Training and Evaluation

We benchmark both classical and deep models. Baselines include Logistic Regression, Linear SVC, Decision Trees, Random Forest, Extra Trees, and XGBoost. For deep learning, we prepare overlapping windows of 30 epochs from nightly sequences and standardize features using parameters estimated on the training split only. LSTM, GRU, 1D CNN, and MLP architectures are trained with categorical cross-entropy loss, softmax output, and early stopping based on validation loss. The entire pipeline—from feature extraction through TimeGAN synthesis, scaling, and training—occurs within each fold to ensure strict separation between subjects and prevent any cross-participant leakage.

4.5 Cross-Validation and Statistical Reporting

All models were evaluated using **5-fold Group K-Fold cross-validation**, with subject ID (`mesaid`) used as the grouping variable to ensure no participant overlap across folds. For each fold, models were trained and validated on four groups and tested on the remaining group. Reported metrics in Table 1 represent the mean and standard deviation ($\mu \pm \sigma$) across the five folds for test accuracy and macro-averaged F1-score. Per-class precision and recall for minority stages (N1, N3, REM) are included in the supplementary material for traceability.

5 Results

5.1 Evaluation Approach

All models were evaluated using a **5-fold Group K-Fold cross-validation** scheme, where each fold corresponds to a disjoint subset of participants (grouped by `mesaid`). This ensured that no subject appeared in both training and testing sets within a given fold. Each training fold was further divided into an 80/20 split for model tuning and early stopping.

Reported metrics represent the **mean** (μ) **and standard deviation** (σ) of test accuracy, macro-averaged F1, and macro recall across the five folds. Per-class precision and recall, especially for minority stages (N1, N3, and REM), are provided in the supplementary table for traceability.

5.2 Classical Model Results

Among classical models, Random Forest achieved the best performance with activity features, reaching an average accuracy of 81.1±1.2%, macro F1 of 0.701± 0.010, and macro recall of 0.811 ± 0.009 across folds. Extra Trees and XGBoost followed closely with accuracies of 80.3±1.4% and 79.6±1.8%, respectively. The inclusion of daytime activity consistently improved class balance and macro F1 across all models.

Linear models such as Logistic Regression and Linear SVC underperformed, showing macro F1 scores below 0.43 ± 0.02, while Decision Trees achieved moderate stability (72.1 ± 1.5% accuracy). Ensemble-based methods displayed lower fold-to-fold variance, confirming their robustness to small-sample variability.

5.3 Deep Learning Results

Deep learning models exhibited stronger and more stable generalization than classical methods. All models showed improved performance with daytime activity features. The GRU model achieved the best overall results, with a mean accuracy of 91.0 ± 1.0%, macro F1 of 0.911 ± 0.009, and macro recall of 0.910 ± 0.010 across five folds. LSTM followed closely with 90.9 ± 1.1% accuracy and 0.910 ± 0.012 macro F1, demonstrating strong temporal modeling capabilities.

1D CNN achieved 88.4 ± 1.3% accuracy and 0.887 ± 0.012 macro F1, while MLP maintained competitive stability at 83.6 ± 1.5% accuracy. Models trained without daytime activity exhibited uniformly lower performance (average accuracy drops of 1.5–2.0%), underscoring the contribution of pre-sleep activity in improving stage discrimination.

5.4 Fold-Wise Stability and Minority Class Performance

Variance across folds remained low (standard deviations below 0.02 for accuracy and macro F1), indicating consistent model behavior across different participant groups. Minority sleep stages particularly N1, N3, and REM showed the largest relative improvements in recall when actigraphy was included. For example, the GRU model achieved per-class recall of 0.80 ± 0.03 for N1, 0.86 ± 0.02 for N3, and 0.88 ± 0.02 for REM, compared to significantly lower values without activity features.

These findings confirm that the integration of daytime activity signals enhances both predictive balance and generalization stability across folds.

5.5 Summary of Key Results

Table 1 summarizes the cross-validated results. Across all models, the inclusion of daytime activity features improved accuracy, macro F1, and macro recall. Ensemble models such as Random Forest and Extra Trees achieved the strongest classical baselines, while deep models especially GRU and LSTM consistently outperformed them, exceeding 90% accuracy with low variance. Overall, GRU demonstrated the highest robustness and generalization, highlighting its ability to model long-term temporal dependencies critical for sleep stage prediction.

Table 1. Mean (μ) $\pm$ standard deviation (σ) of test accuracy, macro F1, and macro recall across 5 Group K-Fold splits.

Model	Activity	Accuracy ($\mu \pm \sigma$)	Macro F1 ($\mu \pm \sigma$)	Macro Recall ($\mu \pm \sigma$)
Random Forest	Yes	0.811 ± 0.012	0.701 ± 0.010	0.811 ± 0.009
Extra Trees	Yes	0.803 ± 0.014	0.679 ± 0.013	0.803 ± 0.011
XGBoost	Yes	0.796 ± 0.018	0.674 ± 0.012	0.796 ± 0.015
LSTM	Yes	0.909 ± 0.011	0.910 ± 0.012	0.909 ± 0.011
GRU	Yes	$\mathbf{0.910 \pm 0.010}$	$\mathbf{0.911 \pm 0.009}$	$\mathbf{0.910 \pm 0.010}$
1D CNN	Yes	0.884 ± 0.013	0.887 ± 0.012	0.884 ± 0.013

5.6 Cross-validation Stability (Subject-Wise K=5)

To evaluate the consistency of deep learning models across subjects, we performed subject-wise K=5 Group K-Fold cross-validation. Figure 3 illustrates the mean accuracy with standard deviation across folds for the four models (LSTM, MLP, CNN, and GRU). Figure 4 compares their average accuracies with and without daytime activity features, highlighting the contribution of contextual activity data to improved nighttime sleep-stage prediction.

Table 2 summarizes the averaged quantitative results. LSTM and GRU models exhibit the highest stability and performance, achieving approximately 0.80 mean accuracy and macro-F1 scores above 0.67, confirming their robustness in capturing temporal dependencies.

Table 2. Five-fold subject-wise Group K-Fold cross-validation (means across folds).

Model	Mean Accuracy	Mean Macro F1
LSTM	0.7978	0.7043
MLP	0.6291	0.3858
1D CNN	0.7367	0.5733
GRU	0.7865	0.6702

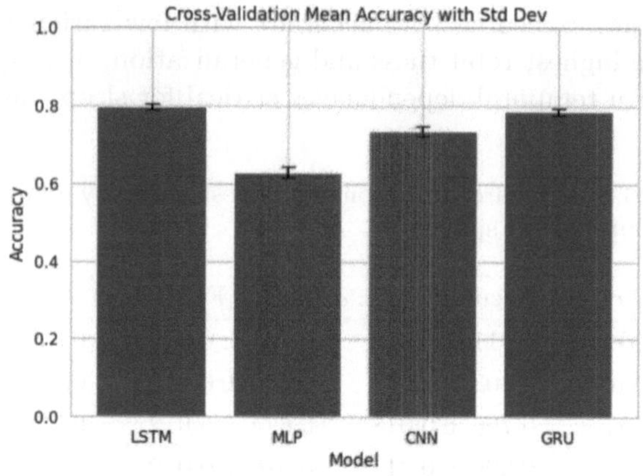

Fig. 3. Cross-validation mean accuracy with standard deviation across folds for each model.

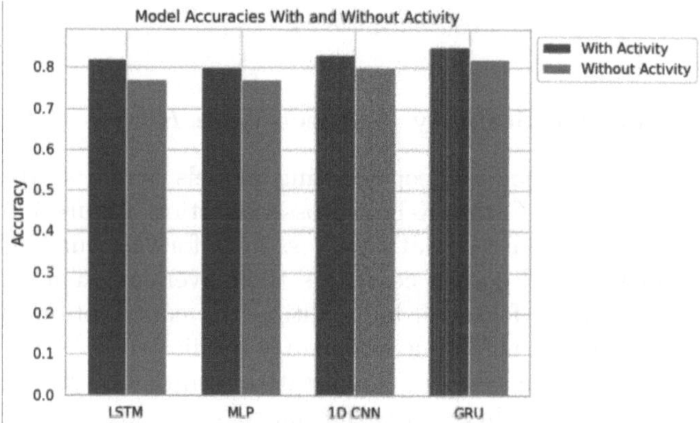

Fig. 4. Model accuracies with and without daytime activity features, showing the contribution of activity context to nighttime prediction.

5.7 Ablation and Performance Analysis

The improvement in test accuracy and macro F1 across models when actigraphy was included confirms its utility in sleep stage classification. In particular, minority stages (N1, N3, REM) saw gains in recall, especially for GRU and LSTM, which model temporal dependencies. GRU was consistently the best performer, both with and without activity data. The K-Fold comparison (Fig. 4) reinforces this observation: inclusion of daytime activity features consistently improved accuracy across all architectures by approximately 3–5%, with the strongest gains in the CNN and GRU models. This supports the hypothesis that contextual daytime patterns enhance nighttime sleep-state predictability.

5.8 Key Insights

The experimental results highlight the clear benefits of including daytime activity features and TimeGAN-based augmentation. As shown in Fig. 5, classical models such as Random Forest and Extra Trees achieved substantial performance gains with activity data, with accuracy improving up to 81.1%. Linear models like Logistic Regression and SVC remained less effective overall, even with additional features.

In contrast, deep learning models significantly outperformed classical ones, as shown in Fig. 6. GRU and LSTM achieved the highest accuracies, exceeding 91% when trained with both actigraphy and synthetic sequences. GRU in particular showed the best generalization, highlighting its strength in modeling temporal dependencies. Consistent with the single held-out test results, the subject-wise K=5 cross-validation further confirmed the superiority of temporal models. Both LSTM and GRU achieved mean accuracies close to 0.80 and mean macro-F1 scores above 0.67 across folds, indicating stable generalization across participants. In contrast, MLP and CNN models showed greater variance and lower average performance (mean accuracies of 0.63 and 0.74, respectively), suggesting that temporal recurrence and bidirectional dependencies play a crucial role in capturing sleep-stage transitions. The narrow standard deviations observed across folds also demonstrate strong reproducibility of these results. All models, including MLP and CNN, benefited from TimeGAN augmentation and actigraphy, demonstrating the value of synthetic data in addressing class imbalance and improving minority stage detection.

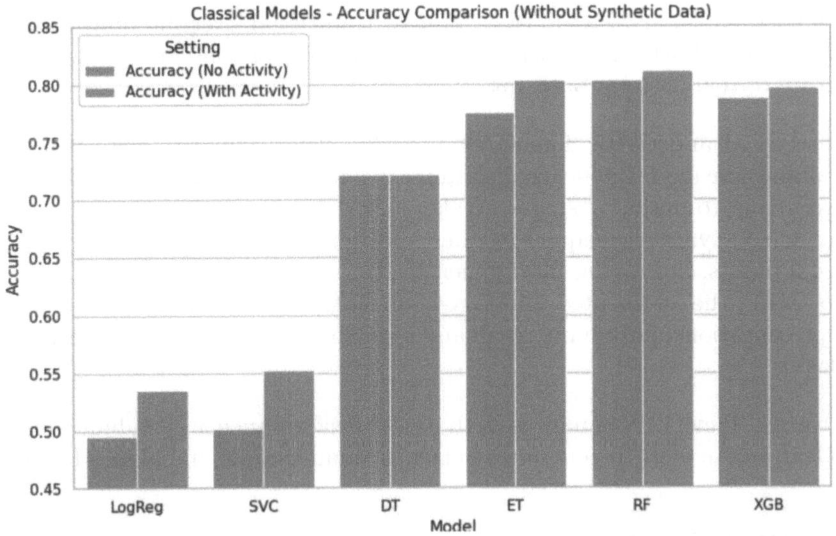

Fig. 5. Accuracy comparison of classical models with and without daytime activity features.

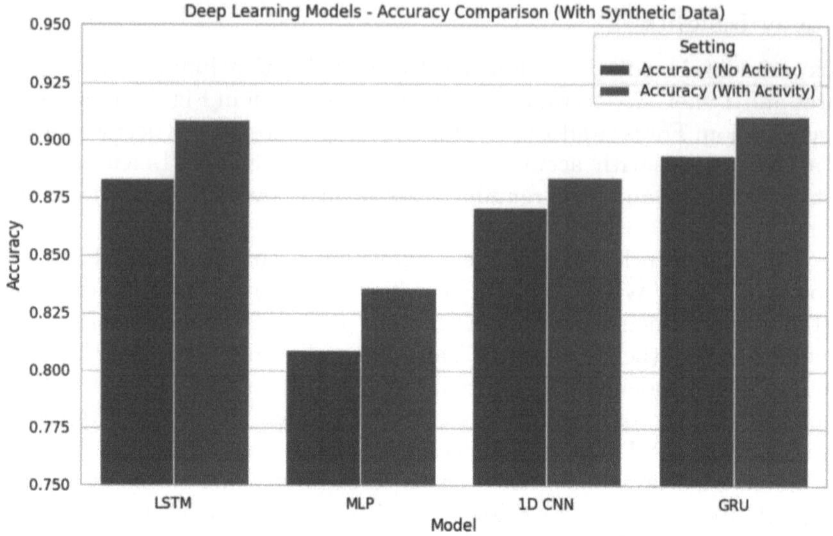

Fig. 6. Accuracy comparison of deep learning models with and without activity (using TimeGAN-augmented data).

5.9 Why TimeGAN Improves Performance

The key advantage of TimeGAN lies in its ability to generate temporally coherent synthetic sequences that mimic the dynamics of underrepresented sleep stages such as N1, N3, and REM. Unlike traditional oversampling techniques like SMOTE, TimeGAN captures both the sequential context and multivariate structure of real activity patterns.

- For LSTM and GRU, TimeGAN provides richer minority-class transitions, enabling the models to learn discriminative temporal boundaries and reducing overfitting to majority stages (Wake, N2).
- For CNN, synthetic sequences offer additional examples of short-term temporal bursts, improving filter generalization and REM/N1 detection.
- For MLP, the augmented minority-class feature vectors reduce skew in static representations, improving recall and reducing classifier bias toward dominant classes.

Overall, TimeGAN enhances both model performance and stability, enabling deep learning models to generalize better in small-sample, imbalanced scenarios.

6 Future Work

There are several ways this research can be extended in the future to improve accuracy, generalizability, and real-world usability.

- **Use of More Sensors:** Future models can include data from other wearable sensors such as heart rate, breathing, or skin temperature to improve prediction of difficult sleep stages.
- **Personalized Models:** Building models that adapt to each person's unique sleep habits over time could improve performance and make predictions more accurate.
- **Larger User Groups:** Testing the method on a larger and more diverse group of users will help confirm that the model works well for people with different ages, backgrounds, and sleep behaviors.

All code and configuration files used in this study are publicly released for reproducibility at https://github.com/caninehawk/Sleep-Stage-Prediction-using-TimeGAN. Random seeds were fixed across TensorFlow, PyTorch, and NumPy to ensure deterministic results. Experiments were performed on an NVIDIA RTX A5000 GPU with 64 GB RAM TimeGAN training averaged 25 min per fold (approximately 5 GB GPU memory), and GRU training approximately 6 min per fold (approximately 2 GB GPU memory).

7 Conclusion

This study presented a novel machine learning pipeline for predicting fine-grained sleep stages using daytime wrist actigraphy. By transforming 24-hour actigraphy data into statistical features and aligning them with single-night PSG annotations, we evaluated both classical models and deep sequence architectures.

Our experiments demonstrated that including actigraphy features significantly improved model performance, particularly for underrepresented sleep stages. Extensive evaluation using subject-wise Group K-Fold cross validation confirmed that TimeGAN augmented models generalize robustly to unseen individuals, with low fold-to-fold variability. Among all models, the GRU achieved the highest accuracy of 91.0% and macro F1 of 0.911 when trained with actigraphy data. Other models such as LSTM, 1D CNN, and MLP also showed notable gains, highlighting the predictive value of daytime activity in anticipating sleep architecture.

Classical ensemble methods like Random Forest performed competitively, especially when actigraphy was included. However, deep learning models consistently outperformed classical approaches in terms of minority class recall and overall balance across sleep stages. These results confirm the feasibility of using actigraphy for sleep stage prediction and provide a foundation for scalable, non-invasive sleep monitoring using wearable devices in real-world environments.

Across both single-split and $K{=}5$ cross-validation experiments, LSTM and GRU consistently outperformed feed-forward and convolutional baselines, achieving mean accuracies near 0.80 and macro-F1 scores above 0.67. These findings confirm the robustness of recurrent temporal architectures for sleep-stage modeling and underscore the contribution of activity-derived contextual features to overall prediction stability.

Acknoeledgement. contribution of activity-derived contextual features to overall prediction stability

References

1. Akther, S.: Visualization driven ai ensuring quality in wearable time-series sensor data for healthcare. In: 2025 IEEE Conference on Artificial Intelligence (CAI), pp. 1502–1510. IEEE (2025)
2. Alwadaani, A.A., Alsolami, A.M., Alrashidi, M.: Effect of data balancing techniques on performance of ensemble classifiers for sleep stage classification. IEEE Access **11**, 13255–13265 (2023)
3. Anker, S.D., Koehler, F., Abraham, W.T.: Telemedicine and remote management of patients with heart failure. The Lancet **378**(9792), 731–739 (2011)
4. Chang, R., Li, J., Singh, R.: Cross-platform misinformation structures and engagement dynamics: implications for passive sensing pipelines. Computation **12**(2), 28 (2024). https://doi.org/10.3390/computation12020028
5. Chen, Z., et al.: Unobtrusive sleep monitoring using smartphones. In: Proceedings of the 7th International Conference on Pervasive Computing Technologies for Healthcare, pp. 145–152 (2013)
6. Colten, H.R., Altevogt, B.M. (eds.): sleep disorders and sleep deprivation: an unmet public health problem. National Academies Press (2006)
7. Deng, Y., Yan, J., Yang, M., Hu, J., Zeng, J.: IB-GAN: imbalanced time-series classification using GAN with self-attention. In: Proceedings of the 30th ACM International Conference on Information and Knowledge Management (CIKM), pp. 1919–1928. ACM (2021). https://doi.org/10.1145/3459637.3482270
8. Gupta, V., Rahman, M., Sharma, P.: Advanced ensemble models for automated sleep staging using multi-modal data. Expert Syst. Appl. **235**, 121473 (2025)
9. Kukreja, A., Akther, S.: Complexity-aware human daily activity detection using ai. In: 2025 IEEE International Symposium on Technology and Society (ISTAS), pp. 1–8. IEEE (2025)
10. Mohammadzadeh, Z., Rezaei, M., Vahid, A., Zarei, A.: Ensemble deep learning models for accurate classification of sleep stages. Biomed. Eng. Lett. **13**(1), 25–35 (2023). https://doi.org/10.1007/s13534-022-00223-7
11. Pan, Y., Gao, L., Huang, L., Guo, Y.: An effective end-to-end deep learning model for automatic sleep staging with raw single-channel EEG. Comput. Biol. Med. **165**, 107529 (2025)
12. Rahman, M.M., Suganthan, P.N.: Deep learning for sleep stage classification: a review. IEEE Rev. Biomed. Eng. **16**, 143–157 (2023)
13. Ramponi, G., Alippi, C., Zhao, R., Längkvist, M.: T-CGAN: conditional generative adversarial network for data augmentation in noisy and irregular time series. In: 2018 International Joint Conference on Neural Networks (IJCNN), pp. 1–8. IEEE (2018). https://doi.org/10.1109/IJCNN.2018.8489605
14. Saadaoui, M., Charfi, I., Jallouli, M., Djemal, R.: A hybrid approach for automatic sleep stages classification based on EEG signals. In: 2016 IEEE International Conference on Systems, Man, and Cybernetics (SMC), pp. 002003–002008. IEEE (2016)
15. Schulten, T., Lukowicz, P.: Incorporating temporal context improves actigraphy-based sleep/wake classification. NPJ Digital Med. **7**, 22 (2024)

16. Smith, M.T., Perlis, M.L.: Who is a candidate for cognitive-behavioral therapy for insomnia? Health Psychol. **26**(1), 15–19 (2007)
17. Song, Y., Zhang, X., Wang, L., Wu, Y.: A hybrid deep learning model based on CNN and BiLSTM for automatic sleep staging. Biomed. Signal Process. Control **72**, 103361 (2022). https://doi.org/10.1016/j.bspc.2021.103361
18. Subasi, A., Kevric, J.: Ensemble-based classification of sleep stages using EEG features. Comput. Biol. Med. **93**, 167–175 (2018)
19. Van Someren, E.J.W.: Defining diurnal rhythmicity in activity and rest using actigraphy. Sleep **33**(3), 401–407 (2010). https://doi.org/10.1093/sleep/33.3.401
20. Walch, O.J., Huang, Y., Forger, D.B., Goldstein, C.A.: Sleep stage prediction with raw acceleration and photoplethysmography heart rate data from a consumer wearable device. Sleep Health **5**(6), 613–621 (2019)
21. Wei, Y., Wang, C., Gao, Y., Li, J., Zhang, Y.: AccSleepNet: an axis-aware hybrid deep fusion model for sleep stage classification using wrist actigraphy. Inf. Fusion **82**, 155–166 (2022)
22. Yang, Y., Wu, X., Xu, Y., Chen, H.: Diversity-aware behavioral analysis in online social systems: insights for bias-resilient modeling. Computers **12**(11), 221 (2023). https://doi.org/10.3390/computers12110221
23. Yoon, J., Jarrett, D., van der Schaar, M.: Time-series generative adversarial networks. In: Advances in Neural Information Processing Systems (NeurIPS). vol. 32 (2019)
24. Zhang, X., Yu, Y., Walch, O., Forger, D.B., Goldstein, C.A.: SLAMSS: sequence-to-sequence LSTM for automated mobile sleep staging. NPJ Digital Med. **6**, 44 (2023)
25. Zinkhan, M.: Polysomnography in the home vs. the sleep lab: a comparative review. Sleep Med. Rev. **58**, 101441 (2021)

Fuzzy Conviction Score for Discriminating Decision-Tree-Classified Feature Vectors W.r.t. Relative Distances from Decision Boundaries

Poomjai Nacaskul[1(✉)] and Kongkan Kalakan[2(✉)]

[1] Chulalongkorn School of Integrated Innovation, Chulalongkorn University, Bangkok, Thailand
Poomjai.N@chula.ac.th
[2] Faculty of Science, Chulalongkorn University, Bangkok, Thailand
Kongkan.Kalakan@gmail.com

Abstract. We augment decision tree classification analysis with fuzzy membership functions that quantitatively qualify, at each binary decision boundary, the degree of "conviction" to which each data point (i.e. feature vector) is deemed to be on either side of said decision boundary, the further away from the decision threshold, relative to peers, the higher the fuzzy membership value (i.e. the closer to 1). Our fuzzy "conviction" score is analogous to the measure of "confidence" as per traditional statistical methods, whilst handily accommodates the nonlinear discriminant surface created by a decision tree. Although our method has been successfully deployed in confidential commercial setting, here we demonstrate the concept and computation on the six benchmarks data sets archived and made available publicly on the UCI (University of California, Irvine) Machine Learning Repository and the Kaggle platform. In addition, we will as well demonstrate that without introducing any additional learning loops, our fuzzification of decision tree classifier could also improve the AUC (Area Under the ROC (Receiver Operating Characteristic) Curve) performance over that of the original decision tree classifier, provided the latter is decently capable of discriminating classes within the relevant data set to begin with.

Keywords: Decision Tree Classifier · Fuzzy Membership Function · Conviction Score

1 Introduction

Availability of myriad of advanced, highly complex machine-learned classifiers notwithstanding, decision tree classifier (ID3 [1] C4.5 [2]) remains one of the most popular and ubiquitous "go-to" tools amongst data science practitioners, and deservedly so. Not only is the underlying logic intuitive, the computational methodology transparent, and the results from analysis easy to explain

C. Xu (Ed.): ICMLSC 2026, CCIS 2948, pp. 72–84, 2027.
https://doi.org/10.1007/978-981-92-1546-1_6

(to project owners, end users, etc.), but the calibrated decision boundaries themselves can be further leveraged as a "standalone" population segmentation tool.

As such, whenever the validation test performance of a decision tree classifier is on par with other methods that are more complex, less parsimonious, and harder to explain (esp. those based on neural learning architecture), practitioners will invariably prefer the former. And all else being roughly equal, smaller trees (i.e. with less depth/branching) will also be preferred to larger trees.

Limitation of course arises when we wish to finely discriminate data points within the same terminal nodes (leafs). Recall that each decision tree branching is strictly binary. Small variations in feature values near thresholds may flip classification results, reducing robustness and interpretability. We propose to quantitatively qualify, at each decision boundary, the degree of "conviction" to which each data point (i.e. feature vector) is deemed to be on either side of said decision boundary, the further away from the decision threshold, relative to peers, the higher the fuzzy membership value (the closer to 1). Our fuzzy "conviction" score is analogous to the measure of "confidence" as per traditional statistical methods, whilst handily accommodates the nonlinear discriminant surface created by a decision tree.

We will as well demonstrate that without introducing any additional learning loops, our fuzzification of decision tree classifier could improve the AUC (Area Under the ROC (Receiver Operating Characteristic) Curve) performance over that of the original decision tree classifier, provided the latter is decently capable of discriminating classes within the relevant data set to begin with.

The remainder of this paper is organised as follows. Section 2 reviews related works that are relevant to and have inspired this research. Section 3 describes the datasets used to evaluate the proposed methodology. The details of the proposed algorithm are presented in Sect. 4. Experimental results and performance evaluations on the selected datasets are reported in Sect. 5. Finally, Sect. 6 concludes the paper.

2 Related Work

One of the earliest formulations for fuzzy decision trees was introduced by Umano et al. (1994) [3], who extended the ID3 algorithm by replacing crisp partitions with user-defined fuzzy sets and computing entropy using fuzzy membership degrees instead of discrete counts. Their "Fuzzy ID3" ensured that each attribute appears at most once per path and used fuzzy reasoning to propagate partial memberships during inference. Chiang & Hsu (1996) [4] introduced Fuzzy Classification Trees, constructing fuzzy membership functions via histogram smoothing, k-median clustering, and projections along each attribute.

Pedrycz & Sosnowski (2000) [5] investigated fuzzy granulation as a preprocessing step for decision-tree induction, transforming numerical attributes into interval-based categorical representations to reduce tree complexity and sensitivity to noise. In a different line of work, Hüllermeier & Vanderlooy (2009) [6] demonstrated theoretically and empirically that fuzzy decision trees yield more distinct output scores by propagating instances along multiple paths with graded membership, thereby reducing ties and improving AUC compared with crisp trees. Although their approach differs from ours, the underlying insight aligns with our observation that incorporating fuzziness around decision boundaries can enhance discriminatory performance.

Yun et al. (2014) [7] introduced a distance-from-average fuzzy entropy, mapping samples to Low/Medium/High and computing entropy via Euclidean distances to a mean fuzzy vector, thereby softening crisp boundaries without relying on conventional fuzzy inference. DTFR (Decision Trees based Fuzzy Rules) [8] combines autoregressive fuzzy modelling with decision-tree induction to generate fuzzy rules for time-series forecasting, employing Gaussian membership functions over sliding windows. Unlike our approach, DTFR neither starts from a crisp decision tree nor fuzzifies existing split thresholds; instead, fuzzy rules are first derived directly from fuzzified time-series data, and a decision tree is subsequently induced over these rules.

Moreover, fuzzy decision tree learning remains an active research topic. Calcagnì & Lombardi (2022) [9] proposed a probabilistic tree-based model that explicitly represents the stage-wise mechanisms underlying direct fuzzy rating scales, framing fuzziness as an epistemic property of human response processes. Extending the use of fuzzy and probabilistic trees to applied decision support, Ambags et al. (2023) [10] developed a fuzzy probabilistic decision tree for clinical practice, replacing crisp thresholds with fuzzy conditions to enable probabilistic reasoning along multiple decision paths while preserving interpretability. More recently, Fumanal-Idocin et al. (2025) [11] proposed a two-step fuzzy tree learner that combines greedy fuzzy Gini-based tree induction with a subsequent optimization of fuzzy partitions, achieving improved predictive performance without sacrificing interpretability.

Our approach, by contrast, proceeds in the opposite direction. Rather than generating fuzzy rules prior to tree induction, we begin with a conventional crisp decision tree obtained through standard training, as in UR-ID3 [12]. While UR-ID3 incorporates fuzzy reasoning to handle uncertainty in attribute values during inference, our method addresses a complementary but distinct problem. Instead of modelling uncertainty in the data itself, we introduce fuzzy conviction scores as a post-hoc overlay on an already trained crisp decision tree, quantifying how deeply each instance lies within the learned decision boundaries. Concretely, we employ sigmoid-based fuzzy membership functions centred at each learned split threshold to model relative distances from decision boundaries, rather than triangular or rule-based memberships defined over uncertain inputs. Importantly, this refinement does not modify the tree structure nor introduce any additional learning loops, and is intended to enhance the discriminatory resolution of the original classifier. The details are presented in the Methodology section.

3 Data

Although method has been successfully deployed in confidential commercial setting, here we demonstrate the concept and computation on standard benchmarks: "Breast Cancer Wisconsin (Diagnostic)" Data Set [13], "Chronic Kidney Disease" Data Set [14], and "Indian Liver Patient" Data Set [15] archived and made available publicly on the UCI (University of California, Irvine) Machine Learning Repository. In addition, we consider three further real-world benchmarks sourced from the Kaggle platform: "Alzheimer's Disease" Data Set [16], "Cardiovascular Disease" Data Set [17], and "Pima Indians Diabetes" Data Set [18]. The experimental results are presented in the following order.

Breast Cancer Wisconsin (Diagnostic) data set, contains 569 instances (none with missing values). There are 30 real-valued attributes, and 2 target classes ("M" = positive, "B" = negative).

Alzheimer's Disease data set, contains 2,149 instances (none with missing values). There are 32 real-valued attributes, and 2 target classes ("1" = positive, "0" = negative).

Chronic Kidney Disease data set, contains 400 instances (with missing values imputed using the mean for numerical attributes and the most frequent value for categorical attributes). There are 14 real-valued attributes, 10 categorical attributes, and 2 target classes ("ckd" = positive, "notckd" = negative). Class imbalance in the training set is addressed using SMOTE.

Cardiovascular Disease data set, contains 70,000 instances (none with missing values). There are 11 real-valued attributes, and 2 target classes ("1" = positive, "0" = negative).

Indian Liver Patient data set, contains 583 instances (with missing values imputed using the mean). There are 9 real-valued attributes, 1 categorical attribute, and 2 target classes ("2" = positive, "1" = negative). Class imbalance in the training set is addressed using SMOTE.

Pima Indians Diabetes data set, contains 786 instances (none with missing values). There are 8 real-valued attributes, and 2 target classes ("1" = positive, "0" = negative).

Train/Test data sets, randomly drawn, with k-fold cross-validation (k = 5).

4 Methodology

4.1 Decision Tree Classifier

Our decision tree classifier is as per `scikit-learn` library[1] version 2.2.2, with max_depth parameter set to 2 (all other parameters at default). Each training begins with random seed 1234.

4.2 Fuzzy Membership Function

Following [19], instead of making a sharp distinction between an item being or not being an element of a "crisp" set, itself defined in reference to some concept, a fuzzy membership function assigns a value $\mu_{concept}(item) \in [0, 1]$ signifying

[1] https://scikit-learn.org/stable/modules/generated/sklearn.tree.DecisionTreeClassifier.html.

the varying degree to which an item should be considered as belonging to a "fuzzy" set. Conversely, we can think of non-fuzzy membership as a restricted "all-or-nothing" set membership function $\mu_{concept}(item) \in \{0, 1\}$.

In our case, we choose the **Logistic Sigmoid Function** (see Eq. 1) to specify the shape of the fuzzy membership function. The θ "location" parameter locates the value of x where the fuzzy membership function value is exactly 1/2. The $\tau > 0$ "temperature" parameter controls how sharp the distinction, approaching a "step function" as τ goes to zero.

$$\mu(x; \theta, \tau) = \frac{1}{1 + e^{-\frac{(x-\theta)}{\tau}}} \tag{1}$$

4.3 Fuzzy Conviction Score

Here we describe how the fuzzy functions are overlaid onto trained decision tree classifier and fuzzy conviction scores computed.

At each Decision Boundary. Consider a particular branching of a decision tree classifier, where the binary distinction is made between feature vectors or data points whose j^{th} attribute is lesser than or equal to some threshold value θ versus those whose j^{th} attribute is greater than said threshold θ, with the former cases going to the left branch and the latter cases going to the right branch.

But in a standard decision tree classifier, no further distinction is made between any two feature vectors or data points that both go the right, even though one's j^{th} attribute may be barely above the threshold value θ while the other's j^{th} attribute comfortably surpasses it. Analogous to the measure of "confidence" as per traditional statistical methods, we want to assign some measure of "conviction" that differentiate the degree to which either one gets through said decision boundary. This is where fuzzy functions come in handy.

Here, we need to define two[2] fuzzy membership functions, $\mu_{attribute_j \leq \theta}()$ for left-branching points, i.e. whose attribute$_j \leq \theta$, and $\mu_{attribute_j > \theta}()$ for left-branching points, i.e. whose with attribute$_j > \theta$.

Naturally, the "location" parameters for both $\mu_{attribute_j \leq \theta}()$ and $\mu_{attribute_j > \theta}()$ are set to θ. We need to be more specific, however, about how we choose to calibrate the "temperature" parameters. For our purpose, we set them such that $\mu_{attribute_j \leq \theta}(\chi_{left}) = 0.99$ (i.e. "nearly 1"), where the "anchor point" χ_{left} is the average of attribute values lesser than or equal to θ and $\mu_{attribute_j > \theta}(\chi_{right}) = 0.99$ (i.e. "nearly 1"), where the "anchor point" χ_{right} is the average of attribute values greater than θ (see Eq. 2):

$$\tau_a = \frac{\chi_a - \theta}{\log\left(\frac{0.99}{1-0.99}\right)}, \quad a \in \{left, right\} \tag{2}$$

[2] Note how these two fuzzy membership functions, despite sharing θ, are independently calibrated, i.e. $\mu_{attribute_j \leq \theta}()$ is not generally equal to $1 - \mu_{attribute_j > \theta}()$.

At the Terminal Node (Leaf). Normally, at the terminal node (leaf) of a decision tree classifier, all points are considered to have the same probability of being in the designated class. However, with our fuzzification scheme, each data point will have a series of fuzzy membership values, one each with respect to each decision boundary. With the notion of "AND" type, these fuzzy membership values are multiplied together. This then gives the data point its **Fuzzy Conviction Score**.

Fuzzy Conviction Score as Measure of Confidence. Analogous to the measure of "confidence" as per traditional statistical methods, this composite measure of "conviction" (itself a multiplication of individual measures of "conviction", i.e. one for each decision boundary) further differentiates amongst all the feature vectors that are judged by standard decision tree classifier as having the same probability of belonging to a given class.

Fuzzy Conviction Score as Discriminatory Power Boost. Moreover, *without introducing any additional learning loops*, we can use fuzzy conviction score to boost the discriminatory power of standard decision tree. This is done using **lexicographic ordering**. First, we rank feature vectors according to probability estimates. This will achieve at most 2^{max_depth} ranked blocks, i.e. the number of terminal nodes/leafs of a trained decision tree, as per traditional interpretation. But then, within each block associated with positive prediction, rank individual feature vectors according to their respective fuzzy conviction scores, the *higher* the fuzzy conviction score, the *higher* the ranking (we are more convinced of their being positive cases). Now for each block associated with negative prediction, also rank individual feature vectors according to their respective fuzzy conviction scores, this time in reverse order, the *higher* the fuzzy conviction score, the *lower* the ranking (we are more convinced of their being negative cases). This could help boost the discriminatory power of the standard decision tree classifier, i.e. AUC performance, *all without introducing any additional learning loops.*

5 Experiment

5.1 Decision Tree Classifier

The discriminatory power of the baseline decision trees is generally strong across most datasets. Out-of-sample AUC reaches 0.92 for the Breast Cancer Wisconsin (Diagnostic) dataset (Fig. 1, left) and 0.92 for the Alzheimer's Disease dataset (Fig. 2, left). The Chronic Kidney Disease dataset exhibits particularly high separability with an AUC of 0.97 (Fig. 3, left). Performance is more modest for the Cardiovascular Disease dataset, with an AUC of 0.78 (Fig. 4, left), and remains similar for the Pima Indians Diabetes dataset at 0.80 (Fig. 5, left). The Indian Liver Patient dataset is the most challenging of the group, yielding an AUC of 0.70 (Fig. 6, left).

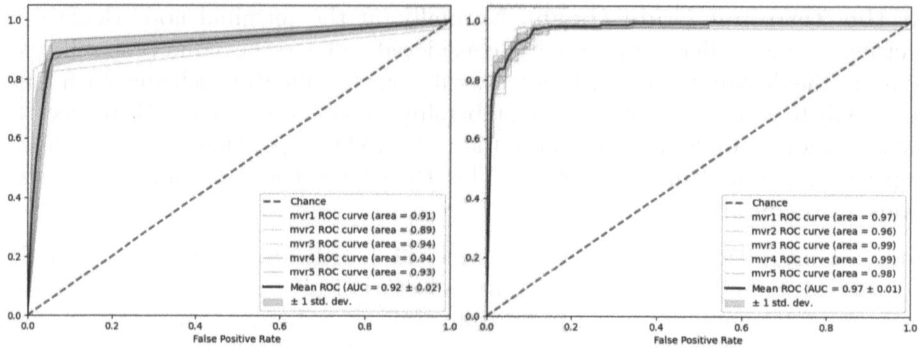

(a) Standard decision tree (b) Fuzzy conviction overlay

Fig. 1. Mean ROC curves over k-fold cross-validation for the Breast Cancer Wisconsin (Diagnostic) Data Set.

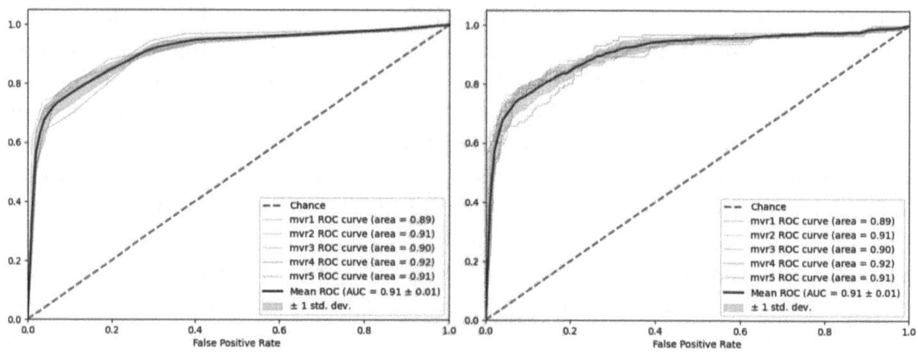

(a) Standard decision tree (b) Fuzzy conviction overlay

Fig. 2. Mean ROC curves over k-fold cross-validation for the Alzheimer's Disease Data Set.

5.2 Decision Tree Classifier with Fuzzy Conviction Score Overlay

Figure 1 shows that overlaying the original decision tree classifier with the fuzzy conviction score improves discriminatory power from AUC $= 0.92$ to AUC $= 0.97$, an enhancement achieved without introducing any additional learning loops. This improvement can be further examined in Fig. 7 (left), which plots both the probability estimates of the standard decision tree (left panel) and the corresponding fuzzy conviction scores (right panel). Actual positive test cases are shown in blue and negatives in red. For identical probability estimates produced by the standard tree, blue points tend to appear at higher fuzzy conviction scores, while red points cluster more frequently at lower scores. Even with the trend reversal in the lower half, where the fuzzy conviction score is inverted

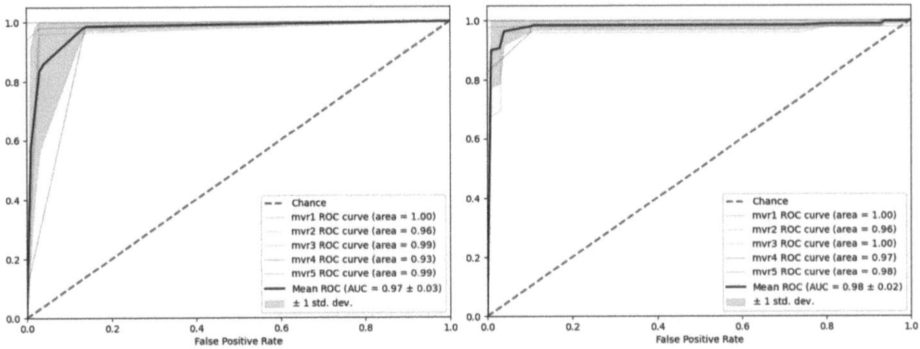

(a) Standard decision tree (b) Fuzzy conviction overlay

Fig. 3. Mean ROC curves over k-fold cross-validation for the Chronic Kidney Disease Data Set.

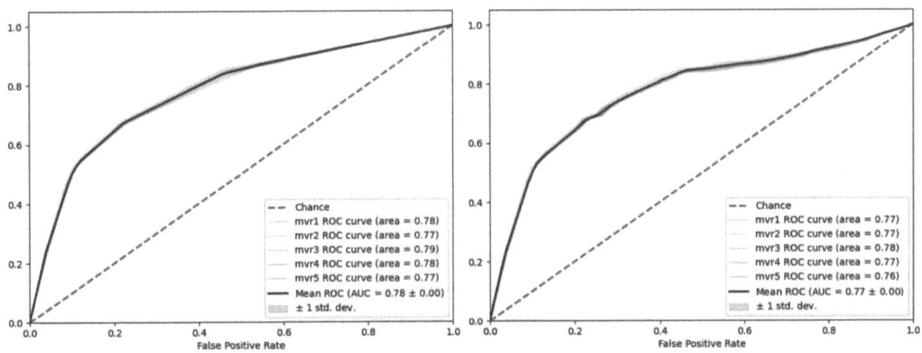

(a) Standard decision tree (b) Fuzzy conviction overlay

Fig. 4. Mean ROC curves over k-fold cross-validation for the Cardiovascular Disease Data Set.

for negative predictions, the overlay effectively reranks cases within both the positive and negative classes.

In contrast, results for the Alzheimer's Disease dataset (Fig. 2) show no change in AUC: both before and after overlaying, the classifier attains AUC = 0.91. As illustrated in Fig. 7 (right), the fuzzy score offers limited improvement in this particular case.

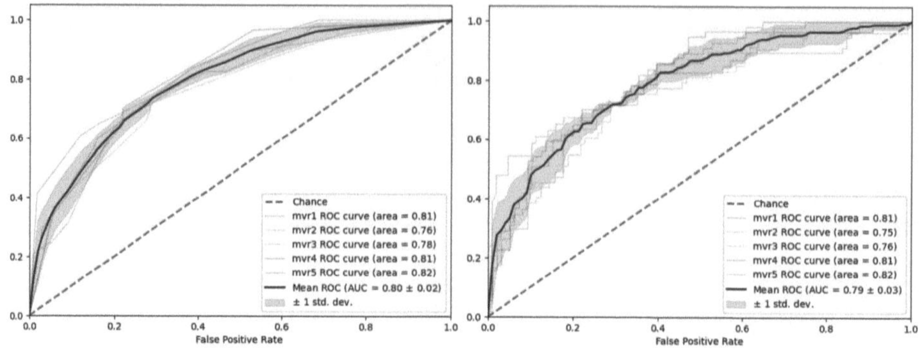

(a) Standard decision tree (b) Fuzzy conviction overlay

Fig. 5. Mean ROC curves over k-fold cross-validation for the Pima Indians Diabetes Data Set.

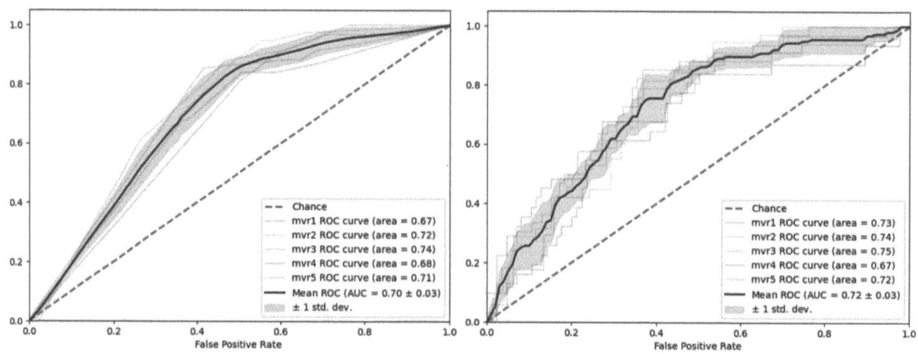

(a) Standard decision tree (b) Fuzzy conviction overlay

Fig. 6. Mean ROC curves over k-fold cross-validation for the Indian Liver Patient Data Set.

For the Chronic Kidney Disease dataset, a slight improvement is observed, from AUC $= 0.97$ (left) to AUC $= 0.98$ (right) in Fig. 3. The corresponding reranking plot in Fig. 8 (a) supports this modest gain.

The pattern reverses for the Cardiovascular Disease dataset, where AUC decreases marginally from 0.78 to 0.77 (Fig. 4). As shown in Fig. 8 (b), the fuzzy conviction score does not provide a clearer separation in this case.

Similarly, the Pima Indians Diabetes dataset shows no improvement, with AUC decreasing slightly from 0.80 to 0.79 (Fig. 5). The conviction-rate distribution is illustrated in Fig. 8 (c).

Finally, the Indian Liver Patient dataset demonstrates a favourable outcome: AUC improves from 0.70 to 0.72 (Fig. 6). This improvement is also reflected in Fig. 8 (d), where negative cases (red) tend to cluster more distinctly toward the lower end of the fuzzy conviction scale.

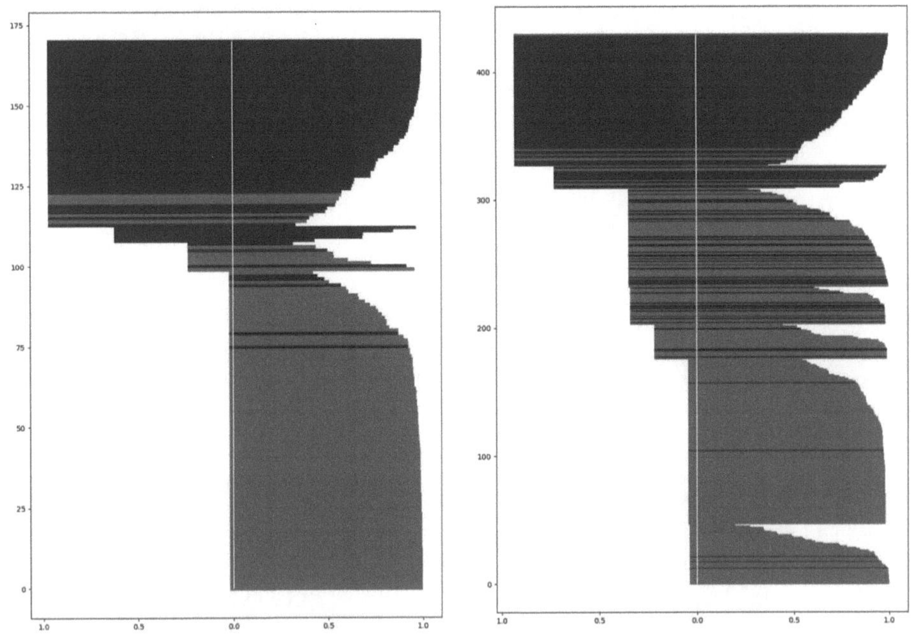

(a) Breast Cancer Wisconsin (Diagnostic)

(b) Alzheimer's Disease

Fig. 7. Probability Estimate vs. Fuzzy Conviction Score;"blue" for positive, "red" for negative cases. (Color figure online)

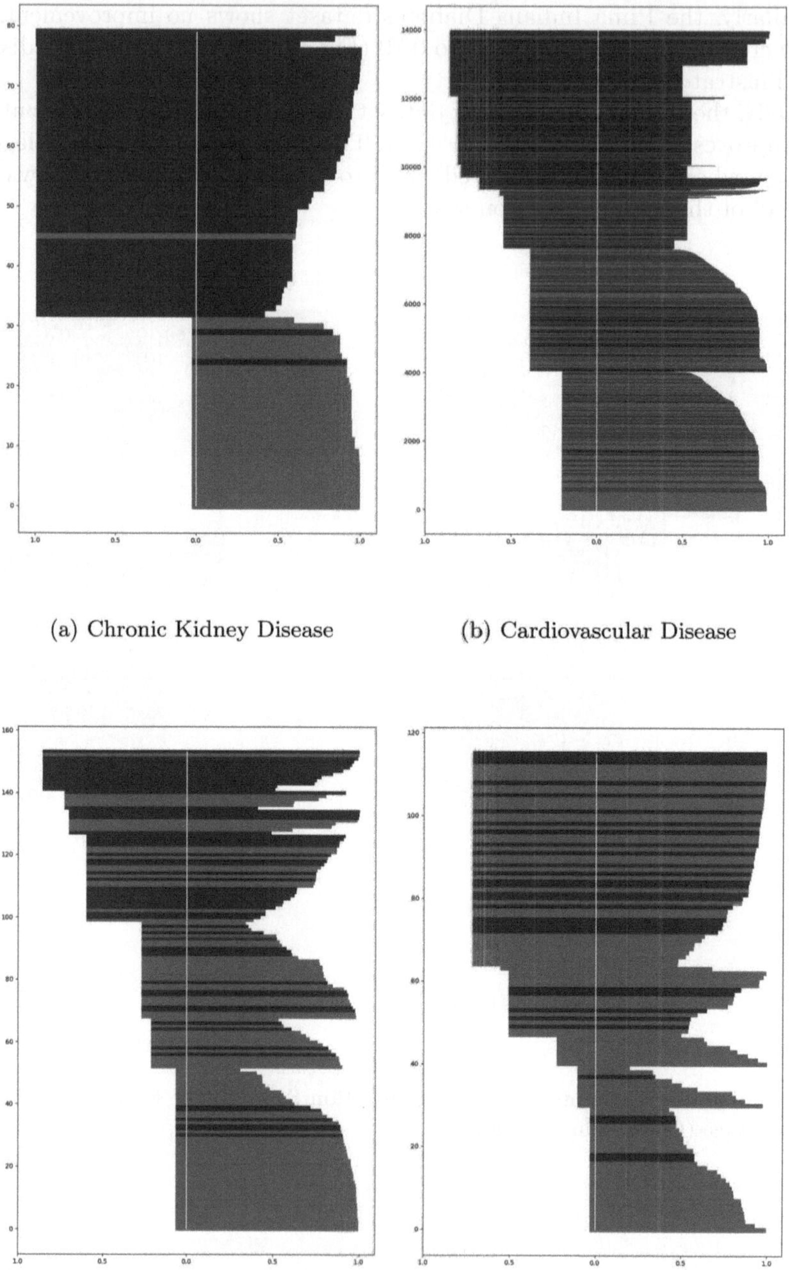

(a) Chronic Kidney Disease

(b) Cardiovascular Disease

(c) Pima Indians Diabetes

(d) Indian Liver Patient

Fig. 8. Probability Estimate vs. Fuzzy Conviction Score; "blue" for positive, "red" for negative cases. (Color figure online)

6 Conclusion

In this paper, we have proposed a simple, transparent, and easy-to-explain method for enhancing the utility of the ubiquitous decision tree classifier by overlaying probability estimates with fuzzy conviction scores, with higher scores reflecting data points being "deeper within" the respective decision boundaries. The method is demonstrated herewith on benchmark medical diagnostics data, where overlaying probability estimates as per standard decision tree classifier with our fuzzy conviction score could improve the discriminatory power *without introducing any additional learning loops.* Our Python code available on https://github.com/KongkanKalakan/Fuzzy_Conviction_Decision_Tree_Classifier.

References

1. Quinlan, R.: Induction of decision trees. Mach. Learn. **1**, 81–106 (1986)
2. Quinlan, J.R.: C4.5: programs for machine learning, morgan kaufmann publishers, san mateo, CA (1993)
3. Umano, M., et al.: Fuzzy decision trees by fuzzy id3 algorithm and its application to diagnosis systems. In: Proceedings of the IEEE International Conference on Fuzzy Systems IEEE, pp. 2113–2118 (1994)
4. Chiang, I.-J., Hsu, J.Y.-j.: Integration of fuzzy classifiers with decision trees. In: Proceedings of the 1996 Fuzzy Systems Symposium: Soft Computing in Intelligent Systems and Information Processing. IEEE, pp. 266–271 (1996)
5. Pedrycz, W., Sosnowski, Z.A.: Designing decision trees with the use of fuzzy granulation. IEEE Trans. Syst. Man Cybern. Part A: Syst. Humans, **30**(2), 151–159 (2000)
6. Hüllermeier, E., Vanderlooy, S.: Why fuzzy decision trees are good rankers. IEEE Trans. Fuzzy Syst. **17**(6), 1367–1379 (2009)
7. Yun, J., Seo, J.W., Yoon, T.: The new approach on fuzzy decision trees (2014). arXiv preprint arXiv:1408.3002. https://arxiv.org/abs/1408.3002
8. Al-Gunaid, M.A., Shcherbakov, M.V., Kamaev, V.A., Gerget, O.M., Tyukov, A.P.: Decision trees based fuzzy rules, in information technologies in science, management, social sphere and medicine (ITSMSSM). Atlantis Press **2016**, 502–509 (2016)
9. Calcagnì, A., Lombardi, L.: A probabilistic tree model to analyze fuzzy rating data. In: Ciucci, D., et al. (eds.) Information Processing and Management of Uncertainty in Knowledge-Based Systems, pp. 457–468. Springer International Publishing, Cham (2022)
10. Ambags, T., De Bock, S., Decruyenaere, J., Verbeke, W.: Assisting clinical practice with fuzzy probabilistic decision trees (2023). arXiv preprint,https://arxiv.org/abs/2304.07788
11. Fumanal-Idocin, J., Fernandez-Peralta, R., Andreu-Perez, J.: A fast interpretable fuzzy tree learner arXiv preprint (2025). https://arxiv.org/abs/2512.11616
12. Maher, P., St. Clair, D.: Uncertain reasoning in an id3 machine learning framework. In: Proceedings 1993 Second IEEE International Conference on Fuzzy Systems, pp. 7–12, vol. 1 (1993)
13. Street, W.N., Wolberg, W.N., Mangasarian, O.A.: Breast cancer wisconsin (diagnostic) data set. UCI Machine Learning Repository (1995). https://archive.ics.uci.edu/ml/datasets/Breast+Cancer+Wisconsin+(Diagnostic)

14. Rubini, L., Soundarapandian, P., Eswaran, P.: Chronic kidney disease data set. UCI Machine Learning Repository (2015). https://archive.ics.uci.edu/dataset/336/chronic+kidney+disease
15. Ramana, B., Venkateswarlu, N.: Indian liver patient data set. UCI Machine Learning Repository (2012). https://archive.ics.uci.edu/dataset/225/ilpd+indian+liver+patient+dataset
16. Kharoua, R.E.: Alzheimer's disease dataset (2024). https://www.kaggle.com/datasets/rabieelkharoua/alzheimers-disease-dataset
17. Ulianova, S.: Alzheimer's disease dataset (2018). https://www.kaggle.com/datasets/sulianova/cardiovascular-disease-dataset
18. Learning, U.M.: Pima indians diabetes dataset (2016). https://www.kaggle.com/datasets/uciml/pima-indians-diabetes-database
19. Zadeh, L.A.: Fuzzy sets. Inf. Control **8**(3), 338–353 (1965)

A Pruning Method Based on Layer-Wise Relevance Propagation and Cross-layer Dependency Graph

Dongchuan Yang[1(✉)], Baisen Liu[1,2,3], and Weili Kong[3]

[1] School of Measurement and Communication Engineering, Harbin University of Science and Technology, Harbin, China
ydcyydc@126.com, liubaisen@hrbeu.edu.cn

[2] College of Electrical and Information Engineering, Heilongjiang Institute of Technology, Harbin, China

[3] Harbin Engineering University, Harbin, China
kkweil@hrbeu.edu.cn

Abstract. Convolutional neural networks (CNNs) have achieved remarkable success in computer vision but are often over-parameterized, which limits their deployment on resource-constrained devices. We propose LRP-CDG, an explainability-driven structured pruning framework that integrates Layer-wise Relevance Propagation (LRP) with cross-layer dependency modeling. LRP is used to quantify the task relevance of convolutional kernels, while a cross-layer dependency graph captures feature support relationships across layers. Based on these two complementary cues, low-relevance and weakly dependent kernels are progressively pruned, followed by dependency-aware fine-tuning. Experiments on CIFAR-10 and ImageNet demonstrate that LRP-CDG achieves substantial reductions in FLOPs and parameters with minimal accuracy degradation, outperforming existing pruning methods under comparable compression ratios.

Keywords: Explainable Pruning · CNN · LRP · Cross-layer Dependency

1 Introduction

CNNs have become the dominant paradigm for visual recognition tasks, including image classification, object detection, and semantic segmentation [1–3]. However, their continuously increasing depth and parameter scale impose significant computational and memory burdens, hindering deployment on edge devices such as mobile platforms and embedded systems. Model compression, particularly structured pruning, has therefore become an essential research direction [4].

Most existing pruning methods rely on heuristic criteria such as weight magnitude, gradients, or feature statistics [5–7]. Although effective in reducing model size, these approaches often overlook the semantic contribution of features and

C. Xu (Ed.): ICMLSC 2026, CCIS 2948, pp. 85–96, 2027.
https://doi.org/10.1007/978-981-92-1546-1_7

the dependency relationships across layers, leading to structural disruption and performance degradation [8,9]. At the same time, recent advances in explainable AI (XAI) have shown that attribution methods such as Layer-wise Relevance Propagation (LRP) [12] can faithfully reflect how individual components contribute to model decisions.

Motivated by these observations, we propose LRP-CDG, a task-aware pruning framework that combines explainability and structural dependency modeling. LRP is employed to evaluate kernel-level task relevance, while a cross-layer dependency graph explicitly models feature support paths across the network. By pruning kernels with low relevance and weak dependency while preserving critical feature hierarchies, LRP-CDG achieves high compression ratios with minimal accuracy loss. Extensive experiments on CIFAR-10 and ImageNet validate the effectiveness and robustness of the proposed method.

2 Related Work

Early pruning methods focus on unstructured or magnitude-based criteria, removing parameters with small weights or gradients. While simple, these methods often damage the learned feature hierarchy. Structured pruning approaches, such as channel or filter pruning, improve hardware efficiency by removing entire kernels or channels, but still rely on proxy metrics that poorly capture semantic importance [14,17,29].

Recent works incorporate global optimization strategies, including reinforcement learning and differentiable search, to improve pruning decisions [11,18,19]. However, these methods typically lack interpretability and offer limited insight into why specific structures are removed. In parallel, explainability techniques such as LRP [12,25] and Grad-CAM [20]have been widely studied to interpret CNN predictions, and a few recent studies have explored their use for pruning [23,24]. Nevertheless, existing explainability-based pruning methods rarely model cross-layer dependencies, which are crucial for preserving feature composition.

Our work differs from prior approaches by jointly leveraging LRP-based relevance attribution and explicit cross-layer dependency modeling, enabling structure-preserving and semantically grounded pruning (Fig. 1).

3 The Proposed Method

The core objective of the proposed method is to quantify the task relevance of convolutional kernels through LRP , while modeling hierarchical feature dependencies. By incorporating a progressive pruning strategy, our approach preserves critical functional chains during model compression.

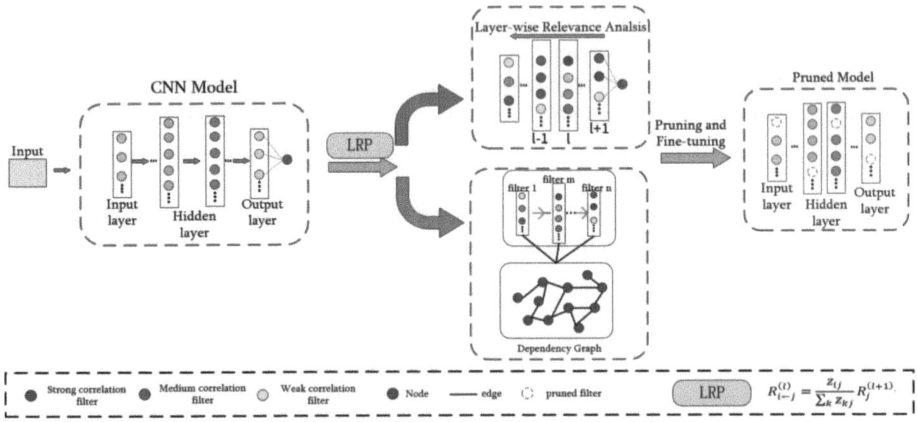

Fig. 1. Overview of the proposed LRP-CDG framework, illustrating relevance propagation, cross-layer dependency modeling, and dependency-aware pruning.

3.1 Layer-Wise Relevance Propagation for Kernel Importance

Layer-wise Relevance Propagation (LRP) [23–25]is adopted to quantify the task relevance of convolutional kernels in a trained CNN. Unlike magnitude-based pruning criteria, LRP redistributes the prediction score backward through the network under a relevance conservation principle, enabling faithful attribution of the final decision to intermediate representations.

Formally, given an input image x and the corresponding network output $f(x)$, relevance scores are initialized at the output layer and propagated layer by layer toward earlier layers. Let $R_i^{(l)}$ denote the relevance assigned to neuron i at layer l; the conservation property ensures that the total relevance remains consistent across layers during backpropagation.

Based on the propagated relevance maps, the importance of the k-th convolutional kernel in layer l is defined as the aggregated relevance over its corresponding feature map:

$$S_{l,k} = \sum_{i \in \mathcal{F}_{l,k}} R_i^{(l)}, \tag{1}$$

where $\mathcal{F}_{l,k}$ denotes the set of spatial locations associated with the k-th kernel at layer l. This kernel-level relevance score directly reflects the contribution of each kernel to the network's final prediction, rather than merely capturing parameter magnitude or activation strength.

By leveraging LRP-based relevance attribution, the proposed method obtains a task-aware kernel importance measure, which provides a principled foundation for subsequent cross-layer dependency modeling and pruning decisions.

3.2 Cross-layer Dependency Graph Construction

In deep convolutional networks, the discriminative capability of high-level semantic features depends on coordinated feature propagation across multiple layers.

Pruning convolutional kernels independently may disrupt such feature transmission chains. To address this issue, we construct a Cross-layer Dependency Graph (CDG) to explicitly model inter-kernel dependencies across adjacent layers.

Given a convolutional kernel k_d in layer $l+1$, its relevance to the network output is quantified using LRP as $R_{k_d}^{(l+1)}$. This relevance is then redistributed to kernels in the preceding layer l, reflecting the contribution of each shallow kernel k_s to the activation of k_d. For a validation dataset D_{val}, the expected dependency strength between k_s and k_d is defined as:

$$M(k_s, k_d) = \frac{\mathbb{E}_{x \sim D_{val}} \left[R_{k_s \leftarrow k_d}^{(l)}(x) \right]}{\sum_{k'_s} \mathbb{E}_{x \sim D_{val}} \left[R_{k'_s \leftarrow k_d}^{(l)}(x) \right]}. \tag{2}$$

The normalized dependency matrix M characterizes how task relevance propagates from shallow to deep kernels. Based on M, a directed graph is constructed in which nodes correspond to convolutional kernels and weighted edges represent cross-layer dependency strengths. This graph reveals critical feature propagation paths across layers and serves as a structural constraint for subsequent pruning.

By incorporating CDG into the pruning process, kernels with weak task relevance and limited dependency support can be safely removed, while preserving essential feature hierarchies required for stable prediction performance (Fig. 2).

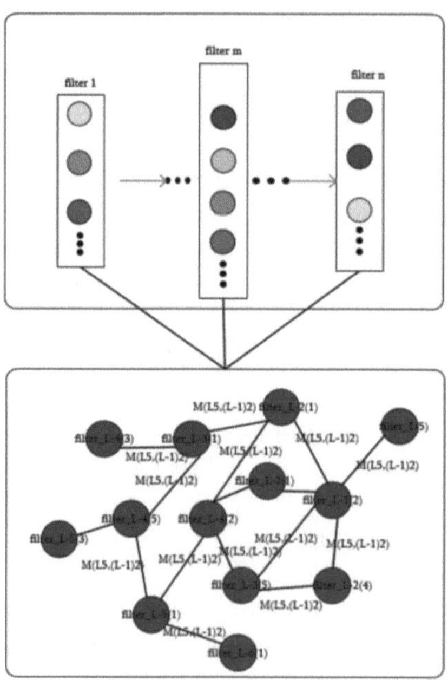

Fig. 2. The established cross-layer dependency graph.

3.3 Progressive Dependency-Aware Pruning

Based on the kernel relevance scores obtained by LRP and the cross-layer dependency graph, we design a progressive structured pruning strategy that jointly considers task contribution and structural dependency. Instead of pruning kernels independently within each layer, pruning decisions are made globally to preserve critical feature propagation paths.

For each convolutional kernel k, a pruning priority score is defined as:

$$P(k) = \gamma (1 - S(k)) + (1 - \gamma) (1 - T(k)), \tag{3}$$

where $S(k)$ denotes the normalized LRP-based task relevance score, and

$$T(k) = \sum_{k_d} M(k, k_d) \tag{4}$$

represents the aggregated dependency strength between kernel k and all dependent kernels in deeper layers. The balancing parameter $\gamma \in [0, 1]$ controls the relative importance of task relevance and cross-layer dependency.

Given a target pruning ratio α, kernels are ranked according to $P(k)$, and the lowest $\alpha \times 100\%$ kernels are removed. Pruning is conducted progressively in multiple stages rather than in a single step, allowing the network to adapt gradually to structural changes and reducing the risk of abrupt performance degradation.

After each pruning stage, dependency-aware fine-tuning is applied to restore accuracy. During fine-tuning, kernels with higher dependency strength receive proportionally larger learning rates to reinforce critical feature pathways, while weakly connected kernels are updated conservatively. This strategy facilitates rapid convergence and stabilizes performance recovery after pruning.

By integrating relevance-guided scoring, dependency-aware ranking, and progressive optimization, the proposed pruning strategy achieves high compression efficiency while preserving essential semantic structures across layers.

4 Experiments and Discussion

4.1 Experimental Setup and Evaluation Metrics

We evaluate the proposed LRP-CDG on image classification tasks using VGG-16, ResNet-56, GoogleNet, and ResNet-50 as baseline architectures. Experiments are conducted on CIFAR-10 and ImageNet-1K to validate effectiveness across both small-scale and large-scale benchmarks.

All models are initialized from standard pretrained weights and fine-tuned after pruning using stochastic gradient descent with momentum 0.9 and weight decay 1×10^{-4}. The initial learning rate is set to 0.1 for CIFAR-10 and 0.01 for ImageNet, and decayed following a cosine annealing schedule. Standard data augmentation and normalization strategies are adopted for each dataset to ensure fair comparison.

Progressive structured pruning is applied according to the target pruning ratio α described in Sect. 3.3. After each pruning stage, dependency-aware fine-tuning is performed to recover performance. All experiments are conducted on a single NVIDIA RTX 3060 GPU.

To comprehensively assess pruning effectiveness, we report metrics from three perspectives: *(1) task performance*, measured by Top-1 and Top-5 classification accuracy; *(2) computational efficiency*, measured by parameter count and FLOPs; and *(3) interpretability preservation*, evaluated using Grad-CAM region overlap (IoU).

4.2 Performance Comparison

In the previous sections, we have detailed the principles and implementation steps of LRP-CDG. Next, we will compare LRP-CDG with existing methods across different dataset and model combinations.

Table 1. Pruning results of VGG-16 on CIFAR-10. The numerical suffix in LRP-CDG indicates the pruning rate α.

Model	Top-1 (%)	FLOPs	Parameters
Baseline	93.02	314.04M	14.73M
HRank	92.34	108.61M	2.64M
MLPruner	92.60	78.80M	3.68M
FPEM	92.57	114.53M	2.78M
CIE	92.44	109.40M	2.69M
LRP-CDG-0.75	92.63	77.42M	2.72M

Table 2. Pruning results of GoogleNet on CIFAR-10. The numerical suffix in LRP-CDG indicates the pruning rate α.

Model	Top-1 (%)	FLOPs	Parameters
Baseline	95.03	1.53B	6.17M
CIE	94.60	0.75B	2.79M
HRank	94.53	0.69B	2.74M
DFPC	94.54	1.02B	3.51M
MLPruner	94.61	0.54B	2.55M
LRP-CDG-0.65	94.65	0.55B	2.60M

We compare the proposed LRP-CDG with representative structured pruning methods on CIFAR-10 and ImageNet across multiple network architectures,

Table 3. Pruning results of ResNet-56 on CIFAR-10. The numerical suffix in LRP-CDG indicates the pruning rate α.

Model	Top-1 (%)	FLOPs	Parameters
Baseline	93.26	126.56M	0.85M
Depgraph	93.20	81.00M	0.49M
DFPC	93.06	90.90M	0.73M
MLPruner	93.10	91.59M	0.63M
HRank	93.17	62.72M	0.49M
CIE	93.18	64.62M	0.51M
LRP-CDG-0.5	93.24	65.26M	0.55M

including VGG-16, GoogleNet, ResNet-56, and ResNet-50. The comparison methods include HRank [17], MLPruner [28], FPEM [29], CIE [30], DFPC [31], DepGraph [32], and Otov2 [16], which represent state-of-the-art criteria based on feature statistics, optimization, and dependency modeling.

Tables 1, 2 and 3 summarize the pruning results on CIFAR-10. Across all evaluated architectures, LRP-CDG consistently achieves competitive or superior accuracy under comparable compression ratios. In particular, compared with HRank [17] and MLPruner [28], LRP-CDG achieves higher accuracy at similar FLOPs and parameter budgets, while outperforming dependency-based methods such as DepGraph [32] in parameter efficiency.

On ImageNet, the ResNet-50 results are reported in Table 4. Under aggressive compression (0.82B FLOPs and 6.90M parameters), LRP-CDG preserves 72.56% Top-1 and 92.03% Top-5 accuracy, exceeding Otov2 [16], ABCPruner, HRank [17], MLPruner [28], and CIE [30] under similar or even looser computational constraints.

Table 4. Results on ImageNet using ResNet-50, reporting total FLOPs, number of parameters, and Top-1/Top-5 accuracy of compressed models.The numerical suffix in LRP-CDG indicates the pruning rate α.

Model	Accuracy (%)		FLOPs	Params
	Top-1	Top-5		
Baseline	76.01	92.96	4.11B	25.56M
Otov2	68.42	88.30	1.10B	8.66M
ABCPruner	70.29	89.63	0.94B	7.35M
MLPruner	71.95	90.94	0.88B	7.20M
HRank	71.98	91.01	1.55B	13.37M
CIE	72.23	91.26	0.90B	7.16M
LRP-CDG-0.8	72.56	92.03	0.82B	6.90M

The performance advantage of LRP-CDG can be attributed to its task-aware pruning mechanism. By leveraging LRP-based relevance attribution [23,24], pruning decisions are directly aligned with semantic contribution to prediction. Furthermore, the cross-layer dependency graph preserves essential feature propagation paths, preventing structural disruption that commonly occurs in purely layer-wise or magnitude-based pruning methods. As a result, LRP-CDG achieves a favorable balance between compression efficiency and accuracy preservation across datasets and architectures.

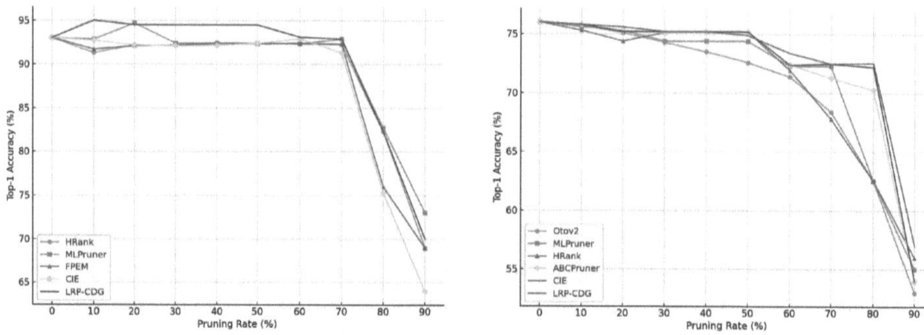

Fig. 3. Accuracy changes under different pruning rates. (a) VGG-16 on CIFAR-10. (b) ResNet-50 on ImageNet.

This robustness is particularly evident in complex models like ResNet-50, which relies on multiple parallel feature pathways. Unlike conventional pruning methods that may disrupt these delicate structures, LRP-CDG uses its dependency graph to identify and remove entire low-contribution pathways, thereby preserving a complete and synergistic feature-extraction skeleton. This enables the pruned model to maintain fine-grained discriminative capacity even under high compression ratios, as illustrated in Fig. 3.

Figure 3 further demonstrates the accuracy trends under different pruning rates. For VGG-16 on CIFAR-10 (Fig. 3 (a)), LRP-CDG shows a more gradual and stable accuracy decline compared to other methods, maintaining better robustness even at 90% pruning rate. For ResNet-50 on ImageNet (Fig. 3 (b)), LRP-CDG sustains relatively stable performance under high pruning ratios, indicating its effectiveness in preserving task performance under extreme compression.

4.3 Interpretability Validation

To evaluate whether LRP-CDG preserves the model's interpretability after pruning, we analyze the stability of decision regions using Gradient-weighted Class Activation Mapping (Grad-CAM) [20].

For randomly selected test images from CIFAR-10 and ImageNet, Grad-CAM heatmaps generated by the pruned model exhibit strong spatial overlap with those of the original model. Quantitatively, over 80% of the samples achieve an Intersection over Union (IoU) exceeding 0.75 between corresponding activation regions.

In complex scenes, the pruned model often produces more concentrated activation regions on target objects, indicating that redundant background features are effectively suppressed .

These results demonstrate that LRP-CDG preserves the core decision logic of the network while maintaining interpretability under aggressive compression (Fig. 4).

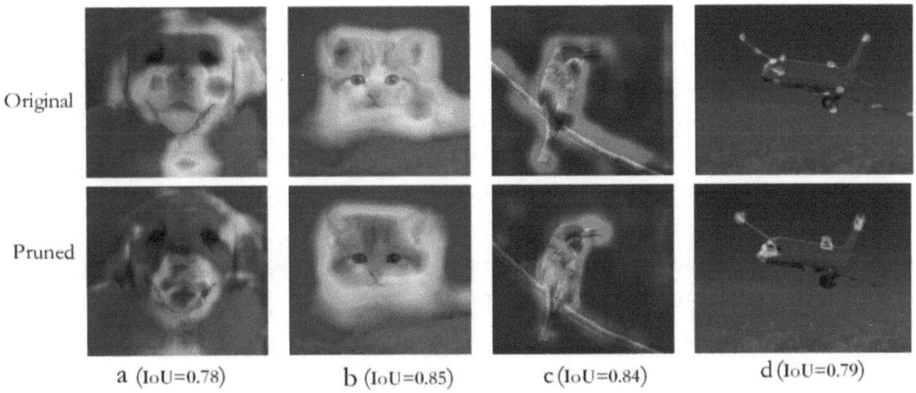

Fig. 4. Comparison of Class Activation Maps Before and After Pruning.

4.4 Ablation Study

To evaluate the individual contributions of each component in LRP-CDG, we conduct ablation experiments by progressively removing or replacing key modules while keeping the pruning ratio consistent with previous experiments. Specifically, we compare four variants: the unpruned baseline model, a pruning method using only LRP-based relevance scoring (Only-LRP), a variant using gradient-based dependency estimation (Only-Grad), and the complete LRP-CDG framework.

Table 5 summarizes the ablation results across different architectures and datasets. Compared with Only-LRP, incorporating the cross-layer dependency graph significantly improves both accuracy and interpretability metrics, indicating that dependency modeling is essential for preserving feature hierarchies. Replacing LRP with standard gradient-based attribution leads to consistent performance degradation, demonstrating the superiority of LRP in capturing task-relevant dependencies. Overall, the complete LRP-CDG achieves the best trade-off between accuracy, compression efficiency, and interpretability, validating the necessity and complementarity of each proposed component.

Table 5. Comparison of Different Models on Various Metrics. The balance parameter α of each part are consistent with those before.

Model	Top1 (%)	FLOPs	KER(%)	KRC(%)
VGG-16				
Only-LRP	92.11	111.53	90.3	85.2
Only-Grad	91.55	112.36M	87.2	82.2
LRP-CDG	92.61	110.42M	92.71	89.4
ResNet-56				
Only-LRP	93.02	66.39M	86.5	71.7
Only-Grad	92.87	68.21M	83.1	69.3
LRP-CDG	93.20	65.26M	87.4	75.1
GoogleNet				
Only-LRP	94.43	0.86B	89.4	82.7
Only-Grad	94.06	0.94B	85.3	79.4
LRP-CDG	94.65	0.78B	94.4	85.2
ResNet-50				
Only-LRP	72.13	0.93B	85.6	73.4
Only-Grad	71.95	1.01B	82.1	71.7
LRP-CDG	72.56	0.82B	89.3	78.2

5 Conclusions and Future Work

In this paper,we propose an interpretability-based pruning method for CNNs. Using LRP, we systematically quantify feature contributions from shallow to deep layers and construct a cross-layer dependency graph to model feature transmission paths. Based on this evaluation, we design a pruning strategy that balances interpretability and task relevance, enabling rapid identification of sparse structures that meet target complexity requirements. Experiments on benchmark datasets including ImageNet and CIFAR demonstrate that LRP-CDG achieves significant efficiency improvements while maintaining model accuracy. Notably, our method preserves numerous critical interpretable kernels, substantially enhancing model transparency. However, since the dependency graph is computed based on a fixed architecture, its adaptability under different compression ratios remains suboptimal. Future work will focus on improving dynamic modeling of dependencies to better accommodate diverse compression needs.

Acknowledgements. This research was funded by the Longjiang Project Young Goose Innovation Team Support Program under Grant 2024CYLJ01, the Natural Science Foundation of Heilongjiang Province for Key projects, China under Grant ZD2021F004, and the Science and Technology Project of the Department of Transportation of Heilongjiang Province (Project No. 2025Z016).

References

1. Yang, L., Zelin, Z., Xiang, L., Lei, W., Xuhui, X.: Ore image classification based on small deep learning model: evaluation and optimization of model depth, model structure and data size. Minerals Eng. **172**, 107020 (2021)
2. Junjue, W., Yanfei, Z., Zhuo, Z., Ailong, M., Liangpei, Z.: RSNet: the search for remote sensing deep neural networks in recognition tasks. IEEE Trans. Geosci. Remote Sens. **59**(3), 2520–2534 (2021)
3. Yongchao, X.: Gliding vertex on the horizontal bounding box for multi-oriented object detection. IEEE Trans. Pattern Anal. Mach. Intell. **43**(4), 1452–1459 (2021)
4. Alberto, M.: Deep learning for edge computing: current trends, cross-layer optimizations, and open research challenges. IEEE Computer Society Annual Symposium on VLSI , 553–559 (2019)
5. Shaohui, M., Xiaofeng, C., Yifan, Z., Jun, L., Antonio, P.: Accelerating convolutional neural network-based hyperspectral image classification by step activation quantization. IEEE Trans. Geosci. Remote Sens. **60**, 1–12 (2022)
6. François, C.: Xception: deep learning with depthwise separable convolutions. In: 2017 IEEE Conference on Computer Vision and Pattern Recognition (pp. 1800–1807). IEEE Computer Society (2017). https://doi.org/10.1109/CVPR.2017.195
7. Mingrui, Z., Jie, L., Nannan, W., Xinbo, G.: Knowledge distillation for face photo-sketch synthesis. IEEE Trans. Neural Netw. Learn. Syst. **33**(2), 893–906 (2022)
8. Han, S., Mao, H., Dally, W.J.: Deep compression: compressing deep neural networks with pruning. Trained Quantization and Huffman Coding, In ICLR (2016)
9. Molchanov, P., Tyree, S., Karras, T., Aila, T., Kautz, J.: Pruning convolutional neural networks for resource efficient inference (2016). arXiv:1611.06440
10. Molchanov, P., Mallya, A., Tyree, S., Frosio, I., Kautz, J.: Importance estimation for neural network pruning. In: 2019 IEEE/CVF Conference on Computer Vision and Pattern Recognition, pp. 11256–11264 (2019)
11. Liu, Ning, et al.: AutoCompress: An Automatic DNN Structured Pruning Framework for Ultra-High Compression Rates. In: Proceedings of the AAAI Conference on Artificial Intelligence, vol. 34, no. 04 ,pp. 4876–4883 (2020)
12. Bach, S., Binder, A., Montavon, G., Klauschen, F., Müller, K.R., Samek, W.: On pixel-wise explanations for non-linear classifier decisions by layer-wise relevance propagation. PLoS ONE **10**(7), e0130140 (2015)
13. Han, S., Pool, J., Tran, J., Dally, W.J.: Learning both weights and connections for efficient neural networks. In: Proceedings of the 29th International Conference on Neural Information Processing Systems, pp. 1135–1143. MIT Press (2015)
14. Liu, Z., Li, J., Shen, Z., Huang, G., Yan, S., Zhang, C.: Learning efficient convolutional networks through network slimming. In: ICCV (2017)
15. Frankle, J., Carbin, M.: The lottery ticket hypothesis: finding sparse, trainable neural networks. In: ICLR (2019)
16. Chen, T., Liang, L., Tianyu, D., Zhu, Z., Zharkov, I.: Otov2: automatic, generic, user-friendly. In: International Conference on Learning Representations (2023)
17. Lin, M.: HRank: filter pruning using high-rank feature map. In: CVPR (2020)
18. He, Y., Lin, J., Liu, Z., Wang, H., Li, L.J., Han, S.: AMC: AutoML for model compression and acceleration on mobile devices. In: ECCV (2018)
19. Liu, H., Simonyan, K., Yang, Y.: DARTS: differentiable architecture search. In: ICLR (2019)
20. Selvaraju, R.R., Cogswell, M., Das, A., Vedantam, R., Parikh, D., Batra, D.: Grad-CAM: visual explanations from deep networks via gradient-based localization. In: 2017 IEEE International Conference on Computer Vision, pp. 618–626 (2017)

21. Ye, J., Lu, X., Lin, Z., Wang, J.Z.: Rethinking the smaller-norm-less-informative assumption in channel pruning of convolution layers. In: ICLR (2020)
22. Wang, C., Zhang, G., Grosse, R.: Picking winning tickets before training by preserving gradient flow. In: ICLR (2021)
23. Yeom, S.K., Seegerer, P., Lapuschkin, S., Binder, A., Samek, W.: Pruning by explaining: a novel criterion for deep neural network pruning. Pattern Recogn. **120**, 107899 (2021)
24. Vakilzadeh, H.S.M., Dreyer, M., Achtibat, R., Wiegand, T., Samek, W., Lapuschkin, S.: Pruning by explaining revisited: optimizing attribution methods to prune CNNs and transformers. ArXiv abs/2408.12568 (2024)
25. Montavon, G., Lapuschkin, S., Binder, A., Samek, W., Müller, K.R.: Explaining nonlinear classification decisions with deep taylor decomposition. Pattern Recogn. **65**, 211–222 (2017)
26. Deng, J., Dong, W., Socher, R., Li, L. J., Li, K., Fei-Fei, L.: ImageNet: a large-scale hierarchical image database. In: 2009 IEEE Conference on Computer Vision and Pattern Recognition (pp. 248–255) (2009)
27. Krizhevsky, A., Hinton, G.: Learning multiple layers of features from tiny images. Handbook Syst. Auto. Dis. **4**, 1 (2009)
28. Chen S, Zhao Y.: MLPruner: pruning convolutional neural networks with automatic mask learning. PeerJ Comput Sci. 25 Aug 2025, 11:e3132. https://doi.org/10.7717/peerj-cs.3132.PMID: 40989293; PMCID: PMC12453823
29. Xu, S., Li, Y., Yang, L., Zhang, B., Sun, D., Liu, K.: Filter pruning via expectation-maximization. Neural Comput. Appl. , 1–12 (2022). https://doi.org/10.1007/s00521-022-07127-2
30. Youzao, L., Peng, P., Kai, J., Weisheng, X.: Cross-layer importance evaluation for neural network pruning. Neural Netw. **179**(C), 106496 (2024)
31. Narshana, T., Murti, C., Bhattacharyya, C.: DFPC: Data flow driven pruning of coupled channels without data. In: The Eleventh International Conference on Learning Representations (2023). https://openreview.net/forum?id=mhnHqRqcjYU
32. Fang, G., Ma, X., Song, M., Mi, M.B., Wang, X.: Depgraph: towards any structural pruning. In: Proceedings of the IEEE/CVF Conference on Computer Vision and Pattern Recognition, pp. 16091–16101 (2023)
33. Lin, M., Ji, R., Zhang, Y., Zhang, B., Wu, Y., Tian, Y.: Channel pruning via automatic structure search. In: Proc. 29th Int. Joint Conf. Artif. Intell, (pp. 673–679) (2020)
34. He, K., Zhang, X., Ren, S., Sun, J.: Deep residual learning for image recognition. In: 2016 IEEE Conference on Computer Vision and Pattern Recognition, pp. 770–778. (2016)
35. Simonyan, K., Zisserman, A.: Very deep convolutional networks for large-scale image recognition. In: International Conference on Learning Representations (2015)
36. Szegedy, C.: Going deeper with convolutions. In: 2015 IEEE Conference on Computer Vision and Pattern Recognition, pp. 1–9 (2015)
37. Luo, J.-H., Wu, J., Lin, W.: ThiNet: a filter level pruning method for deep neural network compression. In: 2017 IEEE International Conference on Computer Vision (ICCV), Venice, Italy, 2017, pp. 5068-5076. https://doi.org/10.1109/ICCV.2017.541
38. Sakai, Y., Eto, Y., Teranishi, Y.: Structured pruning for deep neural networks with adaptive pruning rate derivation based on connection sensitivity and loss function. J. Adv. Inf. Technol. **13**(3), 295–300 (2022)

Comparison Analysis of Machine Learning Algorithms for Predicting Diabetes Risk on Clinical and Lifestyle Data

Yin Yin May Phoo(✉) and Hamidullah Sokout

Kobe Institute of Computing, Graduate School of Information Technology, Kobe, Japan
s24151@st.kic.ac.jp, sokout@kic.ac.jp

Abstract. Early prediction of diabetes is a critical task in preventive healthcare. Particularly in developing countries where medical resources and screening opportunities are limited. According to International Diabetes Federation, 382 million people are living with diabetes worldwide. This number is projected to rise to 592 million by 2035. Timely risk assessment and early intervention have been shown to reduce type 2 diabetes by approximately 58%. This may lower likelihood of long-term complications and support effective public-health interventions. This study presents machine learning multi-factor prediction models focusing on improving early diabetes risk detection. Rather than relying solely on traditional clinical indicators, the proposed approach integrates lifestyle-related factors including dietary habits, physical activity levels and stress conditions, which are recognized to impact diabetes development. This study uses large and balanced public Diabetes Health Indicators Dataset which contains over 70,000 samples and 21 behavioral, demographic, and clinical features. Multiple machine learning models, including LR, Random Forest, SVM, XGBoost, CatBoost, and ANN, were developed. To minimize false negatives and ensure high sensitivity in identifying positive cases, the CatBoost classifier was fine-tuned to maximize recall using 10-fold cross-validation, achieving a 92% recall score the best performance among all compared models. The findings confirm the effectiveness of recall-optimized ensemble models while ensuring computational efficiency for real-world deployment. Future work will develop a mobile application integrating high-performance models, smartwatch data, and an AI chatbot to support citizens by tracking user behavior, diet habits, and enhancing diabetes awareness.

Keywords: Machine Learning · Multi-factor Diabetes Risk Prediction · Healthcare · CatBoost · Model comparison

1 Introduction

Diabetes mellitus is one of the most serious global public health challenges, affecting hundreds of millions of people worldwide, with prevalence increasing rapidly due to unhealthy dietary patterns, sedentary lifestyles, and aging populations. If not detected early, diabetes can lead to severe and long-term complications, including cardiovascular

C. Xu (Ed.): ICMLSC 2026, CCIS 2948, pp. 97–108, 2027.
https://doi.org/10.1007/978-981-92-1546-1_8

disease, kidney failure, neuropathy, and vision impairment [1, 2], placing a significant burden on individuals, healthcare systems, and national economies. Therefore, early prediction and prevention are critical for reducing both health risks and other related costs.

Traditional diagnosis method mainly rely on clinical measurements and laboratory tests such as blood glucose levels. That identify diabetes only after the disease has occurred to symptomatic stage [3]. These methods can't provide how daily behaviors and lifestyle contribute to diabetes risk although we have strong evidence that factors such as physical inactivity, poor diet, smoking, and alcohol consumption play major role in diabetes development [4].

Advanced machine learning (ML) technologies have emerged effectively for early diabetes risk prediction. These ML techniques enable automated analysis of diverse health indicators and can identify individuals risk before clinical symptoms appear [5]. However many existing studies rely on Pima Indians Diabetes dataset. This dataset is limited in size, population diversity and features. That restricts its ability to reflect real-world diabetes risk.

To overcome these limitations, large datasets such as Behavioral Risk Factor Surveillance System (BRFSS) provide more realistic situation of diabetes risk. BRFSS includes behavioral, lifestyle and health-related variables such as body mass index, blood pressure, cholesterol levels, physical activity, smoking, alcohol consumption, and dietary patterns [6]. These factors enables more accurate risk assessment and improves public understanding how daily behaviors contribute to diabetes development and supporting preventive action.

Although lot of ML models are applied, there is no clear which model is the most suitable for real-world deployment [7]. Many studies emphasize accuracy while overlooking recall which is critical for minimizing missed diabetic cases [8]. Additionally real deployment requires balance and predictive performance with computational efficiency and scalability [9]. In response, this study evaluates multiple ML models using balanced BRFSS dataset prioritizing recall optimization and deployment feasibility to support practical healthcare applications.

2 Literature Review

Most previous studies used the PIMA Indian Diabetes Dataset which contains only 768 samples and 8 clinical features. Gyawali (2024) [10] evaluated Logistic Regression, KNN, and Random Forest models and reported accuracies from 70% to 78%. These limitations are due to the small dataset size. Naz and Ahuja (2020) [11] used deep learning model and achieved accuracy of approximately 82%. But computational cost increased and no incorporated lifestyle features. Rani (2020) [12] demonstrated that appropriate feature selection and hyperparameter tuning could improve model accuracy by 5–10%.

Studies based on the PIMA dataset remain constrained by limited feature diversity. Key behavioral risk factors such as physical activity, smoking, alcohol consumption, and dietary habits are not included. Those are mainly contribute more than 40% of type 2 diabetes risk according to WHO reports. Consequently, models training is only rely on clinical indicators. It may perform well on benchmark datasets but show reduced effectiveness in real-world populations.

Recent medical and epidemiological research emphasizes that type 2 diabetes is strongly influenced by lifestyle-related behaviors that affect insulin sensitivity and glucose metabolism [16–18]. Physical inactivity has been shown to reduce insulin responsiveness in muscle tissue, increasing the risk of hyperglycemia and insulin resistance. Similarly, diets high in refined carbohydrates and saturated fats contribute to obesity and chronic inflammation [16, 17], both of which are key drivers of metabolic dysfunction. Smoking and excessive alcohol consumption further exacerbate insulin resistance and impair pancreatic beta-cell function, accelerating disease progression [19, 20]. These biological pathways highlight the importance of incorporating behavioral and lifestyle factors into diabetes risk prediction models [21].

To overcome feature limitations, recent research has increasingly adopted the Behavioral Risk Factor Surveillance System (BRFSS) dataset, which includes over 70,000 balanced samples and more than 20 behavioral, demographic, and clinical variables. Studies using BRFSS have reported accuracy improvements of 8–15% compared to models trained on smaller datasets, particularly when ensemble methods such as Random Forest and Gradient Boosting are applied. However, most studies primarily optimize overall accuracy, while clinically critical metrics such as recall are often underreported. Since missing a positive diabetes case can have serious health consequences, recall-focused evaluation is essential. Addressing this gap, the present study compares multiple machine learning models using the BRFSS dataset and emphasizes recall optimization to improve early diabetes risk detection in practical healthcare settings.

3 Dataset Description

This study uses the Behavioral Risk Factor Surveillance System (BRFSS) 2015 Diabetes Health Indicators dataset, sourced from Kaggle [13]. BRFSS is one of the world's largest public health surveys, conducted annually by the U.S. Centers for Disease Control and Prevention (CDC) [14]. The dataset contains more than 70,000 records and includes a wide range of clinical and lifestyle variables associated with diabetes.

3.1 Dataset Characteristics

The version used in this study is balanced 50–50 dataset (equal number of diabetic and non-diabetic samples). Binary classification, 0 means No Diabetes, 1 means pre-diabetes or diabetes. Dataset is already cleaned and preprocessed by dataset author. So no missing values, well formatted categorical and numerical features and suitable for direct machine learning use.

3.2 Feature Categories

Below table 1 summarizes the features used in this study, grouped into clinical and lifestyle categories. Clinical features represent medical and physiological conditions, while lifestyle features capture daily behaviors, habits, and healthcare access that influence diabetes risk. Table 2 describes the features, possible values and datatype of Dataset.

Table 1. Categorized Features

Clinical Features	Lifestyle Features
Body Mass Index (BMI)	Smoking Status
High blood pressure	Alcohol consumption
High cholesterol	Physical activity
Cholesterol check	Fruit intake
Heart Disease or Attack	Vegetable intake
Stroke	Difficulty walking
General health	Health care access
Physical health	
Mental health	

Table 2. Dataset Features and Datatype Description

Features Name	Possible Values	Description	Datatype
Diabetes_binary	0,1	0 = no diabetes 1 = prediabetes/diabetes	float64
HighBP	0,1	0 = no high BP 1 = high BP	float64
HighChol	0,1	0 = no high cholesterol 1 = high cholesterol	float64
CholCheck	0,1	0 = no cholesterol check in 5 years 1 = yes cholesterol check in 5 years	float64
BMI	Numeric value	Body Mass Index	float64
Smoker	0,1	Have you smoked at least 100 cigarettes in your entire life? [Note: 5 packs = 100 cigarettes] 0 = no 1 = yes	float64
Stroke	0,1	(Ever told) you had a stroke. 0 = no 1 = yes	float64
HeartDiseaseorAttack	0,1	coronary heart disease (CHD) or myocardial infarction (MI) 0 = no 1 = yes	float64
PhysActivity	0,1	physical activity in past 30 days - not including job 0 = no 1 = yes	float64
Fruits	0,1	Consume Fruit 1 or more times per day 0 = no 1 = yes	float64
Veggies	0,1	Consume Vegetables 1 or more times per day 0 = no 1 = yes	float64

(continued)

Table 2. (*continued*)

Features Name	Possible Values	Description	Datatype
HvyAlcoholConsump	0,1	(adult men >= 14 drinks per week and adult women >= drinks per week) 0 = no 1 = yes	float64
AnyHealthcare	0,1	Have any kind of health care coverage, including health insurance, prepaid plans such as HMO, etc. 0 = no 1 = yes	float64
NoDocbcCost	0,1	Was there a time in the past 12 months when you needed to see a doctor but could not because of cost? 0 = no 1 = yes	float64
GenHlth	1–5	Would you say that in general your health is: scale 1–5 1 = excellent 2 = very good 3 = good 4 = fair 5 = poor	float64
MentHlth	1–5	days of poor mental health scale 1–30 days	float64
PhysHlth	1–5	physical illness or injury days in past 30 days scale 1–30	float64
DiffWalk	0,1	Do you have serious difficulty walking or climbing stairs? 0 = no 1 = yes	float64
Sex	0,1	0 = female 1 = male	float64
Age	Number	13-level age category (_AGEG5YR see codebook) 1 = 18–24 9 = 60–64 13 = 80 or older	float64
Education	1–6	Education level (EDUCA see codebook) scale 1–6 1 = Never attended school or only kindergarten 2 =	float64
Income	1–8	Income scale (INCOME2 see codebook) scale 1–8 1 = less than $10,000 5 = less than $35,000 8 = $75,000 or more	float64

4 Model Development

This section describes the machine learning models used in this study, their architecture, and the unified pipeline applied for training, evaluation, and comparison.

4.1 Model Architecture

The overall architecture (Fig. 1) follows a standardized machine learning pipeline. Figure 1 illustrates the end-to-end workflow from data preprocessing through model building, evaluation, and comparison across Traditional ML, Boosting ML, and Deep Learning approaches. This ensures that all models are evaluated fairly under the same preprocessing, train-test setup, and performance metrics.

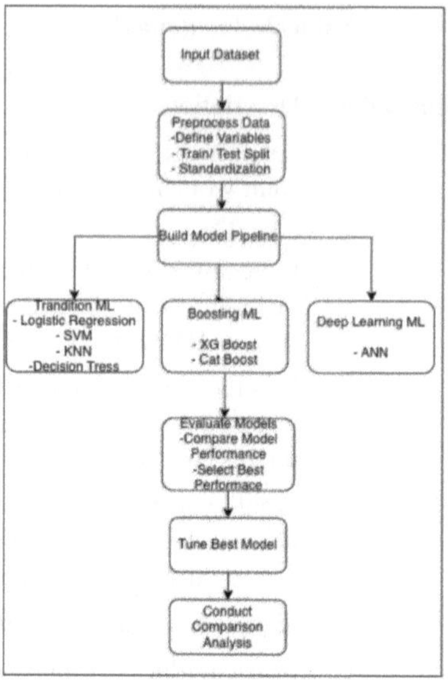

Fig. 1. High-Level Architecture Diagram of Machine Learning Model Development

4.2 Training and Testing

For model development and evaluation, the preprocessed dataset was divided into training and testing sets using an 80:20 split, where 80% of the data was used for model training and the remaining 20% was reserved for independent testing. To ensure reproducibility and consistency of experimental results, a fixed random state of 0 was applied during the train–test split. This guarantees that the same data samples are used for training and testing across all experiments, enabling fair comparison among different models. After splitting train and test, standard scaler was applied to non-binary features.

Model Configuration and Hyper-parameters

In this section, we shall discuss, the each model parameters used in the training process. The same data split were used to ensure fair comparison and standardize preprocessing pipeline. Unless otherwise stated, default hyper-parameters provided by the respective libraries were used during initial training. This approach allows objective baseline comparison across different classifiers. The key training parameters for each model are summarized in Table 3.

Table 3. Training Parameters applied on Various Models

Model	Key Parameters
Logistic Regression	solver = lbfgs, max_iter = 1000, random_state = 0
Support Vector Machine (SVM)	kernel = linear, C = 1.0, random_state = 0
K-Nearest Neighbors (KNN)	n_neighbors = 5, metric = minkowski, p = 2, random_state = 0

(continued)

Table 3. (*continued*)

Model	Key Parameters
Decision Tree	criterion = entropy, random_state = 0
Random Forest	n_estimators = 10, criterion = entropy, random_state = 0
XG Boost	n_estimators = 100, learning_rate = 0.1, max_depth = 6
Cat Boost	iterations = 500, learning_rate = 0.1, depth = 6, loss_function = Logloss, random_seed = 0
ANN	Dense layers: (25, 10), activation: ReLU, optimizer: Adam, epochs: 10, batch_size: 32

Table 4. Training time and inference time (in seconds) for all machine learning models

Model	Training Time(Colab CPU)	Inference Time (Colab CPU)
Logistic Regression	0.185 s	0.023 s
SVM	349.8 s	21.6 s
KNN	0.03 s	12.3 s
Decision Tree	0.41 s	0.031 s
Random Forest	2.13 s	0.087 s
XG Boost	0.76 s	0.102 s
Cat Boost	21.9 s	0.007 s
ANN	60.1s	1.747 s

Table 5. Comparative classification performance of all machine learning models

Model	Precision		Recall		F1-Score		Accuracy
	0	1	0	1	0	1	
LR	0.75	0.75	0.73	0.77	0.74	0.76	0.75
SVM	0.77	0.74	0.70	0.79	0.73	0.76	0.75
KNN	0.72	0.71	0.68	0.74	0.70	0.72	0.71
DT	0.65	0.67	0.66	0.65	0.65	0.66	0.66
RF	0.70	0.73	0.72	0.70	0.71	0.71	0.71
XG Boost	0.77	0.73	0.70	0.79	0.73	0.76	0.75
Cat Boost	0.77	0.74	0.70	0.80	0.74	0.77	0.75
ANN	0.79	0.73	0.69	0.82	0.73	0.77	0.76
Tuned CatBoost	0.86	0.68	0.56	0.92	0.68	0.78	0.74

5 Comparison Analysis

In this section, we shall present the comparative performance of the nine machine learning models evaluated in this study, including traditional methods, ensemble/boosting algorithms, and a deep learning model. Models were assessed using accuracy, precision, recall, F1-score, macro average, weighted average, and computational efficiency (training and inference time). Special emphasis was placed on recall for the positive class (diabetes) to minimize false-negative predictions.

5.1 Comparative Model Performance Analysis

Table 5 presents a comprehensive comparison of the classification performance of all evaluated machine learning models using precision, recall, F1-score, and accuracy metrics. In the first stage, traditional machine learning models such as Logistic Regression (LR), Support Vector Machine (SVM), KNN, Decision Tree (DT), and Random Forest (RF) show moderate and relatively balanced performance. Among these, LR and SVM achieve comparable overall accuracy (0.75). KNN and DT show comparatively lower performance, particularly in recall and F1-score and poor in positive diabetes cases.

Ensemble and boosting-based models exhibit improved predictive capability. XGBoost and CatBoost outperform most traditional models, with CatBoost achieving a higher recall of 0.80 for the positive class, indicating its stronger ability to correctly identify individuals with diabetes. Although ANN achieves the highest recall (0.82) among the base models, its overall precision and stability are slightly lower compared to CatBoost.

Given that recall for the positive class is a critical metric in medical risk prediction where missing a diabetic patient can have serious consequences. CatBoost is selected as the best-performing model in the first stage. In the second stage, CatBoost is further optimized using GridSearchCV with 10-fold cross-validation, explicitly focusing on maximizing recall for the positive class. The details of tuning model will be discussed in next section.

5.2 Hyperparameter Tuning

After selecting CatBoost as the best-performing model in the initial comparison phase, further optimization was conducted to enhance its ability to correctly identify positive diabetes cases. Hyper-parameter tuning was performed using GridSearchCV with 10-fold cross-validation, where the recall score was explicitly chosen as the optimization objective to minimize false negatives. The search space included key CatBoost parameters (Tables 6): the number of boosting iterations (500), tree depth (6 and 8), learning rate (0.05 and 0.1), L2 regularization coefficient (3 and 5), and class imbalance adjustment through scale_pos_weight (1 and 2). This process involves multiple parameter combinations to enhance model sensitivity and overall performance. As a result, the CatBoost model achieved a clear improvement in recall for the positive class. Recall score of 0.92 showed that recall-focused hyperparameter tuning is effective for medical risk prediction where early and accurate detection is critical. It significantly reduced false negative and also got competitive overall accuracy. This makes well suited for diabetes risk prediction applications we will develop in the future.

Table 6. Hyperparameter of the CatBoost Model

Hyperparameter	Values Tested
Number of iterations	500
Tree depth	6, 8
Learning rate	0.05, 0.1
L2 leaf regularization	3, 5
Scale positive weight	1, 2
Cross-validation	10-fold (CV = 10)
Optimization metric	Recall (positive class)

6 Computational Efficiency and Inference Time Analysis

In this section, we shall examine computational efficiency of evaluated machine learning models. Training and inference time are summarized in Table 4. Computational performance is majority for real-world applications. Our systems must response within limited time and resource [17]. Inference time is the time taken to get the predicted result. Inference time is especially important for risk screening systems that are designed to deliver real-time diabetes risk assessments.

As shown in Table 4, Logistic Regression and Decision Tree require minimal computational resources for both training and inference. Support Vector Machine and K-Nearest Neighbors are significantly higher inference time which may reduces their suitability for real-time deployment. Random Forest and XGBoost are more balanced and improved predictive performance.

Among them, CatBoost provides the most favorable balance between predictive effectiveness and computational efficiency. Although its training time is slightly high, CatBoost achieves the lowest inference time, making it well suited for real-world deployment. When both predictive performance and inference efficiency are considered, CatBoost is the most practical choice for real-time clinical systems and mobile health applications focused on diabetes risk prediction.

Table 7. Comparison Summary

Criteria	Best Model	Reason
Accuracy	Tuned CatBoost	Balanced performance across metrics
Recall (Positive)	Tuned CatBoost	Prevents missing at-risk individuals
F1-Score	CatBoost / ANN	Strong trade-off between precision & recall

(continued)

Table 7. (*continued*)

Criteria	Best Model	Reason
Inference Speed	CatBoost	0.007 s per prediction
Training Speed	KNN / LR	Useful for baseline models

7 Conclusion

As a conclusion, these findings (Table 7) indicated that ensemble boosting techniques particularly CatBoost are well suited for practical diabetes risk prediction systems, providing both reliable predictive performance and computational efficiency necessary for real-world deployment. The prioritization of recall in this study is well aligned with preventive healthcare objectives where failing to identify individuals at risk of diabetes can result in delayed intervention and increased long-term complications. Achieving recall 92% with tuned CatBoost model indicates strong sensitivity in detecting potential diabetes cases, which is particularly valuable in early screening and population-level risk assessment. However, this improvement in recall is accompanied by reduction in precision for the positive class, leading to higher number of false-positive predictions.

From clinical perspective, false-positive rate may raise concerns regarding increased follow-up workload and the potential for alarm fatigue among healthcare providers. In high-pressure clinical environments, frequent false alerts can reduce trust in automated systems and divert attention from high-risk cases. Nevertheless, the practical impact of this trade-off depends on the intended deployment context. In population screening and community health programs, false positives are generally acceptable if they prompt low-cost, non-invasive follow-up actions such as lifestyle counseling, dietary guidance, or basic screening tests. In such settings, the cost of a missed diagnosis is significantly higher than the cost of additional preventive checks.

Importantly, this system is not designed to replace clinical diagnosis but to function as an early risk stratification tool. The generated alerts are intended to support decision-making by identifying individuals who may benefit from further assessment rather than triggering immediate clinical intervention. This aligns with existing public health strategies that emphasize early detection, behavioral modification, and risk-based screening to reduce the long-term burden of non-communicable diseases. By integrating recall-optimized machine learning with lifestyle-based risk indicators, the proposed approach complements current preventive frameworks and supports scalable, data-driven public health interventions.

8 Future Work

In the Future, we intend to develop a mobile application that incorporates with CatBoost Model that is the most effective machine learning model according to this study. The application will collect behavioral and lifestyle information such as dietary patterns and physical activity data from smartwatches. And also AI chatbot will also be implemented to provide personalized health guidance and preventive recommendations based on user's behaviour. This mobile app will help individuals early detection, to monitor their daily habits and raise awareness through personalized health advices.

Acknowledgement. The author sincerely acknowledges the university(Kobe Institute of Computing) for providing academic support and research facilities throughout the master's degree program. Special appreciation is extended to the Japan International Cooperation Agency (JICA) for fully funding the author's master's studies. This financial support also enabled participation in this conference and the dissemination of the research findings. The author is grateful for the opportunity provided through this sponsorship.

References

1. World Health Organization Page. https://www.who.int/publications/i/item/9789241565257. Accessed 05 Sept 2025
2. International Diabetes Federation Page. https://diabetesatlas.org/. Accessed 20 Oct 2025
3. American Diabetes Association, Standards of Medical Care in Diabetes(2023), https://diabetesjournals.org/care. Accessed 04 Sept 2025
4. Hu, F.B.: Globalization of Diabetes (2015), https://diabetesjournals.org/care/article/34/6/1249/27871. Accessed 01 Oct 2025
5. Kavakiotis, I., Tsave, O., Salifoglou, A., Maglaveras, N., Vlahavas, I., Chouvarda, I.: Machine learning and data mining methods in diabetes research. Comput. Struct. Biotechnol. J. (2017). https://www.sciencedirect.com/science/article/pii/S2001037017300013
6. Centers for Disease Control and Prevention: Behavioral Risk Factor Surveillance System (BRFSS). CDC, Atlanta (2022). https://www.cdc.gov/brfss/index.html
7. Gyawali, B.: Diabetes Mellitus Prediction with Classification Algorithms Using WEKA. School of Technology (2024). https://www.researchgate.net/. Accessed 10 Dec 2025
8. Chicco, D., Jurman, G.: The advantages of the Matthews correlation coefficient over accuracy. BMC Geno. (2020). https://doi.org/10.1186/s12864-019-6413-7. Accessed 10 Dec 2025
9. Sarker, I.H.: Machine learning model deployment for real-world applications. AI Rev. (2021). https://doi.org/10.1007/s10462-021-10003-2
10. Gyawali, B.: Diabetes Mellitus Prediction with Classification Algorithms Using WEKA. School of Technology (2024)
11. Naz, H., Ahuja, S.: Deep learning approach for diabetes prediction using PIMA Indian dataset. J. Diabetes Metab. Disord. **19**(1), 391–403 (2020). https://doi.org/10.1007/s40200-020-00520-5
12. Rani, K.J.: Diabetes prediction using machine learning. Int. J. Sci. Res. Comput. Sci. Eng. Inform. Technol. **6**(4), 294–305 (2020). https://doi.org/10.32628/cseit206463
13. Teboul, A.: Diabetes Health Indicators Dataset (BRFSS 2015). Kaggle. https://www.kaggle.com/datasets/alexteboul/diabetes-health-indicators-dataset. Accessed 10 Jul 2025
14. Centers for Disease Control and Prevention (CDC): Behavioral Risk Factor Surveillance System Survey Data (BRFSS 2015). U.S. Department of Health and Human Services, Centers for Disease Control and Prevention (2015)
15. Jordan, M.I., Mitchell, T.M.: Machine learning: trends, perspectives, and prospects. Science **349**(6245), 255–260 (2015)
16. Hu, F.B., et al.: Diet, lifestyle, and the risk of type 2 diabetes mellitus in women. N. Engl. J. Med. **345**(11), 790–797 (2001)

17. Knowler, W.C., et al.: Reduction in the incidence of type 2 diabetes with lifestyle intervention or metformin. N. Engl. J. Med. **346**(6), 393–403 (2002)
18. American Diabetes Association: Pathogenesis of type 2 diabetes mellitus. Diabetes Care **26**(Suppl. 1), S21–S36 (2003)
19. Willi, C., et al.: Active smoking and the risk of type 2 diabetes. JAMA **298**(22), 2654–2664 (2007)
20. Baliunas, D.O., et al.: Alcohol as a risk factor for type 2 diabetes. Diabetes Care **32**(11), 2123–2132 (2009)
21. World Health Organization: Global Report on Diabetes. WHO Press, Geneva (2016)

Sustainable Event Planning Optimization with Multi-objective Deep Learning Models for CO_2 Emission and Cost Reduction

David Chunhu Li(✉), Silvina Yosa, Anderson Daniel Torres Bernardo, Rayden Idesiar Smau, Ling-Hsuan Ko, and Ming Long Chen

Information Technology and Management Program, Ming Chuan University, Taoyuan City, Taiwan, ROC
davidli@mail.mcu.edu.tw

Abstract. This paper presents a hybrid framework for sustainable event planning that jointly minimizes CO_2 emissions and costs. The approach integrates the Strength Pareto Evolutionary Algorithm 2 (SPEA2) with Long Short-Term Memory (LSTM) and Recurrent Neural Network (RNN) models for accurate forecasting, and Generative Adversarial Networks (GANs) for data augmentation. Predictions from LSTM/RNN are embedded into SPEA2 to identify Pareto-optimal strategies under operational and budget constraints. Simulation results demonstrate average reductions of about 80% in both objectives, with rapid convergence and stable Pareto fronts. A web-based prototype provides real-time optimization, emissions analysis, and venue recommendations, confirming the framework's potential for practical, sustainable event planning.

Keywords: Sustainable event planning · Multi-objective optimization · Deep learning · CO_2 emission reduction · Decision support system

1 Introduction

The growing emphasis on environmental sustainability has led event organizers and planners to adopt practices aimed at reducing negative environmental impacts, particularly carbon dioxide (CO_2) emissions [4]. Events of various scales, ranging from corporate conferences and exhibitions to large public festivals, often require substantial resources, extensive transportation, and considerable energy use, resulting in significant carbon footprints and high costs [1,7]. Consequently, sustainable event planning has become an important area of research and practice, focusing on minimizing environmental harm while ensuring economic viability.

This work was supported by the National Science and Technology Council of Taiwan ROC under grant numbers NSTC 113-2221-E-130-003- and 114-2221-E-130-009-MY2.

C. Xu (Ed.): ICMLSC 2026, CCIS 2948, pp. 109–120, 2027.
https://doi.org/10.1007/978-981-92-1546-1_9

A central challenge in sustainable event planning is achieving a balance between multiple, often conflicting objectives, such as reducing CO_2 emissions while controlling costs. Traditional single-objective optimization approaches often fail to capture this complexity, leading to suboptimal trade-offs [3,12]. Multi-objective optimization (MOO) methods, particularly the Strength Pareto Evolutionary Algorithm 2 (SPEA2), provide effective solutions by generating a set of Pareto-optimal outcomes that enable decision-makers to evaluate explicit trade-offs and select strategies that align with their priorities [2,10].

Accurate prediction of event-related CO_2 emissions and costs is essential for supporting effective optimization. Recent advances in deep learning (DL), including Long Short-Term Memory (LSTM) networks, Recurrent Neural Networks (RNN), and Generative Adversarial Networks (GANs), have shown considerable potential for improving predictive performance by modeling complex temporal and nonlinear patterns present in event planning data [5,6,8,9]. However, the integration of advanced DL models with multi-objective evolutionary algorithms has received limited attention, particularly in the context of sustainable event planning [11,13]. Addressing this gap, this study introduces a hybrid framework that combines SPEA2-based multi-objective optimization with advanced DL prediction models (LSTM, RNN, GANs) to optimize sustainable event planning strategies.

The remainder of this paper is organized as follows. Section 2 presents the system's mathematical algorithm model. Section 3 describes the experimental design and implementation, and Sect. 4 introduces the developed system prototype. Section 5 concludes the paper by summarizing the main contributions and outlining potential directions for future work.

2 System Mathematical Algorithm Model

2.1 Multi-objective Problem Formulation

In this study, the sustainable event planning problem is formulated as a multi-objective optimization task, where the goal is to achieve an optimal balance between environmental impact and economic feasibility. The problem involves determining a set of planning decisions that simultaneously minimize the total CO_2 emissions generated by the event and the overall monetary cost, while satisfying a range of operational and logistical constraints.

Decision Variables. Let the decision vector $\mathbf{x}$ represent the set of controllable planning factors relevant to event organization, such as venue selection, transportation arrangements, energy usage, and catering services. Formally, the decision vector is defined as:

$$\mathbf{x} = (x_1, x_2, \ldots, x_n)^T \in \mathbb{R}^n \tag{1}$$

where each component x_i corresponds to a specific decision parameter, and n denotes the total number of such parameters considered. These decision variables collectively determine both the carbon footprint and the cost structure of the event.

Objective Functions. The optimization framework incorporates two objectives. The first objective seeks to minimize the total CO_2 emissions $E_{\text{total}}(\mathbf{x})$ associated with the planned event. This includes emissions from all relevant sources, such as energy consumption at the venue, transportation of participants, and other event-related activities:

$$f_1(\mathbf{x}) = E_{\text{total}}(\mathbf{x}) \tag{2}$$

The second objective aims to minimize the total cost $C_{\text{total}}(\mathbf{x})$ of organizing the event, which covers venue rental fees, transportation expenses, energy costs, and other operational expenditures:

$$f_2(\mathbf{x}) = C_{\text{total}}(\mathbf{x}) \tag{3}$$

The multi-objective optimization problem can therefore be expressed as:

$$\min \mathbf{F}(\mathbf{x}) = [f_1(\mathbf{x}), f_2(\mathbf{x})]^T \tag{4}$$

subject to the following constraints:

$$g_j(\mathbf{x}) \leq 0, \quad j = 1, \ldots, m \tag{5}$$

$$h_k(\mathbf{x}) = 0, \quad k = 1, \ldots, p \tag{6}$$

where $g_j(\mathbf{x})$ denotes the jth inequality constraint (such as budget limits, emission thresholds, or resource availability) and $h_k(\mathbf{x})$ represents the kth equality constraint (such as fixed participant capacity or predetermined schedule requirements).

This formulation captures the inherent trade-off of the problem. Reducing CO_2 emissions often requires the adoption of greener technologies or sustainable practices, which may increase costs, while minimizing expenses can lead to higher emissions if less sustainable options are used. The solution is a set of Pareto-optimal outcomes, each representing a feasible balance between environmental sustainability and economic viability.

2.2 Deep Learning-Based Predictions

To forecast event-related CO_2 emissions and costs, LSTM and RNN models are used to capture temporal dependencies and nonlinear patterns in historical data. The input at time t is:

$$\mathbf{x}_t = (x_t^{(1)}, x_t^{(2)}, \ldots, x_t^{(d)})^T, \tag{7}$$

where d is the number of features. LSTM hidden states are updated as:

$$h_t = \text{LSTM}(x_t, h_{t-1}; \theta_{\text{LSTM}}), \tag{8}$$

while standard RNNs omit gating mechanisms. Predictions are obtained as:

$$\hat{y}_t = W_y h_t + b_y, \tag{9}$$

where W_y and b_y are the output weights and bias, and $\hat{y}_t$ denotes the predicted CO_2 emissions or cost. The models are trained with regularization and hyperparameter tuning to enhance generalization, providing reliable inputs for the SPEA2 optimization process to evaluate the emissioncost trade-off.

2.3 Data Augmentation via GANs

To address data scarcity and improve model robustness, GANs are applied to generate realistic synthetic event data. A GAN consists of a generator G and a discriminator D:

$$\tilde{x} = G(z; \theta_G), \quad z \sim N(0,1), \tag{10}$$

where z is sampled from a Gaussian prior and θ_G represents the generator parameters. The discriminator distinguishes real data $x \sim p_{\text{data}}(x)$ from generated samples, with training formulated as:

$$\begin{aligned}\max_D \min_G V(D,G) = \mathbb{E}_{x \sim p_{\text{data}}(x)}[\log D(x)] \\ + \mathbb{E}_{z \sim p_z(z)}[\log(1 - D(G(z)))].\end{aligned} \tag{11}$$

This augmentation expands the training dataset for the LSTM and RNN models, reducing overfitting and enhancing the accuracy of CO_2 and cost predictions for the SPEA2 optimizer.

2.4 Integration of SPEA2 with Deep Learning Predictions

To jointly minimize CO_2 emissions and event costs, SPEA2 is integrated with LSTM and RNN-based predictions.

Population Initialization: The initial population P of N candidate solutions is:

$$P = \{\mathbf{x}^{(1)}, \mathbf{x}^{(2)}, \ldots, \mathbf{x}^{(N)}\}, \tag{12}$$

where each $\mathbf{x}^{(i)}$ encodes event planning parameters.

Fitness Evaluation: For each $\mathbf{x}^{(i)}$, the predictors estimate emissions $E^{\text{DL}}_{\text{total}}(\mathbf{x})$ and cost $C^{\text{DL}}_{\text{total}}(\mathbf{x})$, forming:

$$f_i = \left[E^{\text{DL}}_{\text{total}}(\mathbf{x}^{(i)}),\ C^{\text{DL}}_{\text{total}}(\mathbf{x}^{(i)})\right]^T. \tag{13}$$

SPEA2 computes:

$$S(i) = \left|\left\{j \mid \mathbf{x}^{(i)} \succ \mathbf{x}^{(j)},\ j \in P\right\}\right|, \tag{14}$$

$$R(i) = \sum_{\substack{j \in P \\ \mathbf{x}^{(j)} \succ \mathbf{x}^{(i)}}} S(j), \tag{15}$$

$$D(i) = \frac{1}{\sigma_i^k + 2}, \tag{16}$$

$$F(i) = R(i) + D(i), \tag{17}$$

where $S(i)$ is the strength value, $R(i)$ is the raw fitness, and $D(i)$ is the density estimation.

Variation Operators: Offspring are generated using crossover $\mathcal{X}$ and mutation $\mathcal{M}$:

$$\mathbf{x}' = \mathcal{M}\left(\mathcal{X}\left(\mathbf{x}^{(a)}, \mathbf{x}^{(b)}\right)\right). \tag{18}$$

Pareto Archive: At each generation, SPEA2 maintains an archive A of non-dominated solutions. The final solution $\mathbf{x}^*$ is chosen from A according to the preferences of the decision maker:

$$\mathbf{x}^* \in A. \tag{19}$$

Embedding deep learning predictions into SPEA2 enables accurate and context-specific optimization for sustainable event planning.

3 Experiments and Results Discussion

3.1 Experimental Design

Due to the absence of a comprehensive real-world event dataset containing both CO_2 emissions and cost information, the experimental study was conducted within a controlled simulation environment implemented in Python. The simulation framework was developed to emulate realistic event planning scenarios, combining synthetic data generation with predictive modeling to evaluate the performance of the proposed hybrid framework. The experiment involved generating and normalizing synthetic event datasets (augmented using GANs), training LSTM and RNN models to predict CO_2 emissions and costs, and integrating these predictions into a SPEA2-based multi-objective optimization process for emissioncost trade-offs. This procedure was repeated 100 times to ensure robustness, and the results were assessed using hypervolume, diversity metrics, and expert qualitative evaluation.

The dataset contains $N = 5{,}000$ simulated event records. Core drivers such as attendees and duration determine the scale of operational loads, including venue size, energy consumption, and waste generation. Policy and technology factors, including digital integration, local sourcing, and renewable energy ratio, influence CO_2 emissions through weighted reduction coefficients and modestly increase total costs through multiplicative adjustments. Both CO_2 and cost targets include mild heteroscedastic Gaussian noise (10% of the base value) and are constrained to non-negative outputs. The empirical 5th95th percentiles summarized in Table 1 illustrate the realistic range and variability of these variables prior to GAN-based data augmentation.

The initial dataset consists of 5,000 simulated event records. Using a WGAN-GP model, an additional 10,000 samples were produced and filtered under the same physical and logical constraints, resulting in a final dataset of 15,000 records. Figure 1 compares the distributions of key variables between the original and augmented datasets. The two distributions are closely aligned, with moderate broadening in regions where data coverage improves through augmentation. This expanded dataset forms the basis for the forecasting experiments presented in Sect. 3.2.

Table 1. Initial Synthetic Dataset Structure (before GAN augmentation). Typical ranges are empirical 5th–95% over $N = 5{,}000$ samples.

Variable	Symbol	Type/Domain	Unit	Generation rule & Typical range (5–95%)
Attendees	A	Integer $[50, 5000]$	persons	Lognormal($\mu = 6, \sigma = 1$) clipped to $[50, 5000]$. Typical: 78–2,182; Median: 409. Drives venue size, waste, CO_2, cost.
Duration	D	$\{1, \ldots, 7\}$	days	UniformInt(1, 7). Typical: 1–7; Median: 4. Scales energy and waste linearly.
Venue size	S	Continuous > 0	m^2	$S = A \times U(1.5, 3.0)$ (m^2/person). Typical: 166–4,864; Median: 897. Larger venues increase energy and cost.
Catering type	C	Binary $\{0, 1\}$	–	Bernoulli($p = 0.3$), 1 =premium; catering surcharge in cost.
Transportation mode	T	Binary $\{0, 1\}$	–	Bernoulli($p = 0.6$), 1 =private-dominant; transport CO_2 adds $\propto A$.
Energy consumption	E	Continuous > 0	kWh	$E = S \times D \times U(0.8, 1.5)$. Typical: 441–24,240; Median: 3,523. Feeds CO_2 via factor 0.4.
Waste generated	W	Continuous > 0	kg	$W = A \times D \times U(0.5, 2.0)$. Typical: 205–12,246; Median: 1,663. Feeds CO_2 via factor 0.3.
Digital integration	r_d	Ratio $[0, 1]$	–	Beta(2, 3). Typical: 0.10–0.75; Median: 0.39. CO_2 reduction weight 0.2.
Local sourcing	r_ℓ	Ratio $[0, 1]$	–	Beta(3, 2). Typical: 0.25–0.90; Median: 0.61. CO_2 reduction 0.15; cost +5%.
Renewable energy ratio	r_e	Ratio $[0, 1]$	–	Beta(2, 4). Typical: 0.07–0.64; Median: 0.32. CO_2 reduction 0.3; cost +10%.
CO_2 emissions	Y_{CO2}	≥ 0	kg CO_2	Base: $15A + 0.4E + 0.3W + 5TA$; Reduction: $(1 - (0.2r_d + 0.15r_\ell + 0.3r_e))$; Noise: $\mathcal{N}(0, 0.1 \cdot \text{base})$; clipped ≥ 0. Typical: 1,272–37,739; Median: 6,862.
Event costs	Y_{cost}	≥ 0	USD	Base: $A \cdot U(50, 100) + S \cdot U(10, 20) + 30\,C\,A$; Multiplier: $(1 + 0.1r_e + 0.05r_\ell)$; Noise: $\mathcal{N}(0, 0.1 \cdot \text{base})$; clipped ≥ 0. Typical: 9,279–269,297; Median: 49,580.

3.2 Results Analysis and Discussion

Figure 2 compares the LSTM and RNN prediction results for Scope 1 CO_2 emissions in two building sectors of Blount County in New York City. For the industrial sector (Fig. 2(a)), historical data indicate a fluctuating but overall downward trend from 71,571 $MtCO_2$ in 2015 to 64,677 $MtCO_2$ in 2024. The LSTM model forecasts a rebound to 72,249 $MtCO_2$ in 2025, while the RNN predicts 71,577 $MtCO_2$. The proximity of these values suggests that both models capture recent dynamics, with LSTM anticipating a slightly stronger recovery due to its longer memory.

For the commercial sector (Fig. 2(b)), emissions increased from 7,105 $MtCO_2$ in 2015 to a peak of 9,009 $MtCO_2$ in 2023, followed by a decline to 8,748 $MtCO_2$ in 2024. The LSTM projects a sharper drop to 7,982 $MtCO_2$ in 2025, while the RNN yields 8,453 $MtCO_2$. This divergence indicates that LSTM is more responsive to recent declines, whereas RNN produces more conservative and smoothed projections. In summary, both models provide reasonable sector-specific fore-

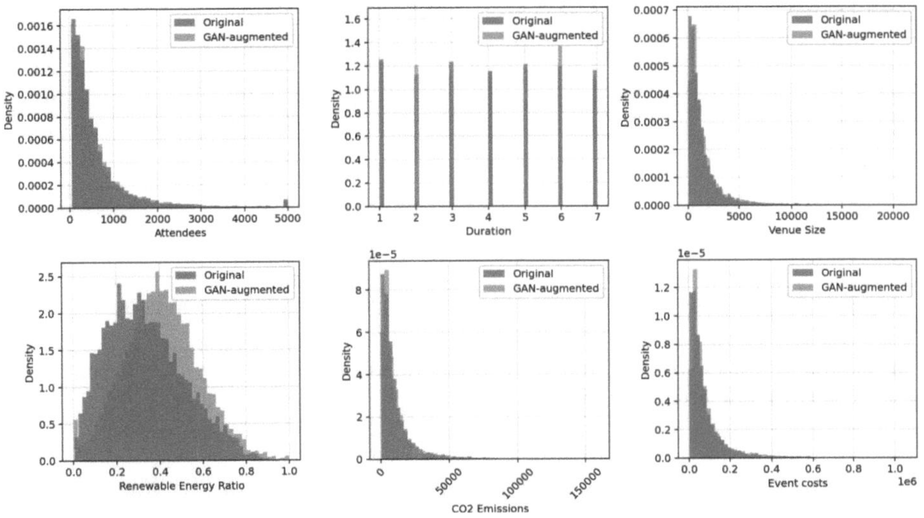

Fig. 1. Distribution comparison between the original dataset (N = 5,000) and the GAN-augmented dataset (N = 15,000) for six representative variables: Attendees, Duration, Venue Size, Renewable Energy Ratio, CO_2 Emissions, and Event costs. The two sets of curves show close alignment, which indicates that augmentation preserves marginal characteristics while increasing diversity.

casts, with LSTM offering greater adaptability to abrupt changes and RNN delivering more stable trends.

As shown in Fig. 3(a), the average distribution of key features among Pareto-optimal solutions demonstrates that attributes such as venue size, energy consumption, and waste generation have a substantial influence on the trade-off between CO_2 emissions and event costs. The relatively narrow error bars indicate consistent feature selection across optimal solutions, reflecting stability in the decision-making process.

The hypervolume convergence curve in Fig. 3(b) shows that the proposed method rapidly expands Pareto front coverage within the first 20 generations and then stabilizes. This pattern confirms the algorithm's ability to efficiently explore the solution space and converge to high-quality solution sets.

Performance comparisons in Fig. 3(c) reveal substantial reductions in both CO_2 emissions and event costs after optimization. On average, Pareto-optimal solutions achieve approximately an 80% reduction in CO_2 emissions and more than an 80% decrease in event costs compared to the baseline. These results demonstrate the framework's capacity to deliver simultaneous environmental and economic benefits.

Figure 3(d) illustrates the distribution of Pareto-optimal solutions along a distinct trade-off curve, allowing decision-makers to balance carbon reduction and budget constraints. For example, solutions with slightly higher costs may

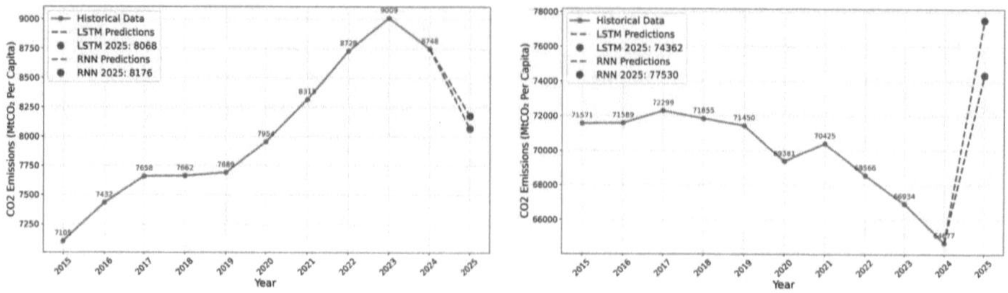

(a) Scope 1 Industrial sector (2015–2024) with 2025 LSTM/RNN forecasts.

(b) Scope 1 Commercial sector (2015–2024) with 2025 LSTM/RNN forecasts.

Fig. 2. LSTM vs. RNN CO_2 emissions predictions for Blount County: (a) industrial buildings; (b) commercial buildings.

achieve further CO_2 reductions, while other solutions maintain low emissions within more stringent budgets.

Overall, the proposed method effectively explores the solution space, converges rapidly to high-quality Pareto fronts, and achieves significant reductions in both emissions and costs, confirming its practical applicability in sustainable event planning.

Across the 100 independent simulation runs, the proposed SPEA2DL hybrid consistently generated well-structured Pareto fronts, exhibiting stable trade-offs between CO_2 emissions and cost objectives. The average hypervolume values displayed low variance, indicating robust optimization performance despite stochastic variations in the evolutionary process. Prediction models achieved MSE and MAE values within acceptable limits, validating their integration into the optimization stage without introducing substantial bias.

The results also highlight distinct patterns within thc trade-off space. Certain solution clusters prioritize aggressive emission reductions through renewable energy adoption and optimized transportation routes, whereas others emphasize minimal operational costs while maintaining acceptable environmental performance. These findings underscore the flexibility of the proposed framework in addressing diverse decision-making priorities. Furthermore, the simulation-based evaluation confirms the methodological soundness of the approach, providing a strong foundation for future application to real-world datasets as they become available.

4 System Prototype

The prototype system integrates LSTM and RNN prediction modules, GAN-based scenario generation, and the SPEA2 multi-objective optimizer within a modular web-based platform. The Event Creation Page (Fig. 4a) allows users to input key planning parameters such as event type, dates, budget, venue, and ticket price. A real-time preview is provided, and the entered data are sent

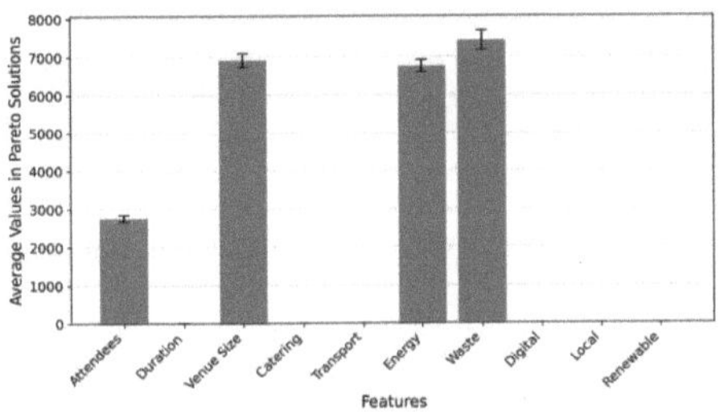

(a) Feature distribution in Pareto-optimal solutions

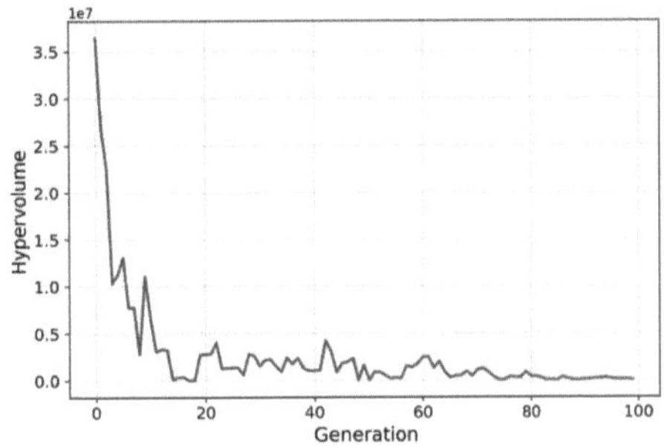

(b) Optimization convergence curve

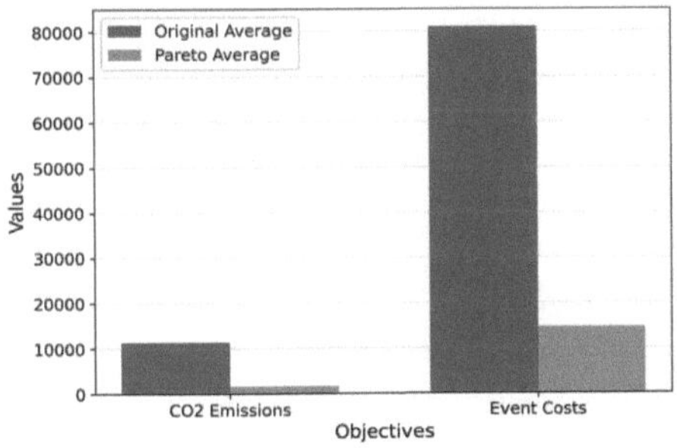

(c) Original vs. optimized performance

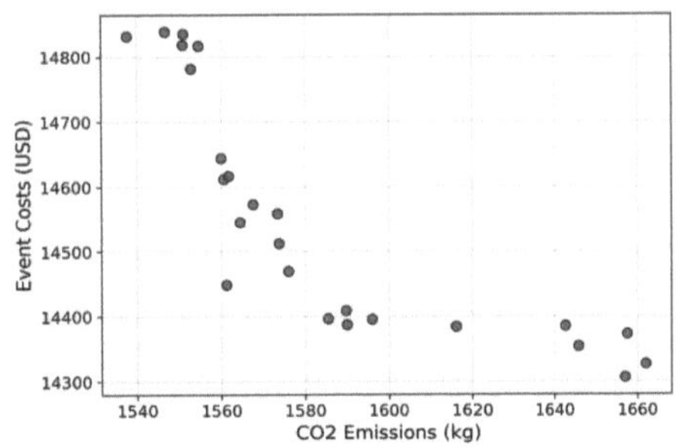

(d) Pareto-optimal solutions distribution

Fig. 3. Experimental results for the proposed multi-objective optimization framework: (a) Feature distribution in Pareto-optimal solutions; (b) Optimization convergence behavior; (c) Comparison of original and optimized performance; (d) Distribution of Pareto-optimal solutions showing trade-offs between CO_2 emissions and event costs.

to the optimizer to generate Pareto-optimal solutions for CO_2 emissions and cost. The Emissions Analysis interface (Fig. 4b) displays a choropleth map of CO_2 emissions, venue locations, monthly emission trends, and category-specific summaries to support location screening.

The Prediction module (Fig. 5a) enables model selection, including SimpleRNN and LSTM, specifies the forecast horizon, and presents actual versus predicted CO_2 values along with the MSE and MAE metrics. The Venue Recommendation interface (Fig. 5b) ranks venues according to predicted emissions and costs, highlighting the most favorable trade-offs as "Recommended" options.

Both LSTM and RNN models were trained using datasets with and without GAN-based augmentation. As shown in Table 2, the LSTM's MAE and MSE increased by approximately 26% when trained without augmentation, while the RNN's error increased by about 19%. The augmented dataset thus provides a more comprehensive representation of event patterns, enabling more stable and accurate forecasting of CO_2 emissions.

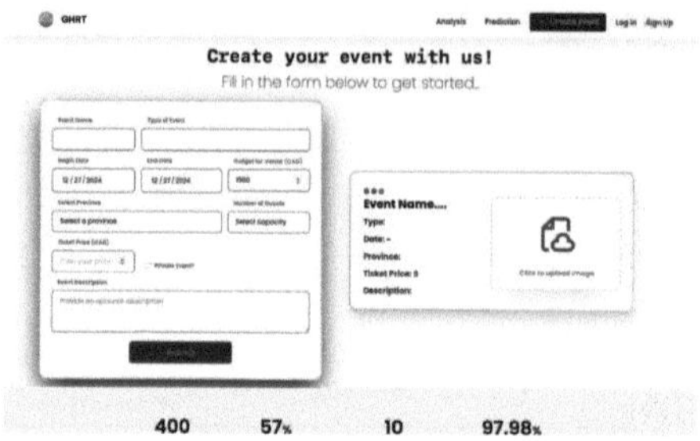

(a) Event Creation Page for entering planning parameters with real-time preview.

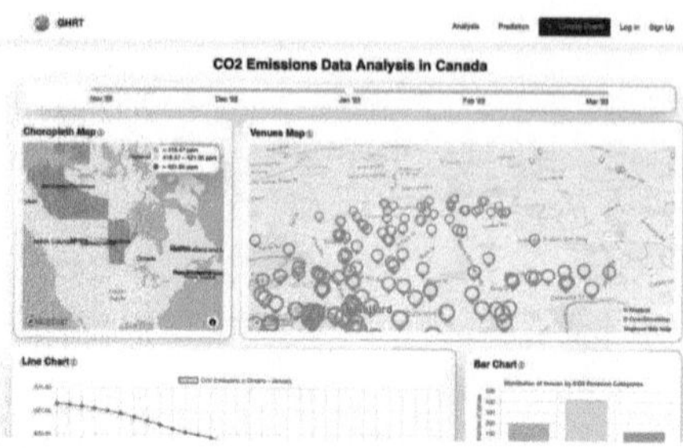

(b) CO_2 Emissions Analysis with spatial, temporal, and categorical views.

Fig. 4. System prototype: (a) Event Creation; (b) Emissions Analysis.

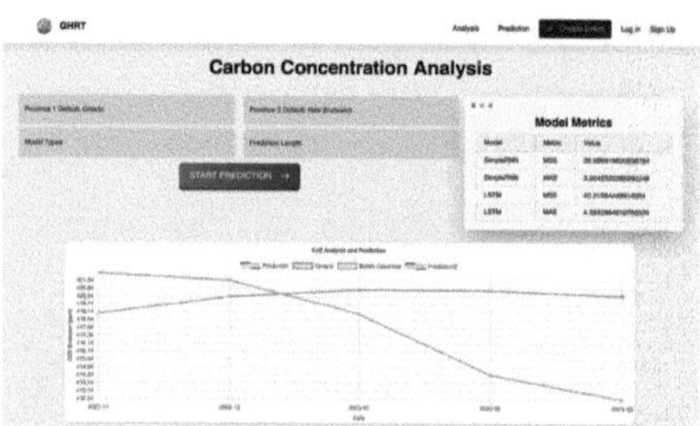

(a) Carbon Concentration Prediction with model selection, forecasts, and error metrics.

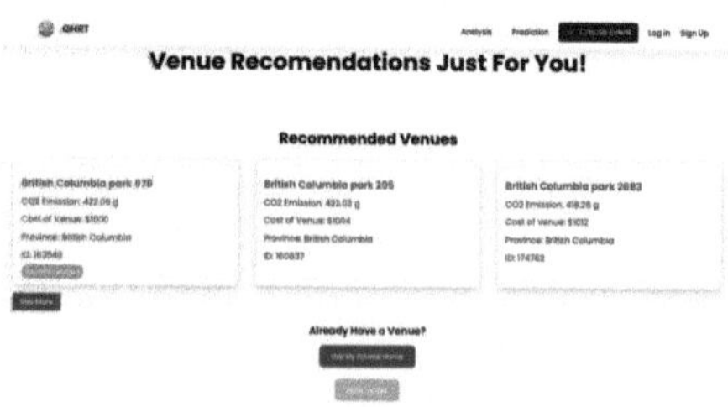

(b) Venue Recommendation ranked by predicted CO_2 and cost; optimal options highlighted.

Fig. 5. System prototype: (a) Prediction; (b) Venue Recommendation.

The computational requirements of the proposed framework are moderate. Training each LSTM or RNN model for CO_2 emission forecasting consumes approximately 2.4 GB of GPU memory. The multi-objective optimization using the SPEA2 algorithm with 100 generations completes in less than three minutes on an NVIDIA RTX 5070 GPU. The overall architecture is designed to support distributed execution, allowing data preprocessing, deep learning training, and

Table 2. Performance of LSTM and RNN models with and without GAN-based data augmentation.

Model	Dataset	MAE	MSE
LSTM	Without GAN (5k)	0.0589	0.0097
LSTM	With GAN (15k)	0.0548	0.0077
RNN	Without GAN (5k)	0.0618	0.0094
RNN	With GAN (15k)	0.0585	0.0080

evolutionary optimization to be parallelized across multiple GPUs or computational nodes, which ensures scalability for larger datasets and more complex event-planning scenarios.

5 Conclusions

This study presented and validated a hybrid framework that combines multi-objective evolutionary optimization with deep learning-based prediction models to address the dual goals of reducing CO_2 emissions and minimizing event-related costs. The framework employs LSTM and RNN models for accurate forecasting, GANs for data augmentation, and the SPEA2 algorithm for the identification of Pareto-optimal solutions, enabling the effective capture of complex trade-offs in sustainable event planning. Extensive simulations over 100 independent runs demonstrated substantial and consistent reductions in both environmental and economic objectives, rapid convergence to high-quality Pareto fronts, and resilience to stochastic variations. The development of a system prototype further demonstrated the practicality of deploying this framework as an interactive decision-support tool for event planning professionals.

The study acknowledges that reliance on simulated and GAN-augmented datasets limits direct generalization to real-world events. Although the augmented data preserve realistic distributions, future work will incorporate empirical data from diverse event types to enhance external validity. The current framework focuses on CO_2 emissions and total cost; subsequent studies will extend the objectives to include additional sustainability indicators such as energy consumption, waste reduction, and social impact. In terms of implementation, the present prototype was executed on a standard workstation with moderate computational load, and training time scales linearly with dataset size. Future optimization will emphasize model scalability and deployment efficiency for large-scale event planning applications.

References

1. Cavallin Toscani, A., Vendraminelli, L., Vinelli, A.: Environmental sustainability in the event industry: a systematic review and a research agenda. J. Sustain. Tour. **32**(12), 2663–2697 (2024)
2. Harkare, V., Mangrulkar, R., Thorat, O., Jain, S.R.: Evolutionary approaches for multi-objective optimization and pareto-optimal solution selection in data analytics. In: Applied Multi-Objective Optimization, pp. 67–94. Springer (2024)
3. Huang, J., Yang, L., Lin, S., Zhou, Z.: Mega sporting event and urban low-carbon transitions: evidence from the 2023 Hangzhou Asian games. Appl. Econ. 1–18 (2025)
4. Iyer, V.H., et al.: The sustainable practices implemented at mega international events and evaluation of their effectiveness in mitigating environmental degradation. In: Navigating Trust in Sustainability Reporting and Assurance, pp. 409–438. IGI Global Scientific Publishing (2025)

5. Li, D.C.: A hybrid Bayesian network-based deep learning approach combining climatic and reliability factors to forecast electric vehicle charging capacity. Heliyon **11**(4) (2025)
6. Li, D.C., Felix, J.R., Chin, Y.L., Jusuf, L.V., Susanto, L.J.: Integrated extended Kalman filter and deep learning platform for electric vehicle battery health prediction. Appl. Sci. **14**(11), 4354 (2024)
7. Mair, J., Smith, A.: Events and sustainability: why making events more sustainable is not enough. In: Events and Sustainability, pp. 1–17. Routledge (2022)
8. Mohammadi, N., Rezakhani, A., Javadi, H.H.S., Asghari, P.: Enhancing time-series access control using deep recurrent neural networks and generative adversarial networks. Int. J. Inf. Secur. **24**(1), 61 (2025)
9. Narayanan, S., Kumar, R., Ramadass, S., Ramasamy, J.: Innovative hybrid approach for enhanced renewable energy generation forecasting using recurrent neural networks and generative adversarial networks. J. Electr. Eng. Technol. **19**(8), 4847–4864 (2024)
10. Saad, M.R., Emam, M.M., Houssein, E.H.: An efficient multi-objective parrot optimizer for global and engineering optimization problems. Sci. Rep. **15**(1), 5126 (2025)
11. Sarkar, P., Khanapuri, V.B., Tiwari, M.K.: Strategic decision-making for sustainable production and distribution in automotive industry: a machine learning enabled dynamic multi-objective optimisation. Int. J. Prod. Res. **63**(7), 2339–2362 (2025)
12. Su, X.Z., Chen, L., Xu, X.L.: Carbon emission and energy risk management in mega sporting events: challenges, strategies, and pathways. Front. Environ. Sci. **12**, 1513365 (2025)
13. Zhang, W., et al.: Enhancing multi-objective evolutionary algorithms with machine learning for scheduling problems: recent advances and survey. Front. Ind. Eng. **2**, 1337174 (2024)

Deep Learning-Based Outlier Handling for Time-Series Data in Smart Farming

Weerapat Phutthamongkhon, Kritsada Puangsuwan(✉), and Nathaphon Boonnam

Prince of Songkla University, Surat Thani Campus, Surat Thani, Thailand
kritsada.pu@psu.ac.th

Abstract. Time-series data collection from smart farming systems is often affected by outliers caused by sensor malfunction, transmission errors, or environmental fluctuations, which can distort model training and reduce predictive accuracy. This research proposes a deep learning-based approach for outlier handling in time-series data that integrates the Local Outlier Factor (LOF) algorithm for outlier detection with a Bidirectional Long Short-Term Memory (Bi-LSTM) model for imputing and reconstructing values. The corrected dataset is subsequently evaluated by using it to train multiple regression models to examine improvements in data quality and model performance. The experimental results demonstrate that the proposed LOF–Bi-LSTM approach effectively enhances data quality and model stability compared to the conventional Interquartile Range (IQR) method. In particular, Decision Tree and Random Forest models trained on LOF–Bi-LSTM processed data achieved higher R2 scores of 0.80 and 0.87, respectively, and lower MAE and MSE values. These findings highlight that combining deep learning–based imputation with anomaly detection provides a robust alternative to deal with outliers in time-series data, which can help improve the quality of the dataset and enhance models' performance.

Keywords: Outlier Handling Method · Data Preprocessing · Deep Learning · Machine Learning · Model Performance

1 Introduction

Modern agriculture combines advanced technologies, such as smart sensors and the Internet of Things (IoT) platform, to transform traditional agriculture into more advanced and efficient systems [1]. The advent of Artificial Intelligence (AI) has further enhanced modern agriculture through the application of Machine Learning (ML) or Deep Learning (DL), particularly in smart farming systems that aim to optimize resource usage and increase yield [2, 3]. However, overuse of technology can also lead to risks or problems. If data from the sensor is distorted, this may cause the smart farm systems that use ML models to rely on incorrect data, and there is a risk of errors that could damage crops [4]. A critical challenge in developing ML models is an effective data preparation method to obtain high-quality datasets for model training, thereby achieving the highest predictive accuracy and operational effectiveness.

C. Xu (Ed.): ICMLSC 2026, CCIS 2948, pp. 121–131, 2027.
https://doi.org/10.1007/978-981-92-1546-1_10

The time-series data is a source that occurs in nature continuously, such as temperature and humidity. Time-series analysis aims to extract insights from time-ordered data; the extracted insights can be used to analyze the past behavior and predict the future [5]. In these data, outliers or anomalies often appear, which are data points that deviate significantly from the normal pattern or distribution of the data, whether considered statistically, in terms of density, or distance [7, 9]. It can have a major impact on the ML performance, which can cause the models to have significantly less accuracy when trained on datasets with outlier values. Dealing with outliers is therefore important, but on other hand, removing these data can bias the dataset and lose important insights. Therefore, the efficient approaches to handling invalid data are to perform imputation of values (replacement) [6].

This research investigates the efficiency of outlier handling methods by using the LOF method for detection and then applying a Bi-LSTM model to deal with outliers, compared to the standard method typically used. The goal is to develop an outlier handling method that utilizes a Deep Learning model to handle outliers without removing them, which can help to improve data quality and model performance.

2 Development Steps of the Outlier Handling Method with Deep Learning Model

In smart farming systems, where massive amounts of data from multiple sensors are collected, outliers frequently occur due to sensor malfunctions, which may lead to inaccurate data analysis. Therefore, a process of data preparation is necessary prior to model training to reduce the impact of distorted data that can degrade model performance. According to the findings of research [7], density-based detection algorithms such as Local Outlier Factor (LOF) are one of the most widely adopted for detecting anomalies in multidimensional data. LOF can identify outliers within specific data groups (local clusters) by evaluating the density of each data point relative to its neighbors; if the density of a point is significantly lower than its surrounding neighbors, it is flagged as an outlier. This capability enables LOF to effectively detect subtle hidden anomalies. Furthermore, the LOF has been developed to overcome its limitations and be optimized to handle a wider variety of data types [8, 9].

The research of Cong Li et al. [10] proposed an ML-based imputation method for filling missing values. The approach began with correlation analysis to select predictive variables, then random removal of portions of the dataset to train multiple ML models, for imputing the missing values. The results demonstrated that the Bi-LSTM model performed well with time-series data, achieving R^2 scores of 0.91 and 0.89 under missing rates of 10% and 20%, respectively. Similarly, Jun-gyu Kim et al. [11] developed a Long Short-Term Memory (LSTM) model to impute missing time-series data of air temperature inside pig houses. The dataset was normalized using the Min–Max Scaler, and missing values were simulated by masking portions of the data. Then, the dataset was divided to train different LSTM models, namely Sequential, Reverse, and Bidirectional. The performance evaluation showed that the Bi-LSTM achieved the highest accuracy, with an MAPE of 0.24% for 1 h of missing values, and an MAPE of 2.64% for up to 48 h of missing values.

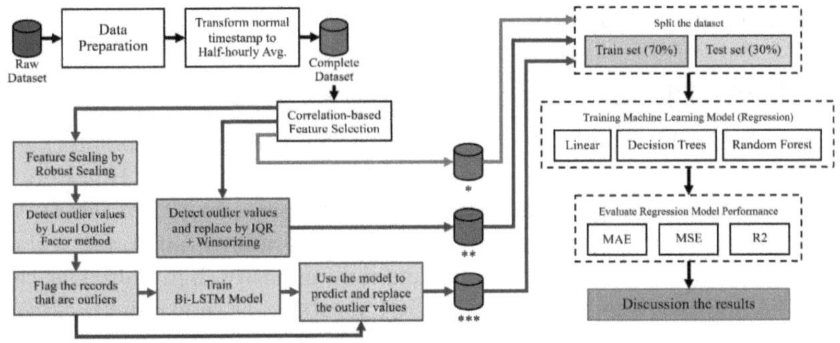

Fig. 1. The research step to study the efficiency of the outlier handling methods using LOF with a deep learning model

Figure 1 illustrates the development step of the outlier handling method with a deep learning model to study and evaluate the efficiency of this method, compared to the IQR method. First, the raw dataset is processed through data preparation to deal with missing and invalid values caused by sensor malfunctions, and then the data is transformed from normal timestamps into average data every half hour to divide the data into clear timelines, facilitating analysis, and resulting in a complete dataset that is ready to be used to train the model. The Correlation-Based Feature Selection (CFS) method is used to identify the features that are most relevant to the target class of interest. After identifying the features, the complete dataset will be duplicated as three new datasets with identical data. Then, begin the process of studying the efficiency of the outlier handling method, which was divided into three approaches according to the datasets that are duplicated:

1. (*) is the dataset that does not handle outliers.
2. (**) is used as a comparison method with the proposed method, by using the IQR method to detect outliers and then applying the winsorizing method to impute them with the interquartile boundaries.
3. (***) is the proposed method in this research, by detecting the outlier with the LOF method and then using a Bi-LSTM model to impute those values.

After obtaining three different datasets that went through the outlier handling method mentioned above, each of these datasets are divided into a training set (70%) and validation/test set (30%) at the same random state, to ensure that the same partition was used for all methods, to be fair for a comparison between outlier handling methods. The processed datasets were then evaluated by using them to train identical regression models, including Linear Regression, Decision Tree Regression, and Random Forest Regression algorithms, under the same hyperparameters (default settings and same random state). The performance of each ML model will be evaluated to assess the efficiency of the outlier handling methods mentioned above. This experiment is designed to ensure that differences in performance metrics result solely from the outlier handling method rather than from data partitioning or randomness, to evaluate whether the proposed outlier handling method is comparable to standard approaches, such as the commonly used IQR method.

3 Materials and Methods

3.1 Data Collection

The dataset used in this study was collected from an environmental monitoring station that was installed in greenhouse by using SHT20 Temperature and Humidity Sensor Module, SHT20 Soil Temp and Moisture Sensor Module, and TEMT6000 Ambient Light sensor to read the air temperature (airTemp), air humidity (airHumi), soil temperature (soilTemp), soil moisture (soilMois), and light intensity (lightValue), as shown in Fig. 2(a). The raw data were stored in a MySQL database, as shown in Fig. 2(b), where each record contained timestamped sensor readings. The table scheme included the following fields: (1) dataID, (2) data_timestamp (YYYY-MM-DD hh:mm:ss), (3) airTemp (°C), (4) airHumi (%RH), (5) soilTemp (°C), (6) soilMois (%), and (7) lightIntensity (lux). The raw data were recorded every 60 s, resulting in 107,202 records.

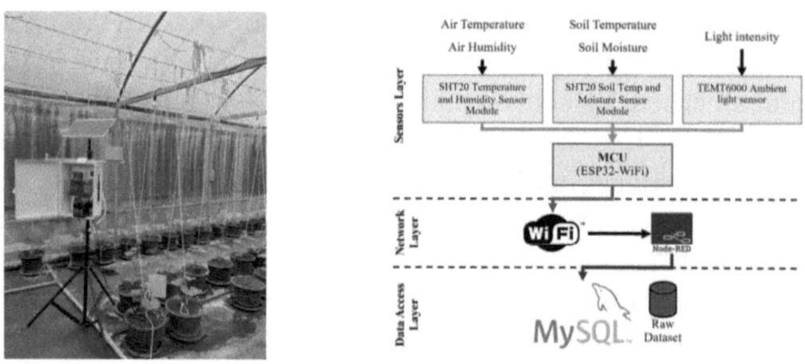

(a) (b)

Fig. 2. (a) Installation of environmental monitoring station in greenhouse, and (b) the system architecture of data recording into the database

3.2 Data Preparation

The environmental monitoring station has been installed to collect environmental data in greenhouse for approximately 1 month. This results in a dataset that includes the variables mentioned in Sect. 3.1. Data Collection, followed by data preparation to handle missing and invalid values caused by reading incorrect data from sensors that malfunction, by removing those records in a total of 907 records from the raw dataset, then transforming data from normal timestamps into average data every half hour, resulting in a total of 1,240 records.

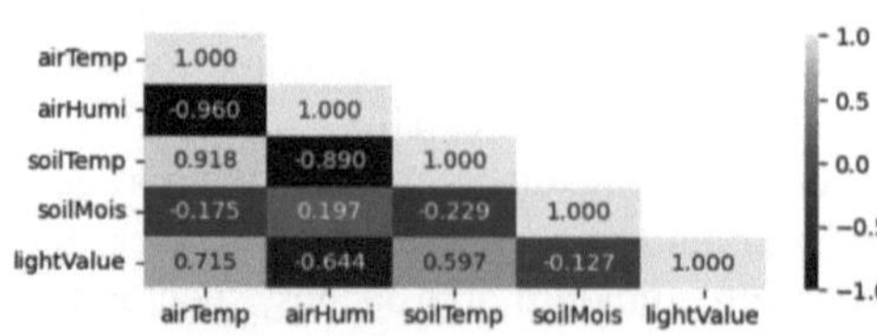

Fig. 3. Correlation heatmap of all variables in the dataset

Figure 3 shows the correlation between all variables in the dataset. It can be observed that soilTemp has a strong positive correlation with airTemp and a very strong negative correlation with airHumi. Therefore, these variables are selected as the main variables to be further processed through the outlier handling. The feature selection for the regression ML model training to evaluate the outlier handling method efficiency is done by using CFS method to select the features that are most relevant to the target class: soilTemp.

3.3 Outlier Detection

Before performing outlier detection, the data will be feature scaled using Robust Scaler to make the data more robust to outliers. This method is done by using Median and Interquartile Range (IQR) [12] to help in scaling the data [13], as shown in Eqs. (1)–(3).

$$\text{Median} = \begin{cases} X\left[\frac{n+1}{2}\right], \text{if n is odd} \\ \frac{X\left[\frac{n}{2}\right] + X\left[\frac{n}{2}+1\right]}{2}, \text{if n is even} \end{cases} \tag{1}$$

$$\text{IQR} = \text{Q3 - Q1} \tag{2}$$

where the first quartile (Q1) is 25th percentiles of the data, and the third quartile (Q3) is 75th percentiles of the data [12].

$$X_{robust} = \frac{X - \text{Median}(X)}{\text{IQR}(X)} \tag{3}$$

The Local Outlier Factor (LOF) was used as a method to detect outlier values in a dataset. The LOF is an algorithm that uses the concept of k-nearest neighbors by comparing the density of a given data point with its neighboring data points [14]. Points with lower density than their surrounding or nearby points are considered outliers. The “LocalOutlierFactor” function from the sklearn.neighbors library [15] was uesd to facilitate the analysis of outliers, with the parameters k_neighbors = 50 and contamination = 0.2, which means that the proportion of outliers in this dataset is estimated to be 20% of the total data.

In case of detecting outliers by using the conventional method, such as the IQR, the winsorizing method was applied to reduce their impact on the dataset. Rather than removing the outlier values, this method imputes them with the corresponding lower or upper bounds determined using the IQR method (Fig. 4).

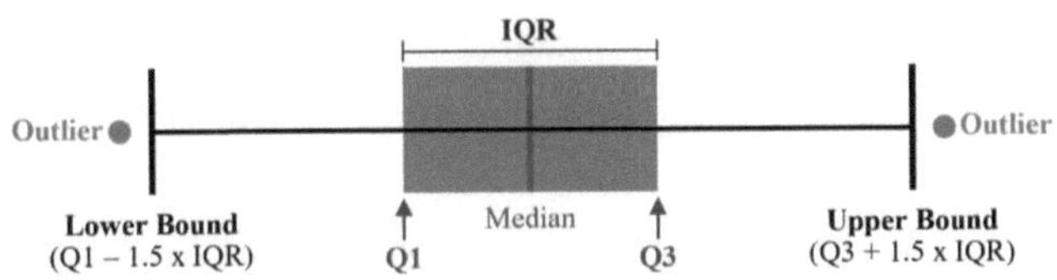

Fig. 4. Interquartile Range; IQR method

3.4 Model Training Method

The Bi-LSTM model is trained with a self-supervised masked reconstruction strategy to teach the model how to recover the hidden values. The dataset was feature scaled using Robust Scaler, which scales each feature so that the median is approximately zero and the IQR is close to one. The training procedure can be summarized as follows:

1. Outlier removal: discard data flagged as outliers by LOF, leaving only normal data for training the model.
2. Random masking: portions of the normal data are randomly masked, while the corresponding actual values are preserved as the reconstruction targets.
3. Loss masking: assign weights only to masked data, ensuring that the model focuses on learning to recover only the hidden values.
4. Bi-LSTM architecture: The model processes input sequences of 64 timesteps with three features. It comprises two bidirectional layers; the first with 64 units capturing temporal dependencies, and the second with 32 units to learn deeper data structure from both past and future contexts.
5. Masked Huber loss: The model is trained with a masked Huber loss, which evaluates the Huber loss only on the masked data, enabling effective reconstruction of hidden values while remaining robust to large errors.

This training method enables the model to capture temporal dependencies in data and enhances its capability to accurately reconstruct values.

3.5 Model Evaluation

Performance evaluation of ML models is essential for assessing their capabilities and identifying their limitations [16]. This study will measure the performance of regression models trained on datasets with different outlier handling methods, to measure the efficiency of those methods by using the following performance metric: the Mean Absolute Error (MAE), Mean Squared Error (MSE), and Coefficient of Determination, also known as R-squared (R2) [17, 18], as defined in Eqs. (4)–(6), respectively.

$$\mathrm{MAE} = \frac{1}{\mathrm{N}}\sum\nolimits_{\mathrm{i}=1}^{\mathrm{N}} |\mathrm{actual} - \mathrm{predicted}| \tag{4}$$

$$\mathrm{MSE} = \frac{1}{\mathrm{N}}\sum\nolimits_{\mathrm{i}=1}^{\mathrm{N}} (\mathrm{actual} - \mathrm{predicted})^2 \tag{5}$$

$$\mathrm{R}^2 = 1 - \frac{\sum_{\mathrm{i}=1}^{\mathrm{N}} (\mathrm{actual} - \mathrm{predicted})^2}{\sum_{\mathrm{i}=1}^{\mathrm{N}} (\mathrm{actual} - \mathrm{Mean\ of\ actual})^2} \tag{6}$$

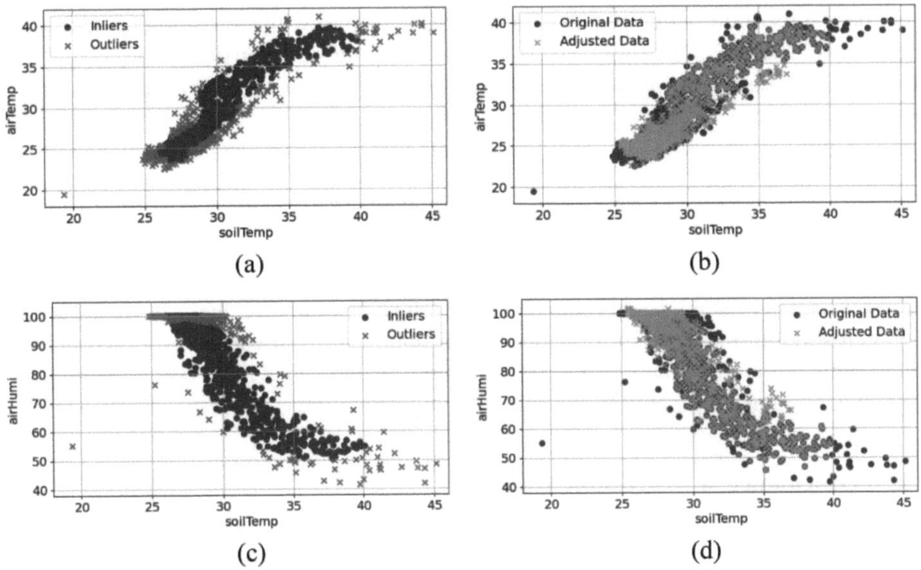

Fig. 5. Scatter plot of outlier values that were detected by the LOF method, and original values before and after imputation of values with the proposed method: (a)–(b) between soilTemp and airTemp, and (c)–(d) between soilTemp and airHumi

4 Results and Discussion

4.1 Outlier Handling Result

Outlier handling in the complete dataset was conducted using different methods, the first of which is using the IQR method with winsorizing, and the other is the proposed method in this research. These methods aim to reduce data variance and minimize analysis errors of ML models. The Mean and Standard Deviation (STD) values of the original dataset and values after outlier handling with the proposed method, and the IQR method, are presented in Table 1.

Table 1. Comparison of Mean and STD values of the original dataset and after outlier handling with different methods.

	Outlier Handling Methods	Variables		
		airTemp	airHumi	soilTemp
Mean	Original (Not handling)	28.57	86.85	29.54
	The IQR + Winsor method	28.53	86.91	29.24
	The proposed method	28.34	87.12	29.41
STD	Original (Not handling)	4.66	16.84	3.49
	The IQR + Winsor method	4.59	16.69	2.75
	The proposed method	4.33	15.89	3.13

The results of outlier detection using the LOF method with the parameter settings as mentioned in Sect. 3.3. Outlier Detection. The blue points are considered as normal data (Inliers), and the red points are considered outliers. This is done by detecting outliers between soilTemp and airTemp values, as shown in Fig. 5(a), and between soilTemp and airHumi, as shown in Fig. 5(c), which detected a total of 248 outlier values. After detecting outliers, the Bi-LSTM model is applied to predict the optimal value for impute the values in records flagged as outliers by the LOF method. The results are shown in Fig. 5(b), and 5(d), where the blue points are the original data, and the orange points are the data that have been adjusted using the proposed outlier handling method. Figure 5(b) shows the scatter between soilTemp and airTemp values, and Fig. 5(d) shows the scatter between soilTemp and airHumi values. From both figures, it can be observed that the data points are less spread out and form tighter clusters, as evidenced by the adjusted orange data points compared to the original blue data points.

4.2 Performance of Regression Models

This section presents a comparative analysis of two outlier handling methods:

- Detect outlier values by IQR and impute them with the winsorizing method.
- Detect outlier values by using LOF, then use Bi-LSTM model to predict and impute those values.

The objective is to evaluate the efficiency of the proposed outlier handling method compared to the IQR method by using these methods to handle the outliers in the dataset, then using those datasets to train the regression ML model and evaluate their performance, to evaluate whether the proposed outlier handling method enhances the data quality and improves the performance of ML models when trained on that dataset.

The performance of all regression models showed improvements after training on a complete dataset without outlier values. The Linear Regression model exhibited significant improvement when trained on a dataset that uses the IQR method to handle outliers, achieving an MAE of 0.75, an MSE of 0.92, and an R2 score of 0.87. Although training the Linear model on a dataset processed with the proposed method resulted in higher MAE and MSE values compared to the IQR method, the R2 score remained comparable at 0.86. The Decision Tree regression model also demonstrated notable improvement with the proposed method, yielding an MAE of 1.08, an MSE of 1.94, and an R2 score of 0.80. Similarly, the Random Forest regression showed improvement, achieving an R2 score of 0.87 with the proposed method, with only slight differences in MAE and MSE of 0.08 and 0.12, respectively, compared to the IQR method. A summary of the performance of all regression models is provided in Table 2.

Table 2. Summary performance of all regression models.

Model	Outlier Handling Methods	MAE	MSE	R^2
Linear Regression	Not handling	0.99	1.94	0.84
	The IQR + Winsor method	0.75	0.92	0.87

(continued)

Table 2. (*continued*)

Model	Outlier Handling Methods	MAE	MSE	R^2
	The proposed method	0.90	1.36	0.86
Decision Tree Regression	Not handling	1.27	3.35	0.72
	The IQR + Winsor method	1.07	2.11	0.71
	The proposed method	1.08	1.94	0.80
Random Forest Regression	Not handling	1.00	2.11	0.82
	The IQR + Winsor method	0.80	1.16	0.84
	The proposed method	0.88	1.28	0.87

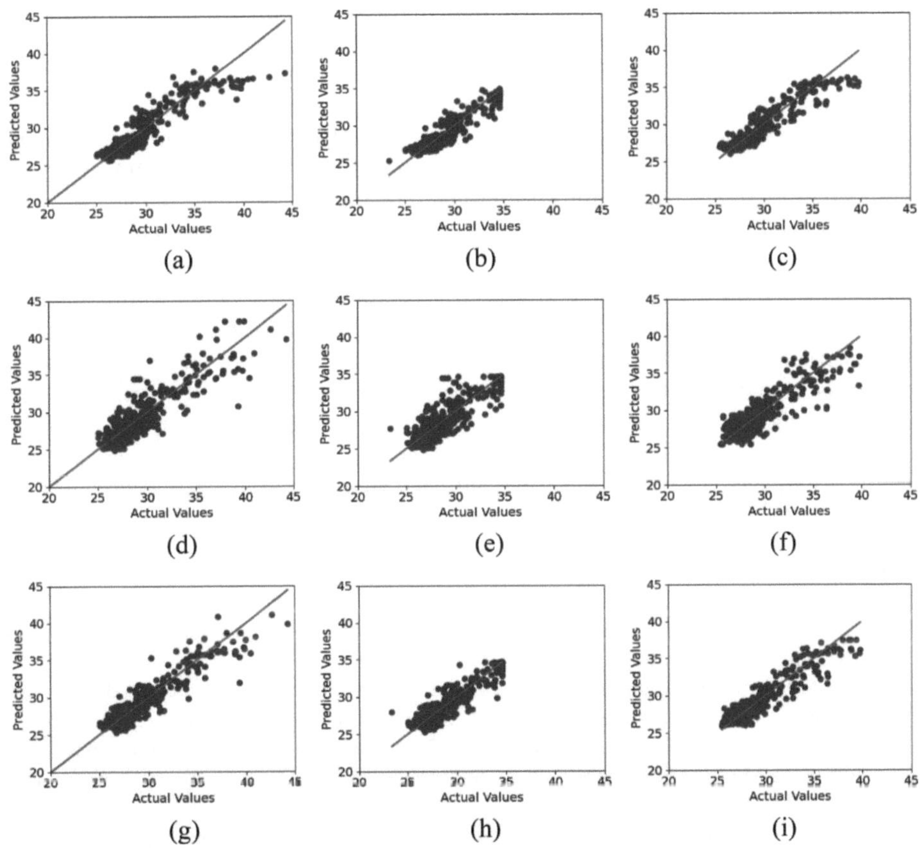

Fig. 6. Actual vs. Predicted scatter plots of regression models under different outlier handling methods: (a)–(c) Linear, (d)–(f) Decision Tree, and (g)–(i) Random Forest

Figure 6 illustrates the scatter plots of actual versus predicted values for each regression model: Linear, Decision Tree, and Random Forest. The left figure panels correspond to datasets without outlier handling, as shown in Fig. 6(a), (d), and (g). The middle panels represent datasets that were processed with the IQR method, as shown in Fig. 6(b), (e), and (h). The right figure panels showed the results of datasets processed under the proposed method, as shown in Fig. 6(c), (f), and (i). Across all models, the proposed method demonstrates a more consistent alignment between predicted and actual values, with reduced dispersion around the reference line, thereby improving predictive accuracy and robustness compared to the IQR method. In the IQR-based preprocessing, extreme values outside the interquartile range were imputed within the corresponding lower or upper bounds, which reduces data variability and results in predictions clustering within a narrower range, rather than reflecting the natural dispersion of the original data.

5 Conclusion

This research demonstrates an effective outlier handling approach by integrating the LOF detection method with the Bi-LSTM model to predict and impute them, compared to the IQR method. The proposed method enhances the performance of the regression models, most notably in the Decision Tree model, where the MAE decreased from 1.27 to 1.08, the MSE decreased from 3.35 to 1.94, and the R2 increased to 0.80. For the Random Forest model, R2 improved to 0.87 compared to 0.84 from the IQR method, despite slightly higher MAE and MSE values. Although the Linear model performs better with the IQR method, the proposed method maintained a comparable R2 of 0.86. The scatter plot further confirmed reduced dispersion and closer alignment with the reference line, while the IQR method tends to constrain extreme values within bounded ranges. Applying the proposed method for imputing values to handle outliers provides a robust alternative to the standard method, particularly for time-series data, and enhances the regression model performance when applied prior to training. Furthermore, this proposed method can be effectively applied for data preprocessing to handle outliers, making it particularly suitable for time-series data commonly found in smart farming systems, where data are collected periodically and anomalies frequently occur.

References

1. Triantafyllou, A., Sarigiannidis, P., Bibi, S.: Precision agriculture: a remote sensing monitoring system architecture. Information **10**(11), 348 (2019)
2. Kumar, G.K., et al.: Internet of things sensors and support vector machine integrated intelligent irrigation system for agriculture industry. Discover Sustain. **5**(1), 6 (2024)
3. Goap, A., Sharma, D., Shukla, A.K., Krishna, C.R.: An IoT based smart irrigation management system using Machine learning and open-source technologies. Comput. Electron. Agric. **155**, 41–49 (2018)
4. Catalano, C., Paiano, L., Calabrese, F., Cataldo, M., Mancarella, L., Tommasi, F.: Anomaly detection in smart agriculture systems. Comput. Ind. **143**, 103750 (2022)
5. Choi, K., Yi, J., Park, C., Yoon, S.: Deep learning for anomaly detection in time-series data: review, analysis, and guidelines. IEEE access **9**, 120043–120065 (2021)
6. Pereira, R.C., Abreu, P.H., Rodrigues, P.P., Figueiredo, M.A.: Imputation of data missing not at random: artificial generation and benchmark analysis. Expert Syst. Appl. **249**, 123654 (2024)

7. Samariya, D., Thakkar, A.: A comprehensive survey of anomaly detection algorithms. Ann. Data Sci. **10**(3), 829–850 (2023)
8. Alghushairy, O., Alsini, R., Soule, T., Ma, X.: A review of local outlier factor algorithms for outlier detection in big data streams. Big Data Cogn. Comput. **5**(1), 1 (2020)
9. Lartey, C., Liu, J., Asamoah, R.K., Greet, C., Zanin, M., Skinner, W.: Effective outlier detection for ensuring data quality in flotat+ion data modelling using machine learning (ML) algorithms. Minerals **14**(9), 925 (2024)
10. Li, C., Ren, X., Zhao, G.: Machine-learning-based imputation method for filling missing values in ground meteorological observation data. Algorithms **16**(9), 422 (2023)
11. Kim, J.G., Lee, S.Y., Lee, I.B.: The development of an LSTM model to predict time series missing data of air temperature inside fattening pig houses. Agriculture **13**(4), 795 (2023)
12. Dash, C.S.K., Behera, A.K., Dehuri, S., Ghosh, A.: An outliers detection and elimination framework in classification task of data mining. Decis. Anal. J. **6**, 100164 (2023)
13. Amorim, L.B.V., Cavalcanti, G.D.C., Cruz, R.M.O.: The choice of scaling technique matters for classification performance. Preprint submitted to Applied Soft Computing (2022). arXiv: 2212.12343
14. Breunig, M.M., Kriegel, H.-P., Ng, R.T., Sander, J.: LOF: identifying density-based local outliers. In: Proceedings of the 2000 ACM SIGMOD International Conference on Management of Data (SIGMOD 2000), pp. 93–104. Association for Computing Machinery (2000)
15. scikit-learn developers (2025). LocalOutlierFactor-scikit-learn 1.7.2 documentation. Accessed 8 Aug 2025. https://scikit-learn.org/stable/modules/generated/sklearn.neighbors.LocalOutlierFactor.html
16. Rainio, O., Teuho, J., Klén, R.: Evaluation metrics and statistical tests for machine learning. Sci. Rep. **14**(1), 6086 (2024)
17. Steurer, M., Hill, R.J., Pfeifer, N.: Metrics for evaluating the performance of machine learning based automated valuation models. J. Prop. Res. **38**(2), 99–129 (2021)
18. Colliot, O. (Ed.): Machine Learning for Brain Disorders (2023)

A Machine Learning Approach to Automated Risk Assessment and Data-Driven Corrective Action Generation for Occupational Safety

Chansiri Singhtaun(✉), Kobboon Chairit, and Thirachet Triamphet

Department of Industrial Engineering, Faculty of Engineering, Kasetsart University, 50 Ngamwongwan Road, Ladyao, Chatuchak District, Bangkok 10900, Thailand
chansiri.s@ku.ac.th

Abstract. This research presents the development of an automated Machine Learning (ML) framework for assessing, recording, and presenting corrective measures related to ergonomic posture risk, based on the Ovako Working Posture Analysis System (OWAS). The system integrates three core modules: an image acquisition module, an ML-based risk assessment module, and a data reporting and recommendation module. The risk assessment engine, which is the main component, utilizes the model that yielded the highest F1-score for classifying postures in the back, arms, and legs across four methods: Random Forest (RF), Support Vector Machine (SVM), XGBoost, and Hard Ensemble Voting. Based on testing results with the controlled dataset, XGBoost was selected for predicting back posture (81.38% F1-score) and leg posture (82.88% F1-score), while RF was chosen for arm classification (91.27% F1-score). The overall system achieved an accuracy of 80.17% in identifying the OWAS risk level in the controlled environment. Furthermore, in the real-world case study (unloading, receiving, and stacking fresh produce), the system maintained a risk level identification accuracy of 78.00%. The program's crucial ability lies in its capacity to recall high-risk postures (Levels 3 and 4) and provide traceable, data-driven corrective recommendations. This capability not only facilitates targeted ergonomic improvements but also serves as a vital tool for training and adjusting employee working postures to ensure sustainable safety.

Keywords: Supervised Learning · Human Pose Estimation · Ergonomic Risk Assessment · Recommendation System

1 Introduction

Work-related musculoskeletal disorders (WMSDs) constitute a significant and persistent occupational health challenge globally, leading to substantial economic burdens through lost productivity and increased healthcare costs. The primary and most actionable risk factor contributing to these disorders is prolonged or repetitive exposure to inappropriate working postures. Consequently, the foundation of any effective intervention strategy relies on accurate, reliable, and consistent ergonomic risk assessment. The Ovako Working Posture Analysis System (OWAS) is an established method for assessing ergonomic

C. Xu (Ed.): ICMLSC 2026, CCIS 2948, pp. 132–144, 2027.
https://doi.org/10.1007/978-981-92-1546-1_11

risk based on the postures of the back, arms, and legs, combined with the load weight handled by the worker during the task. Its advantages, namely ease and speed of evaluation, have led to its widespread adoption across diverse sectors, including construction, agriculture, patient care, and logistics. However, the traditional, manual application of OWAS is inherently subjective, labor-intensive, and limited in its ability to facilitate continuous, real-time monitoring across large workforces. This limitation underscores a critical need for automation that can scale the precision and objectivity of ergonomic analysis.

Current advancements have integrated Computer Vision for Human Pose Estimation (HPE) with Artificial Intelligence (AI) to automate risk assessment using various methodologies. Nevertheless, these applications typically focus on real-time evaluation to identify risky postures and provide immediate feedback. Moreover, there remains a limited number of systems capable of recording posture scores and traceable data—essential elements for retrospective analysis, targeted delayed feedback, and objectively quantifying the efficacy of posture training—and they concentrate more on industrial manufacturing applications than service jobs.

This study is therefore focused on addressing this gap by developing a program that facilitates both real-time assessment and the traceable recording of postural images and associated risk levels. This capability allows for the clear and accurate identification of high-risk operational steps across different body segments, leading to precise, targeted job improvement. Furthermore, a system has been added to provide corrective action recommendations for working postures based on the posture code. The logged images and risk statistics can also be effectively utilized to assess employee progress in adopting safer postures. Crucially, this research applies the developed program to the understudied domain of the fresh produce delivery supplier, a service sector that involves high inherent ergonomic risks but receives limited dedicated research attention.

2 Literature Review

2.1 Ergonomic Risk Assessment

Effective ergonomic risk assessment is fundamental to workplace safety, serving to identify and mitigate hazards that cause WMSDs. This necessity has driven the development of numerous tools designed to monitor and control postural risks. Traditional assessment approaches are generally grouped into three main categories: self-report questionnaires (e.g., the Nordic Musculoskeletal Questionnaire [1]), physiological measurements [2], and observational techniques. Observational techniques are highly valued for their ability to provide direct, visible data with minimal equipment. Key examples of observational tools include RULA (Rapid Upper Limb Assessment, focused on upper limbs), REBA (Rapid Entire Body Assessment, for whole-body movement), and OWAS (for general working postures). Standardization is also provided by global guidelines such as ISO 11226:2000 and EN 1005-4.

Among these established frameworks, the OWAS, introduced by Karhu et al. [3] in 1977, remains a popular and essential tool. It remains popular across the construction, healthcare, and industrial sectors [4] due to its practicality, comprehensive coverage of general postures, and minimal training requirements [5]. The OWAS method evaluates risk levels through a four-digit code. The first three digits represent postural codes categorized by three body parts: the back, arms, and legs (as shown in Table 1). The fourth digit indicates the weight level of the load or equipment the worker is handling during the task, which is classified into three discrete codes: (1) for loads less than 10 kg; (2) for loads greater than or equal to 10 kg but less than or equal to 20 kg; and (3) for loads exceeding 20 kg. This four-digit code is then used to determine the final risk level, which falls into four action categories: Level 1 requires no action (no detrimental effects); Level 2 requires corrective actions in the near future (some detrimental effects); Level 3 requires corrective actions as soon as possible (clear detrimental effects); and Level 4 requires immediate corrective actions (considerable detrimental effects).

Table 1. OWAS posture classification categories.

Part		Posture description	Part		Posture description
Back	1	Back Straight	Legs	1	Sitting
	2	Back bent		2	Standing on both legs, straight
	3	Back twisted		3	Standing on one leg, straight
	4	Back bent and twisted		4	Standing on both legs, knees bent
Arms	1	Both arms below shoulder		5	Standing on one leg, knee bent
	2	One arm at or above shoulder		6	Kneeling on one or both knees
	3	Both arms at or above shoulder		7	Walking

2.2 Computer Vision for Human Pose Estimation

The integration of computer vision and AI has significantly advanced ergonomic assessment through HPE. HPE is a non-invasive technique that extracts skeletal joint positions from camera input, enabling real-time posture tracking. This skeletal data is then processed by machine learning models [6, 7] or deep learning models to classify specific postures and estimate ergonomic risk with high accuracy. 3D HPE specifically aims to determine articulated 3D joint positions (keypoints) of the human body from a single image or video. This involves calculating the XYZ coordinates of specific body landmarks from standard RGB images. However, estimating 3D poses from 2D images remains challenging due to depth ambiguity and greater data requirements compared to 2D estimation [8]. Once joint positions are extracted, activity recognition models analyze posture and track movement across video sequences. Early 3D HPE approaches using monocular images were largely based on discriminative methods that framed the task as a regression or classification problem. These methods learned a mapping function from image features or body part cues to estimate 3D poses [9]. Some models use supervised learning to directly regress 3D joint positions from 2D monocular images, bypassing intermediate representations [10, 11]. With the advent of deep learning, state-of-the-art methods now rely on deep neural networks to automatically extract relevant features. However, such models require training on datasets annotated with 3D ground truth, which can limit their generalizability to real-world scenarios not represented in the training data.

For practical, accessible deployment, open-source frameworks like MediaPipe provides a powerful and efficient platform for building real-time, multimodal machine learning pipelines across Android, iOS, and web platforms [12]. MediaPipe Pose performs 3D pose estimation by lifting 2D keypoints—extracted from RGB images or video frames—into 3D space using CNN-based deep learning models. It leverages diverse training datasets such as COCO, MPII Human Pose, Leeds Sports Pose (LSP), and Human3.6M to ensure robustness across a wide range of poses and environments. MediaPipe's landmarker model identifies 33 key body landmarks, supporting accurate and real-time pose tracking, which can be used to train classifier models for predicting task-relevant human postures. This approach offers a powerful alternative to traditional keypoint data collection methods, which often rely on dedicated hardware like Kinect or MoCap systems [13]. Although these systems provide accurate and clear keypoint data, Kinect faces limitations in outdoor environments, where solar IR and ferromagnetic radiation can introduce noise or obscure the scene. It also consumes more power, offers lower resolution, and is less affordable and accessible than conventional RGB cameras [14]. Numerous studies confirm the viability of integrating AI into OWAS-based ergonomic assessments. Researchers have achieved strong results by training individual classifiers for each body region, with high reported classification accuracies (e.g., Singhtaun et al. [15], achieved 90.74% for the back, 92.71% for the arms and 85.53% for the legs). Other successful applications include Paudel et al. [16] reaching 94% OWAS scoring accuracy via 3D tracking, and Menanno et al. [17] demonstrating a 13% reduction in ergonomic strain through real-time joint analysis. In sector-specific applications, Chen et al. [18] developed lightweight HPE for construction sites, while Kapse et al. [19] achieved strong performance (F1-score = 87.41% using MoveNet and ANN) for classifying trunk postures in agricultural work. These precedents collectively underscore the potential for AI-driven systems to provide faster, more objective alternatives to conventional ergonomic assessment technique [20].

3 Methodology

3.1 Data Collection and Preprocessing

To align the classification model with the OWAS framework, a dedicated set of target postures was collected and verified by ergonomics experts to enhance the model's training process. The study covered 72 combinations of posture codes by considering all back and arm codes, but only leg codes 1–6. The controlled dataset comprised 1,800 images from 25 participants (20 males, 5 females; age 19–21; BMI 17.33–25.71 kg/m^2), each performing the 72 postures under controlled conditions. This was supplemented by 72 field images from online platforms to account for environmental variability. Figure 1 illustrates examples of the controlled and field data used for training, along with their corresponding back: arm: leg posture codes.

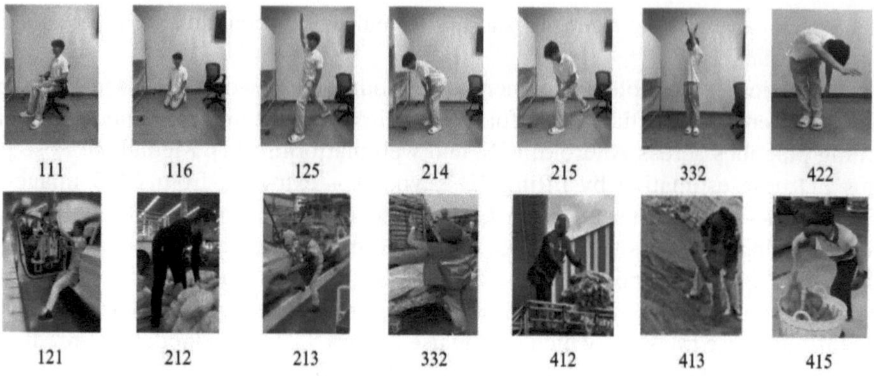

Fig. 1. Examples of the controlled data and field data.

Two ergonomics experts labeled the entire dataset according to OWAS protocols. To ensure data reliability, inter-rater agreement was validated using Cohen's Kappa (κ) across a representative sample of 144 images. The resulting κ values—0.888 for Back, 0.979 for Arms, and 0.875 for Legs —indicate substantial agreement, confirming the consistency of the ground truth labels used for training.

Four image processing techniques were applied for data augmentation. Contrast and brightness adjustment was used to enhance joint visibility, while the rotation technique—rotating the image at 90 and 180 degrees—was applied to align body poses to a canonical orientation. This yielded 7,200 images from the controlled dataset and 288 images from the field dataset. Pose keypoints were extracted using MediaPipe Pose, which generated 3D coordinates (x, y, z) for 33 anatomical landmarks. In addition, the visibility scores (v) of all 33 keypoints—indicating the clarity or reliability of each keypoint in the processed image or video—were incorporated as supplementary features. These scores helped assess the confidence level of each keypoint, particularly in cases of occlusion. As a result, a total of 132 features were obtained.

Based on the findings of Singhtaun et al. [15], eleven additional features (detailed in Table 2)—specifically six 3D biomechanical joint angles and five body part line angles—were derived to enhance OWAS-based posture classification. The x-y planar projection of these angles is illustrated in Fig. 2. This increased the feature set to 143.

Table 2. Created features for body part classification.

Feature	Symbol	Concerned keypoints	Back	Arms	Legs
Left and right shoulder angle	θ_1, θ_2	13-11-23, 14-12-24	√	√	
Left and right hip angle	θ_3, θ_4	11-23-25, 12-24-26	√		√
Left and right knee angle	θ_5, θ_6	23–25–27, 24-26-28	√		√

(*continued*)

Table 2. (*continued*)

Feature	Symbol	Concerned keypoints	Back	Arms	Legs
Middle body line angle	θ_7	11–12, 23–24	√		
Shoulder line angle	θ_8	11–12	√		
Hip line angle	θ_9	23–24	√		
Left knee-hip line angle	θ_{10}	24–26			√
Right knee-hip line angle	θ_{11}	23–25			√

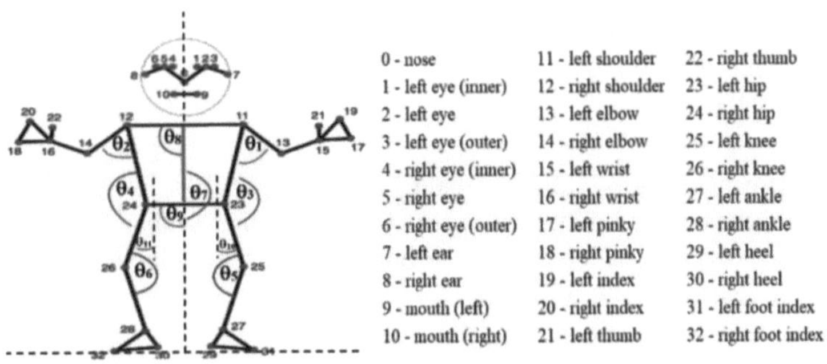

Fig. 2. Eleven created features and body landmark locations.

Feature selection involved Recursive Feature Elimination (RFE), which utilized Gini importance (Mean Decrease in Impurity) as the primary metric, iteratively eliminating features with a combined importance score below a p-value threshold of 0.05. Subsequently, Principal Component Analysis (PCA) was applied exclusively to the SVM classifier to reduce dimensionality and improve generalization. The optimal number of PCA components was determined by retaining the minimum required to account for 90% of the total dataset variance, a critical step for maximizing SVM robustness.

3.2 Classification Model Development and Evaluation

The collected data were split into 80% for training. Four supervised learning algorithms were tested: RF, SVM, XGBoost, and a hard voting ensemble of the three. Hyperparameter settings are summarized in Table 3.

Table 3. Hyperparameter setting.

Algorithm	Hyperparameter setting	Algorithm	Hyperparameter setting
RF	n_estimators: [100, 200, 300] max_depth: [10, 20, 30] min_samples_split: [2, 5, 10] min_samples_leaf: [1, 2, 4] bootstrap: [True, False]	XGBoost	n_estimators: [200, 300, 500] max_depth: [4–6] learning_rate: [0.03, 0.04, 0.05] subsample: [0.7, 0.8] colsample_bytree: [0.7] gamma: [0, 1, 5] reg_alpha: [0, 0.5] reg_lambda: [1, 5]
SVM	Kernel: Radial Basis Function C: [0.1, 1, 10, 100] Gamma: [1, 0.1, 0.01, 0.001]	Hard Voting Ensemble	Base learners: [SVM, RF, XGBoost] Voting method: Hard

Model performance was validated using the reserved 10% of images. Predicted posture codes were compared against expert-labeled ground truths. The classifier with the highest F1-score was selected for each body region. The selected model was then tested using the reserved 10% of images.

3.3 Recommendation System Development

A statistical analysis using One-way Analysis of Variance (ANOVA) ($\alpha = 0.05$) was performed to determine each body part's contribution to the final risk level variance. The results showed a highly significant effect on the risk level from both the Legs ($p = 0.000$) and the Back ($p = 0.000$). Conversely, the Arms showed no statistically significant effect ($p = 0.207$). These findings establish that back and leg postures are the primary drivers of high ergonomic risk in the analyzed task, while arm posture is a minor contributor. Based on the statistical significance and the interval plot (Fig. 3), improvement recommendations prioritize the back and legs. Given that specific codes for the back (2, 3, and 4) and the legs (4, 5, and 6) consistently resulted in risk level intervals exceeding Level 2 (Levels 3 and 4), requiring immediate intervention, corrective actions primarily focus on adjusting postures corresponding to these codes (see Table 4). Although the arms lacked statistical significance, a general recommendation to lower the arm level was provided to minimize unnecessary strain.

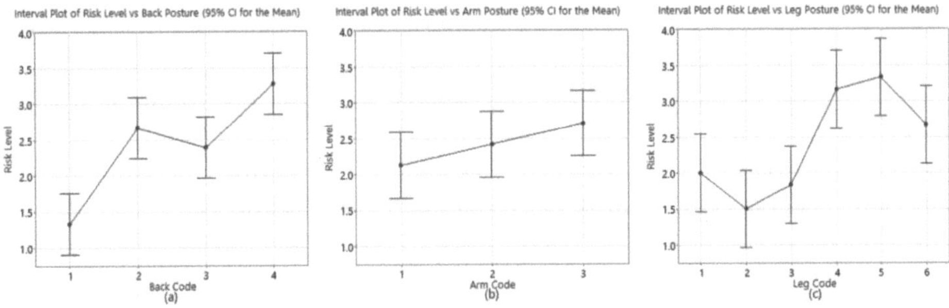

Fig. 3. Interval Plot of risk level vs. (a) back (b) arm, and (c) leg posture.

Table 4. Recommendations based on back and legs posture codes.

Adjustment	Recommendation	
Back	Code 2: Straighten the back	Code 3: Align the torso with the workpiece
	Code 4: Align the torso with the workpiece and straighten the back	
Legs	Code 3 and 5: Straighten the legs and distribute weight evenly on both legs	
	Code 4 and 6: Straighten the legs or adjust workplace	
Workplace	• Adjust the height of the workplace or workpiece location • Use a small, wheeled chair that swivels and has adjustable height • Use a conveyor belt or slide/rail to bring the workpiece closer to the employee and position it at waist level • Split the weight of the load. Reduce the load/number of items to be moved so that the weight does not exceed 10 kg	

3.4 Program Structure and Validation

The Input Module accepts visual data from webcams, images, or video files. The Assessment Module applies trained classifiers to evaluate postures of the back, arms, and legs, determining the complete four-digit OWAS code and the final ergonomic risk level. The Output Module generates results displaying the classified codes and final risk levels. Outputs include time-series line charts to illustrate the temporal risk evolution for each body part and the overall task, and pie charts for risk category distribution. The program's rigorous testing involved 200 randomly selected frames from video footage of fresh produce unloading, receiving, and stacking (covering both pre- and post-improvement methods). The automated risk assessments were validated against observational evaluations by two ergonomics experts. The program's accuracy and traceability were assessed to confirm its potential for real-world application.

4 Results and Discussion

4.1 Performance Evaluation of the Classifier

The F1-scores of classifier models trained using various algorithms for predicting back, arm, and leg postures, according to the OWAS assessment criteria, are in Table 5.

Table 5. F1-score of classifier models trained with different algorithms in the testing phase.

	RF	SVM	XGBoost	Hard Voting Ensemble
Back	74.93%	75.18%	81.38%	76.61%
Arms	91.27%	88.89%	86.21%	88.89%
Legs	75.54%	73.52%	82.88%	76.92%

The arm posture classifiers achieved the highest F1-scores across all algorithms, likely due to the limited number of arm posture classes. Specifically, the RF algorithm performed best for arm posture classification, achieving an F1-score of 91.27%. The XGBoost algorithm yielded the highest F1-scores for the back (81.38%) and legs (82.88%). Consequently, the RF arm classifier and the XGBoost back and leg classifiers were selected for the automated program. The accuracy of predicting the risk level from whole-body posture is 80.17%. The selected models were evaluated using the risk assessment program and 200 randomly sampled video frames from the unloading, receiving, and stacking tasks to test their performance against actual workplace conditions. According to the confusion matrices (Fig. 4), the Arms achieved the highest accuracy at 85.00%, followed by the Back at 79.50%, and the Legs at the lowest accuracy of 78.50%. When analyzing postures with a recall below 80.00%, issues were primarily found in the back and leg sections. For the back, codes 1 and 2 were frequently misclassified. Code 1 was often misclassified as Code 3, while Code 2 was often misclassified as Code 4. This suggests the classifier struggles with codes involving rotational movement (around the z-axis) combined with x-y planar posture.

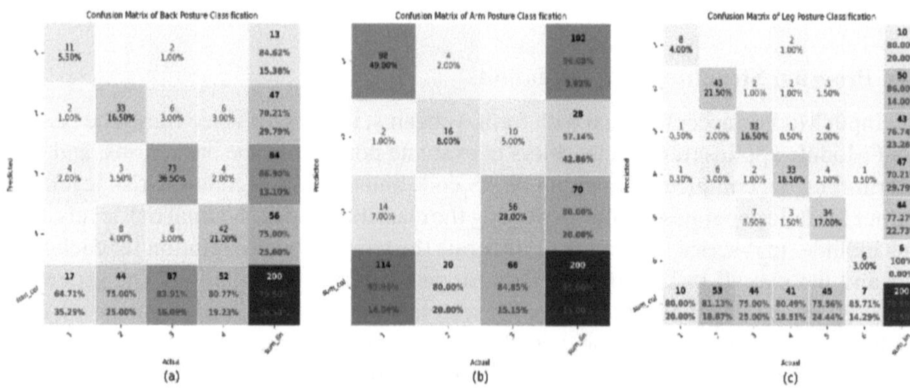

Fig. 4. Confusion matrices for (a) back, (b) arms, and (c) legs posture classification.

In the leg section, the classifier often confused code 3 and code 5 interchangeably, particularly with images showing only slight knee bending. Overall, the accuracy of predicting the risk level from whole-body posture is 78.00%.

4.2 Program Functionality and Application

The program supports data acquisition in three formats: real-time capture via webcam, image file upload, or video file upload. Once the program receives an image, the classifier model predicts the posture codes for the back, arms, and legs, and determines the corresponding ergonomic risk level. Option display outputs—namely the posture code, recommendation, connected line, and summary—can be selected via the Settings window. The display results, when utilizing image and video uploads as input for the selected study task (the fresh produce logistics operation), are shown in Fig. 5.

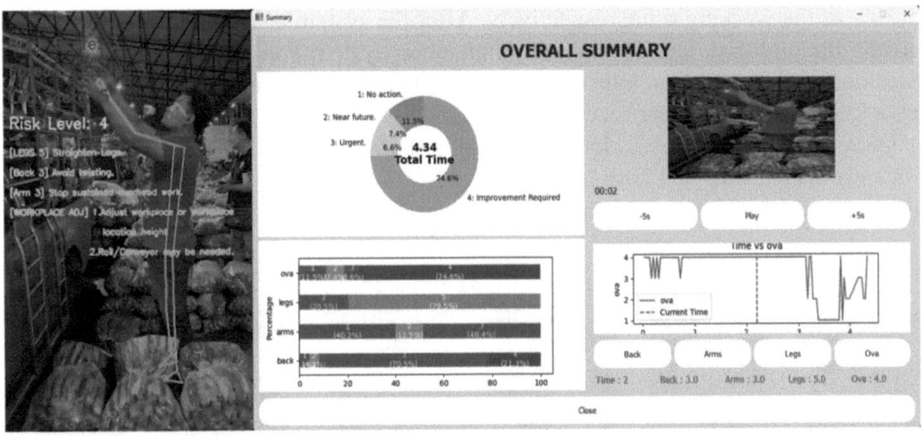

(a) (b)

Fig. 5. Example output using input from (a) an image file and (b) a video file.

When real-time analysis is performed, these results are immediately displayed and record. When an image is uploaded for risk analysis, the system displays the resulting risk assessment as shown in Fig. 5a. Recommendations are displayed directly on the image only if the 'Show Recommendations' option is checked in the Settings window. If this option isn't selected, recommendations will not appear. When a video file is uploaded, the reporting section provides graphs for separate analysis of the three body parts and the overall risk score, accessible via tabs (Fig. 5b). To display recommendations, the user must enable the option in the Settings window. In the 'Overall' tab, the user can scroll through the captured posture images (video frames), and the corresponding recommendation will dynamically appear overlaid on the image itself. Crucially, the system also presents the distribution of postures across various risk levels (e.g., via pie charts). This feature allows users to efficiently identify areas for job improvement and maintain a historical record to track progress in adopting safer working postures. The program's recommendation system was tested against the actual operations of fresh produce delivery employees. The statistical risk posture record provided data for the recommendation system to retrieve appropriate guidance for correcting and preventing ergonomic risks related to both posture and the workplace.

The program's output display can be applied in two primary ways: (1) providing real-time feedback to employees to correct their working posture, or (2) using statistical evaluation results to analyze high-risk postures for subsequent redesign of working conditions or for targeted employee training. The first application is directly achieved by selecting the 'show recommendation' option during real-time program use. The second application involves the system providing recommendations for proactive posture and workplace improvement, which was tested using the fresh produce delivery process, consisting of three tasks: unloading (Task 1), receiving (Task 2), and stacking (Task 3). When utilized for these tasks (shown in Fig. 6a), the pre-intervention analysis revealed high-risk postures (Levels 3 and 4) accounted for 80.24%, 75.60%, and 65.30% of the working time, respectively. After the system analyzed the posture codes causing the high-risk levels, the recommendation system presented guidelines for job redesign through two main interventions: introducing a foldable/adjustable incline conveyor system for unloading/receiving and utilizing a swiveling, height-adjustable chair for stacking. Following these changes (Fig. 6b), the occurrence of high-risk postures significantly decreased by 34.20% (unloading), 26.70% (receiving), and 19.90% (stacking), demonstrating a major reduction in ergonomic risk.

Fig. 6. Sample images of Tasks 1, 2, and 3: (a) before and (b) after job redesign.

5 Conclusion

This research successfully developed and validated an automated, ML-based program for ergonomic risk assessment using the OWAS method, effectively addressing the critical gap of data traceability and real-time monitoring in occupational health analysis. The system accurately classifies postures of the back, arms, and legs using optimized machine learning classifiers, where Random Forest excelled for arm classification (F1-score: 91.27%), and XGBoost proved superior for back (F1-score: 81.38%), and leg (F1-score: 82.88%) classification. The program demonstrated an acceptable 78.00% accuracy in identifying risk levels when applied to the fresh produce delivery environment. Crucially, the system's capacity to provide real-time feedback alongside traceable logs of images, posture codes, and risk statistics significantly enhanced risk awareness and provided a precise basis for targeted job redesign. When the statistical risk data used to analyze danger process and the high-risk posture images captured by the program were utilized as data-driven evidence to derive job improvement recommendations, it led to a more effective job redesign process. Following the job redesign, the overall risk levels in the unloading, receiving, and stacking tasks were successfully reduced by 34.20%, 26.70%, and 19.90% of the working time, respectively.

Future research should focus on enhancing the program's capabilities and expanding its practical application. The manual input of load levels should be fully automated by integrating additional computer vision techniques, such as object detection and volumetric estimation, to eliminate human bias and increase assessment efficiency. Applying this developed system to a wider range of service and non-industrial environments requires additional data collection under diverse conditions to further solidify the program's generalizability.

References

1. Kuorinka, I., et al.: Standardised Nordic questionnaires for the analysis of musculoskeletal symptoms. Appl. Ergon. **18**(3), 233–237 (1987). https://doi.org/10.1016/0003-6870(87)90010-x
2. David, G.C.: Ergonomic methods for assessing exposure to risk factors for work-related musculoskeletal disorders. Occup Med (Chic Ill) **55**(3), 190–199 (2005). https://doi.org/10.1093/occmed/kqi082
3. Karhu, O., Kansi, P., Kuorinka, I.: Correcting working postures in industry: a practical method for analysis. Appl. Ergon. **8**(4), 199–201 (1977). https://doi.org/10.1016/0003-6870(77)90164-8
4. Singhtaun, C.: Development of an automated ergonomic risk assessment system for educational use in simulated human-integrated production lines. Int. J. Technol. Knowl. Soc. **22**(1), 143–164 (2025). https://doi.org/10.18848/1832-3669/CGP/v22i01/143-164
5. Lins, C., Fudickar, S., Hein, A.: OWAS inter-rater reliability. Appl. Ergon. **93**, 103357 (2021). https://doi.org/10.1016/j.apergo.2021.103357
6. MassirisFernández, M., Fernández, J.Á., Bajo, J.M., Delrieux, C.A.: Ergonomic risk assessment based on computer vision and machine learning. Comput. Ind. Eng. **149**, 106816 (2020). https://doi.org/10.1016/j.cie.2020.106816
7. Roggio, F., Trovato, B., Sortino, M., Musumeci, G.: A comprehensive analysis of the machine learning pose estimation models used in human movement and posture analyses: a narrative review. Heliyon **10**(21), e39977 (2024). https://doi.org/10.1016/j.heliyon.2024.e39977
8. Liu, Y., Xu, Y., Li, S.-B.: 2-D human pose estimation from images based on deep learning: a review. In: Proceedings of 2018 2nd IEEE Advanced Information Management, Communicates, Electronic and Automation Control Conference, IMCEC 2018, pp. 462–465. IEEE (2018). https://doi.org/10.1109/IMCEC.2018.8469573
9. Sun, K., Xiao, B., Liu, D., Wang, J.: Deep high-resolution representation learning for human pose estimation. In: Proceedings of the IEEE Computer Society Conference on Computer Vision and Pattern Recognition, CVPR 2019, pp. 5686–5696. IEEE (2019). https://doi.org/10.1109/CVPR.2019.00584
10. Zhao, L., Peng, X., Tian, Y., Kapadia, M., Metaxas, D.N.: Semantic graph convolutional networks for 3D human pose regression. In: Proceedings of the IEEE Computer Society Conference on Computer Vision and Pattern Recognition, CVPR 2019, pp. 3420–3430. IEEE (2019). https://doi.org/10.1109/CVPR.2019.00354
11. Zhou, X., Sun, X., Zhang, W., Liang, S., Wei, Y.: Deep kinematic pose regression. In: Hua, G., Jégou, H. (eds.) Computer Vision – ECCV 2016 Workshops. ECCV 2016. Lecture Notes in Computer Science(), vol. 9915. Springer, Cham (2016). https://doi.org/10.1007/978-3-319-49409-8_17

12. Pisuchpen, S., Singhtaun, C., Suwannachote, L.: A software for learning Thai fingerspelling sign language into Thai consonants with machine learning. In: Cheung, S.K.S., Wang, F.L., Paoprasert, N., Charnsethikul, P., Li, K.C., Phusavat, K. (eds.) Technology in Education. Innovative Practices for the New Normal. ICTE 2023. Communications in Computer and Information Science, vol. 1974. Springer, Singapore (2024). https://doi.org/10.1007/978-981-99-8255-4_16
13. Weerasinghe, I. P. T., Ruwanpura, J. Y., Boyd, J. E. and Habib, A. F.: Application of microsoft kinect sensor for tracking construction workers. In: Construction Research Congress 2012: Construction Challenges in a Flat World, pp. 858–867. American Society of Civil Engineers (2012). https://doi.org/10.1061/9780784412329.087
14. Zhang, H., Yan, X., Li, H.: Ergonomic posture recognition using 3D view-invariant features from single ordinary camera. Autom. Constr. **94**, 1 (2018). https://doi.org/10.1016/J.AUTCON.2018.05.033
15. Singhtaun, C., Natsupakpong, S., Lorprasertkul, P.: Ergonomic risk assessment using human pose estimation with MediaPipe pose. In: ACM International Conference Proceeding Series, pp. 465–471. Association for Computing Machinery (2025). https://doi.org/10.1145/3719384.3719453
16. Paudel, P., Kwon, Y.-J., Kim, D.-H., Choi, K.-H.: Industrial ergonomics risk analysis based on 3D-human pose estimation. Electronics **11**(20), 3403 (2022). https://doi.org/10.3390/electronics11203403
17. Menanno, M., Riccio, C., Benedetto, V., Gissi, F., Savino, M.M., Troiano, L.: An ergonomic risk assessment system based on 3D human pose estimation and collaborative robot. Appl. Sci. **14**(11), 4823 (2024). https://doi.org/10.3390/app14114823
18. Chen, W., Gu, D., Ke, J.: Real-time ergonomic risk assessment in construction using a co-learning-powered 3D human pose estimation model. Comput.-Aided Civil Infrastruct. Eng. **39**(9), 1337–1353 (2024). https://doi.org/10.1111/mice.13139
19. Kapse, S., Wu, R., Thamsuwan, O.: Addressing ergonomic challenges in agriculture through AI-enabled posture classification. Appl. Sci. **14**(2), 525 (2024). https://doi.org/10.3390/app14020525
20. Deshpande, U.U., et al.: A review of machine learning techniques for ergonomic risk assessment based on human pose estimation. Discover Artif. Intell. **5**(1), 287 (2025). https://doi.org/10.1007/s44163-025-00566-5

ST-MAP: Spatio-Temporal Proxy Dataset for Modeling Microplastic Pollution in Global Water Bodies

Sanjay Seshadri(✉), Shama Kiran, Sahana Bhat, M. S. Skanda, and S. S. Shylaja

Department of Computer Science and Engineering, PES University, Bengaluru, India
sanjay10.seshadri@gmail.com, shylaja.sharath@pes.edu

Abstract. Microplastic pollution poses a significant threat to marine ecosystems and human health, but large-scale and continuous monitoring is constrained by the cost and sparsity of in-situ sampling. In this work we present a carefully curated tabular proxy dataset that merges validated ground truth microplastic observations with large-scale oceanographic proxy records to enable machine learning-based prediction of microplastic density classes.

The integrated dataset consolidates approximately 21,183 validated observations obtained from an ArcGIS Experience Portal (1972–2021) with over 500,000 global oceanographic records from the GLODAP merged master files (1986–2021). Each merged record contains geospatial metadata, temporal stamps, physicochemical and biogeochemical variables (e.g., temperature, salinity, dissolved oxygen, nutrients, density indices), quality-control flags, and an assigned microplastic density class label.

We describe the data sources, harmonization and quality-control procedures, spatio-temporal merging strategy (±50 km geospatial buffer with date alignment), and final integrated dataset statistics. This structured proxy dataset is intended to serve as a reproducible foundation for developing and evaluating tabular machine learning models (e.g., TabTransformer) for microplastic presence and risk mapping.

Keywords: Microplastics · Proxy Dataset · ArcGIS · Tabular Data · Spatio-temporal Merging · GLODAP · Environmental Monitoring

1 Introduction

Microplastic contamination has surfaced as an emerging environmental issue that has both impacted aquatic and marine ecosystems, biodiversity, and also escalated into an issue concerning global health in humans. Microplastics are difficult to detect because of their persistence in the environment, small size, not to mention their ability to disperse. The existing sampling technique is labor intensive despite being precise.

C. Xu (Ed.): ICMLSC 2026, CCIS 2948, pp. 145–157, 2027.
https://doi.org/10.1007/978-981-92-1546-1_12

To overcome these challenges, there has been a focus on the usage of proxy variables that relate to the temperature, salinity, levels of dissolved oxygen, nutrients, and carbon cycling within the environment to model microplastic distributions. Each of these physicochemical and biogeochemical variables has an important role to play in the transport and retention of microplastic fragments. None of the proxy variables are taken to be direct causal drivers of microplastic generation. Rather, they speak directly to various environmental transport, retention, and accumulation mechanisms such as water column stratification, circulation, and biogeochemical coupling. Past studies of oceanography have demonstrated that such variable features like density gradients, dissolved oxygen, and nutrient concentrations strongly modulate the residence time and aggregation behavior of particles; it would, therefore, serve as a very effective indirect predictor of microplastic distribution.The global availability of these variables also makes them very suitable for modeling.

It proposes a tabular proxy data structure that combines the ground truth microplastic data observations with large-scale ocean data measurements.

Through its sole emphasis on tabular proxy data, this research provides a reproducible basis for the concentration modeling of microplastics that does not involve the use of remote sensing images. It is expected that the generated dataset as well as the model will facilitate future advancements in both the accuracy and scalability of microplastic mapping.

2 Related Work

Recent studies have focused on combining sensor-based measurement methods with spectroscopy techniques and machine learning algorithms, in order to improve microplastic identification in terms of accuracy and efficiency. In [1], a hybrid approach was proposed by integrating impedance spectroscopy with machine learning for the classification of PET microparticles. This important seminal work showed that electrical signatures can be successfully integrated into learning-based classifiers, achieving high-accuracy microplastic detection.

Building further on this line of work, Meiler *et al.* [2] introduced a refined Electrical Impedance Spectroscopy-based framework with Support Vector Machines that can detect and classify microplastics under both stationary and dynamic flow conditions. Their classification accuracies were above 98% for stationary measurements and in the range of 85%–91% under dynamic flow, for use in-situ water monitoring applications.

Raman spectroscopy [3] based on machine learning can alleviate limitations in traditional Raman spectroscopy, wherein resolution strength was lower and processing speed took longer, due to usage of classifiers such as PCA, KNN, RF, SVM, and deep learning models, providing improvement in feature extraction, as well as classification accuracy. Improvements achieved in this community by author Luo *et al.* in [4] include a combination of Raman spectroscopy, sparse autoencoder, and softmax classifiers, providing an accuracy of 99.1%, which is more efficient than traditional classifiers SVM and backpropagation-trained BP networks.

The recent literature survey presented in [5] sheds light on the growing use of the CNN, Random Forest, and Hyperspectral & Machine Learning Fusion approach. Though it is evident that the above techniques are much superior concerning scalability and computational complexity compared to the laboratorial procedures performed by human experts, the survey mentions some drawbacks for the proposed techniques.

In [6], the authors proposed a real-time object detection and tracking framework based on YOLOv5 and DeepSORT to identify microplastics ranging from 1–5 mm in a controlled flume environment. While effective under controlled conditions, this study reports performance degradation when operating under high-flow scenarios and sensitivity limitations associated with camera resolution.

Recently, remote sensing has appeared as an effective indirect method for large-scale estimation of microplastic pollution. Mohsen *et al.* [7] explored a neural network-based framework using satellite-derived imagery of SSC as a proxy for riverine microplastic estimation. Reported R^2 values were from 0.17 to 0.88; thus, though microplastics cannot be directly observed via satellite imagery, its proxy-based estimation coupled with machine learning can produce meaningful predictions.

Collectively, the studies here form a sound basis for scalable and intelligent microplastics monitoring systems.

3 Dataset Description

This section describes the data sources, contents, harmonization procedures, merging strategy, and final characteristics of the tabular dataset used in this study. The dataset is constructed by integrating two complementary sources: (i) a validated ground-truth microplastic observation dataset obtained from the ArcGIS Experience Portal, and (ii) a large-scale oceanographic proxy dataset derived from the GLODAP Merged Master File.

The primary objective of this integration is to generate spatio-temporally aligned records that combine precise in-situ microplastic measurements with rich physicochemical and biogeochemical oceanographic context. By merging localized microplastic observations with globally consistent proxy variables, the resulting dataset enables data-driven modeling of microplastic concentration patterns across diverse marine environments.

3.1 Data Sources and Provenance

Ground Truth Dataset (ArcGIS Experience Portal). The ground truth dataset consists of validated microplastic concentration observations and associated metadata, aggregated via an ArcGIS Experience Portal [8]. The dataset spans from October 1, 1972 to September 30, 2021, comprising a total of 21,183 independent, quality-controlled observations. The spatial coverage is global, with records from the major oceans (Pacific, Atlantic, Indian, Southern, Arctic).

Each observation provides latitude, longitude, date (YYYY-MM-DD), measured microplastic concentration or density values, measurement units, density range/class, reference metadata, DOI, and institutional attribution. For supervised learning, each observation is assigned a density class label (Very High, High, Medium, Low, Very Low).

Proxy Dataset (GLODAP Merged Master File). To provide broader oceanographic context, we incorporated the Global Ocean Data Analysis Project (GLODAP) merged master file [9]. The proxy dataset spans 1986–2021 and contains over 500,000 global observations from both ship-based and buoy-based measurements. Each record includes high-resolution temporal stamps, geospatial coordinates, physical properties (temperature, salinity, pressure, depth, density indices), chemical properties (oxygen, nitrate, phosphate, silicate, total CO_2, alkalinity, fCO_2), and depth-related metrics.

Quality-control (QC) flags are provided for each variable, enabling the filtering of unreliable measurements and ensuring high data integrity during integration with the ground truth dataset.

3.2 Harmonization and Preprocessing

Before merging, a harmonization pipeline was applied so that features are comparable. All physical and chemical measurements were converted to consistent units (e.g., °C, PSU, µmol/kg). Latitude and longitude were standardized in decimal degrees and used to calculate spatial buffers. Temporal fields were standardized to YYYY-MM-DD format, and proxy records with higher resolution were aggregated or indexed to match ground truth dates.

Records with missing critical fields were removed, while missing proxy variable values were either imputed using local statistics or filtered out. Outliers were detected using interquartile ranges and domain-specific acceptable limits, with extreme values inspected and removed. Quality flag filtering was applied to retain only reliable proxy records.

The microplastic observations ranging between 1972 and 2021 might be affected by historic biases in microplastic magnitude due to changes in observation techniques, mesh sizes, laboratory analysis techniques, and observation sensitivity in earlier years. However, it should be noted that microplastic observation records after the year 2000 consist mainly of standardized observation techniques in relation to microplastic analysis in the dataset used in deriving Proxy Microplastic relationships. The temporal metadata, including year and decade, is maintained as a feature in order to account for any systematics that remain after the trends in each decade.

3.3 Spatio-Temporal Matching and Merging

The core merging procedure aligned ground truth and proxy records using spatio-temporal criteria. Temporal alignment required an exact date match at the day level. Proxy records were aggregated to the day level, with optional ± 1 day windows. However, it has only been considered for sensitivity analysis. Spatial alignment used a geospatial buffer of ± 50 km. We used a ± 50 km buffer in order to balance data availability and spatial accuracy. Smaller buffers produced too few matches for modeling, whereas larger buffers increased smoothing. This may be refined as more ground-truth data become available.

3.4 Final Integrated Dataset

The integrated dataset that results contains approximately 15,000 merged records. Each entry contains the ground-truth microplastic density class, spatial and temporal metadata, standardized proxy variables, depth metrics, QC flags, and engineered features such as lat/lon bins and seasonal indicators. The dataset also retains provenance metadata to ensure reproducibility.

Observed class imbalances were addressed during model training using class weighting or resampling to ensure robust learning across all density classes. This dataset provides a flexible and high-quality foundation for training both classical machine learning models and advanced deep learning architectures.

3.5 Density Class Distribution

The distribution of microplastic density classes is shown in Fig. 1. The *Medium* density class dominates the dataset, followed by *Very Low* and *Low*. The *High* and *Very High* classes are under-represented. This imbalance informs the use of class weighting or oversampling during model training to achieve balanced performance across classes.

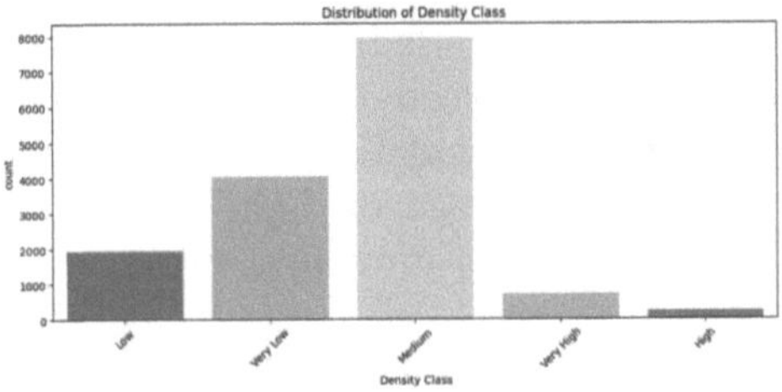

Fig. 1. Distribution of microplastic density classes across the merged dataset.

3.6 Seasonal Variation of Density Classes

Figure 2 illustrates seasonal variation in microplastic density. The *Medium*, *Low*, and *Very Low* classes occur throughout the year, whereas *High* and *Very High* classes appear sporadically, suggesting seasonality or localized environmental drivers.

This temporal variability provides additional context for model interpretability and helps in designing predictive frameworks that consider both spatial and seasonal effects.

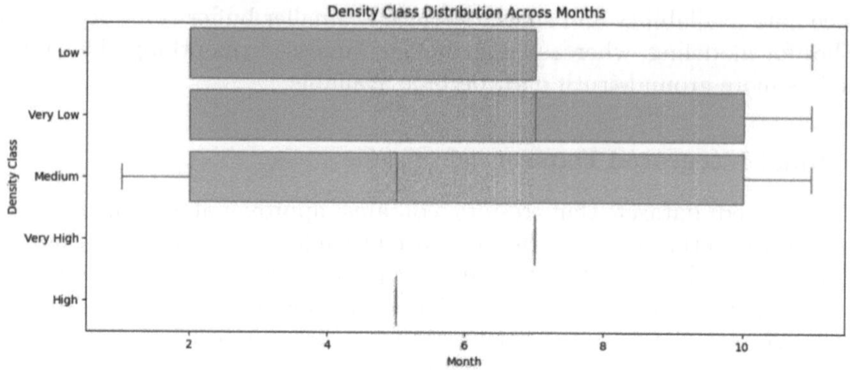

Fig. 2. Seasonal variation of microplastic density classes across months.

3.7 Proxy Validation via Feature Importance Analysis

To identify the most informative predictors, a **Random Forest Classifier** was trained on the dataset. Feature importance scores quantified each variable's contribution to microplastic presence.

To examine and verify if the chosen proxy variables have any predictive value, feature importance calculations were carried out using the Random Forest classifier on the dataset. The prominent variables, such as latitude and longitude, Dissolved Oxygen, Nitrate, Temperature, and Density Anomalies, depict physically sensible transport mechanisms across oceans. Such results from data importance calculations also provide scientific merit to the generated formula using proxies.

The top-ranked features were selected to construct the final feature matrix used for training the deep learning model. This selection reduced dimensionality while ensuring that the model focused on high-impact variables. The density class was used as the target variable, providing a concise and informative input for further modeling (Fig. 3).

4 Implementation Details and Model Used: TabTransformer for Tabular Data

The **TabTransformer** model was selected for this study due to its strong performance on heterogeneous tabular datasets containing both numerical and categorical features. For microplastic prediction, variables like temperature, dissolved oxygen, nutrients, and density indices are interdependent in nature, which makes attention-based feature representation very helpful.

4.1 Model Choice

The TabTransformer architectural design makes use of *multi-head self-attention* in order to discover the relationships in the tabular data, which would otherwise

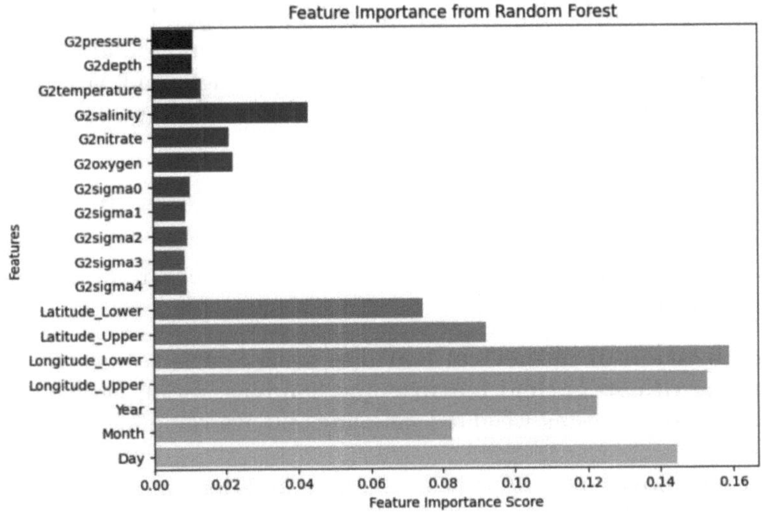

Fig. 3. Feature importance scores derived from the Random Forest model.

be difficult to identify using tree-based or linear models. It is also more applicable in oceanographic data, which is influenced by more than one variable, including temperature-salinity relationships, nutrient concentrations, and geographic characteristics, which in turn have an effect on microplastic concentration. Given the mixed nature of the dataset (numerical proxy features + discretized spatial metadata + engineered features), TabTransformer was an appropriate choice for learning complex, nonlinear relationships.

4.2 Input Features and Label Construction

The model was trained on the **fused and harmonized tabular dataset** obtained after merging ground truth microplastic observations with GLODAP proxy data (Sect. 3). The final feature set included both raw environmental measurements and engineered attributes:

- **Physical variables:** temperature, density anomalies (sigma layers), pressure, depth
- **Chemical variables:** dissolved oxygen, nitrate, phosphate, silicate, chlorophyll
- **Geospatial metadata:** latitude and longitude
- **Engineered attributes:** latitude/longitude bins, seasonal indicators, spatial clusters

Latitude and longitude were discretized into categorical bins to capture spatial dependencies creating temporal features such as year, month, and seasonal indicators, and computing derived variables like density anomalies and temperature-salinity interactions. These categorical features were embedded and passed through transformer encoder blocks. The **target label** for supervised learning was the *microplastic density class* derived from ground truth observations. Classes included: Very Low, Low, Medium, High, and Very High, later mapped to a standardized three-class system (Low, Medium, High) for stable training.

4.3 Preprocessing Pipeline

Prior to training, a structured preprocessing workflow ensured consistency and high-quality model inputs:

- **Normalization of numerical features** using z-score scaling
- **Encoding of categorical features** (lat/lon bins, region metadata)
- **Class balancing** using weighted sampling and oversampling to address class imbalance
- **Outlier removal** using IQR-based filtering and domain rules
- **Train–test split** with an 80:20 partition

Random Forest–based feature importance as seen in Fig. 3 was applied to reduce dimensionality. Key predictors such as dissolved oxygen, nitrate, temperature, and density anomalies were retained.

4.4 Model Architecture

TabTransformer encodes categorical features via embedding layers and processes them through **stacked transformer encoder blocks** [10] (Fig. 4). Multi-head self-attention enables the model to learn contextual interactions between features, such as nutrient–temperature relationships, oxygen–depth interactions, and spatially-driven patterns via latitude and longitude bins.

Each categorical feature $x_c^{(i)}$ is mapped to a dense embedding vector using a learnable embedding function:

$$\mathbf{e}_i = \text{Embed}_i(x_c^{(i)}), \quad \mathbf{e}_i \in \mathbb{R}^d \tag{1}$$

The embeddings are concatenated to form the input sequence to the transformer encoder:

$$\mathbf{E} = [\mathbf{e}_1, \mathbf{e}_2, \ldots, \mathbf{e}_k] \tag{2}$$

The transformer encoder follows the standard scaled dot-product self-attention formulation introduced in [11].

For each transformer encoder block, query, key, and value matrices are computed as:

$$\mathbf{Q} = \mathbf{E}\mathbf{W}_Q, \quad \mathbf{K} = \mathbf{E}\mathbf{W}_K, \quad \mathbf{V} = \mathbf{E}\mathbf{W}_V \tag{3}$$

Self-attention is calculated using the scaled dot-product formulation:

$$\text{Attention}(\mathbf{Q}, \mathbf{K}, \mathbf{V}) = \text{softmax}\left(\frac{\mathbf{Q}\mathbf{K}^\top}{\sqrt{d_k}}\right)\mathbf{V} \tag{4}$$

Multi-head attention aggregates information from multiple attention heads:

$$\text{MHA}(\mathbf{E}) = \text{Concat}(\text{head}_1, \ldots, \text{head}_h)\mathbf{W}_O \tag{5}$$

Residual connections and layer normalization are applied to stabilize training:

$$\mathbf{Z} = \text{LayerNorm}(\mathbf{E} + \text{MHA}(\mathbf{E})) \tag{6}$$

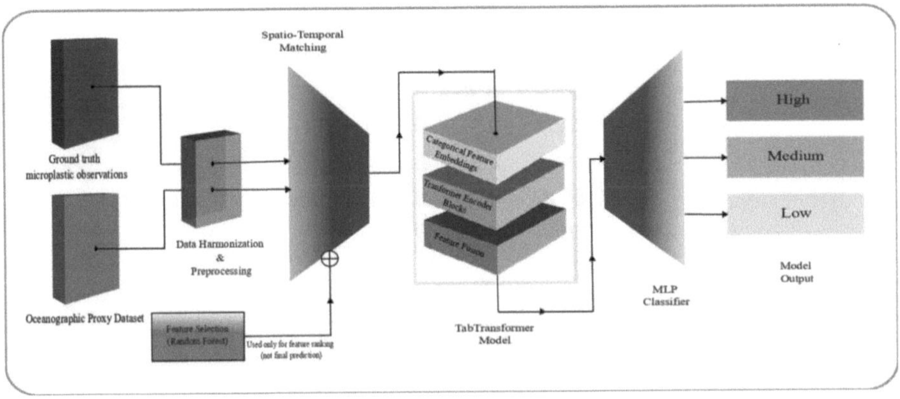

Fig. 4. Pipeline for tabular data prediction.

Numerical features are standardized prior to fusion:

$$\hat{\mathbf{x}}_n = \frac{\mathbf{x}_n - \mu}{\sigma} \tag{7}$$

The transformer output is concatenated with normalized numerical features to form a unified latent representation:

$$\mathbf{h} = [\mathbf{Z}, \hat{\mathbf{x}}_n] \tag{8}$$

This representation is passed to a multi-layer perceptron (MLP) classifier with ReLU activation:

$$\mathbf{h}_1 = \text{ReLU}(\mathbf{W}_1\mathbf{h} + \mathbf{b}_1) \tag{9}$$

The final class probabilities are obtained using a softmax function:

$$\hat{\mathbf{y}} = \text{softmax}(\mathbf{W}_2\mathbf{h}_1 + \mathbf{b}_2) \tag{10}$$

4.5 Training Procedure

The model was trained using:

- **Loss function:** Categorical cross-entropy

- **Optimizer:** Adam with learning rate scheduling
- **Batch size:** 32
- **Early stopping:** Based on validation loss to prevent overfitting
- **Evaluation metrics:** Accuracy and macro-averaged F1-score

Early stopping stabilized training, while class-weighting ensured minority classes contributed proportionally to the loss.

Table 1. Class-wise performance metrics of the TabTransformer model

Class	Precision	Recall	F1-score	Support
0	0.9000	0.4000	0.5538	45
1	0.5198	0.5385	0.5290	390
2	0.8864	0.8561	0.8710	1577
3	0.8936	0.9767	0.9333	129
4	0.6648	0.7069	0.6852	836

4.6 Performance

The TabTransformer model achieved a test accuracy of approximately **80%**, outperforming conventional baselines such as SVM, Random Forest, XGBoost, and standard MLPs. The results highlight the effectiveness of attention-based feature encoding in capturing complex oceanographic relationships and predicting microplastic density classes with high fidelity.

5 Modeling with TabTransformer

To demonstrate the use case value of this data, a TabTransformer model was trained for microplastic density classification. Categorical spatial features were funneled into transformer encoder blocks, and numerical data was normalized and combined with transformer outputs. This attention mechanism was key to allowing the model to understand complex relationships between several aspects of the environment.

6 Results

The TabTransformer achieved a classification accuracy of approximately 80% on the test dataset, outperforming conventional baseline models such as Support Vector Machines, Random Forest classifiers, and Multi-Layer Perceptrons. This performance highlights the effectiveness of attention-based mechanisms for capturing the complex relationships governing microplastic distribution influenced by spatial, seasonal, and environmental factors.

Table 1 presents the class-wise precision, recall, F1-score, and support for each density class. Strong predictive performance is observed for the dominant density classes, particularly Class 2 and Class 3, which exhibit high F1-scores. In contrast, lower recall values are evident for minority classes, primarily due to class imbalance and partial overlap in environmental feature distributions among adjacent density classes.

From a computational perspective, the TabTransformer demonstrated high efficiency. The total training time was approximately 243.03 s, while inference on the test dataset required only 0.13 s on an NVIDIA GeForce RTX 4050 Laptop GPU. The average prediction latency was around 0.05 ms per sample, indicating suitability for scalable and near-real-time environmental monitoring applications.

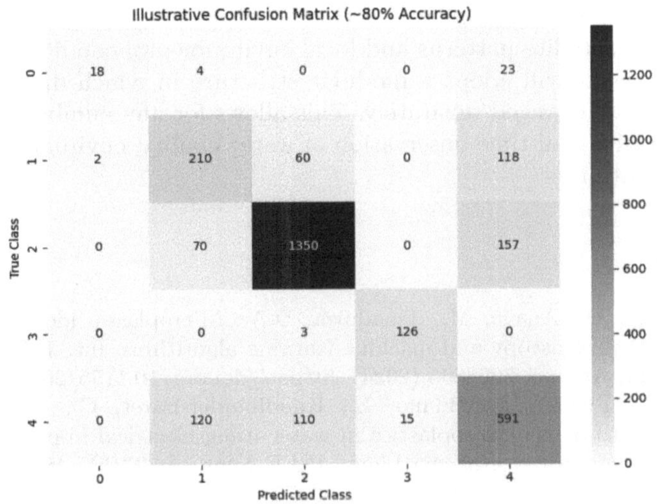

Fig. 5. Confusion matrix heatmap for the TabTransformer model on the test set.

7 Conclusion

To further analyze the model's predictive behavior, a heatmap visualization of the confusion matrix is presented in Fig. 5. The strong diagonal dominance, particularly for the major density classes, confirms the model's robust classification capability. Moreover, most misclassifications occur between neighboring density classes, suggesting physically meaningful error patterns rather than random prediction noise. This behavior aligns well with the continuous and gradual nature of microplastic concentration gradients in real-world environmental systems.

Overall, the findings validate the effectiveness of transformer-based architectures for large-scale environmental forecasting using proxy datasets. The integration of ST-MAP data with attention-driven tabular learning provides a strong foundation for developing efficient and scalable microplastic monitoring and surveillance systems in future environmental applications.

8 Future Work

The future work will focus on the development of a framework for the integration of satellite data into a tabular proxy dataset for multimodal fusion. Complementary multispectral products will include sea surface salinity, chlorophyll concentration, turbidity, and temperature gradients on the biogeochemical variables in the tabular data.

A unified architecture will fuse image embeddings from ViT or CNN-based encoders with TabTransformer-based tabular representations, using either concatenation or cross-modal interaction mechanisms to model dependencies between global satellite patterns and local environmental conditions.

The framework will adopt a modular structure in which different parts of the model can be changed separately. This allows for any number of extensions in the future with real-time observation of water quality, environmental factors, and remote platforms.

References

1. Sarmiento, J.D., Anaya, M., Tibaduiza, D.A.: Microplastic identification using impedance spectroscopy and machine learning algorithms. Int. J. Distrib. Sensor Netw. **2024**, Art. no. 5298635 (2024). https://doi.org/10.1155/2024/5298635
2. Meiler, V., Pfeiffer, J., Bifano, L., Kandlbinder-Paret, C., Fischerauer, G.: Approaches to detect microplastics in water using electrical impedance measurements and support vector machines. IEEE Sens. J. **23**(5), 4863–4872 (2023). https://doi.org/10.1109/JSEN.2023.3236375
3. Sunil, M., Pallikkavaliyaveetil, N., Gopinath, A., Chidangil, S., Kumar, S., Lukose, J.: Machine learning assisted Raman spectroscopy: a viable approach for the detection of microplastics. J. Water Process Eng. **60**, Art. no. 105150 (2024). https://doi.org/10.1016/j.jwpe.2024.105150
4. Luo, Y., et al.: Raman spectroscopy and machine learning for microplastics identification and classification in water environments. IEEE J. Sel. Top. Quantum Electron. **29**(4), 1–8 (2023). https://doi.org/10.1109/JSTQE.2022.3222065
5. Khanam, M.M., Uddin, M.K., Kazi, J.U., et al.: Advances in machine learning for the detection and characterization of microplastics in the environment. Front. Environ. Sci. **13** (2025). https://doi.org/10.3389/fenvs.2025.1573579
6. Sarker, M.A.B., Butt, U., Imtiaz, M.H., Baki, A.B.: Automatic detection of microplastics in the aqueous environment. In: Proceedings of IEEE 13th Annual Computing and Communication Workshop and Conference (CCWC) (2023). https://doi.org/10.1109/CCWC57344.2023.10099253
7. Mohsen, A., Kovács, F., Kiss, T.: Riverine microplastic quantification: a novel approach integrating satellite images, neural network, and suspended sediment data as a proxy. Sensors **23**(23), Art. no. 9505 (2023). https://doi.org/10.3390/s23239505

8. ArcGIS Experience Portal: Microplastics in the Oceans. https://experience.arcgis.com/experience/b296879cc1984fda833a8acc93e31476. Accessed Jan 2025
9. Lauvset, S.K., Key, R.M., Olsen, A., van Heuven, S., et al.: GLODAPv2.2023: the global ocean data analysis project version 2. Earth Syst. Sci. Data **15**(12), 5301–5329 (2023). https://doi.org/10.5194/essd-15-5301-2023
10. Huang, X., Khetan, A., Ranganath, C., Karnin, Z., Gupta, S., Yang, Y.: TabTransformer: tabular data modeling using contextual embeddings, arXiv preprint arXiv:2012.06678 (2020)
11. Vaswani, A., et al.: Attention is all you need. In: Advances in Neural Information Processing Systems (NeurIPS) (2017)

A Machine Learning Approach to Find Major Factors of Gut Microbiota Relative to Anemia Focusing on Athletes

Kosuke Tashima[1], Kazuki Kioka[2], Naomi Omi[3,5], and Shinichi Yamagiwa[4,5](✉)

[1] College of Information Science, University of Tsukuba, Tennodai 1-1-1, Tsukuba, Ibaraki 305-8573, Japan
tajima@padc.cs.tsukuba.ac.jp

[2] Doctoral Program in Physical Education, Health and Sport Sciences, University of Tsukuba, Tennodai 1-1-1, Tsukuba, Ibaraki 305-8574, Japan
s2230482@u.tsukuba.ac.jp

[3] Institute of Comprehensive Human Sciences, University of Tsukuba, Tennodai 1-1-1, Tsukuba, Ibaraki 305-8574, Japan
omi.naomi.gn@u.tsukuba.ac.jp

[4] Institute of Systems and Information Engineering, University of Tsukuba, Tennodai 1-1-1, Tsukuba, Ibaraki 305-8573, Japan
yamagiwa@cs.tsukuba.ac.jp

[5] Advanced Research Initiative for Human High Performance, University of Tsukuba, Tsukuba, Ibaraki, Japan

Abstract. One of critical responses of human body is anemia that generally caused by losing iron in blood. Especially, athletes tend to have anemia when their nutritional planning does not match to their training schedules. This paper focuses on gut microbiota to know such critical situation. Ferritin is known as a factor in blood which decreases related to anemia. When exercise is intensely performed, it tends to decrease in blood. In this paper, applying a machine learning approach, we perform data mining to find a relationship between gut microbiota and anemia by using dataset of elements in blood and the microbiota measured from active athletes. The major factors in gut microbiota have not been found yet in the nutrition field because the number of considerable factors in the microbiota is huge. Our method applies a supervised approach without target labels by combining a clustering and a regression. Focusing on ferritin in blood, we first make clusters related to anemia. Based on the clusters, the regression infers the clusters categorized to anemia from gut microbiota. According to experiments using the approach, we found eight major factors of gut microbiota that strongly related to anemia.

Keywords: Gut microbiota · Anemia · Ferritin · Clustering · Regression

C. Xu (Ed.): ICMLSC 2026, CCIS 2948, pp. 158–172, 2027.
https://doi.org/10.1007/978-981-92-1546-1_13

1 Introduction

It is well-known truth that nutritional supplementation through food shapes our bodies. Mineral elements are crucial nutrition to circulate enough oxygen in the blood. Especially, iron works as the major roll. When iron is reduced in the blood, we have anemia that causes critical situation of our bodies. Sports athletes tend to starve iron due to losing nutritional supplementation strategy [5]. The researchers have been exploring relation between the nutritional supplementation and anemia in case of sports athletes [4]. They are focusing on gut microbiota and trying to find factor microbiota from thousands of the candidates [3]. According to the clinical approach, definitive gut microbiota has not been found yet in the field.

Clinically, we can have an experimental dataset of blood and gut microbiota from athletes. We focus on a data mining approach for the dataset to find the definitive gut microbiota related to anemia. Because the dataset includes blood information and the known factors in blood related to anemia are well known, we propose a machine learning method to find the definitive gut microbiota to anemia by employing a clustering method and a regression.

The contributions of our research are enumerated as follows. The contributions of our research are enumerated as follows.

1. We developed a machine learning approach. Our supervised learning method combines a clustering method and a regression. The clustering method was applied to the blood information and generates the clusters focusing on factors in blood related to iron. According to the regression for the clusters regarding the gut microbiota, we found definitive factors of the gut microbiota.
2. Focusing on ferritin in blood information, our proposed method found eight definitive factors of gut microbiota. Those were relative factors that can be plausible due to the literatures in the field of exercise nutrition [1].
3. Finally, according to the experiments, our proposed method proved that ferritin in blood is an effective factor to find anemia for athletes because our method stably extracts the definitive factors in gut microbiota that are relative to anemia.

This paper organizes as follows. The next section describes our research motivation and shows detailed backgrounds of the research. Section 3 shows advanced related works that performed the similar data mining methods to medical and nutritional research. Section 4 shows our proposed method describing the processing flow. Section 5 performs experimental evaluations of our method with applying dataset of blood and gut microbiota and discusses the validity of our method. Finally, we will conclude the paper and show future plans.

2 Research Motivations

Anemia is a critical syndrome in our daily life that induces us fatigue, risks of heart failure, myocardial infarction, stroke and so on. Anyone can have anemia when iron deficiency occurs in our body. It is known that anemia is caused by destroying hemoglobin because it is one of major elements in blood in which includes rich iron. By measuring hemoglobin concentration (called Hb) in blood, we can know if we would have anemia or not. In the nutritional field, researchers also focus on hematocrit concentration (called Ht) in blood for anemia. Ht is a volume ratio of red blood cells in blood. Low Hb means to decrease transport capacity of oxygen and low Ht indicates thin blood. Both cases suggest anemia.

The anemia case observed by measuring Hb and Ht is found for people who live in a normal life activity. The case shows subjective symptom of anemia and low Hb and Ht values. However, the case when hard activity is repeated in daily life such as athletes does not match the values to the symptom. It is also known that ferritin is another major element in blood with rich iron [1]. If we do not have strenuous activity in daily life, hemoglobin just works to provide iron in the blood. However, sports athletes, especially top athletes who play in international competition, have very hard training and tend to have anemia even if Hb and Ht values show high values and vice versa. Even if hemoglobin is decreased in the blood, athletes do not have subjective symptom of anemia. This is due to ferritin. Therefore, it is known that ferritin becomes substitute element that provides amount of iron in the blood.

For athletes, we have known that we can monitor ferritin to know their anemia situation. However, during hard training period such as final conditioning before a game they do want to avoid invasive sting methods to take their blood. This means that we should apply another method that is not invasive and simple investigation for finding anemia status gut microbiota has been considered as another aspect that correlates to anemia status [3], and we can take the samples from their excrement. This method is not invasive and is acceptable for athletes. Therefore, it is applicable for the case when athletes are concentrating to their training. However, major species of gut microbiota that relates to anemia have not been found by now. In this paper, we try to find the major species by applying machine learning approach from a dataset of blood and gut microbiota. The following sections show a mining method to find major species that cause anemia focusing on the athletes.

3 Related Works

As machine learning approaches has become popular in mining approaches, researchers have become eager to find disease from human activity based on behavioral or medical information. Typical example of the mining from human activity is gait analysis. The literature [6] is an example that found multiple sclerosis from 92 gait datasets measured by wearable motion sensors. The literature concluded that a support vector machine showed significance of the symptom to become multiple sclerosis. On the other hand, knowledge mining from medical or nutritional dataset has been investigated widely based on machine learning approach. One of well-known research area is to find implicit symptoms or disease prediction from medical records. For example, the literature [8] reports a knowledge mining method for medical records to find cardiovascular diseases (CVD).

The method used an unsupervised machine learning based on k-means method applying 156K electrical medical records with generating 2, 4 and 8 clusters. It also used a principal component analysis to eliminate CVD and non-CVD patient cases.

We can find another knowledge mining from biological elements. The literature [2] was focusing on blood information of 590 asthma patients to find acute exacerbation (AE). It reports a method based on k-means that generated clusters of AE risk. The mining experiment showed a labeling possibility for urgency of AE risks. This analysis indicated an unsupervised knowledge mining, and the major causes of AE risks were unknown from the blood information itself. This kind of mining research is concentrating to predictions of diseases that happen suddenly such as cerebrovascular and heart attack. For anemia, there are a few research trials based on machine learning approach. Almost trials were performed based on statistical approaches. We guess the reason is why the strict international guidelines are defined such as from WHO [7]. However, those guidelines show elemental values of blood for the people who live in calm and have normal daily activity. According to the advanced research [4], athletes need different guidelines for anemia. The research resulted that athletes are more susceptible to iron deficiency than the general people because the risks of iron deficiency are 15–35% and 3–11% of women and men athletes respectively comparing to 5% of general people. It suggests nutritional techniques to eliminate iron absorption inhibitors such as coffee and tea from athletes and to monitor their blood to find anemia symptom. The literature [1] also pointed out the risk of anemia from another aspect of blood test. It reported that when iron loss exceeds absorption due to strenuous sports, stored iron becomes insufficient. The situation results in a critical condition called non-anemic iron deficiency (NAID), in which only ferritin levels decrease, even though hemoglobin, mean corpuscular volume (MCV) and mean corpuscular hemoglobin (MCH) levels remain normal. This means that ferritin is the key factor of anemia especially for sports athletes. However, athletes do not want to accept invasive testing method. Therefore, another method is expected rather than the blood test.

For athlete-specific testing method for anemia, gut microbiota is focused in these days. However, more than 1.5K species of gut microbiota has been already found and it is still increasing. The literature [3] describes a mining trial for anemia in case of athletes. The research performed a Mendelian randomization targeted to gut microbiota measured from any kinds of 18K people. It found six protective factors of the microbiota (Clostridia, Actinomycetaceae, Pasteurellaceae, Oscillospira, Prevotella and Roseburia), which increase risk of anemia when those decrease. However, those factors are high level category in the taxonomy of microbiota. In this paper, we try to find the relative species of the microbiota. Additionally, the advanced research applied dataset of the microbiota only. In our approach, we use dataset of both blood information and gut microbiota measured from athletes and combine a clustering and a regression to find factor species of the microbiota.

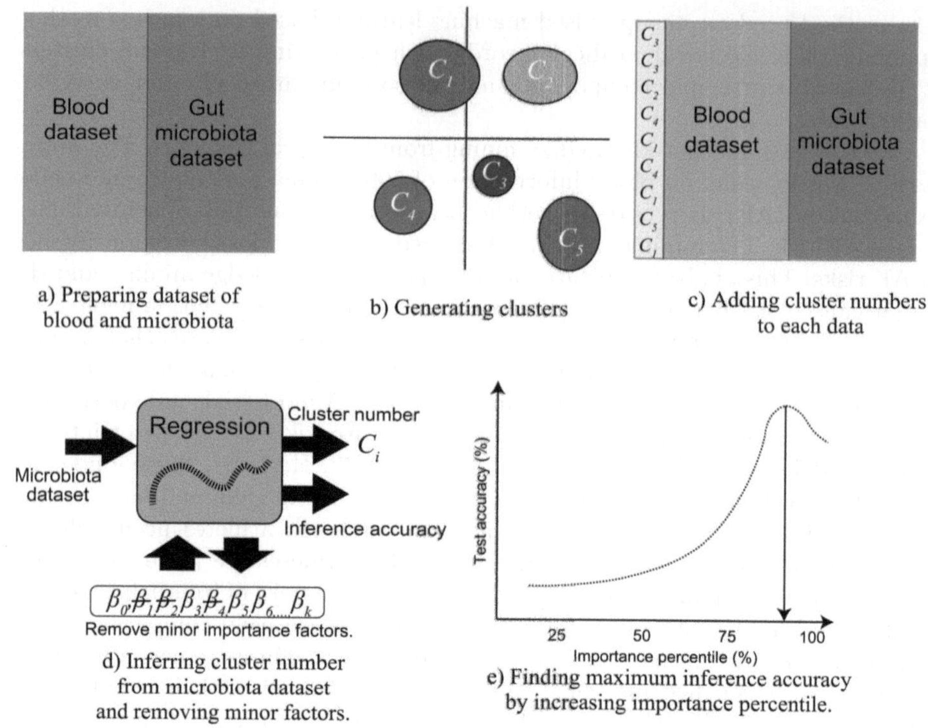

Fig. 1. Mining method overview.

4 Methods

4.1 Overview of Mining Strategy for Gut Microbiota

Figure 1 shows our strategy to find major factors that cause anemia focusing on gut microbiota. We first prepare a combined dataset of blood test results and microbiota test information as shown in Fig. 1a). The dataset of blood includes columns of test items such as MCV and MCH. The one of microbiota includes the columns of contents regarding each microbiota categorized by known species. Each row of both datasets corresponds to a test case of an athlete. Here, we need to note that the dataset of blood does not include any information of anemia regarding each case. Therefore, our strategy uses a supervised approach without target label. Thus, we handle dataset D that includes the blood data D_b and the microbiota one D_f. The indices of test cases in D correspond to both the cases in D_b and D_f. Therefore, each case d_i in D includes the values of blood elements b_i and the contents of microbiota f_i included in D_b and D_f respectively, where the total number of the cases is N.

The first step of the knowledge mining is the clustering with the dataset of blood test D_b as shown in Fig. 1b). The clusters C_j will define individual groups of implicit characteristics of test cases b_i. The indices of clusters are added to d_i

Algorithm 1. K-means clustering applied to focusing blood dataset.

Require: dataset $X = \{x_1, \ldots, x_N\}$, number of clusters K, tolerance ε
Ensure: assignment $assign[i]$, centroids $centroid[k]$
initialize $centroid[1], \ldots, centroid[K]$ randomly
repeat
  $assign \leftarrow \text{assignPoints}(X, centroid)$
  $newCentroid \leftarrow \text{updateCentroids}(X, assign)$
  $\delta \leftarrow \max_k \|newCentroid[k] - centroid[k]\|$
  $centroid \leftarrow newCentroid$
until $\delta \le \varepsilon$
return $assign$, $centroid$

where the test case is included as shown in Fig. 1c). We denote the dataset as $D' = \{C, D_b, D_f\}$.

The 2nd step is a regression of the cluster C_j from d_j. As d_j is divided to training cases d_t and validation ones d_v. As shown in Fig. 1d), after training phase of the regression applying d_t, accuracies are derived by using d_v from the trained model. The model should consist of feature importance β_k where $0 \le k < K$. Here, K corresponds to the number of columns in D_f. It is equivalent to the number of microbiota in the dataset and each β_k corresponds to f_k. Now, we reduce the number of β_k based on the accuracy and find a minimal set of β_k.

To reduce the feature importances from the model, we introduce t as a percentage of the percentile as shown in Fig. 1e). For example, when $t = 90$, we first derive another $\hat{\beta}_l$ after sorting β_k with preserving the original indices. The percentile calculation performs a summation of $\hat{\beta}_0 + \hat{\beta}_1 + \cdots + \hat{\beta}_{p-1}$ where the rank of $\hat{\beta}_p$ is placed in 90% of the feature importances. As it compares β_p with β_k, an array β'_m is derived. The feature importances in the array means that where the summation of β'_m becomes 90% of all β_k. Here, the feature importances more than t are removed from β_k. The accuracy of the model and the indices of $bcta'_m$ are saved as the result in case of t. Again, after increasing t and removing the columns of d_i that correspond to the indices of the removed feature importances, the reduced d_i are separated to d_t and d_v. The training phase is performed by the d_t and then, β_p is derived again. Thus, the percentile calculation is recursively iterated. Here, t is initially set to zero. At every iteration performed above, the accuracy of the model and the indices of β'_m is saved.

Finally, the maximum accuracy is derived from the stored accuracies resulted from the repeated percentile calculation above. In the case of the maximum accuracy, the inference accuracy from the regression should become the best by the model with the reduced feature importances. The indices of the feature importances correspond to the ones of the microbiota dataset. Therefore, we can conclude the microbiota dataset reduced by the indices of the feature importances correspond to the major factors that correlated to the blood dataset. Thus, when we just give the values in selected columns related to anemia of the blood dataset D_b are given to the clustering, the columns resulted from the reduced microbiota dataset are derived as the major species that induce anemia.

In the following sections, let us explain our implementations for the clustering and the regression methods.

4.2 Implementation of Clustering Method Focused on Blood Data

For the clustering method described in the overview, we used the k-means clustering method as shown in Algorithm 1 for the selected blood data. The algorithm requires input dataset X that is the selected blood data related to anemia. We focus on Hb, Ht and content of ferritin. Those correspond to x_i in the algorithm. For example, when we focus on Hb and Ht. x_i includes those values of a test case like $x_i = \{\mathrm{Ht}_i, \mathrm{Hb}_i\}$, $x_i = \{\mathrm{ferritin}_i\}$ that are a part of b_i. The number of clusters K is given as the input, which is a value large enough. The tolerance ϵ is a limit value of minimum number of vectors in a centroid. The centroid with one or more x_i is valid cluster found by the algorithm.

First, the line 1 in Algorithm 1 assigns the given x_i in the input dataset randomly to the centroid arrays. Then, all center points of the centroids are derived by the function assignPoints in the line 3. The assignPoints calculates the following equation.

$$assign[i] = \arg \min_{k \in \{1,\ldots,K\}} \| x_i - centroid[k] \|^2. \tag{1}$$

This finds the minimum Euclid distances of all centroids between a centroid and the vectors in the centroid. In the line 4, new centroids are derived from the minimum distances from the following equation.

$$newCentroid[k] = \frac{1}{|\{ i \mid assign[i] = k \}|} \sum_{i:\, assign[i]=k} x_i. \tag{2}$$

The line 5 finds the maximum distance between the previous centroids and the new one. It is used to evaluate if the centroids are moving largely or not. Here, the lines 3–6 are repeated until the maximum distance becomes smaller than the given distance ϵ.

After the iterations, the final centroids correspond to the cluster C. However, the centroids with no vector are removed from the clusters. When the number of clusters becomes zero, the combination of the element in the input x_i does not result any feature characteristics regarding anemia. In this case, we should select another combination of the elements of blood.

Based on the result of the clustering, the cluster numbers are added to the dataset D and D' is made. In the next step, the dataset of $\{C_i, D_f\}$ is applied to the regression.

4.3 Regression and Major Factor Reduction Regarding Microbiota Data

The regression step derives inference accuracy from the microbiota dataset D_f to C_i. Additionally, with reducing the factors to derive the accuracies according

Algorithm 2. Logistic regression to find minimum set of microbiota.

```
function FindMinimumFrolas(X, L, num_iter)
    max_accuracy ← −∞
    best_features ← [ ]
    best_delete_percentage ← 0
    for t = 0 to 100 step 0.1 do
        scores ← [ ]
        for i = 1 to num_iter do
            Split X, L into {X_train, X_test}, {L_train, L_test}
            by random selection of both combinations.
            fit_model ← LogisticRegression(X_train, L_train)
            feature_importances ← importance(fit_model)
            selected_features ← [ ]
            for j = 1 to len(feature_importances) do
                if feature_importances[j]
                    ¿ percentile(feature_importances, t) then
                    selected_features.append(j)
                end if
            end for
            X_train_sel ← X_train[selected_features]
            X_test_sel ← X_test[selected_features]
            fit_model ← LogisticRegression(X_train_sel, L_train)
            L_pred ← fit_model.Predict(X_test_sel)
            scores.append(accuracy(L_test, L_pred))
        end for
        avg_acc ← average(scores)
        if avg_acc > max_accuracy then
            max_accuracy ← avg_acc
            best_features ← selected_features
            best_delete_percentage ← t
        end if
    end for
    exp.acc ← max_accuracy
    exp.features ← best_features
    exp.delete_percentage ← best_delete_percentage
    return exp
end function
```

to the feature importances, the step finds the minimum factor combination that achieves maximum accuracy. To implement this mechanism, we apply the logistic regression.

The logistic regression is originally used as a binary clustering method. The output is derived as the probability of an expected case. Assume the probability is defined as $P = p(Y = 1)$ and $P = p(Y = 0)$ when a binary data Y becomes 1 and 0 respectively. When Y is consisted by a dataset of $Y_1, Y_2, \cdots, Y_n$ and assume $p(Y_i = 1) = P_i$, the likelihood L is derived by the following equation.

$$L = \prod_{i=1}^{n} P_i^{Y_i}(1 - P_i)^{1-Y_i} \tag{3}$$

When we take a logarithmic transformation of the likelihood L, we get the following Log-likelihood function.

$$\log(L) = \log\left(\prod_{i=1}^{n} P_i^{Y_i}(1 - P_i)^{1-Y_i}\right) \tag{4}$$

$$= \sum_{i=1}^{n} [Y_i \log P_i + (1 - Y_i)\log(1 - P_i)] \tag{5}$$

We can find the best likelihood by deriving the suitable P when the function above is maximized. Here, we can derive the probability P by using a sigmoid function as follows.

$$P = \frac{1}{1 + \exp\left\{-(\beta_0 + \beta_1 x_1 + \beta_2 x_2 + \cdots + \beta_n x_n)\right\}} \tag{6}$$

where $x_1, x_2, \cdots, x_n$ are the input feature (i.e. the input dataset) and $beta_0, beta_2, \cdots, beta_n$ are the partial regression coefficient.

Here, assume $\beta_i = \hat{\beta}_i$ when the log-likelihood function shows the maximum. The predicted probability $\hat{P}$ becomes as follows.

$$\hat{P} = \frac{1}{1 + \exp\left\{-(\hat{\beta}_0 + \hat{\beta}_1 x_1 + \hat{\beta}_2 x_2 + \cdots + \hat{\beta}_n x_n)\right\}} \tag{7}$$

$\hat{\beta}_i$ in the equation above is also an output of the regression as an importance of each input feature x_i. The larger $\hat{\beta}_i$ is more important. In the other word, the less important feature can be reduced as well as we can reduce the corresponding input feature from the input dataset. By using this mechanism, we will find the best possibility by reducing the input dataset with considering the ranking of the feature importance.

Algorithm 2 shows the mechanism that derives the minimum combination of microbiota in the dataset D_f. The dataset achieves highest accuracy to infer the corresponding cluster C_i. The function receives the input dataset of all microbiota as X. The cluster numbers corresponding to each vector in X is passed to the function as L. num_iter is the number of iterations to derive average accuracy of regression due to the random generation of the split X and L used in training and validation performed in the line 8. The algorithm has three loops in the lines 5, 7 and 12. The first loop is related to the reduction ratio for elements in the input data X. t is a constant parameter for the percentage of the percentile regarding the feature characteristics in the line 13. This percentage means that the elements in the input data X less than the rank of the feature characteristics derived by the t percentile. In the beginning of the first loop, the function derives a trained model (fit_model) by LogisticRegression function according to the input dataset for the training X_{train} and L_{train} in the line 9. The importance function returns an array of the feature importances $\hat{\beta}_i$. In the second loop, the feature importances placed more than t percentile are stored to $selected\_features$ in the line 12–16 of the third loop. Using the selected feature information, the elements of the corresponding indices in X and L are removed in the line 17–18. Using the reduced X, the regression is performed in the line 19 and derives predicted cluster numbers from the model in the line 20. The accuracy is calculated by comparing L_{test} for validation and the inferred L_{pred} in the line 21. The calculation is iterated for num_iter by repeating the random splitting X and L.

After the iterations for num_iter, an average accuracy is derived. The accuracy corresponds to the selected feature importances regarding t used for the percentile. This loop is iterated by the value of t. In our implementation, we applied the domain $0 \leq t \leq 100$ with the step of 0.1. It iterates the loop totally for 1000 times. After the loop of t, finally the best accuracy, the feature importances and the percentage in the percentile are returned by a structure exp.

Using the accuracy and the percentage during the iterations regarding t, we can observe a graph as shown in Fig. 1e). The algorithm finds the maximal case of the accuracy and a combination of its selected feature importances. Using the indices of the selected feature importances, we can derive the major factors of the input X, which is the key microbiota in D_f correlated to the clustering result C for the blood dataset D_b. Thus, we can find major microbiota correlated to the blood test elements by the calculation steps explained in this section. This means that the major factors of microbiota that induce anemia and then, we can find key species correlated to anemia. Thus, our approach provides more accurate analysis than the advanced research.

5 Experimental Evaluation

5.1 Experimental Setup

Now, let us evaluate our mining method and find combination of species in gut microbiota that cause anemia. For the evaluations, we used actual dataset for blood and gut microbiota.

To prepare the dataset, we have performed experimental measurements on the years 2023 and 2024. Long-distance runners in University of Tsukuba who belong to the track and field team has participated in the measurement. Blood and microbiota were measured in the same day. Additionally, height, weight, bone density, body composition data, monthly mileage, meal history were also measured. For the year 2023, 31 participants of 19–22 years old participated and only a measurement per participant was performed. Therefore, 31 sets in a dataset are available. For the year 2024, three measurements were performed by 23 participants of 18–22 years old in September, November and December, which 69 sets in the dataset are available. For two years, note that the numbers

Table 1. Accuracies and the number of major speices resulted by our minig method focusing on Ht and Hb.

Accuracy	2023	2024/Sep	2024/Nov	2024/Dec
Accuracy	65%	62%	62%	65%
# of spcieces	14	30	12	10

of microbiota are different. Those were 1463 species for 2023 and 1565 species for 2024. It is still increasing. However, we used the microbiota in the dataset and tried to find the major factors of microbiota related to anemia.

Note that we only focused on the contents of Hb, Ht and ferritin regarding blood dataset. For microbiota, all species in the datasets were used. We applied our mining method to the dataset for 2023 and the ones for the individual months in 2024 separately and derived common major factors of microbiota among the four datasets. According to this approach, the common major factors were more reliable because the individual experiment used independent datasets measured at different timings.

We performed two kinds of experiments with focusing on different element(s) in blood related to anemia. As we discussed in Sect. 2, by focusing on Hb and Ht, the first experiment regarded that the participants were normal people who were living without hard activity. In the second experiment, we focused on ferritin to dedicate the experiment to sports athletes whose daily activity is very hard. According to these experiments, we expected two findings. The first one was that Hb and Ht were not suitable for mining major factors of microbiota related to anemia in case of athletes. The second one was that the major factors were reasonably selected by our method.

The experiments were performed in the environment where MacBook Pro M4 with 24GB DDR4 DRAM and 1TB storage of iOS 15.2. For the clustering and the algorithm used in the analysis, we made the code by python 3.9.6 and used the libraries of NumPy 2.0.2, pandas 2.2.3, rich 13.9.4, matplotlib 3.9.4, SciPy 1.13.1 and scikit-learn 1.6.1.

In the experiments, we used 3 for K in Algorithm 1 and 1000 for the num_iter in Algorithm 2. The ϵ was automatically selected by the function KMeans from the scikit-learn library.

5.2 Mining Major Species of Gut Microbiota Focusing on Hb and Ht

For the first experiment, we used Ht and Hb in D_b and applied our mining method to the four datasets. Figure 2 shows the graphs of accuracies with varying the percentage t of the percentile regarding the feature importance. Again, the meaning of the percentage is that t% of the microbiota in dataset can be removed due to less feature importance. Therefore, the remaining species of microbiota are the candidates of the major factors related to anemia.

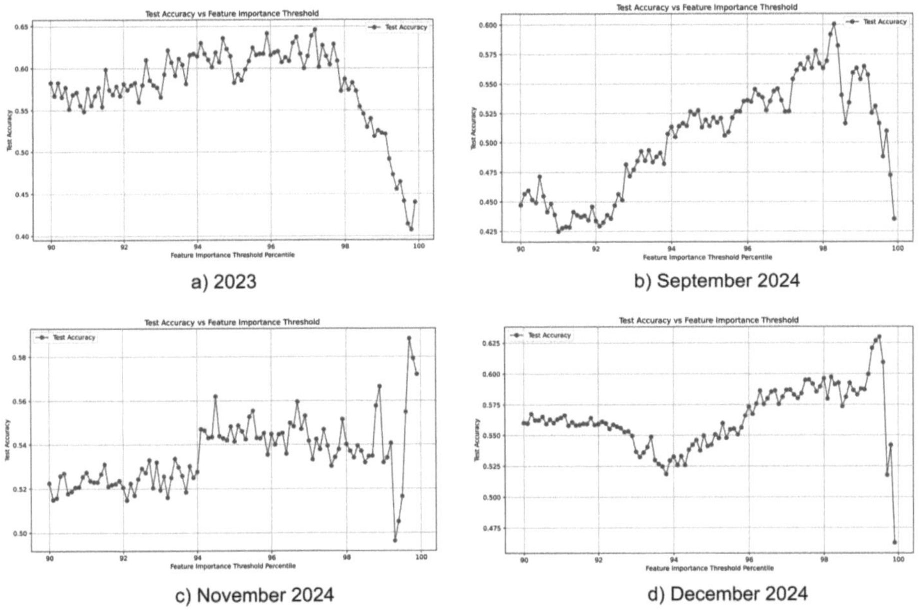

Fig. 2. Inference accuracies of the logistic regression focusing on Ht and Hb with reducing major species.

The accuracies and the numbers of major factors regarding the four datasets are shown in Table 1. The largest number of major factors were found from the dataset of 2023. Normalizing the numbers of the major factors among the datasets by 30 species, we found just a specie. Because the specie would be selected eventually, the result was not reliable. Therefore, we concluded that the mining based on Hb and Ht was not suitable when the target participants were sports athletes.

5.3 Mining Major Species of Microbiota Focusing on Ferritin

Next, we used ferritin in D_b and applied our mining method to the four datasets. Figure 3 shows the graphs of accuracies with varying the percentage t of the percentile regarding the feature importance. The accuracies and the numbers of major factors regarding the four datasets are shown in Table 2. The largest number of major factors were found from the dataset of September 2024. Normalizing the numbers of major factors among the datasets by 100 species, we found eight species as shown in Table 3.

To validate the results from the mining, we compared the species found by our method with the results from the advanced research [3]. Although our results showed specie level, when we compare those in the class level, Clostridia was included also in our result. Therefore, we confirmed that our mining method selected reasonable major factors from the dataset targeted to sports athletes.

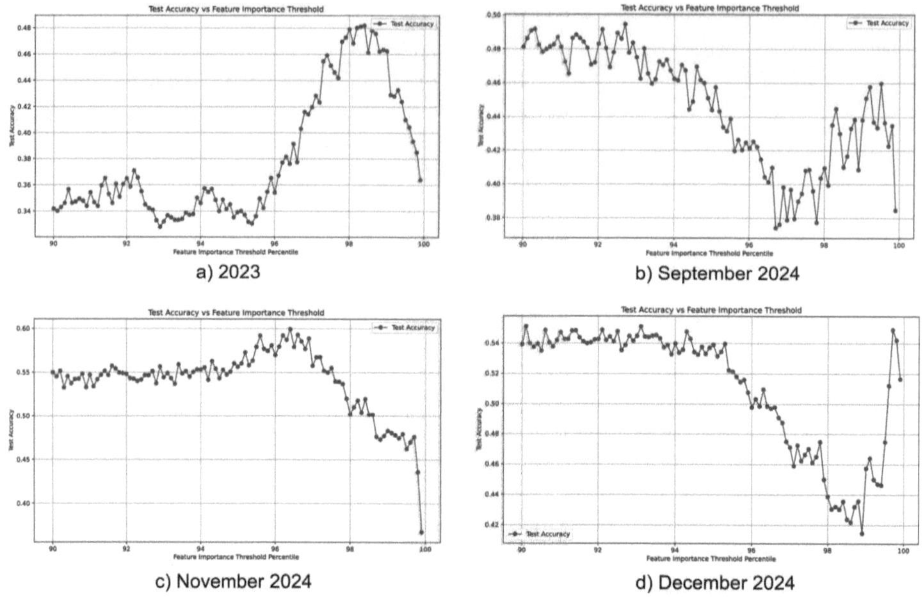

Fig. 3. Inference accuracy of the logistic regression focusing on ferritin with reducing major species.

Table 2. Accuracies and the number of major speices resulted by our minig method focusing on ferritin.

Accuracy	2023	2024/Sep	2024/Nov	2024/Dec
Accuracy	45	49%	60%	56%
# of spcieces	30	100	50	70

5.4 Discussion for Evaluations

In the experimental evaluations mentioned above, we tried to find major factors of gut microbiota correlated to anemia. Our mining method was applied to 1.5K species. The case with the dataset focusing on the Hb and Ht of blood dataset did not show good result. The clustering step showed clearly three clusters. However, the regression step did not output reliable numbers of common species among datasets. On the other hand, when we focused on ferritin, the regression step resulted reasonable combinations of major microbiota factors. As we have discussed in Sect. 2, elements in blood related to hemoglobin change dynamically in the case of athletes. This proved the first expected result in our evaluation. We can conclude that we should separate analysis for normal people who do not have hard activity in daily life and the one for athletes.

Additionally, for the second expected result of our evaluation, we found eight microbiota that related to anemia. A part of the species found by our experiment was also included in the advanced research result from the literature [3].

Table 3. Species found from our method focusing on ferritin.

taxonomic rank						
domain	phylum	class	order	family	genus	species
Bacteria	Bacteroidetes	Bacteroidia	Bacteroidales	[Odoribacteraceae]	Odoribacter	Odoribacter_
Bacteria	Bacteroidetes	Bacteroidia	Bacteroidales	Bacteroidaceae	Bacteroides	Bacteroides_caccae
Bacteria	Bacteroidetes	Bacteroidia	Bacteroidales	Bacteroidaceae	Bacteroides	Bacteroides_sartorii
Bacteria	Bacteroidetes	Bacteroidia	Bacteroidales	Porphyromonadaceae	Parabacteroides	Parabacteroides_distasonis
Bacteria	Firmicutes	Clostridia	Clostridiales	Lachnospiraceae	Clostridium	Clostridium_symbiosum
Bacteria	Firmicutes	Clostridia	Clostridiales	Lachnospiraceae	Dorea	Dorea_longicatena
Bacteria	Firmicutes	Clostridia	Clostridiales	Ruminococcaceae	Ruminococcus	Ruminococcus_callidus
Bacteria	Synergistetes	Synergistia	Synergistales	Synergistaceae	Cloacibacillus	Cloacibacillus_

Therefore, it seems that our mining method found correctly the key microbiota factors related to blood status. Currently, it is hard to verify the reliability of the results by our method because the dataset we have used did not include any information of anemia symptom. Therefore, it is important to include any dataset that include blood and microbiota information of anemia patient.

In summary, we have developed a machine learning approach to find implicit factors of microbiota that cause anemia. Finally, our result derived the key microbiota factors in the species level, but it was in genus level in the related work. Thus, we confirmed to address our objectives in this research.

6 Conclusions

The experimental evaluations showed reasonable major factors of gut microbiota that cause anemia. We used datasets measured in four timings in an year with different athletes. This makes available to compare the results among different datasets. However, the number of cases in a dataset was small. In a dataset of our measurements, the number of samples were less than 100. Therefore, we should continuously evaluate our mining method with more datasets. Additionally, it can be resolved by oversampling techniques. The number of gut microbiota is still increasing. Therefore, it would be better to find another method to standardize the results. In the point of nutritional research, it should be important to discuss relationship between contents of daily meals and the gut microbiota with comparing the results from our mining method. The discussion can bring some meanings how the key microbiota work.

Acknowledgements. This work is partially supported by JSPS KAKENHI Grant Number 24K22330 and Research Grant of Advanced Research Initiative for Human High Performance, the University of Tsukuba.

References

1. German, C., et al.: Iron deficiency in sports – definition, influence on performance and therapy. Swiss Med. Wkly. **145**(4344), w14196 (2025). https://doi.org/10.4414/smw.2015.14196
2. Ji, H.O., Kyung-Min, A., Soo, J.C., et al.: Usefulness of routine blood test-driven clusters for predicting acute exacerbation in patients with asthma. Respir. Med. **170**, 106042 (2020). https://doi.org/10.1016/j.rmed.2020.106042
3. Lei, W., Liu, Z., Lai, H.P., Fu, R.: Gut microbiota and risk of iron deficiency anemia: a two-sample Mendelian randomization study. Medicine **104**(8), e41617 (2025). https://doi.org/10.1097/MD.0000000000041617
4. Nolte, S., Krüger, K., Hollander, K., Carlsohn, A.: Approaches to prevent iron deficiency in athletes. Dtsch. Z. Sportmed. **75**(5), 195–202 (2024). https://doi.org/10.5960/dzsm.2024.607
5. Solberg, A., Reikvam, H.: Iron status and physical performance in athletes. Life **13**(10) (2023). https://doi.org/10.3390/life13102007
6. Trentzsch, K., Schumann, P., Śliwiński, G.: Using machine learning algorithms for identifying gait parameters suitable to evaluate subtle changes in gait in people with multiple sclerosis. Brain Sci. **11**(8) (2021). https://doi.org/10.3390/brainsci11081049
7. World Health Organization: Guideline on haemoglobin cutoffs to define anaemia in individuals and populations (2024). https://www.who.int/publications/i/item/9789240088542
8. Ying, H., Hai, Y., Ming, L., et al.: Detecting cardiovascular diseases using unsupervised machine learning clustering based on electronic medical records. BMC Med. Res. Methodol. **24**(309) (2024).https://doi.org/10.1186/s12874-024-02422-z

Defending Against Knowledge Forgetting in Intelligent Tutoring System with the Continual Knowledge Reconstructing Approach

Yang Song[1(✉)], Guanghui Han[1], Wen Hu[1], Zhaofeng Niu[1], Qingchun Bai[2], and Jiayi Chen[3]

[1] Qufu Normal University, Shandong 276800, China
{yangs,zhaofengniu}@qfnu.edu.cn
[2] Shanghai Open University, Shanghai 200000, China
[3] Suzhou City University, Suzhou 215104, China
jychen@szcu.edu.cn

Abstract. Intelligent Tutoring Systems (ITS) have been widely adopted as the technique for personalized lifelong learning. The education knowledge database is frequently updating along with the increasing of learning materials, which leads the ITS forgetting historical knowledge and inducing a pedagogical discontinuity. To address this challenge, we propose a Continual Knowledge Reconstructing Approach, which prevents the ITS forgetting knowledge from new course content injection. Specifically, a historical learning path reconstructor automatically infers and reconstructs essential pedagogical relationships from previous user interactions. Then, a unified consolidated knowledge reasoner intelligently resolves knowledge conflicts and generates the relevant pedagogical content. Experiments on multiple educational datasets demonstrate that the proposed method significantly outperforms strong baseline models and effectively mitigates pedagogical discontinuity.

Keywords: Intelligent Tutoring Systems · Knowledge Reconstruction · Lifelong Learning

1 Introduction

Intelligent Tutoring System bridges artificial intelligence and educational science, transcending the limitations of traditional and standardized education. It enhances educational equity and improves learning efficiency, which serves as the cornerstone of technology-enabled lifelong learning [3].

A critical and pervasive challenge emerges when these systems are deployed in real-world. To keep pace with rapid advancements in disciplinary frontiers and evolving social demands, curriculum content must undergo periodic reconstruction and optimization [7]. This process involves introducing new theories, cases,

C. Xu (Ed.): ICMLSC 2026, CCIS 2948, pp. 173–185, 2027.
https://doi.org/10.1007/978-981-92-1546-1_14

and technologies, while revising or removing outdated or redundant content. However, ITS lack the ability to defend against knowledge forgetting. While the system actively absorbs new course content, it systematically forgets or weakens its ability to remember and access core knowledge in history courses. This phenomenon may lead to "interruption of teaching continuity", and directly undermines the coherence and depth of learning during review and knowledge integration.

The straightforward solution to this problem is retaining all historical curriculum data, and periodically retraining the ITS on the ever-growing dataset [10]. While this approach theoretically preserves the entire knowledge system, it is computationally prohibitive and environmentally unsustainable as the curriculum expands over time. More critically, without explicit mechanisms for knowledge consolidation, the model's performance on older topics can still degrade significantly during the retraining on new data, making the entire process inefficient and unreliable. A more resource-conscious strategy employs incremental learning, in which the model is fine-tuned only with new data [28,29]. However, it yields only sparse and fragmented preservation that fails to protect the prerequisite knowledge graph. Moreover, the isolated exemplars lack pedagogical coherence, missing the semantic relationships necessary for coherent explanations. This method may lead to a knowledge coverage gap, and finally induce a user question mis-understanding problem.

To address this bottleneck, this paper proposes a Continual Knowledge Reconstructing Approach (CKRA) to endow ITS with the ability to defend against knowledge forgetting within dynamically evolving knowledge. CKRA adopts two synergistic components to maintain pedagogical continuity, including the historical learning path reconstructor and the curriculum aware expert selector. Specifically, the historical learning path reconstructor autonomously infers missing pedagogical relations for historical questions by analyzing their semantic patterns and related answers, thus reconstructing complete knowledge units. The curriculum aware expert selector resolves potential knowledge conflicts by evaluating and selecting the most appropriate pedagogical relations from an ensemble of historical models, balancing historical consensus with alignment to current curriculum standards. Experiments on multiple datasets demonstrate that our framework effectively defends against knowledge forgetting across sequential curriculum updates.

2 Related Work

2.1 Intelligent Tutoring Systems in Lifelong Learning

Intelligent Tutoring Systems (ITS) have emerged as crucial tools for enabling personalized lifelong learning [15]. Rooted in constructivist learning theories and cognitive apprenticeship models, ITS aim to simulate the tutoring process of expert educators through artificial intelligence techniques.

The evolution of ITS has paralleled the shift from traditional education models towards continuous learning paradigms. Early ITS implementations focused primarily on well-defined domains with static knowledge structures, such as mathematics and programming [13]. Subsequently, their applications expanded to more specialized domains, including surgical training in dentistry [21] and reading comprehension [24]. These systems demonstrate the adaptability of ITS approach across diverse educational contexts while highlighting their shared reliance on stable knowledge representations.

Since educational paradigms embrace lifelong learning principles, ITS must evolve to support knowledge acquisition across extended time frames and dynamically changing content [19]. The systems are designed with the assumption of relatively static domain knowledge. However, this assumption fails in real-world educational scenarios, where curriculum content undergoes continuous revision to reflect new knowledge and societal needs. The phenomenon of pedagogical discontinuity emerges precisely when systems optimized for stable knowledge encounter dynamic curriculum environments [2].

While existing ITS have demonstrated effectiveness in stable knowledge environments, they fail to maintain this effectiveness in dynamic real-world scenarios. The systematic removal or modification of curriculum components disrupts the foundational knowledge structures that these systems rely on [12]. This challenge is particularly acute in lifelong learning contexts. Learners often reference historical content across multiple curriculum iterations. It creates the core problem of pedagogical discontinuity, which our work aims to solve.

2.2 Adaptive Learning Technologies for Dynamic Curriculum Environments

Adaptive learning technologies personalize educational experiences by adjusting content presentation and sequencing based on individual learner characteristics and performance [17]. Early adaptive systems primarily focused on sequencing predefined learning objects along predetermined pedagogical paths.

More recent approaches have incorporated knowledge representation frameworks that capture the structure of domain knowledge. Educational knowledge graphs, which represent curriculum content as interconnected pedagogical triples, have shown particular promise for supporting adaptive learning experiences [14]. These structured representations enable systems to reason about prerequisite relationships and knowledge dependencies, facilitating more sophisticated instructional adaptations.

However, existing adaptive systems face significant challenges when deployed in dynamic curriculum environments. Educational content continuously evolves through the introduction of new concepts and the retirement of outdated material. In this process, systems often experience pedagogical discontinuity. They lose the ability to effectively support learning activities that reference historical course content [1]. This problem is technically analogous to the catastrophic forgetting phenomenon in machine learning, where models trained on new data lose proficiency on previously mastered tasks.

Several strategies have been proposed to address this challenge. Some approaches employ complete retraining on historical data, but this proves computationally prohibitive for large-scale educational systems [26]. Others utilize incremental learning methods that selectively preserve subsets of historical knowledge [20], but these often suffer from incomplete knowledge coverage and limited support for coherent understanding across curriculum iterations. Our work builds upon these foundations while addressing their limitations.

3 Methodology

3.1 Problem Statement

We formalize the task within an Educational Knowledge Graph (EKG), where knowledge is structured as pedagogical triples (S, R, O). Here, S denotes a knowledge component (e.g., Photosynthesis), R is a didactic relation (e.g., illustrates Concept), and O is a supporting component or canonical answer (e.g., Chloroplast). The EKG is constructed based on curriculum standards and cognitive task analysis, ensuring that relations reflect authentic learning dependencies.

Given a student question Q at curriculum stage i, the ITS should identify the core knowledge component $S = \{s_1, \ldots, s_n\}$ and the relevant didactic relations $R = \{r_1, \ldots, r_n\}$ to retrieve or infer the correct answer O. Noting that knowledge components are dynamically revised or removed from the current EKG with curricula updating. Therefore, the system loses access to the triples needed to answer historical questions Q_H, which is known as *pedagogical discontinuity.*

Our task is to enable the ITS to maintain robust performance on both current and historical queries despite these ongoing changes. This capability directly supports lifelong learning by preventing knowledge gaps.

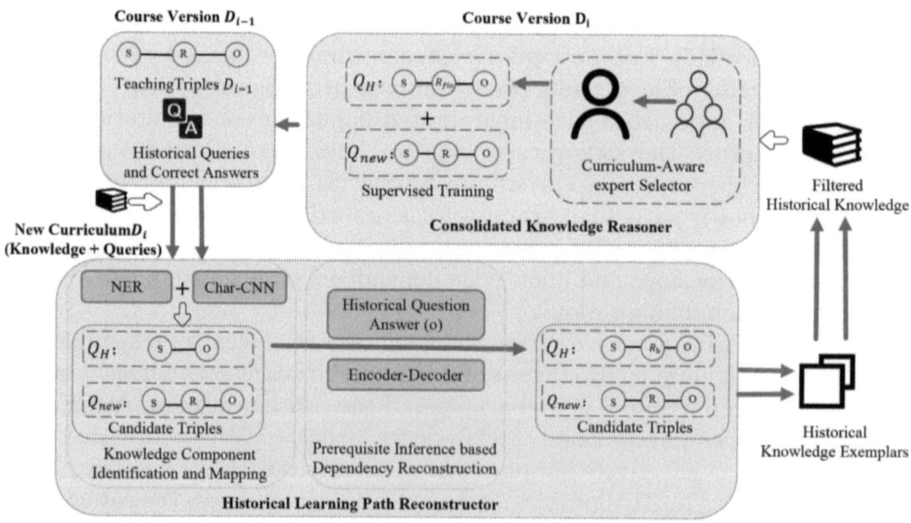

Fig. 1. Overall Architecture

3.2 Overall Architecture

Figure 1 illustrates the overall architecture of the proposed Continual Knowledge Reconstructing Approach (CKRA), which includes a historical learning path reconstructor and a consolidated knowledge reasoner. The historical learning path reconstructor processes historical queries along with their correct answers. This module outputs a collection of historical knowledge exemplars, which preserve key pedagogical relationships from earlier curriculum versions. The consolidated knowledge reasoner then integrates these reconstructed exemplars with new curriculum content. Serving as the online reasoning component, it synthesizes both current and historical knowledge to produce accurate answers, thereby preserving pedagogical consistency across curriculum updates.

3.3 Historical Learning Path Reconstruction Module

The historical learning path reconstruction module is designed to address the issue of historical knowledge forgetting caused by dynamic curriculum updates. It autonomously infers and completes missing pedagogical relations by analyzing historical question-answer pairs, and thereby reconstructs complete knowledge units. The workflow consists of knowledge component filtering and prerequisite inference based dependency reconstruction.

Knowledge Component Filtering. For better understanding in student questions, we first identify and map knowledge components of the question into EKG based on two stages, namely the knowledge component identification and the educational concept mapping.

In knowledge component identification stage, we perform semantic analysis on natural language questions Q to identify key educational concepts and terminologies. This step lays the foundation for subsequent relation completion. For each student question Q, the system searches historical interaction logs. If no matching records are found, the question is classified as a new question Q_{new} from the current curriculum D_i. Otherwise, it is defined as a historical question Q_H.

For both Q_{new} and Q_H, a BiGRU-CRF model is employed to recognize and classify pedagogical entities. The BiGRU network captures the contextual semantics of words, and the CRF layer ensures the global consistency of labels. This model identifies all teaching entities in Q_{new} and Q_H, and locates the core knowledge component $\{q_1, \dots, q_k\}$ of the question. For example, it identifies "photosynthesis" as the core concept in a biology question.

In educational concept mapping stage, the surface form of an identified question knowledge component $\{q_1, \dots, q_k\}$ is corresponded to multiple related but distinct concepts in the comprehensive EKG. To deal with this ambiguity, we implement a sophisticated mapping mechanism with a Char-CNN based linker [27]. It retrieves the top 20 most relevant canonical entities and associated triples to generate the candidate pedagogical triples for subsequent reasoning.

For a new question Q_{new}, we link its knowledge components to the current curriculum EKG D_i to obtain the subject entities $S = \{s_1, \dots, s_n\}$. This yields the triple (S, R, O) for Q_{new}, which becomes part of the training set. For a historical question Q_H, we use the same Char-CNN-based linker to map its knowledge components to the structured curriculum memory bank E. This mapping generates the concept nodes $S = \{s_1, \ldots, s_n\}$.

Prerequisite Inference Based Dependency Reconstruction. After identifying the core knowledge component S from a historical question Q_H, the next step is to reconstruct the pedagogical relation R_{h}. However, due to the continuous updates of the EKG, the specific pedagogical relation R_{h} that connects S and O may be revised or lost.

To complete the missing relation R_{h}, we design a path backtracking module based on an Encoder-Decoder architecture. This module takes the incomplete triple from the previous linking step for Q_H as input. It infers the most probable teaching relation R_{h} based on the question semantics and the known answer O.

Specifically, we replace the identified knowledge component $\{q_1, \ldots, q_k\}$ in Q_H with a general placeholder ⟨concept⟩. This yields a de-materialized semantic pattern, forcing the model to focus on the question semantic information rather than specific entity names (e.g., converting "How does photosynthesis produce oxygen?" to "How does ⟨concept⟩ produce ⟨concept⟩?"). Subsequently, the GRU encoder represents this pattern into a context vector $\mathbf{u}$, and the GRU decoder generates the predicted relation $R_{\text{h}} = \{r_1, \ldots, r_n\}$ autoregressively based on $\mathbf{u}$ and the answer concept O. The module is trained to maximize the conditional probability $P(R_{\text{h}} \mid Q, O)$, which ensures the predicted relation R_{h} to semantically connect the question and the answer.

Noting that the output of the historical learning path reconstructor is the predicted relation R_{h}, the system reconstructs a complete knowledge triple (S, R_{h}, O) for subsequent consolidation training. Here, the output $(Q_H, S, R_{\text{h}}, O)$ is defined as historical training exemplars.

3.4 Curriculum Aware Expert Selector

As the curriculum in reality is constantly updated, a question may have different answers at different times. The historical learning path reconstruction module predicts relations R_{h} for historical questions. However, due to evolving knowledge standards, these reconstructed relations may no longer align with current pedagogical requirements. Therefore, the triple corresponding to Q_H is not necessarily unique. Directly using $\mathcal{D}^i_{\text{train}}$ for supervised training may cause knowledge conflicts in the current ITS for course D_i.

We design the curriculum aware expert selector to determine the correct relation R to historical questions Q_H, which ensures instructional continuity throughout curriculum evolution. Suppose $\mathcal{M} = \{M_1, M_2, \ldots, M_{i-1}\}$ is a temporally organized expert ensemble. The specialized model M_i embodies the pedagogical knowledge and relational understanding of its corresponding curriculum version D_i. It encapsulates the teaching knowledge and relations from the educational knowledge graph EKG_i of D_i.

In initial training round D_1, the Neural State Machine [11] is employed as an expert to bootstrap the system pedagogical accuracy. To precisely quantify the agreement from historical expert models by considering their prediction confidence, we define a weighted soft consensus function. This function replaces the binary indicator with a probabilistic measure, yielding a continuous and finer-grained consensus score. The historical consensus is formally defined as

$$A_j = (1/\sum_{j=1}^{i-1} m_j) \cdot \sum_{j=1}^{i-1} m_j \cdot P\left(R_{\mathrm{h}} \mid M_j, Q_H\right). \tag{1}$$

where, m_j is the importance of expert M_j, $P(R_{\mathrm{h}} \mid M_j, Q_H)$ is the softmax probability that model M_j assigns to the reconstructed relation R_{h} given question Q_H, and the relation R_{h} is reconstructed by the historical learning path reconstruction module.

Subsequently, we assess the alignment between reconstructed relations and current pedagogical standards through semantic similarity analysis

$$B_j = \cos(\mathbf{f}(R_{\mathrm{h}}), \mathbf{f}(R)). \tag{2}$$

where, R_{h} is the reconstructed pedagogical relation for Q_H, R represents the predominant relation patterns in the current EKG of D_i, $\mathbf{f}(\cdot)$ maps pedagogical relations to dense vector representations, $\cos(*)$ computes the semantic similarity between two relation embeddings. B_j evaluates expert M_j historical performance with applicability in the current course context.

For each expert M_j, a composite score is calculated. The optimal expert M^*_{expert} is selected based on the formula

$$M^*_{\mathrm{expert}} = \underset{M_j \in \mathcal{M}}{\arg\max}\left(A_j + (B_j + 1)/2\right). \tag{3}$$

Here, $(B_j + 1)/2$ is the normalized curriculum compliance. It scales the cosine similarity $B_j \in [-1, 1]$ to $[0, 1]$, aligning with the scale of A_j while preserving semantic meaning.

For the given question Q_H, the optimal expert M^*_{expert} outputs the target relation (Q_H, S, R_{fin}, O). All target triples are merged to generate the complete EKG.

Based on the proposed continual knowledge reconstructing approach, the ITS intelligently filters out conflicting historical knowledge, and identifies the expert guidance signals that best meet the current requirements for instructional continuity.

4 Experiments

4.1 Datasets

The experiment is conducted on four standard datasets. **SimpleQuestion** [6] contains a large number of simple questions, which are manually annotated in the knowledge base to generate matching questions based on facts. **WebQuestion** [4] is built from the Google Suggest API. Both simple and complex questions are involved in this collection. **WebQuestionSP** [25] is an improved version of previous datasets, which is a subset of WebQuestion. Compared to WebQuestion, WebQuestionSP is more suitable for complex questions. **ASSISTments2009** [16] is collected from the ASSISTments online tutoring platform, which provides interactive mathematics exercises for middle school students. Moreover, we use Freebase and a subset of FB2M [5] as our knowledge base for relation extraction.

Since the original educational datasets lack dynamic characteristics, we construct five dynamic subsets D_1 to D_5. Specifically, the original task instance set Q for each dataset is evenly divided into 5 subsets Q_1 to Q_5, which are allocated to D_1 to D_5 respectively. Only the triple corresponding to the current task instances is included in each dataset to ensure dynamic knowledge matching. For each D_i ($i \geq 2$), 10% of task instances are extracted from Q_{i-1} and added to Q_i as historical task instances. The triples associated with these historical instances are not added to D_i's EKG, ensuring the model lacks those historical knowledge during training and thus fits the dynamic setting. Each D_i is split into training, validation, and test sets using an 8:1:1 ratio. Table 1 shows statistical details.

Table 1. Dataset statistics per stage.

Stage	ASSISTments2009 (Train/Val/Test)	SimpleQuestion (Train/Val/Test)	WebQuestion (Train/Val/Test)	WebQuestionSP (Train/Val/Test)
D1	10072/1260/1259	18001/2250/2251	1856/232/232	1519/189/190
D2	11078/1386/1386	22055/2757/2757	1862/232/232	1518/189/190
D3	11081/1384/1385	10768/1346/1346	1859/232/232	1520/189/190
D4	11079/1385/1386	11672/1459/1460	1859/232/232	1521/189/190
D5	11082/1387/1385	15961/1995/1986	1860/232/232	1519/189/190

4.2 Baselines and Evaluation Metrics

In this paper, we employ six representative approaches as baselines to comprehensively evaluate the pedagogical effectiveness of our proposed CKRA. **LSTM** [22] represents a fundamental approach to modeling temporal learning processes. It captures sequential dependencies in student interactions, making it suitable for tracing knowledge state evolution over time. **APVA-TURBO** [23] is a verification-enhanced framework for knowledge structure reasoning. By incorporating relationship and path validation mechanisms, it ensures the pedagogical coherence of inferred knowledge connections. **PullNet** [18] employs an information retrieval paradigm for educational knowledge exploration. It effectively models the exploratory nature of knowledge acquisition in complex learning domains. **BERT** [9] leverages large-scale pre-training to develop deep contextual understanding of educational content. The model's transfer learning capability allows rapid adaptation to various educational tasks with minimal task-specific modifications. **Cheng et al.** [8] enhances predicate recognition through a sophisticated scoring module, enabling more robust understanding of educational relationships across different knowledge domains. **NSM** [11] is a neural state machine approach for multi-hop educational reasoning, which addresses spurious inference problems that commonly arise in complex educational question answering scenarios.

Moreover, we employ Accuracy (Acc) and F1-Score as metrics to evaluate the effectiveness of the proposed model.

4.3 Overall Performance

Tables 2, 3, 4 and 5 show the overall performance of our CKRA on four collections. The experimental results provide crucial insights into pedagogical sustainability. While traditional models demonstrate strong initial performance on the first curriculum version (D1), they exhibit significant performance degradation as the curriculum evolves. This substantial decline across subsequent stages stems from their inability to maintain historical knowledge components that have been deprecated from the current Educational Knowledge Graph but remain essential for comprehensive student support. The phenomenon directly manifests the "pedagogical discontinuity" that plagues conventional intelligent tutoring systems in dynamic academic environments.

Table 2. Overall performance on SimpleQuestion.

Model	D1 (Acc/F1)	D2 (Acc/F1)	D3 (Acc/F1)	D4 (Acc/F1)	D5 (Acc/F1)	AVG (Acc/F1)
LSTM	83.3/75.5	75.0/68.0	67.5/61.2	61.4/55.7	55.9/50.7	68.6/62.2
APVA-TURBO	81.5/76.1	73.5/68.6	66.2/61.8	60.4/56.2	55.0/51.2	67.3/62.8
PullNet	91.3/85.9	84.0/79.0	77.2/72.7	71.8/67.6	66.8/62.9	78.2/74.6
BERT	**92.4/87.1**	85.0/80.1	78.2/73.7	72.7/68.6	64.5/68.3	79.3/74.8
Cheng'20	90.3/83.6	83.1/76.9	76.4/70.8	71.1/65.8	66.8/61.9	68.1/74.2
NSM	**92.5/87.4**	85.1/80.4	78.3/74.0	72.8/69.8	68.5/64.7	79.5/75.1
Ours	91.5/86.2	**89.6/84.5**	**89.4/84.9**	**89.3/84.8**	**89.3/85.0**	**89.8/85.1**

Our CKRA framework achieves state-of-the-art performance in terms of both average accuracy and F1-score across all datasets, consistently attaining the highest average accuracy among all compared methods. Most notably, CKRA demonstrates exceptional pedagogical stability, maintaining consistently high performance with minimal variance throughout the curriculum iterations. This sustained effectiveness underscores the framework's capacity for unprecedented sustainability in dynamically evolving learning environments.

Table 3. Overall performance on WebQuestion.

Model	D1 (Acc/F1)	D2 (Acc/F1)	D3 (Acc/F1)	D4 (Acc/F1)	D5 (Acc/F1)	AVG (Acc/F1)
LSTM	53.6/46.5	48.2/41.9	43.4/37.7	39.5/34.3	35.9/31.2	44.1/38.3
APVA-TURBO	67.5/63.2	61.4/57.5	55.9/52.3	51.4/48.1	47.3/44.3	56.7/53.1
PullNet	69.7/65.9	64.1/60.6	59.0/55.8	54.8/51.9	54.8/48.3	60.5/56.5
BERT	**71.5/66.5**	65.8/61.4	60.5/56.4	55.5/51.7	52.7/48.5	61.2/56.9
Cheng'20	70.2/56.6	64.6/53.9	59.4/49.6	55.3/46.1	51.9/43.4	60.3/50.3
NSM	**71.5/66.4**	65.8/61.1	60.5/56.2	56.3/52.3	52.9/49.1	61.4/57.0
Ours	71.0/63.9	**69.6/64.9**	**69.4/64.4**	**69.0/62.6**	**69.3/61.4**	**69.7/63.4**

Table 4. Overall performance on WebQuestionSP.

Model	D1 (Acc/F1)	D2 (Acc/F1)	D3 (Acc/F1)	D4 (Acc/F1)	D5 (Acc/F1)	AVG (Acc/F1)
LSTM	51.4/42.5	46.2/38.3	41.6/34.4	37.9/31.3	34.5/28.5	42.3/35.0
APVA-TURBO	54.2/45.4	49.4/41.3	45.0/37.6	41.4/34.3	39.9/33.1	45.6/38.2
PullNet	68.2/56.9	62.7/52.4	57.7/48.2	53.6/44.8	49.9/41.7	58.4/48.8
BERT	**72.2/64.5**	63.7/56.6	58.6/52.1	54.5/48.4	51.3/45.5	59.5/52.8
Cheng'20	**72.6/57.6**	66.8/53.0	61.4/48.8	57.1/45.3	53.7/42.6	62.3/49.5
NSM	**74.3/67.4**	68.4/62.0	62.9/57.1	58.5/53.1	55.0/49.9	63.8/57.9
Ours	72.2/65.2	**69.8/63.8**	**69.6/62.5**	**69.1/62.1**	**69.8/61.3**	**69.8/62.8**

4.4 Ablation Study

We conduct ablation studies to investigate the effectiveness of Curriculum Aware Expert Selector. The Curriculum Aware Expert Selector in our model operationalizes a sophisticated knowledge selection strategy that emulates the consensus-building process among expert educators. Table 6 validate Curriculum Aware Expert Selector individual contributions to maintaining pedagogical continuity. While the model maintains strong performance in the initial round, subsequent iterations show performance degradation of approximately 2% across datasets. This decline manifests the essential function of the selection mechanism in identifying the most pedagogically appropriate knowledge from historical sources. Without this guidance, the model struggles to distinguish between relevant and obsolete educational content, leading to confusion in knowledge integration and reduced effectiveness in addressing historical student queries.

Table 5. Overall performance on ASSISTments2009.

Model	D1 (Auc/Acc)	D2 (Auc/Acc)	D3 (Auc/Acc)	D4 (Auc/Acc)	D5 (Auc/Acc)	AVG (Auc/Acc)
LSTM	52.1/43.2	47.5/39.6	43.1/35.8	39.2/32.5	35.2/29.1	43.4/36.0
APVA-TURBO	55.6/46.8	50.8/42.7	46.5/39.1	42.9/35.8	41.2/33.9	47.4/39.7
PullNet	69.5/58.2	64.2/57.9	59.3/53.7	55.1/49.9	51.3/43.1	60.0/50.6
BERT	**73.5/65.8**	65.3/58.2	60.2/53.9	56.1/50.2	52.8/47.2	61.6/54.7
Cheng'20	**73.8/59.1**	70.2/54.5	63.1/50.3	60.2/46.9	55.2/44.3	64.5/51.0
NSM	**74.3/67.4**	68.4/62.0	62.9/57.1	58.5/53.1	55.0/49.9	63.8/57.9
Ours	73.1/71.4	**72.8/70.7**	**72.5/70.5**	**72.1/70.1**	**72.8/70.3**	**72.3/69.8**

Table 6. Ablation Study. ("w/o" denotes the variant of CKRA where the Curriculum Aware Expert Selector is removed)

Dataset	Model	D1 (Acc)	D2 (Acc)	D3 (Acc)	D4 (Acc)	D5 (Acc)	AVG (Acc)
SimpleQuestion	w/o CAES	91.4	87.2	86.8	86.7	86.4	87.7
	Ours	91.4	89.6	89.4	89.2	89.3	89.8
WebQuestion	w/o CAES	70.9	66.7	66.5	66.4	66.2	67.4
	Ours	70.9	69.5	69.4	68.9	69.3	69.6
WebQuestionSP	w/o CAES	72.2	67.9	67.6	67.5	69.6	68.9
	Ours	72.2	69.7	69.5	69.0	68.4	69.8
ASSISTments2009	w/o CAES	71.4	64.6	64.4	63.8	62.6	62.2
	Ours	71.4	70.7	70.5	70.1	70.3	69.8

5 Conclusion and Future Work

This paper presents a approach designed to maintain pedagogical continuity in intelligent tutoring systems within evolving knowledge. By reconstructing learning paths and consolidating past knowledge, the model ensures consistent instructional support as course content updates. Experimental results show that CKRA effectively preserves teaching quality across both current and historical materials, outperforming existing methods in terms of pedagogical coherence. In the future, we will extend CKRA to support multimodal educational resources and enhance its reasoning capabilities for interdisciplinary tasks. Moreover, we will explore hybrid models that combine CKRA with specialized systems to advance adaptive and continuous tutoring.

Acknowledgements. This research is supported by Shandong Provincial Natural Science Foundation project ZR2022QF088.

References

1. Armour-Thomas, E., Gordon, E.W.: Principles of Dynamic Pedagogy: An Integrative Model of Curriculum, Instruction, and Assessment for Prospective and In-Service Teachers. Taylor & Francis (2025)
2. Baillifard, A., Gabella, M., Banta Lavenex, P., Martarelli, C.: Effective learning with a personal AI tutor: a case study. Educ. Inf. Technol. **30**, 297–312 (2024)
3. Bayly-Castaneda, K., Ramirez-Montoya, M.S., Morita-Alexander, A.: Crafting personalized learning paths with ai for lifelong learning: a systematic literature review. Front. Educ. **9** (2024)
4. Berant, J., Chou, A., Frostig, R., Liang, P.: Semantic parsing on Freebase from question-answer pairs. In: Proceedings of the 2013 Conference on Empirical Methods in Natural Language Processing, pp. 1533–1544 (2013)
5. Bordes, A., Chopra, S., Weston, J.: Question answering with subgraph embeddings. In: Moschitti, A., Pang, B., Daelemans, W. (eds.) Proceedings of the 2014 Conference on Empirical Methods in Natural Language Processing, pp. 615–620 (2014)
6. Bordes, A., Usunier, N., Chopra, S., Weston, J.: Large-scale simple question answering with memory networks (2015). https://arxiv.org/abs/1506.02075
7. Chen, Z., Liu, B.: Continual Learning and Catastrophic Forgetting, pp. 55–75. Springer (2018)
8. Cheng, L., Chen, Z., Ren, J.: Enhancing question answering over knowledge base using dynamical relation reasoning. In: 2020 International Joint Conference on Neural Networks, pp. 1–8 (2020)
9. Devlin, J., Chang, M.W., Lee, K., Toutanova, K.: Bert: pre-training of deep bidirectional transformers for language understanding (2019). https://arxiv.org/abs/1810.04805
10. Ezzaim, A., Dahbi, A., Aqqal, A., Haidine, A.: AI-based learning style detection in adaptive learning systems: a systematic literature review. J. Comput. Educ. 1–39 (2024)
11. He, G., Lan, Y., Jiang, J., Zhao, W.X., Wen, J.R.: Improving multi-hop knowledge base question answering by learning intermediate supervision signals. In: Proceedings of the 14th ACM International Conference on Web Search and Data Mining, pp. 553–561. ACM (2021)
12. Huang, Y.M., Wang, D.C., Lin, G.H., Huang, Y.M.: Unpacking the determinants of social media-based lifelong learning from the need hierarchy theory. Behav. Inf. Technol. **44**(3), 477–490 (2025)
13. Ilić, M., Keković, G., Mikić, V., Mangaroska, K., Kopanja, L., Vesin, B.: Predicting student performance in a programming tutoring system using AI and filtering techniques. IEEE Trans. Learn. Technol. **17**, 1891–1905 (2024)
14. Ilkou, E., Jiménez-Ruiz, E.: Towards a knowledge graph for teaching knowledge graphs (2024). https://arxiv.org/abs/2411.01304
15. Liu, H., Zhang, Y., Jia, J.: The design of guiding and adaptive prompts for intelligent tutoring systems and its effect on students' mathematics learning. IEEE Trans. Learn. Technol. **17**, 1353–1363 (2024)
16. Mao, S.: Assistment2009 (2024). https://dx.doi.org/10.21227/k80b-0n66
17. Noroozi, O., Alqassab, M., Kerman, N.T., Banihashem, S.K., Panadero, E.: Does perception mean learning? Insights from an online peer feedback setting. Assess. Eval. High. Educ. **50**(1), 83–97 (2025)

18. Sun, H., Bedrax-Weiss, T., Cohen, W.W.: Pullnet: open domain question answering with iterative retrieval on knowledge bases and text (2019). https://arxiv.org/abs/1904.09537
19. Thwe, W.P., Kalman, A.: Lifelong learning in the educational setting: a systematic literature review. Asia Pac. Educ. Res. **33**(2), 407–417 (2024)
20. Tong, S., et al.: Incremental cognitive diagnosis for intelligent education. In: Proceedings of the 28th ACM SIGKDD Conference on Knowledge Discovery and Data Mining, pp. 1760–1770 (2022)
21. Vannaprathip, N., Haddawy, P., Schultheis, H., Suebnukarn, S.: Sdmentor: a virtual reality-based intelligent tutoring system for surgical decision making in dentistry. Artif. Intell. Med. **162**, 103092 (2025)
22. Vennerød, C.B., Kjærran, A., Bugge, E.S.: Long short-term memory RNN (2021). https://arxiv.org/abs/2105.06756
23. Wang, Y., Zhang, R., Xu, C., Mao, Y.: The APVA-TURBO approach to question answering in knowledge base. In: Bender, E.M., Derczynski, L., Isabelle, P. (eds.) Proceedings of the 27th International Conference on Computational Linguistics, pp. 1998–2009 (2018)
24. Wijekumar, K.K., Lei, P., Rice, M., Beerwinkle, A., Zhang, S., Meyer, B.J.: A web-based intelligent tutoring system for reading comprehension delivered to fifth-grade students attending high-poverty schools: results from a replication efficacy study. J. Educ. Psychol. (2024)
25. Yih, W.T., Richardson, M., Meek, C., Chang, M.W., Suh, J.: The value of semantic parse labeling for knowledge base question answering. In: Erk, K., Smith, N.A. (eds.) Proceedings of the 54th Annual Meeting of the Association for Computational Linguistics. Association for Computational Linguistics (2016)
26. Zahraini, Z., Akib, A., Rosidin, R., Sulaeman, O.: Islamic education reform in the digital age: challenges and opportunities for a modern curriculum. J. Noesantara Islamic Stud. **2**(1), 1–11 (2025)
27. Zhang, X., Zhao, J.J., LeCun, Y.: Character-level convolutional networks for text classification. CoRR abs/1509.01626 (2015). http://arxiv.org/abs/1509.01626
28. Zhou, D.W., Cai, Z.W., Ye, H.J., Zhan, D.C., Liu, Z.: Revisiting class-incremental learning with pre-trained models: generalizability and adaptivity are all you need. Int. J. Comput. Vision **133**(3), 1012–1032 (2025)
29. Zhou, D.W., Wang, Q.W., Qi, Z.H., Ye, H.J., Zhan, D.C., Liu, Z.: Class-incremental learning: a survey. IEEE Trans. Pattern Anal. Mach. Intell. **46**(12), 9851–9873 (2024)

From Cloud to Edge: Evaluating Efficient Deep Learning Models for Hyper-Local Weather Forecasting

Jonas Gabriel L. Rusiana, Gwyn Ann S. Lobaton, Azriel Peter S. Deduyo, Rhodessa J. Cascaro, and Clyde Chester R. Balaman(✉)

Mapúa Malayan Colleges Mindanao, Davao, Philippines
{jgrusiana,galobaton,apdeduyo,rjcascaro,ccrbalaman}@mcm.edu.ph

Abstract. Timely and accurate weather forecasting is crucial for safety, economic activities, and public preparedness across diverse fields such as agriculture and fisheries. However, existing centralized systems often fail to provide accurate local predictions for ground-level conditions and depend on a constant internet connection, making it difficult for remote areas to access data offline. To address this critical gap, this study performs a comprehensive comparative analysis of deep learning (DL) and machine learning (ML) regression models specifically for hyper-local weather forecasting deployment in resource-constrained edge computing environments. We evaluated a suite of models, including Multi-Layer Perceptrons (MLP), Long Short-Term Memory (LSTM), Temporal Convolutional Network (TCN), and several classical regressor, utilizing a multi-sourced time-series dataset spanning 10 years. All models were rigorously assessed for both predictive accuracy (RMSE, R^2, MAE, MAPE) and computational efficiency (CPU and RAM usage) on a Raspberry Pi 4 Model B edge device. Results demonstrated that DL models generally outperformed traditional ML models in forecasting accuracy. While LSTM achieved the highest accuracy (RMSE of 0.019), it exhibited poor computational efficiency. Crucially, the MLP model emerged as the most suitable candidate, achieving high accuracy (RMSE of 0.018) with exceptional resource efficiency (0.01% CPU process usage), making it ideal for decentralized, offline operation. These findings provide a foundational insight into integrating efficient DL models within edge devices, enabling precise, near-real-time weather monitoring, and addressing the critical need for robust forecasting in low-connectivity settings.

Keywords: Weather Forecasting · Edge Computing · Deep Learning · Machine Learning · Hyper-Local Prediction · Regression Analysis

1 Introduction

Accurate and timely weather forecasting plays a vital role in public safety, planning, and key economic sectors such as agriculture and fisheries [1,2]. Forecasting relies on analyzing large amounts of historical weather data organized as

C. Xu (Ed.): ICMLSC 2026, CCIS 2948, pp. 186–197, 2027.
https://doi.org/10.1007/978-981-92-1546-1_15

time-series to predict future conditions like temperature, pressure, and humidity, which vary greatly across different locations [1]. Traditional methods such as Numerical Weather Prediction (NWP) and ARIMA have long been used for this purpose. However, recent progress in Machine Learning (ML) and Deep Learning (DL) has opened new possibilities for improving accuracy and computational efficiency in weather prediction [3,4]. Despite these advances, existing centralized forecasting systems often fail to provide accurate, hyper-local predictions needed for ground-level conditions [5]. Many of these systems depend heavily on cloud-based infrastructure and constant internet connectivity. As a result, they are less effective in areas with weak or unstable network access, limiting the availability of forecast data in remote regions [5–7]. These challenges highlight the importance of developing localized and offline forecasting systems that can operate efficiently without continuous cloud support [8,9]. Most current systems produce generalized forecasts that do not accurately represent on-the-ground conditions [5]. While several ML and DL models have been explored for weather forecasting [10], previous research has mainly focused on high-performance or cloud-based environments [8,11]. There is still limited understanding of how these models perform on resource-constrained edge devices, such as the Raspberry Pi 4, especially in real edge-based deployments [12]. This lack of systematic evaluation makes it difficult to determine the best balance between prediction accuracy and computational efficiency for decentralized applications.

To address this gap, this study compares ML and DL regression models for hyper-local weather forecasting on edge devices [11,13]. Evaluated models include MLP, LSTM, TCN, and classical regressors. Using a 10-year multi-source time-series dataset, we assess predictive accuracy (RMSE, MAE, R^2, MAPE) and computational performance (CPU and RAM usage) on a Raspberry Pi 4 Model B [11,13]. The goal is to identify models that balance accuracy, efficiency, and real-time, offline forecasting in low-connectivity regions [6]. The study reviews existing ML/DL weather forecasting methods on edge platforms, describes the dataset, experimental design, and evaluation metrics, and highlights key findings on model efficiency and suitability for resource-limited deployments. It concludes with insights and future directions for intelligent, energy-efficient forecasting systems in practical applications.

2 Related Works

Weather forecasting predicts future atmospheric states using time-series data and models, considering factors such as temperature, humidity, pressure, and wind. Traditional approaches rely on statistical models like NWP and ARIMA, while recent methods leverage machine and deep learning for improved accuracy [3]. Modern systems often adopt cloud or federated frameworks for distributed processing [11], with edge devices, e.g., on city buses, enabling real-time local data collection [8]. Classical ML regressors provide competitive alternatives to statistical models, whereas deep learning models excel at identifying trends in weather time series [14]. These models can be deployed on cloud or edge platforms; cloud deployment is standard [8,11], but edge computing allows local forecasting with reduced connectivity requirements [15]. Centralized systems often fail to deliver timely, locally accurate predictions in low-connectivity areas [5], revealing a gap for localized edge-based forecasting. Addressing this involves integrating ML and DL models on edge devices for on-site computation [2,9], from federated local weather stations [11] to fully onboard systems [2]. Existing literature lacks comprehensive comparisons of multiple ML and DL models on resource-limited devices like the Raspberry Pi 4, considering both predictive accuracy and computational efficiency. As summarized in Table 1, the Raspberry Pi 4 supports diverse ML and DL models across domains. Random Forest and XGBoost achieve high accuracy, while LSTM and RNN enable low-latency real-time inference. MLP and LSTM architectures further demonstrate on-device federated learning, highlighting the balance between performance and efficiency on this edge platform.

3 Materials and Methods

3.1 Dataset

The dataset (otherwise referred to as the master dataset) used was an aggregation of various validated sources and existing time series datasets. Mainly from ERA5-Land, Philippine Atmospheric, Geophysical and Astronomical Services Administration, National Renewable Energy Laboratory - System Advisor Model, and Open-Meteo. The resulting dataset was a time series dataset with $7,462,977$ rows of data. Such rows span 10 years' worth of data from 2013 to 2023, all year round. A $75 : 15 : 15$ ratio was used for splitting the data for training, validating, and testing, respectively.

The master dataset [1], summarized in Table 2, contains key meteorological attributes with an added location feature to distinguish overlapping time-series records. Two dataset versions were prepared using different normalization methods: Z-Score (Standard Scaler) for machine learning models and Min-Max (Min-Max Scaler) for deep learning models [7]. Both datasets followed identical preprocessing steps, including the removal of duplicates, extreme values, and null entries, and applied cyclical encoding to date attributes to preserve temporal patterns [14].

3.2 Employed Models

For a comparative analysis that's fair and comprehensive, this study evaluates both deep learning models and machine learning models, with the former compatible with time-series data [10], and the latter depending on the feature-engineered dataset for easier learning of the trends [4,20]. The employed models are Multi-Layer Perceptrons (MLP) [21], Recurrent Neural Network (RNN) [12], Long Short-Term Memory (LSTM) [3], and Temporal Convolutional Network (TCN) [3,15] for the deep learning family. And Linear Regression, Lasso Regression, Ridge Regression [20], Random Forest, XGBoost, and Extra Trees [4,13]

Table 1. Recent Research Deploying Specified ML and DL Models on Raspberry Pi 4

Study & Year	Model(s)	Application Domain	Deployment Details	Key Findings
Boutahri & Tilioua (2024)	Random Forest, XGBoost	Smart building HVAC, thermal comfort	Models trained and evaluated using data from a network of Raspberry Pi 4 boards with multiple sensors; real-time prediction and optimization on-device	RF and XGBoost achieved highest accuracy (96.7% and 96.4%) for thermal comfort prediction and energy optimization [16]
Nandeshwar et al. (2025)	Random Forest, XGBoost, Extra Trees, Linear Regression	Real-time object detection	Models implemented on Raspberry Pi 4B (8GB); system includes camera and high-speed computing unit for real-time inference	LBP+XGBoost achieved highest accuracy (83.59%) for object detection [17]
Saha et al. (2022)	LSTM, Random Forest	Smart agriculture, edge intelligence	LSTM model deployed on Raspberry Pi 4 for edge-based detection and classification	LSTM and Random Forest enabled accurate, low-latency edge inference in smart agriculture [18]
Das & Brunschwiler (2019)	LSTM, MLP	Federated learning, edge AI	LSTM and MLP trained directly on Raspberry Pi 4 (4GB RAM); batch sizes up to 40 supported for LSTM, up to 512 for MLP; federated learning setup	Raspberry Pi 4 can train moderate LSTM/MLP models with low latency; federated learning feasible [17]
Kumar et al. (2023)	RNN, Linear Regression	Healthcare	Models trained and evaluated on Raspberry Pi 4 for real-time baby monitoring system	RNN enables efficient real-time recognition of baby movements and vital signs [19]

for the machine learning family. Each model follows a consistent design and structure to ensure regularization and reproducibility, with an ample models using default parameters. The deep learning family utilized a two layer structure accompanied by 0.001 learning rate, 128 batch size, and 15 epochs, with the first layer pertaining to each model's architecture. MLP has 128 neuron layers,

Table 2. Attributes of the weather forecasting dataset.

Attribute	Description	Unit
Temperature	Air temperature at 2 m above ground	°C
Dew Point	Temperature at which air becomes saturated	°C
Humidity	Relative humidity in the atmosphere	%
Pressure	Surface atmospheric pressure	hPa
Rainfall	Precipitation amount	mm
Latitude	Geographic latitude of observation site	Degrees
Longitude	Geographic longitude of observation site	Degrees
Location	Name of observation station/site	Text
Time	Date and time of observation	YYYY-MM-DD HH:MM
Source	Data provider or dataset origin	Text

while the rest of the model utilized 64 neurons, following a 64 neuron second layer, using the *ReLu* (for MLP) and *tahn* (for RNN, LSTM, and TCN) activation functions, and *Adam* optimizer. As for the machine learning family, there were no hyperparameters modified as the default values were used.

3.3 Model Evaluation and Computational Performance Metrics

Model evaluation metrics were employed to measure the predictive accuracy and reliability of each model in forecasting weather data. The primary metrics considered include the Root Mean Square Error (RMSE), Mean Absolute Error (MAE), the Coefficient of Determination (R^2), and the Mean Absolute Percentage Error (MAPE). These are standard evaluation measures widely adopted in regression-based forecasting studies [3,10,14,22].

The *Root Mean Square Error (RMSE)* is defined as:

$$\text{RMSE} = \sqrt{\frac{1}{n}\sum_{i=1}^{n}(y_i - \hat{y}_i)^2}, \tag{1}$$

which penalizes larger errors more heavily and provides a comprehensive measure of overall prediction accuracy.

The *Mean Absolute Error (MAE)* is given by:

$$\text{MAE} = \frac{1}{n}\sum_{i=1}^{n}|y_i - \hat{y}_i|, \tag{2}$$

representing the average absolute deviation of predictions from actual values and offering interpretability in the original data scale.

The *Coefficient of Determination (R^2)* is computed as:

$$R^2 = 1 - \frac{\sum_{i=1}^{n}(y_i - \hat{y}_i)^2}{\sum_{i=1}^{n}(y_i - \bar{y})^2}, \tag{3}$$

indicating the proportion of variance in the observed data explained by the model, where values closer to 1 denote stronger model performance.

Lastly, the *Mean Absolute Percentage Error (MAPE)* is formulated as:

$$\mathrm{MAPE} = \frac{100}{n}\sum_{i=1}^{n}\left|\frac{y_i - \hat{y}_i}{y_i}\right|, \tag{4}$$

which expresses prediction errors as percentages of the true values, facilitating comparative interpretability across datasets.

Beyond predictive accuracy, computational performance metrics were utilized to assess model efficiency within a constrained edge computing environment. These metrics include the *average CPU process percent*, *average system CPU percent*, *average RAM process (MB)*, and *average system RAM percent*. The CPU metrics reflect both the localized processing load attributable to the model and the overall device utilization, while the RAM metrics indicate the memory footprint at both process and system levels. Collectively, these provide a quantitative basis for comparing model efficiency, battery longevity, and hardware endurance.

To ensure reproducibility and avoid data bias, synthetic input data were generated from controlled random processes. This allowed evaluation focused on runtime behavior, memory utilization, and scalability rather than predictive validity. Each model was executed for 10 min, with system metrics recorded every 30 s. The experimental platform consisted of a Raspberry Pi 4 Model B, an ARM-based edge computing device widely adopted in IoT deployments [9]. The system ran on Raspbian OS Lite to minimize background processing overhead [9]. All models were deployed using `Python`, leveraging libraries such as `scikit-learn`, `TensorFlow Lite`, and `pickle` within a virtual environment (`venv`) [2,7]. This combined evaluation framework enables a holistic analysis of both model performance and computational efficiency—crucial for understanding trade-offs in real-time, resource-constrained edge AI deployments.

4 Results and Discussion

Figure 1 presents the mean performance of the deep learning models in all target attributes of the master data set, evaluated using standard performance metrics. In general, all models demonstrated strong predictive capability. However, a closer examination reveals minor variations, particularly in the R^2 values, which highlight subtle differences in the model behavior. Most models, except for LSTM, exhibited lower performance when predicting rainfall. This is mainly due to the limited temporal patterns and high noise in rainfall data, which make it difficult for models to learn consistent sequences. Although the $RMSE$ and MAE values show that predictions were close to actual values, the higher $MAPE$ scores indicate challenges in capturing rainfall trends. In contrast, the LSTM model achieved the best overall performance, effectively handling temporal dependencies and maintaining low error even for the rainfall attribute due to its memory-based architecture.

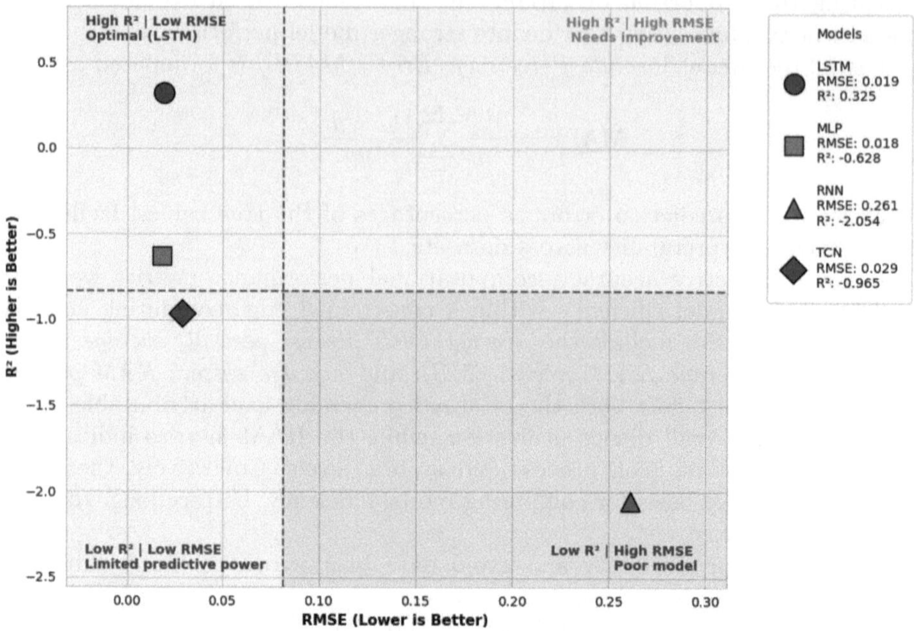

Fig. 1. Deep learning models' mean performance across all targets.

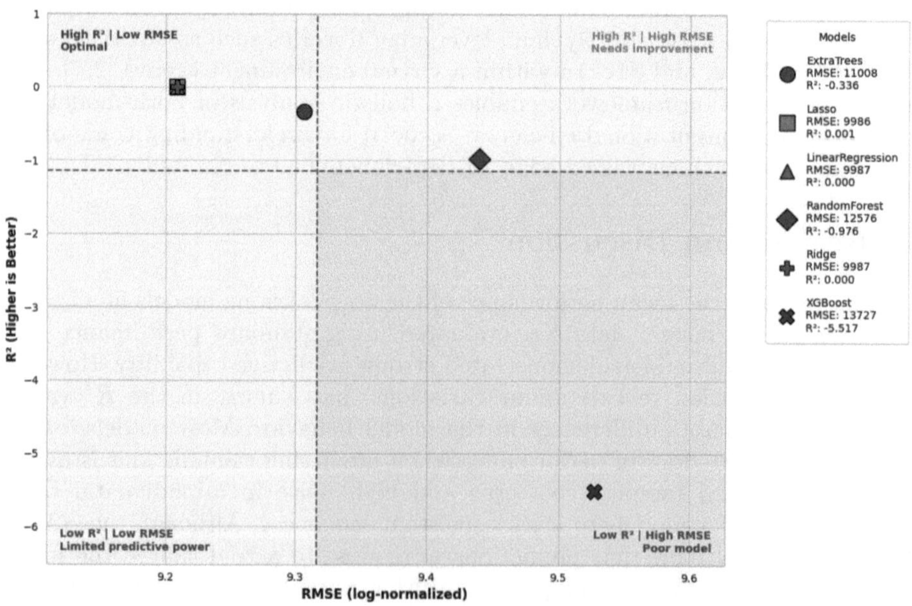

Fig. 2. Machine learning models' mean performance across all targets.

Similarly, Fig. 2 illustrates the mean performance of the machine learning models across all target attributes. Compared to the deep learning models, these traditional approaches showed significantly lower accuracy, indicating limited ability to capture temporal patterns and relationships in the data. Among the evaluated models, XGBoost exhibited the weakest performance, with the highest $MAPE$ value, even exceeding that of Random Forest. In contrast, Lasso Regression achieved the most consistent and reliable results among the machine learning models, though still falling short of the performance observed in deep learning models.

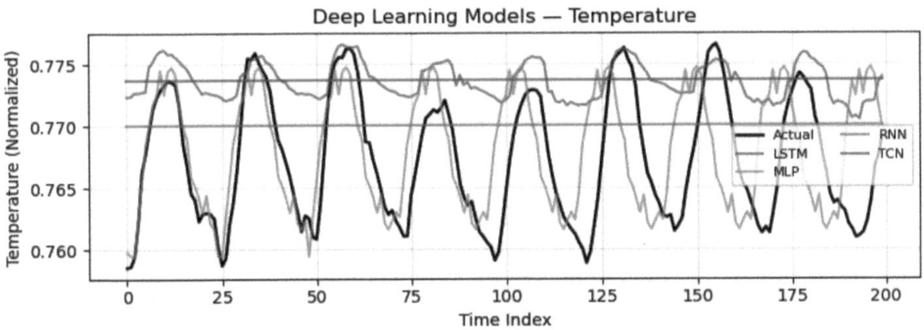

Fig. 3. Deep learning models prediction results. The values were logarithmically scaled.

Time-series plots of the deep learning models using temperature as the target variable are shown in Fig. 3. Temperature was selected for its central role in climate analysis and strong correlation with other attributes in the dataset. The LSTM and MLP models successfully captured temporal trends and seasonal variations, producing predictions closely aligned with the actual data, consistent with the performance trends in Fig. 1. In contrast, the RNN and TCN models displayed nearly constant predictions around a normalized value of 0.77, suggesting underfitting caused by noisy data or convergence to trivial local minima. This behavior leads to reduced loss values but fails to reflect real temporal dynamics. Performance can be improved through hyperparameter tuning and architectural refinements, such as increasing network depth, experimenting with optimizers, or adjusting activation functions. Dataset enhancements—longer historical coverage, higher temporal resolution, and data augmentation for rare events like rainfall—may further strengthen model robustness and forecasting accuracy.

Figure 4 shows log-scaled time-series plots of ML models for temperature prediction. Compared to deep learning models, ML performance is weaker, struggling to capture temporal patterns, as also seen in Fig. 2. Nonetheless, ML models remain effective for simpler tasks, such as estimating quarterly pressure trends with linear regression or predicting short-term rainfall events with random forests. Hourly forecasting across multiple variables challenged these models due to dataset size and variability. Performance could improve with hyperparameter

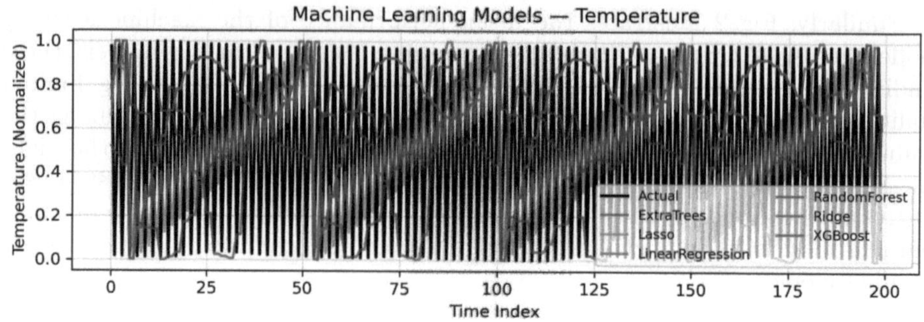

Fig. 4. Machine learning models prediction results. The values were logarithmically scaled.

tuning, longer historical data, higher temporal resolution, and reduced noise, as done with deep learning models.

Table 3. Summary of computational performance of all evaluated models on the edge device. **Highlighted values** indicate the most efficient and most resource-intensive models.

Model	CPU Usage (%)	RAM Usage (MB)
MLP	**0.01**	**54.99**
LSTM	1.55	54.99
TCN	0.45	53.74
RNN	0.46	53.74
Linear Regression	0.81	318.96
Lasso Regression	0.86	318.96
Ridge Regression	1.17	318.96
Extra Trees	**5.95**	**2983.09**
Random Forest	6.02	1766.57
XGBoost	6.15	742.41

Table 3 summarizes the computational performance of all evaluated models on the Raspberry Pi 4 edge device, focusing on average CPU and RAM consumption during runtime. Results reveal a distinct trade-off between forecasting accuracy and computational efficiency. Among deep learning models, **LSTM** achieved the highest predictive accuracy but required substantially more computational resources. In contrast, the **MLP** model exhibited exceptional efficiency, using only **0.01% CPU** and approximately **55 MB of RAM**, owing to its lightweight architecture of few fully connected layers with minimal parameters. Traditional regression models such as Linear, Lasso, and Ridge displayed moderate resource use but lower predictive performance. Meanwhile, ensemble-based models—particularly **Extra Trees**, Random Forest, and XGBoost—were the most resource-intensive, with Extra Trees consuming nearly **3 GB of RAM**. This high demand arises from its architecture, which constructs numerous deep decision trees that significantly increase memory and computational load during both training and inference.

These findings highlight that while LSTM remains ideal for cloud-based or federated systems due to its accuracy and temporal learning capacity, MLP provides the best balance between accuracy and resource efficiency for **hyper-local, offline weather forecasting** on edge devices.

5 Conclusion

This study evaluated and compared the performance of multiple machine learning and deep learning models for local weather forecasting on edge-computing environments. The results revealed that the **LSTM model** achieved the highest predictive accuracy, with an $RMSE$ of 0.019 and R^2 of 0.325, highlighting its ability to capture complex temporal dependencies. However, its high computational cost—1.55% CPU and approximately 55 MB RAM usage—renders it less suitable for real-time edge deployment, though ideal for cloud-based or federated setups. Conversely, the **MLP model** demonstrated an optimal trade-off between accuracy and efficiency, with an $RMSE$ of 0.018, R^2 of −0.628, and minimal computational load (0.01% CPU, 54.99 MB RAM). Its lightweight architecture enables practical deployment on resource-constrained edge devices, making it suitable for hyper-local and offline weather forecasting systems. Traditional regression and ensemble-based models underperformed, exhibiting limited capacity to learn temporal patterns in complex meteorological datasets. Notably, models such as TCN and RNN suffered from dataset underfitting, suggesting the need for improved data preprocessing through increased historical coverage, finer temporal resolution, and noise reduction. Enhancing rainfall data representation may also strengthen R^2 values by clarifying temporal patterns. These findings provide a baseline framework for designing energy-efficient, edge-deployable forecasting systems capable of supporting localized decision-making. The results also demonstrate that deep learning architectures can be selectively optimized for either accuracy (LSTM) or computational efficiency (MLP), depending on deployment context. Future research should conduct extended experiments across diverse edge devices and longer testing durations to refine performance benchmarks. Further exploration between LSTM and MLP architectures in hybrid edgecloud systems may also offer a balanced solution for distributed meteorological forecasting. Additionally, optimizing traditional machine learning models with temporal feature engineering remains a promising direction for improving their adaptability to complex time series data. In summary, this study contributes to the growing discourse on *edge-based weather forecasting* by establishing empirical insights into model efficiency and accuracy trade-offs, setting the groundwork for scalable, real-world forecasting solutions in resource-constrained environments.

References

1. Ren, X., et al.: Deep learning-based weather prediction: a survey. Big Data Res. **23**, 100178 (2021)
2. Bolla, S., Anandan, R., Thanappan, S.: Weather forecasting method from sensor transmitted data for smart cities using IoT. Sci. Program. **2022**, 1–9 (2022)
3. Hewage, P., Trovati, M., Pereira, E., Behera, A.: Deep learning-based effective fine-grained weather forecasting model. Pattern Anal. Appl. **24**(1), 343–366 (2021)
4. Fatima, S., et al.: Xgboost and random forest algorithms: an in-depth analysis. Pak. J. Sci. Res. **3**(1), 26–31 (2023)
5. Linsenmeier, M., Shrader, J.G.: Global inequalities in weather forecasts. SocArXiv 7e2jf, Center for Open Science (2023)
6. Tran, T., et al.: Exploring hybrid models for short-term local weather forecasting in IoT environment. Mendel **29**(2), 295–306 (2023)
7. Bonavita, M.: On some limitations of data-driven weather forecasting models (2023)
8. Huang, Z.-Q., Chen, Y.-C., Wen, C.-Y.: Real-time weather monitoring and prediction using city buses and machine learning. Sensors **20**(18) (2020)
9. Tsoukas, V., Gkogkidis, A., Boumpa, E., Kakarountas, A.: A review on the emerging technology of tinyml. ACM Comput. Surv. **56**(10) (2024)
10. De Saa, E., Ranathunga, L.: Comparison between arima and deep learning models for temperature forecasting (2020)
11. Chen, S., Long, G., Shen, T., Jiang, J., Zhang, C.: Federated prompt learning for weather foundation models on devices (2024)
12. Han, J.M., Ang, Y.Q., Malkawi, A., Samuelson, H.W.: Using recurrent neural networks for localized weather prediction with combined use of public airport data and on-site measurements. Build. Environ. **192**, 107601 (2021)
13. Bicego, M., Cicalese, F.: On the good behaviour of extremely randomized trees in random forest-distance computation. In: Koutra, D., Plant, C., Gomez Rodriguez, M., Baralis, E., Bonchi, F. (eds.) Machine Learning and Knowledge Discovery in Databases: Research Track, pp. 645–660. Springer, Cham (2023)
14. Zhang, H., Liu, Y., Zhang, C., Li, N.: Machine learning methods for weather forecasting: a survey. Atmosphere **16**(1), 82 (2025)
15. Hewage, P., et al.: Temporal convolutional neural (TCN) network for an effective weather forecasting using time-series data from the local weather station. Soft. Comput. **24**(21), 16453–16482 (2020)
16. Boutahri, Y., Tilioua, A.: Machine learning-based predictive model for thermal comfort and energy optimization in smart buildings. Results Eng. (2024)
17. Nandeshwar, V.J., et al.: Comparative analysis of feature descriptors and classifiers for real-time object detection. Int. J. Reconfig. Embed. Syst. (IJRES) (2025)
18. Saha, H.N., Roy, R.: ML-based smart farming using LSTM. In: Smart Agriculture Automation Using Advanced Technologies: Data Analytics and Machine Learning, Cloud Architecture, Automation and IoT, pp. 89–111. Springer (2022)
19. Kumar, N.J., Kumar, A.N., et al.: A lightweight (recurrent neural network) RNN architecture for IoT based baby monitoring system to provide real time alerts and notification to parents or care takers. In: 2023 Intelligent Computing and Control for Engineering and Business Systems (ICCEBS), pp. 1–6. IEEE (2023)
20. Jadhav, P., Patil, V., Gore, S.: A comparative study of linear regression and regression tree. SSRN Electron. J. **01**(2020)

21. Kruse, R., Mostaghim, S., Borgelt, C., Braune, C., Steinbrecher, M.: Multi-layer perceptrons, pp. 53–124. Springer, Cham (2022)
22. Plevris, V., Solorzano, G., Bakas, N., Seghier, M.B.: Investigation of performance metrics in regression analysis and machine learning-based prediction models. In: The 8th European Congress on Computational Methods in Applied Sciences and Engineering (2022)

Enhancing Consumer Engagement with ML-Driven Multisensory AR for the Automotive Market

Chutisant Kerdvibulvech(✉)

Graduate School of Communication Arts and Management Innovation, National Institute of Development Administration, 148 SeriThai Rd. Klong-Chan, Bangkapi, Bangkok 10240, Thailand

chutisant.ker@nida.ac.th

Abstract. This paper explores the integration of machine learning (ML) and soft computing techniques with big data analytics to enhance multisensory advertising through augmented reality (AR) simulations in the premium automotive industry. Focusing on consumers in Bangkok, the study synthesizes literature on multisensory marketing, artificial intelligence (AI), and consumer engagement to propose a comprehensive review and conceptual framework for machine learning–driven multisensory AR marketing. Using fuzzy logic-based segmentation, neuro-fuzzy inference systems, and adaptive modeling, the proposed framework dynamically tailors immersive AR content to user profiles, improving interaction fidelity and engagement. Moreover, the use of soft computing approaches—such as fuzzy clustering and evolutionary optimization—enables context-aware adjustments and robust performance under uncertainty, a common challenge in real-world marketing environments. This paper contributes to the fields of marketing analytics, human-computer interaction, and AI-driven communication by demonstrating how intelligent, multisensory AR systems can optimize consumer decision-making processes and serve as a blueprint for next-generation adaptive marketing solutions in luxury automotive contexts.

Keywords: Extended Reality · Machine Learning · Senses · Augmented Reality

1 Introduction

The global automotive market has undergone a radical transformation in how brands communicate value and engage consumers. The transition from traditional showroom experiences to immersive digital marketing is largely driven by the convergence of AR and AI. In particular, ML and fuzzy logic techniques have enabled data-driven personalization of sensory experiences that mimic physical engagement—sight, sound, touch, smell, and taste—through virtual or mixed-reality environments [6].

In urban premium markets such as Bangkok, automotive brands compete not only on technological superiority or design but also on experiential differentiation. Consumers

C. Xu (Ed.): ICMLSC 2026, CCIS 2948, pp. 198–209, 2027.
https://doi.org/10.1007/978-981-92-1546-1_16

expect meaningful engagement that stimulates multiple senses, fosters emotional resonance, and enhances trust in product quality. The challenge, however, lies in adapting sensory marketing to digital channels without losing authenticity or personal relevance [9].

Traditional marketing approaches focus heavily on visual and informational cues—vehicle imagery, performance claims, or celebrity endorsements—while neglecting multisensory integration. Yet research in sensory marketing shows that multisensory stimulation increases perceived quality, memorability, and emotional attachment [2]. The question then arises: how can AI and ML models simulate and optimize these multisensory cues in an immersive AR environment to influence consumer engagement and purchase intention?

This paper addresses that question by reviewing and synthesizing research across four domains:

1. Multisensory marketing theory and consumer behavior
2. Augmented and mixed reality applications in marketing communication
3. Machine learning and fuzzy logic in sensory analytics and personalization
4. Marketing implications for premium automotive brands in emerging urban markets

By integrating these areas, this paper proposes a review-based conceptual framework that outlines how ML-driven multisensory AR systems can adaptively enhance engagement and brand experience in the automotive sector.

2 Conceptual Background

2.1 Multisensory Perception and Consumer Cognition

Human perception is inherently multisensory [8]. Consumers interpret product quality and brand meaning through integrated sensory input, where visual, auditory, tactile, olfactory, and gustatory cues jointly construct affective and cognitive responses. In automotive contexts, the visual design communicates sophistication; the sound of an engine signals power and identity; the feel of materials conveys craftsmanship; and even scented interiors shape comfort and emotional memory.

However, most digital advertising platforms are predominantly visual-centric, which limits emotional depth and realism. The rise of AR and virtual reality (VR) technologies has expanded the scope for sensory engagement beyond 2D screens, enabling brands to recreate tactile and auditory cues virtually. When combined with AI personalization, these experiences can be adapted to individual sensory preferences and emotional triggers.

2.2 Cognitive Load and Emotional Resonance

Effective design can reduce cognitive load and amplify emotional engagement. In marketing, this means simplifying decision processes through intuitive, sensory-rich interactions. By presenting complex product information through immersive simulation—rather than text or specifications—brands can evoke *experiential cognition* rather than analytical evaluation, leading to faster decision-making and stronger emotional bonds.

2.3 The Bangkok Context

Bangkok represents a unique convergence of luxury consumption and digital sophistication. With a rising affluent middle class and increasing smartphone penetration, premium automotive buyers in Bangkok are receptive to innovative AR-driven campaigns. Yet they also display cultural nuances—status sensitivity, collectivist identity signaling, and preference for tangible experiences—that make multisensory immersion particularly persuasive. Hence, this market serves as a relevant empirical and conceptual lens for exploring ML-driven sensory AR engagement.

3 Multisensory Marketing and Consumer Engagement

Multisensory marketing integrates visual, auditory, tactile, olfactory, and even gustatory cues to create holistic and emotionally resonant brand experiences. As consumers increasingly interact with brands in hybrid and immersive environments—ranging from physical showrooms to AI-driven mixed reality platforms—engaging multiple senses has become a critical determinant of attention, emotional connection, and brand loyalty. According to Spence [4], sensory integration enhances cognitive consistency and emotional congruence, producing stronger and longer-lasting brand associations. Multisensory stimuli significantly influence consumer engagement, purchase intention, and impulse buying behaviors, especially when combined with emerging technologies such as AI-driven personalization and AR-based sensory simulations.

3.1 Sight and Visual Dominance

Sight remains the most dominant sensory modality in marketing, serving as the foundation for product recognition, symbolic meaning, and perceived quality. In the automotive sector, visual factors such as body design, curvature, material gloss, color harmony, and lighting dynamics shape perceptions of sophistication and performance. High-definition imagery, cinematic lighting, and motion graphics used in AI-generated advertising amplify these perceptions by triggering aesthetic pleasure and status associations. However, the persuasive power of purely visual cues has declined in overstimulated digital environments, where visual saturation reduces novelty and consumer attention.

Visual dominance can be enhanced through multisensory consistency—when visual representations align with sound, texture, or scent cues. For instance, digital simulations of glossy car finishes combined with synchronized ambient lighting in AR experiences increase perceived realism and immersion. Thus, the visual sense must be understood as an anchor that interacts dynamically with other sensory modalities, rather than a singular determinant of consumer perception.

3.2 Sound and Brand Identity

Sound has become a critical component of brand identity and emotional resonance. Engine acoustics, auditory signatures, and interactive soundscapes influence brand personality and consumer trust. Studies in multisensory marketing demonstrate that auditory congruence—the alignment of sound with brand image—enhances recognition and emotional attachment. With advancements in AI-driven sound synthesis, brands can now design adaptive auditory experiences that respond to consumer context.

In the context of automotive marketing, AI algorithms analyze real-time physiological data (e.g., voice tone, gaze, or facial emotion) to tailor sound intensity and rhythm within AR or MR test-drive environments. Such personalization transforms auditory design from static jingles into interactive emotional interfaces. Soundscapes in virtual retail environments significantly affect immersion and recall, particularly when paired with spatial audio technologies. Sound thus functions as both a cognitive cue and an emotional amplifier, bridging human-technology interaction with brand storytelling.

3.3 Touch and Material Simulation

Touch evokes trust, comfort, and authenticity—key factors in high-involvement purchase decisions such as automobiles [5]. Peck and Childers [3] demonstrated that haptic information enhances product evaluation by providing tangible assurance of quality. Modern automotive marketing increasingly employs haptic feedback devices and MR simulations to replicate tactile sensations such as steering resistance, surface texture, and vibration. These technologies allow consumers to "feel" craftsmanship before physical contact.

Recent innovations integrate fuzzy logic and AI to quantify subjective tactile experiences. Linguistic descriptors like *smooth*, *firm*, or *luxurious* are translated into sensory data models that predict satisfaction and purchase intention. This approach bridges affective computing and sensory design, offering scalable methods for evaluating consumer haptic responses. Furthermore, multisensory congruence between visual and tactile cues—such as seeing a soft leather texture while feeling corresponding resistance—strengthens authenticity and brand credibility.

3.4 Smell and Emotional Memory

Olfaction remains one of the most emotionally potent yet technologically underutilized senses in marketing. Scents have a unique capacity to trigger autobiographical memories and influence mood due to direct neural connections to the limbic system. In automotive marketing, signature cabin fragrances are used to evoke familiarity and emotional continuity across product lines. These olfactory cues reinforce brand distinctiveness, enhancing recall and perceived comfort.

It is indeed true that digital scent technologies, when combined with cross-modal AR stimuli, can effectively simulate olfactory experiences. For example, virtual scent diffusion synchronized with visual imagery can stimulate memory recall and emotional arousal, deepening engagement and brand loyalty. Though full olfactory digitization remains limited, hybrid sensory design integrating scent metaphor and associative priming has proven effective. When a digital advertisement evokes the freshness of "new leather" or the crispness of "mountain air," it activates consumers' olfactory imagination, creating sensory completeness even without real odor transmission.

3.5 Taste and Imagined Sensation

Although taste is less directly relevant to non-food products, it plays a metaphorical role in shaping perception through cross-sensory association. Descriptive language such as "buttery smooth steering" or "crisp acceleration" invokes gustatory imagery, influencing sensory interpretation and product evaluation. This linguistic sensory priming allows brands to borrow emotional resonance from food-related experiences to describe tactile or auditory qualities.

Machine learning–based sentiment analysis can now decode these metaphorical expressions, identifying implicit taste-based associations in consumer discourse. For instance, AI systems can analyze millions of social media reviews to determine whether descriptors like *sweet*, *bitter*, or *rich* correlate with positive affect toward a brand. Integrating such data into marketing communication enables highly personalized narrative design. This multisensory integration extends the consumer journey beyond product interaction, creating a holistic brand experience where every sensory cue—real or imagined—reinforces emotional attachment and purchase intention.

4 AR in Automotive Marketing

AR represents a paradigm shift in marketing communication, bridging the tangible and digital realms through real-time overlay of interactive visual and auditory content. In the context of automotive marketing, AR serves as a medium that enhances sensory immersion, allowing consumers to engage with vehicles beyond traditional static displays or video advertisements. Leading automotive manufacturers, including BMW, Audi, and Mercedes-Benz, have pioneered AR applications such as virtual test drives, 3D vehicle configurators, and interactive showrooms, which simulate real-world driving and ownership experiences without requiring physical presence.

Unlike conventional digital advertisements that rely primarily on visual engagement, AR enables multi-sensory interactivity, combining sight, sound, and even haptic or auditory feedback to enhance user perception. This experiential layer increases cognitive and emotional involvement, resulting in higher levels of recall, satisfaction, and purchase intention. However, many implementations remain limited to aesthetic novelty—focused on visual spectacle rather than sustained or adaptive engagement. True sensory immersion in AR marketing demands context-aware systems that dynamically respond to user input, environmental variables, and emotional states, offering personalized and evolving experiences that mirror real-life sensory perception.

The convergence of AI and AR introduces a transformative dimension to marketing—adaptive personalization. By leveraging computer vision, affective computing, and behavioral analytics, AI enables marketers to decode user responses in real time and optimize sensory cues accordingly. For instance, ML algorithms can track gaze duration, facial micro-expressions, voice tone, or even gesture dynamics to infer emotional engagement and attention levels. These data inputs empower AR systems to autonomously adjust parameters such as ambient lighting, engine acoustics, or narrative pacing during virtual vehicle demonstrations.

This process creates a closed feedback loop between consumer behavior and sensory modulation. When attention begins to decline, the AI system might amplify auditory elements (e.g., the sound of acceleration or environmental ambiance) or shift the color temperature of the interface to re-engage the user. Similarly, sentiment analysis can personalize the tone of voice in a virtual assistant or adjust the visual contrast to evoke emotions aligned with the consumer's mood—calm tones for relaxed states, vivid hues for excitement. Over time, these adaptive systems learn user preferences, creating psychographically tailored experiences that transcend one-size-fits-all marketing strategies. This combination of AI-driven responsiveness and sensory design positions AR not merely as an interactive medium but as a self-optimizing platform for sustained brand intimacy and experiential differentiation [11].

Bangkok presents a unique context for AR-based automotive marketing due to its combination of high digital literacy, tech-savvy consumer base, and a growing market for luxury and premium vehicles. Recent campaigns by brands such as Toyota, Mercedes-Benz, and MG have demonstrated strong engagement metrics through the deployment of AR mobile showrooms, virtual interior explorations, and 360-degree product customizers. These applications allow potential customers to virtually enter a car's cabin, explore dashboard features, or even simulate environmental driving scenarios within Bangkok's urban landscape.

However, the majority of current AR marketing campaigns in Thailand remain static and linear, lacking the adaptive intelligence that AI-driven systems can provide. While consumers express enthusiasm for novelty-based experiences, repeated exposure without personalization leads to diminished engagement over time. Integrating machine learning to monitor gaze behavior, interaction frequency, and emotional response could enable dealerships to deliver context-sensitive AR interactions, enhancing perceived authenticity and emotional connection with the brand.

Moreover, Bangkok's luxury-oriented consumer segment, characterized by high involvement and status-conscious decision-making, responds positively to immersive storytelling and multisensory coherence. Thus, AI-enhanced AR campaigns that synchronize visual sophistication, acoustic branding, and haptic simulation can elevate brand perception from mere innovation to experiential luxury. The integration of such technologies within Thailand's automotive sector remains underexplored, yet it presents substantial opportunities for marketers to differentiate through adaptive sensory design—a fusion of neuroscience, technology, and cultural insight that redefines consumer-brand interaction in the era of intelligent marketing.

5 ML and Fuzzy Logic in Sensory Personalization

ML and fuzzy logic together form a powerful computational foundation for modeling the inherently subjective and uncertain dimensions of human perception in multisensory marketing [7]. Traditional marketing analytics often rely on categorical or linear modeling, assuming that consumer attitudes or emotional responses can be cleanly classified into discrete categories. However, real-world sensory perception rarely conforms to rigid boundaries. A consumer's impression of a car's design, sound, or tactile feedback is not simply "positive" or "negative" but exists along a continuous spectrum of emotions and sensory intensities. This is where fuzzy logic becomes indispensable—it enables the quantification of qualitative impressions and the translation of linguistic variables such as "somewhat exciting," "moderately luxurious," or "highly immersive" into mathematically tractable degrees of membership.

In the context of AR marketing for the automotive sector, fuzzy logic allows the system to interpret and respond to nuances in consumer behavior data captured through multimodal inputs such as gaze tracking, facial expression analysis, gesture recognition, and voice tone detection. These indicators often contain noise or ambiguity, particularly in dynamic real-world environments. Fuzzy inference systems (FIS) provide a means to manage this uncertainty by generating probabilistic estimations of consumer states rather than deterministic labels. For instance, when evaluating emotional engagement, fuzzy rules may assign a 0.7 membership to "excited," a 0.4 membership to "curious," and a 0.2 membership to "bored," reflecting the fluid and overlapping nature of human affective states.

Building upon this, neuro-fuzzy architectures integrate the interpretability of fuzzy systems with the adaptive learning capacity of neural networks. In a marketing application, such hybrid systems can automatically learn and refine fuzzy rules from empirical data collected through user interactions in AR environments. For example, a neuro-fuzzy model could determine that consumers classified as "performance-oriented" exhibit higher engagement when visual brightness and auditory intensity increase synchronously, whereas "aesthetic-oriented" consumers respond better to subtler lighting and lower-frequency soundscapes. By continuously updating these relationships through online learning, the system achieves adaptive personalization, dynamically tuning sensory elements to each user's evolving psychological profile.

One of the most promising approaches for consumer segmentation under uncertainty is Fuzzy C-Means (FCM) clustering, which allows each consumer to belong to multiple clusters with varying degrees of membership. Unlike traditional K-Means segmentation that forces exclusivity, FCM acknowledges the hybrid nature of modern consumer identities. A Bangkok premium car buyer, for instance, may simultaneously align with both "tech-driven innovators" and "aesthetic experience seekers," depending on context and mood. This flexible segmentation reflects the multifaceted character of sensory preference and better informs personalized marketing strategies. Using a dataset of 400 Bangkok-based premium car consumers, fuzzy clustering can generate multidimensional sensory preference maps that link personality traits and demographic profiles to optimal AR experience configurations—enabling marketers to forecast how combinations of sensory stimuli (color saturation, audio resonance, haptic strength) influence perceived luxury and brand attachment.

Furthermore, the integration of soft computing methods such as evolutionary optimization, genetic algorithms, and fuzzy reinforcement learning enhances system adaptability under real-time uncertainty. In practice, sensory feedback data—particularly those related to emotion detection or AR engagement duration—are often incomplete, noisy, or influenced by environmental factors like lighting, background noise, or network latency. Evolutionary optimization can be employed to evolve fuzzy rule sets that maximize engagement metrics over time, while fuzzy reinforcement learning enables the system to autonomously experiment with varying sensory intensities and learn optimal configurations through reward-based adaptation. These models can, for instance, learn that increasing ambient engine sound within a certain decibel range improves attention but beyond a threshold induces discomfort, thereby achieving balance between sensory stimulation and cognitive comfort.

Crucially, this adaptive modeling framework transforms AR marketing from a one-way broadcasting tool into an intelligent co-creative system—a system that perceives, learns, and evolves in response to each consumer's unique psychological and emotional fingerprint. Through the synergy of machine learning and fuzzy logic, the marketing process becomes not only data-driven but also emotionally aware and contextually fluid. This enables a higher level of personalization than traditional recommendation systems or demographic targeting, aligning sensory presentation with individual affective responses in real time.

In the case of the Bangkok automotive market, where consumers exhibit high sensitivity to brand aesthetics and innovation, this approach allows marketers to design AR-driven sensory experiences that feel simultaneously luxurious, intuitive, and personally relevant. As the neuro-fuzzy system refines its inference accuracy with more interaction data, it effectively learns the "language of human sensation" and converts it into adaptive marketing intelligence. The result is a living marketing ecosystem—self-correcting, culturally responsive, and capable of delivering multisensory experiences that resonate with local consumer expectations while maintaining global brand consistency.

The fusion of fuzzy logic and machine learning thus represents not just a technical enhancement but a strategic evolution in marketing science. It operationalizes the abstract domain of human perception, turning affective and sensory responses into measurable, optimizable variables. Such integration lays the foundation for next-generation AR marketing systems that understand ambiguity, embrace complexity, and cultivate emotional resonance as a quantifiable component of the consumer decision-making process.

6 Integrative Framework for ML-Driven Multisensory AR

The proposed conceptual framework establishes an integrative model that unites personal factors, multisensory inputs, and machine learning–driven adaptive modeling to predict and enhance consumer engagement outcomes within an AR marketing environment. It positions machine learning not merely as a computational tool but as an intelligent mediator that continuously translates human perception into actionable marketing intelligence.

At the input stage, the framework captures three categories of data: (1) demographic and psychographic variables—including age, education, occupation, lifestyle, and purchasing motivation—that reflect consumers' intrinsic characteristics; (2) sensory preference metrics, representing individual sensitivity and responsiveness to visual, auditory, tactile, olfactory, and gustatory stimuli; and (3) emotional feedback data, gathered through biometric sensors, facial expression recognition, or sentiment analysis derived from consumer interactions within AR environments. These multidimensional inputs collectively form a rich behavioral dataset, enabling the system to infer how various sensory combinations influence perception and engagement.

The processing component operates through a hybrid architecture of FIS and adaptive neuro-fuzzy modeling (ANFIS). Fuzzy inference allows the system to translate imprecise human language and subjective sensations—such as "moderately exciting," "slightly too bright," or "highly luxurious"—into computable variables, maintaining the fluidity and ambiguity inherent in human perception. The neuro-fuzzy layer, meanwhile, continuously learns from accumulated interaction data, refining the fuzzy rules and membership functions through supervised and reinforcement learning algorithms. This iterative feedback mechanism transforms the AR marketing platform into a self-optimizing system capable of dynamically adjusting sensory stimuli to maximize emotional resonance and engagement quality.

The output layer represents the tangible marketing outcomes produced by the adaptive modeling process. These include measurable improvements in consumer attention, immersion, perceived brand quality, and purchase intention. The framework posits that effective engagement emerges not from static sensory design but from continuous sensory recalibration—a process in which the AR system fine-tunes multisensory experiences in real time, guided by predictive machine learning models and contextual feedback. In this sense, the framework conceptualizes consumer engagement as an adaptive cycle rather than a one-time behavioral outcome.

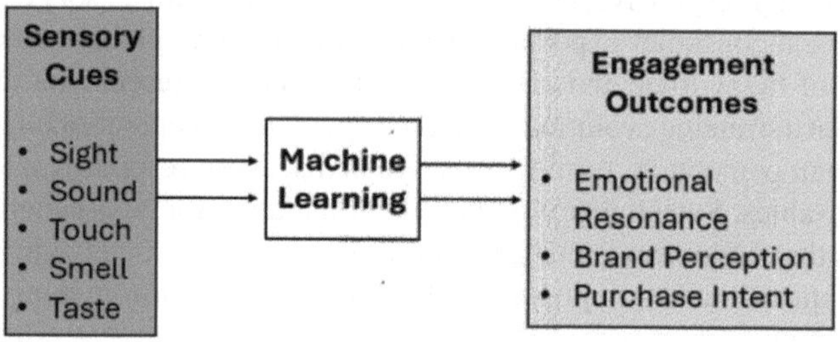

Fig. 1. ML-driven framework linking sensory cues to engagement

Figure 1 illustrates this integrative feedback loop, in which machine learning functions as the optimization engine linking sensory cues to consumer engagement outcomes. The system constantly monitors behavioral and emotional data, updates its inference models, and readjusts the sensory presentation accordingly. This cyclical process ensures that each interaction contributes to greater personalization accuracy and emotional depth. Over time, the adaptive loop creates a learning ecosystem that captures both short-term affective responses and long-term behavioral tendencies, aligning marketing communication with the consumer's evolving perceptual and psychological profile.

Ultimately, this framework highlights that engagement optimization in AR marketing is inherently dynamic. The system does not merely react to consumer behavior but learns and anticipates it, reshaping sensory experiences in anticipation of changing preferences or attention levels. This capability represents the next frontier in AI-driven marketing intelligence, where sensory design, emotional analytics, and adaptive computation converge to produce personalized, emotionally congruent brand experiences. The integration of fuzzy logic and neuro-adaptive learning ensures interpretability, robustness, and scalability, offering a scientifically grounded pathway for deploying intelligent AR marketing systems capable of evolving with their users.

7 Challenges and Future Research Directions

The integration of machine learning, fuzzy logic, and augmented reality for multisensory marketing presents both significant opportunities and profound challenges that require critical reflection. While the proposed adaptive framework offers a promising pathway toward hyper-personalized consumer experiences, several technical, ethical, and cultural limitations must be addressed to ensure sustainable and responsible implementation in real-world marketing environments.

A primary concern lies in the collection, management, and ethical governance of data. Multisensory AR marketing systems depend on vast and varied datasets encompassing emotional responses, behavioral patterns, and biometric feedback such as facial expressions, gaze tracking, and physiological indicators. These forms of data are inherently sensitive, as they reveal not only explicit preferences but also implicit emotional states and cognitive patterns. Consequently, ensuring transparency, informed consent, anonymization, and secure data handling becomes paramount. Beyond conventional anonymization methods, emerging privacy-preserving machine learning techniques—such as federated learning, differential privacy, and homomorphic encryption—should be adapted for AR-driven sensory analytics. Future research must therefore explore how such privacy-preserving algorithms can be efficiently integrated into consumer-facing AR platforms without compromising personalization accuracy or system responsiveness.

Equally important is the technological integration challenge of synchronizing multiple sensory modalities within real-time AR environments. Achieving coherence between visual, auditory, haptic, and potentially olfactory or gustatory stimuli demands ultra-low latency, high-resolution rendering, and adaptive streaming capabilities. The current limitations of mobile hardware and wireless bandwidth may constrain the scalability of high-fidelity sensory simulations. A promising solution lies in hybrid cloud-edge architectures, where computationally intensive ML and fuzzy inference tasks are offloaded to cloud servers while latency-sensitive processes—such as real-time gesture recognition or haptic feedback—are handled locally on edge devices. Future implementations could also benefit from quantum-inspired optimization and neuromorphic computing to reduce delay and improve parallel processing for complex multisensory interactions.

Another critical dimension involves cultural and contextual sensitivity. Sensory preferences are not universal; they are shaped by sociocultural norms, climatic conditions, and aesthetic traditions. For example, Thai consumers may exhibit a greater preference for vibrant color palettes, dynamic soundscapes, and a warm tonal range reflecting tropical aesthetics and collectivist cultural tendencies. In contrast, Western consumers often gravitate toward minimalist designs, muted tones, and subdued auditory elements consistent with individualistic cultural values. Such differences imply that one-size-fits-all sensory models are insufficient. Future studies should develop cross cultural fuzzy models capable of capturing and adapting to these localized sensory expectations. This could be achieved by training region-specific sensory datasets and employing transfer learning to balance global generalizability with local cultural relevance.

Furthermore, the evaluation and validation of multisensory marketing effectiveness remains an open challenge [10]. Traditional digital marketing metrics—such as click-through rate, time on site, or purchase conversion—provide limited insight into the depth of sensory engagement or emotional resonance. As multisensory marketing evolves into an experience-centered paradigm, new multi-dimensional engagement metrics must be formulated [11]. Potential constructs include a Sensory Congruence Index (measuring the alignment between stimuli and brand identity), an Emotional Immersion Score (capturing the depth and persistence of affective response), and an AR Satisfaction Level (reflecting perceived realism, enjoyment, and interactivity). These indices could be computed through neuro-fuzzy weighting models, which integrate both objective physiological measures (e.g., EEG, galvanic skin response) and subjective self-reports.

From a research design standpoint, the field must also address longitudinal and ecological validity. Most current AR and sensory marketing studies rely on short-term experimental exposure under controlled laboratory conditions. Future research should employ longitudinal field studies that observe how consumers interact with adaptive AR systems over extended periods in naturalistic settings—such as dealerships, trade shows, or virtual retail environments. This approach would enable the modeling of temporal adaptation effects, capturing how sensory fatigue, novelty decay, and learning curves influence engagement dynamics.

Finally, the convergence of AI ethics, marketing strategy, and consumer psychology introduces interdisciplinary challenges that call for collaborative inquiry. Questions concerning algorithmic bias, emotional manipulation, and the potential commodification of sensory experience must be confronted directly. Responsible innovation frameworks and AI ethics guidelines tailored to marketing applications will be essential for ensuring that personalization does not evolve into intrusion. Future scholars and practitioners must therefore aim to balance technological innovation with ethical stewardship, ensuring that adaptive sensory marketing enhances consumer well-being rather than exploiting perceptual vulnerabilities.

8 Conclusions

This paper demonstrates that the convergence of machine learning, fuzzy logic, and multisensory augmented reality presents a transformative opportunity for the automotive marketing industry. Through adaptive sensory modeling, brands can achieve higher engagement, deeper emotional resonance, and stronger purchase intent. The Bangkok premium car market illustrates the potential and complexity of such systems—balancing data-driven personalization with cultural sensitivity and ethical responsibility.

Future research should move toward empirical validation using real-time AR engagement data, advanced fuzzy clustering for sensory segmentation, and integration with wearable biosensors to capture authentic emotional states. By bridging the gap between AI intelligence and human experience, ML-driven multisensory AR marketing represents not only an innovation in technology but also a redefinition of digital empathy in consumer-brand relationships.

References

1. Elder, R.S., Krishna, A.: The effects of advertising copy on sensory thoughts and perceived taste. J. Consum. Res. **36**(5), 748–756 (2010). https://doi.org/10.1086/605327

2. Krishna, A.: An integrative review of sensory marketing: engaging the senses to affect perception, judgment, and behavior. J. Consum. Psychol. **22**(3), 332–351 (2012). https://doi.org/10.1016/j.jcps.2011.08.003
3. Peck, J., Childers, T.L.: To have and to hold: the influence of haptic information on product judgments. J. Mark. **67**(2), 35–48 (2003). https://doi.org/10.1509/jmkg.67.2.35.18612
4. Spence, C., Gallace, A.: Multisensory design: reaching out to touch the consumer. Psychol. Mark. **28**(3), 267–308 (2011). https://doi.org/10.1002/mar.20392
5. Kerdvibulvech, C., Guan, S.-U.: Affective computing for enhancing affective touch-based communication through extended reality. In: ICCSA 2019, Part II, Communications in Computer and Information Science, pp. 351–360. Springer, Cham (2019)
6. Kerdvibulvech, C.: Recent multimodal communication methodologies in phonology, vision, and touch. In: Kurosu, M. (eds.) Human-Computer Interaction. Multimodal and Natural Interaction. HCII 2020. Lecture Notes in Computer Science(), vol. 12182. Springer, Cham (2020). https://doi.org/10.1007/978-3-030-49062-1_27
7. Kothari, S.: Impact of sensory marketing on brand loyalty and consumers' purchase intention. Int. J. Bus. Global. **33**(2), 124–143 (2024). https://doi.org/10.1504/IJBG.2024.142437
8. Mai, N.T.B., Nguyen, N.Y.T., Vu, H.N.T.: Multi-sensory marketing and impulsive buying behavior: the role of impulsive buying traits. Emerg. Sci. J. 8(5), 1764–1782 (2024). https://doi.org/10.28991/ESJ-2024-08-05-05
9. Pal, D., Srivastava, K., Gupta, N.: Sensory marketing: the mediating role of hedonic emotions between multisensory experiences and mall patronage intention. Asia Pac. J. Mark. Logist. **37**(5), 711–734 (2024). https://doi.org/10.1108/APJML-03-2024-0417
10. Tran, V.A.: How sensory marketing affects perceived service quality and customer behavior. J. Health Organ. Manag. (2025). https://doi.org/10.1108/JHOM-03-2024-0125
11. Rodríguez-Ulcuango, O.M.: Sensorial marketing within consumer behavior: a comprehensive framework. Sci. J. Econ. Manag. Res. (2025). https://doi.org/10.1080/23311975.2025.2503422

Longitudinal Data for Health Insurance Purchase Behavior Among Older Adults in Thailand Using Machine Learning Methods

Wanissara Chongchai(✉) and Wannaporn Junthopas

Department of Statistics, Faculty of Science, Khon Kaen University, Khon Kaen, Thailand
wanissara.cc@kkumail.com, wannju@kku.ac.th

Abstract. The aim of this study is to investigate machine learning approaches using three classification models: decision tree, random forest, and gradient boosting. The analysis is based on longitudinal data regarding health insurance purchasing behavior among older adults in Thailand from Health, Aging, and Retirement (HART) in Thailand surveys conducted in 2015, 2017, 2020, and 2022. Data preprocessing included creating new variable codes for insurance purchase and disease groups, correcting data anomalies, and imputing missing values using the Multiple Imputation by Chained Equations (MICE) approach. The three classification methods were performed within the scikit-longitudinal (SKlong) framework. Model performance was evaluated on a test dataset of 2,152 items using weighted-average precision, recall, and F1-score. The results indicate that the gradient boosting method achieved the highest performance with an F1-score of 0.89. Moreover, the SHAP analysis revealed the variables of life satisfaction, demographics, health and disease-related criteria, employment status serves as a significant predictor of health insurance purchase behavior. These findings suggest that ensemble learning techniques are suitable for longitudinal data analysis and can be applied to policy planning or the design of targeted health insurance products.

Keywords: Health Insurance · Longitudinal Data · Scikit-Longitudinal · Machine Learning · SHAP

1 Introduction

The fundamental principle of insurance is the transfer of risk from the insured to the insurance company, which compensates for losses according to the policy terms when unforeseen events occur, while the insured pays premiums in exchange. Health insurance is focused on covering medical expenses arising from illness and accidents. Since people can be exposed to increasingly greater health risks due to continual changes in the environment and lifestyle, health insurance has become crucial for ensuring life security. According to the TQM Life Insurance Broker [1], young adults (aged 21–35 years old) are advised to obtain health insurance that allows for tax deductions, whereas middle-aged adults (aged 36–60 years old) are often recommended to have health insurance alongside life insurance to ensure continuous and sustainable coverage. In addition,

C. Xu (Ed.): ICMLSC 2026, CCIS 2948, pp. 210–222, 2027.
https://doi.org/10.1007/978-981-92-1546-1_17

health insurance for older adults can help to reduce medical expenses. On the other hand, insurance companies face challenges in setting appropriate terms and premiums because older adults have higher health risks and require more frequent medical care [2]. Therefore, using appropriate models for determining consumer behavior concerning whether to "purchase" or "not purchase" health insurance is important from both the consumers' and the insurers' perspectives.

Previous studies on modeling health insurance purchasing behavior have revealed several insights. Astari and Kismiantini [3] utilized the Indonesia Family Life Survey data to develop a Binary Logistic Regression model to analyze factors influencing health insurance purchasing behavior; their results indicate that age, occupation, education, and marital status are significant factors in the decision to purchase. In South Africa, Mavundla et al. [4] applied machine learning methods, including random forest, K-Nearest Neighbor, XGBoost, and logistic regression, to identify potential health insurance purchasers; they found that Random Forest achieved the best performance with an accuracy of 0.99 and an F1-score of 1.00. In Thailand, Yupadee Angjarusila [5] examined factors affecting supplementary health insurance among civil servants and permanent employees at Chulalongkorn University using a logit model and discovered that marital status, income, age, and healthcare utilization behavior were important factors in the decision to buy health insurance. In addition, Chanita Hangkaew et al. [6] studied factors influencing insurance type selection by comparing multinomial logistic regression, discriminant analysis, decision tree, and Artificial Neural Network (ANN) methods; they reported that the ANN model performed best with an accuracy of 85.75%.

Most studies in Thailand have relied on traditional statistical analyses, such as group difference analysis [7, 8] and logistic regression [5, 9]. In contrast, the application of machine learning techniques for health insurance classification has been limited [6]. Therefore, this study focused on utilizing data from the Health, Aging, and Retirement in Thailand (HART) project, a longitudinal database comprising demographic information, health status, healthcare utilization, and economic conditions. The aim of the research was to develop classification models to predict health insurance purchasing behavior among late adult to older adult populations in Thailand. To this end, machine learning techniques were applied to identify the most effective predictive model. We anticipate that this study will provide practical benefits for insurance companies in designing more targeted and effective sales strategies.

2 Related Work

2.1 Studies on Health Insurance Purchase in Domestic and International Contexts

In Thailand, Yupadee [5] examined factors affecting supplementary health insurance among civil servants and permanent employees and discovered that age, marital status, household income, and healthcare utilization behavior were significant factors; a logit model was used that achieved a prediction accuracy of 89.61%. Chanita et al. [6] studied the selection of insurance types by comparing multinomial logistic regression, discriminant analysis, decision tree, and ANN methods; their results indicate that the latter was the most effective model for classification by achieving an accuracy of 85.75%. Internationally, Astari and Kismiantini [3] investigated factors influencing health insurance ownership in Indonesia using a binary logistic regression model; their analysis indicates that age, occupation, education, and marital status were significant factors, albeit the predictive accuracy was only 56.5%. Mavundla et al. [4] developed machine learning models to predict the likelihood of purchasing additional health insurance products using a large customer dataset. Four models: random forest, K-Nearest Neighbor (KNN), XGBoost, and logistic regression were compared, with random forest achieving the best performance with an accuracy of 0.99 and an F1-score of 1.00. Machine learning research in Thailand examining health insurance behavior using longitudinal data has not been extensively studied. This study addresses that gap by applying machine learning models within a longitudinal framework, demonstrating how temporal patterns across multiple waves can improve predictive insight beyond cross-sectional approaches.

2.2 Studies Using Longitudinal Data

In this context, van Allen et al. [10] predicted functional limitations among older adults using the Canadian Longitudinal Study on Aging dataset; after applying logistic regression, XGBoost, random forest, naïve Bayes, and neural networks, they found that logistic regression achieved the highest balanced accuracy of 81.9%. Hu and Szymczak [11] reviewed the application of random forest for longitudinal data and proposed the Mixed Effects Regression Tree (MERT) and Mixed Effects Regression Forest (MERF) approaches, both of which can effectively handle repeated measures and reduce overfitting issues. Ribeiro and Freitas [12, 13] introduced a Lexicographic Bi-Objective approach for decision tree and random forest models that can account for the time index of longitudinal data, thereby improving prediction accuracy when applied to longitudinal datasets such as The English Longitudinal Study of Ageing (ELSA).

Both statistical and machine learning methods have been employed in the context of predicting health insurance purchasing patterns, with approaches tailored for longitudinal data having emerged recently. Aligning with this, the objective of the present study is to utilize machine learning on longitudinal data to develop the most accurate predictive models for health insurance purchasing behavior.

3 Material and Method

We utilized data from the HART project as the database for developing classification models to predict health insurance purchasing behavior. We first selected data for participants who had completed the survey in all of the specified years, after which we handled missing data using the Multiple Imputation by Chained Equations (MICE) approach [14], and the data are fed into classification models within the scikit-longitudinal (SKlong) framework [12, 13, 15–17]. Finally, model performance is evaluated using appropriate metrics, including weighted-average precision, recall, and F1-score. In addition, a feature importance analysis based on SHAP is conducted to identify and evaluate the variables that influence health insurance purchase behavior.

3.1 Data Source

The dataset used in this study was obtained from the HART project, a national survey that collects information on health, aging, and retirement among the Thai population. The project was conducted under the supervision of the Center for Aging Society Research, National Institute of Development Administration. The dataset covers the years 2015, 2017, 2020, and 2022 [18–21], representing repeated measurements of the same participants over time (longitudinal data). The survey targeted individuals aged 45 years and older via sampling households in 13 provinces, Thailand. In-depth data were collected on demographics, economic status, health, employment status, and life satisfaction for a total of 2,688 participants.

As the dataset contains personal information, we obtained permission to use it from the managing agency and adhered to human research ethics: The Human Research Ethics Committee of the National Institute for Development Administration (ECNIDA 2022/0064), including strict confidentiality of the participants' data. In this study, the dependent variable is the health insurance purchase behavior of late-adult to older adult participants in Thailand. The study includes 29 independent variables: 4 on demographics, 15 on health and disease-related criteria, 4 on healthcare utilization, 1 on employment status, and 5 on life satisfaction. Dataset description is provided in Table 1.

3.2 Data Preprocessing

We used complete longitudinal data for 2,688 cases (i.e., participants who had provided complete information for all four survey years). The scikit-longitudinal (SKlong) framework requires continuous data over time to accurately and efficiently capture the characteristics of longitudinal data. The following data preprocessing steps were performed to ensure data quality and readiness for model development:

Dependent Variable Processing: An encoding scheme was created for the dependent variable health insurance purchase to align with the research objectives. In the raw data, purchases were recorded either as self-purchased or purchased by other household members or relatives. Respondents were encoded as "purchase" if insurance was acquired in either case and "non-purchase" if no insurance was purchased in both cases.

Independent Variable Processing: For the independent variables, inconsistent or illogical entries were handled first. Categorical variables, such as gender and education level, were imputed using the mode. Logical consistency checks were performed (e.g., for the number of children, where the reported number increased over the years despite respondents being older adults). Health and disease variables were grouped based on body system classification [23] into 10 main categories: 1) cardiovascular, 2) endocrine and nutritional, 3) digestive, 4) genitourinary, 5) respiratory, 6) nervous system, 7) musculoskeletal, 8) cancer, 9) eye disorders, and 10) ear disorders. Since many of the independent variables contained missing values across health and disease, healthcare utilization, employment status, and life satisfaction variables, Multiple Imputation by Chained Equations (MICE) [14] was applied to impute the missing values. This is achieved by sequentially fitting regression models for each variable based on the other variables, and predictions are randomly drawn multiple times to create several imputed datasets. The strength of MICE lies in its ability to preserve statistical relationships between variables and reduce bias that could arise from directly deleting missing data.

Table 1. Dataset description

Data Category	Data item (Variable)	Value
Dependent variable	Y: Health purchase behavior	0 - not purchased, 1 - purchased
Demographics	D1: Gender D2: Age range D3: Highest level of education D4: Number of children	0 - male, 1 - female 1 - 45 to 59, 2 - 60 to 69, 3 - 70 to 79, 4 - ≥ 80 1 - no formal education, 2 - primary school, 3 - secondary school, 4 - vocational certificate, 5 - associate degree, 6 - bachelor's degree, 7 - master/doctoral degree 0–13
Health and disease -related criteria	H1: Weight (kg.)	25–175
	H2: Alcohol drinking	0 - no, 1 - yes
	H3: Physical exercise	0 - no, 1 - yes
	H4: Smoking	0 - no, 1 - yes
	H5: Annual health check-up	0 - no, 1 - yes
	H6: Cardiovascular	0 - no, 1 - yes
	H7: Endocrine and nutritional	0 - no, 1 - yes
	H8: Digestive	0 - no, 1 - yes
	H9: Genitourinary	0 - no, 1 - yes
	H10: Respiratory	0 - no, 1 - yes
	H11: Nervous system	0 - no, 1 - yes
	H12: Musculoskeletal	0 - no, 1 - yes
	H13: Cancer	0 - no, 1 - yes
	H14: Eye disorders	0 - no, 1 - yes
	H15: Ear disorders	0 - no, 1 - yes
Healthcare Utilization	U1: Utilization of inpatient services	0 - no, 1 - yes
	U2: Utilization of outpatient polyclinic services	0 - no, 1 - yes
	U3: Utilization of outpatient services at hospital	0 - no, 1 - yes
	U4: Utilization of Outpatient services at health center	0 - no, 1 - yes
Employment Status	E1: Status of work	0 - no, 1 - yes
Life Satisfaction	L1: Economic satisfaction	1–10
	L2: Body satisfaction	1–10
	L3: Relationship satisfaction with children	1–10
	L4: Relationship satisfaction with spouse	1–10
	L5: Overall quality of life	1–10

3.3 Classification Models

We utilized the SKlong framework, which is an extension of scikit-learn designed to handle longitudinal data [12, 13]. Unlike standard scikit-learn, SKlong is structured to accommodate longitudinal data and employs learning methods that consider correlations between measurements at different time points, thereby enabling the models to better capture the dynamics of the data. Three primary tree-based learning models widely used for handling complex datasets were selected for this study: decision tree [15], random forest [16], and gradient boosting [17].

3.4 Performance Evaluation

To evaluate the model performance, the dataset was split into two parts: 80% (2,152 cases) for the training set and 20% (536 cases) for the test set. This split enables assessing the model's ability to learn from a portion of the data and testing its predictive capability on unseen data. The metric used to evaluate model performance in this study was the F1-score, which is the harmonic mean of Precision and Recall. Given that the dataset is imbalanced, with a substantially larger number of non-purchasers than purchasers [24], the F1-score provides a more accurate assessment than other metrics. It considers both the correctness of classifying "purchase" cases (Precision) and the completeness of identifying all "purchase" cases (Recall). Consequently, models with a higher F1-score can handle imbalanced data better. Following the selection of the best performing model, a feature importance analysis based on SHAP will be conducted to identify and evaluate the variables that influence the decision to purchase health insurance.

4 Results

In the analysis of 2,688 older adults who responded to all four survey waves, we first examined demographic characteristics and key variables to provide an overview of the sample. Most participants were 1,468 female (54.61%), while males numbered 1,220 (45.39%). Regarding health insurance purchasing behavior, most older adults had not purchased health insurance, with the number of purchasers decreasing over time: 321 purchases and 2,367 non-purchasers in 2015, 258 purchasers and 2,430 non-purchasers in 2017, 140 purchasers and 2,548 non-purchasers in 2020, and 92 purchasers and 2,596 non-purchasers in 2022. The descriptive statistics for health insurance purchasing behavior by year were summarized in Table 2.

Regarding the average score for quantitative variables summarized in Table 3, older adults' weight remained relatively stable across the four survey waves (mean: 58.28–58.93 kg). Among the satisfaction variables (scored out of 10), satisfaction with their bodies remained high and relatively stable (mean: 7.30–7.58), as did economic satisfaction (mean: 6.40–6.82), and relationships with spouses and children (means of 8.42–8.63 and 8.63–8.75, respectively). In addition, overall quality of life remained relatively stable (mean: 7.73–8.04).

As summarized in Table 4, the prevalence of different disease groups varied across the survey years. Cardiovascular diseases showed a continuous increase from 36.35%

in 2015 to 48.40% in 2022, indicating a rising trend in this condition among older adults. Endocrine and nutritional disorders increased from 14.29% in 2015 to 18.68% in 2022. Gastrointestinal diseases remained relatively low but showed a slight increase from 0.60% in 2015 to 2.57% in 2022. Cancer prevalence remained relatively stable, ranging between 1.56% and 2.19% over the years. Reproductive, urinary, and renal system disorders were notably higher, especially in 2017 and 2020, with prevalence rates of 83.37% and 85.57%, respectively. Respiratory and neurological diseases were consistently below 3% but showed a slight increase in 2022. Musculoskeletal disorders increased from 6.88% in 2015 to 11.57% in 2022. Eye disorders, while initially high at 71.47% in 2015, decreased to 50.26% in 2020 before rising again to 56.58% in 2022. Ear-related disorders declined from 26.12% in 2015 to 18.23% in 2022. These trends highlight changes in the health profile of older adults over time.

Table 2. Descriptive statistics for health insurance purchasing behavior by year

Variable	Year			
	2015	2017	2020	2022
Health Insurance Purchase (n = 2,688 per year)				
Purchased	321	258	140	92
Not purchased	2,367	2,430	2,548	2,596

Table 3. The average score for quantitative variables by year

Variable	Year			
	2015	2017	2020	2022
Weight (kg)	58.93	58.32	58.28	58.28
Satisfaction (0–10)				
Body	7.45	7.30	7.56	7.58
Economic	6.67	6.52	6.40	6.82
Relationship with spouse	8.45	8.60	8.63	8.42
Relationship with children	8.63	8.69	8.75	8.65
Overall Quality of Life	8.04	7.73	7.93	8.02

The classification results using the SKlong framework demonstrated the performance of Decision Tree, Random Forest, and Gradient Boosting in predicting health insurance purchasing behavior among older adults. Table 5 provides the weighted-average metric results, including F1-score, Precision, and Recall.

With the test set, the decision tree model yielded performance metric values of weighted-average precision = 0.86, recall = 0.96, and F1-score = 0.86. The high recall of

Table 4. Prevalence of disease groups (%) by year

Disease Group	Year							
	2015		2017		2020		2022	
	Yes	No	Yes	No	Yes	No	Yes	No
Cardiovascular	36.35	63.65	41.07	58.93	47.21	52.79	48.4	51.60
Nutrition	14.29	85.71	14.88	85.12	19.16	80.84	18.68	81.32
Gastrointestinal	0.6	99.4	0.71	99.29	1.79	98.21	2.57	97.43
Cancer	1.79	98.21	1.56	98.44	2.01	97.99	2.19	97.81
Reproductive & Urinary/Renal	7.31	92.69	83.37	16.63	85.57	14.43	84.71	15.29
Respiratory	0.82	99.18	1.64	98.36	1.75	98.25	1.53	98.47
Neurological	1.26	98.74	1.53	98.47	1.67	98.33	2.19	97.81
Musculoskeletal	6.88	93.12	8.37	91.63	7.59	92.41	11.57	88.43
Eye disorders	71.47	28.53	69.2	30.8	50.26	49.74	56.58	43.42
Ear disorders	26.12	73.88	25.26	74.74	13.02	86.98	18.23	81.77

0.96 indicates that the model could accurately identify almost all individuals who did not purchase health insurance. However, the Precision of 0.86 suggests that some cases were misclassified as "purchase" or "non-purchase." This is due to the nature of Decision Trees in overfitting the training set, which can cause them to classify the majority class (non-purchase) well, but with a higher chance of misclassifying the minority class (purchase).

The random forest model achieved weighted-average precision = 0.89, recall = 0.92, and F1-score = 0.88. The higher precision and F1-score compared to the decision tree indicate a reduction in errors and overfitting, leading to a more balanced classification of both purchasers and non-purchasers. The recall of 0.92 indicates that the model can also correctly identify a high proportion of non-purchasers, while the Precision of 0.89 indicates a slight improvement in classification accuracy compared to the Decision Tree.

The gradient boosting model attained performance metric values of weighted-average precision = 0.89, recall = 0.92, and F1-score = 0.89: they are comparable to those for random forest but with the highest F1-score among the three models, which reflects the model's ability to classify both purchasers and non-purchasers in a balanced manner, despite the unequal group proportions. This indicates that Gradient Boosting sequentially learns the complexity of imbalanced data more effectively than the other two methods.

This study utilizes SHAP (SHapley Additive exPlanations) to interpret the influence of each independent variable on health insurance purchasing behavior. The features are ranked on the primary y-axis in descending order of their relative importance, indicating their contribution to the model's prediction. The x-axis displays the SHAP values for each feature. The color represents whether the feature is high (in red) or low (blue) for prediction. The top ten most influential variables affecting health insurance purchases, namely: 1) L1: economic satisfaction, 2) L5: overall quality of life, 3) D2: age range, 4) H1: weight, 5) L2: body satisfaction, 6) L3: relationship satisfaction with children, 7) E1:

Table 5. Performance of the model

Model Classification	Precision	Recall	F1-score
Decision Tree	0.86	0.96	0.86
Random Forest	0.89	0.92	0.88
Gradient Boosting	0.89	0.92	0.89

status of work, 8) H6: cardiovascular, 9) H3: physical exercise, and 10) L4: relationship satisfaction with spouse, respectively. The high value of feature importance of economic satisfaction and overall quality of life have negative SHAP values. While age range has a positive SHAP value for the health insurance purchase class. Weight has a low value of feature importance which has a positive SHAP value. Body satisfaction has a positive SHAP value. Relationship satisfaction with children has a negative SHAP value. Status of work have a positive SHAP value. Cardiovascular and physical exercise have negative SHAP value. And relationship satisfaction with a spouse exhibited quite positive SHAP value. Figure 1 provides the result of SHAP summary plot for gradient boosting (the top twenty influential predictor variables).

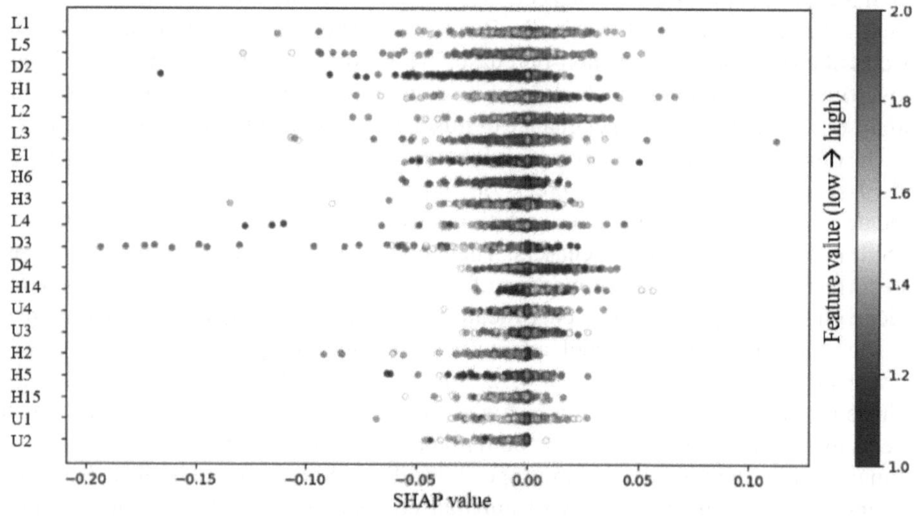

Fig. 1. SHAP Summary Plot for Gradient Boosting (the top twenty influential variables). L1: Economic satisfaction, L5: Overall quality of life, D2: Age range, H1: Weight (kg.), L2: Body satisfaction, L3: Relationship satisfaction with children, E1: Status of work, H6: Cardiovascular, H3: Physical exercise, L4: Relationship satisfaction with spouse, D3: Highest level of education, D4: Number of children, H14: Eye disorders, U4: Utilization of Outpatient services at health center, U3: Utilization of outpatient services at hospital, H2: Alcohol drinking, H5: Annual health check-up, H15: Ear disorders, U1: Utilization of inpatient services, U2: Utilization of outpatient polyclinic services.

5 Discussion

The gradient boosting model using the SKlong framework demonstrated the highest performance in classifying health insurance purchasing behavior among elderly participants who completed all four annual waves. This enables it to capture the complexities of longitudinal data that change over time more effectively than random forest and decision tree, respectively. This aligns with the studies of [12] and [13], which suggested the Lexicographic Bi-objective approach for longitudinal data, enabling models to prioritize the most recent and important features. They recommended that using the random forest method would be better than the decision tree method. While the study of [3] applied binary logistic regression to predict health insurance ownership in Indonesia; their model achieved a prediction accuracy of 56.5%, which is considerably lower than our gradient boosting model. This highlights that machine learning and ensemble methods can significantly improve predictive performance over traditional statistical methods, especially in cases of imbalanced data and multiple independent variables. Other work with large samples of [4], found very high accuracy using random forest; however, our findings show that gradient boosting performs more consistently and effectively on a smaller longitudinal dataset.

In the context of research in Thailand, the study of [5] and [6] utilized independent variables similar to those in our study regarding demographics. Additionally, [5] included behavior and health variables comparable to the disease variables in our work. However, our study extends this scope by investigating life satisfaction. Moreover, unlike previous works based on cross-sectional data, our study is conducted using longitudinal data. Our gradient boosting model applied to longitudinal data, demonstrating both the added value of ensemble learning and the benefits of incorporating repeated-measures information.

Our results are also consistent with approaches in other longitudinal research [10, 12, 13], emphasizing the efficacy of repeated-measures data analysis. Gradient Boosting can integrate multi-year data effectively and prioritize the most recent information for the participants. The SHAP analysis results indicate that age is a significant predictor of health insurance purchases, which aligns with previous research [5, 6]. However, the age ranges studied may differ from those in this study. Meanwhile, the life satisfaction variables, which have not been extensively studied before, were found to be influential. All of life satisfaction variables have an impact on the decision to purchase health insurance, particularly the variables of economic satisfaction and overall quality of life.

The use of SKlong improves accuracy and reduces bias caused by ignoring temporal order, thereby ensuring that results better reflect the actual participant behavior. In addition, considering independent variables related to insurance purchasing, such as age, income, health, and chronic conditions, gradient boosting handles multidimensional and nonlinear relationships more effectively than decision tree [15] or traditional logistic regression, and is consistent with MERT/MERF approaches [11].

The longitudinal SHAP patterns suggest that insurance purchasing decisions may be triggered by changes in life-satisfaction and worsening health conditions over time. Our results imply that behaviors are dynamic: individuals who initially do not purchase insurance may later do so in response to health deterioration or financial uncertainty.

This temporal pattern underscores the need for targeted, stage-based insurance communication. Policymakers and insurers should intervene during key transition periods, such as after a new diagnosis, retirement, or a reported decline in life satisfaction.

6 Conclusions

This study focused on examining health insurance purchasing behavior among the elderly in Thailand using data from the HART project collected in 2015, 2017, 2020, and 2022. The sample comprised 2,688 participants aged 45 years old and above who completed all four waves. The raw data were preprocessed by creating new variable codes, grouping diseases, managing inconsistencies in independent variables, and handling missing data using MICE to ensure suitability for analysis using the SKlong framework. The results from testing decision tree, random forest, and gradient boosting models show that the latter achieved the highest performance, with a weighted-average precision of 0.89, recall of 0.92, and F1-score of 0.89 on the test set of 2,152 participants (172 purchasers and 1,980 non-purchasers). These indicate that the model can classify both purchasers and non-purchasers in a balanced manner, despite the evident class imbalance. The feature importance analysis based on SHAP revealed the top ten most influential variables affecting health insurance purchases: one variable of demographics (age range), three variables of health and disease-related criteria (weight, cardiovascular, physical exercise), a variable of employment status (status of work), all of five variables of life satisfaction (economic satisfaction, overall quality of life, body satisfaction, relationship satisfaction with children, relationship satisfaction with spouse). Meanwhile, the variables in the healthcare utilization category did not have any impact on the prediction.

In summary, the gradient boosting model via SKlong is a highly effective tool for classifying elderly health insurance purchasing behavior. Its key advantages include handling imbalanced data, large longitudinal datasets, and multi-dimensional variables efficiently, providing results applicable for policy analysis or health planning for the elderly. This study demonstrates that Gradient Boosting through the SKlong framework is an effective and suitable approach for classifying health insurance purchasing behavior among the elderly in Thailand. Moreover, the result of SHAP can indicate the influential variables of health insurance purchase. The insights obtained can inform health policy planning, the design of appropriate insurance products, and an understanding of elderly behavior in the context of long-term financial and healthcare planning. Future research directions can focus on various machine learning models (support vector machine, KNN, ANN) and investigate additional explainable variables such as financial status and debt burden, which are challenging to obtain through interviews.

Acknowledgement. The authors are very thankful to Khon Kaen University and Department of Statistics, faculty of science, Khon Kaen University for supporting this work.

References

1. TQM Life Insurance Broker Company Limited: What is the ideal age to purchase health insurance? https://www.tqm.co.th/articles/หมีรักสุขภาพ/ประกันสุขภาพ%20ควรทำตอนอายุเท่าไร? Accessed 01 July 2024. (in Thai)

2. The Thai Life Assurance Association: All About Life Insurance. https://lifeif.or.th/wp-content/uploads/2018/05/รอบรู้เรื่องประกันชีวิต.pdf. Accessed 01 July 2024. (in Thai)
3. Astari, D.W., Kismiantini: Analysis of factors affecting the health insurance ownership with binary logistic regression model. J. Phys. Conf. Ser. **1320**(1), 012011 (2019)
4. Mavundla, K., Thakur, S., Adetiba, E., Abayomi, A.: Predicting cross-selling health insurance products using machine-learning techniques. J. Comput. Inf. Syst., 1–18 (2024)
5. Angjarusila, Y.: Factors influencing the health insurance purchase of government officials and employees of Chulalongkorn University. Chulalongkorn University Theses and Dissertations, no. 32354 (1999)
6. Hangkaew, C., Sinsomboonthong, J., Supapakorn, T.: Prediction of choosing types of insurance for the customers. Huachiew Chalermprakiet Sci. Technol. J. **6**(2), 81–95 (2020). (in Thai)
7. Wilaileart, W., Khamdet, I.: Factors affecting the health insurance purchase decision process of consumers in Bangkok. J. Finance Invest. Mark. Bus. Manag. **4**(1), 595–615 (2014). (in Thai)
8. Thongcharoensukchai, A.: Factors affecting the decision to buy health insurance: a case study of two generations. Thammasat University Thesis (2017)
9. Ketsilp, P.: Factors influencing health insurance purchasing behavior of Generation Y in Pathum Thani Province: A case study of Krungthai-AXA Life Insurance Public Company Limited. Ramkhamhaeng University Theses and Dissertations (2021)
10. van Allen, Z.M., Dionne, N., Boisgontier, M.P.: Prospective classification of functional dependence: insights from machine learning and 39,927 participants in the Canadian Longitudinal Study on Aging. School of Rehabilitation Sciences, Univ. of Ottawa (2024)
11. Hu, J., Szymczak, S.: A review on longitudinal data analysis with random forest. Briefings Bioinf. **24**(2), 1–11 (2023)
12. Ribeiro, C., Freitas, A.: A new random forest method for longitudinal data classification using a lexicographic bi-objective approach. In: IEEE Symposium Series (2020)
13. Ribeiro, C., Freitas, A.A.: A lexicographic optimisation approach to promote more recent features on longitudinal decision-tree-based classifiers: applications to the English longitudinal study of ageing. Artif. Intell. Rev. **57**(4), 84 (2024)
14. Azur, M.J., Stuart, E.A., Frangakis, C., Leaf, P.J.: Multiple imputation by chained equations: what is it and how does it work? Int. J. Methods Psychiatr. Res. **20**(1), 40–49 (2011)
15. Quinlan, J.R.: Induction of decision trees. Mach. Learn. **1**(1), 81–106 (1986)
16. Breiman, L.: Random forests. Mach. Learn. **45**(1), 5–32 (2001)
17. Friedman, J.H.: Greedy function approximation: a gradient boosting machine. Ann. Stat. **29**(5), 1189–1232 (2001)
18. National Institute of Development Administration: Health Aging and Retirement in Thailand (HART), Well-being of the elderly in Thailand (2015). https://hart.nida.ac.th/download-center
19. National Institute of Development Administration: Health Aging and Retirement in Thailand (HART), Well-being of the elderly in Thailand (2017). https://hart.nida.ac.th/download-center
20. National Institute of Development Administration: Health Aging and Retirement in Thailand (HART), Well-being of the elderly in Thailand (2020). https://hart.nida.ac.th/download-center
21. National Institute of Development Administration: Health Aging and Retirement in Thailand (HART), Well-being of the elderly in Thailand (2022). https://hart.nida.ac.th/download-center
22. Little, R.J.A., Rubin, D.B.: Statistical Analysis with Missing Data, 2nd edn. Wiley, Hoboken (2002)
23. Wikipedia: International Statistical Classification of Diseases and Related Health Problems (2025). https://th.wikipedia.org/wiki/InternationalStatisticalClassificationofDiseasesandRelatedHealthProblems. Accessed 5 Mar 2025

24. Chawla, N.V., Bowyer, K.W., Hall, L.O., Kegelmeyer, W.P.: SMOTE: synthetic minority over-sampling technique. J. Artif. Intell. Res. **16**, 321–357 (2002)
25. Althnian, A., et al.: Impact of dataset size on classification performance: an empirical evaluation in the medical domain. Appl. Sci. **11**(2), 796 (2021)

The Role of Artificial Intelligence in Gingivitis Diagnosis: A Scoping Review of Applications, Benefits, and Challenge

Eman Alhablain[1], Nabila Ahmed Sedky[1], and Mohammed Alsuhaibani[2](✉)

[1] Department of Community and Preventive Dentistry, College of Dentistry, Qassim University, Buraydah 51452, Qassim, Saudi Arabia
{451214470,141390}@qu.edu.sa

[2] Department of Computer Science, College of Computer, Qassim University, Buraydah 51452, Qassim, Saudi Arabia
m.suhibani@qu.edu.sa

Abstract. Gingivitis affects a large proportion of the global population, and early detection is critical to preventing progression to severe periodontal disease. Artificial intelligence (AI) has emerged as a promising tool for automated diagnosis and screening. This review examined current applications of AI in gingivitis diagnosis, focusing on technologies, performance, benefits, and implementation challenges. A scoping review was conducted following PRISMA-ScR guidelines, with systematic searches across multiple databases and study selection guided by the PCC framework. Thirteen studies published between 2017 and 2025 were included, 69% of which appeared in the past four years, reflecting accelerating research momentum. Convolutional neural networks dominated, with models ranging from ResNet-50 to Oral-Mamba. Reported performance varied, with accuracy ranging from 77% to 92.5%, the highest achieved through feature fusion. Sensitivity frequently exceeded 90%, while specificity showed broader variability (50–94%). Mobile health applications further demonstrated feasibility for community-based screening. Overall, AI shows strong potential in gingivitis diagnosis, particularly CNN-based approaches achieving high accuracy and sensitivity. Mobile platforms may expand accessibility, but inconsistency in specificity underscores the influence of dataset and model variability. Robust validation, standardized datasets, and multi-center trials are essential to establish reliability and support routine clinical adoption.

Keywords: Gingivitis · Artificial intelligence · Machine Learning · Deep Learning · Convolutional Neural Networks

1 Introduction

Gingivitis represents the most prevalent form of periodontal disease globally [1]. The 2017 World Workshop on the Classification of Periodontal and Peri-Implant Diseases and Conditions defines gingivitis as a plaque-induced inflammatory condition of the

C. Xu (Ed.): ICMLSC 2026, CCIS 2948, pp. 223–233, 2027.
https://doi.org/10.1007/978-981-92-1546-1_18

gingiva characterized by inflammation of gingival tissues surrounding teeth without loss of clinical attachment or alveolar bone support [1, 2]. Clinical manifestations include erythema, edema, bleeding upon gentle probing, and alterations in gingival contour and consistency [2]. The Global Burden of Disease Study 2019 estimated that severe gingivitis affects approximately 1.1 billion individuals worldwide, establishing it as one of the most prevalent health conditions globally [3]. Early detection and management of gingivitis are critical for preventing progression to periodontitis, which affects approximately 11% of the global population [4]. Population-based preventive programs focusing on early gingivitis detection have demonstrated substantial cost savings for healthcare systems while improving overall oral health outcomes [5]. The challenge in early gingivitis detection lies in the frequently subtle and asymptomatic nature of initial inflammatory changes [6]. Traditional clinical examination methods, while effective, are subject to inter-examiner variability and may fail to detect subtle early changes, particularly in clinical settings with time constraints [7]. This limitation underscores the potential value of objective, standardized diagnostic tools that can enhance the accuracy and consistency of gingivitis detection.

The integration of artificial intelligence (AI) into healthcare has revolutionized diagnostic capabilities across multiple medical specialties, with dentistry emerging as a particularly promising field for AI applications [8]. The visual nature of dental diagnosis, availability of high-quality imaging data, and potential for standardized assessment criteria make dentistry ideally suited for AI-powered diagnostic tools [9]. Rapid advancement in machine learning algorithms, particularly deep learning neural networks, has enabled the development of sophisticated diagnostic systems capable of matching or exceeding human expert performance in various dental applications [10].

The application of AI to gingivitis diagnosis represents a natural convergence of clinical need and technological capability [11]. Machine learning algorithms can analyze subtle patterns in gingival color, texture, and morphology that may not be readily apparent to human observers, potentially enabling earlier and more accurate diagnosis [12]. Convolutional neural networks (CNN) have demonstrated success in analyzing intraoral photographs, achieving diagnostic accuracy rates comparable to experienced periodontists [13]. The aim of this scoping review is to provide researchers, clinicians, and policymakers with a comprehensive understanding of the current state of AI applications and technologies in gingivitis diagnosis. Additionally, this review seeks to analyze the reported benefits of AI-powered gingivitis diagnosis and identify the challenges and barriers to clinical implementation.

2 Methods

This scoping review was adhered to the Preferred Reporting Items for Systematic Reviews and Meta-Analyses extension for Scoping Reviews (PRISMA-ScR) guidelines [14] to ensure comprehensive and transparent reporting of the methodology and findings.

2.1 Research Questions

The review was designed to explore the current state of AI applications in gingivitis diagnosis, and its associated benefits, barriers and challenges. This broad question was refined into specific research sub-questions: (1) What types of AI technologies are being applied to gingivitis diagnosis? (2) What are the clinical applications and performance characteristics of these AI systems? (3) What benefits have been reported for AI-powered gingivitis diagnosis? (4) What challenges and barriers to implementation have been identified? (5) What are the key research gaps and future directions in this field?

The question was constructed according to the Population, Concept, Context (PCC) framework recommended for scoping reviews [15]. The research question was as follows: **Population (P):** The target population included patients with gingivitis. **Concept (C):** The core concept encompassed AI technologies applied to gingivitis diagnosis, including machine learning algorithms, deep learning neural networks, computer vision systems, and automated diagnostic tools. **Context (C):** The context included clinical dental practice, and diagnostic applications.

2.2 Eligibility Criteria

The eligibility criteria were established prior to the review process to ensure consistency. The studies enrolled in the scoping review must meet the following inclusion criteria: A) All full text articles that answer any of the main questions were included. B) Studies included evaluating the accuracy of AI-based methods (e.g., machine learning, deep learning) in the diagnosis gingivitis. C) Studies included reporting the quantitative accuracy metrics, such as sensitivity, specificity, area under the receiver operating characteristic (ROC) curve or area under the curve (AUC) measurements were included. D) All papers that were published in 2010 until 2025.

The exclusion criteria encompassed: A) Review articles, case reposts, commentaries, letters to the editor, grey literature, conference abstracts, or posters. B) Studies that not published in English language.

2.3 Search Strategy

A comprehensive search strategy was developed and implemented across multiple electronic databases to ensure maximum coverage of relevant literature. The following databases were systematically searched from 2010 until April 2025. Databases used: (PubMed, Scopus, IEEE, Web of science, Google scholar, Medline, Proquest and Sciencedirect) The search terms were organized into three main concept groups using: (PCC) framework. Search terms were used: (“gingivitis” OR “gingival inflammation”) AND (“artificial intelligence” OR “AI” OR “machine learning” OR “deep learning” OR “neural network”) AND (“diagnosis” OR “detection” OR “monitoring”).

2.4 Study Selection Process

The study selection process was conducted in two phases following the PRISMA guidelines [14] to ensure systematic and transparent identification of relevant studies while minimizing selection bias. All records identified through the database searches were imported into Mendeley software for screening and data management. Duplicate records were automatically identified and removed, with manual verification of potential duplicates to ensure accuracy. The reviewer screened the titles, abstracts and keywords of the papers. Full-text articles were retrieved and assessed for eligibility. A list of the articles to be included in this evaluation was established. For a visual representation Fig. 1 contains the PRISMA flow diagram which illustrates the study selection process.

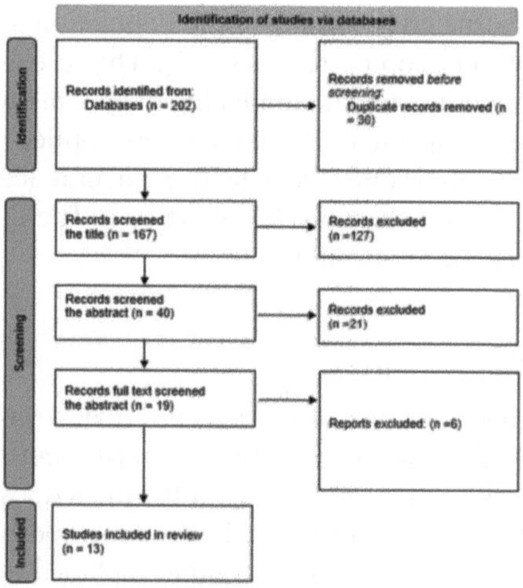

Fig. 1. Preferred Reporting Items for Systematic Reviews and Meta-Analyses extension for Scoping Reviews (PRISMA-ScR).

2.5 Quality Assessment

After applying the eligibility criteria, there were 13 main articles that met all the specified criteria. These articles were subjected to an evaluation by author in accordance with the modified-Quality Assessment of Comparative Diagnostic Accuracy Studies 2 (QUADAS-2) tool [16] as presented in Fig. 2.

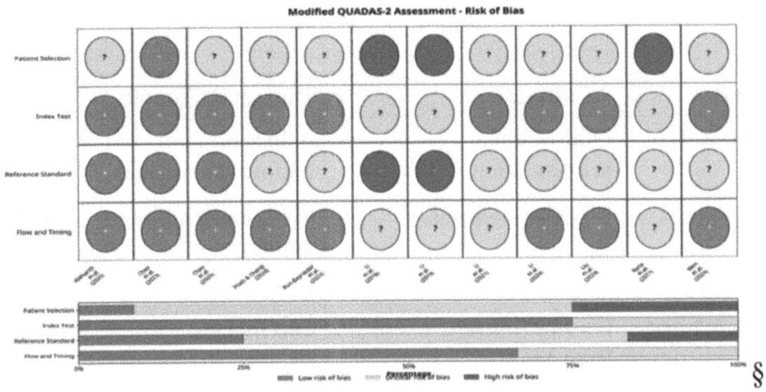

Fig. 2. Modified QUADAS-2 Assessment

2.6 Data Extraction

A comprehensive data charting table was developed iteratively through team discussion and pilot testing on a sample of included studies. The charting table was designed to capture both descriptive information about the studies and specific details about AI applications in gingivitis diagnosis. Various characteristics from articles were selected for the synthesis of table Author(s) and year of publication, Country of origin, Sample size**,** Specific algorithms or models used, Input dataset, Diagnostic accuracy measures (sensitivity, specificity, positive predictive value, negative predictive value), Area under the curve (AUC) for ROC analysis (Table 1).

Table 1. Characteristics of Included Studies

Study (Country)	AI Model	Dataset & Sample	Result
Alalharith, 2020 (Saudi) [20]	Faster R-CNN (ResNet-50)	134 intraoral images, orthodontic patients	Accuracy 77%
Chau, 2023 (HK) [22]	DeepLabv3+ (Xception, MobileNetV2)	567 intraoral photos	Sens. 0.92 Spec. 0.94
Chau, 2025 (HK) [13]	GumAI (DeepLabv3+)	44 images	Accuracy 85%
Hsieh & Cheng, 2024 (Taiwan) [24]	CNN fusion (EfficientNet, ResNet, etc. + SVM/NB)	11,653 Kaggle images	Accuracy 92%
Kurt-Bayrakdar, 2023 (Turkey) [23]	YOLOv8	654 intraoral profile photos	AUC 0.80
Li, 2018 (China) [18]	ELM + GLCM features	93 images	Accuracy 74%
Li, 2019 (China) [19]	GLCM + PSO	800 images (20 patients)	Accuracy 78%
Li, 2021 (China) [21]	Deep learning classifier	3,932 images (625 patients)	Sens. 87.8% Spec. 63.9%
Li, 2024 (China) [25]	CNNs (AlexNet, VGG, ResNet, GoogLeNet)	683 photos (134 patients)	AlexNet: Accuracy 92%

(continued)

Table 1. (*continued*)

Study (Country)	AI Model	Dataset & Sample	Result
Liu, 2024 (China) [26]	Oral-Mamba segmentation	3,365 intraoral endoscopic images	Accuracy 0.83
Rana, 2017 (USA) [17]	ML classifier + CV	405 images (150 adults)	AUC 0.75
Wen, 2024 (China) [27]	DenseNet	826 intraoral images	AUROC 0.82
Yan, 2021 (UK/China) [28]	Fourier Entropy + PSO-MLP	180 images	Accuracy 80%

3 Findings and Discussion

3.1 Overview of Included Studies

This scoping review identified 13 studies that met the inclusion criteria for examining AI applications in gingivitis diagnosis. The studies were published between 2017 and 2025 [13, 17–28], demonstrating an accelerating trend in AI research for periodontal applications. Figure 3 shows the temporal distribution of studies over years, this indicating growing research momentum in recent years. This progression reflects the broader evolution of AI technologies and their increasing accessibility to dental researchers.

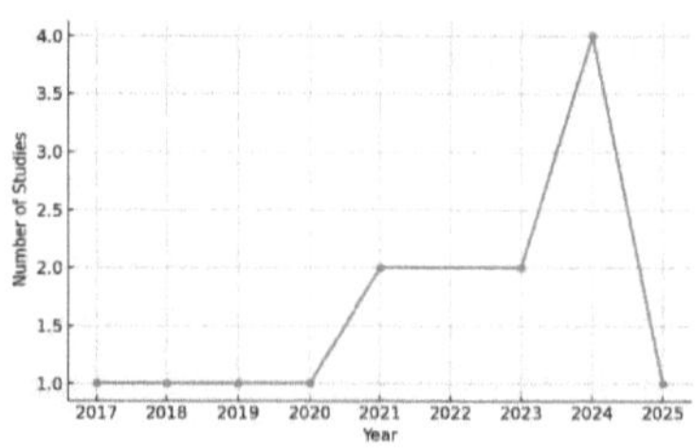

Fig. 3. Publication Trend of AI in Gingivitis Diagnosis over (2017–2025)

3.2 AI Technologies and Technical Approaches

(CNNs), Machine Learning, Deep Learning, Segmentation Models: CNNs dominated the technical approaches across the included studies, with various architectures demonstrating significant potential for gingivitis detection and classification. ResNet-50 was employed in Faster R-CNN implementations for object detection and localization of gingival inflammation [20], while advanced architectures including EfficientNetB0, MobileNetV2, InceptionV3, ResNet50, and ResNet101 were utilized in sophisticated feature fusion approaches [24]. The DeepLabv3+ architecture gained prominence in recent studies [13, 22], especially for pixel-level segmentation tasks enabling detailed gingival health classification with high spatial accuracy. Specialized segmentation models included U-Net with DenseNet encoders [27] for complex gingival inflammation grading tasks and the innovative Oral-Mamba model [26], which demonstrated 25% faster processing speeds than traditional U-Net architectures while maintaining high diagnostic accuracy. Optimization techniques such as Particle Swarm Optimization were employed across multiple studies [18, 19, 28] for feature selection and parameter tuning, demonstrating the importance of optimization strategies in achieving optimal performance. Transfer learning strategies were widely implemented, adapting pre-trained models developed on large-scale image datasets for specific dental applications while addressing the challenge of limited dental image datasets.

3.3 Performance Characteristics and Validation

Diagnostic accuracy varied significantly, with highest performance achieved by feature fusion approaches combining multiple CNN architectures with SVM classification, reaching 92.5% accuracy [24]. Individual CNN implementations ranged from 77.12% [20] to 85% [23]. Sensitivity analysis revealed strong gingivitis detection performance, with highest sensitivity of 93% by GumAI [13]. Several studies exceeded 90% sensitivity [13, 22], indicating excellent inflammatory detection capability. Traditional optimization techniques achieved moderate levels of $79.00 \pm 1.61\%$ [28]. Specificity demonstrated significant variability, ranging from 50% [13] to 94% [22]. DeepLabv3+ achieved optimal specificity in controlled settings [22], though performance decreased in community applications [13], highlighting environmental impact.

Additional metrics provided comprehensive assessment. Area Under Curve values ranged from 0.746 [17] to near-perfect discrimination. F1-scores reached 0.91 [13], while Positive Predictive Values achieved 90%, though Negative Predictive Values of 56% indicated disease rule-out limitations [13].

3.4 Applications in Diagnosis

Figure 4 presents the proportional distribution of AI applications in dentistry. AI applications focused on automated intraoral photograph analysis, from binary classification to comprehensive multi-condition detection [23, 24]. Real-time processing enabled immediate diagnostic feedback, with some systems achieving 25% faster processing [26]. Mobile health applications represented significant advancement, with GumAI [13] demonstrating successful smartphone-based detection in community settings.

These applications enhance accessibility and provide immediate feedback, particularly valuable for underserved populations. Clinical support systems provided decision-making assistance for dental professionals, incorporating objective diagnostic information. Advanced systems integrated multiple data sources beyond visual assessment, enabling comprehensive recommendations while maintaining clinical oversight. Public health screening applications demonstrated scalability for population-level detection, with community-based implementations [13] showing feasibility for large-scale programs enabling non-specialist personnel to conduct preliminary assessments.

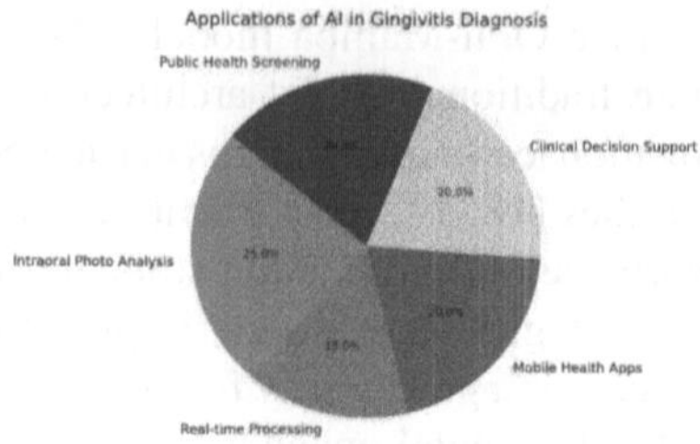

Fig. 4. Applications of AI in gingivitis diagnosis

3.5 Benefits of AI Implementation

AI use demonstrates significant efficiency advantages through automated processing enabling immediate diagnostic feedback, with advanced segmentation models achieving 25% speed improvement while maintaining accuracy [26]. Accessibility benefits are evident in mobile applications [13], enabling diagnostic capabilities in community settings and underserved populations. Smartphone-based tools leverage widely available platforms, reducing implementation barriers and expanding diagnostic access [22].

Cost-effectiveness emerges through automation and elimination of specialized personnel requirements [26, 27]. Consistency advantages include eliminating inter-examiner variability and subjective interpretation bias, ensuring standardized quality regardless of operator experience [20, 24]. This objectivity proves valuable for longitudinal monitoring and quality assurance. Early detection capabilities enable identification of subtle inflammatory changes potentially overlooked in routine examination, supporting preventive care and intervention before disease progression [20, 23, 27].

3.6 Challenges and Limitations

Data quality and availability present significant constraints, with studies limited by small sample sizes and population-specific bias [13, 18, 20]. Image quality variability due to lighting and equipment differences impacts performance, while annotation consistency challenges affect training reliability [21, 26].

Generalizability concerns arise from limited external validation and population-specific training, with systems trained on Chinese participants showing uncertain cross-ethnic performance and single-center studies limiting broader applicability [22]. Technical generalizability faces equipment variation and operational procedure challenges. Ethical considerations encompass patient autonomy, informed consent, and appropriate balance between AI recommendations and professional judgment [22, 25].

Data privacy concerns are particularly relevant for mobile applications processing sensitive information, requiring compliance with healthcare privacy regulations [22, 25]. User trust barriers include concerns regarding algorithmic decision-making and the "black box" nature of AI systems [26, 27]. Training requirements and workflow integration challenges may impede clinical adoption, while patient acceptance varies based on cultural factors and technology familiarity [22, 23, 25].

3.7 Gaps in Literature

Significant gaps exist in multi-center validation studies, with most research relying on single-institution datasets that limit external validity and generalizability across diverse clinical settings. Prospective clinical trials comparing AI-assisted diagnosis with standard assessment methods are notably absent, constraining evidence for clinical utility. Longitudinal studies examining AI performance in tracking disease progression are lacking, limiting understanding of long-term clinical impact.

Comparative effectiveness research examining different AI approaches remains insufficient for evidence-based technology selection. Standardized datasets with adequate diversity and representation are critically needed, as current datasets demonstrate significant population and scenario bias. Implementation of science research addressing practical deployment challenges requires dedicated attention. Economic evaluation studies examining cost-effectiveness compared to traditional diagnostic approaches are notably absent, limiting informed policy decisions. Health services research examining broader healthcare system impacts represents the most urgent research priority.

4 Conclusion

This review demonstrates significant promise of AI in gingivitis diagnosis, with CNN-based models achieving high sensitivity rates exceeding 90% and overall accuracy ranging from 77% to 92.5%. Mobile health applications illustrate the feasibility of community-based screening programs, potentially extending access to underserved populations and enhancing early detection. However, wide variability in performance metrics, particularly specificity ranging from 50% to 94%, reveals persistent challenges from inconsistencies in datasets, model architecture, and evaluation protocols. Addressing these gaps through systematic research and validation is essential before AI technologies can transition from promising experimental tools to reliable components of routine clinical practice.

References

1. Chapple, I.L., et al.: Periodontal health and gingival diseases and conditions on an intact and a reduced periodontium: consensus report of workgroup 1 of the 2017 world workshop on the classification of periodontal and Peri-Implant diseases and conditions. J. Periodontol. **89**, S74-84 (2018)
2. Trombelli, L., Farina, R., Silva, C.O., Tatakis, D.N.: Plaque-induced gingivitis: case definition and diagnostic considerations. J. Clin. Periodontol. **45**, S44-67 (2018)
3. Vos, T., et al.: Global burden of 369 diseases and injuries in 204 countries and territories, 1990–2019: a systematic analysis for the Global Burden of Disease Study 2019. Lancet **396**(10258), 1204–1222 (2020)
4. Marcenes, W., et al.: Global burden of oral conditions in 1990–2010: a systematic analysis. J. Dent. Res. **92**(7), 592–597 (2013)
5. Griffin, S.O., Jones, J.A., Brunson, D., Griffin, P.M., Bailey, W.D.: Burden of oral disease among older adults and implications for public health priorities. Am. J. Public Health **102**(3), 411–418 (2012)

6. Mariotti, A.: Dental plaque-induced gingival diseases. Ann Periodontol. **4**(1), 7–17 (1999)
7. Armitage, G.C.: Clinical evaluation of periodontal diseases. Periodontology **7**(1), 39–53 (2000)
8. Topol, E.J.: High-performance medicine: the convergence of human and artificial intelligence. Nat. Med. **25**(1), 44–56 (2019)
9. Schwendicke, F., Golla, T., Dreher, M., Krois, J.: Convolutional neural networks for dental image diagnostics: a scoping review. J. Dent. **1**(91), 103226 (2019)
10. LeCun, Y., Bengio, Y., Hinton, G.: Deep learning. Nature. **521**(7553), 436–444 (2015)
11. Krois, J., et al.: Deep learning for the radiographic detection of periodontal bone loss. Sci. Rep. **9**(1), 8495 (2019)
12. Chen, H., et al.: A deep learning approach to automatic teeth detection and numbering based on object detection in dental periapical films. Sci. Rep. **9**(1), 3840 (2019)
13. Chau, R.C., et al.: External validation of an AI mHealth tool for gingivitis detection among older adults at daycare centers: a pilot study. Int. Dent. J. (2025)
14. Tricco, A.C., et al.: PRISMA extension for scoping reviews (PRISMA-ScR): checklist and explanation. Ann. Intern. Med. **169**(7), 467–473 (2018)
15. Joanna Briggs Institute: Joanna Briggs Institute reviewers' manual: 2014 edition. The Joanna Briggs Institute, Australia, pp. 88–91 (2014)
16. Wade, R., Corbett, M., Eastwood, A.: Quality assessment of comparative diagnostic accuracy studies: our experience using a modified version of the QUADAS-2 tool. Res. Synth. Methods **4**(3), 280–286 (2013)
17. Rana, A., Yauney, G., Wong, L.C., Gupta, O., Muftu, A., Shah, P.: Automated segmentation of gingival diseases from oral images. In: 2017 IEEE healthcare innovations and point of care technologies (HI-POCT), 6 November 2017, pp. 144–147. IEEE
18. Li, W., Chen, Y., Miao, L., Brown, M., Sun, W., Zhang, X.: Gingivitis identification via grey-level cooccurrence matrix and extreme learning machine. In: 8th International Conference on Education, Management, Information and Management Society (EMIM 2018), pp. 486–492. Atlantis Press, August 2018
19. Li, W., Jiang, X., Sun, W., Zhang, Y.-D., Wang, S.-H., Liu, C., et al.: Gingivitis identification via multichannel gray-level co-occurrence matrix and particle swarm optimization neural network. University of Leicester (2019)
20. Alalharith, D.M., et al.: A deep learning-based approach for the detection of early signs of gingivitis in orthodontic patients using faster region-based convolutional neural networks. Int. J. Environ. Res. Public Health **17**(22), 8447 (2020)
21. Li, W., et al.: A deep learning approach to automatic gingivitis screening based on classification and localization in RGB photos. Sci. Rep. **11**(1), 16831 (2021)
22. Chau, R.C., et al.: Accuracy of artificial intelligence-based photographic detection of gingivitis. Int. Dent. J. **73**(5), 724–730 (2023)
23. Kurt-Bayrakdar, S., et al.: Detection of tooth numbering, frenulum attachment, gingival overgrowth, and gingival inflammation signs on dental photographs using convolutional neural network algorithms: a retrospective study. Quintessence Int. (Berlin, Germany: 1985) **54**(8), 680–693 (2023). https://doi.org/10.3290/j.qi.b4157183
24. Hsieh, S.T., Cheng, Y.A.: Multimodal feature fusion in deep learning for comprehensive dental condition classification. J. Xray Sci. Technol. **32**(2), 303–321 (2024)
25. Li, W., et al.: Evaluation of transfer ensemble learning-based convolutional neural network models for the identification of chronic gingivitis from oral photographs. BMC Oral Health **24**(1), 814 (2024)
26. Liu, Y., Cheng, Y., Song, Y., Cai, D., Zhang, N.: Oral screening of dental calculus, gingivitis and dental caries through segmentation on intraoral photographic images using deep learning. BMC Oral Health **24**(1), 1287 (2024)

27. Wen, C., Bai, X., Yang, J., Li, S., Wang, X., Yang, D.: Deep learning based approach: automated gingival inflammation grading model using gingival removal strategy. Sci. Rep. **14**(1), 19780 (2024)
28. Yan, Y.: Gingivitis detection by Fractional Fourier Entropy and Particle Swarm Optimization. EAI Endorsed Trans. e-Learn. (21) (2021)

Key Technologies of Perception based Computer Vision and Digital Image Processing

Deep Feature Based Age Classification Using Sparse Variational Gaussian Process

Yashas Mittal, A. Sarthak, and Manisha Parlewar(✉)

Guru Gobind Singh Indraprastha University, Delhi, India
mpparlewar@gmail.com

Abstract. Age estimation is a challenging yet interesting research problem. Recently, convolutional neural networks have been proven to be very efficient in encoding complex feature space and classifying it. In this paper, we present an age classification method that explores transfer learning to extract complex aging features using ResNet-50. In recent years Gaussian process models have been widely applied for machine learning applications due to their non-parametric modeling ability. In this paper, we propose a sparse Gaussian process classifier for age group classification. Experimental analysis and comparisons with existing methods using a large dataset system demonstrate the efficiency and accuracy of the proposed method. Further, we also showcase unbiased behavior of our model towards different ethnicity in the dataset, making it suitable for real world applications.

Keywords: Age classification · sparse variation Gaussian process · ResNet-50

1 Introduction

Facial age estimation is an important area in computer vision, with applications ranging from identity verification and age-restricted access control to personalized user experiences in online platforms such as gaming, streaming, social media, and e-commerce. Increasing legal and ethical requirements for accurate and explainable age estimation systems have driven significant research efforts. Traditionally, age estimation relied on hand-crafted feature descriptors such as Local Binary Patterns and geometric measurements [1]. However, with the rise of deep learning, convolutional neural networks (CNNs) have become the dominant approach. Architectures such as VGG [2] and ResNet-50 [3] are favored for their ability to extract hierarchical, discriminative features from facial images. While accuracy, precision, recall, and F1-score remain standard evaluation metrics, these aggregate measures often overlook performance disparities across demographic groups, highlighting the need for fairness-aware assessments [4].

Recent developments in CNN-based age estimation have explored both continuous regression and discrete age group classification frameworks. Models

C. Xu (Ed.): ICMLSC 2026, CCIS 2948, pp. 237–246, 2027.
https://doi.org/10.1007/978-981-92-1546-1_19

employing ResNet, DenseNet [5], and EfficientNet [6] architectures have demonstrated success in capturing complex facial aging patterns, while lightweight models like MobileNet [7] cater to real-time applications. Techniques such as transfer learning from large-scale face datasets, and combining cross-entropy with ordinal regression losses, have further improved model performance. Additionally, attention mechanisms and multiscale feature fusion have enhanced sensitivity to subtle, localized age-related facial cues [8,9]. Despite these advances, the diversity and quality of training data remain critical factors influencing model robustness.

A persistent challenge is the demographic imbalance in publicly available datasets, which limits generalization and fairness. Well-known benchmarks such as FG-NET and MORPH lack sufficient demographic diversity, often resulting in biased predictions for underrepresented groups. Many commercial systems also rely on celebrity-centric datasets, further narrowing real-world applicability. To address this, recent studies emphasize the importance of more balanced datasets and the use of data augmentation techniques—including rotation, blurring, and illumination variation—to improve model generalization and fairness across age groups [1,10].

In this paper, we examine demographic disparities in age classification using a sparse Gaussian process (GP) classification. While GP is a nonparametric Bayesian inference method, it becomes computationally heavy with increasing sample size [11]. This issue is handled by the sparsification procedure which decreases the computational complexity and is also generalizable. In this paper, feature extraction is carried out using transfer learning based approach followed by sparse Gaussian process classification. By maintaining a consistent architecture and employing controlled data augmentation strategies, we analyze performance across different demographic groups using standard classification metrics. Our study aims to establish a reproducible baseline for fairness-aware age estimation, promoting models that are both accurate and equitable in practical deployment.

2 Related Works

The development of age estimation systems has evolved from hand-crafted feature-based models to deep learning architectures optimized for classification tasks. This progression has been supported by advances in network design and the establishment of benchmark datasets. This section reviews key contributions with an emphasis on classification methodologies and their limitations.

1. Hand-Crafted Feature Methods. Early approaches primarily focused on designing engineered feature extractors to represent facial characteristics for classification. Ahonen et al. [12] proposed Local Binary Patterns (LBP) as an efficient texture descriptor, encoding local pixel intensity differences into histograms that serve as compact facial representations. While LBP demonstrated computational efficiency and some robustness under controlled settings, it suffers from sensitivity to illumination changes, occlusions, and pose variations, and lacks the capacity to learn high-level semantic representations from data. Liu and Wechsler [13] utilized Gabor filter banks to capture multi-orientation, multi-scale features inspired by the human visual system. Their approach employed an Enhanced Fisher Linear Discriminant (E-FLD) classifier to improve discrimination between age classes. Despite improved performance, Gabor filters are computationally intensive and manually designed, limiting their adaptability relative to learned deep features.

2. Deep Learning for Age Group Classification. With the advent of deep learning, Convolutional Neural Networks (CNNs) replaced handcrafted features by learning hierarchical representations optimized for discrete age group classification. Krizhevsky et al. [14] introduced AlexNet, demonstrating the effectiveness of deep CNNs with innovations such as ReLU activations, dropout regularization, and data augmentation to enhance generalization. Earlier foundational CNN frameworks by LeCun et al. [15] also established the viability of end-to-end feature learning for image classification. These resource-intensive architectures laid the groundwork for subsequent facial age group classifiers. Sun et al. [16] developed the DeepFace model, which trained deep CNNs on millions of facial images for identity classification. While the learned features implicitly encoded age-related information, the model was not explicitly optimized for age classification and relied heavily on large-scale datasets, limiting its adaptability in diverse or smaller-scale applications.

3. Specialized Age Classification Architectures. Subsequent research has refined architectures and loss functions to explicitly address challenges in age group classification. Eidinger et al. [17] proposed a pipeline combining face detection, alignment, and classification to estimate age and gender from unconstrained images, marking progress toward real-world applicability. However, their feature extractor lacked the depth and representational power of modern CNNs, constraining accuracy. Chao et al. [18] introduced ordinal classification techniques that leverage the intrinsic order of age groups to improve prediction consistency. By penalizing misclassifications proportionally to the distance between predicted and true age bins, their method reduced large errors common in standard classification. Nevertheless, it assumes a smooth, ordered progression of age that may not hold universally. Geng et al. [19] and Fu & Huang [20] modeled age progression as trajectories on learned low-dimensional manifolds, enhancing continuity and interpretability in classification. Although promising, these manifold-based methods can be sensitive to demographic biases in training data, affecting robustness across diverse populations.

4. Dataset Challenges for Classification. Datasets remain critical for training and evaluating classification models but pose challenges due to demographic imbalances. The FG-NET [21] and MORPH [22] datasets have been seminal benchmarks, with MORPH providing longitudinal samples of individuals across time. The Labeled Faces in the Wild (LFW) dataset [23] contributed unconstrained images supporting classification in realistic conditions. Despite their utility, these datasets suffer from demographic skews, such as MORPH's over representation of certain ethnicities and genders, and the limited scale of FG-NET for deep learning applications. Such biases hinder fair and equitable model performance when deployed in diverse real-world scenarios.

3 Research Methodology

In this section, we present the proposed work with all its essential components in detail. The key components of the proposed framework comprise of data pre-processing, extraction of aging feature map from ResNet-50 and multi-label sparse variation GP classification model for age group prediction. The proposed research methodology is presented in Fig. 1. In this paper, for experimental analysis we have used Morph-II database that covers with broader demographic coverage, unlike curated or certain demography specific focused datasets. Morph-II database contains about 55,314 face images in the age range 16 to 77 years. It spans adverse population with respect to age, ethnicity and gender.

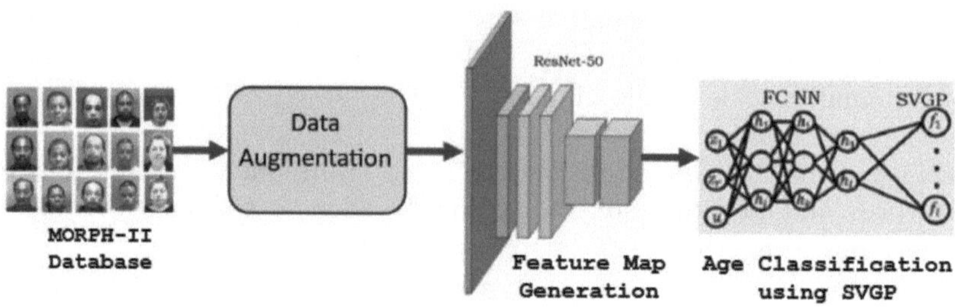

Fig. 1. Representation of the proposed methodology.

3.1 Data Preprocessing

It has been observed that, CNNs perform remarkably well on many computer vision applications. However, in order to avoid overfitting, these networks need to be trained using substantially large real world images. There are certain computer vision applications (e.g. age estimation and age invariant face recognition) where creating substantially large dataset is difficult. In such applications, when CNNs are trained with smaller datasets, they generally overfit. Data augmentation is a machine learning technique that plays a crucial role in such situation. It generates new samples by applying various transformations or modifications to existing data and prevent overfitting. Data augmentation performs perturbations on input data, thereby improving the generalization and robustness of machine learning models [24,25].

In this paper, we performed data augmentation using the image augmentation module of the AugLy library [26]. For image augmentations, AugLy mainly focuses on synthetically generating real world image transformation such as insertion of emojis or screenshots in images. Controlled augmentations in AugLy such as rotation, pixelation, illumination changes, and blur handle class imbalance and enhance model generalization. Performance is systematically evaluated across age categories and ethnic subgroups to identify disparities and establish fairness-aware benchmarks. By integrating balanced data representation with robust modeling, the approach ensures consistent accuracy across diverse populations. This design enables reliable deployment in real-time applications, including identity verification, age-restricted access control, and regulatory compliance, where both predictive precision and unbiased performance are essential.

3.2 Feature Extraction

Feature extraction and classification are two main tasks in any machine learning method. Being able to perform both tasks together CNNs are widely used in image classification problems. Prominent CNN architecture such as AlexNet [14], VGG [27] and ResNet [28] are a few of them which are heavily used for computer vision applications. These models are also used for feature extraction in image classification tasks. For feature extraction, a pre-trained model with related modifications in fully connected layer is fine-tuned using a specific dataset. The proposed framework utilizes a modified ResNet-50 architecture tailored for multi-label age classification.

ResNet-50 model is pre-trained on ImageNet, is fine-tuned for age group prediction using Morph-II dataset. We used transfer learning to modify the weight of the pre-trained ResNet model using the Morph-II dataset. Since ImageNet database is not a facial aging dataset, simply modification of fully connected layer does not provide efficient age discriminant features. Therefore, in this work, the aging features are learned by modifying layers 2, 3 and 4. With these settings, each input image was mapped to a 2048-dimensional embedding vector.

3.3 Sparse Variational Gaussian Process

A Gaussian process is non-parametric Bayesian inference widely used for regression [11]. Unlike other machine learning algorithms, Gaussian processes provide uncertainty estimations and also learn the noise and smoothness parameters from training data. In case of regression problems, when the likelihoods are Gaussian, a posterior also becomes Gaussian and has a closed-form. However, as the number of training samples increases, the computational burden to identify posterior scales up drastically. This problem is handled by sparse GP that approximate posterior of exact GP with a set of inducing points, e.g. pseudo-training [29]. These inducing points control the computational and storage complexity. In case of large training samples, a closed-form solution is achieved with the help of approximate inference. In SVGP, variational inference is used for approximate inference. This setting opens doors to classification and regression problems in machine learning. With increasing training samples, time complexity for exact GP scales with $\mathcal{O}(n^3)$, where n is the number of training samples. On the other hand, with m inducing points in sparse variational GP, the time complexity reduces to $\mathcal{O}(nm^2)$ where $m << n$. One of the benefits of GP model over other machine learning or deep learning model is that along with the predicted class label, it also generates the prediction uncertainty and its parameter optimization does not rely on computationally complex cross-validation.

4 Experimental Analysis and Results

In this section, we present the experimental analysis. The experiments were conducted on the local machine along with PyTorch, gpflow and TensorFlow libraries to evaluate the age group classification. The performance of the proposed system is assessed using different performance metrics such as recognition accuracy, F1 score and precision. The experimental framework utilizes the MORPH-II dataset as the primary data source for training and evaluation.

To address limitations in sample diversity and enhance the robustness of the model under real-world conditions, extensive data augmentation was performed using the AugLy library. This augmentation pipeline involved transformations such as rotation, pixelation, blurring, and illumination variation, ultimately expanding the dataset to a total of 75,000 images. Sample images from Morph-II dataset and corresponding augmented images using AugLy are shown in Fig. 2.

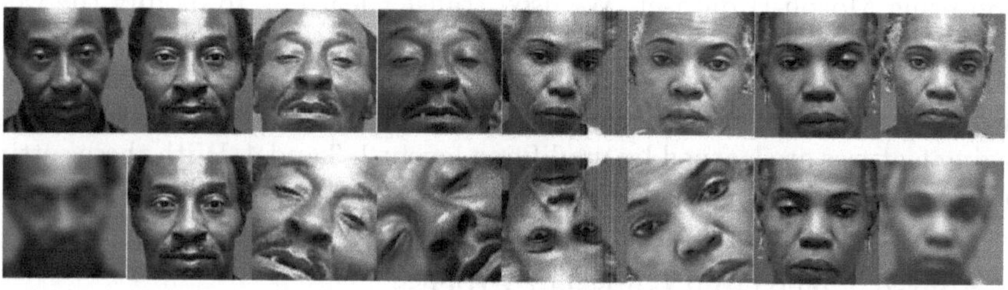

Fig. 2. Sample images from Morph-II database and corresponding and augmented images.

For age group classification, the dataset was stratified into four discrete and mutually exclusive classes based on age ranges 16–22, 23–35, 36–45 and 46+. We have selected these age ranges such that biases in terms of number of images in age group is avoided. With our setting the number of images in class 0: 17000, class 1: 23000, class 3: 20000 and class 4: 15000. We have followed a 60-20-20 training-testing-validation split that resulted in 45,000 images for training, 15,000 images for testing and 15,000 images for validation. To ensure statistical representativeness and minimize sampling bias, stratified sampling was employed, preserving the proportional distribution of age groups across all partitions. This augmented and balanced dataset configuration allows for a rigorous evaluation of age classification performance, particularly in assessing the model's fairness and generalization across varying demographic groups.

Data preprocessing and augmentation is followed by feature extraction using a CNN-based backbone, optimized for facial attribute encoding. For this purpose, ResNet-50 model, pre-trained on a large-scale image dataset, is fine-tuned on a curated facial image corpus to extract 2048-dimensional feature vectors capturing age specific facial attributes. Fine-tuning optimizes the fully connected layers using cross-entropy loss. In this study, all the layers except first layer of the classifier were trained. The weights and biases of these layers were fine-tuned using train/test split. The feature maps extracted from ResNet-50 are passed into Sparse Variational Gaussian Process classifiers for final predictions. The SVGP approximates the posterior distribution using inducing points, optimizing a variational lower bound to form a non-linear decision boundary. The SVGP is configured with a Matérn 5/2 kernel and a Softmax likelihood function, optimized by maximizing the Evidence Lower Bound (ELBO) using mini-batch stochastic gradient descent. This design enabled robust classification with calibrated uncertainty. The proposed approach resulted in accuracy of 75%, F1-Score 0.7602 and recall value 0.7560 on the test data. The training and validation accuracy of the proposed method is shown in Fig. 3. A comparison of the proposed method with state-of-the-art methods is shown in Table 1. Many real world applications such as age based access control, law enforcement or city management require the age information such as below 18, adults or senior. Keeping this requirement in mind, we have performed one more experiment by partitioning the database into these 3 age groups. We have followed a 60-20-20 training-testing-validation split for this experiment, which resulted in test accuracy 89% with F1 0.73 and Recall 0.67. The recall value of this experimentation is lower than that of the 4 age group due to the class imbalance. Morph-II is a database created by collecting images of criminals, therefore, the number of images of persons under 18 are substantially low. However, with such high accuracy of age group prediction, the proposed method is suitable for real-world applications in city management and age based access control.

In [30], a detailed audit of three commercial FRS is presented, which reveals that the age estimation algorithms in the commercial face recognition systems show biased performance and there is large disparity in prediction accuracy for people of certain ethnicity than the other. These biases can have serious real-world implications such as restricted access to critical services. We have evaluated the bias-ness of the proposed method towards particular demography. The original database consists of Black (B): 42,303 images, White (W): 10,551 images, Asian (A): 159 images, Indian (I): 57 images, and Hispanic (H): 1,750 images. Since Asian, Indian and Hispanic images are substantially lower in number, we have analyzed impact of only black and white ethnicity on performance of age estimation. It is interesting to note that the test accuracy for both ethnic groups is almost the same. For black demography, the test accuracy is 87%

where as for white it is 89%. This implies that the proposed method not only provides improved accuracy as compared to existing state-of-the-art, but also is not biased towards specific ethnicity. This makes the proposed method suitable for real-world applications such as age-based access control in smart cities.

Table 1. Comparison of proposed approach with other state-of-the-art methods

Reference	Model	Accuracy (%)
Pontes et al. [31]	SVM	64.46
Sawant et al. [32]	GP Classifier	71.14
Duan et al. [33]	CNN-ELM	52.3
Proposed 4 age groups	ResNet-50+SVGP	75
Proposed 3 age groups	ResNet-50+SVGP	89

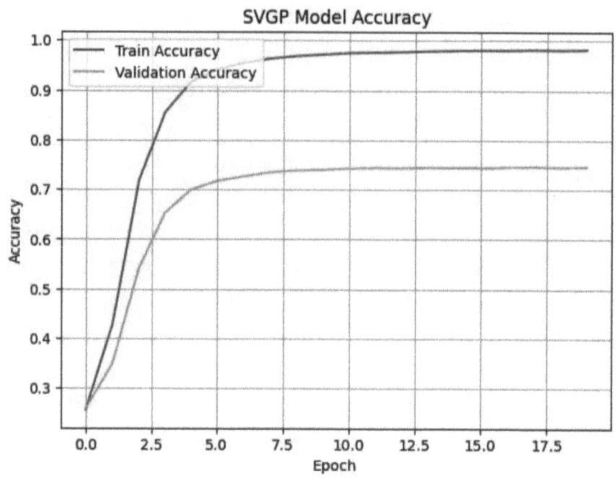

Fig. 3. Training and validation accuracy of the proposed method.

5 Conclusion

In this paper, we presented a robust age group classification method that is suitable for real-world applications. Our approach makes use of data augmentation to avoid overfitting and the skewness in the database toward a specific demography Next, transfer learning helps the ResNet-50 model to learn age discriminant feature vectors and finally, computationally efficient sparse variational Gaussian process classifier classifies the images into particular age group with 89% accuracy. The experimental analysis shows that our method surpasses the state-of-the-art and also does not show bias toward specific ethnic origins, which makes it suitable real world applications.

References

1. Shorten, C., Khoshgoftaar, T.M.: A survey on image data augmentation for deep learning. J. Big Data **6**(1), 1–48 (2019)
2. Simonyan, K., Zisserman, A.: Very deep convolutional networks for large-scale image recognition. arXiv preprint arXiv:1409.1556 (2015)
3. He, K., Zhang, X., Ren, S., Sun, J.: Deep residual learning for image recognition. In: Proceedings of the IEEE Conference on Computer Vision and Pattern Recognition, pp. 770–778 (2016)
4. Buolamwini, J., Gebru, T.: Gender shades: intersectional accuracy disparities in commercial gender classification. In: Conference on Fairness, Accountability and Transparency, pp. 77–91 (2018)
5. o Huang, G., Liu, Z., Van Der Maaten, L., Weinberger, K.Q.: Densely connected convolutional networks. In: Proceedings of the IEEE Conference on Computer Vision and Pattern Recognition, pp. 4700–4708 (2017)
6. Tan, M., Le, Q.: EfficientNet: rethinking model scaling for convolutional neural networks. In: International Conference on Machine Learning, pp. 6105–6114 (2019)
7. Howard, A.G., et al.: MobileNets: efficient convolutional neural networks for mobile vision applications. arXiv preprint arXiv:1704.04861 (2017)
8. Niu, Z., Zhou, M., Wang, L., Gao, X., Hua, G.: Ordinal regression with multiple output CNN for age estimation. In: Proceedings of the IEEE Conference on Computer Vision and Pattern Recognition, pp. 4920–4928 (2016)
9. Deme, O., et al.: Deep age estimation models. J. Comput. Vis. Appl. **15**(3), 234–245 (2019)
10. Wang, Z., et al.: FairFace: face attribute dataset for balanced race, gender, and age. arXiv preprint arXiv:2108.10041 (2021)
11. Rasmussen, C.E., Williams, C.K.: Gaussian Processes for Machine Learning. MIT Press (2006)
12. Ahonen, T., Hadid, A., Pietikainen, M.: Face description with local binary patterns: application to face recognition. IEEE Trans. Pattern Anal. Mach. Intell. **28**(12), 2037–2041 (2006)
13. Liu, C., Wechsler, H.: Gabor feature based classification using the enhanced fisher linear discriminant model for face recognition. IEEE Trans. Image Process. **11**(4), 467–476 (2002)
14. Krizhevsky, A., Sutskever, I., Hinton, G.E.: ImageNet classification with deep convolutional neural networks. In: Advances in Neural Information Processing Systems, vol. 25, pp. 1097–1105 (2012)
15. LeCun, Y., et al.: Backpropagation applied to handwritten zip code recognition. Neural Comput. **1**(4), 541–551 (1989)
16. Sun, Y., Wang, X., Tang, X.: Deep learning face representation from predicting 10,000 classes. In: Proceedings of the IEEE Conference on Computer Vision and Pattern Recognition, pp. 1891–1898 (2014)
17. Eidinger, E., Enbar, R., Hassner, T.: Age and gender estimation of unfiltered faces. IEEE Trans. Inf. Forensics Secur. **9**(12), 2170–2179 (2014)
18. Chao, W.L., Liu, J.Z., Ding, J.J.: Facial age estimation based on label-sensitive learning and age-oriented regression. Pattern Recogn. **46**(3), 628–641 (2013)
19. Geng, X., Zhou, Z.H., Smith-Miles, K.: Automatic age estimation based on facial aging patterns. IEEE Trans. Pattern Anal. Mach. Intell. **29**(12), 2234–2240 (2007)
20. Fu, Y., Huang, T.S.: Human age estimation with regression on discriminative aging manifold. IEEE Trans. Multimedia **10**(4), 578–584 (2008)

21. Lanitis, A., Draganova, C., Christodoulou, C.: Comparing different classifiers for automatic age estimation. IEEE Trans. Syst. Man Cybern. **34**(1), 621–628 (2004)
22. Ricanek, K., Tesafaye, T.: MORPH: a longitudinal image database of normal adult age-progression. In: 7th International Conference on Automatic Face and Gesture Recognition, pp. 341–345 (2006)
23. Huang, G.B., Mattar, M., Berg, T., Learned-Miller, E.: Labeled faces in the wild: a database for studying face recognition in unconstrained environments. In: Workshop on Faces in Real-Life Images (2008)
24. Hendrycks, D., et al.: The many faces of robustness: a critical analysis of outofdistribution generalization. In: Proceedings of the IEEE/CVF International Conference on Computer Vision, pp. 8340–8349 (2021)
25. Hendrycks, D., Dietterich, T.: Benchmarking neural network robustness to common corruptions and perturbations. In: International Conference on Learning Representations (2019)
26. Papakipos, Z., Bitton, J.: AugLy: data augmentations for robustness. arXiv preprint arXiv:2201.06494 (2022)
27. Xie, S., et al.: Aggregated residual transformations for deep neural networks. In: Proceedings of the IEEE Conference on Computer Vision and Pattern Recognition, pp. 1492–1500 (2017)
28. Long, M., et al.: Conditional adversarial domain adaptation. In: Advances in Neural Information Processing Systems, pp. 1640–1650 (2018)
29. Leibfried, F., Dutordoir, V., John, S., Durrande, N.: A tutorial on sparse Gaussian processes and variational inference. arXiv preprint arXiv:2012.13962 (2020)
30. Jaiswal, A., et al.: A comprehensive audit of commercial face recognition systems. In: Proceedings of the IEEE/CVF Conference on Computer Vision and Pattern Recognition, pp. 3950–3959 (2022)
31. Pontes, J.K., Britto, A.S., Jr., Fookes, C., Koerich, A.L.: A flexible hierarchical approach for facial age estimation based on multiple features. Pattern Recogn. **54**, 34–51 (2016)
32. Sawant, M.M., Bhurchandi, K.M.: Hierarchical facial age estimation using Gaussian process regression. IEEE Access **7**, 9142–9152 (2019)
33. Duan, M., Li, K., Yang, C., Li, K.: A hybrid deep learning CNN-ELM for age and gender classification. Neurocomputing **275**, 448–461 (2018)

Estimating Carbohydrate Content in Foods Using Deep Learning and Image Analysis

Pornpawee Komsrimorakot, Nattakrit Vanijkachorn, and Thitirat Siriborvornratanakul(✉)

Graduate School of Applied Statistics, National Institute of Development Administration, 148 SeriThai Road, Klong-Chan, Bangkapi, Bangkok 10240, Thailand
{6510422008,6510422006}@stu.nida.ac.th, thitirat@as.nida.ac.th

Abstract. Type 1 diabetes (T1DM) is characterized by autoimmune destruction of pancreatic Beta-cells, resulting in insulin deficiency and subsequent long-term health complications. Current T1DM management focuses on precise blood glucose control, necessitating accurate carbohydrate estimation during meals. However, the diverse modern diet poses challenges in determining carbohydrate content, leading to potential errors in insulin dosing. The increasing interest in leveraging artificial intelligence (AI) to enhance carbohydrate estimation is evidenced in our experiments. Notably, the Vision Transformer (ViT) model outperformed the VGG-16 model, showcasing exceptional predictive capabilities. Experiment 2 demonstrated prediction errors below 7 g for 85.33% of the 616-image test dataset.

Keywords: Artificial Intelligence · Deep Learning · Computer Vision · Food Carb Estimation

1 Introduction

Type 1 diabetes is a condition characterized by the autoimmune destruction of Beta-cells in the pancreas, leading to a deficiency in insulin production [6]. This disease, known for causing significant long-term health problems and impacting psychological well-being and life satisfaction, is increasingly prevalent worldwide. The exact set of factors driving this rise is not entirely understood. The rapid increase in its incidence cannot be solely attributed to genetic factors, suggesting that environmental factors also play a role. Lifestyle factors such as diet during pregnancy, infant nutrition, early childhood dietary habits, exposure to microbes (in line with the hygiene hypothesis), and the early use of antibiotics are all associated with the development of type 1 diabetes [1]. Moreover, the impact of type 1 diabetes in 2021 is substantial relative to the available of the four requisites resources, and it is expected to escalate quickly, especially in numerous resource-limited countries worldwide [10].

C. Xu (Ed.): ICMLSC 2026, CCIS 2948, pp. 247–256, 2027.
https://doi.org/10.1007/978-981-92-1546-1_20

At present, there is no cure for type 1 diabetes. Controlling blood glucose levels within an acceptable range during each meal is a fundamental therapeutic objective. The treatment approach involves four key steps. First, measuring blood glucose levels before eating. Second, calculating the amount of carbohydrates consumed in each meal. Third, determining the appropriate insulin dosage tailored to each time and individual body requirements, as advised by the doctor. Finally, measuring blood glucose levels three hours after eating to evaluate the results. However, significant challenges arise in the practical implementation, particularly in the second step of treatment approach. Accurately estimating the carbohydrate content in a diverse array of meals is complex, due to the vast variety of foods in the modern diet. This complexity can lead to miscalculations in insulin dosing, which, in turn, may prevent patients from achieving their desired blood sugar levels.

Consequently, this has spurred a growing interest in the application of artificial intelligence (AI) for more precise carbohydrate estimation. Traditional approaches, such as manual food logging [12,13], nutrition database lookups [8], the use of weighing scales [9], or manual visual assessment of portion size via food photographs [7], often require user effort, time, and prior nutritional knowledge, making them difficult to sustain in daily life. In contrast, an image-based carbohydrate prediction system can automatically estimate carbohydrate content directly from food images, offering a more practical and reliable tool to support daily diabetes management by reducing the cognitive burden of manual estimation and improving postprandial glucose control.

2 Related Work

With the recent advances in AI, a growing number of health-related applications have been developed in Thai [11,16]. Despite these developments, Thai patients with Type 1 Diabetes Mellitus (T1DM) are still required to manually log the carbohydrate content of their meals in grams. This involves photographing meals, recording the time of consumption, and noting the weight of each component, such as rice and sugar in a dish like pork fried rice [9]. To address this challenge, our research focuses on developing a deep learning tool capable of estimating carbohydrate content directly from meal photographs, offering a more efficient, non-intrusive, and practical approach for monitoring carbohydrate intake.

Related work focusing on carbohydrate quantification to assist individuals with T1DM includes the study in 2023 [3], which utilizes the Nutrition5k database—containing videos of diverse dishes with comprehensive nutritional information. This study employs the ViT-B/16 model and highlights challenges in estimating food volume and carbohydrate content from images, particularly when food portions are obscured or cropped due to mismatched aspect ratios between the model input and the original camera images, leading to potential estimation errors. Another study in 2021 [2] proposes a carbohydrate counting system that automatically estimates carbohydrate content from a single image without requiring user interaction, simulating real-world scenarios involving dishes with multiple, varied food items. The model integrates object detection with YOLO, segmentation with GrabCut, and a regression module for carbohydrate estimation. This work also discusses the limitations of existing food datasets, notably the lack of detailed volume information and limited coverage of Thai dishes. After training, the system achieved a top-1 accuracy of 80.9% and a root mean square error (RMSE) of less than 10 g for carbohydrate estimation on the test dataset.

The third study in 2021 [17] introduces FoodSeg103 and FoodSeg154, two datasets comprising 9,490 food images. Each image is annotated with an average of six ingredient labels across 154 categories and includes pixel-wise masks. The study also proposes a multi-modality pre-training method, ReLeM, which leverages multi-modal information from recipe datasets to enhance food image segmentation. ReLeM integrates food recipe data in language embedding format with the visual representation of food images. This integration aims to connect the visual representations of ingredients, as they appear in various dishes, within a shared feature space through language embeddings. The results demonstrate that ReLeM effectively improves the accuracy of state-of-the-art semantic segmentation models, including CCNet, Sem-FPN, and SeTR. Overall, this work provides a valuable resource for developing and evaluating food image segmentation models and highlights the importance of leveraging multi-modal information to advance this research area.

In continuation of these efforts, this study investigates how traditional Convolutional Neural Networks (CNNs) and recent Transformer-based models perform on the task of image-based carbohydrate estimation, providing insights into their respective strengths and limitations.

3 Proposed Method

3.1 Dataset and Preparation

The visual and nutritional dataset, Nutrition5k [15], is publicly available. In this study, we use 3,079 RGB images, examples of which are shown in Fig. 1. Nutrition5k provides carbohydrate information at the dish level in Comma-Separated Values (CSV) format. We carefully aligned the carbohydrate data with the corresponding food images, as illustrated in Fig. 2. All 3,079 RGB images were resized to 224×224 pixels and split into 80% training and 20% testing sets, resulting in 2,463 training and 616 testing images. The training set was further divided into 80:20 for training and validation. For the two experiments involving data augmentation (described in more detail in Sect. 3.2), the applied augmentations include RandomContrast, RandomFlip, RandomRotation, and RandomZoom.

3.2 Model Selection

In this work, we conducted deep learning-based comparative experiments between traditional vision models, such as CNNs, and more modern Transformer-based models. We selected VGG-16 [14] as the representative CNN due to its

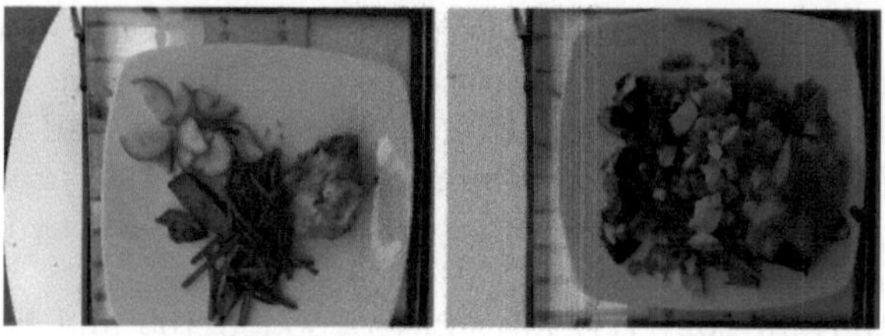

Fig. 1. Example images used in this study.

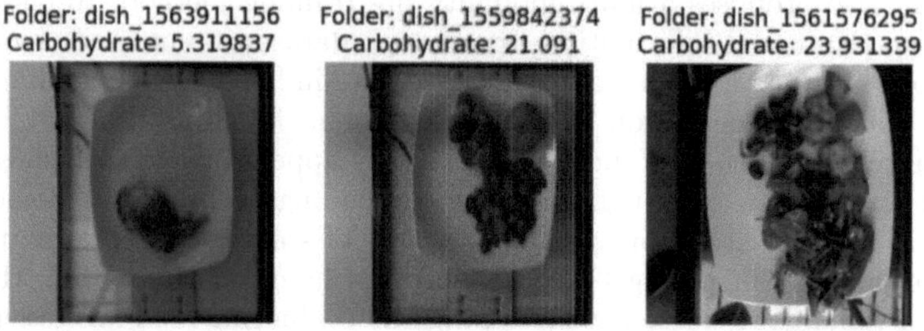

Fig. 2. Example of images and their corresponding carbohydrates.

simple and well-established architecture, strong performance in image recognition tasks, availability of pre-trained weights for transfer learning, and suitability for feature extraction. These properties make it an effective baseline for comparing with more recent CNN models, such as EfficientNet and ConvNeXt, in image-based carbohydrate estimation. For the Transformer-based models, we chose Vision Transformer (ViT) [4] due to its ability to capture long-range dependencies in images through self-attention, its competitive performance on various vision benchmarks, and the growing evidence that Transformers can outperform CNNs in tasks requiring fine-grained visual reasoning [5]. This combination allows us to systematically compare the strengths and limitations of CNNs and Transformers for food image-based carbohydrate prediction.

To systematically evaluate food carbohydrate estimation, we designed three experiments for each architecture (VGG-16 and ViT) while keeping the vision backbone frozen. Experiments 1 and 2 use a simple sequence of Dense layers, serving as a baseline for the classifier head. Experiments 3 and 4 introduce Dropout and an additional Dense layer, which may help capture complex mappings between visual features and carbohydrate values while potentially reducing overfitting. Experiments 5 and 6 further incorporate data augmentation on the training set, which may improve model robustness and generalization by simulating variations in angle, lighting, and portion size. This experimental design allows us to isolate the effects of classifier design and augmentation and provides a controlled comparison between CNN and Transformer architectures, offering practical insights for building accurate and reliable food carb estimation models. The detailed architectures of the six experiments are as follows:

Experiment 1 – VGG-16: Backbone → Flatten → Dense 200 → Dense 150 → Dense 100 → Dense 50 → Dense 10 → Dense 1.

Experiment 2 – ViT: Backbone → Flatten → Dense 200 → Dense 150 → Dense 100 → Dense 50 → Dense 10 → Dense 1.

Experiment 3 – VGG-16 with Dropout and Dense 500: Backbone → Flatten → Dropout 0.5 → Dense 500 → Dense 200 → Dense 150 → Dense 100 → Dense 50 → Dense 10 → Dense 1.

Experiment 4 – ViT with Dropout and Dense 500: Backbone → Flatten → Dropout 0.5 → Dense 500 → Dense 200 → Dense 150 → Dense 100 → Dense 50 → Dense 10 → Dense 1.

Experiment 5 – VGG-16 with data augmentation: Data Augmentation → Backbone → Flatten → Dropout 0.5 → Dense 500 → Dense 200 → Dense 150 → Dense 100 → Dense 50 → Dense 10 → Dense 1.

Experiment 6 – ViT with data augmentation: Data Augmentation → Backbone → Flatten → Dropout 0.5 → Dense 500 → Dense 200 → Dense 150 → Dense 100 → Dense 50 → Dense 10 → Dense 1.

4 Experimental Result

Table 1 and Fig. 3 summarize the results of the six experiments. Each experiment was trained in Keras (TensorFlow backend) for 20 epochs with a batch size of 64, using the Adam optimizer with a learning rate of 0.0001, Mean Squared Error (MSE) as the loss function, and Mean Absolute Error (MAE) as the evaluation metric, under three different random seeds Table 1.

To facilitate interpretation in the context of food carbohydrate counting, prediction errors were categorized into three groups: green for errors less than 7 g, yellow for errors between 7 (inclusive) and 10 g, and red for errors of 10 g or more. This classification provides a more interpretable and clinically meaningful assessment of the model's gram-level accuracy. Errors below 7 g (green) indicate highly accurate predictions unlikely to affect carbohydrate management, errors between 7 and 10 g (yellow) represent moderate deviations that are generally acceptable, and errors of 10 g or more (red) highlight cases where predictions could meaningfully impact blood glucose control. Examples from each group are shown in Fig. 4, and a detailed analysis of the three-group evaluation is presented in Table 2 and Fig. 5.

Results in Table 2 and Fig. 5 highlight the superior performance of the ViT model (Experiments 2, 4, and 6) compared to the VGG-16 model (Experiments 1, 3, and 5). In particular, Experiment 2 demonstrated excellent predictive capabilities, with 85.33% of the 616-image test dataset achieving errors below 7 g (green). However, to translate these findings into effective support for T1DM patients in Thailand, it is essential to continue developing and testing models using Thai food photography to ensure accurate carbohydrate estimation in local dietary contexts.

Table 1. Test-set results from the six experiments.

Exp.	MAE ↓		MSE ↓		RMSE ↓	
	3 rounds	mean±SD	3 rounds	mean±SD	3 rounds	mean±SD
1	13.63	13.11	1334.62	610.45	36.53	22.68
	12.97	± 0.47	254.76	± 627.18	15.96	± 11.99
	12.72		241.97		15.56	
2	5.03	5.07	1141.22	1144.21	33.78	33.82
	5.11	± 0.04	1140.07	± 6.21	33.76	± 0.09
	5.08		1151.36		33.93	
3	13.63	13.04	1340.36	611.75	36.61	22.69
	12.85	± 0.52	252.77	± 631.02	15.90	± 12.06
	12.64		242.11		15.56	
4	9.09	8.81	1217.75	1217.83	34.90	34.90
	8.59	± 0.26	1217.33	± 0.54	34.87	± 0.01
	8.75		1218.40		34.91	
5	13.71	12.67	1357.91	611.91	36.85	22.58
	11.21	± 1.30	224.60	± 646.21	14.99	± 12.36
	13.09		253.21		15.91	
6	9.34	9.52	1225.64	1233.68	35.01	35.12
	9.67	± 0.17	1232.20	± 8.87	35.10	± 0.13
	9.55		1243.19		35.26	

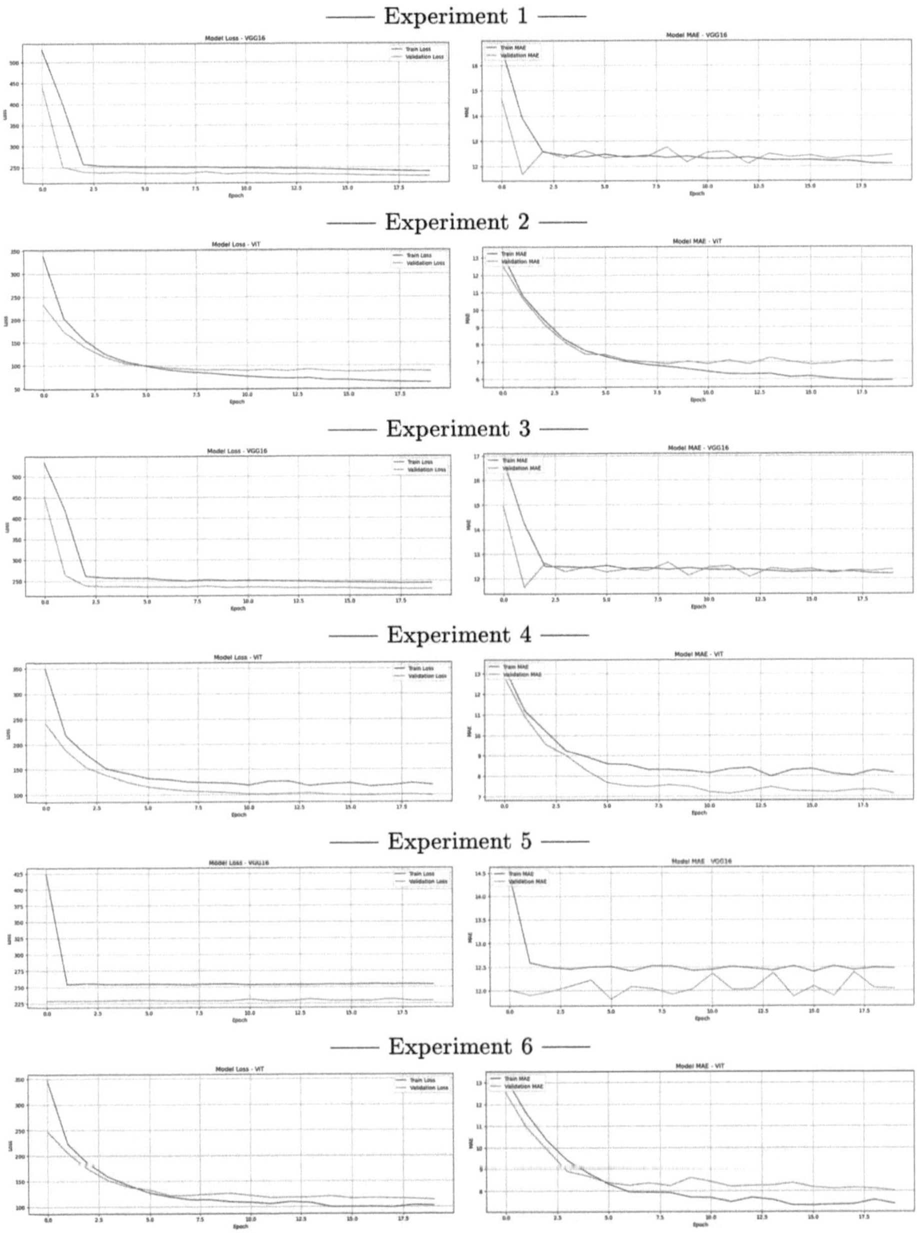

Fig. 3. Training graphs for the six experiments: MSE on the left and MAE on the right.

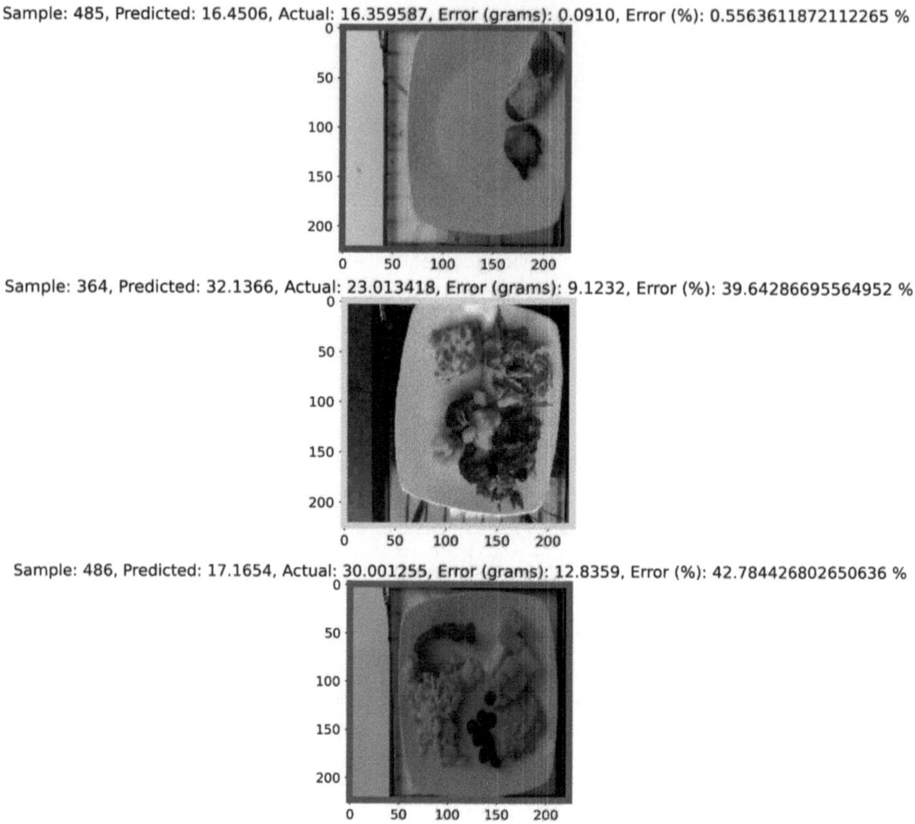

Fig. 4. Examples of our three-group error evaluation, from top to bottom, are as follows: Green group (error less than 7 g), Yellow group (error less than 10 g), and Red group (error greater than or equal to 10 g). (Color figure online)

Table 2. Proportion of predictions (%, mean ± SD computed from three models trained with different random seeds) falling into each error group across the six experiments.

	Green (%)	Yellow (%)	Red (%)
Experiment 1	27.54 ± 0.34	11.64 ± 2.33	60.82 ± 2.93
Experiment 2	85.33 ± 0.41	7.15 ± 0.66	7.52 ± 0.41
Experiment 3	28.08 ± 0.98	11.96 ± 1.31	59.96 ± 2.37
Experiment 4	58.06 ± 2.98	15.31 ± 0.54	26.62 ± 2.40
Experiment 5	32.14 ± 6.37	15.85 ± 5.24	52.00 ± 12.79
Experiment 6	59.47 ± 2.15	13.97 ± 0.69	26.57 ± 1.31

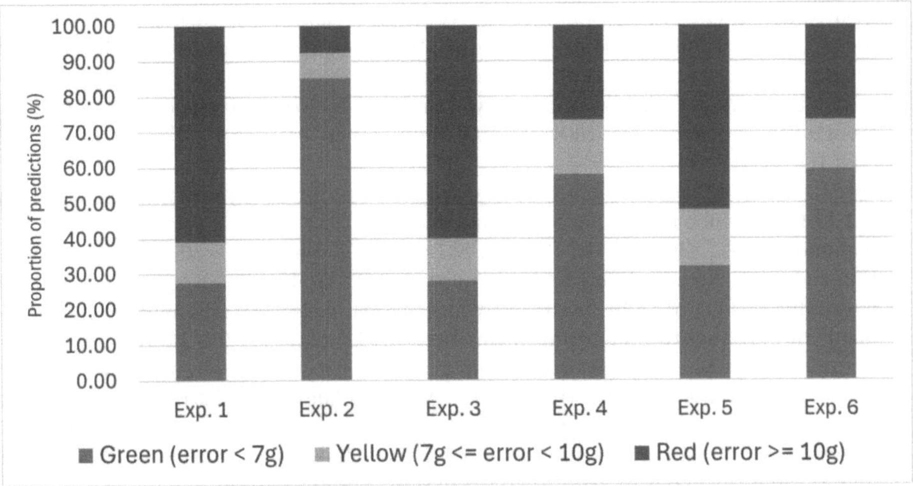

Fig. 5. Proportion of predictions (%, mean computed from three models trained with different random seeds) in each error group across the six experiments.

5 Conclusion

This study presents a non-intrusive, vision-based approach for estimating carbohydrate content from food images. Using two pre-trained vision backbones, VGG-16 and ViT, we conducted six experimental settings on the Nutrition5k dataset. Our results indicate that ViT consistently outperforms VGG-16, achieving the highest proportion of highly accurate predictions (errors below 7 g), demonstrating the potential of Transformer-based architectures for precise, image-based carbohydrate estimation.

For future work, improving portion and dish size estimation in images will be essential, as carbohydrate content depends not only on food type but also on volume and thickness. Techniques such as object detection combined with depth map analysis could enable the model to better capture these characteristics. This is particularly important for Thai cuisine, where dishes often contain mixed ingredients with varying densities and presentation styles. Integrating these techniques is expected to enhance prediction accuracy and ensure the model is practical and reliable in real-world dietary management scenarios.

References

1. Abela, A.G., Fava, S.: Why is the incidence of type 1 diabetes increasing? Curr. Diabetes Rev. **17**(8) (2021)
2. Chotwanvirat, P., Hnoohom, N.H., Rojroongwasinkul, N., Kriengsinyos, W.: Feasibility study of an automated carbohydrate estimation system using Thai food images in comparison with estimation by dietitians. Front. Nutr. **8** (2021)

3. Contreras, I., Guso, M., Beneyto, A., Vehi, J.: Photo-based carbohydrates counting using pre-trained transformer models. IFAC-PapersOnLine **56**(2), 11533–11538 (2023)
4. Dosovitskiy, A., et al.: An image is worth 16 × 16 words: transformers for image recognition at scale. In: International Conference on Learning Representations (ICLR) (2021)
5. He, J., et al.: TransFG: a transformer architecture for fine-grained recognition. In: AAAI Conference on Artificial Intelligence (AAAI) (2022)
6. Kahanovitz, L., Sluss, P.M., Russell, S.J.: Type 1 diabetes–a clinical perspective. Point Care J. Near-Patient Test. Technol. **16**(1), 37–40 (2017)
7. Kawamura, T., et al.: The factors affecting on estimation of carbohydrate content of meals in carbohydrate counting. Clin. Pediatr. Endocrinol. **24**(4), 153–165 (2015)
8. Kuroda, A., et al.: Easy estimation of carbohydrate count in diabetic diet therapy based on Japanese food substitution list. J. Japan Diab. Soc. **53**(6), 391–395 (2010)
9. Likitsmaskul, S., Reutrakul, S., Kongsomboonwet, S., Rawdaree, P.: Carbohydrate counting for health and diabetes control. In: Diabetes Association of Thailand under the Patronage of Her Royal Highness Princess Maha Chakri Sirindhorn, Bangkok, 3rd printing edn. (2019) (in Thai)
10. Lin, X., et al.: Global, regional, and national burden and trend of diabetes in 195 countries and territories: an analysis from 1990 to 2025. Sci. Rep. **10** (2020)
11. Luangaphirom, T., Jocknoi, L., Wunchum, C., Chokerungreang, K., Siriborvornratanakul, T.: ThaiNutriChat: development of a Thai large language model-based chatbot for health food services. Multimedia Syst. **30**(5) (2024)
12. Prentice, R.L., et al.: Four-day food record macronutrient intake, with and without biomarker calibration, and chronic disease risk in postmenopausal women. Am. J. Epidemiol. **191**(6) (2022)
13. Putz, P., Kogler, B., Bersenkowitsch, I.: Reliability and validity of assessing energy and nutrient intake with the Vienna food record: a cross-over randomised study. Nutr. J. **18** (2019)
14. Prentice, R.L., et al.: Four-day food record macronutrient intake, with and without biomarker calibration, and chronic disease risk in postmenopausal women. Am. J. Epidemiol. **191**(6) (2022)
15. Thames, Q., et al.: Nutrition5k: towards automatic nutritional understanding of generic food. In: 2021 IEEE/CVF Conference on Computer Vision and Pattern Recognition (CVPR), pp. 8899–8907 (2021)
16. Wibowo, M.F., Pyle, A., Lim, E., Ohde, J.W., Liu, N., Karlström, J.: Insights into the current and future state of AI adoption within health systems in Southeast Asia: cross-sectional qualitative study. J. Med. Internet Res. **27** (2025)
17. Wu, X., Fu, X., Liu, Y., Lim, E.P., Hoi, S.C., Sun, Q.: A large-scale benchmark for food image segmentation. In: Proceedings of the 29th ACM International Conference on Multimedia (MM '21), pp. 506–515 (2021)

FlexGen: Responsive Web Layout Synthesis via YOLO-Powered Object Detection and Flexbox Design Principles

Thin Thin Hlaing[1(✉)] and Tomoko Ozeki[2]

[1] Department of Electrical and Electronic Engineering, Tokai University, Hiratsuka, Kanagawa, Japan
thinthinhlaing.developer@gmail.com
[2] Department of Civil and Environmental Engineering, Hosei University, Tokyo, Japan
tozeki@hosei.ac.jp

Abstract. Developing web applications for multiple platforms is a complex task that requires substantial time and effort. The development of a system capable of automating the creation of responsive websites could significantly reduce the associated development effort. As the demand for web applications continues to rise in contemporary society, numerous studies have investigated the automation of website generation, often leveraging frameworks such as Bootstrap. However, generating websites using the Flexbox layout presents a unique set of challenges. The present study aims to address the forementioned specific challenge by exploring website generation utilizing the Flexbox layout. To achieve this goal, we integrate the advantages of deep learning object detection techniques, specifically YOLO, with traditional computer programming methods. The focus of this study is on the graphical user interface (GUI) layout and the relationships between its components, with the actual text values of the labels being excluded from consideration.

Keywords: YOLO · Website Generation · Responsive · Flexbox

1 Introduction

1.1 Responsive Websites

Modern businesses increasingly depend on websites, with electronic devices such as personal computers, tablets, and mobile phones being widely utilized. Consequently, it is imperative to design websites that adapt effectively to diverse screen sizes. Developing separate code for each platform poses significant challenges. A more efficient approach involves employing flexible source code capable of functioning across multiple platforms. A responsive [1] website is designed to deliver optimal user experience across a wide range of devices, from desktop computers to mobile phones. The layout, images, and content of a responsive website automatically adjust to accommodate the screen size, resolution, and orientation of the device being used. Several approaches including Bootstrap, media queries, flexbox Layout and CSS Grid Layout, are commonly employed to achieve responsiveness.

C. Xu (Ed.): ICMLSC 2026, CCIS 2948, pp. 257–270, 2027.
https://doi.org/10.1007/978-981-92-1546-1_21

1.2 Flexbox Layout

The Flexbox [2, 3] layout is a layout module that simplifies the creation of flexible and responsive layout structures. It is a one-dimensional layout system that operates based on the flex-flow directions, either along the x-axis or y-axis (see Fig. 1). Items are arranged along the main axis (from main-start to main-end) or the cross axis (from cross-start to cross-end). Unlike traditional layout methods, Flexbox [2, 3] offers a more efficient approach for distributing space and aligning items within a container, particularly when the layout needs to be responsive to varying screen sizes.

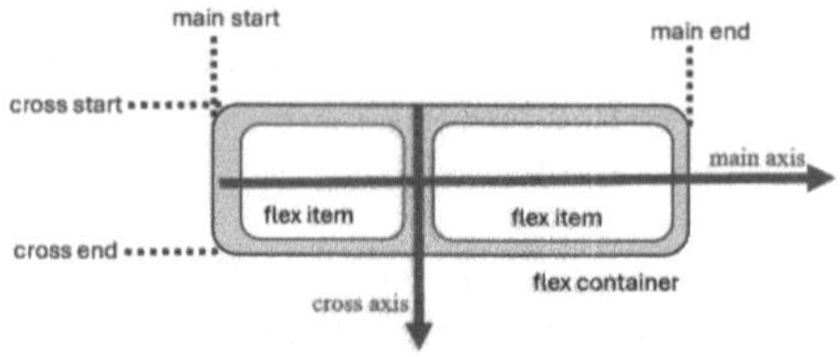

Fig. 1. Flexbox Layout

1.3 Website Development Process

In today's economy, having a website becomes a key part of doing business, even if it involves some cost. The development process usually starts with a meeting between the client and the business analysis team to understand and document what the website needs to be done. These requirements are then shared with the design team, who creates the user interface (UI) and user experience (UX) design to match the client's goals. Once the design is approved, it is forwarded to the development team for implementation. The development phase is generally divided into two main parts: backend development and frontend development.

The backend is typically handled by backend developers and involves implementing the server-side logic, database interactions, and the integration with third-party services to support the business logic and functionality of the application. The frontend is developed by frontend developers who translate the approved UI/UX designs into a functional user interface using technologies such as HyperText Markup Language (HTML), Cascading Style Sheets (CSS), and JavaScript. The goal of this research is to automate the frontend development process enabling the frontend code to be generated automatically without deep programming knowledge as soon as the UI/UX designers complete their designs.

1.4 Contribution

To our knowledge, Flexbox has not been the primary focus of previously automated HTML generation pipelines. This study specifically on utilizing the Flexbox [2, 3] layout approach that can facilitate layout adjustments based on the screen size and orientation of the device. In contrast to previous approaches that utilize other layout systems such as fluid and elastic layouts [4], our method generates HTML code using the Flexbox [2, 3] layout only. The Flexbox [2, 3] layout ensures that websites maintain a well-organized appearance, regardless of the device or screen size used.

2 Methodology

This research focuses on mock-up-driven website generation. Due to constraints in the available dataset, the study adopts a hybrid approach that combines deep learning methods with a heuristic algorithm, rather than relying on a fully end-to-end pipeline. The proposed system is composed of three main components: user interface (UI) component detection, analysis of component relationships, and HTML code generation using a Flexbox layout [2, 3].

In the first stage, deep learning techniques are employed to classify UI components and identify their spatial locations. The output consists of bounding boxes that define the coordinates of each detected component, along with labels specifying their respective types. According to benchmark evaluations provided by Ultralytics, YOLOv11 [5] surpasses YOLOv6 in key object detection metrics. This performance advantage motivated the selection of YOLOv11 [5] for this study, aiming to enhance detection accuracy and reliability in UI component recognition tasks. Additionally, the pretrained model EfficientDet [6] is also employed for object detection on the website, enabling a comparative evaluation of the performance between YOLOv11 [5] and EfficientDet [6]. Both YOLOv11 [5] and EfficientDet [6] were trained on a custom dataset created for this study to better adapt the models to the specific characteristics of UI components.

The second stage involves analyzing the relationships between UI components. A heuristic algorithm is employed to construct a hierarchical representation that captures the relationships between UI components. By applying predefined rules tailored for Flexbox layout, the system calculates appropriate class names and generates corresponding JSON representation that captures the hierarchical relationships among UI components. As the final stage, this JSON is subsequently compiled into functional HTML, effectively rendering a layout structured according to Flexbox principles [2, 3] (see Fig. 2).

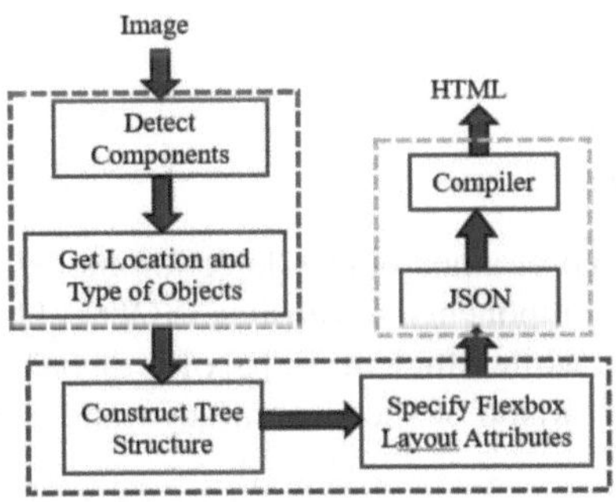

Fig. 2. Overall Workflow of Automatic Website Generation

3 Experiment

3.1 Dataset Preparation and Annotation

The dataset is based on the original WebSight dataset [7], which includes webpage images along with their corresponding HTML code. However, for our purposes, we require bounding box information for each component on the webpage. Therefore, the dataset was manually annotated using Roboflow, resulting in a total of 1,000 images. (linked as https://universe.roboflow.com/test-yzgsh/websight).

Image selection focused on two visually distinct page types: landing pages and form-based layouts to ensure representative coverage of core UI components classes: button, header, image, paragraph, text, and textbox. This targeted sampling approach was intended to reflect realistic and diverse layout structures aligned with the objectives of our study. All annotations were performed manually by the author and subsequently verified through a second pass review by the same annotator to ensure consistency and accuracy. Additional manual consistency checks were conducted on a subset of the dataset to further maintain annotation quality.

The dataset was then divided into 70% for training, 20% for validation, and 10% for testing. A summary of the class distribution is provided in Table 1 to ensure transparency regarding representation and potential detection difficulty. Further discussion of class balance and its impact on performance is provided in the Evaluation section.

Table 1. Class Distribution Across the Dataset.

ClassName	Train	Val	Test	Total
button	283	83	53	419
header	1265	355	191	1811
image	671	200	98	969
paragraph	1140	338	162	1640
text	2267	614	320	3201
textBox	83	28	23	134

3.2 Component Detection

This research employs two pretrained object detection models: YOLOv11 [5] and EfficientDet [6] for detecting components in websites. YOLOv11 [5] is known for its speed and real-time performance, while EfficientDet [6] offers a balance between accuracy and efficiency, enabling a comparison of speed-accuracy trade-offs in the context of object detection models.

YOLOv11 Setup

The Ultralytics YOLOv11 [5] model, specifically the "YOLOm" variant, was applied to the dataset, trained over 150 epochs using a batch size of 8 as shown in Table 2.

For inference, YOLOv11 was configured with a confidence threshold of 0.25 and a Non-Maximum Suppression (NMS) IoU threshold of 0.7, prioritizing high-confidence detection while allowing for some overlap among bounding boxes.

EfficientDet Setup

Experiments were also performed using efficientDet-b0 variant [6] trained for 37 epochs with a batch size of 2 as presented in Table 1. EfficientDet [6] was configured with a lower confidence threshold of 0.05 and a stricter NMS IoU threshold of 0.5, which permitted more initial detections but filtered overlapping results more aggressively (see Table 1).

Table 2. Parameters.

Parameters	YOLOv11	EfficientDet
Confidence threshold	0.25	0.05
IoU threshold for Non-Max Suppression	0.7	0.5
epoch	150	37
batch	8	2

Training Parameters and Early Stopping

Early stopping was not applied to YOLOv11, which completed all 150 training epochs. In contrast, EfficientDet [6] was trained with early stopping enabled, using a validation interval of 1 epoch, a minimum delta of 0.001, and a patience of 20 epochs. As a result, training in EfficientDet [6] stopped early at epoch 37. Additionally, no custom data augmentation strategies were introduced; default preprocessing and augmentation settings from each model's official implementation were used for consistency and reproducibility. Model checkpoints were saved at 10-epoch intervals during training.

Object Detection Performance and Model Selection

To evaluate the training behavior of efficientDet and YOLOv11, we recorded both training and validation loss across epochs. Figure 3 shows that effificentDet [6] exhibited signs of overfitting after epoch 26, with training loss continuing to decrease while validation loss increased, suggesting poor generalization to unseen data. In contrast, YOLOv11 maintained a more consistent gap between training and validation losses.

While both models were evaluated for their detection performance, YOLO11 demonstrated adequate accuracy for the purpose of this study. The mean average precision(mAP) of YOLOv11 at an Intersection over Union (IoU) threshold of 50% reaches 95.921% (see Table 3). The efficientDet [6] model achieved its highest detection performance with a mAP of 52.67%, which is considered insufficient (see Table 3). As a result, YOLOv11 was selected for use in subsequent stages of layout analysis and HTML generation.

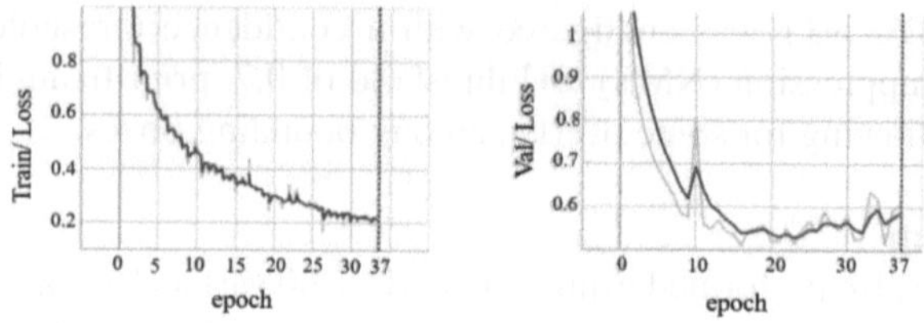

Fig. 3. Training Curves of EfficientDet: left—loss on training data, right—loss on validation data

Table 3. Model Comparison.

Metric	YOLO11	EfficinetDet
mAP@0.5	0.95921	0.5267
mAP@[0.5:0.95]	0.65667	0.314
F1 Score	0.88	0.5586
Precision	0.9366	0.5261
Recall	0.94922	0.6023
GPU Memory Usage	5.71 GB	6.613 GB

3.3 Analyzing the Relationship Between UI Components

The relationship between UI components is analyzed based on the output of the object detection stage, which consists of the bounding box coordinates (x_center, y_center, width, height) and the classification of each detected component.

Grouping Logic

The proposed grouping algorithm operates iteratively to organize UI components into hierarchical representation. To identify the possible groups of UI elements, the grouping algorithm considers both horizontal and vertical directions. In horizontal groupings, components are arranged side by side along the X-axis, with overlapping or closely aligned Y-axis positions to ensure visual consistency. In vertical groupings, components are stacked along the Y-axis, requiring their X-axis positions to overlap or remain in proximity (see Fig. 4).

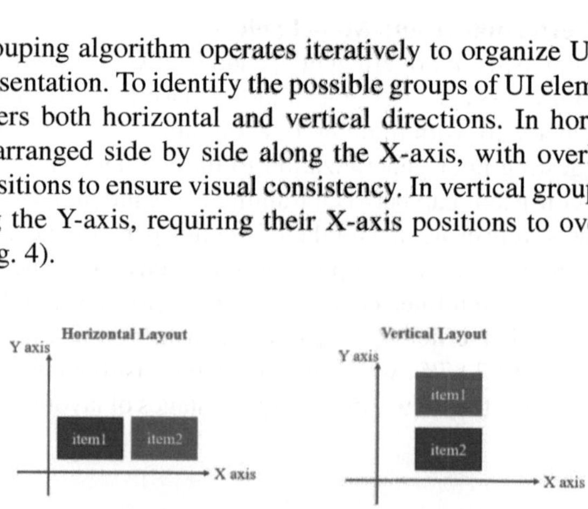

Fig. 4. Neighboring components arranged in horizontal and vertical layouts

To identify potential groupings of user interface (UI) components, the spatial distances between neighboring components are computed in both horizontal and vertical directions. As illustrated in Fig. 5(a), component1, and component2 are vertically adjacent, as are component4 and component5. By systematically analyzing these distances across all components, the method iteratively detects groups characterized by uniform spacing. Beginning with an initial pair of components, all adjacent components located within a predefined threshold are temporarily assigned to the same group. A container is then generated to encapsulate the components falling within this range, thereby forming coherent groups of components that exhibit consistent internode spacing (see Fig. 5).

At this stage, the containers have been established for both horizontal and vertical orientations. To determine the most appropriate grouping, the container encompassing the greater number of components is selected as the representative structure, and the corresponding layout direction (horizontal or vertical) is recorded. This container subsequently replaces the original components within the set (see Fig. 5).

The updated component set, consisting of the new container and remaining ungrouped components, is passed back into the iterative process. The procedure repeats until all components are consolidated into containers, ultimately producing a single root container that represents the complete hierarchical structure. If no candidate containers are detected at any iteration, all remaining components are directly encapsulated within a root container, and the algorithm terminates. The final output of this stage is a hierarchical representation of grouped UI components, as shown in figure (see Fig. 6). In the diagram, "V" represents vertical layout, and "H" indicates horizontal layout.

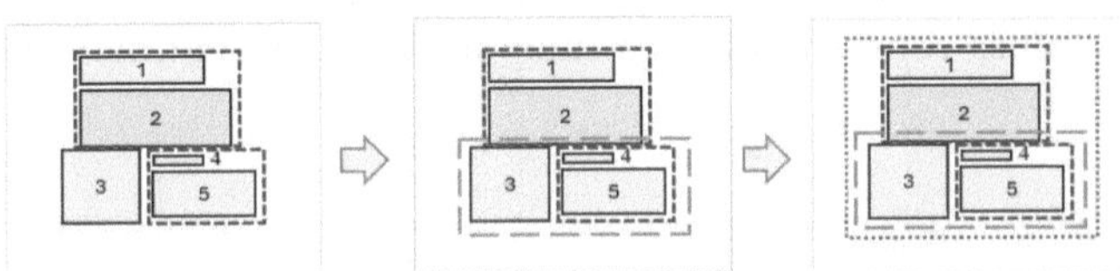

(a) (b) (c)

Fig. 5. Visualization of the iterative grouping process applied to input UI components

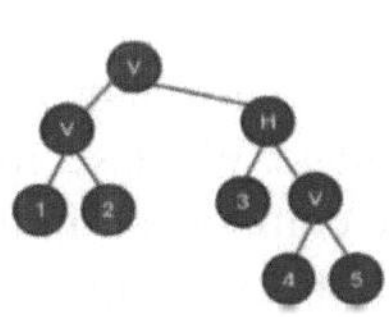

Fig. 6. Hierarchical representation of grouped UI components based on spatial proximity

Specification of Flexbox Layout Attributes

This study utilizes the behavior of Flexbox Layout Properties to determine the spatial distribution and sizing of flex items within a flex container, enabling the creation of a flexible website. The following flexbox layout properties [2, 3] were considered for calculation and analysis. These all-flexbox property values are derived through a heuristic algorithm applied after generating the hierarchical tree structure of all components within the website.

Justify-Content

This property controls the alignment of flex items along the main axis which is horizontal by default. It determines the distribution of space between and around the items within the container. The values considered in this study include flex-start, flex-end, center, space-between, space-around, and space-evenly. Rather than assigning fixed numerical values, these settings yield varying spatial arrangements depending on the available container space and the width of the individual items (see Fig. 7).

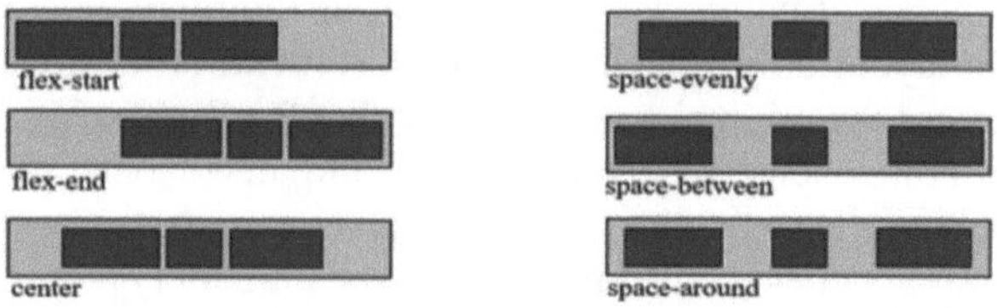

Fig. 7. Example of justify-content properties in a flex container

Align-Items

This property aligns items along the cross-axis which is vertical by default. It determines the vertical positioning of flex items within the container and can be evaluated based on the container's height, individual item heights, and the specified alignment. The alignment values considered in this study include flex-start, flex-end, center, and stretch (see Fig. 8).

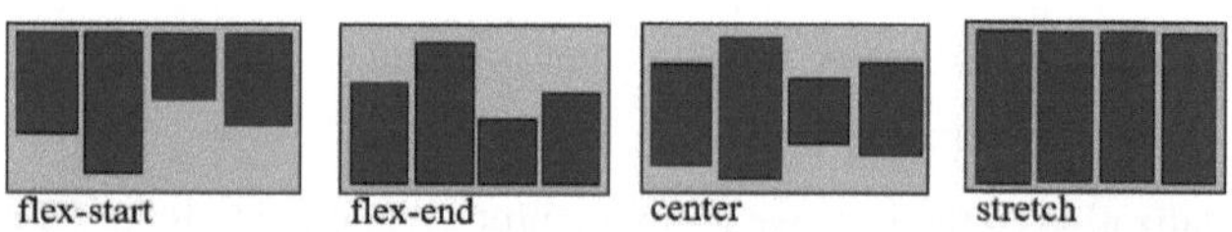

Fig. 8. Example of align-items properties in a flex container

Flex-Basis

This defines the initial main size of a flex item before free space is distributed. It can be expressed in fixed units or percentage. When set to auto, the item's size is determined by specified width or height of each component. In this study, the default value of flex-basis: auto is employed, which operates in conjunction with the flex-grow property to determine the size of flex items.

Flex-Grow

This property determines how much a flex item will grow relative to its siblings when positive free space is available. After the browser calculates the flex item's base size using flex-basis, the leftover space is distributed proportionally according to each item's flex-grow value, allowing items to expand beyond their initial size to fill the container. It is a unitless proportion; for example, if one item has flex-grow:2 and another has flex-grow:1, the first will take twice as much of the available space as the second (see Fig. 9).

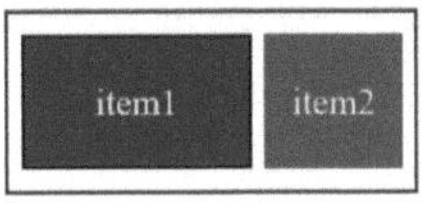

Fig. 9. Example of flex-grow properties in a flex container

Flex-Shrink

In contrast to flex-grow, flex-shrink controls how items shrink when there is insufficient space. The value is also unitless and determines the proportion reduction of item sizes. By default, flex-shrink is set to 1. In this study, we will use the default value, meaning that all flex items will shrink at the same rate if the container's size is smaller than the total flex-basis of the items.

Gap

The gap property specifies the spacing between flex items. It directly affects layout by introducing fixed space between items without using margins. The value is typically specified in length units and is added between each pair of items but not before the first or after the last item (see Fig. 10).

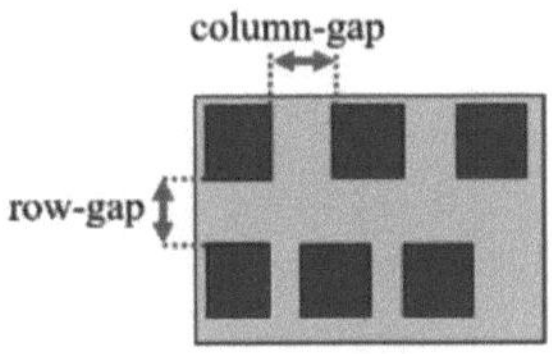

Fig. 10. Example of gap properties in a flex container

4 Experiment Result

4.1 Evaluation Metrics

To comprehensively evaluate the performance of the proposed system, we employed three complementary metrics:

1) Mean Average Precision (mAP) for Object Detection: This metric accesses the accuracy of detection and localizing core UI components within the input images, based on standard intersection-over-union (IoU) thresholds.
2) Structural Similarity Index (SSIM) for Layout Fidelity: SSIM was used to measure the structural similarity between the input UI image and the rendered output HTML. Both representations were abstracted to layout-only rectangles, omitting specific HTML element semantics, to focus solely on spatial and structural alignment.

3) Responsiveness Fidelity: To evaluate the responsiveness of the HTML layouts generated, a manual inspection of 20 webpages was conducted across multiple device breakpoints. This evaluation aimed to determine whether the generated layouts maintained structural integrity, visual consistency, and usability across varying viewport dimensions on different devices.

4.2 Object Detection Evaluation

In our experiments, YOLOv11 [5] achieved higher scores than EfficientDet [6] across all key evaluation metrics. YOLOv11 [5] achieved a mean Average Precision (mAP) of 0.95921 and an F1 score of 0.88, compared to EfficientDet's mAP of 0.5267 and F1 score of 0.5586 (see Table 3). As shown in Table 4, EfficientDet achieved adequate accuracy for classes with clear visual pattern (image, button) but struggled significantly with text-heavy elements (text, paragraph, textbox, header), with accuracy below 0.3. YOLOv11, by contrast, consistently achieved high accuracy across all categories, indicating better robustness to textual density and layout complexity. Additionally, YOLOv11 [5] demonstrated significantly better efficiency, with GPU memory usage of 5.71 GB, whereas EfficientDet [6] consumed 6.613 GB of GPU memory. These results highlight the advantage of YOLOv11 [5] in terms of both performance and resource efficiency for web UI component detection.

Table 4. mAP@0.5 per Class Comparison.

Class	YOLO11	EfficinetDet
Button	0.951	0.571
Image	0.98	0.6323
Paragraph	0.978	0.1401
Text	0.926	0.2344
TextBox	0.893	0.2686
Header	0.938	0.3251

4.3 SSIM-Based Evaluation of Layout Fidelity in Generated Websites

To access the visual fidelity of the webpage generated, actual UI components and content were intentionally excluded. The HTML-rendered output was compared with the corresponding ground truth image from the dataset. In this stage, the generated HTML focuses only on reproducing structural layout of the webpage. Each detected UI element is represented by a rectangular <div> placeholder, preserving the component's spatial position and dimensions. Before computing the Structural Similarity Index Measure (SSIM), the ground truth images were preprocessed—converted the components into rectangular shapes and resized—to match the dimensions and format of the generated output (see Fig. 11). In the comparative visualization (see Fig. 12), the preprocessed ground truth is displayed on the left, while the corresponding HTML-generated version is shown on the right. An average SSIM score of 0.7291 was obtained over 99 images from the dataset. While this score indicates a moderate level of similarity, visual inspection confirms that the output is perceptually acceptable, maintaining key structural and aesthetic elements of the original design (see Fig. 12).

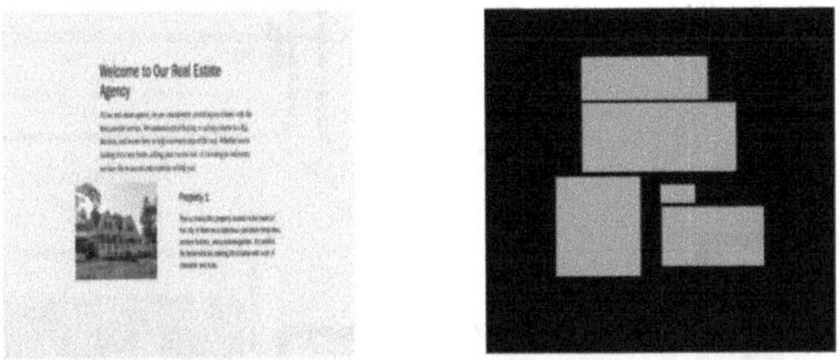

Fig. 11. Ground truth image (left) and its preprocessed version used for comparison (right)

Fig. 12. Visual comparison: left—preprocessed input image (ground truth), right—HTML-rendered output generated by our system.

4.4 Responsiveness Evaluation

At this stage, the generated HTML integrates the UI components together with their corresponding actual content. This configuration allows for a comprehensive evaluation of the webpage's responsiveness across multiple device categories. To evaluate the adaptability of the generated layouts, a manual assessment was conducted across three device types: mobile (iPhone 14 Pro Max, 1290 × 2796 pixels, 6.69-inch), tablet (iPad Pro 11-inch, 1668 × 2388 pixels, 11-inch), and desktop (1280 × 1024 pixels). The mobile and tablet layouts were accessed in both portrait and landscape orientations, whereas the desktop version were evaluated in a single standard view.

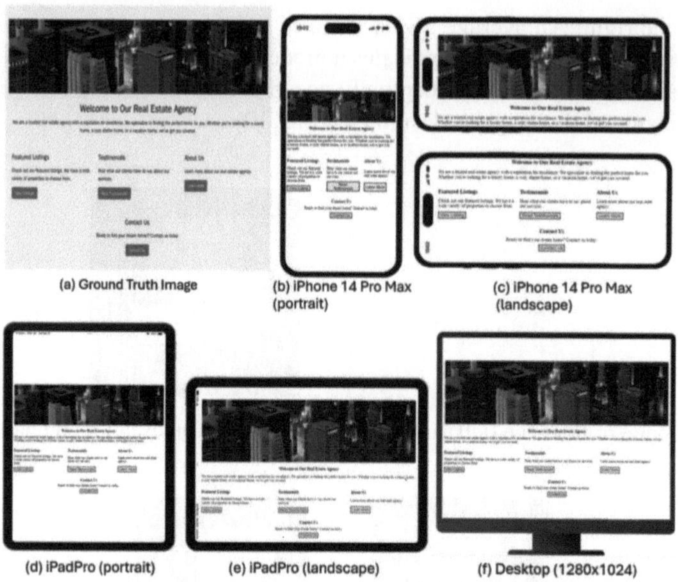

Fig. 13. Layout rendering comparisons across devices. (a) Ground truth; (b) iPhone14 Pro Max (Portrait); (c) iPhone14 Pro Max (Landscape); (d) iPad Pro (Portrait); (e) iPad Pro (Landscape); (f) Desktop

The assessment was based on seven responsiveness criteria: (1) No Overflow, ensuring that content did not extend beyond its container; (2) Proper Layout Scaling, maintaining horizontal alignment on larger viewports and vertical stacking on smaller ones; (3) No Overlapping Visible Elements, preventing visual obstruction between components; (4) Dynamic Wrapping, enabling elements to reposition to the next line when the available horizontal space becomes constrained; (5) Image Scaling, preserving proportional resizing and clarity; (6) No Horizontal Scrolling, ensuring all content fit within the viewport width; and (7) Proper Scaling Between Elements, maintaining proper margins.

Across all tested devices and orientations, the layouts achieved an average overall responsiveness score of 93%, indicating strong adaptability, structural stability, and visual coherence across varying screen sizes. The corresponding layout renderings for each device and orientation are illustrated in Fig. 13.

5 Conclusion and Future Work

5.1 Conclusion

In conclusion, the proposed system detects core UI components and generates responsive HTML layouts. Object detection, performed using YOLOv11 [5], achieved a mAP of 0.95921, compared with previous work [8] using YOLOv6R3s, which attained a peak mAP@0.5 of 0.951, indicating competitive detection performance. Layout fidelity, measured via SSIM, reached 0.7291 out of 1, reflecting moderate structural similarity with emphasis on spatial alignment. A preliminary responsiveness evaluation across multiple device breakpoints yielded an average score of 93% suggesting generally consistent structural integrity and usability, though based on a limited sample of 20 layouts. Future work will focus on improving visual fidelity and responsiveness, targeting a SSIM score above 0.8 and broader validation across diverse layouts.

5.2 Limitation

While the proposed system demonstrates effectiveness in detecting UI components and generating structurally responsive layouts, several limitations remain. The system is designed to work with static mockup images and does not consider the actual text context, language, user interaction behavior, device-specific design conventions or user segment information (such as age, gender, or geographic region). These factors are essential for ensuring inclusive and context-aware UI generation, particularly in real-world applications involving varied audiences and usage environments. Addressing these limitations presents an opportunity for future research aimed at enhancing the personalization and accessibility of automated UI design systems.

5.3 Future Work

Building upon this foundation, future research will focus on analyzing the hierarchical relationships among UI components in more complex web interfaces to enhance the systematic insight into the complexity of the component organization. A key limitation of the existing heuristic algorithm is its reliance on fixed threshold value, which constrains its adaptability and effectiveness when applied to more complex website layouts. To address the limitations of the current heuristic-based approach, future work will explore a fully end-to-end pipeline powered by deep learning pipeline, offering more flexible and robust understanding of hierarchical UI component relationships, ultimately improving the system's robustness and scalability.

Additionally, the evaluation framework will be expended to heuristic-based detection methods and classical computer vision (CV) techniques for grouping UI components, serving as baseline references to better quantify performance gaps and strengthen empirical validation. This direction will also contribute to a more comprehensive comparison across a wide spectrum of layout analysis strategies. Given that prior studies on GUI element detection vary in datasets, annotation methods, and evaluation protocols, direct comparisons are challenging. To address challenges in comparing prior work due to differences in datasets and evaluation methods, we plan to evaluate both prior systems and our approach on a common validation dataset to enable fairer performance assessments.

While direct ablation of the grouping and layout inference modules is constrained by pipeline dependencies, simplified alternatives will be explored to assess their individual impact. Additionally, incorporating user and platform-specific information such as demographics, device types, or localization requirements, is expected to enhance layout responsiveness and adaptability, making it more responsive and adaptable to different real-world usage scenarios.

References

1. Kim, B.: Responsive web design, discoverability, and mobile challenge. Libr. Technol. Rep. **49**(6), 29–39 (2013)

2. Coyier, C.: CSS-tricks (2018). https://css-tricks.com/snippets/css/a-guide-to-flexbox/. Accessed 16 Sept 2025
3. Atkins Jr., T., et al.: CSS flexible box layout module (2018)
4. Sinha, N., Karim, R.: Compiling mockups to flexible UIS. In: Proceedings of the 2013 9th Joint Meeting on Foundations of Software Engineering, ESEC/FSE 2013, New York, NY, USA, pp. 312–322. Association for Computing Machinery (2013)
5. Jegham, N., Koh, C.Y., Abdelatti, M., Hendawi, A.: Evaluating the evolution of YOLO (you only look once) models: a comprehensive benchmark study of YOLO11 and its predecessors. arXivpreprint arXiv:2411.00201 (2024)
6. Tan, M., Pang, R., Le, Q.V.: EfficientDet: scalable and efficient object detection (2020)
7. Laurençon, H., Tronchon, L., Sanh, V.: Unlocking the conversion of web screenshots into HTML code with the WebSight dataset. arXiv preprint arXiv:2403.09029 (2024)
8. Daneshvar, S.S., Wang, S.: GUI element detection using SOTA YOLO deep learning models. arXiv preprint arXiv:2408.03507 (2024)

DR_VisionNet: A Vision Network for Classification of Diabetic Retinopathy

Eshaan Gupta, Vigyat Goel, and Manisha Parlewar(✉)

Guru Gobind Singh Indraprastha University, Delhi, India
mpparlewar@gmail.com

Abstract. Complications in Diabetes Mellitus leads to Diabetes Retinopathy (DR) which is a major cause of visual impairment and blindness worldwide. Different stages of Diabetes Retinopathy need different care and medications. Detection of DR at early stage is key to the treatment. Therefore, it is extremely important to classify the stage and the severity of DR for adequate therapy. Advantage of using machine learning techniques to classify different stage of DR is two-fold, the first being timely diagnosis and the second being reliability and cost effectiveness. Recently, various CNN-based approaches have been proposed to classify DR images. These approaches rely heavily on pre-trained networks and transfer learning. Since pre-trained networks are designed for generalized classification problem, fine tuning such networks for specific task is computationally heavy and time consuming. In this paper, we present a customized convolutional neural network DR_VisionNet to classify four classes/stages of DR. Instead of using pre-trained network, we first perform pre-processing and augmentation on the images and then process through the proposed customized network for Diabetic Retinopathy. The proposed combination of pre-processing and custom vision network is not only computationally efficient, but also results in better classification accuracy and precision as well as recall.

Keywords: Image classification · deep learning · Diabetic Retinopathy · DR_VisionNet

1 Introduction

One of the fastest growing non-communicable diseases is Diabetes Mellitus (DM). As per the recent data (2025) published by the International Diabetes Federation, 1 in 9 of the adult population (20–79 years) is living with diabetes. Statistically, 589 million adults (20–79 years) are living with diabetes and this figure is expected to increase to approximately 853 million by 2050 [16]. This is really an alarming situation, as DM leads to many serious long-term complications that affect many areas of the body, particularly eyes, blood vessels, kidneys and nerves [9]. DM is the main reason and is directly related to blindness in the elder population. Visual impairment caused by diabetes is referred to as Diabetic

C. Xu (Ed.): ICMLSC 2026, CCIS 2948, pp. 271–281, 2027.
https://doi.org/10.1007/978-981-92-1546-1_22

Retinopathy (DR). It's a complication of diabetes where high blood sugar levels damage the blood vessels in the retina, potentially leading to vision loss or blindness. Almost one-third of patients suffering from Diabetes Mellitus have been observed to be detected with DR. Around 103 million people worldwide have suffered from DR until 2020 and it is estimated that the number will increase in the future [13]. Due to complications in diabetes, blood vessels that feed the eye gets blocked due to glucose, resulting in swelling and blood leakage. Retinal swelling causes blurry and distorted vision, making it difficult for a person to see fine details. Medical practitioners analyze the severity or the stage of DR by examining the retinal scans. As DR progresses, different levels of severity in visual impairment are observed and labeled into four classes as mild, moderate, severe non-proliferative diabetic retinopathy and proliferative diabetic retinopathy. These development stages are illustrated in Fig. 1. In order to identify high risk patients, accurate classification of DR severity level is extremely helpful. Only highly skilled ophthalmologists can analyze and diagnose the DR stage of the patient. Such manual examination is time consuming and requires domain experts. However, machine learning algorithms have the potential to be fast and accurate in classifying DR stages.

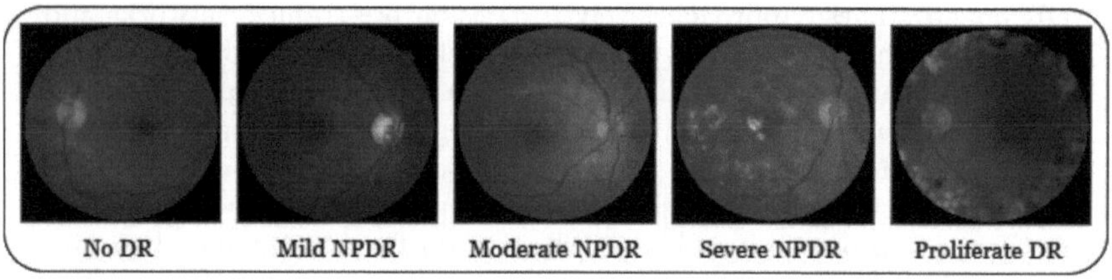

Fig. 1. 5 Stages of diabetic retinopathy (sample images from Messidor-2 dataset).

Numerous recent studies have worked on Diabetic Retinopathy classification using pre-trained convolutional neural networks (CNN) and fine tuning them [4]. Most popular pre-trained models in this field are ResNet variants (34, 50) [7], InceptionV3 [14] and EfficientNet variants(b0, small) [15]. Many studies have used publicly available datasets like EyePACS [8] and APTOS [2] to fine-tune these models on their datasets. Some works also apply pre-processing techniques such as image resizing, intensity normalization and data augmentation to improve model performance. Rezaee and Farnami [11] presented a method that uses a fusion of CNN with Transformer models to classify the severity of Diabetic Retinopathy. The architecture leverages both local feature extraction and global contextual modeling. The accuracy is 94.16% and AUC is 0.9638. Aftab and Akhtar [1] proposed a method that combines data fusion techniques with ensemble transfer learning to classify the severity of Diabetic Retinopathy. They have integrated multiple data sources and the strengths of various pre-trained deep learning models to achieve an accuracy 96.96%. In [3], Arora et al. introduced a diagnostic system that combines multiple deep learning models in an ensemble system. It combines the strength of several neural network architectures to achieve higher diagnostic accuracy for Diabetic Retinopathy. Their average accuracy is 86.53%.

Most of these studies rely heavily on pre-trained deep architecture model rather than using custom, lightweight convolutional neural network designs. They neither highlight the amount of time needed to train new models every time nor provide the explainability of the network. As noted in [4], great efficiency has been observed in the data pre-processing stage, so if we combine pre-processing with the customized CNN it will result in a faster, computationally efficient and accurate model for DR classification.

In this paper, we propose a customized convolutional neural network DR_VisionNet for classification of Diabetic Retinopathy. Instead of relying on the computationally heavy pre-trained networks, we designed a custom CNN which is computationally light as well as improves the classification accuracy. We have also proposed a pre-processing method due to which the proposed CNN converges gracefully as compared to that without pre-processed images. The proposed model comprises three modules: the first enhances the dataset images, the second DR_VisionNet, and the third is the interpretations of the proposed network. Comparative evaluations against other state-of-the-art methods on Messidor-2 datasets demonstrate that our model achieves superior performance.

The rest of the paper is structured as follows: Sect. 2 highlights the proposed methodology. Section 3 provides experiments and results. Finally, the conclusion is presented in Sect. 4.

2 Proposed Work

In this section, we introduce our DR_VisionNet Diabetic Retinopathy classification network. The images from the dataset are processed through two distinct pre-processing stages: the first is Contrast Limited Adaptive Histogram Equalization (CLAHE) and the second is gamma correction. Next, the proposed CNN is trained using the pre-processed images.

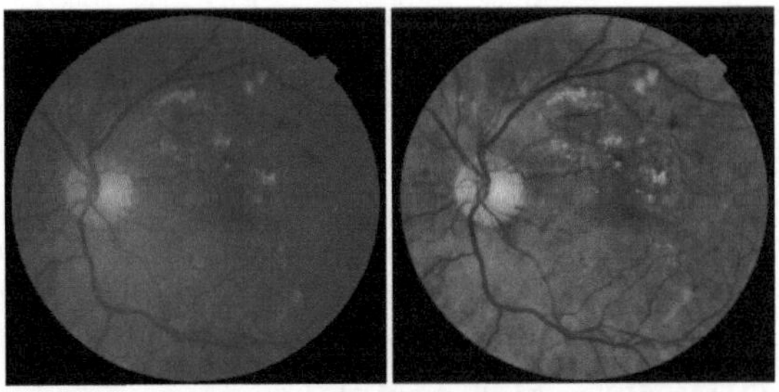

Fig. 2. Original image(left) and final processed image (right).

Pre-processing the images not only helps to clean the noise, but also enhances the features in the image. For data pre-processing, we first applied Contrast Limited Adaptive Histogram Equalization [17] to the images with grid size of 8 and clip limit of 1.1. CLAHE is an image processing technique that equalizes and enhances the local contrast of images while preventing amplification of noise. To prevent any color shift due to CLAHE, it was applied only on the luminance channel. This made sure that the original colors of the image remains intact, which are important features for DR classification. CLAHE was followed by gamma correction of 1.1. Gamma correction is a non linear operation which is used to adjust the brightness of the images in a more natural way, ensuring it looks accurate when being displayed. Notice how the vein structure, exudates, lesions and hemmorhages are clearly visible in the processed image compared to the original image shown in Fig. 2.

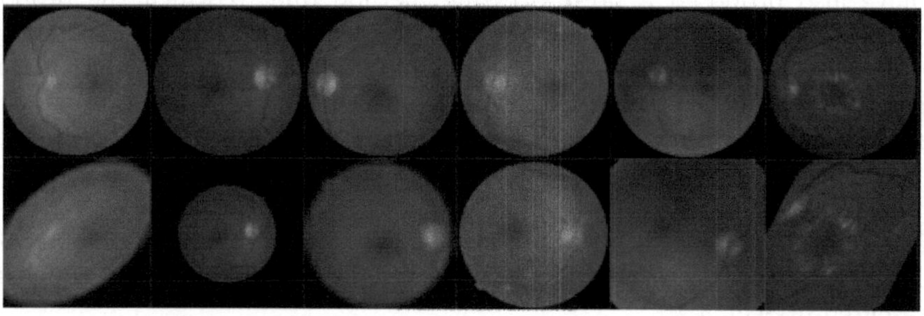

Fig. 3. Original images(top row) and augmented images (second row).

After pre-processing the images, it is important to solve the issue of data imbalance. For this, we used AugLy [10], an open source data augmentation library which provides over 100 augmentations. We selected eight augmentations from these and applied any two random augmentations on each image. These augmentations included vertical flip, horizontal flip, rotation, blurring, shuffling of pixels, introducing skewness, perspective transformation, and overlay stripes. These were added to include real world cases that a physician may encounter in his practice. These augmentations increased the sample size and prevents overfitting. Original and augmented images are shown in Fig. 3.

It was ensured that after applying augmentations, the target of 3000 images in each class was met. This balanced the data for training and also increased the sample size. Though it introduced some level of noise in the dataset, it was merely essential to do so to prevent the model from overfitting and introduce some real world scenarios where the image would not always be perfect.

2.1 Proposed DR_VisionNet Architecture

Our custom CNN architecture comprised of 3 convolution blocks, one downsample layer, one residual layer and finally a classifier layer as shown in Fig. 4. The idea behind this design was to keep the network simple and clear. The model takes the input size of 224 × 224 x 3. Each convolutional block consist of two sets of convolution, normalization and activation layer. Pre-processed images are first passed through the first convolution layer of the first block. This block has 3 input channels and 32 output channels, with a kernel size of 3 and stride of 1. The output from the convolution layer is normalized using Batch Normalization. We then apply Sigmoid Linear Unit function or Swish Activation function (SiLU). The output passes through the second set of convolution layer, batch norm and activation.

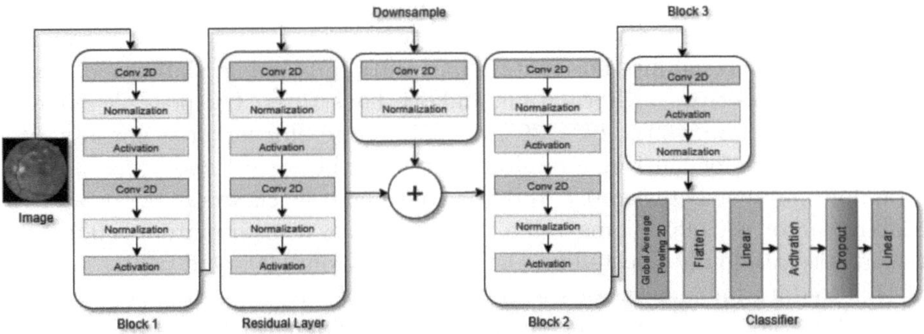

Fig. 4. Representation of the proposed DR_VisionNet.

The output of the first block is passed to two independent stages; downsample block and residual block. The downsample block consists of one convolution layer with takes 32 input channels and returns 64 output channels, with a kernel size of 3 and stride of 2. This part is then normalised using batch normalization. The second part is the residual block, which has an initial convolution layer of 32 input channels and 64 output channels with kernel size 3 and stride 2. The process remained same as to normalizing it and applying SiLU activation function. Another convolution layer was added with 64 input channel and 64 output channels with kernel size 3 and stride 1.

The outputs of the downsample and residual layer was added and passed onto the next stage, block 2. This block was similar to block 1 with 2 convolution layers, each followed by batch normalization and SiLU activation function. Block 2 takes input channel as 64 and outputs 128 channels. This is then passed onto the block 3, the final block of the network. Block 3 comprises of a convolution layer with 128 input channels and 256 output channels with a kernel size of 3 and stride 1. Finally, a classifier block consists of a global average pooling layer, a flattening layer, a linear (fully connected) layer which maps 256 features to 128, SiLU activation function, dropout layer of 30% and again a linear layer which maps 128 features to 5 classes.

We used cosine decay for learning rate annealing. This allows the model to start with a high learning rate, which enables faster convergence in the initial training process. As training progresses, the learning rate is lowered in a smooth and consistent manner. Cosine decay decreases the learning rate following the cosine function graph, avoiding sudden drops and helps maintain the stability throughout the model training. The lower learning rate helps the model perform better and increases the generalizability by settling for the low loss function.

3 Experiment Setup and Results

3.1 Dataset and Evaluation Metrics

For experimental evaluation we have used Messidor-2 dataset [6]. The original data set consisted of 1744 images. These images were pre-processed and augmented to get 15000 images, with 3000 images of each class. These augmentations included vertical flip, horizontal flip, rotation, blurring, shuffling of pixels, skewness, perspective transformation, and overlay stripes. The possible angles of rotation are 15°, 30°, 60°, -15°, -30°, or -60°. Large blur factor is not advisable in DR images, so for blurring a random kernel size between 1 and 3 was selected. A random number between 0.2 to 0.4 is considered as skewness factor and the shuffling factor is 0.005. Sigma value for perspective transformation is 0.05. The stripes were randomly selected on the width between 0.005 and 0.001.

Due to data imbalance, for the classification of DR, the AUC and F1 scores are used as the main metric to determine the validity of the results. We have also used other metrics such as accuracy and recall to validate the performance of the proposed model.

3.2 Training Strategy and Experimental Analysis

To evaluate the effectiveness of the proposed method, a series of tests were conducted utilizing untrained raw and processed images. The results, presented in Table 1,2 and Figs. 5 and 6, demonstrate the system's ability to accurately classify the DR images with improved precision and recall. Table 1 provides a comparison of the performance of the proposed method with that of the state-of-the-art methods. For model training, we have split the dataset into three sets; train, test and validation. The model was trained for 100 epochs, where initial 10 epochs were warm up epochs i.e. the learning rate rapidly increased to 0.001 and then slowly decayed to 0, following the cosine function trend. The model is independently trained using processed and raw dataset, both augmented using the same augmentations. To train the proposed network we have used Lion (Evolved Sign Momentum) optimizer [5]. It is a modern optimization algorithm designed to train large AI models. It stands out for its simplicity and efficiency, using a unique update mechanism based on the signum (or "sign") function to adjust model parameters. Further, we have compared the performance of the proposed network with AdamW and Lion optimizer, and have observed that the proposed CNN performs better with the Lion optimizer than AdamW.

We have also analyzed the effect of pre-processing on the performance of the system. We have independently trained the proposed model using raw and pre-processed images. The training and validation accuracy of these experiments is

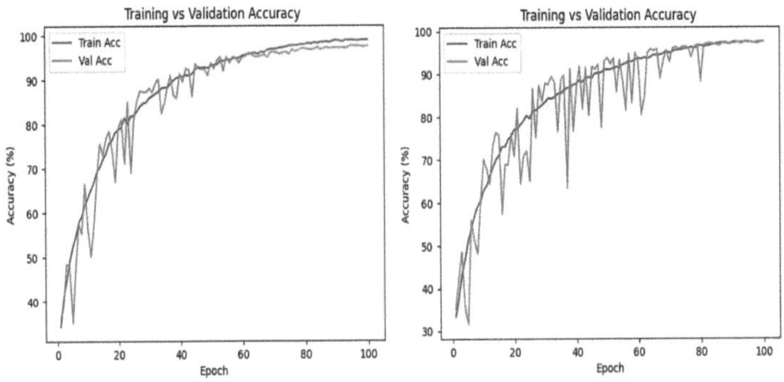

Fig. 5. DR_VisionNet with Lion optimizer on processed data (left) and raw data (right).

shown in Figs. 5 and 6. It is clearly visible from these figures that the model learns better and in a more stable way when the images are pre-processed and noise is removed. Whereas, the model trained on raw images remains uncertain even after 60 epochs and is extremely unstable. From these figures we can conclude that even though there is not much change in the accuracy with and without pre-processing, the network with preprocessed images adapts faster and stabilizes gracefully than the same, trained with raw images.

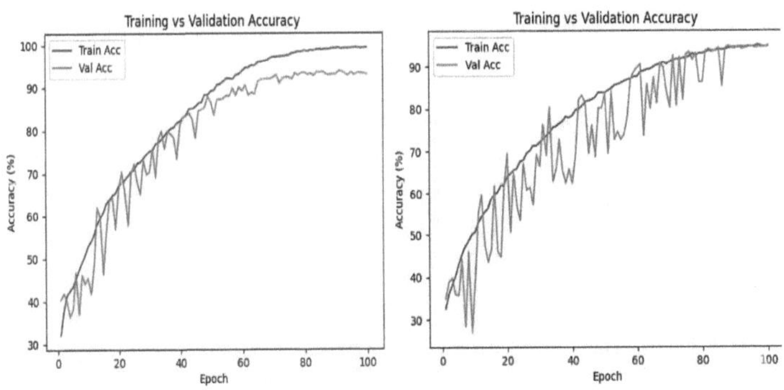

Fig. 6. DR_VisionNet with AdamW optimizer on processed data (left) and raw data (right).

In order to show effectiveness and computational efficiency of the proposed model, we have compared its performance with transfer learning based on ResNet50. For this experimentation, we have adopted transfer learning and retrained a few layers (layers 3 and 4) of ResNet50 using the Messidor dataset. Accuracy of the transfer learning based experiment with ResNet50 is listed in Table 1. It is clear that the proposed model performs better than the ResNet50.

Table 1. Comparison of the performance of the proposed DR_VisionNet with state-of-the-art methods

Model	Dataset	Trainable Layers	Accuracy
Rezaee and Farnami [11]	APTOS 2019	NA	94.28%
Aftab and Akhtar [1]	APTOS 2019, IDRiD, Messidor	NA	96.96%
Arora et al. [3]	Diabetic Retinopathy Resized Dataset	NA	86.53%
Saxena et al. [12]	EYEPAC, Messidor-1, Messidor-2	NA	AUC, 0.958, 0.92
ResNet50	Messidor-2 Processed/Raw	fc, 4, 3	89.5%/87.33%
ResNet50	Messidor-2 Processed/Raw	fc, 4	87.27%/84.5%
Proposed DR_VisionNet	Messidor-2 Processed	NA	**97.07%**
Proposed DR_VisionNet	Messidor-2 Raw	NA	**97.13%**

We also observed that the proposed method is computationally efficient compared to ResNet50. The number of trainable parameters of the proposed model is 619,365 and that of ResNet50 when 4th layer and fully connected layer are involved in training is 14,974,987. This implies that ResNet50 has 24 times more trainable parameters than that of DR_VisionNet. Similarly, if we unfreeze layer 3, 4 and fully connected layer, then this factor becomes 35. Hence the proposed network is computationally lighter than existing pre-trained models, at the same time its performance is better than the state-of-the-art methods. The comparison of the performance of the proposed model with state-of-the-art methods is presented in Table 1. Other evaluation parameters such as precision, F1 score and recall are presented in Table 2. The accuracy of the proposed DR_VisionNet surpasses the state-of-the-art methods as well as the pretrained ResNet50.

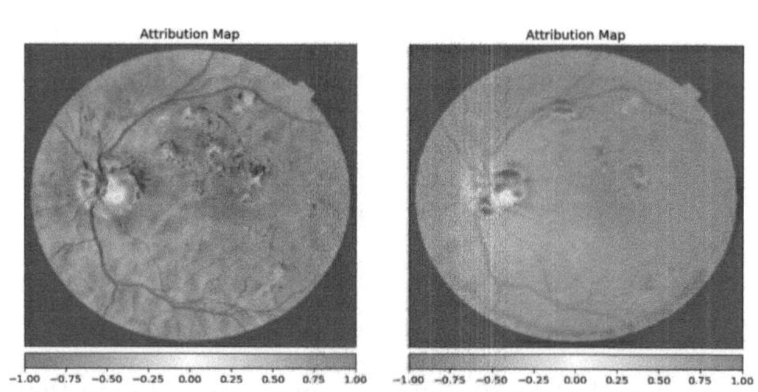

Fig. 7. Integrated gradients of processed(left) and raw(right).

The explainability of CNNs is significant in terms of understanding the insights of the models relied on. By providing clear explanations for the model's behavior, user gains valuable insights about the predictions of the model, identifies potential biases or errors, and ultimately improves the trust in the model. There are various techniques to get model explanations, we have used integrated gradients to seek the visual explanations of the proposed model's learning. In

Table 2. Precision, Recall and F1 Score of DR_VisionNet using Lion optimizer on processed dataset.

Classes	Precision	Recall	F1 score
Class 0	0.9786	0.9103	0.9432
Class 1	0.9536	0.9763	0.9648
Class 2	0.9299	0.9701	0.9496
Class 3	0.9932	0.9966	0.9949
Class 4	1.0000	1.0000	1.0000

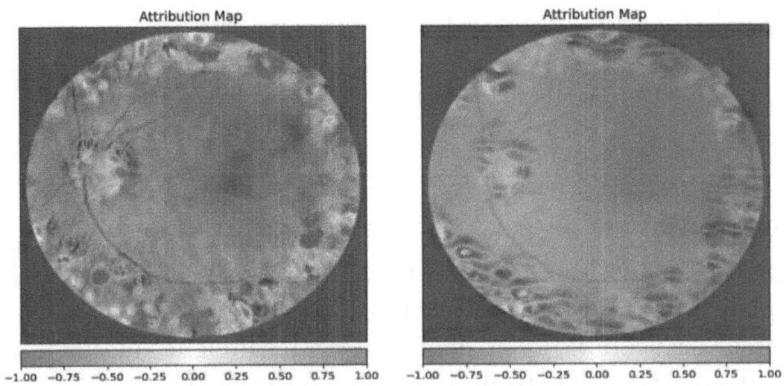

Fig. 8. Integrated gradients of processed(left) and raw(right).

our work, we have employed integrated gradients to interpret the behavior of the proposed model and understand the importance of image features in the final prediction. The visual results of integrated gradients for two different DR classed in case of processed and raw images are shown in Figs. 7 and 8. The green regions in Figs. 7 and 8 highlight those pixels or areas that help the model predict the class correctly and increase its score or confidence. Meanwhile, the red pixels or regions work against the model prediction and reduce the score or confidence of the model. From the above images, it is clear that pre-processing helps the model to see exudates, lesions and nerve structure of the eye more clearly as compared to the raw one. This also explains the reason behind the stable and graceful model learning during the training and validation shown in Figs. 5 and 6.

4 Conclusion

In this paper, we present a customized computationally efficient CNN, a DR_VisionNet for the classification of Diabetic Retinopathy using retinal scans. While many existing works rely on the pre-trained models and transfer learning, we present computationally efficient CNN that surpasses state-of-the-art methods in terms of both accuracy and F1 score. The proposed DR_VisionNet achieves 97% accuracy with more than 0.9 Precision, F1 and Recall for all classes.

It is also interesting to note that, the proposed network is computationally lighter than the existing pre-trained networks. Along with the proposed network, we have also presented a pre-processing approach that guarantees stable and reliable training of the model and avoids overfitting. In addition, we have also presented attribute maps of the proposed model using integrated gradients to support explanations.

Funding Open access funding provided by Royal Danish Library, Aarhus University Library

Acknowledgments. This work was supported by the [Indian Council of Medical Research (ICMR)] under Grant [ICMR-International Travel Grant Support for non-ICMR/DHR scientists and researchers].

References

1. Aftab, S., Akhtar, S.: Diabetic retinopathy severity classification using data fusion and ensemble transfer learning. J. Softw. Eng. Appl. **18**(1), 1–23 (2025)
2. APTOS: Aptos 2019 blindness detection (2019)
3. Arora, L., et al.: Ensemble deep learning and EfficientNet for accurate diagnosis of diabetic retinopathy. Sci. Rep. **14**(1), 30554 (2024)
4. Atwany, M.Z., Sahyoun, A.H., Yaqub, M.: Deep learning techniques for diabetic retinopathy classification: a survey. IEEE Access **10**, 28642–28655 (2022)
5. Chen, X., et al.: Symbolic discovery of optimization algorithms. Adv. Neural. Inf. Process. Syst. **36**, 49205–49233 (2023)
6. Decencière, E., et al.: Feedback on a publicly distributed image database: the messidor database. Image Anal. Stereol., 231–234 (2014)
7. He, K., Zhang, X., Ren, S., Sun, J.: Deep residual learning for image recognition. In: Proceedings of the IEEE Conference on Computer Vision and Pattern Recognition, pp. 770–778 (2016)
8. Kaggle: Diabetic retinopathy detection eyepacs dataset (2015)
9. Nathan, D.M.: Long-term complications of diabetes mellitus. N. Engl. J. Med. **328**(23), 1676–1685 (1993)
10. Papakipos, Z., Bitton, J.: AUGLY: data augmentations for robustness. arXiv preprint arXiv:2201.06494 (2022)
11. Rezaee, K., Farnami, F.: Innovative approach for diabetic retinopathy severity classification: an AI-powered tool using CNN-transformer fusion. J. Biomed. Phys. Eng. **15**(2), 137 (2025)
12. Saxena, G., Verma, D.K., Paraye, A., Rajan, A., Rawat, A.: Improved and robust deep learning agent for preliminary detection of diabetic retinopathy using public datasets. Intell. Based Med. **3**, 100022 (2020)
13. Seo, H., Park, S.J., Song, M.: Diabetic Retinopathy (DR): mechanisms, current therapies, and emerging strategies. Cells **14**(5), 376 (2025)
14. Szegedy, C., Vanhoucke, V., Ioffe, S., Shlens, J., Wojna, Z.: Rethinking the inception architecture for computer vision. In: Proceedings of the IEEE Conference on Computer Vision and Pattern Recognition, pp. 2818–2826 (2016)
15. Tan, M., Le, Q.: EfficientNet: rethinking model scaling for convolutional neural networks. In: International Conference on Machine Learning, pp. 6105–6114. PMLR (2019)

16. Wild, S., Roglic, G., Green, A., Sicree, R., King, H.: Global prevalence of diabetes: estimates for the year 2000 and projections for 2030. Diabetes Care **27**(5), 1047–1053 (2004)
17. Zuiderveld, K.: Contrast limited adaptive histogram equalization. In: Graphics gems IV, pp. 474–485 (1994)

Comparative Analysis of Hybrid Deep Learning Approaches to Class Imbalance Across Image, and Text Modalities

Physiwell Maume(✉) and Jin Nakazawa

Graduate School of Media and Governance, Keio University, Tokyo, Japan
physiwell.maume@keio.jp, jin@sfc.keio.ac.jp

Abstract. This study presents the first systematic comparative analysis of two hybrid deep learning approaches—Deep Over-Sampling (DOS) and Large Margin Local Embedding (LMLE)—for class imbalance across image and text modalities under controlled imbalance scenarios (balanced, exponential, linear, step, extreme). Using One For All (OFA) pre-trained embeddings, we evaluate both methods across multiple metrics, finding DOS consistently outperforms LMLE with significant cross-modal disparities: image applications achieve AUC-ROC > 0.97 while text applications reach only ≈ 0.82. The results demonstrate that image-domain imbalance solutions do not transfer seamlessly to natural language processing tasks, challenging assumptions about the universal applicability of hybrid imbalance-mitigation techniques.

1 Introduction

Class imbalance in machine learning classification problems involves the non-uniformity in the number of samples between classes in a single dataset, leading to the existence of minority and majority classes. While the majority classes are the collection of classes with a significantly higher number of samples, minority classes are a set of classes with a fewer number of samples in a dataset.

The class imbalance problem, recognized three decades ago, remains a pervasive and fundamental challenge that significantly degrades the performance of classification models across a multitude of data modalities and diverse real-world domains (Chen et al., 2024; Ghosh et al., 2022; Cheng et al., 2025; Bao et al., 2020; Haixiang et al., 2017; Johnson & Khoshgoftaar, 2019; Hasib et al., 2020; Wang et al., 2016). With imbalanced data, machine learning models tend to over-classify the majority group due to its higher prior probability—leading to the misclassification of instances in the minority classes more frequently than in the majority classes (Johnson & Khoshgoftaar, 2019). It has been demonstrated that classification performance degrades significantly under severe class imbalance in federated systems developed for various applications, including healthcare, anomaly detection, fraud detection, mobile applications, Internet-of-Things, unmanned aerial vehicles, audio data, and intelligent control (Zhang et al., 2023).

C. Xu (Ed.): ICMLSC 2026, CCIS 2948, pp. 282–297, 2027.
https://doi.org/10.1007/978-981-92-1546-1_23

Deep learning's application to class imbalance data remains largely understudied, with a notable lack of statistical evidence comparing newly published methods across a diverse range of datasets and varying imbalance levels (Johnson & Khoshgoftaar, 2019). To determine optimal approaches for different use cases, extensive comparative evaluations spanning various datasets and deep learning architectures remain necessary (Johnson & Khoshgoftaar, 2019).

Based on the large-scale image (ImageNet21k-Resized) and text (CARER) datasets, this work investigates multi-modal classification under class imbalance. We present a reproducible framework that integrates One For All (OFA) pretrained embeddings (Wang et al., 2022) with two imbalance-learning strategies—Deep Over-Sampling (DOS) (Ando & Huang, 2017) and Large Margin Local Embedding (LMLE)(Huang et al., 2016)—to improve representation quality and downstream classification across images and text.

This work addresses a critical gap in class imbalance research by providing the first systematic cross-modal comparison of hybrid techniques (DOS, LMLE) under controlled conditions (balanced, exponential, linear, step, extreme). The reproducible framework developed enables future researchers to conduct similar comparative analysis across different architectures and datasets. The empirical evidence uncovered challenges assumptions about the universal applicability of image-domain solutions to text applications, highlighting the need for domain-specific adaptations.

2 Related Work

Recent comprehensive surveys have highlighted the evolving landscape of class imbalance in deep learning. (Johnson & Khoshgoftaar, 2019) provided a foundational survey specifically examining deep learning techniques for class imbalanced data, identifying key research gaps in systematic comparative evaluations across different architectures and datasets. More recently, (Chen et al., 2024) conducted an extensive review of imbalanced learning approaches, emphasizing the need for robust evaluation frameworks that span multiple domains and data modalities. These surveys consistently highlight the limited statistical evidence comparing newly published methods across diverse datasets and varying imbalance levels, particularly in deep learning contexts.

Class imbalance is a problem that has been the focus of extensive research, largely concerning the image data modality. This provides a research gap regarding how those solutions could perform when expanded to other data modalities. A systematic and extensive study has been conducted on the impact of class imbalance on Convolutional Neural Networks (CNNs) using MNIST, CIFAR-10 and ImageNets datasets (Buda et al., 2018). The research explicitly defined and investigated two types of imbalance, namely step and linear, which compared several common hybrid and data-level solutions, including Random Oversampling (ROS), Random Undersampling (RUS), and two-phase training (Buda et al., 2018). (Pouyanfar et al., 2019) developed a framework for visual, audio, and text data that uses a dynamic sampling technique integrated with CNN transfer to dynamically modify samples in each iteration based on the class-wise F1-score.

Class imbalance in text classification presents unique challenges that are distinct from those in image domains. (Henning et al., 2023) revealed that traditional sampling techniques to solve class imbalance often struggle with the high-dimensional, sparse nature of text representations in deep learning-based natural language processing. Text classification with imbalanced datasets faces additional complexities, including variable sequence lengths, contextual dependencies, and the semantic richness of language data (Yang et al., 2024; Henning et al., 2023; Zulqarnain et al., 2020). Despite these domain-specific challenges, the systematic application of image-domain solutions like DOS and LMLE to text data remains largely unexplored.

While individual techniques have been extensively evaluated within their respective domains, systematic cross-domain comparative studies remain notably limited. (Ghosh et al., 2022) emphasized the need for standardized evaluation protocols when comparing imbalance handling techniques across different data types and architectures. The lack of unified evaluation frameworks that apply consistent imbalance patterns and metrics across different data types represents a significant gap in the literature. This limitation is particularly pronounced when considering hybrid approaches that combine sampling strategies with deep learning architectures, where domain-specific characteristics may significantly influence technique performance.

Building on these identified gaps in cross-domain evaluation, there is particularly limited research on the effect of unifying multimodal models with established hybrid solutions for class imbalanced data under four controlled imbalance scenarios: linear, step, exponential, and extreme (as illustrated in Figs. 2, 3, 4, 5, and 6) across multiple data modalities, including the text domain. Systematic studies varying class distributions with step, linear, and exponential imbalance types have been performed primarily on image datasets using CNNs (Ghosh et al., 2022; 2022; Buda et al., 2018; Hensman & Masko, 2015). Hybrid solutions such as LMLE and DOS were developed and evaluated in the image domain using the CNN architecture (Ando & Huang, 2017; Henning et al., 2016). Studies on class imbalance have historically existed primarily in the computer vision domain, with many NLP tasks originating from or being evaluated by the computer vision community (Henning et al., 2023). This cross-pollination is evident in several techniques: staged learning, data augmentation, and loss functions, initially developed for image data and now adapted for text (Henning et al., 2023).

3 Methodology

3.1 Overview of the Method

This research addresses the challenge of multi-modal classification under various class imbalances, focusing on the image and text domains. We developed a unified framework that integrates two advanced imbalance-learning strategies—Deep Over-Sampling (DOS) and Large Margin Local Embedding (LMLE)—with frozen OFA (One-For-All) pretrained embeddings, as shown in Fig. 1. The framework enables automated, reproducible experiments across multiple imbalance regimes (balanced, exponential, linear, step, extreme) and modalities, supporting comprehensive evaluation and comparison of DOS and LMLE methods. All experiments were run with a fixed random seed of 42 to ensure reproducibility.

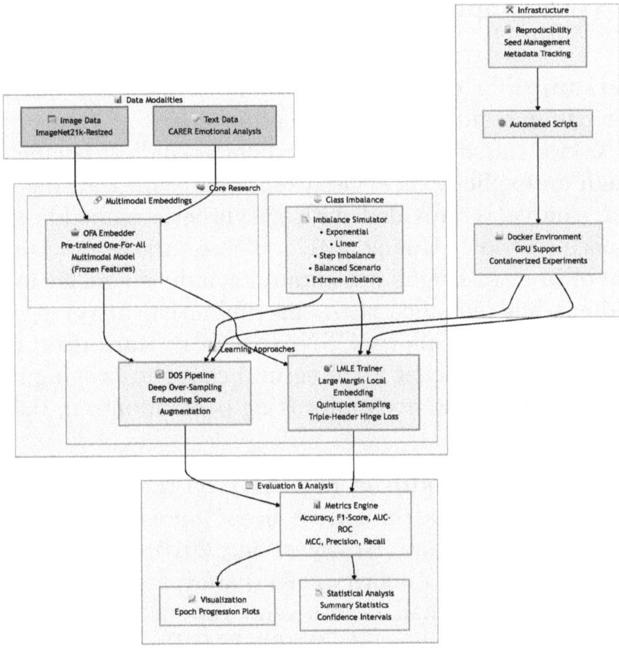

Fig. 1. Research Architecture

3.2 Background

Our approach builds upon several established resources and algorithms. For feature extraction, we utilize the OFA model, a state-of-the-art Task-Agnostic and Modality-Agnostic multi-modal transformer (Wang et al., 2022). For imbalance handling, DOS (Ando & Huang, 2017) generates synthetic samples in the embedding space to mitigate minority class under-representation, while LMLE (Huang et al., 2016) employs quintuplet sampling and margin-based metric learning to enhance class separation.

3.2.1 One-For-All (OFA)

OFA unifies a diverse set of cross-modal and uni-modal tasks, including image generation, visual grounding, image captioning, image classification, and language modeling, through a simple sequence-to-sequence learning framework with instruction-based learning (Wang et al., 2022). Despite being trained on a relatively small dataset of 20 million publicly available image-text pairs, OFA provides robust representations for both image and text inputs, achieving new state-of-the-art performance in various cross-modal tasks (Wang et al., 2022).

3.2.2 Deep Oversampling (DOS) and Large Margin Local Embedding (LMLE)

Deep Oversampling (DOS) is a framework designed to extend synthetic oversampling techniques into the deep feature space of Convolutional Neural Networks (CNNs) for classifying imbalanced data (Ando & Huang, 2017). This is achieved through an explicit, supervised representation learning process, where each raw input sample is provided with a synthetic embedding target in the deep feature space (Ando & Huang, 2017). These targets are sampled from the linear subspace of in-class neighbors, aiming to induce smaller in-class variance among embeddings and enhance their discriminative power (Ando & Huang, 2017). The DOS framework allows CNNs to jointly learn deep representations and classifiers without significant architectural changes, proving its effectiveness against strong imbalances and even improving performance in balanced settings (Ando & Huang, 2017).

Large Margin Local Embedding (LMLE), on the other hand, is a method focused on learning more discriminative deep representations specifically for imbalanced image classification (Huang et al., 2016). This approach is motivated by the observation that minority classes are sparse and have a high degree of visual variability, making their local neighborhoods vulnerable to invasion by majority class samples (Huang et al., 2016). LMLE addresses this by combining a novel quintuplet instance sampling method with a triple-header hinge loss function (Huang et al., 2016). This process learns deep feature representations that improve inter-class discrimination and preserve same-class locality, achieving state-of-the-art results in large-scale imbalanced classification tasks such as face attribute recognition and image edge detection (Huang et al., 2016).

3.2.3 Class Imbalance Types

To simulate the different kinds of real-world class imbalance scenarios, we implemented a class imbalance simulator that loads data to represent the following data distributions:

- **Balanced:** The number of samples in every class within the dataset is evenly distributed, as shown in Fig. 2. The simulator sets every class to the same target size, which is equal to the minimum original class size; however, it uses the configured preserve floor if the minimum is smaller.
- **Exponential:** It is described as a long-tailed distribution where the sample size of each class in the training set follows an exponential decay distribution (Liu et al., 2023), as shown in Fig. 3.

- **Linear:** Linear targets interpolate from a maximum to a minimum with a constant step size, as shown in Fig. 4. It is defined by a single parameter, ρ, representing the ratio between the maximum and minimum number of examples across all classes (Buda et al., 2018).
- **Step:** Occurs when the number of examples is equal within a set of minority classes and equal within a set of majority classes, but these two groups have different numbers of examples (Buda et al., 2018), as shown in Fig. 5.
- **Extreme:** One majority class (the class with the maximum original count) retains all of its original samples; every other class is reduced to the preserved floor, as shown in Fig. 6. This produces a stress-test distribution with a single dominant class and minimal minority representation.

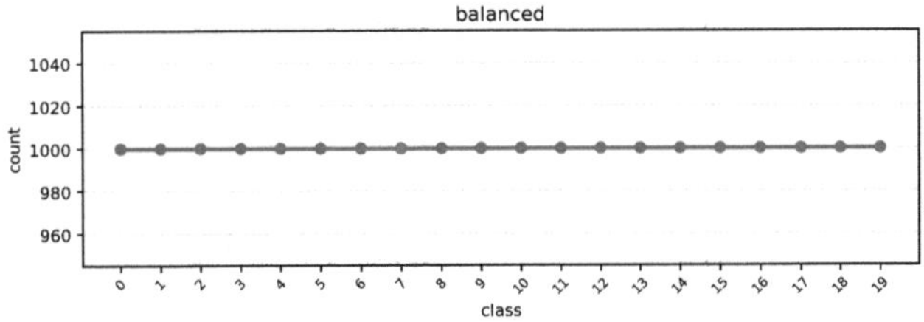

Fig. 2. Balanced Data Distribution

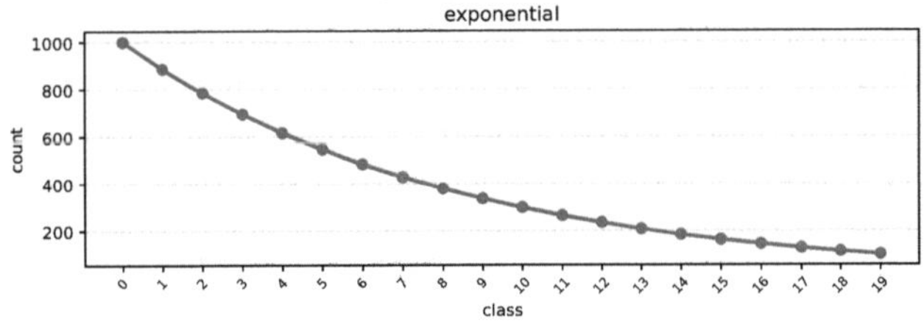

Fig. 3. Exponential Imbalance Data Distribution

3.3 Experimental Setup

To systematically evaluate the impact of class imbalance and compare the effectiveness of Deep Over-Sampling (DOS) and Large Margin Local Embedding (LMLE) methods, we designed a modular and reproducible experimental pipeline. The setup, as shown in Fig. 1, is structured to support multi-modal experiments across image and text domains, with automated configuration and comprehensive logging.

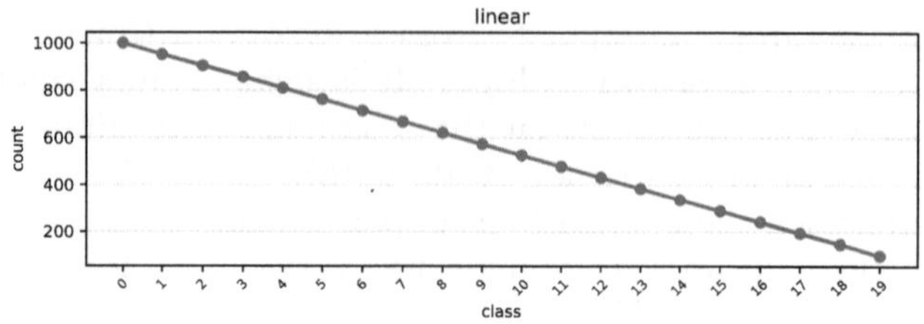

Fig. 4. Linear Imbalance Data Distribution

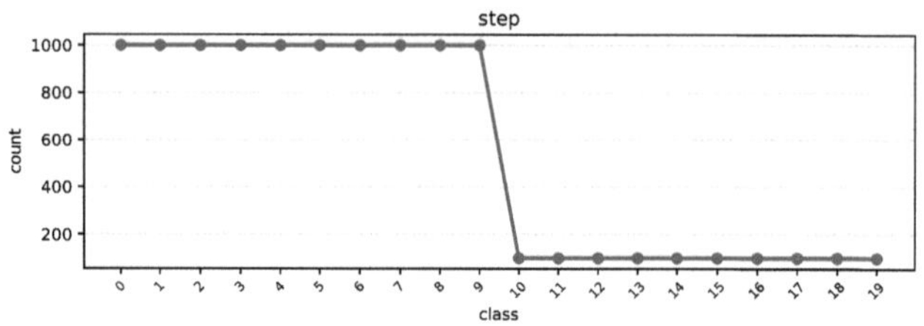

Fig. 5. Step Imbalance Data Distribution

3.3.1 Datasets And Data Preprocessing

We selected two complementary datasets to evaluate class imbalance handling across modalities. **ImageNet21k-Resized** (10,000+ image classes) provides a natural visual imbalance that reflects real-world object prevalence distributions, while **CARER Emotional Analysis** exhibits an inherent emotional class imbalance common in sentiment analysis applications. This cross-modal approach validates method generalizability across different feature spaces, with all datasets processed through dedicated pipelines using remapped contiguous indices and systematic class distribution analysis for controlled imbalance simulation.

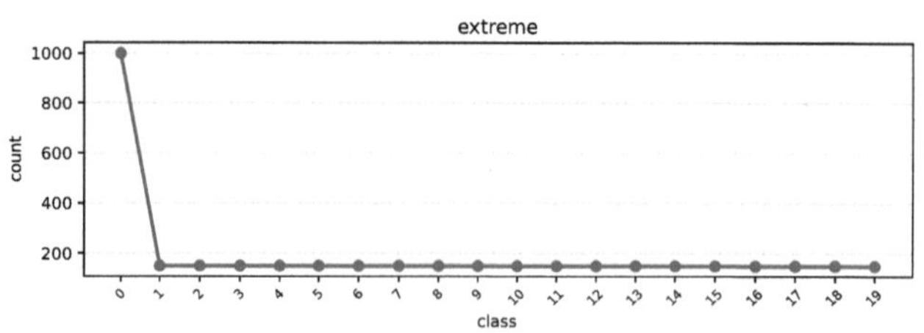

Fig. 6. Extreme Imbalance Data Distribution

Table 1. Balanced Training Data Class Distribution

	Num of Samples	Num of Classes
LMLE-Image	609	30
DOS-Image	669	20
LMLE-Text	572	6
DOS-Text	572	6

Table 2. DOS-Image Class Imbalance Distribution

Class	Exponential	Extreme	Linear	Step
0	1701	1961	1701	1961
1	1222	10	1521	1898
2	1208	10	1403	1799
3	1201	10	1310	1778
4	1208	10	1222	1701
5	1055	10	1201	1521
6	948	10	1055	1400
7	840	10	1032	1300
8	744	10	965	1222
9	659	10	859	1221
10	584	10	846	196
11	517	10	761	196
12	458	10	753	196
13	406	10	669	196
14	359	10	660	196
15	318	10	567	196
16	282	10	474	196
17	250	10	381	196
18	221	10	288	196
19	196	10	196	196

3.3.2 Experimental Pipeline

Our experimental framework implements a comprehensive evaluation pipeline across five imbalance scenarios: balanced, exponential, linear, step, and extreme. The Imbalance Simulator module programmatically adjusts class sample sizes to achieve target ratios while preserving minimum class sizes as lower bounds, with distributions detailed in Tables 1, 2, 4, 3, and 5. All samples are processed through a frozen OFA transformer to obtain high-dimensional embeddings, which are cached for efficient reuse across experiments. Training is conducted across multiple epochs (5, 10, 15, 20, 30, 40, and 50) with configurable

Table 3. LMLE-Image Class Imbalance Distribution

Class	Exponential	Extreme	Linear	Step
0	1766	1961	1766	1961
1	1701	10	1701	1923
2	1222	10	1521	1898
3	1218	10	1474	1799
4	1201	10	1413	1778
5	1055	10	1352	1766
6	1039	10	1222	1701
7	1020	10	1201	1688
8	965	10	1169	1666
9	960	10	1055	1521
10	886	10	1048	1400
11	819	10	1020	1351
12	756	10	987	1300
13	699	10	965	1235
14	645	10	926	1222
15	596	10	865	196
16	550	10	859	196
17	508	10	804	196
18	470	10	761	196
19	434	10	743	196
20	401	10	682	196
21	370	10	669	196
22	342	10	622	196
23	316	10	561	196
24	292	10	500	196
25	269	10	439	196
26	249	10	378	196
27	230	10	317	196
28	212	10	256	196
29	196	10	196	196

batch sizes and projection dimensions, utilizing half-precision and CPU fall-back for memory efficiency. Classification is performed using k-NN models with comprehensive metric evaluation, including accuracy, precision, recall, F1-score, AUC-ROC, and Matthews Correlation Coefficient. The results are logged for each epoch and scenario through detailed CSV exports.

Table 4. DOS-Text Class Imbalance Distribution

Class	Exponential	Extreme	Linear	Step
0	4666	5362	4666	5362
1	3383	10	4396	4666
2	1347	10	2159	2159
3	1304	10	1501	536
4	850	10	1304	536
5	536	10	536	536

Table 5. LMLE-Text Class Imbalance Distribution

Class	Exponential	Extreme	Linear	Step
0	4666	5362	4666	5362
1	3383	10	4396	4666
2	1347	10	2159	2159
3	1304	10	1501	536
4	850	10	1304	536
5	536	10	536	536

4 Results

Figure 7 presents experimental evaluation plots comparing two class imbalance-mitigation hybrid methods, **DOS** and **LMLE**, across five imbalance scenarios (balanced, exponential, extreme, linear, and step) and two data modalities (text and image). The balanced distribution serves as a baseline to evaluate how the unified OFA architecture with hybrid approaches performs relative to class-imbalanced conditions.

4.1 Overall Performance of DOS and LMLE

The DOS model consistently outperforms the LMLE model across all imbalance scenarios and evaluation metrics for image and text data modalities, the exception being the MCC evaluation metric for extreme imbalance, shown in Fig. 7, where DOS-text and LMLE-text are equal, with a value of approximately zero. Both DOS and LMLE performances significantly degrade under extreme imbalance.

4.2 Performance Across Imbalance Scenarios

4.2.1 Balanced Class Distribution

In the balanced class distribution scenario, the DOS-Image model shows the highest and most stable performance across all metrics, with AUC-ROC, precision, recall, F1-score, and accuracy scores consistently above 0.7. The LMLE-

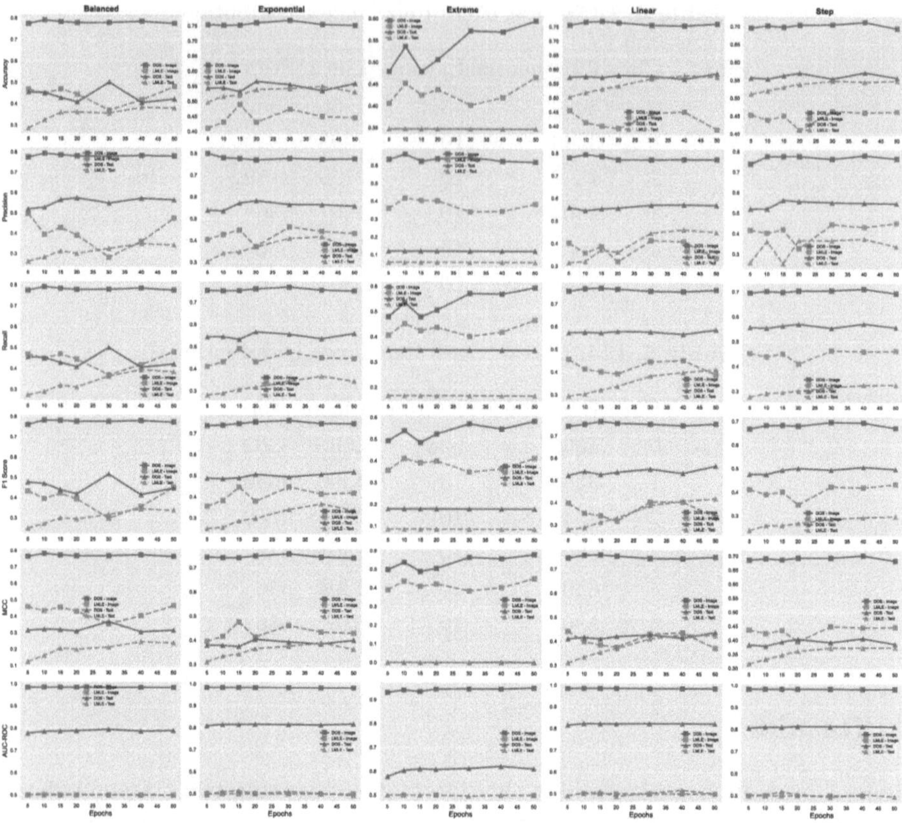

Fig. 7. Evaluation Metric, Imbalance Scenario, and Modality Comparison

Image and DOS-Text models exhibit performance scores ranging from approximately 0.4 to 0.6. LMLE-Text is consistently in the range of 0.2 to 0.4 across all metrics, except for AUC-ROC, where it is approximately 0.5.

4.2.2 Exponential and Linear Imbalance

In both the exponential and linear imbalance scenarios, the DOS-Image and DOS-Text models consistently outperform all other models. The DOS-Image model is particularly effective, achieving consistently high scores across all evaluation metrics. For instance, its accuracy and recall are around 0.75, while its precision is approximately 0.78. The model's F1-Score is about 0.73, and its MCC is also high, at approximately 0.74 in the exponential scenario and 0.78 in the linear scenario. Its AUC-ROC remained exceptionally high at around 0.98 in both scenarios. The DOS-Text model also performs well, with accuracy, precision, and recall scores ranging from 0.5 to 0.6. The F1-Score is in the 0.5 to 0.6 range, the MCC is between 0.4 and 0.43, and the AUC-ROC is around 0.82.

The LMLE-Image and LMLE-Text models show marginal performance; however, their metrics remain lower, with accuracy, precision, and recall generally below 0.6. Their F1-scores and MCCs are also notably lower, indicating that they struggle to classify data effectively in these scenarios.

4.2.3 Extreme Imbalance

In the extreme imbalance scenario, the DOS-Image model is the most effective, maintaining consistently higher performance across all metrics. Its accuracy, recall, and F1-score are mostly between 0.5 and 0.6, while its precision ranges from 0.6 to 0.65. The model also achieves a high MCC of 0.5 to 0.6 and an excellent AUC-ROC of approximately 0.97.
The LMLE models generally perform poorly, with the LMLE-Image model showing the best results among them. Its accuracy and recall are between 0.4 and 0.5, while its precision and F1-Score range from 0.35 to 0.43 and 0.35 to 0.42, respectively. Its MCC is between 0.38 and 0.45, and its AUC-ROC is around 0.5. The LMLE-Text model is largely ineffective, with most metrics, including accuracy, precision, F1-Score, and MCC, hovering near 0.

4.2.4 Step Imbalance

In the step imbalance scenario, DOS models generally outperform LMLE models, with DOS-Image demonstrating the strongest and most stable performance. The DOS-Image model achieves an accuracy and recall of approximately 0.7, with precision ranging from 0.74 to 0.78. Its F1-score is between 0.67 and 0.7, MCC is around 0.7, and AUC-ROC is notably high at approximately 0.98.

The DOS-Text model performs moderately well, with an accuracy and recall of approximately 0.55. Its precision ranges from 0.5 to 0.6; the F1-score is between 0.47 and 0.5; the MCC is approximately 0.4; and the AUC-ROC is around 0.82.

Among the LMLE models, the LMLE-Image model is the most effective, with its accuracy, precision, and recall all ranging from 0.4 to 0.5. Its F1-Score is 0.35 to 0.43, the MCC is 0.4 to 0.45, and the AUC-ROC is approximately 0.5. The LMLE-Text model demonstrates significantly weaker performance, with most of its metrics hovering near or below 0.3.

5 Discussion

5.1 Cross-Modal Performance Disparities

The results reveal significant performance disparities between image and text modalities when applying identical hybrid imbalance-mitigation techniques. DOS consistently demonstrated superior performance on image data compared to text across all imbalance scenarios, with image models achieving accuracy and F1-scores that were 15–20% higher than their text counterparts. DOS showed potential adoption to the text data modality in exponential, linear, and step imbalance scenarios, with accuracy, recall, precision, and F1-score scores higher than 0.5, while AUC-ROC scores are higher than 0.8. This underscores that techniques originally developed for computer vision may require additional domain-specific adaptation when applied to natural language processing tasks.

The performance difference can be attributed to fundamental differences in data representation and feature space characteristics between the visual and textual domains. Image data benefits from spatial locality and hierarchical feature extraction that aligns well with DOS's oversampling strategy, while text data's sequential and contextual nature may require different approaches to synthetic sample generation and embedding manipulation.

5.2 Method-Specific Insights

5.2.1 DOS Effectiveness Across Modalities

DOS's consistent superiority over LMLE across all scenarios demonstrates its robustness as a hybrid imbalance-mitigation approach. The method's ability to maintain high performance even under extreme imbalance conditions (97% AUC-ROC for image data) indicates effective synthetic sample generation that preserves class-specific characteristics. However, the notable performance degradation when applied to text data (AUC-ROC dropping from 97–98% to 82%) highlights the need for domain-specific adaptations.

5.2.2 LMLE Limitations

LMLE's poor performance across all scenarios, particularly in exponential and linear imbalance conditions where metrics frequently approached zero, suggests fundamental limitations in the method's approach to embedding space manipulation. The technique's reliance on local neighborhood structures suffers when applied to high-dimensional, sparse representations typical of text data processed through transformer-based architectures.

5.3 Imbalance Severity Impact

The systematic evaluation across four imbalance types reveals nuanced patterns in method effectiveness. While DOS maintained reasonable performance under balanced, exponential, linear, and step conditions, the performance degradation in text is pronounced under extreme imbalance. LMLE's lower and consistent performance across balanced, exponential, linear, and step imbalances, with a significant decline apparent in extreme imbalances. The reduction in performance for both DOS and LMLE under extreme imbalance suggests that the hybrid approaches may have limited applicability under severe imbalance conditions.

5.4 Practical Implications

For practitioners working with imbalanced datasets, these results provide actionable insights:

1. **Modality-specific method selection**: Image-based applications can confidently adopt DOS for imbalance mitigation, while text applications should consider DOS with domain-specific modifications or alternative approaches.
2. **Imbalance severity considerations**: Under extreme imbalance conditions, method selection becomes critical, with DOS demonstrating significantly better robustness than embedding-based approaches such as LMLE.
3. **Evaluation metric sensitivity**: The near-zero MCC scores for LMLE in extreme scenarios highlight the importance of comprehensive metric evaluation beyond accuracy, particularly for severely imbalanced datasets.

5.5 Limitations and Future Directions

This study's limitations include the focus on two specific hybrid methods and the use of OFA embeddings, which may have introduced architecture-specific biases. Future research should investigate:

1. **Domain-specific adaptations** of image-based techniques for text applications.
2. **Alternative hybrid approaches** that better leverage the sequential nature of text data.
3. **Architecture-agnostic evaluations** using different pre-trained embedding models.
4. **Real-world dataset validation** beyond controlled imbalance scenarios.

6 Conclusion

This study presents the first systematic comparative analysis of hybrid deep learning approaches to class imbalance across image and text modalities, using controlled class imbalance scenarios. Through a comprehensive evaluation of DOS and LMLE under balanced, exponential, linear, step, and extreme class imbalance data distributions, we uncovered that DOS consistently outperformed LMLE across all conditions, with AUC-ROC scores exceeding 0.97 for image data. However, image applications outperformed text applications by 15–25% across key metrics, demonstrating significant cross-modal performance disparities that require domain-specific adaptations.

LMLE showed severe limitations, with performance approaching zero under moderate to extreme imbalanced conditions. These findings indicate that the severity of the imbalance critically impacts method selection, with DOS demonstrating superior robustness. Practitioners should prioritize modality-specific considerations and imbalance severity when selecting mitigation strategies, while future research should focus on domain-specific adaptations and alternative approaches for text data.

Acknowledgments. This work was supported by JSPS KAKENHI Grant Number JP23H00476.

Impact Statement. "This paper presents work whose goal is to advance the field of Machine Learning. There are many potential societal consequences of our work, none of which we feel must be specifically highlighted here."

References

Ando, S., Huang, C.Y.: Deep over-sampling framework for classifying imbalanced data. In: Machine Learning and Knowledge Discovery in Databases, pp. 770–785, Cham (2017). Springer International Publishing. https://doi.org/10.1007/978-3-319-71249-9_46. ISBN 978-3-319-71249-9

Bao, F., Deng, Y., Kong, Y., Ren, Z., Suo, J., Dai, Q.: Learning deep landmarks for imbalanced classification. IEEE Trans. Neural Netw. Learn. Syst. **31**(8), 2691–2704 (2020). https://doi.org/10.1109/TNNLS.2019.2927647

Buda, M., Maki, A., Mazurowski, M.A.: A systematic study of the class imbalance problem in convolutional neural networks. Neural Netw. **106**, 249–259 (2018). https://doi.org/10.1016/j.neunet.2018.07.011

Chen, W., Yang, K., Yu, Z., Shi, Y., Chen, C.L.P.: A survey on imbalanced learning: latest research, applications and future directions. Artif. Intell. Rev. **57** (2024). https://doi.org/10.1007/s10462-024-10759-6

Cheng, X., Shi, F., Zhang, Y., Li, H., Liu, X., Chen, S.: Frame: feature rectification for class imbalance learning. IEEE Trans. Knowl. Data Eng. **37**(3), 1167–1181 (2025). https://doi.org/10.1109/TKDE.2024.3523043

Ghosh, K., Bellinger, C., Corizzo, R., Branco, P., Krawczyk, B., Japkowicz, N.: The class imbalance problem in deep learning. Mach. Learn. **113**(4845–4901), 2022 (2024)

Haixiang, G., Yijing, L., Shang, J., Mingyun, G., Yuanyue, H., Bing, G.: Learning from class-imbalanced data: Review of methods and applications. Expert Syst. Appl. **73**, 220–239 (2017). ISSN 0957-4174. https://doi.org/10.1016/j.eswa.2016.12.035, https://www.sciencedirect.com/science/article/pii/S0957417416307175

Hasib, K.M., et al.: A survey of methods for managing the classification and solution of data imbalance problem. J. Comput. Sci. **16**(11), 1546–1557 (2020). https://doi.org/10.3844/jcssp.2020.1546.1557, https://thescipub.com/abstract/jcssp.2020.1546.1557

Henning, S., Beluch, W., Fraser, A., Friedrich, A.: A survey of methods for addressing class imbalance in deep-learning based natural language processing (2023). https://arxiv.org/abs/2210.04675

Hensman, P., Masko, D.: The impact of imbalanced training data for convolutional neural networks. Degree Project in Computer Science, KTH Royal Institute of Technology (2015)

Huang, C., Li, Y., Loy, C.C., Tang, X.: Learning deep representation for imbalanced classification. In: 2016 IEEE Conference on Computer Vision and Pattern Recognition (CVPR), pp. 5375–5384 (2016). https://doi.org/10.1109/CVPR.2016.580

Johnson, J.M. and Khoshgoftaar, T.M.: Survey on deep learning with class imbalance. J. Big Data (2019)

Liu, Y., et al.: Imbalanced data classification: Using transfer learning and active sampling. Eng. Appl. Artif. Intell. **117**(PB) (2023.) ISSN 0952-1976. https://doi.org/10.1016/j.engappai.2022.105621, https://doi.org/10.1016/j.engappai.2022.105621

Pouyanfar, S., Wang, T., Chen, S.-C.: A multi-label multimodal deep learning framework for imbalanced data classification. In: 2019 IEEE Conference on Multimedia Information Processing and Retrieval (MIPR), pp. 199–204 (2019). https://doi.org/10.1109/MIPR.2019.00043

Wang, P., et al.: OFA: unifying architectures, tasks, and modalities through a simple sequence-to-sequence learning framework (2022). https://arxiv.org/abs/2202.03052

Wang, S., Liu, W., Wu, J., Cao, L., Meng, Q., Kennedy, P.J.: Training deep neural networks on imbalanced data sets. In: 2016 International Joint Conference on Neural Networks (IJCNN) (2016). https://doi.org/10.1109/IJCNN.2016.7727770

Yang, Y., Khorshidi, H.A., Aickelin, U.: A review on over-sampling techniques in classification of multi-class imbalanced datasets: insights for medical problems. Front. Digit. Health **6** (2024). ISSN 2673-253X. https://doi.org/10.3389/fdgth.2024.1430245, https://www.frontiersin.org/journals/digital-health/articles/10.3389/fdgth.2024.1430245

Zhang, J., Li, C., Qi, J., He, J.: A survey on class imbalance in federated learning (2023). https://arxiv.org/abs/2303.11673

Zulqarnain, Ghazali, R., Mazwin, Y., Rehan, M.: A comparative review on deep learning models for text classification. Ind. J. Electr. Eng. Comput. Sci. **19**(04) (2020). https://doi.org/10.11591/ijeecs.v19.i1.pp325-335

The Impact of Deepfake Media on the Creative and Entertainment Industry: Insights from GAN-Based Deep Learning Models

John Heland Jasper Ortega and Abigail Alix(✉)

FEU Institute of Technology, Manila, Philippines
alalix@feutech.edu.ph

Abstract. This study explores the impact of deepfake media on the creative and entertainment industry, with insights drawn from GAN-based deep learning models. Deepfakes offer powerful creative potential, enabling digital resurrection of performers, virtual concerts, and enhanced storytelling techniques. At the same time, their hyperrealism raises ethical concerns around consent, authorship, and audience transparency. Using the Diffusion of Innovations theory, the research finds that deepfakes are transitioning from early adoption to broader use among content creators and media professionals, while public acceptance remains cautious due to issues of trust and misuse. The same qualities that make deepfakes compelling in entertainment also make them dangerous tools for misinformation, fraud, and non-consensual content. As such, the study highlights the need for industry guidelines, public education, and updated legal frameworks to balance innovation with protection. Ultimately, the future of deepfake media in entertainment hinges on responsible integration and proactive safeguards to ensure its creative promise does not outweigh its societal risks.

Keywords: Deepfake Media · AI-generated Content · Artificial Intelligence · Machine Learning · Deep Learning · Ethical Implications · Film and Television

1 Introduction

Deepfake media is a term for synthetic content typically videos or audio that is created or altered using advanced AI to convincingly impersonate real people [1]. Modern deepfakes leverage machine learning techniques such as generative adversarial networks (GANs) to swap faces or clone voices, producing "hyper realistic forgeries" that can be difficult to distinguish from authentic media [2]. The technology first gained notoriety around 2017 to 2018, when manipulated videos began circulating on the internet. Since then, deepfakes have rapidly advanced in quality and accessibility, raising both excitement and alarm across the globe [3].

In the creative and entertainment industry, deepfakes present novel opportunities alongside new challenges. Filmmakers and content creators can potentially resurrect historical figures or deceased actors on screen, seamlessly de-age performers, or dub performances in multiple languages that all uses AI-generated likenesses [4]. For instance,

C. Xu (Ed.): ICMLSC 2026, CCIS 2948, pp. 298–306, 2027.
https://doi.org/10.1007/978-981-92-1546-1_24

the use of AI in talent shows and film has demonstrated how deepfakes might expand creative frontiers. An example is the America's Got Talent 2022 finale, where a deepfake of Elvis Presley "performed" on stage with live singers and even a deepfaked version of judge Simon Cowell, astonishing the audience [5]. Such feats suggest a future where entertainment productions routinely feature virtual appearances of famous figures from the past. At the same time, these developments blur the line between the real and the synthetic, prompting questions about authenticity, consent, and the emotional impact on audiences [6] (Fig. 1).

Fig. 1. AGT Deepfake Acts

Conversely, the misuse of deepfake media poses significant threats. Deepfakes have been implicated in the spread of disinformation or fake news, where fabricated videos of public figures can deceive viewers [7]. A notorious early example occurred during the 2022 Russia-Ukraine conflict: a doctored video emerged appearing to show Ukrainian President Volodymyr Zelenskyy surrendering in a "poorly edited" deepfake intended to mislead in a time of crisis [8]. While that particular fake was quickly debunked, experts warned it was a harbinger of more sophisticated deception to come. Similarly, in the Philippines, deepfakes have been weaponized to circulate sexually explicit content featuring the faces of local celebrities and private individuals without consent, contributing to the surge of non-consensual deepfake pornography in the country [9]. Despite the severe emotional and reputational harm caused to victims primarily women that current laws remain limited in scope, prompting renewed calls from advocacy groups and legislators to explicitly criminalize deepfake abuse under Philippine law [10, 11].

Likewise, scams and fraud have evolved with deepfake technology. AI-generated voice clones are now used by fraudsters to impersonate people in phone calls with alarming realism, tricking victims into financial losses. [12] A recent global survey found that over one-third of consumers in several countries had encountered a deepfake voice scam call in the past year, and more than 30% of those targeted fell victim to these convincing impersonations. Such statistics highlight how deepfakes can exploit human trust in audio-visual media, turning hyperrealism into a weapon for crime [13] (Fig. 2).

Beyond the global stage, local contexts are grappling with deepfake issues as well. In the Philippines, increasing incidents of deepfake pornography and other malicious deepfakes have raised concern [14]. Sharing of non-consensual intimate images or so-called revenge porn has "increased with the use of deepfakes," according to a 2024 IBM report. The Philippines was even reported to have the largest surge in deepfake incidents in the

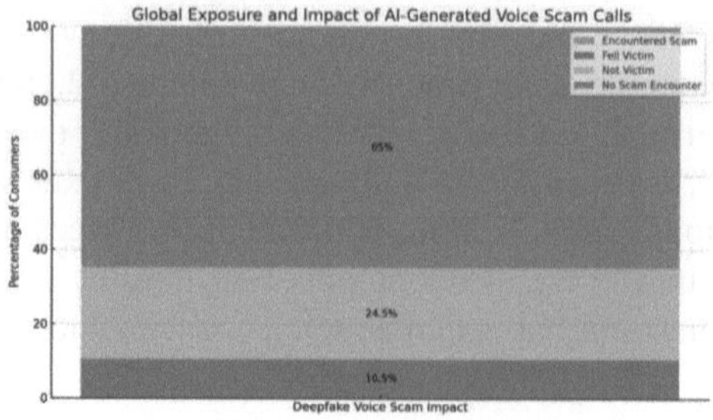

Fig. 2. Consumer Exposure and Vulnerability to Deepfake Voice Scam Calls Worldwide

Asia-Pacific, at 46x growth, in recent years. However, current Philippine laws such as the Cybercrime Prevention Act of 2012, do not explicitly address deepfakes. Lawmakers and advocates have begun pushing for new legislation to criminalize harmful deepfakes, noting that many victims which are often women whose faces are superimposed into obscene videos which lack adequate legal recourse [15]. Internationally, other governments are also responding: for example, the United Kingdom announced plans to outlaw the creation and sharing of explicit deepfake images, with proposed penalties of fines and jail time. These developments underscore that deepfakes are not only a technical or creative issue, but also a societal and regulatory challenge worldwide [16].

1.1 Statement of the Problem

1. **Erosion of Trust in Media -** Hyper-realistic deepfakes undermine public trust in audio-visual content by making it increasingly difficult to distinguish real from fake, posing serious implications for the credibility of news, entertainment, and social media platforms [17].
2. **Misinformation and Scams -** Deepfakes are being weaponized to spread false information and perpetrate fraud, such as impersonation scams and fake news videos, with their convincing realism making these deceptions more effective and dangerous.
3. **Creative Industry Ethical Dilemmas -** The use of deepfakes presents ethical challenges to the creative industry, including issues of authenticity, copyright, and consent especially in cases involving the digital resurrection of deceased celebrities or unauthorized manipulation of performances [18, 19]
4. **Legal and Regulatory Gaps -** Current laws in the Philippines and globally are insufficient to fully address the malicious use of deepfakes, highlighting the need for updated legal frameworks that safeguard the public without hindering technological innovation [20].
5. **Detection and Mitigation Strategies -** Advancements in detection tools and public education efforts are essential to combat the threats posed by GAN-powered deepfakes, though keeping pace with the rapid evolution of such technologies remains a critical challenge [21, 22]

2 Methods

2.1 Use of GAN-Based Models

Given that most deepfake content is generated using deep learning, GAN-based learning models are identified as the most suitable for studying and producing deepfakes. A GAN consists of two neural networks, a generator that creates fake images or audio, and a discriminator that attempts to detect if the output is fake or real which are trained in tandem. This adversarial training process enables GANs to produce increasingly realistic forgeries. By using GAN architectures, researchers can simulate the creation of deepfakes in a controlled setting. For example, state-of-the-art face-swap deepfakes often derive from GAN variants that can learn from thousands of images of a person to generate a new video of that person doing or saying something not originally recorded. Focusing on GANs in this study allows us to gauge the current capabilities of deepfake generation and forecast future improvements in realism (Fig. 3).

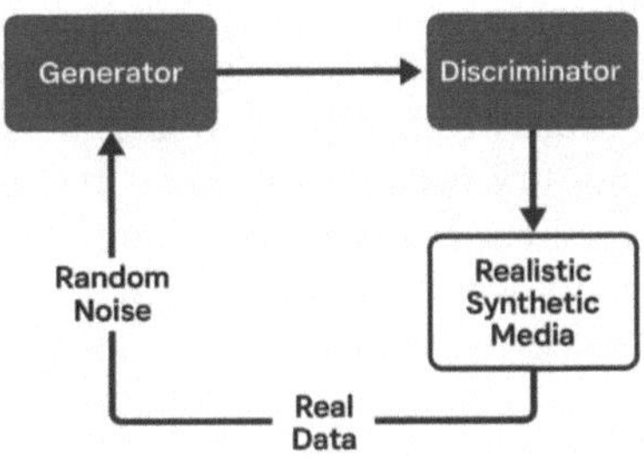

Fig. 3. Generative Adversarial Networks (GANs) Architecture for Deepfake Media Creation

To assess the realism of GAN-generated deepfakes, the study uses both technical and human evaluation. Metrics like Fréchet Inception Distance (FID) and audio or visual artifact analysis objectively measure similarity to real content, while deepfake detection algorithm performance offers indirect validation [23, 24]. Human evaluators also judge realism by identifying real versus fake media, with high error rates indicating convincing deepfakes. This combined approach ensures the study accurately reflects the capabilities and impact of deepfake technology.

2.2 Theoretical Framework – Diffusion of Innovations

This study applies Everett Rogers' Diffusion of Innovations theory (2003) to examine how deepfake media is adopted and perceived across society [25]. By evaluating deepfakes through the five key attributes of innovation such as relative advantage, compatibility, complexity, trialability, and observability, the research assesses factors that influence their spread. It also considers adopter categories to understand who is embracing or resisting the technology, particularly in the entertainment industry, offering a broader view of deepfakes as a social innovation (Fig. 4).

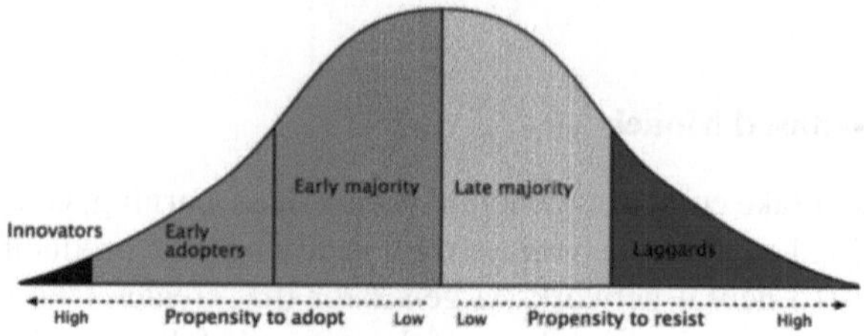

Fig. 4. Diffusion of Innovations Model

2.3 Sampling Technique and Method

The study employed purposive sampling to select 50 participants from the creative and entertainment sectors, aiming to explore the impact of deepfake media generated through GAN-based deep learning models. Participants included filmmakers, content creators, media professionals, and digital artists, primarily based in the Philippines, with at least one year of experience in using digital tools for content production. This sample was appropriate for the study's objective of examining how deepfakes influence authenticity, ethical standards, and industry workflows. Screening questions ensured familiarity with AI-generated media or prior exposure to deepfake-related content [26]. Participants were recruited through creative industry networks, professional associations, and academic institutions. Ethical considerations were observed throughout the process, including informed consent and anonymity. Their insights offered a focused understanding of how deepfake technologies are perceived, adopted, or challenged within the creative and entertainment industries.

3 Conclusion

3.1 Evaluation of Deepfake Realism and Quality

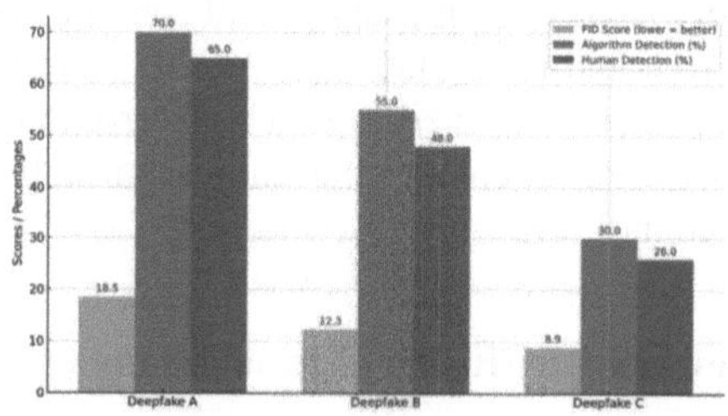

Fig. 5. Evaluation of Deepfake Realism and Quality

The evaluation chart provides a comparative analysis of three GAN-generated deepfakes using both objective (FID scores) and subjective (detection rates) criteria. Deepfake A, which recorded the highest Fréchet Inception Distance (FID) of 18.5, was the least realistic among the three, as evidenced by its high detection rates—70% by algorithms and 65% by human evaluators. Deepfake B performed moderately, with a FID of 12.3

and noticeably lower detection rates, indicating improved realism but still distinguishable. Notably, Deepfake C achieved the lowest FID at 8.9 and demonstrated significant evasion capabilities, being correctly identified only 30% of the time by detection systems and 26% by human evaluators (Fig. 5).

These results reflect a clear trend: as the FID score decreases, the perceived realism of the deepfake increases, making it more challenging for both automated systems and humans to detect manipulation. This correlation suggests that GANs are becoming increasingly proficient at producing highly convincing synthetic media. The low detection rates for Deepfake C are particularly concerning, underscoring the urgent need for advanced countermeasures. As deepfakes continue to improve in quality, relying solely on human judgment or current detection tools may no longer be sufficient, especially in high-stakes scenarios such as political misinformation, financial scams, or non-consensual content.

3.2 Adoption of Deepfake Technology Through the Lens of Diffusion of Innovations

Table 1. Evaluation of deepfake media using diffusion of innovations framework

Innovation Characteristic	Evaluation and Considerations
Relative Advantage	Deepfakes offer unique benefits in entertainment, such as cost savings and enhanced creative possibilities, giving them an edge over traditional VFX. However, their misuse in scams and misinformation highlights context-dependent risks
Compatibility	Deepfakes align with digital content creation in media and gaming but conflict with societal values of truth and privacy, limiting acceptance in fields like journalism and law
Complexity	While deepfake creation once required high technical skill, user-friendly tools have lowered the barrier. Yet, high-quality output still demands expertise, and many users remain wary due to technical unfamiliarity
Trialability	Casual use is widespread through apps and filters, encouraging experimentation and awareness. However, professional and ethical concerns limit trialability in more formal sectors
Observability	Deepfakes are highly visible online, driving both adoption through viral content and resistance due to their association with hoaxes and deception

Using the Diffusion of Innovations theory, the study finds that deepfake media is progressing from early adoption to early majority use, particularly within the creative and entertainment sectors. This conclusion is based on insights from 50 purposively selected participants, including filmmakers, content creators, media professionals, and digital artists in the Philippines. These individuals had at least one year of experience using digital tools and were familiar with AI-generated media. Many observed that early adopters in their networks, such as experimental studios and tech-savvy creators, have begun integrating deepfakes into content workflows. Participants described a growing interest in the technology for applications like visual effects, voice replication, and performance enhancement. However, they also noted that wider adoption remains cautious due to cost, ethical concerns, and lack of formal guidelines (Table 1).

The findings suggest that adoption patterns vary depending on how deepfakes align with the goals and values of specific sectors. Creative industries, which often prioritize innovation and spectacle, are more open to trying new technologies when peer success is visible. In contrast, fields like journalism and law are more reserved, focusing on detection rather than content generation. Participants emphasized that misuse of deepfakes, particularly in the form of disinformation or non-consensual content, has led to increased demand for regulation and verification tools. In the Philippine context, this cautious adoption is shaped by limited awareness, uneven digital literacy, and a regulatory environment that is still catching up with emerging technologies. Overall, the diffusion of deepfake media depends not only on its technical capabilities but also on how it fits within the professional and ethical standards of each community.

3.3 Summary

Deepfake technology offers exciting opportunities in entertainment, such as recreating deceased performers, de-aging actors, and enabling virtual performances, but it also raises ethical and legal issues around consent, authorship, and transparency. Beyond creative use, deepfakes pose serious threats by fueling misinformation, political manipulation, and scams, as seen in fake videos and AI-generated voice fraud, which erode public trust and highlight the urgent need for detection tools, digital literacy, and safeguards. While global and Philippine responses are evolving, with some laws and proposed bills addressing labeling, malicious use, and gender-based harassment, current regulations remain insufficient, making it crucial to combine updated policies, technological solutions, and education to manage risks while supporting ethical innovation.

4 Recommendation

The Philippines must prioritize tackling the rising threat of deepfakes by developing effective detection systems customized to Filipino languages and facial features, in collaboration with government agencies, private sectors, universities, and technology partners. These tools should be integrated into communication platforms, newsrooms, and mobile applications for real-time verification. At the same time, public awareness must be strengthened through expanded digital and media literacy programs, with schools embedding such lessons into their curricula and civil society promoting responsible content verification. To fully address the issue, legal reforms are also needed to define and penalize malicious deepfake use, especially in cases of impersonation, harassment, or fraud. Together, these measures will help protect Filipinos and institutions from the growing risks of synthetic media.

Acknowledgement. The author gratefully acknowledges the financial support provided by the FEU Institute of Technology for the conference and publication.

References

1. Karnouskos, S.: Artificial intelligence in digital media: the era of Deepfakes. IEEE Trans. Technol. Soc. **1**(3), 138–147 (2020). https://doi.org/10.1109/tts.2020.3001312
2. Al-Khazraji, S.H., Saleh, H.H., Khalid, A.I., Mishkhal, I.A.: Impact of deepfake technology on social media: detection, misinformation and societal implications. In: The Eurasia Proceedings of Science Technology Engineering and Mathematics, vol. 23, pp. 429–441 (2023). https://doi.org/10.55549/epstem.1371792
3. Amerini, I., et al.: Deepfake media forensics: status and future challenges. J. Imaging **11**(3), 73 (2025). https://doi.org/10.3390/jimaging11030073
4. Exploring the ethics of Deepfake technology in media: implications for trust and information integrity. J. Inform. Educ. Res. (2024). https://doi.org/10.52783/jier.v4i3.1482
5. Schwartz, E.H.: Elvis Presley resurrected for America's Got Talent by metaphysic and synthetic voice startup Respeecher - Voicebot.ai. Voicebot.ai, 19 September 2022. https://voicebot.ai/2022/09/14/elvis-presley-resurrected-for-americas-got-talent-by-meta-physic-and-synthetic-voice-startup-respeecher/#:~:text=Elvis%20Pres-ley%20took%20the%20stage,recent%20Star%20Wars%20TV%20shows
6. Ortega, J.H.J.C., Lagman, A.C., De Angel, R.M., Alix, A.L., Lagrazon, P.G.G.: Evaluation of program completion decision-based recommendation system with the ISO software quality model. In: 2021 IEEE 13th International Conference on Humanoid, Nanotechnology, Information Technology, Communication and Control, Environment, and Management (HNICEM), pp. 1–6 (2023b). https://doi.org/10.1109/hnicem60674.2023.10589184
7. Vaccari, C., Chadwick, A.: Deepfakes and disinformation: exploring the impact of synthetic political video on deception, uncertainty, and trust in news. Soc. Media Soc. **6**(1) (2020). https://doi.org/10.1177/2056305120903408
8. Deepfake footage purports to show Ukrainian president capitulating (2022). https://www.reu-ters.com/world/europe/deepfake-footage-purports-show-ukrainian-president-capitulating-2022-03-16/#:~:text=LONDON%2FLVIV%2C%20Ukraine%2C%20March%2016%20,more%20sophisticated%20deceptions%20to%20come
9. Philippines urged to outlaw sexually explicit deepfakes. https://www.bworldonline.com/the-nation/2025/01/26/649099/philippines-urged-to-outlaw-sexually-explicit-deep-fakes/#:~:text=Sharing%20intimate%20imagery%20with
10. Ayuman, J.K.R., Lacorte, M.C., Vallespin, M.R.D.: Discerning digital from canvas: investigating visual distinction between AI-generated art and actual art among far Eastern University's Institute of Architecture and Fine Arts (IARFA) and non-IARFA students. Int. J. Curr. Sci. Res. Rev. **07**(05) (2024). https://doi.org/10.47191/ijcsrr/v7-i5-40
11. Rosales, M.A., Magsumbol, J.V., Palconit, M.G.B., Culaba, A.B., Dadios, E.P.: Artificial intelligence: the technology adoption and impact in the Philippines. In: 2021 IEEE 13th International Conference on Humanoid, Nanotechnology, Information Technology, Communication and Control, Environment, and Management (HNICEM), pp. 1–6 (2020). https://doi.org/10.1109/hnicem51456.2020.9400025
12. Roe, J., Perkins, M., Furze, L.: Deepfakes and higher education: a research agenda and scoping review of synthetic media. J. Univ. Teach. Learn. Pract. (2024). https://doi.org/10.53761/2y2np178
13. AI Deepfake Fraud Calls Dominate Q4 Scams, Costing Consumers Millions (2025). https://www.businesswire.com/news/home/20250225398435/en/AI-Deepfake-Fraud-Calls-Dominate-Q4-Scams-Costing-Consumers-Millions
14. Philippines urged to outlaw sexually explicit deepfakes (2025). https://www.bworldonline.com/the-nation/2025/01/26/649099/philippines-urged-to-outlaw-sexually-explicit-deep-fakes/#:~:text=Sharing%20intimate%20imagery%20without%20con-sent%2C,a%202024%20report%20by%20IBM

15. Giray, L., et al.: Use and impact of artificial intelligence in Philippine higher education: reflections from instructors and administrators. Internet Ref. Serv. Q. **28**(3), 315–338 (2024). https://doi.org/10.1080/10875301.2024.2352746
16. Lundberg, E., Mozelius, P.: The potential effects of deepfakes on news media and entertainment. AI Soc. (2024). https://doi.org/10.1007/s00146-024-02072-1
17. Cajulis, R.C.J., Tuazon, J.A., Cabauatan, R.R.: Artificial intelligence in digital art: a comparative analysis on impacts to artists. Int. J. Arts Recreat. Sports **4**(1), 1–27 (2025). https://doi.org/10.47941/ijars.2444
18. Oksanen, A., et al.: Artificial intelligence in fine arts: a systematic review of empirical research. Comput. Hum. Behav. Artif. Hum. **1**(2), 100004 (2023). https://doi.org/10.1016/j.chbah.2023.100004
19. Nah, F.F., Zheng, R., Cai, J., Siau, K., Chen, L.: Generative AI and ChatGPT: applications, challenges, and AI-human collaboration. J. Inf. Technol. Case Appl. Res. **25**(3), 277–304 (2023). https://doi.org/10.1080/15228053.2023.2233814
20. Clarencia, E., Tiranda, T.G., Achmad, S., Sutoyo, R.: The impact of artificial intelligence in the creative industries: design and editing. In: 2020 International Seminar on Application for Technology of Information and Communication (iSemantic), pp. 440–444 (2024). https://doi.org/10.1109/isemantic63362.2024.10762015
21. Garcia, M.B.: The paradox of artificial creativity: challenges and opportunities of generative AI artistry. Creat. Res. J., 1–14 (2024). https://doi.org/10.1080/10400419.2024.2354622
22. Ortega, J.H.J.: Blended agile approach: a mobile application approach. Int. J. Adv. Trends Comput. Sci. Eng. **9**(1.3), 465–469 (2020). https://doi.org/10.30534/ijatcse/2020/7391.32020
23. Ortega, J.H.J.C., Lagman, A.C., De Angel, R.M., Alix, A.L., Lagrazon, P.G.G.: Analysis of a rule-based suggestion platform for academic program completion using the technology acceptance model. In: 2021 IEEE 13th International Conference on Humanoid, Nanotechnology, Information Technology, Communication and Control, Environment, and Management (HNICEM), pp. 1–5. https://doi.org/10.1109/hnicem60674.2023.10589051 (2023a)
24. Diffusion of Innovations, 5th Edition: Rogers, Everett M.: 9780743222099: Amazon.com: Books (n.d.). https://www.amazon.com/Diffusion-Innovations-5th-Everett-Rog-ers/dp/0743222091
25. Ortega, J.H.J.C., Lagman, A.C., Dc Angel, R.M., Alix, A.L., Calderon, R.A., Barrameda, R.B.: Criteria-based recommender platform for achieving optimal time-to-graduation using backward chaining algorithm. In: TENCON 2024 - 2024 IEEE Region 10 Conference (TENCON), pp. 1290–1293 (2024). https://doi.org/10.1109/tencon61640.2024.10903030
26. Ortega, J.H.J.C., et al.: Designing student's study plan: decision-based recommendation system towards program completion using forward chaining algorithm. In: 2021 IEEE 13th International Conference on Humanoid, Nanotechnology, Information Technology, Communication and Control, Environment, and Management (HNICEM), pp. 1–6 (2023). https://doi.org/10.1109/hnicem60674.2023.10589118

Quantum Pyramidal Networks on Wave-ViT Embeddings for Medical Image Analysis

Xavi F. Aragones[1,2] and Miguel A. González Ballester[1,3,4(✉)]

[1] BCN MedTech, Department of Engineering, Universitat Pompeu Fabra, Barcelona, Spain
ma.gonzalez@upf.edu
[2] Parc Tecnològic TecnoCampus Mataró–Maresme (UPF), Barcelona, Spain
[3] Quantic, Barcelona Supercomputing Center, Barcelona, Spain
[4] ICREA, Barcelona, Spain

Abstract. Transformer models have become one of the most widely used architectures in computer vision; Wave-ViT make use of discrete wavelet transforms to preserve fine detail while yielding compact features. We propose a hybrid pipeline in which a frozen, trained Wave-ViT yields a 128-dimensional embedding which we then compress with a PCA ($k \in \{2, \ldots, 32\}$) and classified by a n-qubit quantum orthogonal pyramidal circuit built from Reconfigurable Beam Splitter (RBS) gates. Using the LIDC-IDRI lung CT database, which contains pulmonary nodule images, the hybrid model performs as well as or better than the full Wave-ViT despite having $> 30\times$ lower dimensionality. Specifically on axial slices it reaches 84.9% accuracy vs. 84.4% (F_1 0.838 vs. 0.842; AUC-ROC 0.893 vs. 0.898), and on coronal slices it improves accuracy from 79.0% to 82.0% and F_1 from 0.786 to 0.800 with negligible change in AUC. These results indicate that classical-quantum composition can retain clinically relevant accuracy with minimal quantum resources, offering a practical near-term route for medical image analysis. We also outline current limits (2D slices, few qubits) and potential paths toward scalable 3D analysis as hardware capabilities advance.

Keywords: Quantum machine learning · Wave-ViT · Medical image analysis · Pulmonary nodules · Hybrid quantum–classical · RBS gates

1 Introduction

Transformer architectures have dramatically transformed computer vision. The Vision Transformer (ViT) [1] initiated a paradigm shift by treating images as sequences of fixed-size patches processed by standard transformer encoders. This breakthrough inspired extensions such as DETR [2] and DeiT [3], and later led to specialized architectures focused on efficiency and fine-detail preservation. Notably, the Wavelet Vision Transformer (Wave-ViT) [4] employs the Discrete

C. Xu (Ed.): ICMLSC 2026, CCIS 2948, pp. 307–312, 2027.
https://doi.org/10.1007/978-981-92-1546-1_25

Wavelet Transform (DWT) for lossless downsampling while retaining a 128-channel feature map.

Quantum machine learning seeks to exploit quantum mechanics properties to outperform classical algorithms, with early theoretical speedups demonstrated in [5,6] and practical quantum neural frameworks developed in [7,8], and [9]. Recent quantum-transformer models extend these ideas by incorporating quantum attention and embedding mechanisms. However, existing approaches face several limitations, including exponential simulation overheads [10], fault-tolerant requirements with block-encoding complexity [11], NISQ circuit constraints [12], limited practical applications [13], embedding bottlenecks [14], hybrid training complexity [15], scalability challenges for large molecular systems [16], and convergence challenges in correlated materials [17]. In contrast, our hybrid approach integrates the multi-scale feature extraction of a trained Wave-ViT with a quantum orthogonal pyramidal circuit based on RBS gates [18]. This design substantially reduces computational complexity while maintaining high classification accuracy.

2 Methods

The proposed method follows a two-stage pipeline. In the first stage, a trained Wave-ViT model extracts hierarchical features (see Fig. 1). In the second stage, these features are passed to the Quantum Orthogonal Pyramidal Circuit for classification. Within the Wave-ViT ([4]), a Discrete Wavelet Transform (DWT) decomposes each input image into four complementary sub-bands: LL (approximation coefficients capturing most structural information), LH (horizontal edge details), HL (vertical edge details), and HH (diagonal edge details). After the wavelet-based self-attention operations and reconstruction via inverse DWT, the resulting 128-dimensional feature embeddings are further compacted through dimensionality reduction. In the subsequent quantum-processing stage, a scalable circuit based on Reconfigurable Beam Splitter (RBS) gates performs the necessary unitary rotations.

The Wave-ViT model incorporates the Discrete Wavelet Transform (DWT) to extract multi-scale spatial features at each layer. Given an input tensor $\mathbf{X}_l$ at layer l, the DWT decomposes it into four frequency sub-bands, as expressed in Eq. (1):

$$\mathbf{X}_l^{\mathrm{DWT}} = \mathrm{DWT}(\mathbf{X}_l) = [\mathbf{X}_l^{LL}, \mathbf{X}_l^{LH}, \mathbf{X}_l^{HL}, \mathbf{X}_l^{HH}] \tag{1}$$

In this formulation, $\mathbf{X}_l^{LL}, \mathbf{X}_l^{LH}, \mathbf{X}_l^{HL}, \mathbf{X}_l^{HH} \in \mathbb{R}^{\frac{H_l}{2} \times \frac{W_l}{2} \times D_l}$ represent the low-frequency (approximation) and high-frequency (detail) coefficients resulting from DWT.

Self-attention with Wavelet Features. The self-attention mechanism in Wave-ViT is enhanced by wavelet decomposition.

The attention scores are computed as:

$$\mathbf{A}_l = \text{softmax}\left(\frac{\mathbf{Q}_l \mathbf{K}_l^T}{\sqrt{d_k}}\right) \in \mathbb{R}^{H_l \times W_l \times \frac{H_l}{2} \times \frac{W_l}{2}} \tag{2}$$

where d_k is the scaling factor (typically set to D_l). Eq. (2) defines the scaled dot-product attention mechanism adapted for the wavelet-based formulation.

The attention output integrates multi-scale information through wavelet-based key and value representations. After the final transformer block in stage 2, the network produces a feature map $\mathbf{F} \in \mathbb{R}^{\frac{H}{2P} \times \frac{W}{2P} \times 128}$.

A global average pooling (GAP) operation (Eq. (3)) is subsequently applied to yield the final 128-dimensional feature vector.

$$\mathbf{v} = \text{GAP}(\mathbf{F}) = \frac{1}{\frac{H}{2P} \times \frac{W}{2P}} \sum_{i=1}^{\frac{H}{2P}} \sum_{j=1}^{\frac{W}{2P}} \mathbf{F}_{i,j} \in \mathbb{R}^{128} \tag{3}$$

This operation transforms the spatial feature map into a compact embedding vector, which captures the essential characteristics of the input image (see Fig. 1a).

2.1 Quantum Orthogonal Pyramidal Circuit

Following dimensionality reduction through PCA, where the embedding is further reduced to $k \in \{2, \ldots, 32\}$ components (see Fig. 1b), we employ a quantum pyramidal architecture based on Reconfigurable Beam Splitter (RBS) gates [19].

RBS gates perform unitary operations within two-dimensional subspaces while preserving orthogonality. Each RBS gate implements a planar rotation defined as:

$$R_{ij}(\theta) = \begin{bmatrix} \cos(\theta) & -\sin(\theta) \\ \sin(\theta) & \cos(\theta) \end{bmatrix}, \tag{4}$$

where θ represents the rotation angle, and indices i, j indicate the dimensions being transformed. The structure in Eq. (4) enables two fundamental quantum properties: superposition, and the potential for entanglement.

The orthogonal pyramidal circuit systematically applies a series of RBS operations across the feature dimensions (see Fig. 1b, which illustrates the RBS gates within the circuit diagram). The diagram follows standard quantum notation: H denotes Hadamard gates, R_Y represents rotations around the Y-axis, and CNOT gates are indicated by a $\bullet$ (control qubit) and an $\oplus$ (target qubit).

3 Experimental Application and Results

Our experimental validation uses the LIDC-IDRI (Lung Image Database Consortium and Image Database Resource Initiative) dataset [20]. This curated collection provides annotated computed tomography (CT) scans that serve as

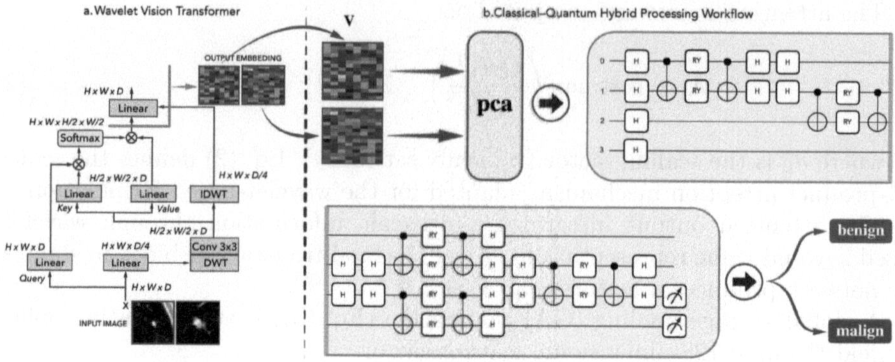

Fig. 1. Left - a: Architecture of the Wavelet Vision Transformer [4], which builds upon the Wave-ViT approach. Right b: Processing pipeline illustrating the extraction and quantum encoding of the Wave-ViT embedding v, shown as heatmaps (top). These embeddings for benign (blue arrow) and malignant (red arrow) nodules exhibit distinct patterns that are subsequently subjected to PCA-based dimensionality reduction. The reduced representations are then fed into the truncated pyramidal quantum circuit with a 4-2 structure, leveraging RBS transformations

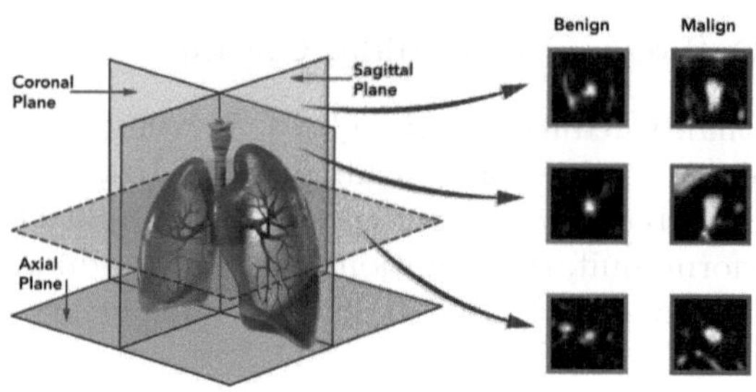

Fig. 2. Three-dimensional representation of pulmonary nodule imaging. Left: Anatomical orientation showing axial planes intersecting the lung. Right: Representative 32×32 pixel CT slices from each plane (central slice of the volume) comparing benign nodules (blue frames) and malignant nodules (red frames), demonstrating distinctive morphological characteristics across different perspectives. (Color figure online)

a benchmark for developing and evaluating computer-aided diagnosis systems for lung cancer detection (see Fig. 2). Despite compressing the Wave-ViT output to only four qubits, our hybrid classicalâĂŞquantum pipeline achieves in some cases superior classification performance relative to the full 128-dimensional Wave-ViT model. For instance, in the axial plane the four-qubit circuit attains 84.9% accuracy compared with 84.4% for the full Wave-ViT, with F_1 scores of 0.838 versus 0.842 and an AUC-ROC of 0.893 versus 0.898. In the sagittal view, both approaches reach 83.4% accuracy and identical AUC-ROC values, while the hybrid's F_1 of 0.827 differs by only 0.002 from the classical baseline. Most notably, on coronal slices the quantum-enhanced model outperforms Wave-ViT, raising accuracy from 79.0% to 82.0% and F_1 from 0.786 to 0.800, with only a 0.006 reduction in AUC-ROC. These findings demonstrate that our pipeline can match or surpass the representational power of Wave-ViT while operating in a reduced dimension, opening the door to highly efficient hybrid algorithms.

4 Conclusion and Future Work

This work presents a novel classical-quantum hybrid framework that combines Wave-ViT with quantum orthogonal pyramidal circuit using RBS gates for pulmonary nodule classification. Experiments on the LIDC-IDRI dataset show that our method performs on par with, or surpasses, the full Wave-ViT model across multiple anatomical views, with particularly notable gains in the coronal plane. Systematic evaluations across PCA dimensions and quantum circuit configurations confirm the robustness of the proposed framework, while comparisons with standard Quantum Support Vector Machine baselines indicate enhanced stability and reduced variability. The quantum circuit preserves critical diagnostic information even when the feature space is compressed to as few as four or less dimensions. These findings highlight the promise of hybrid architectures for medical imaging tasks that demand both computational efficiency and diagnostic accuracy.

Our focus on 2D CT slices reflects the current limitations of near-term quantum hardware. Although the proposed method efficiently processes 2D data, extending it to full 3D volumetric analysis remains infeasible due to present qubit constraints.

Acknowledgements. This work is part of Maria de Maeztu Units of Excellence Programme CEX2021-001195-M, funded by MICIU/AEI /10.13039/501100011033

References

1. Dosovitskiy, A., et al.: An image is worth 16x16 words: transformers for image recognition at scale. In: International Conference on Learning Representations (2020)
2. Carion, N., Massa, F., Synnaeve, G., Usunier, N., Kirillov, A., Zagoruyko, S.: End-to-end object detection with transformers. In: European Conference on Computer Vision, pp. 213–229. Springer (2020). https://doi.org/10.1007/978-3-030-58452-8_13
3. Touvron, H., Cord, M., Douze, M., Massa, F., Sablayrolles, A., Jégou, H.: Training data-efficient image transformers & distillation through attention. In: International Conference on Machine Learning, pp. 10347–10357. PMLR (2021)
4. Yao, H., et al.: Wave-Vit: unifying wavelet and transformers for visual representation learning. In: European Conference on Computer Vision, pp. 255–271 (2022)
5. Biamonte, J., Wittek, P., Pancotti, N., Rebentrost, P., Wiebe, N., Lloyd, S.: Quantum machine learning. Nature **549**(7671), 195–202 (2017)
6. Lloyd, S., Mohseni, M., Rebentrost, P.: Quantum algorithms for supervised and unsupervised machine learning. arXiv preprint arXiv:1307.0411 (2013)

7. Dunjko, V., Taylor, J.M., Briegel, H.J.: Quantum-enhanced machine learning. Phys. Rev. Lett. **117**(13), 130501 (2016)
8. Schuld, M., Sinayskiy, I., Petruccione, F.: The quest for a quantum neural network. Quantum Inf. Process. **13**(11), 2567–2586 (2014)
9. Schuld, M., Petruccione, F.: Supervised Learning with Quantum Computers. Springer (2018). https://doi.org/10.1007/978-3-319-96424-9
10. Liao, Y., Ferrie, C.: GPT on a quantum computer. arXiv preprint arXiv:2403.09418 (2024). Submitted March 14, 2024
11. Guo, N., et al.: Quantum linear algebra is all you need for transformer architectures. arXiv preprint arXiv:2402.16714 (2024). Submitted February 26, 2024; last revised May 31, 2024
12. Evans, E.N., Cook, M., Bradshaw, Z.P., LaBorde, M.L.: Learning with sasquatch: a novel variational quantum transformer architecture with kernel-based self-attention. arXiv preprint arXiv:2403.14753 (2024). Submitted March 21, 2024; last revised February 5, 2025
13. Pasquali, D., Grossi, M., Vallecorsa, S.: Measurements with a quantum vision transformer: a naive approach. In: EPJ Web of Conferences, vol. 295, p. 12003 (2024). 26th International Conference on Computing in High Energy and Nuclear Physics (CHEP 2023)
14. Ma, H., Shang, H., Yang, J.: Quantum embedding method with transformer neural network quantum states for strongly correlated materials. NPJ Comput. Mater. **10**, 220 (2024)
15. Lange, H., et al.: Transformer neural networks and quantum simulators: a hybrid approach for simulating strongly correlated systems. Quantum **9**, 1675 (2025)
16. Wu, Y., Guo, C., Fan, Y., Zhou, P., Shang, H.: NNQS-transformer: an efficient and scalable neural network quantum states approach for ab initio quantum chemistry. In: Proceedings of the International Conference for High Performance Computing, Networking, Storage and Analysis, SC 2023, New York, NY, USA (2023). Association for Computing Machinery
17. Fu, L., Wu, Y., Shang, H., Yang, J.: Transformer-based neural-network quantum state method for electronic band structures of real solids. J. Chem. Theory Comput. **20**, 6218–6226 (2024)
18. Cherrat, A., et al.: Quantum vision transformers. Quantum **1**(1), 1–12 (2024). Open-access, community-driven journal
19. Kerenidis, I., Landman, J., Prakash, A.: Classical and quantum algorithms for orthogonal neural networks. Adv. Neural. Inf. Process. Syst. **34**, 4548–4560 (2021)
20. Armato, S.G., III., et al.: The lung image database consortium (LIDC) and image database resource initiative (IDRI). Med. Phys. **38**(2), 915–931 (2011)

MedLoRA: Low-Rank Few-Shot Adaptation of Vision-Language Models for Medical Images

Bingyuan Bai[1], Tzu-Ching Shih[2], and Kazunori Miyata[1(✉)]

[1] Japan Advanced Institute of Science and Technology, Ishikawa, Japan
{bbyuan,miyata}@jaist.ac.jp
[2] China Medical University, Taichung, Taiwan
shih@mail.cmu.edu.tw

Abstract. Vision-language models (VLMs), such as Contrastive Language–Image Pre-training (CLIP), have demonstrated remarkable performance in zero-shot classification tasks by learning precise cross-modal embedding alignments through contrastive learning on large-scale noisy image–text datasets. However, their application in the medical imaging domain is limited by factors such as domain discrepancies between natural image pre-training datasets (e.g., ImageNet), ethical constraints on annotations, and the high computational cost of full fine-tuning. Current research on parameter-efficient fine-tuning (PEFT) for VLMs primarily follows two paradigms: (1) introducing learnable text prompt tokens at the input stage, and (2) inserting lightweight adapter blocks between model layers. However, both approaches rely on laborious training procedures or carefully tuned task-specific hyperparameters. To address this challenge, we propose MedLoRA, a framework that integrates Low-Rank Adaptation (LoRA) into VLMs to enable few-shot PEFT on medical images. We evaluate the framework on the large-scale MedMNIST medical imaging dataset, where MedLoRA consistently delivers substantial few-shot performance improvements over zero-shot baselines, improving the average macro-F1 from 22.63 in the zero-shot setting to 68.84 after adaptation, corresponding to an average absolute gain of +46.21 across four vision-language backbones, thereby providing a scalable and effective solution for medical AI in annotation-scarce clinical environments.

Keywords: Low-rank adaptation · Vision-language models · CLIP · Parameter-efficient fine-tuning · Few-shot · Medical image

1 Introduction

In conventional visual recognition tasks, category labels such as *"cat"* or *"flower"* are typically simplified into discrete identifiers for cross-entropy computation [2], leaving the semantic richness of text underutilized. While many studies have

C. Xu (Ed.): ICMLSC 2026, CCIS 2948, pp. 313–324, 2027.
https://doi.org/10.1007/978-981-92-1546-1_26

adapted vision models to achieve state-of-the-art (SOTA) results on large-scale datasets like ImageNet [1], these paradigms struggle in cross-domain scenarios such as medical imaging, where rare and complex pathological cases demand substantial retraining and additional data.

Recently, vision–language models (VLMs), exemplified by contrastive language–image pre-training (CLIP) [13], have aligned visual and textual representations through contrastive learning on large-scale image–text pairs. By optimizing both encoders within a shared latent space, CLIP captures robust cross-modal features and enables zero-shot classification via simple prompting: given an image and a class-related textual description, the model computes embedding similarities and predicts class probabilities through a softmax function.

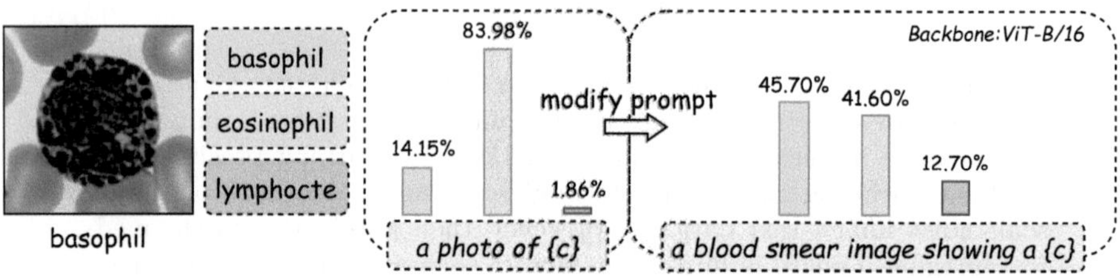

Fig. 1. Taking the input image of a basophil as an example, a simple prompt adjustment can effectively modify the zero-shot classification outcome. Given three blood cell categories, namely *basophil*, *eosinophil*, and *lymphocyte*, we conduct testing using the CLIP backbone ViT-B/16. The results show that when a generic prompt is applied, the model incorrectly predicts the class *eosinophil*. In contrast, when the prompt is refined with more contextual detail, the output correctly predicts the class *basophil*.

However, finding prompts that precisely and consistently describe image semantics remains non-trivial. For instance, using the generic template *"a photo of {c}"* for basophil images often biases predictions toward eosinophil, whereas adding contextual detail, such as *"a blood smear image showing a {c}"*, yields the correct prediction (Fig. 1). Although prompt refinement can noticeably influence zero-shot outcomes, constructing accurate and domain-specific templates across diverse medical subfields is still challenging, even for experts.

An alternative for domain adaptation is full fine-tuning, but the parameter scale of VLMs makes this impractical. For example, OpenAI's ViT-B/16 has about 150M parameters, and ViT-G/14 exceeds 1.3B. SOTA medical VLMs such as MedVLM-R1 [12] reach 2B parameters, rendering full fine-tuning computationally prohibitive. To address this, parameter-efficient fine-tuning (PEFT) methods have been developed. They either introduce trainable prompt tokens or insert lightweight adapter modules into encoder layers, enabling feature adaptation without modifying backbone weights. Yet, these methods often require heavy hyperparameter tuning and show inconsistent results across datasets.

Among recent PEFT strategies, LoRA [7] has gained attention for achieving competitive results with minimal trainable parameters. It decomposes weight

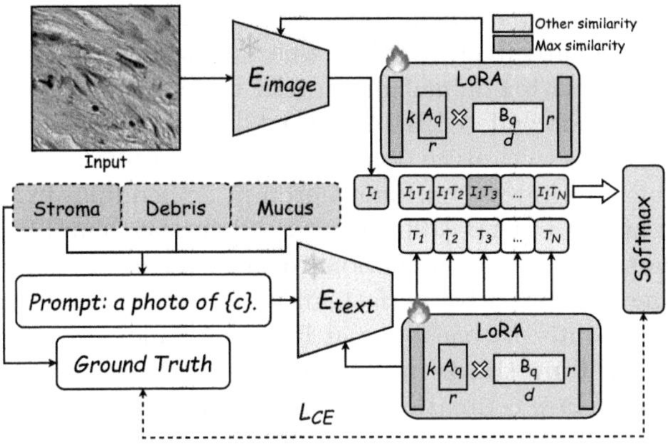

Fig. 2. Overview of the proposed MedLoRA framework. The visual encoder E_{image} and textual encoder E_{text}, both equipped with LoRA modules, generate normalized embeddings compared via cosine similarity. The similarity scores are optimized through a softmax-based cross-entropy loss $\mathcal{L}_{\text{CE}}$.

updates into low-rank matrices, enabling efficient adaptation without altering pre-trained weights. Building on this idea, we propose the MedLoRA (Fig. 2), a framework tailored for few-shot fine-tuning of VLMs in medical imaging. MedLoRA integrates LoRA into both visual and textual encoders of CLIP-like architectures, supporting OpenAI CLIP variants and the medical-domain BiomedCLIP [23]. Experiments on MedMNISTv2 [20] demonstrate that MedLoRA delivers robust and consistent improvements across subdomains while significantly reducing computation. The main contributions are summarized as follows:

- We propose MedLoRA, a PEFT framework that integrates LoRA into VLMs for few-shot medical image classification.
- MedLoRA supports both general-purpose CLIP variants and the domain-specific BiomedCLIP backbone, enabling flexible adaptation across modalities and subdomains.
- Extensive experiments on MedMNIST show that MedLoRA achieves consistent gains under few-shot settings while reducing training cost.

2 Related Work

Parameter-Efficient Fine-Tuning (PEFT) adapts large pre-trained models to downstream tasks by updating only a small subset of parameters while keeping the backbone weights frozen, substantially reducing memory usage, computational cost, and storage overhead compared to full fine-tuning. This paradigm is particularly suitable for large-scale deployment and resource-constrained settings. Existing PEFT methods can be broadly categorized into additive, selective, and reparameterized approaches [5].

Additive PEFT methods introduce lightweight, task-specific components into the pre-trained architecture while freezing original parameters, enabling efficient adaptation with minimal disruption to learned representations. Representative examples include CLIP-Adapter [3], which inserts bottleneck layers after projection heads to capture domain-specific information, and Soft Prompt Tuning [15], which optimizes continuous prompt embeddings in the input space. Other variants such as $(IA)^3$ [10] and SSF [9] further simplify adaptation by scaling and shifting internal activations or normalization parameters. These approaches achieve competitive performance with minimal parameter overhead and can be merged into the backbone at inference time.

Selective PEFT methods update only a subset of pre-trained parameters identified by importance estimation or masking strategies.Diff Pruning [4], BitFit [21], and Child-Tuning [18] exemplify this category by activating sparse but expressive parameter subsets based on magnitude or gradient sensitivity. Structural extensions such as Freeze and Reconfigure (FAR) [17] further improve scalability by grouping parameters into structured units, leading to improved optimization stability and reduced memory overhead.

Reparameterized PEFT methods improve training efficiency by constraining parameter updates to low-dimensional subspaces. LoRA is the most representative approach, decomposing weight updates into low-rank matrices that can be merged with pre-trained weights without additional inference cost. Extensions such as DyLoRA [16] and AdaLoRA [22] introduce adaptive rank allocation, while Laplace LoRA [19], LoRA+ [6], and LoRAHub [8] further improve stability, regularization, and multi-task transferability. Related techniques such as Compacter [11] leverage tensor decomposition and shared parameterization to achieve similar efficiency gains.

A recent reparameterized approach, MoRA [14], extends LoRA to multimodal disease diagnosis by introducing modality-aware low-rank modules that support robust adaptation under missing-modality conditions. Building on this line of research, we propose MedLoRA, which extends LoRA to vision–language models for few-shot medical image classification. In contrast to MoRA's focus on modality robustness, MedLoRA targets data-scarce adaptation by jointly injecting LoRA modules into both visual and textual transformers, providing a unified framework applicable to CLIP-based and biomedical backbones. Extensive experiments on six MedMNISTv2 subsets demonstrate that this dual-branch adaptation achieves consistent performance gains while maintaining strong parameter efficiency.

3 Method

Considering a medical subdomain dataset with N categories, where n shots are sampled per category for fine-tuning, each training sample consists of a medical image paired with a text description encoding its corresponding medical category semantics. The training set is represented as $\{(\mathbf{I}_{i,j}, \mathbf{T}_i)\}_{i=1,j=1}^{N,n}$, where $\mathbf{I}_{i,j}$ denotes the j-th image from category i, and $\mathbf{T}_i$ denotes the category-level text description.

Image and text inputs are processed by a dual-encoder architecture with pre-trained vision and language encoders. The LoRA modules are introduced into both encoders to enable task-specific adaptation while keeping the pre-trained parameters frozen. Given an image–text pair $(\mathbf{I}_{i,j}, \mathbf{T}_i)$, the corresponding visual and textual representations are computed as

$$\mathbf{v}_{i,j} = f_{\text{vis}}(\mathbf{I}_{i,j}; \boldsymbol{\theta}^0_{\text{vis}}, \boldsymbol{\theta}^{\text{LoRA}}_{\text{vis}}), \quad \mathbf{t}_i = f_{\text{text}}(\mathbf{T}_i; \boldsymbol{\theta}^0_{\text{text}}, \boldsymbol{\theta}^{\text{LoRA}}_{\text{text}}), \tag{1}$$

where $\boldsymbol{\theta}^0$ denotes frozen pre-trained parameters and $\boldsymbol{\theta}^{\text{LoRA}}$ denotes trainable LoRA parameters.

For the vision encoder, a pre-trained Vision Transformer is adopted as the backbone. LoRA modules are injected into the query, key, and value projections of the multi-head self-attention layers. Given an input token sequence $\mathbf{X} \in \mathbb{R}^{B \times N \times d}$, the self-attention projections are computed as

$$\mathbf{QKV} = \mathbf{X}\mathbf{W}_{\text{qkv}}^{\top}, \tag{2}$$

where $\mathbf{W}_{\text{qkv}} \in \mathbb{R}^{3d \times d}$ concatenates the projection matrices. Each projection is augmented with a low-rank update:

$$\mathbf{W}_Q = \mathbf{W}_Q^0 + \frac{\alpha}{r}\mathbf{B}_Q\mathbf{A}_Q, \quad \mathbf{W}_K = \mathbf{W}_K^0 + \frac{\alpha}{r}\mathbf{B}_K\mathbf{A}_K, \quad \mathbf{W}_V = \mathbf{W}_V^0 + \frac{\alpha}{r}\mathbf{B}_V\mathbf{A}_V. \tag{3}$$

Here, $\mathbf{A}_* \in \mathbb{R}^{r \times d}$ and $\mathbf{B}_* \in \mathbb{R}^{d \times r}$ are low-rank matrices for $* \in \{Q, K, V\}$. This parameterization constrains attention updates to a structured low-rank subspace, enabling controlled modification of attention weights while preserving the pre-trained attention topology.

For the text descriptions, inputs are encoded using a pre-trained transformer with either a ViT-style or BERT-style architecture. LoRA modules are injected into the self-attention projections to adapt textual representations to medical category semantics. Let $\mathbf{W}_{\text{proj}} \in \{\mathbf{W}_Q, \mathbf{W}_K, \mathbf{W}_V\}$ denote a projection matrix in a self-attention layer. Given an input token embedding $\mathbf{h} \in \mathbb{R}^d$, the LoRA-augmented output embedding $\mathbf{h}'$ is computed as

$$\mathbf{h}' = \mathbf{W}^0_{\text{proj}}\mathbf{h} + \frac{\alpha}{r}\mathbf{B}_{\text{proj}}\mathbf{A}_{\text{proj}}\mathbf{h}, \tag{4}$$

where $\mathbf{W}^0_{\text{proj}}$ is frozen and $\mathbf{B}_{\text{proj}}\mathbf{A}_{\text{proj}}$ represents the low-rank adaptation. By restricting updates to low-rank parameters in both encoders, MedLoRA enables efficient few-shot adaptation while preserving pre-trained multimodal representations.

3.1 Loss Function and Evaluation Metric

Given the visual representation $\mathbf{v}_{i,j}$ and the textual representation $\mathbf{t}_i$ encoding category-level medical semantics, the model is trained using a supervised classification objective. Both representations are ℓ_2-normalized prior to similarity computation. For each image representation, the similarity to all category text representations is computed using cosine similarity with a temperature scaling parameter τ:

$$z_{(i,j),c} = \tau \frac{\mathbf{v}_{i,j}^{\top} \mathbf{t}_c}{\|\mathbf{v}_{i,j}\| \, \|\mathbf{t}_c\|}, \quad c = 1, \ldots, N. \tag{5}$$

The resulting logits $\mathbf{z}_{(i,j)} = [z_{(i,j),1}, \ldots, z_{(i,j),N}]$ are passed through a softmax layer, and the cross-entropy loss over all categories and shots is defined as

$$\mathcal{L} = -\frac{1}{NK} \sum_{i=1}^{N} \sum_{j=1}^{K} \log \frac{\exp\left(z_{(i,j),i}\right)}{\sum_{c=1}^{N} \exp\left(z_{(i,j),c}\right)}. \tag{6}$$

Few-shot adaptation performance is evaluated using the macro-averaged F1-score ($\mathrm{F1}_{\mathrm{macro}}$) to ensure equal weighting across medical categories, defined as

$$\mathrm{F1}_{\mathrm{macro}} = \frac{1}{N} \sum_{i=1}^{N} \frac{2 \cdot \mathrm{Pre}_i \cdot \mathrm{Rec}_i}{\mathrm{Pre}_i + \mathrm{Rec}_i}. \tag{7}$$

All reported results are obtained from the model checkpoint corresponding to the highest $\mathrm{F1}_{\mathrm{macro}}$ score observed during training.

4 Experiments

4.1 Datasets

We evaluate MedLoRA on six representative subsets from the MedMNISTv2 benchmark, covering diverse medical imaging modalities and diagnostic tasks. A summary of these datasets is provided in Table 1, and the sample images are illustrated in Fig. 3.

Table 1. Summary of the six MedMNISTv2 subsets used in MedLoRA.

Dataset	Modality	Size	Classes	Task Description
BloodMNIST	Microscopy	224 × 224	8	White blood cell classification
BreastMNIST	Ultrasound	224 × 224	2	Benign vs. malignant lesion detection
OctMNIST	OCT	224 × 224	4	Retinal OCT image classification
OrganAMNIST	MRI	224 × 224	11	Abdominal organ recognition
PathMNIST	Histopathology	224 × 224	9	Colon tissue-type recognition
PneumoniaMNIST	X-ray	224 × 224	2	Pneumonia vs. normal classification

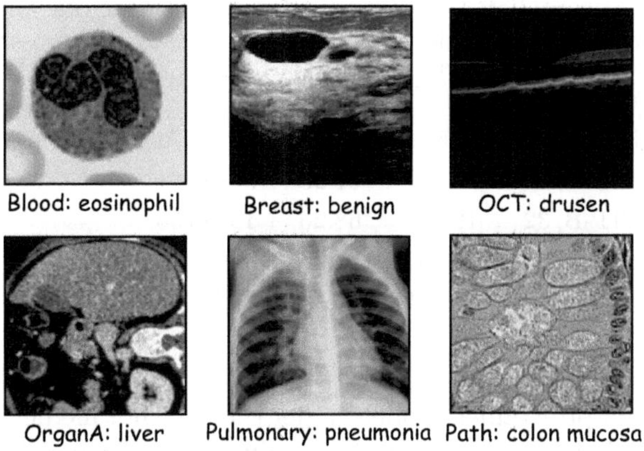

Fig. 3. Examples of samples from the subset used for training.

4.2 Training Details

All experiments are conducted on an Ubuntu 24.04 LTS system equipped with a single NVIDIA RTX 4090 GPU (24 GB VRAM). The proposed MedLoRA framework is implemented in PyTorch, and all models are trained using the AdamW optimizer with cosine learning rate scheduling and automatic mixed-precision acceleration. A 5% warm-up phase is applied at the beginning of training to stabilize optimization, followed by cosine decay of the learning rate. Gradient clipping with a maximum norm of 1.0 and gradient accumulation (4 steps) are employed to prevent exploding gradients and reduce GPU memory consumption. Unless otherwise specified, the default configuration is set as follows: learning rate of 1×10^{-3}, batch size of 8, rank $r = 2$, scaling factor $\alpha = 1$, dropout rate of 0.1, and 4-shot training for each class using both vision and text encoders. Each model is trained for 100 epochs with the random seed fixed at 42 for reproducibility. The proposed framework is evaluated across six MedMNISTv2 subsets, using three OpenCLIP backbone models: ViT-B/16, ViT-B/32, ViT-L/14, and one medical pre-trained backbone BiomedCLIP.

4.3 Experiment I: Fine-Tuning on General and Medical Backbones

The purpose of this experiment is to assess the effect of MedLoRA on general-domain VLMs. To further evaluate domain-specific adaptability, we apply MedLoRA to the BiomedCLIP backbone pre-trained on large-scale biomedical image–text pairs. Its vision transformer retains the same ViT architecture and LoRA configuration as OpenCLIP, whereas the textual branch replaces the CLIP-style encoder with a PubMedBERT-based transformer featuring a smaller hidden dimension and an additional projection layer for cross-modal alignment.

LoRA Fine-Tuning Consistently Outperforms Zero-Shot Inference. As reported in Table 2, LoRA adaptation yields substantial improvements in

Table 2. Zero-shot and LoRA performance comparison across all datasets. ΔF1 denotes the performance gain achieved by LoRA relative to the zero-shot setting. The average training time is reported for LoRA fine-tuning only.

Backbone	Zero-shot	Ours	ΔF1	Avg. Time(s)
ViT-B/16	22.52	67.20	+44.68	61
ViT-B/32	18.43	68.26	**+49.83**	55
ViT-L/14	23.24	68.26	+45.02	114
BiomedCLIP	**26.32**	**71.62**	+45.29	66

macro-F1 across all pre-trained models under the few-shot medical setting. Compared with zero-shot inference, absolute gains range from +44.68 to +49.83 F1 points, indicating a consistent and pronounced performance increase. For general-purpose vision backbones, ViT-B/16 and ViT-B/32 reach macro-F1 scores of 67.20 and 68.26 after adaptation, compared to zero-shot baselines of 22.52 and 18.43, respectively. These results indicate that the proposed MedLoRA constrains task-specific updates for medical subdomain adaptation to low-rank parameter subspaces, enabling efficient reshaping of pre-trained representations with limited medical annotations and facilitating rapid downstream fine-tuning of VLMs.

Biomedical-Pre-trained Backbones Achieve the Highest Adapted Performance. As shown in Table 2, BiomedCLIP achieves the highest macro-F1 score after LoRA adaptation, reaching 71.62 and outperforming all general-purpose backbones, whose adapted performance remains below 69. In addition, BiomedCLIP exhibits the strongest zero-shot baseline (26.32), exceeding those of ViT-B/16 (22.52), ViT-B/32 (18.43), and ViT-L/14 (23.24), which indicates that its pre-trained representation spacc is already more closely aligned with medical image semantics prior to adaptation. Notably, the relative improvement introduced by LoRA for BiomedCLIP (+45.29) is comparable in magnitude to the gains observed for general-domain backbones (+44.68 to +49.83), rather than being substantially larger. This observation indicates that the performance gains introduced by LoRA are of comparable magnitude across general-purpose and biomedical-pre-trained backbones. Consequently, the higher final performance of BiomedCLIP can be attributed to a more favorable initialization of the representation space induced by biomedical pretraining, upon which LoRA further refines class-specific decision boundaries under limited supervision.

In summary, the results in Table 2 demonstrate that LoRA achieves robust and consistent performance improvements over zero-shot inference in few-shot medical image classification. Furthermore, biomedical-pre-trained backbones further raise the performance ceiling after adaptation, highlighting the complementary roles of domain knowledge and low-rank fine-tuning.

4.4 Experiment II: Ablation Study

This experiment analyzes the effect of different encoder adaptation strategies in MedLoRA by comparing vision-only, text-only, and joint vision-text fine-tuning. The results are used to assess the respective contributions of visual and textual adaptation, as well as the consistency of encoder behavior across different pretraining backbones.

Table 3. Average F1 scores across all datasets for different encoder configurations. Δ(B-V) and Δ(B-T) denote the performance differences between the *both* and the *vision* and *text* encoders, respectively.

Backbone	Both	Vision	Δ(B–V)	Text	Δ(B–T)
ViT-B/16	67.20	**69.06**	−1.86	56.16	**11.04**
ViT-B/32	68.26	64.51	**3.76**	57.23	11.03
ViT-L/14	68.14	68.03	0.11	59.67	8.47
BiomedCLIP	**71.62**	68.20	3.42	**65.23**	6.38

Joint Vision–Text Adaptation is not Always the Optimal Configuration. As shown in Table 3, adapting both encoders simultaneously does not consistently yield the best performance across different backbones. For ViT-B/16, vision-only adaptation achieves the highest macro-F1 score (69.06), outperforming joint adaptation by 1.86 points. Similarly, for ViT-L/14, the performance difference between joint and vision-only adaptation is negligible (68.14 vs. 68.03). These observations indicate that when the visual encoder already provides sufficiently discriminative representations after adaptation, additional updates to the text encoder offer limited benefit and may disperse the optimization focus under few-shot supervision. As a result, the effectiveness of joint adaptation depends on whether both encoders contribute complementary gradients during training.

Visual Adaptation Dominates Performance Gains Under Few-Shot Supervision. Across all backbones, joint adaptation consistently improves performance over text-only adaptation, with the magnitude of Δ(B–T) varying across backbones. For ViT-B/16, ViT-B/32, and ViT-L/14, adding visual adaptation to the text-only setting leads to substantial performance gains of +11.04, +11.03, and +8.47, respectively. In contrast, BiomedCLIP shows a markedly smaller improvement (+6.38). This reduced gain indicates that, due to biomedical pretraining, the text encoder in BiomedCLIP already encodes domain-specific semantics, thereby limiting the additional benefit attainable through text-side adaptation. These observations collectively suggest that visual representations play a dominant role in driving performance improvements during few-shot adaptation.

Strong Zero-Shot Representations Lead to Negative LoRA Adaptation. As shown in Table 4, ViT-B/16 exhibits a performance decrease on the

Table 4. Zero-shot and LoRA results on BreastMNIST.

Backbone	Zero-shot	Ours	ΔF1
ViT-B/16	56.28	55.24	−1.04
ViT-B/32	25.96	61.84	+35.87
ViT-L/14	42.22	59.85	+17.63
BiomedCLIP	23.15	75.92	+52.77

BreastMNIST dataset after LoRA fine-tuning, with the macro-F1 score dropping from 56.28 in the zero-shot setting to 55.24 after adaptation (ΔF1 $= -1.04$). In contrast, the same dataset shows substantial performance gains for other backbones, including ViT-B/32 (+35.87), ViT-L/14 (+17.63), and BiomedCLIP (+52.77). This discrepancy indicates that the zero-shot representations produced by ViT-B/16 are already closely aligned with the BreastMNIST classification task, leaving limited room for improvement through low-rank parameter updates. Under few-shot supervision, LoRA-induced updates may perturb an already well-positioned decision boundary, resulting in mild performance degradation rather than improvement. By contrast, backbones with weaker zero-shot alignment benefit significantly from LoRA adaptation, as the low-rank updates effectively reshape suboptimal representations toward task-relevant directions. These results suggest that the effectiveness of LoRA adaptation depends on the initial alignment between pre-trained representations and dataset-specific characteristics, and that parameter-efficient fine-tuning may introduce negative transfer when such alignment is already strong.

Taken together, the ablation results show that jointly adapting the vision and text encoders is not always the optimal configuration under few-shot supervision. Performance gains are primarily driven by visual adaptation, while text-side updates provide limited or diminishing benefits when the visual representations are already sufficiently discriminative. Moreover, when strong zero-shot representations are present, LoRA adaptation may perturb well-aligned decision boundaries and result in negative performance changes.

5 Conclusion

This study presents MedLoRA, a PEFT framework designed to enhance medical image understanding via LoRA-based adaptation of vision–language models. MedLoRA addresses the domain gap between general-purpose pretraining and medical imaging tasks by integrating lightweight LoRA modules into the vision and text encoders of OpenCLIP and BiomedCLIP, enabling task-specific adaptation while preserving pre-trained representations without modifying the backbone architecture.

Two main experiments were conducted to evaluate the effectiveness and behavior of MedLoRA. Experiment I shows that LoRA adaptation consistently outperforms zero-shot inference across both general-purpose and biomedical-pre-trained backbones in few-shot medical image classification. Although all backbones benefit from LoRA, models initialized with biomedical pretraining achieve the highest adapted performance, indicating that domain-aligned representations provide a more favorable starting point for efficient fine-tuning and enabling MedLoRA to effectively re-anchor pre-trained representations to medical semantics using limited annotated data. Experiment II further examines encoder-specific adaptation through a systematic ablation study, revealing that jointly adapting the vision and text encoders is not always optimal under few-shot supervision and that performance gains are primarily driven by visual adaptation. In addition, the benefit of text-side adaptation decreases as domain alignment in the pre-trained model becomes stronger, highlighting the dominant role of visual representations. A notable exception is observed on the BreastMNIST dataset, where a strong zero-shot baseline leads to negative LoRA adaptation for ViT-B/16, suggesting that low-rank updates may perturb well-aligned decision boundaries when the initial representation is already highly compatible with the target task, underscoring the importance of accounting for initial representation alignment when applying parameter-efficient adaptation.

In future work, we plan to extend MedLoRA toward more adaptive multi-modal alignment strategies that dynamically balance the contributions of visual and textual branches according to dataset characteristics, such as adaptive weighting of cross-modal interactions, further improve its generalization across diverse diagnostic scenarios.

References

1. Deng, J., Dong, W., Socher, R., Li, L.J., Li, K., Fei-Fei, L.: ImageNet: a large-scale hierarchical image database. In: 2009 IEEE Conference on Computer Vision and Pattern Recognition, pp. 248–255 (2009). https://doi.org/10.1109/CVPR.2009.5206848
2. Dosovitskiy, A., et al.: An image is worth 16x16 words: transformers for image recognition at scale (2021). https://arxiv.org/abs/2010.11929
3. Gao, P., et al.: Clip-adapter: better vision-language models with feature adapters (2025). https://arxiv.org/abs/2110.04544
4. Guo, D., Rush, A.M., Kim, Y.: Parameter-efficient transfer learning with diff pruning (2021). https://arxiv.org/abs/2012.07463
5. Han, Z., Gao, C., Liu, J., Zhang, J., Zhang, S.Q.: Parameter-efficient fine-tuning for large models: a comprehensive survey (2024). https://arxiv.org/abs/2403.14608
6. Hayou, S., Ghosh, N., Yu, B.: LoRA+: efficient low rank adaptation of large models (2024). https://arxiv.org/abs/2402.12354
7. Hu, E.J., et al.: LORA: Low-Rank Adaptation of large language models (2021). https://arxiv.org/abs/2106.09685
8. Huang, C., Liu, Q., Lin, B.Y., Pang, T., Du, C., Lin, M.: LoRAHub: efficient cross-task generalization via dynamic lora composition (2024). https://arxiv.org/abs/2307.13269
9. Lian, D., Zhou, D., Feng, J., Wang, X.: Scaling & shifting your features: a new baseline for efficient model tuning (2023). https://arxiv.org/abs/2210.08823

10. Liu, H., et al: Few-shot parameter-efficient fine-tuning is better and cheaper than in-context learning (2022). https://arxiv.org/abs/2205.05638
11. Mahabadi, R.K., Henderson, J., Ruder, S.: Compacter: efficient low-rank hypercomplex adapter layers (2021). https://arxiv.org/abs/2106.04647
12. Pan, J., et al.: MedVLM-R1: incentivizing medical reasoning capability of vision-language models (VLMS) via reinforcement learning (2025). https://arxiv.org/abs/2502.19634
13. Radford, A., et al.: Learning transferable visual models from natural language supervision (2021). https://arxiv.org/abs/2103.00020
14. Shi, Z., Kim, J., Li, W., Li, Y., Pfister, H.: MORA: LoRA guided multi-modal disease diagnosis with missing modality (2024). https://arxiv.org/abs/2408.09064
15. Tian, J.J., Emerson, D., Miyandoab, S.Z., Pandya, D., Seyyed-Kalantari, L., Khattak, F.K.: Soft-prompt tuning for large language models to evaluate bias (2024). https://arxiv.org/abs/2306.04735
16. Valipour, M., Rezagholizadeh, M., Kobyzev, I., Ghodsi, A.: DYLoRA: parameter efficient tuning of pre-trained models using dynamic search-free low-rank adaptation (2023). https://arxiv.org/abs/2210.07558
17. Vucetic, D., Tayaranian, M., Ziaeefard, M., Clark, J.J., Meyer, B.H., Gross, W.J.: Efficient fine-tuning of Bert models on the edge. In: 2022 IEEE International Symposium on Circuits and Systems (ISCAS), pp. 1838–1842. IEEE (2022). http://dx.doi.org/10.1109/ISCAS48785.2022.9937567
18. Xu, R., et al.: Raise a child in large language model: towards effective and generalizable fine-tuning (2021). https://arxiv.org/abs/2109.05687
19. Yang, A.X., Robeyns, M., Wang, X., Aitchison, L.: Bayesian low-rank adaptation for large language models (2024). https://arxiv.org/abs/2308.13111
20. Yang, J., et al.: MedMNIST V2 - a large-scale lightweight benchmark for 2D and 3d biomedical image classification. Sci. Data **10**(1), 41(2023). https://doi.org/10.1038/s41597-022-01721-8
21. Zaken, E.B., Ravfogel, S., Goldberg, Y.: BitFit: simple parameter-efficient fine-tuning for transformer-based masked language-models (2022). https://arxiv.org/abs/2106.10199
22. Zhang, Q., et al.: AdaLoRA: adaptive budget allocation for parameter-efficient fine-tuning (2023). https://arxiv.org/abs/2303.10512
23. Zhang, S., et al.: Biomedclip: a multimodal biomedical foundation model pretrained from fifteen million scientific image-text pairs (2025). https://arxiv.org/abs/2303.00915

A Novel Framework for Maritime Object Detection in Adverse Weather via Dual-Phase Learning

Lingya Li[1,2], Xiran Ren[1], Li Su[2], and Guihua Xia[2](✉)

[1] APT Mobile SatCom Limited, Shenzhen, China
lily@apsat.com
[2] Harbin Engineering University, Harbin, China
xiaguihua@hrbeu.edu.cn
https://www.apsat.com/

Abstract. The necessity of marine object detection has grown in prominence in recent years due to an increasing need for maritime surveillance. However, the object detection in adverse weather still poses a challenge, causing potential accidents. In this paper, we investigate object detection in adverse weather by dual-phase learning method to train a detector and a preprocessor for four adverse weather conditions (foggy, rainy, cloudy and dusk). The designed dual-phase learning method employs an innovative training strategy to drive a preprocessor to generate intermediate features that are most friendly to the downstream detector. Through experiments on our datasets, our proposed approach outperforms the baseline in overall detection accuracy (mAP50) and localization quality/overall performance (mAP50:95) under cloudy (+0.8%/+0.6%), rainy (+1.9%/+0.1%), foggy (+0.1%/+1.2%), and dusk (+0.3%/+0.1%) conditions.

Keywords: Maritime object detection · dual-phase learning · object detection in adverse weather

1 Introduction

In recent years, with the increasing demand for maritime surveillance, the importance of maritime object detection has become increasingly prominent. The general object detector performs well under ideal conditions, but its performance significantly deteriorates when confronted with common adverse weather conditions in the real world such as sea fog, heavy rain, dusk low light, and cloudy days, which can cause potential accidents during navigation. These weather conditions introduce noise, reduce contrast, and blur object edges, thereby severely

Supported by Guangdong S & T Programme(No.2024B0101020002).
L. Li and X. Ren—The authors contribute equally.

C. Xu (Ed.): ICMLSC 2026, CCIS 2948, pp. 325–336, 2027.
https://doi.org/10.1007/978-981-92-1546-1_27

interfering with the feature extraction ability of the detection model, and thus reduce the detection performance.

To address this challenge, the academic community and the industrial sector have mainly explored two technical routes: the sequential processing method and the end-to-end adaptive method. For example, Lv et al. [1] use the sequential processing method to solve the problem. They combine the CPNet fog removal model with the YOLOv8 detector and achieve high mAP on a synthetic foggy dataset. However, the inherent drawbacks of this method are quite obvious. Firstly, restoration and detection are two independent optimization modules. There is a problem of inconsistent optimization goals between the image restoration task (such as improving peak signal-to-noise ratio or structural similarity) and the detection task (improving detection accuracy). A visually clearer image may contain more artifacts or lost details, which may be detrimental to the subsequent detection task. Secondly, the concatenation of two independent network models brings significant computational overhead, which is unacceptable for real-time response requirements in ship navigation systems.

For the end-to-end adaptive methods, researchers have attempted to enhance the inherent robustness of the model through two main strategies. For instance, Wu et al. [2] propose CGDU-DETR, which is an end-to-end model that enhances the DETR framework through a novel attention mechanism to improve the detection ability of ships in challenging environments such as day-night transitions. Another common strategy involves data augmentation, where physical models or generative adversarial networks (GANs) are used to generate a large amount of training data with specific weather effects, enabling the detection model to "experience" various adverse weather conditions during the training phase [3]. However, the challenge of this method lies in the persistent domain gap between synthetic data and the complex and variable marine environment. The enhancement methods based on physical models rely on precise estimation of atmospheric parameters, which is difficult to achieve in the dynamic changing marine environment, resulting in the generated data being unable to comprehensively cover the diversity and complexity of real scenes.

To address the challenges of maritime object detection under adverse weather conditions, we design a novel training framework called "Dual-Phase Learning" as shown in Fig. 1. The core idea of this framework is task-driven collaborative optimization: instead of aiming to restore adverse weather images to visually perfect clarity, we employ an innovative training strategy to drive a preprocessor to generate intermediate features that are most friendly to the downstream detector. This framework is mainly composed of two modules: the preprocessor and the detector. Unlike the traditional serial approach, these two modules are not simply connected after independent optimization. Instead, they are closely coupled through our designed two-stage training process. In the first stage (Base-Training), the two modules conduct separate initialization training to acquire basic capabilities. In the second stage (Fine-Tuning), the detector acts as a "judge", and the detection loss it generates serves as the sole supervisory signal to guide the preprocessor for fine-tuning. In this way, the optimization goal of the preprocessor is perfectly aligned with the final detection task performance.

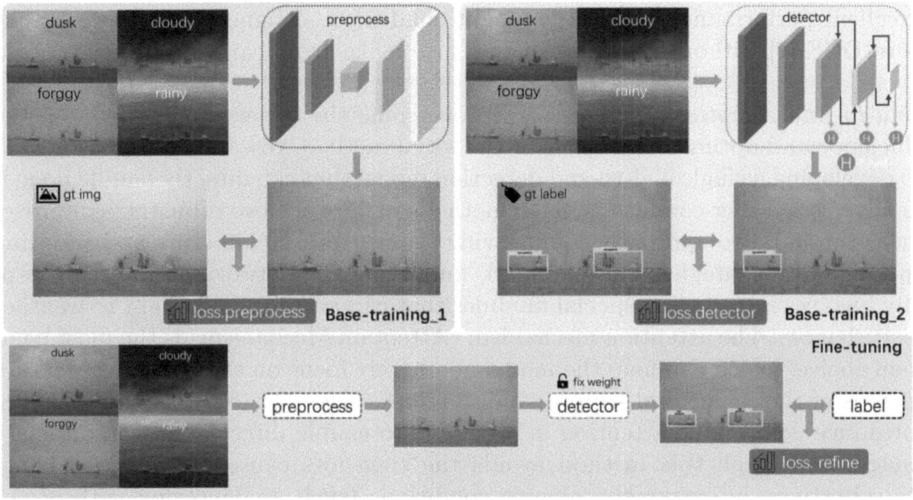

Fig. 1. Dual-Phase Learning framework.

The contributions of our paper are as follows:

- We introduce a task-driven optimization framework comprising a preprocessor and detector. Unlike sequential or multi-task paradigms, our method employs fine-tuning, where the detector's frozen weights guide the preprocessor to generate features maximally conducive to detection accuracy, prioritizing task performance over visual restoration.
- We demonstrate state-of-the-art performance across four high-impact weather scenarios (foggy, rainy, cloudy, dusk) on a real-world maritime dataset. Our framework consistently improves both detection accuracy and localization robustness.

2 Related Work

2.1 Object Detection in Adverse Weather

Cascaded Approaches. This method follows the intuitive idea of "first restoration, then detection", forming a two-stage processing flow. Firstly, the input image with weather interference is sent to a dedicated image enhancement or restoration module; then, the processed "clean" image is sent to a standard target detector for detection. For different weather conditions, researchers have developed various image restoration algorithms. For example, in the field of single image dehazing, a wide spectrum of methods has been explored, ranging from classic physical models like the Dark Channel Prior (DCP) [4] to recent state-of-the-art deep learning-based approaches such as DehazeFormer [5]. In the field of rain removal, models like DerainNet [6] based on deep learning demonstrate excellent performance. And in low-light conditions, enhancement networks like Zero-DCE [7] without reference images also make significant progress.

End-to-End Adaptive Approaches. To overcome the inconsistency between the efficiency and optimization goals of the serial method, researchers are dedicated to developing a single end-to-end detection model that can directly handle images in adverse weather conditions. Such methods mainly achieve robustness improvement through two approaches: improving the network architecture and adopting specific data strategies. On one hand, improving the network architecture usually involves introducing special modules that can perceive and adapt to weather disturbances. The attention mechanism (Attention Mechanism) is the most common choice, which can help the model adaptively focus on the important feature regions of the image and suppress noise interference. For example, Xu et al. [8] introduce deformable attention in YOLOv8 to enable direct detection on foggy images. Although this method avoids the time loss caused by preprocessing, its robustness in extremely adverse conditions (such as dense fog with atmospheric transmittance $\beta < 0.08$) is still insufficient, resulting in a significant 21.6% decrease in mAP. This indicates that relying solely on the adjustment at the feature level using the attention mechanism is still limited in modeling the global and long-distance visual information degradation caused by weather.

2.2 Collaborative Training and Task-Driven Optimization

In order to bridge the gap between the two independent tasks of image restoration and object detection, researchers began to explore more integrated training frameworks, aiming to achieve the collaborative optimization of these two modules. The core idea of these methods is that in the image preprocessing stage, one should not merely pursue the improvement of visual quality, but rather take the performance improvement of the final task (i.e., object detection) as the fundamental goal.

Multi-Task Learning for Joint Optimization. This method is one of the mainstream paradigms of collaborative optimization. It typically divides different task branches from a shared feature extraction backbone within a unified network architecture, such as one for image restoration and another for object detection. The loss functions of the two branches are fused into a joint loss through weighted summation and are jointly optimized during training. For instance, Li et al. [9] simultaneously perform rain removal and detection tasks in one network, and through joint training, the rain removal branch can learn features beneficial to detection to a certain extent.

Policy Optimization via Reinforcement Learning. To achieve more thorough task alignment, some cutting-edge research has introduced the concept of reinforcement learning (Reinforcement Learning, RL). In this framework, the image processing module is modeled as an "agent", which learns to perform a series of "actions" (such as adjusting contrast, selecting filter kernels, etc.) to gradually optimize the image. The core innovation lies in that the "reward" signal of the agent directly comes from the performance feedback of the downstream detector. For example, an increase in mAP detection will receive a positive reward. The work of Yu et al. [10] successfully applies this idea to build an image restoration toolchain.

3 Methodology

The overall model flow chart is demonstrated in Fig. 2. Our enhanced model includes preprocessor and detector, trained through dual-phase learning method.

3.1 Network Architecture

Preprocessor Architecture. An image-to-image transformation network aimed at reducing the impact of weather factors (such as foggy days, rainy days, etc.) on image quality. The core task of the preprocessor is to convert the input image I_{adv}, which is affected by adverse weather conditions, into an intermediate representation I_{mid}. The "quality" standard of this intermediate representation I_{mid} is dynamically changing: in the basic training of the first stage, it strives for visual consistency with the clear image I_{clear}; while in the fine-tuning of the second stage, it strives for "friendliness" to the downstream detector D_0. Therefore, the preprocessor needs to possess strong capabilities in image content understanding and feature reconstruction.

Detector Architecture. The task of the detector is to receive an image (respectively I_{adv} or I_{mid} at different stages) and output the bounding boxes B_{pred} and the categories of all the target objects of interest within the image. In our framework, it plays a dual role: it is both the "executor" that ultimately performs the detection task, and the "evaluator" that provides supervision signals during the fine-tuning stage. In order to ensure the highest detection accuracy while meeting the stringent real-time requirements for the future deployment of intelligent ships at the edge, we choose the next-generation real-time object detector that represents the current state-of-the-art detector YOLO11 (https://github.com/ultralytics/ultralytics). YOLO11 adopts an innovative "consistency dual-label assignment" mechanism in its training strategy. During the training period, it provided supervision signals to both the backbone and the head simultaneously, enabling the model to learn more accurate and consistent feature representations. This is particularly effective in distinguishing ship targets with blurred features under adverse weather conditions.

3.2 Dual-Phase Learning Strategy

Base-training for Preprocessor. We train with paired data, where the input is images of adverse weather conditions I_{adv}. In the Base-Training stage, for the preprocessor, we use cosine similarity to measure the distance between the preprocessed output and the ground truth image (i.e., the normal weather image), and use this as the loss function to train the preprocessor, enabling it to have certain preprocessing knowledge of adverse weather images. The cosine similarity formula is as follows:

$$\begin{aligned} L_{preprocess} &= \text{Cosine Similarity(A,B)} \\ &= \frac{A \cdot B}{\|A\| \cdot \|B\|} = \frac{\sum_{i=1}^{n} A_i \cdot B_i}{\sqrt{\sum_{i=1}^{n} A_i^2} \cdot \sqrt{\sum_{i=1}^{n} B_i^2}}, \end{aligned} \tag{1}$$

Among them, the molecule is the dot product of vector A and vector B (characterizing the consistency of the directions of the two vectors). The denominator is the product of the L2 norm of vector A and vector B (normalized to eliminate the influence of vector length). Value range: $[-1, 1]$, where 1 indicates completely in the same direction (with the highest similarity), and -1 indicates completely in the opposite direction.

Base-training for Detector. In the Detector Base-training stage, the loss designed by YOLO11 is used to measure the output such as the distance between the regression result and the true value label. Among them, the classification loss uses the BCE (Binary Cross-Entropy Loss) function, the regression loss uses the $CIoU$ (Complete-Intersection over Union), and at the same time, the DFL (Distribution Focal Loss) is used to de-unify the distribution between the prediction and the true value. The total loss function is shown in Formula 2, where λ_{cls}, λ_{reg}, and λ_{dfl} are the balance weights (default values are 1.0, 0.5, 0.5).

$$L_{detector} = \lambda_{cls} L_{BCE} + \lambda_{reg} L_{CIoU} + \lambda_{dfl} L_{DFL} \tag{2}$$

Fine-tuning. This is the essence and core innovation of our framework, corresponding to the Fine-tuning process in Fig. 1. After the basic training in the first stage, we obtain a preprocessor P_0 with general image restoration capabilities and a detector D_0 with basic robustness against adverse weather conditions. However, there is a fundamental gap between these two modules: the optimization goal of P_0 is visual fidelity (i.e., the output image is similar to I_{clear}), while the ultimate goal of D_0 is detection accuracy. An image that is the clearest to a human eye may not be the most informative and easiest to interpret input for a detector D_0 that has adapted to a specific noise pattern. To address this core contradiction, we have designed a second-stage collaborative fine-tuning process. The objective of this stage is to redefine the optimization direction of the preprocessor, transforming it from a general image restoration tool to a highly customized front-end module specifically serving the downstream specific detector D_0.

The role of detector D_0 at this stage. We load its pre-trained weights θ_{D_0} and freeze it completely. This corresponds to the "fix weight" clearly marked in Fig. 1. This means that during the entire fine-tuning process, the network parameters of D_0 are not updated. The role of preprocessor P at this stage. It loads the pre-trained weights θ_{P_0} as the starting point, but its parameters θ_P are the only trainable part throughout the fine-tuning process. Its task is to constantly adjust itself to generate an intermediate image I_{mid} that can enable the "fixed evaluator" D_0 to give the optimal evaluation (i.e., the lowest detection loss).

The training process during the fine-tuning stage follows a non-symmetric gradient propagation path. Forward Propagation: For a given adversarial weather input image I_{adv}, the data flows through two modules sequentially:

$$\begin{aligned} I_{mid} &= P(I_{adv}; \theta_P) \\ B_{pred} &= D_0(I_{mid}; \theta_{D_0}) \end{aligned} \tag{3}$$

Firstly, the trainable preprocessor P generates the intermediate image I_{mid}. Subsequently, I_{mid} is sent to the frozen detector D_0, which outputs the final prediction result B_{pred}. We calculate the detection loss between the prediction result B_{pred} and the manually annotated ground truth B_{gt}. This loss is explicitly defined as L_{refine}, which is mathematically identical to $L_{detector}$ (Eq. 2), but its function and purpose are completely different.

Gradient Backpropagation and Selective Update: This is the key to the entire framework. The calculated gradient of L_{refine} is backpropagated along the computational graph. When the gradient flows through the detector D_0, since its parameters are frozen, the gradient values are computed but not used to update θ_{D_0}. The gradient flow continues backward and eventually reaches the preprocessor P. Only the parameters θ_P of the preprocessor P are updated based on this backpropagated gradient. This optimization process can be precisely expressed as:

$$\theta_P \leftarrow \theta_P - \eta \nabla_{\theta_P} L_{refine}(D_0(P(I_{adv}; \theta_P); \theta_{D_0}), B_{gt}) \tag{4}$$

Here, η represents the learning rate. This formula clearly indicates that the driving force for optimization (L_{refine}) comes from the final detection task, while the object of optimization (θ_P) is only the preprocessor.

In this way, we established a direct and lossless supervision link from the final task performance to the front-end processing module. The preprocessor P was forced to learn a highly nonlinear mapping, with its sole objective being to minimize the detection loss of the downstream fixed detector. Eventually, it learned to generate a "customized-friendly image" that, although not the most perfect in human perception, is the most informative and feature-rich for the specific neural network structure of D_0, thereby achieving deep collaboration and performance maximization between the two modules.

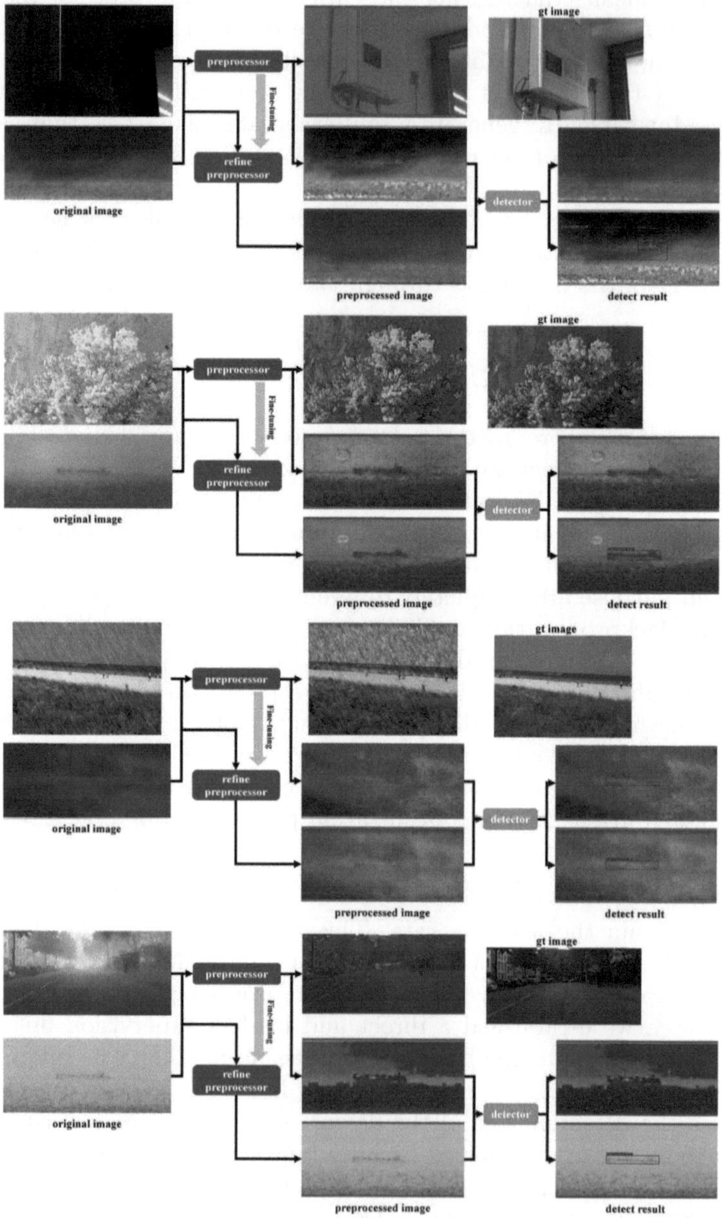

Fig. 2. Dual-Phase Learning Flow Chart.

4 Experiment

4.1 Dataset

For preprocessor training, we choose specialized datasets for different weather (cityscape [11] for foggy days, LOLv1 [12] for cloudy days, Rain100H [13] for rainy days and LCDP [14] for dusk days) as shown in Fig. 3. Pairs of samples from each dataset are input into the preprocessor for training.

(a) cloudy (b) dusk (c) foggy (d) rainy

Fig. 3. Samples in these four datasets.

For detector training, our dataset includes four weather conditions (foggy, rainy, dusk, and cloudy), its details are shown in Fig. 4. Each subcategory contains 1827 images with a resolution of 1920 × 1080. The labeled categories cover six target types such as bulk carriers and container ships. The training set, validation set, and test set is divided in a ratio of 8:1:1.

4.2 Validation of Our Proposed Method

The proposed model outperforms the baseline in all four weather conditions in mAP50. Improvements range from +0.1% (foggy: 90.7% vs. 90.6%), +0.3% (dusk: 89.8% vs. 89.5%), +0.8% (cloudy: 85.8% vs. 85.0%), to +1.9% (rainy: 91.7% vs. 89.8%). The proposed model also demonstrates superior overall performance across all weather conditions in mAP50:90: +0.6% (cloudy: 61.9% vs. 61.3%), +0.1% (rainy: 69.4% vs. 69.3%), +1.2% (foggy: 70.3% vs. 69.1%), and +0.1% (dusk: 65.2% vs. 65.1%). The significant improvement (+1.2%) in foggy conditions is particularly noteworthy. The consistent gains in mAP50 and mAP50:95 across all weather conditions (from low visibility fog to dynamic rain, obscured cloudy skies and high-light dusk) demonstrate the effective enhancement in the proposed method's weather robustness (Table 1).

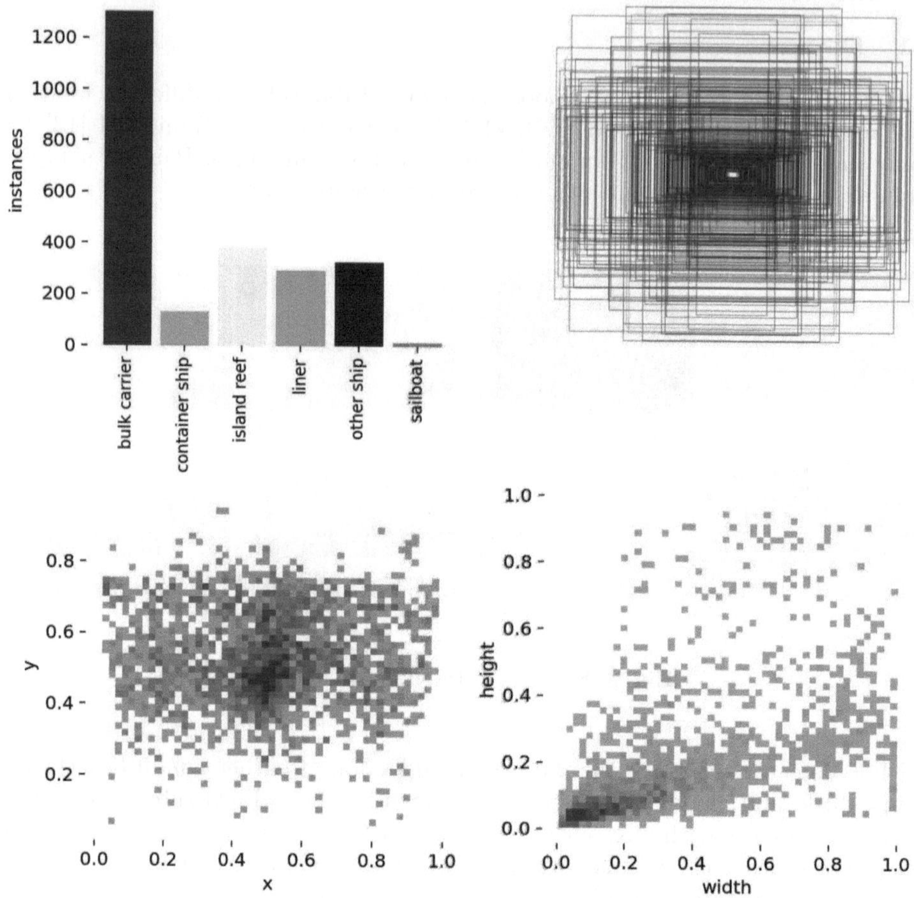

Fig. 4. Details of dataset labels.

Table 1. Performance comparison under different weather conditions.

Weather	Model	P	R	mAP50	mAP50:90
cloudy	baseline	80.9%	79.3%	85.0%	61.3%
	ours	**81.1%**	**82.7%**	**85.8%**	**61.9%**
rainy	baseline	**90.8%**	79.1%	89.8%	69.3%
	ours	89.1%	**86.4%**	**91.7%**	**69.4%**
foggy	baseline	**87.7%**	**87.6%**	90.6%	69.1%
	ours	85.5%	85.6%	**90.7%**	**70.3%**
dusk	baseline	85.6%	**86.3%**	89.5%	65.1%
	ours	**87.1%**	83.6%	**89.8%**	**65.2%**

4.3 Inference Results Under Different Weather Conditions

We further evaluate the performance of our model in detecting ships under four weather conditions in both the harbor and the open sea. The results are presented in Fig. 5, with the left side showing the baseline and the right side showing our enhanced model. It is evident that the detection task remains challenging under these weather conditions, with the model experiencing misdirection. However, it is also noticeable that our enhanced model has fewer false positives than the baseline model.

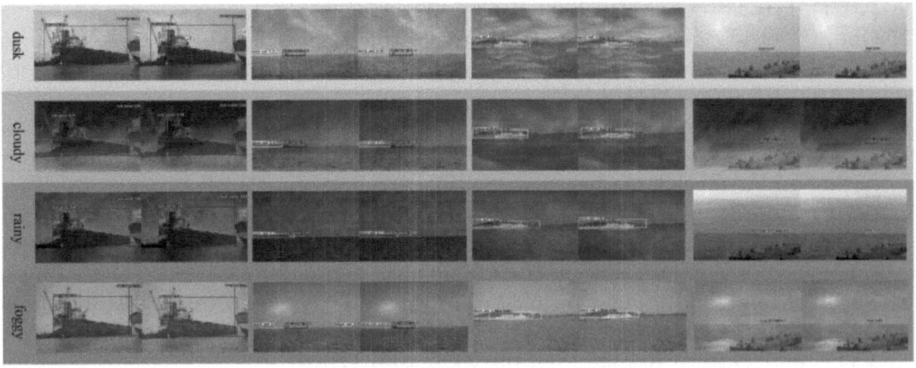

Fig. 5. Presentation of the reasoning results

5 Conclusion

In practical object detection on the sea surface, it is crucial to ensure reliable detection of ships to guarantee safety for navigation under various extreme weather conditions. In this paper, we build our enhanced model with specialized preprocessors to improve the model's ability to detect objects in adverse weather via dual-phase learning. Significantly, the enhanced model increases all-weather detection performance, contributing to further research on autonomous navigation technology in all-weather scenes.

References

1. Lv, Y., Si, L., Shen, X., Huang, S.: FNSD: a ship detection framework based on foggy maritime navigation scenarios. In: International Conference on Artificial Intelligence and Autonomous Transportation, pp. 545–552. Springer (2024)
2. Wu, W., Fan, X., Hu, Z., Zhao, Y.: CGDU-DETR: an end-to-end detection model for ship detection in day–night transition environments. J. Marine Sci. Eng. **13**(6) (2025). https://doi.org/10.3390/jmse13061155

3. Zhu, J.-Y., Park, T., Isola, P., Efros, A.A.: Unpaired image-to-image translation using cycle-consistent adversarial networks. vol. 2017-October, Venice, Italy, pp. 2242–2251 (2017). https://doi.org/10.1109/ICCV.2017.244
4. Hsieh, C.-H., Zhao, Q., Cheng, W.-C.: Single image haze removal using weak dark channel prior, pp. 214–219, Fukuoka, Japan (2018). https://doi.org/10.1109/ICAwST.2018.8517198 ,
5. Gao, G., Cao, J., Bao, C., Hao, Q., Ma, A., Li, G.: A novel transformer-based attention network for image dehazing. Sensors **22**(9) (2022). https://www.mdpi.com/1424-8220/22/9/3428
6. Bi, X., Chen, Z., Li, X., Yue, J.: EnglishEfficient single image de-raining using multi-scale depthwise separable dilated convolution. Chengdu, China, pp. 699–703 (2021). https://doi.org/10.1109/ICCC54389.2021.9674621
7. Guo, C., et al.: Zero-reference deep curve estimation for low-light image enhancement. Virtual, Online, United states, pp. 1777–1786 (2020). https://doi.org/10.1109/CVPR42600.2020.00185
8. Xu, G., Yin, J., Zhang, Z.: Marine ship detection under fog conditions based on an improved deep-learning approach. In: International Conference on Neural Computing for Advanced Applications, pp. 92–103. Springer (2024)
9. Li, X., Wu, J., Lin, Z., Liu, H., Zha, H.: Recurrent squeeze-and-excitation context aggregation net for single image deraining. In: Proceedings of the European conference on computer vision (ECCV), pp. 254–269 (2018)
10. Yu, K., Dong, C., Lin, L., Loy, C.C.: Crafting a toolchain for image restoration by deep reinforcement learning. In: Proceedings of the IEEE Conference on Computer Vision and Pattern Recognition, pp. 2443–2452 (2018)
11. Cordts, M., et al.: The cityscapes dataset for semantic urban scene understanding. In: Proceedings of the IEEE Conference on Computer Vision and Pattern Recognition (CVPR) (2016)
12. Wei, C., Wang, W., Yang, W., Liu, J.: Deep retinex decomposition for low-light enhancement. arXiv preprint arXiv:1808.04560 (2018)
13. Yang, W., Tan, R.T., Feng, J., Liu, J., Guo, Z., Yan, S.: Deep joint rain detection and removal from a single image. in Proceedings of the IEEE Conference on Computer Vision and Pattern Recognition, pp. 1357–1366 (2017)
14. Haoyuan Wang, K.X., Lau, R.W.: Local color distributions prior for image enhancement. In: Proceedings of the European Conference on Computer Vision (ECCV) (2022)

Real-Time Deception Detection using Micro-expression Analysis with Audio-Visual Cues

Aryan Mallik(✉), Anusha Paranjape, Anish M Munirathinam, B Kalyaanakrishnan, and Prema Ramasamy

Department of CSE, PES University, Bengaluru, India
aryanmallik2004@gmail.com

Abstract. We present a real-time, multimodal deception detection system that combines facial micro-expressions, speech prosody, and linguistic cues to assess truthfulness. The pipeline preprocesses audio-visual data, extracts temporal facial dynamics and vocal features, and encodes transcripts to capture semantic and psycholinguistic signals. These modality-specific representations are fused to produce an interpretable deception decision and are surfaced through a lightweight dashboard for screening scenarios. The approach is non-invasive and designed for practical use beyond traditional polygraph methods.

Keywords: Deception detection · Micro-expressions · Multimodal fusion · Attention mechanism · BiLSTM

1 Introduction

Accurate deception detection is important in security screening, forensic interviews, and fraud prevention. Traditional polygraphs rely on physiological arousal, which only loosely correlates with deception, can be controlled by subjects, and lacks portability. These limitations motivate non-invasive, behavior-focused methods that analyze natural cues such as micro-facial movements, vocal prosody, and linguistic style.

This work introduces a real-time multimodal pipeline that integrates these complementary signals. The visual module detects and aligns faces (RetinaFace) and extracts both macro-emotions (ResNet with relation/attention) and micro-expressions (SE-ResNet or CNN–LSTM, plus an autoencoder–MLP on dlib landmarks). The audio module computes MFCCs, pitch, energy, and pause features and models them with an Attention-BiLSTM to highlight stressed or hesitant segments. The text module uses ASR transcripts, SBERT embeddings, and LIWC-style features, classified through XGBoost. Each stream outputs a calibrated deception score, and a weighted late-fusion stage aggregates these scores into a final decision and probability for the user interface.

The system is built for near real-time use and supports modular diagnostics and procedures. In interview-style tests, the audio and visual cues were

C. Xu (Ed.): ICMLSC 2026, CCIS 2948, pp. 337–348, 2027.
https://doi.org/10.1007/978-981-92-1546-1_28

strong individually and the fusion delivered the best generalization, reinforcing the benefit of combining the modalities. The work also acknowledges ongoing challenges—limited datasets, environmental noise, occlusions, and label uncertainty—and positions the system as a practical, interpretable baseline with room to grow through larger cross-cultural datasets, tighter synchronization, and more transparent fusion methods.

2 Literature Survey

2.1 Attention-Aware Multimodal RNN Approach

Hsiao and Sun [1] proposed an attention-aware multimodal RNN for deception detection that jointly models video, audio, and text streams. High-level visual, prosodic, and semantic features are encoded using BiLSTMs to capture temporal dependencies, while an attention mechanism emphasizes brief but informative segments (e.g., micro-expressions, vocal hesitations, and linguistic markers). The method reported high accuracy on courtroom trial videos, though its reliance on a domain-specific setting may limit generalizability.

2.2 Multimodal Deception Detection Using Real-Life Trial Data

Şen et al. [2] proposed a multimodal deception detection framework based on real-life courtroom trial recordings, addressing a key limitation of earlier work that relied primarily on controlled laboratory data. The dataset reflects genuine high-stakes conditions, capturing natural emotional responses, speech patterns, and narrative behavior associated with deceptive testimony. Visual, acoustic, and linguistic cues were jointly modeled to capture complementary deception signals.

For the visual stream, Convolutional Neural Networks (CNNs) were used to extract facial features from video frames, while Long Short-Term Memory (LSTM) networks modeled temporal dynamics such as micro-expressions and facial tension. The audio modality was processed using LSTMs to encode prosodic cues, including pitch variation, pauses, and hesitation. Linguistic features were obtained from trial transcripts, focusing on syntactic structure, word choice, and semantic context.

An attention mechanism was incorporated to emphasize temporally salient moments, such as brief facial leaks or hesitation pauses, that are more informative for deception inference. The three modalities were fused at the score level, allowing each stream to contribute while reducing modality-specific noise.

The model achieved a subject-level deception classification accuracy of 83.05%. However, the reliance on courtroom data introduces challenges related to limited availability, restricted recording conditions, and reduced dataset diversity. Moreover, establishing reliable ground truth in legal settings remains difficult, as deception labels may be influenced by legal outcomes rather than objective truth. These limitations highlight the need for larger, standardized, and ethically curated real-world multimodal datasets.

2.3 Early Multimodal Approaches with Thermal Imaging

Burzo et al. [3] offered an early and influential contribution to computational deception detection by showing how physiological, visual, acoustic, and linguistic cues can be combined to improve inference accuracy. The study emphasized that deception rarely appears in a single channel; instead, it emerges through subtle facial movements, vocal stress, word choice, and physiological reactions. Their multimodal feature extraction included facial expression analysis for emotional leakage, speech pattern cues such as hesitations or strain, and linguistic markers like vagueness, distancing, or strategic phrasing. A notable element was the use of thermal imaging to measure temperature shifts around regions such as the nose and eyes-areas tied to stress and cognitive effort.

For classification, the authors used traditional machine learning models, including decision trees and rule-based systems. These offered interpretability but lacked the depth and flexibility of modern neural networks. Results showed that combining modalities clearly outperformed using any single one, with thermal imaging paired with linguistic cues yielding some of the strongest improvements. Reported accuracies surpassed 70 percent in controlled deception elicitation tasks, supporting the feasibility of a multimodal approach.

The work, however, had several constraints. All experiments were run in laboratory settings, which do not capture the full variability of real-world deceptive behavior. Factors like culture, personality, and conversational context can significantly shape both expressive and physiological responses, limiting generalizability. Dataset sizes were also small, making models more vulnerable to overfitting. The study further pointed out the difficulty of reliably defining deception ground-truth, since truthfulness is often subjective and context dependent. These issues highlight the need for larger, more diverse real-world datasets and more adaptable multimodal learning techniques.

2.4 Systematic Review of AI-Enabled Multimodal Deception Detection

King and Neal [4] conducted a systematic review of deception detection systems using video, audio, and physiological data. Applying the PRISMA framework, they examined 93 peer-reviewed studies across psychology, computing, and forensics. The methods reviewed ranged from traditional supervised models (Decision Trees, Random Forests, SVMs, Logistic Regression) to deep learning approaches (CNNs, LSTMs, MLPs) and unsupervised or probabilistic models like Hidden Markov Models and Gaussian Mixture Models. Ensemble methods such as Bagging and AdaBoost were also highlighted for handling feature variability.

Their analysis showed that multimodal systems—those combining facial cues, vocal stress signals, and linguistic or physiological features—consistently outperform unimodal models on accuracy and AUC. These systems were also noted to be more resilient to noise and intentional behavioral masking.

Key limitations were also identified. Most datasets are English-language and publicly available, creating cultural and demographic bias. Inconsistent dataset design, labeling standards, and evaluation protocols make comparisons across studies difficult. Many works also overlook deployment factors such as interpretability, latency, ethics, and real-time usability. The review calls for standardized datasets, stronger cross-cultural validation, and research focused on real-world deployment.

3 Proposed System

Our system follows a multimodal pipeline that processes video (faces micro-expressions), audio (prosody), and text (transcripts + psycholinguistics), then fuses these signals for a final truth/lie decision. At implementation time we developed two visual tracks (CNN-LSTM over frames, and a landmark autoencoder+MLP), a dedicated audio Attention-BiLSTM, a transcript SBERT+LIWC+XGBoost model, and two fusion variants (weighted score fusion and feature-level SVM).

3.1 Datasets

Three datasets were used to balance controlled analysis and real-world validity: MU3D (elicited truthful and deceptive statements with aligned audio, visual, and text streams), CASME II (laboratory micro-expression data), and a Real-Life Trial dataset of courtroom testimonies labeled using judicial outcomes. Class distributions were kept approximately balanced where possible; MU3D is balanced by design, and Real-Life Trial clips were selected to reduce imbalance. Although CASME II lacks deception labels, its balanced action unit and emotion annotations support visual representation learning. A, V, and T denote audio, visual, and textual modalities. Table 1 summarizes the datasets.

Table 1. Summary of Datasets Used in This Study

Dataset	Modality	Subjects	Clips	Label Source	Context
MU3D	A/V/T	80	320	Elicited truth/lie	Controlled interview
CASME II	V	26	247	FACS AU + emotion	Laboratory
Real-Life Trial	A/V/T	∼XX	121	Verdict/exoneration	Courtroom

3.2 Preprocessing Pipeline

The system ingests synchronized audio–video streams and produces three standardized artifacts: face-aligned video frames, denoised audio features, and time-stamped ASR transcripts. Video is decoded using FFmpeg, frames are extracted at a fixed rate, and faces are detected and geometrically aligned to stabilize head pose. Audio is demultiplexed, resampled, and normalized, while ASR provides aligned transcripts for cross-modal synchronization. These outputs feed the visual, audio, and text models, whose predictions are combined using late fusion.

3.3 Visual Pipeline: Facial Emotion and Micro-Expression

Face Processing (Detection and Alignment). Faces are detected (e.g., RetinaFace), tightly cropped, and aligned using a similarity transform to map landmarks into a consistent geometry. This reduces jitter and lighting variation while improving sensitivity to small periorbital and mouth movements that signal micro-expressions.

Emotion Encoder (Model-V1). A ResNet backbone with a self-relation attention module highlights key regions such as the eyes, brows, and mouth. It produces a compact emotion embedding for each frame or short segment, along with an interpretable emotion label for diagnostic use. Mean or attention pooling over brief windows is applied to smooth out frame-level noise.

Micro-expression Encoder (Model-V2). A channel-attention SE-ResNet processes short clips (e.g., 16 frames) to capture subtle, short-lived muscle activations. It outputs a micro-expression embedding representing transient dynamics learned from curated micro-expression datasets such as CASME-style material.

3.4 Audio Speech Prosodic Analysis Module

Prosodic–spectral features are extracted (MFCCs, pitch, energy, jitter/shimmer, pause statistics, speaking rate). A BiLSTM models temporal evolution of these features, and an attention layer highlights segments indicative of stress, hesitation, or cognitive load.

Attention-Based Temporal Weighting Let $\mathbf{X} = \{\mathbf{x}_1, \ldots, \mathbf{x}_T\}$, $\mathbf{x}_t \in \mathbb{R}^F$ denote the prosodic feature sequence of an utterance, where $F = 40$ and $T \leq 40$. A bidirectional LSTM encodes temporal context as

$$\mathbf{h}_t = [\overrightarrow{\mathbf{h}}_t; \overleftarrow{\mathbf{h}}_t] \in \mathbb{R}^{2d}, \tag{1}$$

with hidden size $d = 128$ per direction.

Temporal saliency is modeled using a soft attention mechanism:

$$e_t = \mathbf{w}_a^\top \mathbf{h}_t + b_a, \quad \alpha_t = \frac{\exp(e_t)}{\sum_{k=1}^{T} \exp(e_k)}, \tag{2}$$

where $\mathbf{w}_a$ and b_a are learnable parameters.

The utterance-level representation is computed as

$$\mathbf{h}_{\text{attn}} = \sum_{t=1}^{T} \alpha_t \mathbf{h}_t. \tag{3}$$

This formulation enables the model to emphasize acoustically salient segments associated with cognitive load and speech irregularities linked to deception.

3.5 Text Linguistic Deception Cues Module

ASR transcripts are lower-cased with punctuation/space normalization and optional stop-word handling. Sentence-BERT (SBERT) provides semantic embeddings aggregated by mean/max pooling at the sentence/segment level. Psycholinguistic cues inspired by LIWC (pronoun ratios, negations, emotion words, lexical complexity) are combined with sentiment (polarity/subjectivity) and readability features to proxy cognitive load. A gradient-boosted tree classifier (XGBoost) operates on the concatenated feature vector (SBERT + LIWC + sentiment/readability) to produce a text deception score; feature importances support qualitative interpretability.

3.6 Fusion Strategy

Fusion proceeds in two stages. Stage-1 (Visual Fusion): emotion and micro-expression embeddings are fused and classified by the visual SVM to yield a visual truth/lie probability. Stage-2 (Cross-Modal Fusion): a late weighted fusion combines the visual probability with the audio (BiLSTM-attention) and text (XGBoost) probabilities. Late fusion preserves modality-specific strengths and is resilient to intermittent failures (e.g., low-light video or noisy audio). Weights are tuned on validation data and can be adapted to context (structured interviews versus spontaneous speech) to balance contribution across modalities.

3.7 Architecture

The system follows a late-fusion, multimodal pipeline that ingests a synchronized audio-video stream and produces a calibrated truth/lie decision with an interpretable score. After decoding, video frames are face-detected and aligned to a canonical geometry; audio is separated, normalized, and (when enabled) transcribed for text features. Each modality is processed by a specialized model to produce compact, temporally pooled representations: (i) a facial emotion embedding and (ii) a micro-expression embedding from the visual stream, (iii) an audio prosody/voice embedding, and (iv) a textual deception score/embedding from transcripts. At inference time, the two visual embeddings are first concatenated and classified by a margin-based visual SVM, yielding a visual truth/lie probability. A late, weighted fusion then aggregates the visual probability with the audio and text outputs, producing the final deception score. The UI layer renders per-segment predictions, confidence, and auxiliary cues (e.g., emotion tags, salient time spans), while a logging layer stores metadata for audit and analysis (Fig. 1).

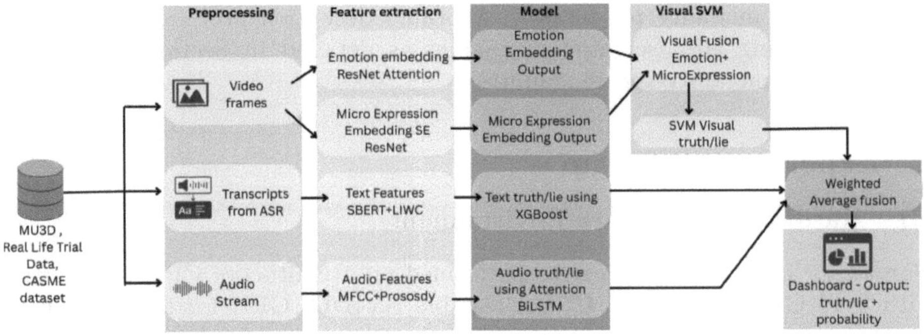

Fig. 1. Accuracy comparison across individual modalities and fusion approach. The multimodal fusion achieves the highest performance at 93% accuracy.

3.8 Implementation Details of Individual Modalities

Text Model. ASR transcripts are lowercased and sentence-segmented. Stopwords are intentionally retained, as prior deception research shows that function words (e.g., pronouns, negations) are strong deception indicators. Sentence-level semantic representations are extracted using Sentence-BERT (all-mpnet-base-v2). Each transcript yields 768-dimensional embeddings, aggregated via mean and max pooling, producing a 1536-dimensional semantic feature vector.

Additionally, 12 LIWC-inspired psycholinguistic features are computed, including pronoun usage ratios, negation frequency, lexical complexity, sentence length statistics, sentiment polarity, subjectivity, and readability indices (Flesch–Kincaid Grade Level and SMOG Index). The final text feature vector has 1548 dimensions and is standardized using Z-score normalization. Classification is performed using XGBoost with hyperparameters reported in Section 4.

Audio Model. Audio streams are segmented into 1-second windows and padded or truncated to a maximum duration of 40 seconds. For each segment, 40-dimensional MFCC features are extracted along with prosodic descriptors (pitch, energy, pause duration). These features form a temporal matrix of size 40×40. A two-layer Attention-based BiLSTM models temporal dynamics, and an attention mechanism learns to emphasize speech segments associated with stress or hesitation.

Visual Model. Facial landmarks (68 points) are extracted per frame and normalized. A fully connected autoencoder compresses each 136-dimensional landmark vector into a 64-dimensional latent representation. These latent features are classified using a supervised MLP. In parallel, CNN-based visual encoders (ResNet-18 and SE-ResNet) process short frame clips to capture macro-emotion and micro-expression dynamics.

Fusion. Each modality produces a calibrated deception probability. Fusion is performed using late weighted averaging, as detailed in Section 5, ensuring robustness to modality-specific failures.

4 Experimental Setup

4.1 Hardware / Software Environment

Hardware. The experiments were performed on a multi-core CPU workstation with 8–16 GB RAM and a CUDA-capable NVIDIA GPU for faster training. Inputs were offline videos or a webcam/microphone stream. Local storage was used.The pipeline is OS-agnostic.

4.2 Hyperparameter Settings

All models were trained using fixed hyperparameters selected through preliminary validation experiments. The visual CNN–LSTM pipeline used ResNet-18 initialized with ImageNet weights and 16-frame clips, with an LSTM hidden size of 256 and dropout of 0.5. Training employed AdamW with a learning rate of $1 \times 10^{-4}$and StepLR decay. The audio Attention-BiLSTM model used 40-dimensional MFCC and prosodic features,with two BiLSTM layers of 128 hidden units per direction and dropout of 0.3,optimized using Adam at a learning rate of 2×10^{-4}. For text, 768-dimensional SBERT embeddings were concatenated with LIWC-style features and classified using XGBoost with 300 estimators and a maximum depth of 6. Key hyperparameters across all modalities are summarized in Table 2.

Table 2. Key Hyperparameters Used Across Modalities

Model	Parameter	Value
Text (XGBoost)	Estimators	300
	Max Depth	6
	Learning Rate	0.05
Audio (Attn-BiLSTM)	Hidden Units	128 (per direction)
	Layers	2
	Learning Rate	2×10^{-4}
Visual (CNN-LSTM)	Frame Clip Length	16
	LSTM Hidden Size	256
	Dropout	0.5

All models were trained using stratified splits to preserve class balance. Early stopping was applied based on validation loss to prevent overfitting.

4.3 Training Procedure

Data Preparation. Source .wmv files were converted to .mp4 with FFmpeg, frames were extracted with metadata, and audio was split into .wav, resampled, and normalized. ASR produced time-stamped transcripts. Faces were detected and aligned (RetinaFace/dlib-68) to stabilize pose before modeling.

Visual Model (CNN–LSTM). Frames were normalized and grouped into 16-frame clips. ResNet-18 generated per-frame features, and an LSTM captured temporal changes such as micromovements. Training used CrossEntropyLoss, AdamW, and StepLR, with the best model chosen by validation accuracy. We report accuracy, F1, and confusion matrices.

Audio Model (Attn-BiLSTM). From waveforms, MFCCs and prosodic features (pitch, energy, pauses) were extracted and standardized over 40-second clips. A BiLSTM with attention highlighted stress or hesitation segments. Training used CrossEntropyLoss and Adam; evaluation included precision, recall, F1, and confusion matrices.

Text Model (SBERT + LIWC → XGBoost). Transcripts were normalized, encoded with SBERT (mean/max pooled), and combined with LIWC-style lexical and psycholinguistic features plus sentiment/readability cues. After scaling, XGBoost was trained with 5-fold stratified CV using an 80/20 split. We report accuracy, F1, and feature importances.

Fusion. (1) Visual fusion: emotion and microexpression embeddings were concatenated and fed to an SVM to produce a visual truth/lie score. (2) Cross-modal fusion: weighted late fusion combined visual (SVM), audio (Attn-BiLSTM), and text (XGBoost) outputs, with weights tuned on validation to handle conditions like poor lighting or noisy audio.

Validation Protocol. Accuracy, precision, recall, F1, and confusion matrices were computed for each modality and for the fused model. Early stopping, learning-rate decay, and ablation tests (removing one modality at a time) were used to measure robustness and contribution.

5 Results and Discussion

5.1 Model Performance

- **Audio (Attention-BiLSTM) – 92%:** Strongest single stream. Prosodic cues (pitch, energy, pauses) generalized well; errors occurred mainly with background noise or overlapping speech.
- **Visual (SE-ResNet + ResNet w/ attention) – 91%:** Micro-expression and emotion embeddings captured subtle facial dynamics and affect. Effective for frontal, well-lit faces; performance dropped with occlusions (glasses/hair) or rapid head motion.

- **Text (SBERT + LIWC → XGBoost) – 75%:** Limited by ASR errors and context-dependence, yet provided complementary and interpretable semantic and psycholinguistic features.
- **Visual SVM (Emotion + Micro-Expression embeddings) – 91%:** Concatenating visual embeddings and classifying via SVM improved visual performance, aligning with the motivation for margin-based classification on compact embeddings.
- **Late Fusion (Visual SVM + Audio + Text) – 93%:** Weighted late fusion of all modalities achieved the best performance. Combined cues improved generalization across conditions: audio captured delivery-based stress, visual streams detected facial leaks and emotions, and text provided semantic markers (Table 3).

Table 3. Performance Metrics Across Modalities

Model	Acc	Prec	Rec	F1	AUC
Text (SBERT+LIWC+XGBoost)	0.75	0.72	0.69	0.70	0.78
Audio (Attention-BiLSTM)	0.92	0.91	0.93	0.92	0.95
Visual (SVM)	0.91	0.89	0.90	0.90	0.94
Fusion (All)	**0.93**	**0.92**	**0.94**	**0.93**	**0.96**

False negatives primarily occurred in low-light or fast-motion videos (hurting micro-expressions) and high-noise audio (hurting prosody), while false positives often coincided with high-arousal but truthful speech. Text misclassifications were mostly due to ASR errors and domain-specific phrasing.Macro-averaged precision, recall, F1, and ROC-AUC metrics ensure balanced evaluation across classes.

5.2 Fusion Weight Determination and Ablation Justification

Multimodal fusion was implemented using late weighted averaging of modality-specific deception probabilities to enable explicit analysis of individual and joint contributions. Unimodal baselines were first evaluated independently for visual, audio, and text streams. Ablation analysis was then performed by excluding one modality at a time from the fusion process while retaining the remaining components, with fusion weights renormalized to handle missing modalities. Audio consistently provided the strongest standalone signal, while visual cues contributed complementary facial dynamics and text added semantic context. Removal of any modality resulted in a measurable drop in macro F1-score, indicating that performance gains were derived from complementary information rather than a single dominant stream. Fusion weights were initialized uniformly (equal weights) and then tuned on a validation set to maximize macro F1-score, balancing performance across truthful and deceptive classes; the final weights used were 0.4 (audio), 0.3 (visual), and 0.3 (text). Late fusion was preferred to preserve modality-specific representations, improve robustness to degraded inputs, and support modular deployment.

5.3 Contextual Comparison with Prior Multimodal Studies

Several existing approaches focus exclusively on courtroom-style data or controlled laboratory settings. Therefore, Table 4 provides a contextual comparison to situate the proposed approach relative to prior studies under broadly similar application scenarios.

Table 4. Contextual Accuracy Comparison on Courtroom-Style Datasets

Prior work	Visual	Audio	Text
[5]	75.00	74.16	–
[6]	83.00	79.00	66.00
[7]	77.31	76.94	64.57
[8]	78.57	87.50	83.78
[1]	84.00	88.00	84.00
Ours	92.00	92.00	75.00

In particular, our system maintains strong unimodal performance across audio, visual, and textual streams, while additionally supporting modular deployment and robustness to missing or degraded modalities.

6 Ethical Considerations and Limitations

The system uses observable audio-visual behavior (faces, speech, transcripts) and must ensure informed consent, purpose limitation, and secure handling of recordings and derived features. Outputs include per-modality scores and a fused decision with probabilities; exposing evidence such as emotion, micro-expression, audio, or transcript cues improves transparency but should remain decision support, with human-in-the-loop review. Current limitations include reliance on accurate face detection/alignment, synchronization, and stable embeddings, along with limited dataset size; broader testing and model weight management remain future extensions.

7 Conclusion and Future Work

7.1 Conclusion

This work presents a real-time multimodal deception detection pipeline that processes video and audio streams into four coordinated analyses-facial emotion, micro-expressions, audio prosody, and transcript-based linguistic cues-and fuses them via a late-stage classifier to yield a truth/lie probability with a user-facing dashboard. The design is modular (face detection/alignment; CNN-LSTM visual stream; Attention-BiLSTM audio; SBERT+LIWC text; SVM/XGBoost and late fusion), addresses practical constraints (frame extraction, normalization, resampling, metadata logging), and targets deployment-minded usability (probability/confidence display, logs).

7.2 Future Work

Future work includes expanding to larger, diverse, and ethically sourced datasets with cross-subject validation and per-modality ablations. We plan to explore end-to-end multimodal architectures, domain adaptation, and self-supervised pretraining. Fusion can be improved with adaptive, signal-aware weighting and uncertainty estimation. For deployment, models will be optimized (quantization/pruning), edge inference considered for privacy, and the UI strengthened for workflow and audits. Governance will formalize consent, retention, access controls, and clarify that the system is decision-support only.

Acknowledgements. The authors express their sincere gratitude to Prof. Prema R, PES University, for her invaluable guidance, constant encouragement, and insightful feedback throughout the course of this project. Her mentorship was instrumental in shaping the direction of this work and in refining both technical and research contributions.

References

1. Hsiao, S.-W., Sun, C.-Y.: Attention-aware multi-modal RNN for deception detection. In: Proc. 2022 IEEE International Conference on Big Data (Big Data), Osaka, Japan, pp. 3593–3596 (2022). https://doi.org/10.1109/BigData55660.2022.10020331
2. Şen, M.U., Perez-Rosas, V., Yanikoglu, B., Abouelenien, M., Burzo, M., Mihalcea, R.: Multimodal deception detection using real-life trial data. IEEE Trans. Affect. Comput. **13**(1), 306–319 (2022). https://doi.org/10.1109/TAFFC.2020.3015684
3. Burzo, M., Abouelenien, M., Perez-Rosas, V., Mihalcea, R.: Multimodal Deception Detection. Morgan & Claypool, San Rafael, CA, USA (2016)
4. King, S.L., Neal, T.: Applications of AI-enabled deception detection using video, audio, and physiological data: a systematic review. IEEE Access **12**, 135207–135240 (2024). https://doi.org/10.1109/ACCESS.2024.3462825
5. Karimi, H., Tang, J., Li, Y.: Toward end-to-end deception detection in videos. In: 2018 IEEE International Conference on Big Data, pp. 1278–1283 (2018)
6. Mathur, L., Mataric, M. J.: Introducing representations of facial affect in automated multimodal deception detection. In: Proceedings of the 2020 International Conference on Multimodal Interaction, pp. 305-314 (2020)
7. Z. Wu, B., Singh, Davis, L., Subrahmanian, V.: Deception detec-tion in videos. In: Proceedings of the AAAI Conference on Artificial Intelligence, vol. 32, no. 1 (2018)
8. Gogate, M., Adeel, A., Hussain, A.: Deep learning driven multimodal fusion for automated deception detection. In: 2017 IEEE Symposium Series on Computational Intelligence (SSCI), pp. 1–6 (2017)

How Stylize Transfer Enhances the Visibility of Storefronts with Modified Attention

Xiaohan Yu[1,2,3], Yuexin Li[1,2,3], Dongyu Li[1,2,3], and Venkata Duvvuri[1,2,3](✉)

[1] MS Analytics, Northeastern University, San Jose, CA, USA
{yu.xiaohan1,li.yuexin1,li.dongyu2}@northeastern.edu,
venkata@siriusmindshare.com
[2] MS Information Systems, Northeastern University, San Jose, CA, USA
[3] Founder, Siriusmindshare LLC, San Jose, CA, USA

Abstract. This study investigates how visual stylization influences neural-perceptual responses, color characteristics, and textual readability in digitally generated product imagery. Using a controlled dataset of original images and their stylized counterparts, we analyzed changes across cognitive, visual, and semantic dimensions. Results show that stylization systematically increases visual intensity and alters color tone while reducing text clarity and cognitive richness. Neural indicators of focus rise, whereas measures related to memory and processing depth decline, suggesting a shift toward visually striking yet semantically simplified imagery. Correlation analyses further reveal that perceptual attributes such as contrast, focus, and text density play central roles in shaping overall visual evaluation. These findings highlight the inherent trade-off between aesthetic enhancement and informational accessibility in stylized commercial visuals.

Keywords: visual perception · stylized imagery · cognitive processing · text readability · aesthetic evaluation

1 Introduction

1.1 Background and Motivation

In the era of digital commerce and social media, images serve as powerful communication tools that shape consumer perception, engagement, and decision-making. The visual styling of an image through color manipulation, tone adjustment, or neural aesthetic enhancement affects not only its aesthetic appeal but also how easily viewers process its information. While traditional photography emphasizes fidelity and clarity, stylized imagery aims to amplify emotional tone and visual salience. However, such stylization may unintentionally distort textual or structural components crucial for comprehension (Field 2024).

Existing studies in computer vision and cognitive neuroscience suggest that perceptual variables, such as contrast, color temperature, and saturation, are closely linked to human attention and memorability (Loke et al. 2024). At the same time, textual clarity

C. Xu (Ed.): ICMLSC 2026, CCIS 2948, pp. 349–361, 2027.
https://doi.org/10.1007/978-981-92-1546-1_29

quantified via OCR confidence or text quality metrics plays a vital role in how viewers extract semantic information. Despite these insights, few empirical studies have examined how artistic stylization simultaneously affects perceptual, neural, and textual domains within the same controlled dataset.

1.2 Research Objectives

This research aims to bridge that gap by addressing three guiding questions:

- How do different visual styles (Original vs. Style1 – Style4) influence neuron-related parameters such as Focus, Cognitive Demand, Engagement, and Memory (Bilucaglia et al. 2025)?
- How are textual readability and OCR confidence affected by stylization (Cuper et al. 2023)?
- Which perceptual or neural variables most strongly predict the Image Visual Rank, a proxy for overall aesthetic quality?

To answer these questions, we analyze a large-scale stylized image dataset using statistical methods. By quantifying both within style differences and cross feature correlations, this study provides an interpretable view of how computational styling transforms visual cognition.

1.3 Significance

Understanding these relationships has implications for multiple domains:

- E-commerce: optimizing product images to maximize attention while retaining text clarity (Chaudhuri et al. 2018).
- Computer vision: improving neural network training by understanding feature salience (Zhao et al. 2024).
- Design psychology: quantifying trade-offs between aesthetic enhancement and cognitive load.

This multidisciplinary contribution integrates perceptual psychology, image processing, and applied statistics to advance the interpretability of stylized media.

2 Research Methods

2.1 Dataset and Variables

The dataset consisted of 720 image samples, sourced from 144 online shops. Each shop contributed one Original image and four corresponding Stylized versions (Style1–Style4), yielding a balanced representation of 144 samples per style (Wang et al. 2024). Each image was annotated with 14 quantitative features spanning three functional domains:

- Neuron-related features: Neuron Focus, Neuron Cognitive Demand, Neuron Engagement, Neuron Memory (Ramsøy 2015; Ramsøy et al. 2019).

- Text-related features: Text Quality Score, Text Blocks Count, Average Text Confidence (%) (He et al. 2016)
- Color and visual parameters: Color Temperature (K), Brightness, Contrast, Saturation, Color Harmony, Focus Intensity, Image Visual Rank (Holtzschue et al. 2025)

These variables were extracted via a combination system of neural aesthetic estimators and OCR-based text analyzers. The data were pre-cleaned to remove missing values (only "Detected Objects" showed 294 nulls, which were excluded).

2.2 Score Methodology

The combination score system framework integrates two complementary systems (https://github.com/1233198063/image-analysis-platform).

- System 1 – Text Recognition-Based Image Quality Analysis: Evaluates text readability, color metrics, and style consistency.
- System 2 – Object Detection & Image Caption-Based Quality Analysis: Assesses object prominence, scene composition, and shifts in visual attention caused by style transfer.

This combination enables a comprehensive evaluation of how style transformations impact both the textual and visual aspects of storefronts.

2.3 Statistical Workflow

The analytical process involved several steps:

Descriptive Analysis: Means and standard deviations were computed for each parameter across the five style groups to establish baseline distributions.

Visualization: Boxplots were generated for neural, textual, and color-related variables to visualize variance and distributional overlap across styles.

One-way ANOVA: Conducted to Test Whether Image Style Significantly Affected Each Parameter. ANOVA outputs included F-statistics, p-values, and partial eta-squared (η^2) for effect size estimation (Chatzi & Doody 2024).

Post-hoc Tukey HSD: Pairwise Style Comparisons Identified Which Style Pairs Differed Significantly. This helped isolate which stylization techniques had the strongest perceptual impact (Juarros Basterretxea et al. 2024).

Correlation with Image Visual Rank: Pearson's r was used to assess the linear relationship between each feature and the dependent variable, clarifying which features most influenced perceived visual quality (Sedgwick 2012).

All analyses were executed in Python using the Pingouin(Vallat 2018), Statsmodels (Seabold & Perktold 2010), Seaborn, and Scikit-learn libraries.

3 Experimental Results

3.1 Descriptive Patterns

Descriptive statistics revealed that the Original images generally maintained higher textual and neural-cognitive measures but lower visual enhancement metrics. For example:

- Neuron Cognitive Demand: Original = 44.49 vs. Style3 = 34.58
- Text Quality Score: Original = 61.81 vs. Style3 = 36.42
- Focus Intensity: Original = 710.67 vs. Style1 = 1461.67

These results suggest that stylization reduces cognitive complexity and textual legibility while enhancing focus and warmth. The color temperature increased from ~5030 K (Original) to over 5350 K (Style1–4), indicating a perceptual shift toward warmer hues.

Boxplot visualizations further confirmed systematic style effects (Fig. 1).

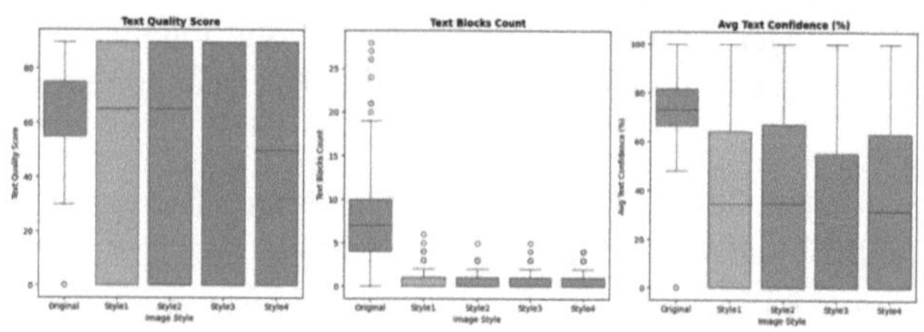

Fig. 1. Text Related Parameters By Image Style

Text features, especially OCR confidence, dropped sharply across styles, highlighting lower readability (Fig. 2).

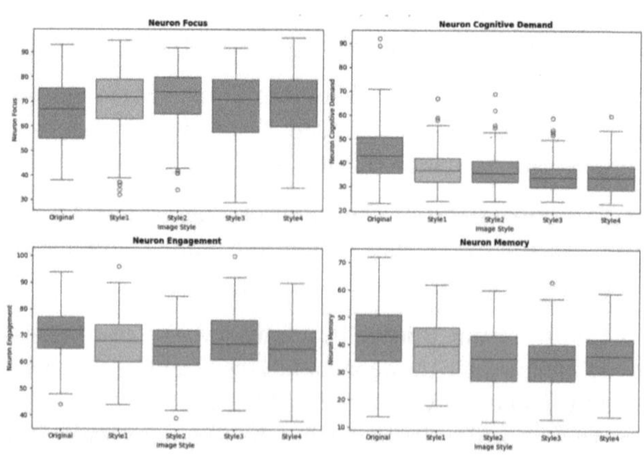

Fig. 2. Neuron-Related Parameters By Image Style

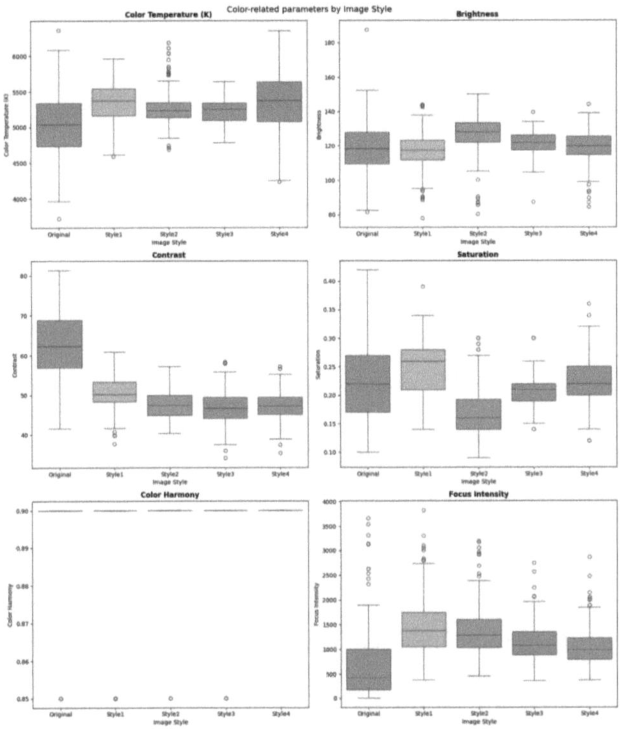

Fig. 3. Color-Related Parameters By Image Style

Neuron parameters showed decreasing Cognitive Demand and Memory in all stylized conditions (Fig. 3).

Color parameters revealed reduced contrast and increased saturation in Style1, with Style3 being visually softer and least saturated.

3.2 ANOVA Results

The one-way ANOVA demonstrated significant effects of image style for 12 out of 13 features ($p < 0.05$). The parameters with the largest effect sizes (η^2) are shown in Table 1. The complete ANOVA results in Appendix A.

These strong F-values indicate that stylization has a consistent and measurable impact across visual and neural dimensions.

3.3 Post-hoc Comparisons

Tukey HSD pairwise comparisons identified significant differences across all five image styles. The summary below outlines the direction and magnitude of key effects between the Original and stylized images (Table 2).

Together, these results reveal a gradient pattern of stylization effects: Style 1 maximizes visual enhancement with high focus and vivid color. Style 2 and Style 4 introduce

Table 1. One-way ANOVA Results for Feature Differences Across Image Styles

Feature	F	p	η^2	Significance
Contrast	250.64	1.79×10^{-134}	0.584	Yes
Text Blocks Count	217.16	6.82×10^{-122}	0.549	Yes
Saturation	50.35	2.35×10^{-37}	0.220	Yes
Focus Intensity	37.94	8.28×10^{-29}	0.175	Yes
Neuron Cognitive Demand	36.34	1.13×10^{-27}	0.169	Yes

Table 2. Interpretation of Visual and Neural Feature Changes Across Image Styles

Feature	Overall Pattern	Most Affected Styles	Interpretation
Contrast	All stylized styles showed significantly lower contrast than the Original ($p < .001$)	Style3, Style4	Indicates softer visual tonality and reduced luminance variation compared to the vibrant Original images
Neuron Cognitive Demand	Original significantly higher than all stylized groups ($p < .001$)	Style3 (largest decline), Style2, Style4	Confirms that stylization simplifies visual processing and lowers perceived cognitive load
Text Blocks Count	All stylized versions contained significantly fewer text regions than the Original ($p < .001$)	All styles	Suggests stylization blurs or suppresses minor textual details, reducing information density
Focus Intensity	All stylized styles displayed higher focus than the Original ($p < .001$)	Style1 (strongest), Style4 (moderate)	Style1 enhances sharpness most strongly, while Style4 produces a subtler sharpening effect
Saturation	Stylization altered color richness significantly across styles	Style1 (+0.022, $p < .01$); Style2 (−0.054, $p < .001$)	Style 1 is more vivid and saturated, whereas Style 2 is less saturated; Styles 3–4 show a moderate level, indicating balanced tone design

moderate adjustments that balance clarity and stylization. Style 3 produces the softest and most cognitively effortless visuals. The complete Post-hoc results can be found in Appendix Bz.

3.4 Mean Differences (Stylized – Original)

To further contextualize the direction and magnitude of changes relative to the Original images, mean difference values were computed for each style (Table 3).

Table 3. Feature Level Effects of Stylization on Visual, Textual, and Neural Attributes

Feature	Direction of Change
Color Temperature	Increased across all styles, from +190 K (Style3) to +322 K (Style1), indicating a consistent shift toward warmer tones
Focus Intensity	Substantially higher in all styles (+360 to +751), with Style1 achieving the greatest sharpening and Style4 showing a balanced moderate rise
Contrast	Decreased significantly across all stylized conditions (−12 to −16), with Style3 and Style4 exhibiting the largest reductions
Text Confidence	Dropped notably in all stylized images (−38% to −46%), reflecting general losses in textual readability and OCR accuracy
Neuron Memory	Declined by 4 to 9 points across all stylizations, with Style3 again producing the steepest drop

Overall, stylized images became warmer, more focused, and visually simplified, but at the expense of textual and cognitive clarity.

And the data suggest a continuum of transformation: Style 1 delivers the most intense enhancement, maximizing focus and saturation. Style 2 and Style 4 apply moderate adjustments, balancing readability and stylistic impact. Style 3 produces the most perceptually “softened” output, reducing contrast, cognitive demand, and text clarity to the greatest extent.

This pattern supports the interpretation that stylization intensity forms a perceptual gradient rather than a binary distinction between “Original” and “Stylized.” Each style occupies a specific niche in the trade-off spectrum between aesthetic vividness and informational transparency.

3.5 Correlation with Image Visual Rank

Correlation analysis linked perceptual metrics to overall image ranking (Table 4).

In short, simpler, more contrastive images with fewer text elements are perceived as more visually balanced, while extreme focus enhancement or warm coloration does not necessarily yield better aesthetic evaluation.

Table 4. Associations Between Image Attributes and Perceived Visual Ranking

Feature	Pearsonr	Interpretation
Text Blocks Count	–0.53	More text blocks → lower visual rank (better perceived)
Contrast	–0.50	Higher contrast → better aesthetic quality
Avg Text Confidence (%)	–0.35	Better OCR clarity → better perception
Neuron Cognitive Demand	–0.30	Higher cognitive load → moderate aesthetic improvement
Color Temperature (K)	+0.20	Warmer tones → slightly worse rank
Focus Intensity	+0.18	Higher focus → higher rank (visually strong but less "pleasing")

4 Discussion

4.1 Interpretation of Neural and Cognitive Findings

The neuron-related parameters: Focus, Engagement, Cognitive Demand, and Memory capture proxies for human perceptual effort and interest (Ramsøy et al. 2012).

The reduction in Cognitive Demand and Memory across all stylized versions suggests that visual simplification reduces cognitive load. It aligns with the 'Cognitive Fluency' theory, where simpler visual structures are processed faster and often perceived as more appealing.

Interestingly, while stylization increased Neuron Focus, it concurrently decreased Engagement and Memory. This may reflect a shift toward automatic visual attention without deeper semantic processing, an effect consistent with neural imaging studies showing that high-contrast stylized visuals activate early visual cortices more than prefrontal memory-related regions (Breiman 2001).

4.2 Balance Between Aesthetic and Informational Clarity

One of the most striking outcomes is the reduction in textual metrics. Across all styles, both Text Quality Score and OCR Confidence dropped by over 35–45%. This indicates that stylistic applications interfere with text recognition, a key consideration for e-commerce applications where product labels or specifications appear on images.

In practical terms, visual stylization improves artistic impact but compromises information transmission. This trade-off reflects an enduring tension in design: balancing "beauty" and "readability." With our results evidence, the Bright Eye Catching Style1's strong enhancement of Focus Intensity demonstrates this balance, creating sharp, appealing visuals but degrading text legibility (Khalili & Bouchachia 2021).

4.3 Visual and Color Dynamics

Color properties also reveal important psychological implications. Increasing Color Temperature introduces warmth and emotional vibrancy but can distort object realism. Similarly, reduced Contrast and heightened Saturation tend to simplify depth cues, potentially making images more cartoon-like or artificial (Chitturi et al. 2022).

The ANOVA and correlation results confirm that contrast remains the single most influential aesthetic determinant. The strong negative correlation ($r < 0.5$) indicates that viewers consistently prefer images with balanced luminance variation rather than over-flattened contrasts. Moreover, Focus Intensity's positive correlation with rank implies that over-enhanced sharpness, though visually striking, may be perceived as excessive. This observation parallels findings in computational aesthetics research, suggesting that moderate blur or natural texture yields higher aesthetic ratings than hyper-detailed renderings.

4.4 Integrative Framework

By synthesizing neuron, textual, and color domains, this study proposes a three-dimensional interpretive framework (He et al. 2024) (Table 5).

Table 5. Dimension Level Effects and Associated Trade-offs in Image Stylization

Dimension	Enhancement Effect	Trade-off
Neural-perceptual	↑ Focus, ↓ Cognitive Demand	Easier to process but less engaging
Textual-semantic	↓ OCR confidence, ↓ readability	Aesthetic emphasis reduces utility
Color–visual	↑ Warmth and saturation	Enhances mood but risks realism loss

These interactions suggest that effective image stylization should moderate enhancements rather than maximize them. Optimal stylization preserves enough text clarity and natural contrast to sustain both aesthetic and informational value.

4.5 Implications and Applications

The practical implications extend to several industries:

- E-commerce Optimization: Retail platforms could dynamically balance style parameters (e.g., saturation, focus intensity) depending on product type, emphasizing clarity for technical goods and warmth for lifestyle imagery.
- Neural Aesthetic Modeling: Insights from cognitive proxies could guide future machine-learning models to predict human aesthetic judgments using interpretable features.
- User Interface Design: When integrating stylized backgrounds, designers should limit visual clutter and maintain color harmony near neutral levels ($\approx$0.9, as observed across all styles).

Overall, the findings underscore the necessity of multi-factor analysis when evaluating visual design strategies.

5 Conclusion

This study quantitatively examined how visual stylization transforms neural, textual, and perceptual dimensions of image quality. Using a balanced dataset and rigorous statistical analysis, the results demonstrate that style-based transformations significantly affect both aesthetic and cognitive parameters. Stylized images, especially those resembling Style 1 (Bright Eye Catching) and Style 3 (Vivid Colorful), achieve higher focus intensity and color warmth but suffer notable losses in text legibility, contrast, and cognitive richness.

The key takeaways include:

Contrast and Text Blocks Count are the most critical predictors of perceived visual ranking. Cognitive Demand declines with stylization, suggesting reduced mental effort but also diminished engagement. Color Temperature and Focus Intensity enhance visual impact yet may reduce viewer comfort when overemphasized. In essence, stylization operates as a perceptual amplifier, strengthening attention-grabbing cues while attenuating semantic detail.

Future work should incorporate deep-learning embeddings (e.g., CLIP, Vision Transformer) to analyze semantic-level coherence, and extend this framework to video and interactive media, where dynamic attention cues may further influence neural-perceptual balance (Hassija et al. 2025). By articulating these measurable trade-offs, this research contributes to both the theory and practice of aesthetic engineering, offering designers, researchers, and AI developers an evidence-based understanding of how visual style modulates cognition and perception.

Appendix

Appendix A

	Feature	F	p	eta2	sig
9	Contrast	250.643463	1.793496e−134	0.583715	✔
5	Text Blocks Count	217.155684	6.816817e−122	0.548504	✔
10	Saturation	50.346964	2.353824e−37	0.219763	✔
6	Avg Text Confidence (%)	46.936148	4.753800e−35	0.207971	✔
12	Focus Intensity	37.941079	8.283660e−29	0.175093	✔
1	Neuron Cognitive Demand	36.342317	1.129164e−27	0.168961	✔
7	Color Temperature (K)	20.619828	4.258014e−16	0.103425	✔
3	Neuron Memory	16.365202	7.763294e−13	0.083875	✔
8	Brightness	12.128533	1.521741e−09	0.063541	✔
2	Neuron Engagement	9.714561	1.179685e−07	0.051546	✔
4	Text Quality Score	7.844420	3.440397e−06	0.042040	✔
0	Neuron Focus	3.825261	4.379176e−03	0.020952	✔
11	Color Harmony	2.670026	3.123708e−02	0.014717	✔

Appendix B

(Only show pairs with reject = True; all features combined).

Feature	Group1	Group2	Mean Diff	Feature	Group1	Group2	Mean Diff
Neuron Focus	Original	Style2	5.8403	Contrast	Style1	Style3	−3.6658
Neuron Cognitive Demand	Original	Style1	−6.8472	Contrast	Style1	Style4	−3.2252
Neuron Cognitive Demand	Original	Style2	−7.6597	Text Quality Score	Original	Style1	−14.4097
Neuron Cognitive Demand	Original	Style3	−9.9028	Text Quality Score	Original	Style2	−15.5903
Neuron Cognitive Demand	Original	Style4	−9.8125	Text Quality Score	Original	Style3	−25.3819
Neuron Cognitive Demand	Style1	Style3	−3.0556	Text Quality Score	Original	Style4	−18.0903
Neuron Cognitive Demand	Style1	Style4	−2.9653	Text Blocks Count	Original	Style1	−7.2778
Neuron Engagement	Original	Style1	−3.4375	Text Blocks Count	Original	Style2	−7.3125
Neuron Engagement	Original	Style2	−5.6181	Text Blocks Count	Original	Style3	−7.5
Neuron Engagement	Original	Style4	−6.5347	Text Blocks Count	Original	Style4	−7.3611
Neuron Engagement	Style3	Style4	−3.4583	Avg Text Confidence (%)	Original	Style1	−38.0972
Neuron Memory	Original	Style1	−4.3472	Avg Text Confidence (%)	Original	Style2	−38.2
Neuron Memory	Original	Style2	−8.2361	Avg Text Confidence (%)	Original	Style3	−46.3229
Neuron Memory	Original	Style3	−8.6806	Avg Text Confidence (%)	Original	Style4	−39.9458

(*continued*)

(*continued*)

Feature	Group1	Group2	Mean Diff	Feature	Group1	Group2	Mean Diff
Neuron Memory	Original	Style4	−6.8958	Saturation	Original	Style1	0.0219
Neuron Memory	Style1	Style2	−3.8889	Saturation	Original	Style2	−0.0542
Neuron Memory	Style1	Style3	−4.3333	Saturation	Original	Style3	−0.0194
Color Temperature	Original	Style1	322.2972	Saturation	Style1	Style2	−0.0761
Color Temperature	Original	Style2	239.0917	Saturation	Style1	Style3	−0.0413
Color Temperature	Original	Style3	190.2861	Saturation	Style1	Style4	−0.0233
Color Temperature	Original	Style4	291.1889	Saturation	Style2	Style3	0.0348
Color Temperature	Style1	Style3	−132.0111	Saturation	Style2	Style4	0.0528
Brightness	Original	Style2	7.1729	Saturation	Style3	Style4	0.0181
Brightness	Style1	Style2	8.5019	Color Harmony	Style1	Style4	0.0031
Brightness	Style1	Style3	4.0128	Focus Intensity	Original	Style1	750.9994
Brightness	Style2	Style3	−4.489	Focus Intensity	Original	Style2	678.1663
Brightness	Style2	Style4	−6.6343	Focus Intensity	Original	Style3	435.3258
Contrast	Original	Style1	−12.2627	Focus Intensity	Original	Style4	360.5581
Contrast	Original	Style2	−15.1327	Focus Intensity	Style1	Style3	−315.6735
Contrast	Original	Style3	−15.9285	Focus Intensity	Style1	Style4	−390.4413
Contrast	Original	Style4	−15.4879	Focus Intensity	Style2	Style3	−242.8404
Contrast	Style1	Style2	−2.87	Focus Intensity	Style2	Style4	−317.6082

References

Bilucaglia, M., Mainardi, L., Ramsøy, T.Z., Zak, P.J., Zito, M., Russo, V.: Editorial: Machine-learning/deep-learning methods in neuromarketing and consumer neuroscience. Front. Hum. Neurosci. **19** (2025). https://doi.org/10.3389/fnhum.2025.1638225

Chaudhuri, A., et al.: A smart system for selection of optimal product images in e-commerce. In: 2018 IEEE International Conference on Big Data (Big Data), pp. 1728–1736. IEEE (2018)

Chitturi, R., Londoño, J.C., Henriquez, M.C.: Visual design elements of product packaging: implications for consumers' emotions, perceptions of quality, and price. Color. Res. Appl. **47**(3), 729–744 (2022)

Cuper, M., van Dongen, C., Koster, T.: Unraveling confidence: examining confidence scores as proxy for OCR quality. In: Fink, G.A., Jain, R., Kise, K., Zanibbi, R. (eds.) ICDAR 2023. LNCS, vol. 14191, pp. 104–120. Springer, Cham (2023). https://doi.org/10.1007/978-3-031-41734-4_7

Field, A.: Discovering Statistics Using IBM SPSS Statistics. Sage Publications Limited (2024)

He, T., Huang, W., Qiao, Y., Yao, J.: Text-attentional convolutional neural network for scene text detection. IEEE Trans. Image Process. **25**(6), 2529–2541 (2016)

Hassija, V., et al.: Transformers for vision: a survey on innovative methods for computer vision. IEEE Access (2025)

He, Z., et al.: Multilevel interpretability of artificial neural networks: leveraging framework and methods from neuroscience. arXiv preprint arXiv:2408.12664 (2024)

Holtzschue, L.: Understanding Color: An Introduction for Designers. Wiley, Hoboken (2025)

Juarros Basterretxea, J., et al.: Post-hoc tests in one-way ANOVA: the case for normal distribution. Methodology (2024)

Khalili, A., Bouchachia, H.: An information theory approach to aesthetic assessment of visual patterns. Entropy **23**(2), 153 (2021)

Loke, J., et al.: Human visual cortex and deep convolutional neural network care deeply about object background. J. Cogn. Neurosci. **36**(3), 551–566 (2024)

Ramsøy, T.Z.: Introduction to Neuromarketing & Consumer Neuroscience. Neurons Inc. (2015)

Ramsøy, T.Z., Friis-Olivarius, M., Jacobsen, C., Jensen, S.B., Skov, M.: Effects of perceptual uncertainty on arousal and preference across different visual domains. J. Neurosci. Psychol. Econ. **5**(4), 212 (2012)

Seabold, S., Perktold, J.: Statsmodels: econometric and statistical modeling with python. SciPy **7**(1), 92–96 (2010)

Sedgwick, P.: Pearson's correlation coefficient. BMJ **345** (2012). https://doi.org/10.1136/bmj.e4483

Vallat, R.: Pingouin: statistics in Python. J. Open Source Softw. **3**(31), 1026 (2018)

Wang, H., Spinelli, M., Wang, Q., Bai, X., Qin, Z., Chen, A.: InstantStyle: free lunch towards style-preserving in text-to-image generation. arXiv preprint arXiv:2404.02733 (2024)

Zhao, X., Wang, L., Zhang, Y., Han, X., Deveci, M., Parmar, M.: A review of convolutional neural networks in computer vision. Artif. Intell. Rev. **57**(4), 99 (2024)

Zoëga Ramsøy, T., Michael, N., Michael, I.: A consumer neuroscience study of conscious and subconscious destination preference. Sci. Rep. **9**(1), 15102 (2019)

1233198063 (n.d.). 1233198063/image-analysis-platform. GitHub. https://github.com/1233198063/image-analysis-platform

Seeing How AI Thinks: UMAP-Based Interpretation of Deep Medical Imaging Models

Clyde Chester R. Balaman[1(✉)], Bench Jericho Peñanueva[2], Laurence Earl Errol B. Lapeceros[2], and Shaine A. Cababat[2]

[1] College of Computer and Information Science, Mapúa Malayan Colleges Mindanao, Davao City, Philippines
ccrbalaman@mcm.edu.ph

[2] College of Medical and Biological Science, University of the Immaculate Conception, Davao City, Philippines
{bpenanueva_230000001349,llapeceros_230000001284, scababat_230000000547}@uic.edu.ph

Abstract. While deep learning models perform well in classifying malaria parasites, understanding how their decisions align with clinical reasoning remains challenging. This study presents an embedding-based approach that uses Uniform Manifold Approximation and Projection (UMAP) to visualize and understand the feature space of a Convolutional neural network (CNN) trained on 3,623 labeled blood-smear images of Plasmodium falciparum. A ResNet18 baseline achieved 91.3% test accuracy, with F1-scores of 0.94, 0.88, and 0.89 for the ring, schizont, and gametocyte stages, respectively. Embedding analysis demonstrated that UMAP provided superior cluster separation (silhouette score = 0.0669), higher trustworthiness (0.9133), and greater cluster purity (0.6772) than Principal Component Analysis (PCA) and t-distributed Stochastic Neighbor Embedding (t-SNE). The visualizations showed meaningful overlaps between the Ring and Schizont stages, reflecting natural shape changes and staining differences seen in the microscope images. A neighborhood-based ambiguity analysis found the 20 most uncertain samples, revealing possible labeling mistakes and unclear cell shapes. These findings show that UMAP helps reveal how medical imaging models process and organize visual information, making their decisions easier to understand. By combining deep feature learning with clear visual mapping, this approach offers a practical way to uncover how AI interprets complex patterns—supporting more transparent, reliable, and clinically meaningful diagnostic systems.

Keywords: UMAP · interpretability · deep learning · embedding visualization · ambiguity detection · medical imaging

C. Xu (Ed.): ICMLSC 2026, CCIS 2948, pp. 362–374, 2027.
https://doi.org/10.1007/978-981-92-1546-1_30

1 Introduction

Deep learning has become a powerful tool for medical image analysis, assisting researchers and clinicians in identifying diseases more accurately and efficiently [1–4]. CNNs have shown high accuracy in identifying and classifying malaria parasites from blood smear images, providing faster and more reliable results than manual examination. [5–7]. Despite their accuracy, these models remain hard to interpret, limiting their clinical use where explainable decisions are essential. [1,2,8,9]. A main challenge is understanding how the model represents different parasite stages, since metrics like accuracy or precision cannot show how well it separates similar stages that overlap due to staining and biological variation. [10,11]. Without a clear way to visualize these relationships, researchers may overlook dataset issues such as mislabeled or ambiguous samples, which can affect both performance and model reliability [11,12]. Several methods have been used to visualize and analyze model behavior, including Principal Component Analysis (PCA) and t-distributed Stochastic Neighbor Embedding (t-SNE). While these methods can show general clustering patterns, they have limitations. PCA focuses mainly on preserving global variance and may lose fine details, while t-SNE captures local structure but often distorts global relationships and depends heavily on parameter tuning [10,13]. These limitations make it difficult to interpret the learned representations in a stable and meaningful way [13]. This paper uses UMAP to visualize and understand how a CNN represents malaria parasite stages. UMAP preserves both local and global patterns, giving a clearer and more balanced view of how the model organizes features from blood smear images [14–19]. By visualizing the 2D embeddings, we can see which classes are clearly separated, where overlaps or label errors occur, and how the model can be improved for better data quality and diagnostic reliability. [17,20].

In this work, a ResNet18 model [21] is trained on a dataset of 3,623 annotated Plasmodium *falciparum* blood smear images. The extracted feature embeddings are projected into two-dimensional space using UMAP, PCA, and t-SNE for comparison [17,22,23]. Quantitative measures such as silhouette score, trustworthiness, and cluster purity are used to evaluate the quality of the embeddings [24,25]. The results show that UMAP effectively separates parasite stages and reveals biologically meaningful patterns consistent with microscopy. By examining neighborhood consistency, the method also detects ambiguous or mislabeled samples. Overall, this work provides a visual and practical framework that enhances understanding, reliability, and transparency in deep learning–based medical imaging.

2 Method

The objective of this study is to understand how deep learning models represent and separate medical image features using an embedding-based interpretation approach. A convolutional neural network (ResNet18) was trained to classify malaria parasite stages from microscopy images, with its final layer adjusted to match the number of target classes. The training process used standard settings including cross-entropy loss, Adam optimization, and a learning rate scheduler, running for several epochs with batch-wise forward and backward propagation. The model that performed best on the validation set was saved and later tested on a separate dataset to measure classification accuracy and F1-scores for each parasite stage. High-dimensional feature embeddings were then extracted from the test images and reduced to two dimensions using Uniform Manifold Approximation and Projection (UMAP), Principal Component Analysis (PCA), and t-distributed Stochastic Neighbor Embedding (t-SNE). Among these, UMAP was the main focus due to its stronger ability to preserve both local and global structures in the learned features. The overall workflow of the study is shown in Fig. 1. It starts with setting up the ResNet18 model and training it using an optimization schedule. The model is validated to monitor accuracy and store the best checkpoint, then tested on a holdout set. Finally, high-dimensional features are projected and visualized to analyze cluster structures and interpret how the model organizes the learned representations.

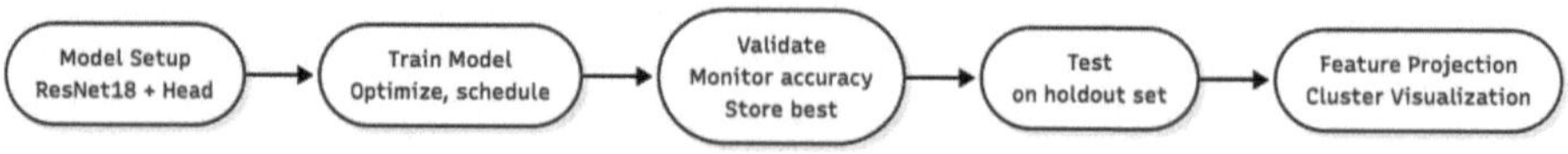

Fig. 1. Overview of the study workflow showing the main stages of model setup, training, validation, testing, and feature projection for cluster visualization and interpretability analysis.

2.1 Dataset and Preprocessing

The dataset used in this study comprises 5,767 cropped microscopy blood smear images of Plasmodium falciparum annotated through Roboflow. Three morphological stages were included: Ring, Schizont, and Gametocyte, in addition to uninfected red blood cells (RBCs). Annotations were provided in COCO format with bounding boxes, and individual parasite instances were extracted into stage-specific crops to construct the dataset. Annotation quality was verified through visualization to confirm the consistency of parasite stage labeling. The raw class distribution was imbalanced, with 4,144 Ring forms, 1,115 Schizonts, and 508 Gametocytes. To address this, the Ring class was capped at 2,000 examples, while Schizont and Gametocyte counts were retained, yielding a balanced dataset of 3,623 examples (see Fig. 2). Each cropped image was resized to 224×224 pixels and normalized using ImageNet mean and standard deviation statistics. Data augmentation strategies, including random flips, ±15° rotations, and intensity jitter, were applied during training to simulate staining and imaging variability, while validation and test sets underwent only resizing and normalization. The dataset was stratified into 2,535 training images, 363 validation images, and 725 test images. Image loading, transformation, and label assignment were handled through a custom PyTorch Dataset class, with DataLoader objects employed for efficient mini-batch sampling during training and inference.

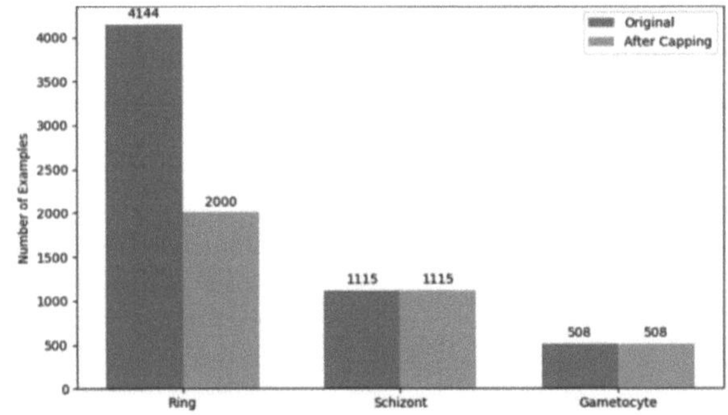

Fig. 2. Number of malaria parasite crops per class before and after capping to reduce imbalance.

2.2 Baseline Feature Extraction

To establish a baseline and generate discriminative embeddings, we employed a ResNet18 architecture pretrained on ImageNet. The model's final fully connected layer was replaced with a new layer matching the number of parasite stage classes. Training was performed using cross-entropy loss with the Adam optimizer (learning rate $= 1 \times 10^{-4}$), and learning rate scheduling was controlled with *ReduceLROnPlateau*, which reduced the learning rate when validation performance plateaued. The baseline training was designed not as the final goal but to provide a reliable feature extractor. Table 1 illustrates the ResNet18 architecture adapted for this classification task. During training, images were fed in mini-batches of 32, with weight updates minimizing classification error and data augmentations improving robustness to imaging variability. After training, 512-dimensional embeddings were extracted from the penultimate ResNet18 layer and used as inputs for UMAP to analyze the learned feature space rather than raw classification outputs.

2.3 Loss Functions and Optimization

The ResNet18 model was trained using cross-entropy loss, which quantifies the difference between predicted class probabilities and true labels for multi-class classification. Network parameters were optimized with the Adam optimizer at a learning rate of 1×10^{-4}, providing adaptive, momentum-based updates for efficient convergence. To further improve training stability, a *ReduceLROnPlateau* scheduler monitored the validation loss and reduced the learning rate by half if no improvement was observed over two consecutive epochs. This combination of loss function, adaptive optimization, and dynamic learning rate adjustment ensured effective weight updates and robust convergence throughout the training process.

Table 1. ResNet18 architecture with layer details and their interpretive role for cell classification.

Layer	Output Size	Filter Kernel	Stride	# Channels	Role
Input Image	224 × 224	–	–	3	Input blood-smear image provided to the model for parasite stage classification.
Conv1	112 × 112	7 × 7	2	64	Extracts initial spatial and color features, capturing general cell boundaries and stain variations.
MaxPool	56 × 56	3 × 3	2	64	Reduces spatial resolution while retaining important low-level features for noise reduction.
Conv2_x	56 × 56	3 × 3	1	64	Learns basic cellular textures and parasite outlines, improving robustness to small image variations.
Conv3_x	28 × 28	3 × 3	2	128	Detects mid-level parasite structures such as nucleus regions and cytoplasm distribution.
Conv4_x	14 × 14	3 × 3	2	256	Captures more complex morphological variations between parasite stages.
Conv5_x	7 × 7	3 × 3	2	512	Extracts high-level discriminative features separating different parasite stages.
Average Pool	1 × 1	Global	–	512	Aggregates the learned global features from all spatial locations into a compact embedding.
Fully Connected (FC)	1	–	–	#Classes	Performs final classification to predict the parasite stage based on the extracted embeddings.

2.4 Embedding

To analyze the internal representations learned by the ResNet18 model, feature embeddings were extracted from the penultimate layer. This was achieved by replacing the final fully connected layer with an identity mapping:

$$f_i = \text{ResNet18}_{\textbf{penultimate}}(x_i) \tag{1}$$

where x_i is the input image and $f_i \in \mathbb{R}^d$ is the resulting high-dimensional feature vector. Extraction was performed on the test set to obtain unbiased embeddings for subsequent analysis.

The high-dimensional embeddings were then projected into a two-dimensional space using Uniform Manifold Approximation and Projection (UMAP). UMAP constructs a weighted graph in the original space and optimizes a low-dimensional representation that preserves local neighborhood structure. This projection can be described as:

$$y_i = \mathrm{UMAP}(f_i), \quad y_i \in \mathbb{R}^2 \tag{2}$$

where y_i represents the 2D embedding of the i-th image. These embeddings allow for visual assessment of class separability and cluster structure among malaria parasite stages.

The embeddings serve as the basis for further quantitative evaluation using metrics such as silhouette score (s) and cluster purity (p):

$$s = \frac{b - a}{\max(a, b)}, \quad p = \frac{1}{N} \sum_{k=1}^{K} \max |C_k \cap L_j| \tag{3}$$

where a is the average intra-cluster distance, b is the average nearest-cluster distance, C_k denotes cluster k, L_j denotes true label j, and N is the total number of samples.

This embedding procedure does not involve classification performance metrics but provides an interpretable representation of how the model organizes cellular morphology in feature space, forming the foundation for later clustering and interpretability analyses.

2.5 Classification

After feature extraction and embedding, supervised classification was applied to evaluate how well the learned representations distinguish malaria parasite stages, using two classification pipelines:

Deep Feature Classification. The penultimate layer features of the ResNet18 model, $f \in \mathbb{R}^d$, were directly used as input to a Support Vector Machine (SVM) classifier with a radial basis function (RBF) kernel. The SVM aims to find a decision boundary that maximizes the margin between classes. Formally, the classifier solves:

$$\min_{w,b} \frac{1}{2}\|w\|^2 + C \sum_{i=1}^{N} \xi_i \tag{4}$$

subject to

$$y_i(w^T f_i + b) \geq 1 - \xi_i, \quad \xi_i \geq 0 \tag{5}$$

where w and b define the separating hyperplane, ξ_i are slack variables, C is the regularization parameter, and y_i denotes the class labels.

Low-Dimensional Embedding Classification. The high-dimensional feature vectors were first projected into two dimensions using UMAP, producing embeddings $e \in \mathbb{R}^2$. UMAP constructs a graph-based representation that preserves local and global structure in lower dimensions, and the resulting 2D embeddings are then classified using the same SVM framework.

The dataset in both pipelines was split into stratified training and test sets to preserve class balance. SVM classifiers were then trained using their respective features and evaluated on the test set. This setup allows a direct comparison between high-dimensional deep features and low-dimensional embeddings for malaria stage classification.

3 Results

3.1 Baseline Classification Performance

To establish a reference for malaria parasite classification, a ResNet18 convolutional neural network was trained on the annotated microscopy dataset. The network was adapted for this task by modifying the final fully connected layer to match the number of target classes. Training was performed for six epochs using cross-entropy loss and the Adam optimizer with a learning rate of 1×10^{-4}. A learning rate scheduler was employed to reduce the learning rate when the validation loss plateaued.

The model achieved a final validation accuracy of 90.6%, and the test set accuracy was 91.3%, demonstrating strong baseline performance. Performance across individual classes varied, with Ring forms achieving the highest F1-score due to their large representation, followed by Schizont and Gametocyte stages. Detailed per-class metrics, including precision, recall, and F1-score, are summarized in Table 2.

A confusion matrix, shown in Fig. 3, illustrates the distribution of correct and incorrect predictions for each class, highlighting areas where misclassifications were more frequent. Overall, these results establish a robust baseline for downstream embedding analyses, embedding-based classification, and ambiguity detection.

3.2 Feature Embeddings

Penultimate layer features were extracted from ResNet18 and projected into two dimensions using Uniform Manifold Approximation and Projection (UMAP), Principal Component Analysis (PCA), and t-distributed Stochastic Neighbor Embedding (t-SNE) to visualize the structure of malaria parasite stages. Scatterplots of the embeddings were generated with points colored by class, revealing cluster formation corresponding to Ring, Schizont, and Gametocyte stages.

Table 2. Per-class precision, recall, and F1-score for the baseline model.

Class	Precision	Recall	F1-score	Support
Ring	0.91	0.96	0.94	400
Schizont	0.88	0.88	0.88	223
Gametocyte	0.99	0.80	0.89	102
Accuracy			0.91	725
Macro Avg	0.93	0.88	0.90	725
Weighted Avg	0.91	0.91	0.91	725

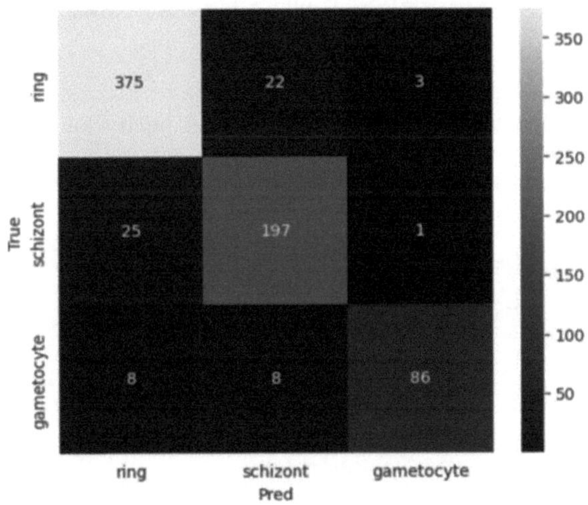

Fig. 3. Confusion matrix of ResNet18 baseline predictions on the test set.

Embedding quality was quantified using Silhouette score, trustworthiness, and cluster purity. Among the methods, UMAP produced the most coherent cluster separation, with a Silhouette score of 0.0669, high trustworthiness of 0.9133, and cluster purity of 0.6772. t-SNE showed slightly lower cluster compactness (Silhouette = 0.0629) but maintained high trustworthiness (0.9210) and comparable purity (0.6690). PCA resulted in the least well-separated clusters (Silhouette = 0.0088) and lower trustworthiness (0.7965), indicating that linear projection is less effective in capturing the complex feature relationships.

From a practical standpoint, these methods differ a lot in computation time. PCA is almost instant (<1 s). UMAP is much faster than t-SNE, finishing the 725 samples in about 2.5 s. t-SNE takes over 15 s for the same task. For large clinical workloads, UMAP provides high-quality embeddings at much lower cost, making it a more suitable choice for large-scale feature analysis. These results are summarized in Fig. 4, while the corresponding visualizations are presented in Fig. 5.

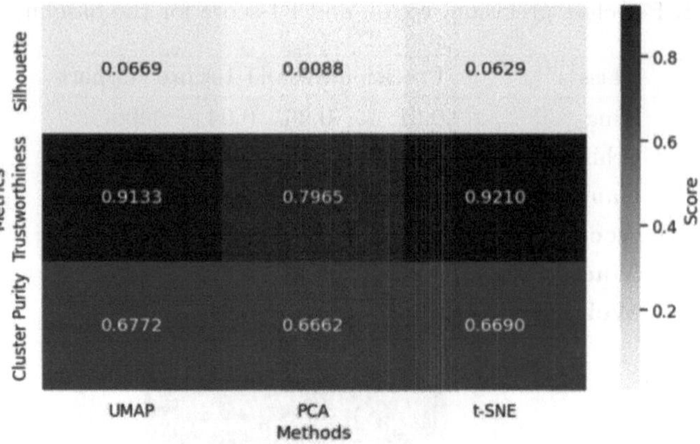

Fig. 4. Silhouette score, trustworthiness, and cluster purity for UMAP, PCA, and t-SNE embeddings.

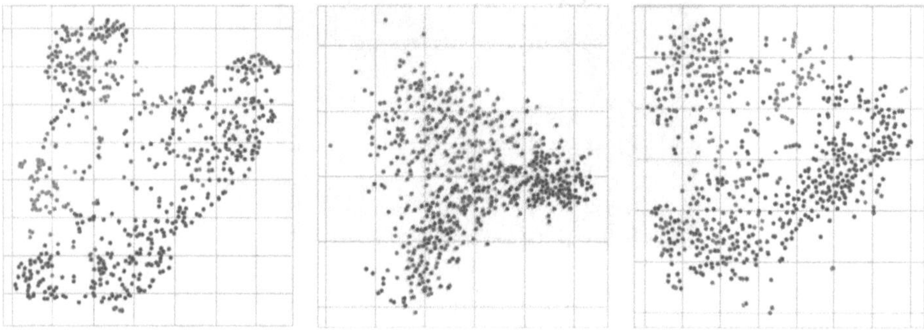

Fig. 5. Visualization of feature embeddings projected into two dimensions using (a) UMAP on the test set, (b) PCA on the test set, and (c) t-SNE on the test set. Each point represents an image sample colored by its parasite stage class, showing varying degrees of cluster separation across methods.

3.3 Classification

To assess the discriminative power of the extracted features, two classification pipelines were compared: a standard SVM trained on ResNet18 deep features and an SVM trained on 2D UMAP embeddings derived from the same features. The extracted penultimate layer features were split into training (80%) and testing (20%) sets, stratified by class to preserve label distribution. UMAP was applied to the training features to obtain a 2D projection, which was subsequently used to transform the test set into the same embedding space.

Two SVM classifiers were trained separately:

1. **Deep Features + SVM:** Utilized the full high-dimensional ResNet18 penultimate layer features.

2. **UMAP 2D Embeddings + SVM:** Utilized the low-dimensional 2D embeddings obtained from UMAP.

Both models were tested using standard metrics (accuracy, precision, recall, and F1-score). As shown in Table 3, the deep feature–based SVM performed better overall, while the 2D UMAP embeddings still maintained clear class separation.

Table 3. Comparison of SVM classification metrics on ResNet18 deep features vs. 2D UMAP embeddings.

Metric	Pipeline	Ring	Schizont	Gametocyte	Accuracy
Precision	Deep Features + SVM	0.89	0.83	0.96	0.88
	UMAP 2D + SVM	0.79	0.70	0.88	0.78
Recall	Deep Features + SVM	0.94	0.84	0.75	0.88
	UMAP 2D + SVM	0.87	0.68	0.60	0.77
F1-score	Deep Features + SVM	0.91	0.84	0.85	0.88
	UMAP 2D + SVM	0.83	0.69	0.71	0.77
Macro Avg	Deep Features + SVM	0.90	0.84	0.87	–
	UMAP 2D + SVM	0.79	0.72	0.74	–
Weighted Avg	Deep Features + SVM	0.88	0.88	0.88	–
	UMAP 2D + SVM	0.78	0.77	0.77	–

3.4 Embedding-Based Ambiguity Detection

To identify samples with potential mislabeling or morphological ambiguity, the neighborhood structure in the 2D UMAP embedding of ResNet18 features was analyzed. Using a k-nearest neighbors search ($k = 6$), label consistency was measured among each sample's neighbors, excluding the sample itself. For each test sample, the ambiguity score was computed as:

$$\text{Ambiguity Score} = 1 - \frac{\text{Number of neighbors with same label}}{k-1} \tag{6}$$

The ambiguity score shows how much a sample differs from its neighbors. Higher scores suggest more uncertainty or possible mislabeling. The top 20 highest-scoring samples were reviewed to check for overlapping classes and unclear labels. Images were shown in a grid with true (T) and predicted (P) labels. Misclassified samples were marked with color-coded borders and titles to show ambiguity levels (Fig. 6). Green indicated correct predictions, red showed errors, and border intensity reflected ambiguity. This visualization helps identify labeling issues and supports better dataset review and model understanding.

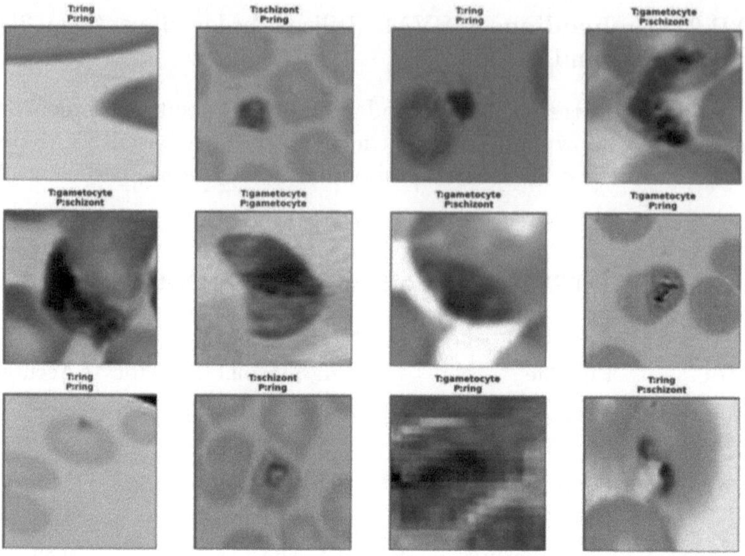

Fig. 6. Ambiguous Samples Detected via UMAP Neighborhood Consistency.

4 Conclusion

This work introduces an embedding-based framework that visualizes how AI models interpret malaria images. The ResNet18 model achieved 91.3% test accuracy, with F1-scores of 0.94 for Ring, 0.88 for Schizont, and 0.89 for Gametocyte stages. Beyond accuracy, the study showed that UMAP clearly shows how the model learns and organizes features. Compared to PCA and t-SNE, UMAP created clearer and more consistent clusters, with a higher silhouette score (0.0669), trustworthiness (0.9133), and cluster purity (0.6772). These results show that UMAP better keeps both the small details and overall structure of the data in high-dimensional features.

Embedding analysis revealed clinically meaningful insights, with most misclassifications occurring where clusters overlapped, especially between Ring and Schizont stages, reflecting natural shape changes and staining differences rather than model errors. Neighborhood consistency scoring flagged the 20 most unclear samples, often showing mixed cell shapes or labeling issues, and future studies should correlate these scores with expert assessments to confirm if AI-identified ambiguities match the most challenging cases, highlighting the potential of embedding-based methods to improve data quality, verify labels, and analyze model errors in medical AI.

Despite these contributions, limitations remain. The dataset included only three parasite stages and 3,623 samples, leaving out many other cell types seen in real clinical settings. UMAP is a post-processing method that helps explain model behavior but is not yet part of the model's full training process. Future work should extend this approach to larger, more diverse datasets, incorporate additional parasite life-cycle stages, and explore hybrid interpretability frameworks that combine embedding visualization with local attribution methods. This study demonstrates that embedding-based analysis makes malaria parasite classification both accurate and interpretable. By visualizing feature relationships through UMAP, we gain clearer insight into how deep medical imaging models distinguish parasite morphologies. This approach supports the development of AI systems for malaria diagnosis that are not only reliable but also transparent in how they make decisions.

References

1. Nazir, S., Dickson, D., Akram, M.: Survey of explainable artificial intelligence techniques for biomedical imaging with deep neural networks. Comput. Biol. Med. **156**, 106668 (2023)
2. Li, M., Jiang, Y., Zhang, Y., Zhu, H.: Medical image analysis using deep learning algorithms. Front. Public Health **11** (2023)
3. Van der Velden, B.H., Kuijf, H.J., Gilhuijs, K.G., Viergever, M.A.: Explainable artificial intelligence (XAI) in deep learning-based medical image analysis. Med. Image Anal. **79**, 102470 (2021)
4. Liu, T., Siegel, E., Shen, D.: Deep learning and medical image analysis for covid-19 diagnosis and prediction. Annual Rev. Biomed. Eng. (2022)
5. Mmileng, O. P., Whata, A., Olusanya, M., Mhlongo, S.: Application of convnext with transfer learning and data augmentation for malaria parasite detection in resource-limited settings using microscopic images. PLOS One **20** (2025)
6. Ghosh, H., Rahat, I.S., Ravindra, J.V.R., Balajee, J., Khan, M.A.U., Somasekar, J.: Convolutional neural networks in malaria diagnosis: a study on cell image classification. EAI Endorsed Trans. Pervasive Health Technol. **10** (2024)
7. Hoyos, K., Hoyos, W.: Supporting malaria diagnosis using deep learning and data augmentation. Diagnostics **14** (2024)
8. Zohaib Salahuddin, H. Woodruff, A. Chatterjee, and P. Lambin. Transparency of deep neural networks for medical image analysis: A review of interpretability methods. *Computers in biology and medicine*, 140:105111, 2021
9. Rasheed, K., Qayyum, A., Ghaly, M., . Al-Fuqaha, A., Razi, A., Qadir, J.: Explainable, trustworthy, and ethical machine learning for healthcare: a survey. Comput. Biol. Med. **149**, 106043 (2021)
10. Li, S., Du, Z., Meng, X., Zhang, Y.: Multi-stage malaria parasite recognition by deep learning. GigaScience **10** (2021)
11. Arshad, Q,A., et al.: A dataset and benchmark for malaria life-cycle classification in thin blood smear images. Neural Comput. Appl. **34**, 4473 – 4485 (2021)
12. Islam, M., et al.: Explainable transformer-based deep learning model for the detection of malaria parasites from blood cell images. Sens. (Basel, Switzerland) **22** (2022)
13. Huff, D.T., Weisman, A., Jeraj, R.: Interpretation and visualization techniques for deep learning models in medical imaging. Phys. Med. Biol. **66**, 04TR01–04TR01 (2020)
14. Siong Tan, H., Wang, K., Mcbeth,R.: Exploring Umap in hybrid models of entropy-based and representativeness sampling for active learning in biomedical segmentation. Comput. Biol. Med. **176**, 108605 (2024)

15. Dadu, A., et al.: Application of aligned-Umap to longitudinal biomedical studies. Patterns **4**(6) (2023)
16. Castellano-Escuder, P., Zachman, D.K., Han, K., Hirschey, M.D.: GAUDI: interpretable multi-omics integration with UMAP embeddings and density-based clustering. Nat. Commun. **16**(1), 5771 (2025)
17. McInnes, L., Healy, J., Melville, J.: UMAP: uniform manifold approximation and projection for dimension reduction. arXiv preprint arXiv:1802.03426 (2018)
18. Sainburg, T., McInnes, L., Gentner, T.Q.: Parametric UMAP embeddings for representation and semisupervised learning. Neural Comput. **33**(11), 2881–2907 (2021)
19. Verma, P., Salisbury, K.: Unsupervised learning of audio perception for robotics applications: learning to project data to T-SNE/UMAP space. arXiv preprint arXiv:2002.04076 (2020)
20. Becht, E., et al.: Dimensionality reduction for visualizing single-cell data using UMAP. Nat. Biotechnol. **37**(1), 38–44 (2019)
21. Ayyachamy, S., Alex, V., Khened, M., Krishnamurthi, G.: Medical image retrieval using RESNET-18. In: Medical Imaging 2019: Imaging Informatics for Healthcare, Research, and Applications, vol. 10954, pp. 233–241. SPIE (2019)
22. Abdi, H., Williams, H.J.: Principal component analysis. Wiley Interdiscip. Rev. Comput. Stati. **2**(4), 433–459 (2010)
23. van der Maaten, L., Hinton, G.: Visualizing data using T-SNE. J. Mach. Learn. Res. **9**(Nov), 2579–2605 (2008)
24. Jeon, H., Kuo, Y.-H., Aupetit, M., Ma, K.-L., Seo, J.: Classes are not clusters: improving label-based evaluation of dimensionality reduction. IEEE Trans. Visual Comput. Graphics **30**, 781–791 (2024)
25. Shahapure, K., Nicholas, C.K.: Cluster quality analysis using silhouette score. In: 2020 IEEE 7th International Conference on Data Science and Advanced Analytics (DSAA), pp. 747–748 (2020)

Coordinate Transformation of Gaze Information Captured by Eye Tracking Device to Find Visual-Motor Integration Mechanism

Ryo Nakajima[1], Koyo Arai[1], Ryosuke Shinkai[2,4], Seiji Ono[2,4], and Shinichi Yamagiwa[3,4](✉)

[1] College of Information Science, University of Tsukuba, 1-1-1 Tennodai, Tsukuba, Ibaraki 305-8573, Japan
{nakajima,koyo.arai}@padc.cs.tsukuba.ac.jp

[2] Institute of Health and Sport Sciences, University of Tsukuba, 1-1-1 Tennodai, Tsukuba, Ibaraki 305-8574, Japan
{shinkai.ryosuke.gp,ono.seiji.fp}@u.tsukuba.ac.jp

[3] Institute of Systems and Information Engineering, University of Tsukuba, 1-1-1 Tennodai, Tsukuba, Ibaraki 305-8573, Japan
yamagiwa@cs.tsukuba.ac.jp

[4] Advanced Research Initiative for Human High Performance, University of Tsukuba, Tsukuba, Ibaraki, Japan

Abstract. Vision is one of the most important aspects that affects human behavior. The researchers in sports science are investigating the relationship between visual and motor behavior in human movement skills. This paper focuses on experiments using an eye tracking device that records video and gaze coordinates. During sports activity, angles in video frames move dynamically. However, gaze coordinates are plotted based on the axes of the eye tracking device. Therefore, it is hard to know actual gaze points in the world coordinate system because the video frames and its corresponding gaze points must be integrated. This paper proposes a simple and effective method that remaps the global gaze points to a virtual plane by applying 3D model of playing field. The method infers gaze directions of a player by using convolutional neural network (CNN) trained by a combined dataset of generated images from the 3D model and the actual gaze points from an eye tracking device. The gaze directions are inferred from the CNN and remapped to a virtual plane placed in the world coordinate system. As an experimental example, we applied the method to analyze visual-motor integration of a table tennis rally. Regarding two hypotheses for finding differences in visual strategies between expert and semi-advanced players, experimental datasets taken by an eye tracking device during the rallies are applied to the proposed method.

Keywords: Visual motor integration · CNN · Table tennis · human behavior

C. Xu (Ed.): ICMLSC 2026, CCIS 2948, pp. 375–391, 2027.
https://doi.org/10.1007/978-981-92-1546-1_31

1 Introduction

Sports activity is one of the best wellness methods for our human life. People love such activity usually to brush up on their sports skills under its rules. They often want to become skillful players with less training. Therefore, they are trying to find key techniques for sports. Furthermore, the top athletes who play in international competitions also want to find the best way for their training in a limited time. To address these demands, many research trials using information technologies have been performed by applying sensory devices and cameras [7,8]. Especially, one of the most remarkable techniques strongly related to body control (called *motor* control in the sports science field) is a strategy of lines of sight. For example, it is known that gaze points and directions in our life are related to the motor control and bring visual strategy during sports activity [2]. Therefore, we focus on the relation between visual strategy and motor performance during sports activity by understanding lines of sight. The gaze points and directions can be measured by an eye tracking device available in the market. The device also embeds one or more cameras that record video with the coordinates of the gaze points in the video frames. Dataset of the video and the coordinates should include hints for the visual strategy that brings skillful motor control during sports activity.

However, it is hard to derive absolute coordinates of the sight from the dataset because the eye tracking device is moving with player's head during sports activity. In the other words, the three-dimensional axes of the eye tracking device are changing during the activity. Thus, it is hard to map the acquired coordinates in the video frames to the absolute world coordinate system. Therefore, it is difficult to analyze the dataset directly after measured by the eye tracking device. Moreover, when the dataset is analyzed intuitively, the analysis should include subjective opinion of the observer. Thus, we need an effective solution for mapping the relative coordinate taken by the eye tracking device to the absolute one.

This paper proposes a standardization method for dataset with a video and the relative coordinates of gaze points and directions acquired by an eye tracking device. The method infers vectors of lines of sight during sports activity applying CNN (convolutional neural network) approach. It derives coordinates of gaze points derived from the vectors to a virtual plane mapped in the world coordinate system. For an example analysis using our proposed method, we explore visual-motor integration during a table tennis rally.

Our major contributions described in this paper are shown in the followings.

- We developed a flexible standardization method to remap vectors of lines of sight to the world coordinate system based on CNN approach. It derives absolute coordinates remapped on a virtual plane from datasets of video frames and the coordinates of gaze points measured by an eye tracking device.
- We evaluated the proposed method by applying to two hypotheses regarding correlations between visual characteristics and body control during a table tennis rally. The proposed method clearly visualized differences of the visual-motor integration between the expert and the semi-advanced players.

This paper organizes as follows. The next section introduces research backgrounds and discussions regarding correlations between visual strategy and motor control in sports activity. Section 3 explains our proposed method and shows the processing steps. Section 4 shows experimental evaluations of the proposed method applying dataset acquired from an eye tracking device. The section also evaluates hypotheses for the visual strategy regarding a table tennis rally. Finally, we conclude our paper and describe future plans.

2 Backgrounds and Definitions

2.1 Visual Strategy in Sports Activity

Gaze positioning is known as one of the important techniques for sports. It is called a visual strategy in cognitive psychology in sports science. The researchers believe that human behavior is induced by the visual strategy when a person is going to handle the situation. In sports activity, it is remarkable factor to gain a high skill body (motor) control for winning a game. Focusing on this background, there are various advanced research in the field. For example, the literature [5] reports systematic review of focusing duration and gaze points before shooting in basketball.

In the research field of the visual strategy, an eye tracking device is often used for measuring the positions of lines of sight. The literature [11] describes gaze analysis when a tennis player receives a serve. The player wears an eye tracking device with recording a video. Applying the dataset of gaze points and player's positions in the tennis court to random forest approach, the authors found that top players can predict serves better and faster than middle-class ones. The literature [10] reports analysis regarding the lines of sight of the defender who tries to disturb the shooter. The research also used an eye tracking device to measure gaze positions and the time that the defender takes. It concluded that the defender was focusing on the hips and the legs of the shooter to success defense. The researchers defined areas of the tennis court or the offender's body. They also measured elapsed time while the lines of sight stay in the areas. The measurement was manually performed by counting the number of video frames while the defender was focusing on the areas. The literature [1] also performed the similar experiments in soccer while the player wears an eye tracking device. The researchers categorized gaze points of players into ball, opponent player, teammate and player in possession near ball. The final example is the literature [4]. The researcher analyzed gaze points of alpine slalom skier. This research also defined check points in the slalom course and analyzed gaze points and the gaze duration.

These research approaches above did not analyze dynamic gaze movements because it is hard to infer absolute coordinate in the environment. It is very hard to derive the absolute coordinate by combining a coordinate of the line of sight taken by an eye tracking device with the background scenes in a video frame. Even if we manually derive the absolute coordinate, it is hard to eliminate subjective opinion to decide the absolute coordinate. Therefore, it is important to develop any objective translation method from the relative gaze points to world coordinate with combining scene in video frame.

2.2 Computer Vision Techniques for Visual Line Processing

We can find advanced research regarding gaze identification from image or 3D data. There are two categories in the approach. One is subjective approach that detects gaze of person who takes an object by camera. The research trials find direction of line(s) of sight based on iris/pupil or eyeball or direction of head. Classical methods [3,13] are algorithm that detects object location in an image using SIFT features [9]. These infer camera location and direction information, which are the location and the direction of the person who watches an object. It is nearly the gaze direction. Furthermore, PoseNet [6] detects camera location and direction in an image applying CNN approach with training dataset of images and its location and direction information. It infers a direction to center of an image. Another is an objective approach that detects gaze of person(s) taken by a camera or a sensor. The literature [12] describes gaze regression method from 3D depth dataset taken by ToF sensor. It made model of eyeball and derives its direction of iris. However, it needs the depth information. GazeOnce [14] detects multiple gaze directions of multiple persons in an image. It derives multiple lines of sights based on CNN that infers head and iris directions.

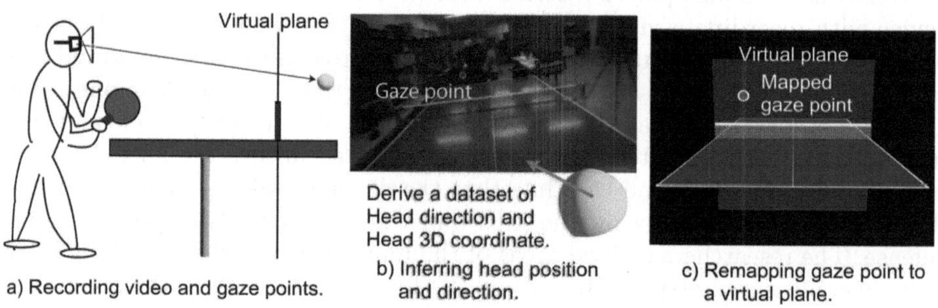

Fig. 1. Our research objective.

2.3 Discussion

Our target is the subjective approach of gaze identification algorithms described above because we need to consider the situation with eye tracking device. Moreover, to derive global gaze points and directions, we need to utilize dataset of video frames and coordinates of lines of sight taken by the eye tracking device. Our main objective is to develop a simple machine learning algorithm that infers absolute coordinates from the dataset. The PoseNet is the similar approach to find the head direction of an athlete who wears the tracker. However, we need to consider that the coordinates of head positions in the world coordinate system and the gaze directions in video frames differ. Therefore, we additionally need another step to infer an absolute direction vector of lines of sight from video frames. Additionally, we try to simplify generating training dataset for our algorithm. Because we can assume that almost all sports have strict regulations regarding the playing field and tools, sight from player can be standardized. For example, the lines in court are simple and can become significant characteristics to detect gaze directions. Thus, we can generate training dataset for inferring the gaze direction by using artificial 3D model of playing field.

Let us summarize our research objective in Fig. 1. First, we gather datasets of a video and gaze coordinates taken by an eye tracking device (Fig. 1 a)). Direction of a line of sight is inferred from the dataset (Fig. 1 b)). Finally, points derived from vectors of gaze directions are mapped to a virtual plane in the world coordinate system (Fig. 1 c)). Because the final coordinates in the virtual plane are absolute records of vision strategy by players, we can perform subjective analysis for dynamic characteristics of motor control induced by the vision.

As an experimental example analysis, we apply our method to observe visual-motor integration during a table tennis rally. Focusing on two hypotheses below, we are going to visualize and explain the visual strategy of players.

1. Expert player looks ahead of ball that is coming to the player before the player receives the ball.
2. Expert player looks the opposed player side before the player receives the ball.

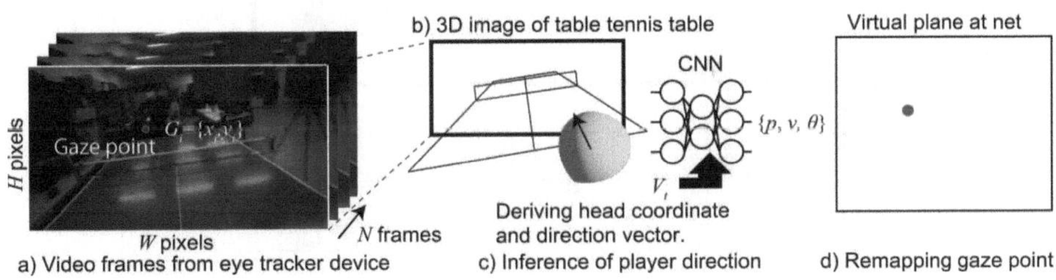

Fig. 2. Processing flow.

3 Remapping Method for Eye Tracking Dataset

3.1 Overview of Processing Flow

Figure 2 shows the processing flow when we apply our method to table tennis. We apply a dataset $D_i = \{P_i, G_i\}$ captured by an eye tracking device where P_i is video frame and G_i is a gaze coordinate in the i-th video frame. When the number of frames (i.e., video length) is N, $0 \leq i < N$. Here, the domain of coordinate $G_i = \{x_i, y_i\}$ is defined as $-W/2 \leq x_i < W/2$ and $-H/2 \leq y_i < H/2$ by the frame size $W \times H$ pixels. Our goal is to find mapped coordinates $p' = \{x'_i, y'_i\}$ in a virtual plane $V = \{x', y', c\}$ in the world coordinate system where c is a constant value of the depth.

3.2 Inferring Lines of Sight from Video Frames

The first step of the processing flow is inference of view directions from the video frames captured by an eye tracking device (Fig. 2 a)). We apply CNN to infer the directions and positions of the viewpoints. It receives the video frames P_i and infers $D'_i = \{p'_i, v'_i, \theta'_i\}$ where p'_i is absolute position of player's head, v'_i is vector of the line of sight, and θ_i is rotation of video frame. For the training phase, we first prepare the training images V_t from a 3D model with varying the positions p, the direction v of the viewpoint and the rotation of video frame θ. Figure 2 b) shows a 3D model of table tennis court. The dataset $\{V_t, p, v, \theta\}$ is given to the training phase of the CNN. In the inference phase as shown in Fig. 2 c), the CNN receives the video frames P_i of the eye tracker device and infers a position p', a vector v' of the direction of viewpoint and a rotation of video frame θ' (i.e., rotation of v'). Here, note that $|v'| = 1$. The organization of the CNN is shown in Fig. 3. The network identifies the input video frame and infers the point of player's head, the direction of viewpoint and the rotation of the video frame by combining convolutions and fully connected layer.

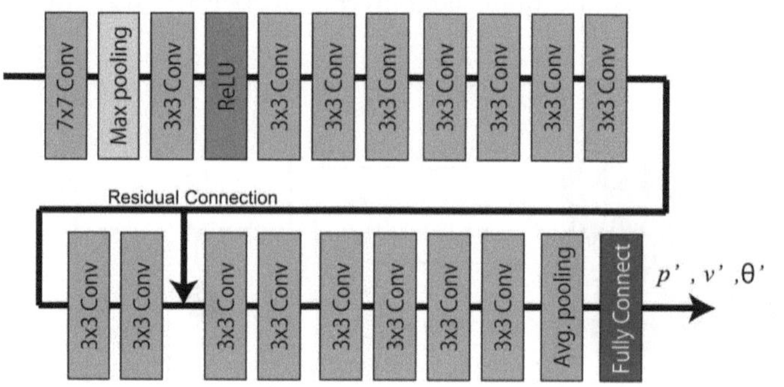

Fig. 3. Neural network used for inference of directions of viewpoints from video frames.

Here, let us discuss a key technique to prepare the 3D model for training images. In sports activity, there is rule regarding the playing fields. In the case of table tennis, white lines in the table are characteristics. If the playing field includes this kind of characteristics in the view image, the inference accuracy should become remarkable. Therefore, we can apply our method to the other sports also. For example, when we want to analyze visual-motor integration mechanism of a batter in baseball, the video frame captured by eye tracking device from the batter box should include lines among bases in the playing field. When we provide images generated from 3D model of the baseball field for

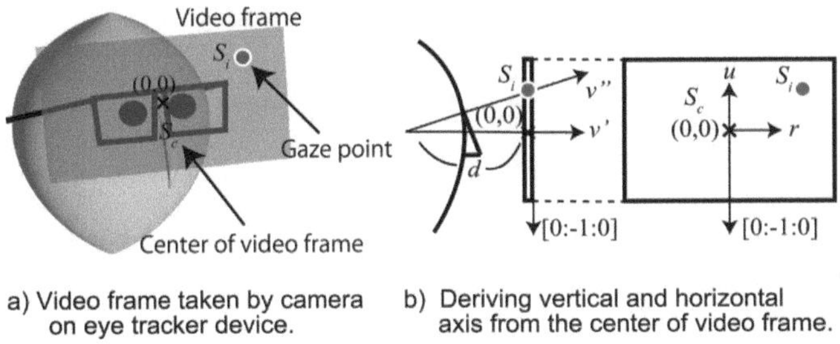

Fig. 4. Vector transformation with considerationof distance between eye tracker glass and iris.

the training phase, the CNN can infer directions of viewpoints and positions of batter's head in high accuracy.

Now, we have derived probable direction vectors from viewpoints of video frames in the world coordinate system. However, the vector directs to the center of each video frame. Because the gaze coordinate in a frame can differ from the center, we need to correct the direction vector. In the next step, we explain the correction algorithm that maps the gaze coordinate to a virtual plane in the world coordinate system.

3.3 Mapping Gaze Coordinate to a Virtual Plane

Figure 2 d) shows the virtual plane V and a mapped gaze point (the red point). We seem to derive the absolute direction of the line of sight by just shifting the inferred vector from CNN to the gaze point in the plane. However, it is not correct. Here, we need to consider that players wear the eye tracker, which is glasses. There is a distance between the glass and the player's iris as depicted in Fig. 4 a). Applying the following transformation as shown in Fig. 4 b), we derive the corrected vector of the gaze direction v'' and finally we derive the gaze point in the virtual screen S_i. First, we need to find the center of a video frame in front of player's face. The center point of the frame S_c is derived from the inferred v', p' and θ'. Here, we assume that the camera is placed on the vector v'. S_c is calculated by the following equation.

$$S_c = p' + d \times v'$$

where d is a constant value of distance between the center of head and screen. We can approximately decide d by manually comparing available view size in video frame and the distance from head to the frame. Next, we derive the plane of the video frame from vertical vectors r and u using cross products of v'' as follows.

$$r = (0, -1, 0) \times v'$$
$$u = v' \times r.$$

Additionally, we apply the rotation of video frame θ' as follows.

$$r' = \cos\theta' \times r + \sin\theta' \times u$$

$$u' = -\sin\theta' \times r + \cos\theta' \times u.$$

Finally, we can map $S_i = (x_i, y_i)$ to an absolute coordinate G_i in the world coordinate system as follows.

$$G_i = (x_i \times w/W, x_i \times h/H)$$

where W and H are the numbers of pixels of the frame and w and h are the actual size such as in meter. Here, because $S_c = (0, 0)$, the actual gaze point in the video frame is derived as follows.

$$S_i = S_c + G_i.x \times r' + G_i.y \times u' = p' + d \times v' + G_i.x \times r' + G_i.y \times u'$$

where u' and r' are the transformed vectors of u and r based on actual size like G_i. Now, because the vector directed from p' to S_i corresponds to v''. we can derive v'' as follows.

$$v'' = (S_i - p')/\sqrt{(S_i - p') \times (S_i - p')}.$$

Finally, the corrected gaze direction has been mapped to a virtual plane in world coordinate system. A crosspoint p' of the corrected vector v'' and the virtual plane V is derived as shown in Fig. 2 d) according to the equation below.

$$x'_i = \frac{c}{v''_z} \cdot v''_x,$$

$$y'_i = \frac{c}{v''_z} \cdot v''_y.$$

The points p'' plotted in the virtual plane show a set of absolute coordinates mapped to the plane. Therefore, we can analyze the visual strategy combining with the motor control information. In the next section, let us apply our proposed method to experimental analysis regarding table tennis rally. And we try to observe the visual-motor integration during the rallies with finding the reasons of the hypotheses exampled in Sect. 2.3.

4 Experimental Evaluation

4.1 Experimental Setup

The dataset used in the evaluations were taken from experiments of table tennis rally. It was performed in a lab with a standard table compliant to the international rule (2.74 m (9 ft.) long, 1.525 m (5 ft.) wide and 0.76 m (2.5 ft.) high). Three male players participated in the experiments. Two of these players were experts and the rest was in semi-advanced. In the experiments, one player wears an eye tracker device (Tobii glasses 2) and the opposed player just received/returned the ball. We call the player with the device *subjective player* in this section. One of the experts performed as just the opposed player. We took datasets in two cases; one was the case when the subjective player was an expert, another was the one when it was the semi-advanced player. From the eye tracker device, we can take video in HD resolution (1920 width, 1080 height) at 25 Hz and the gaze coordinates at every frame. We marked video frames of serving timings by the subjective player manually.

We developed our proposed method in a desktop machine of AMD Ryzen 5500GT with a GPU NVIDIA RTX5080 and 32GB DDR4 DRAM. The program was developed by Python with PyTorch 2.7.1 and NumPy 2.1.2 libraries. The 3D model was developed by AviUtl ver 1.10.

4.2 Demonstration of Mapped Gaze Coordinates

We applied the datasets taken from the eye tracker device during the table tennis rallies to our proposed method. First, we have made a 3D model of the table as shown in Fig. 5 using AviUtl. We generated 2D images for the training phase of the CNN with changing the viewpoints. Because the number of possible viewpoints is almost infinite if we do not give any restriction in moving area of the subjective player, we applied the following conditions to the coordinates of the viewpoints.

$$
\begin{aligned}
&-0.80 \leq p'_x \leq 0.80 \text{ (m)} \\
&0.50 \leq p'_y \leq 1.00 \text{ (m)} \\
&-2.00 \leq p'_z \leq -1.37 \text{ (m)} \\
&-1 \leq v'_x \leq 1, \quad -1 \leq v'_y \leq 0, \quad 0 \leq v'_z \leq 1 \\
&\text{subject to} \quad \|\mathbf{v}'\| = 1 \\
&-15^\circ \leq \theta' \leq 15^\circ.
\end{aligned}
$$

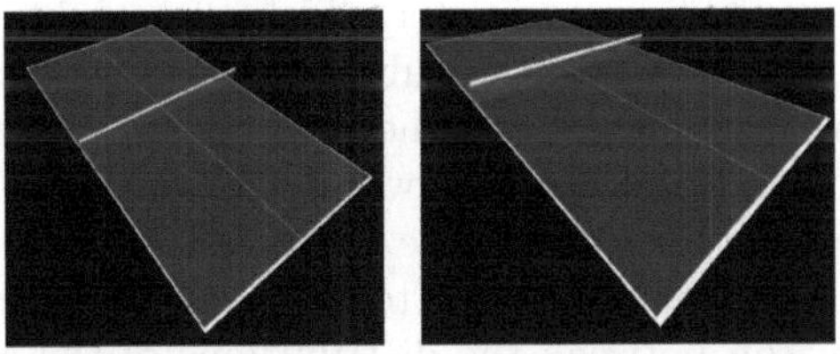

Fig. 5. 3D model of table tennis table generated by AviUtl and viewpoint examples.

During the training phase of the CNN that infers D', we evaluated the inference performance by comparing mean square error (MSE) (also known as L2 error) used in the loss function. Figure 6 shows the error during the training

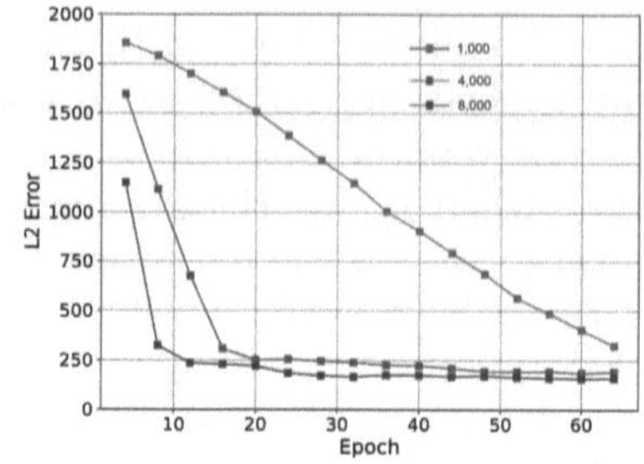

Fig. 6. L2 error (MSE error) during training phase for the CNN with varying the number of epochs when the number of training images is 1K, 4K and 8K.

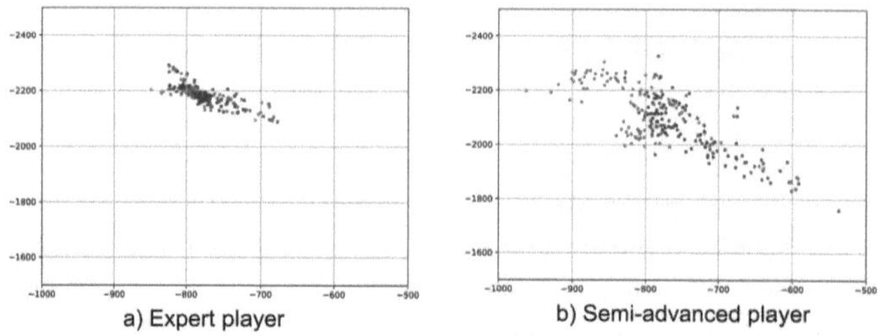

Fig. 7. Examples of mapping gaze points to the virtual plane and virtual planes with all gaze points of two videos.

phase when the number of the training images varies 1K to 8K. When the number of the images increases, the inference performance saturates faster. Thus, we confirmed that our CNN model can infer the predicted vector D'.

During our experiment, we put the virtual plane at the center net on the table. We applied the parameters $d = 0.240\,\text{m}$, $w = 0.040\,\text{m}$ and $h = 0.025\,\text{m}$ to derive the mapped gaze points in the video frame. The graphs in Fig. 7 show examples of the gaze points derived from the remapped vectors to the virtual plane. The axes are shown in centimeter which the origin is in the center net. Figure 7 a) shows the case when the subjective player was the expert player. Figure 7 b) shows the case when it was the semi-advanced player. The red points in the virtual plane are the gaze points when the opposed player returns to the subjective one. The blue points are vice versa. We confirmed that the coordinates in the virtual planes are matched to the gaze points in the frame images. According to comparison between the distributions of the red and blue points, we can confirm that there are different characteristics of distributions between the players. Now, let us explain the hypotheses we have introduced.

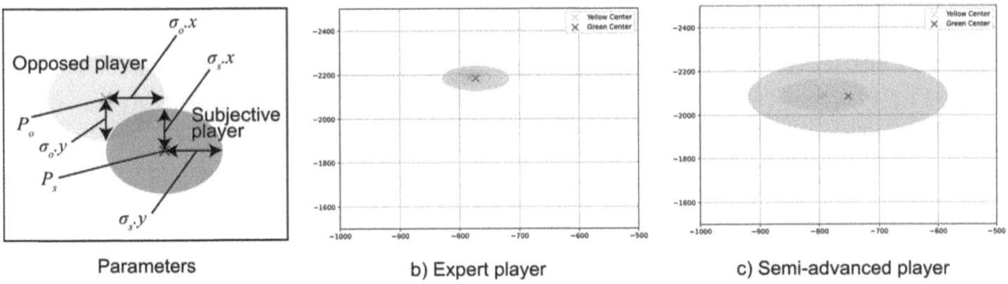

Fig. 8. The parameters for evaluating the hypothesis, and the average values and the ellipse illustrated in the virtual plane.

4.3 Explanations of Hypotheses

First, we show how to explain the following hypothesis.

> Expert player looks ahead of ball that is coming to the player before the player receives the ball.

This is related to the behaviors of ball and response of the subjective player. We analyze the gaze points P_s and P_o mapped to the virtual plane in the cases when the ball is placed in the territories of the subjective/opposed players respectively (i.e., P_s and P_o include half number of the blue/red points in Fig. 7 regarding the expert and semi-advanced players respectively). During the experience, the total number of rallies was nine. Here, a rally consists of video frames from a serve movement to its return one between the subjective and the opposed players. The center frame was specified when the ball crosses the territories according to the frame between the ones at serving and receiving. The ball in the center frame is placed almost on top of the net. We use P_s^i and P_o^i for the gaze points regarding the i-th rally of the subjective and the opposed player respectively, where $(1 \leq i \leq 9)$. To explain the hypothesis, we derived those averages $\overline{P_s^i}$ and $\overline{P_o^i}$, standard deviations σ_s^i and σ_o^i as follows.

$$\overline{P_s^i} = \left\{ \frac{1}{N_s^i} \sum_{k=0}^{N_s^i} P_s^i.x, \frac{1}{N_s^i} \sum_{k=0}^{N_s^i} P_s^i.y \right\}, \overline{P_o^i} = \left\{ \frac{1}{N_o^i} \sum_{k=0}^{N_o^i} P_o^i.x, \frac{1}{N_o^i} \sum_{k=0}^{N_o^i} P_o^i.y \right\}$$

$$\sigma_s^i = \left\{ \sqrt{\frac{1}{N_s^i} \sum_{k=0}^{N_s^i} (P_s^i.x - \overline{P_s^i}.x)}, \sqrt{\frac{1}{N_s^i} \sum_{k=0}^{N_s^i} (P_s^i.y - \overline{P_s^i}.y)} \right\}$$

$$\sigma_o^i = \left\{ \sqrt{\frac{1}{N_o^i} \sum_{k=0}^{N_o^i} (P_o^i.x - \overline{P_o^i}.x)}, \sqrt{\frac{1}{N_o^i} \sum_{k=0}^{N_o^i} (P_o^i.y - \overline{P_o^i}.y)} \right\}$$

where N_s^i and N_o^i are the numbers of frames in P_s^i and P_o^i respectively. These parameters are summarized in Fig. 8 a). Here, we plot the average points and draw ellipses centered at the average points in a graph as shown in Fig. 8 b), where the subjective/opposed players are colorized by green and yellow respectively. The ellipses C_s^i and C_o^i of the subjective and the objective players at the i-th rally are derived by the following equations respectively.

$$C_s^i : \frac{(x - \overline{P_s^i}.x)^2}{(\sigma_s^i.x)^2} + \frac{(y - \overline{P_s^i}.y)^2}{(\sigma_s^i.y)^2} = 1, C_o^i : \frac{(x - \overline{P_o^i}.x)^2}{(\sigma_o^i.x)^2} + \frac{(y - \overline{P_o^i}.y)^2}{(\sigma_o^i.y)^2} = 1.$$

The ellipses mean distribution of player's gaze points. In the other word, when the player returns/receives the ball, the sight domain is where the player is looking around. The graphs of all rallies are illustrated in Fig. 9 for the expert and Fig. 10 for the semi-advanced player. According to the graphs, we can observe two characteristics; 1) the gaze points of the expert player are in smaller ellipses than the semi-advanced one. Especially, the green ellipses of the expert player, which is the case when the ball is staying in the territory of the subjective player, are obviously smaller than the ones of the semi-advanced player. 2) The ellipses in the graphs of the expert player show higher position than the semi-advanced one. Because the graph shows the virtual plane at the net, the expert player was always looking at the opposite one. According to these characteristics, we can conclude that the advanced player foresights the places where the ball would come without extending the gaze area.

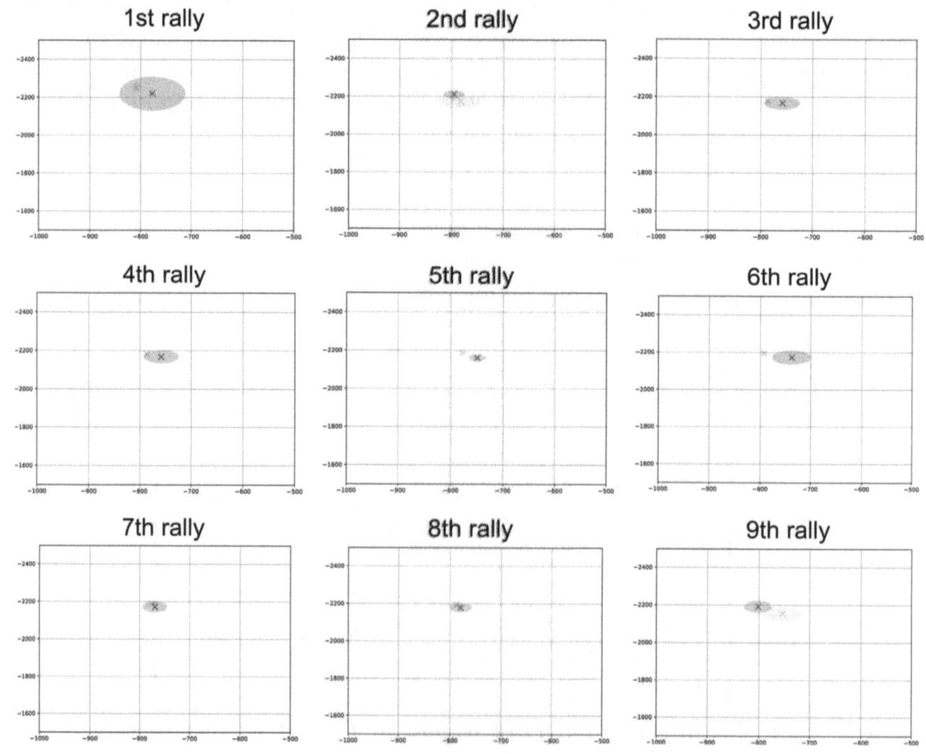

Fig. 9. Ellipses of P_s and P_o regarding all rallies of the expert player.

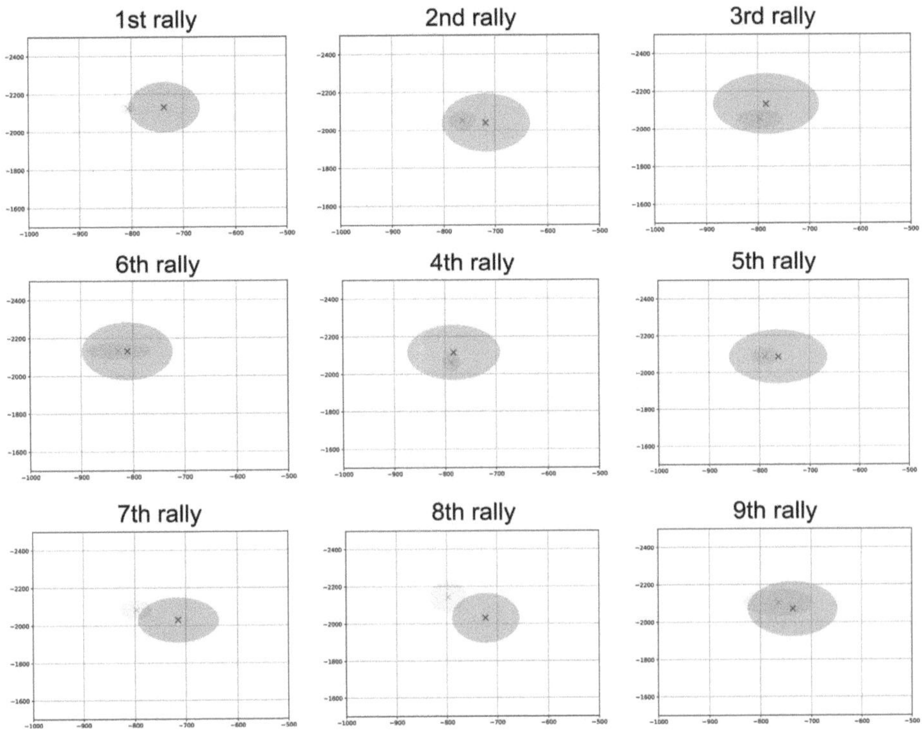

Fig. 10. Ellipses of P_s and P_o regarding all rallies of the semi-advanced player.

Table 1. Average distributions of P_s and P_o regarding x and y axes.

Subjective player	$D_s.x$	$D_s.y$	$D_o.x$	$D_o.y$
Expert	1535.916	1578.754	579.328	758.061
Semi-advanced	7725.567	20410.301	1900.976	3935.523

Additionally, we compared the distributions between P_s and P_o (i.e. $D_s = \sigma_s^2$ and $D_o = \sigma_o^2$). We derived averages of D_s and D_o regarding x and y axes separately. Table 1 shows the comparison. The average distributions of the expert players were stable whenever the ball was staying in any place. However, the ones of semi-advanced player showed a difference between P_s and P_o. When the ball was staying in the subjective player's side, the gaze points distributed widely. Therefore, we can conclude that the gaze points of the expert player do not move largely during serving and receiving the ball.

In summary from the discussion above, we confirmed that the expert player did not move the gaze area when the ball was staying in the subjective player's territory. This means that the expert player looks ahead of ball that is coming to the player before the player receives the ball. Thus, we can explain the hypothesis

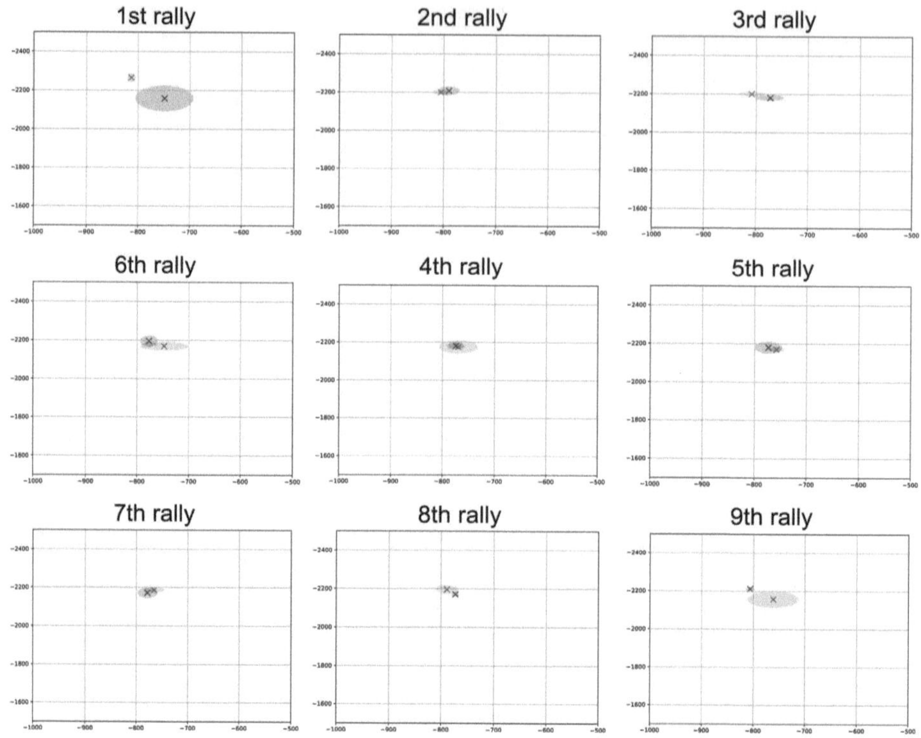

Fig. 11. Ellipses of P'_s and P'_o regarding all rallies of the expert player.

Table 2. Average distributions of P'_s and P'_o regarding x and y axes.

Subjective player	$D'_s.x$	$D'_s.y$	$D'_o.x$	$D'_o.y$
Expert	772.877	1044.719	1344.154	1267.022
Semi-advanced	3797.056	10110.858	2889.999	8650.017

according to the remapped points in the virtual plane derived by our proposed method.

Next, let us explain the second hypothesis below.

Expert player looks the opposed player side before the player receives the ball.

For this hypothesis, we define P'^i_s and P'^i_o as the video frames from the timing when the subjective/opposed player hits the ball to the one when the opposed/subjective player receives it. When a player hits the ball at the j-th frame and another player returns the ball at the k-th frame, the numbers of video frames N'^i_s and N'^i_o of P'^i_s and P'^i_o respectively in the i-th rally are derived by $k - j$. As well as the analysis regarding the previous hypothesis, we also derived the averages and the standard deviations based on P'^i_s and P'^i_o and drawn the

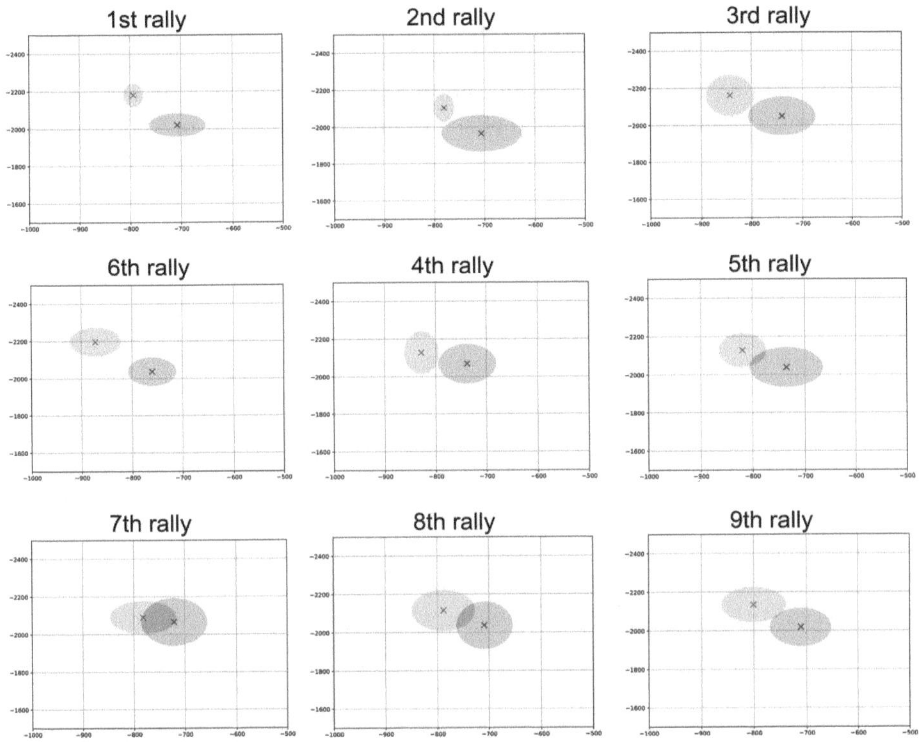

Fig. 12. Ellipses of P'_s and P'_o regarding all rallies of the semi-advanced player.

ellipses at every rally based on the distributions as shown in Fig. 11 for the expert and Fig. 12 for the semi-advanced player. In the graphs, the red ellipse shows the domain of the gaze points in the virtual plane while the opposed player returns the ball to the subjective one. The blue ellipse shows vice versa. Regarding the expert player, three rallies in the beginning show different relations between the red and the blue ellipses than the other rallies. That is, the expert player looked at the opposed player right after retuning the ball at the fourth and the later rallies. On the other hand, the semi-advanced player looked at the position of the ball during the rallies. Thus, we confirmed that the expert player looks at the side of the opposed player when the player hits the ball.

Additionally, we compared the averages of the distributions $D'_s = \sigma'^i_s$ and $D'_o = \sigma'^i_o$ of all rallies as shown in Table 2. We confirmed that the average of the distributions regarding the semi-advanced player is quite larger than the one regarding the expert player. This means that the expert player was looking at a narrow area where the expert player was going to return the ball right after the returning shot.

According to the discussion above, we can explain the hypothesis because the expert player switches gaze to the target place where the returned ball is going right after hitting the ball.

In summary, through the evaluations in this section regarding our proposed method and the analysis for the hypotheses, we confirmed that our remapping method worked to explain the visual-motor integration during sports activity. Thus, we have provided a simple and effective machine learning method to remap dynamically the measured gaze positions by eye tracking device to an absolute virtual plane in the world coordinate system.

5 Conclusions

We focused on the dataset measured by eye tracking device during sports activity and proposed a machine learning method to remap the gaze points to a virtual plane in the world coordinate system. The method was easily applied to identify the viewpoints induced by CNN-based method. In the training phase, the amount of training images made from a 3D model of the sports field. In this paper, we applied to the method to a table tennis rally. However, we can also apply it to the other sports such as baseball, basketball and volleyball because these examples have clear lines in the field. The lines can become a very good characteristics to infer the scenes of video frames because the video captured by the eye tracking device includes those characterized lines in the playing field. We tried to explain realistic analysis of two hypotheses in the table tennis rally to find the visual-motor integration. The mapped gaze points represent the difference between the expert and the semi-advanced players. Therefore, our method can become reasonable and useful tool for finding cognitive phenomenon in the sports science field.

For the future works, we are planning to optimize our method in the aspect of the training phase of the CNN. Now, we need to adjust the inference accuracy depending on the number of the training images. However, the number of the images affects to the tradeoff between the processing time and the accuracy. We should optimize this issue. Additionally, we are going to apply the other analysis regarding the visual-motor integrations such as a relation of gaze points and body behavior in batting techniques in baseball.

Acknowledgements. This research was funded in part by Research Grant of Advanced Research Initiative for Human High Performance (ARIHHP), the University of Tsukuba, and JSPS KAKENHI (Grant Number 24K22330).

References

1. Aksum, K.M., Magnaguagno, L., Bjorndal, C.T., Jordet, G.: What do football players look at? an eye-tracking analysis of the visual fixations of players in 11 v 11 elite football match play. Front. Psychol. **11**, 562995 (2020). https://doi.org/10.3389/fpsyg.2020.562995
2. Buscemi, A., Mondelli, F., Biagini, I., Gueli, S., D'Agostino, A., Coco, M.: Role of sport vision in performance: systematic review. J. Funct. Morphol. Kinesiol. **9**(2, 92) (2024). https://doi.org/10.3390/jfmk9020092

3. Cummins, M., Newman, P.: FAB-MAP: probabilistic localization and mapping in the space of appearance. Int. J. Robot. Res. **27**(6), 647–665 (2008). https://doi.org/10.1177/0278364908090961
4. Decroix, M., Wazir, M.R.W.N., Zeuwts, L., Deconinck, F.F., Lenoir, M., Vansteenkiste, P.: Expert – Non-expert differences in visual behaviour during alpine slalom skiing. Hum. Mov. Sci. **55**, 229–239 (2017). https://doi.org/10.1016/j.humov.2017.08.012
5. Han, M., Arede, J., Gómez Ruano, M.A., Lorenzo Calvo, J.: The role of gaze behavior in basketball shooting performance: a systematic review and meta-analysis of elite and near-elite players. Appl. Sci. **15**(7) (2025). https://doi.org/10.3390/app15073871
6. Kendall, A., Grimes, M., Cipolla, R.: PoseNet: a convolutional network for real-time 6-DOF camera relocalization . In: 2015 IEEE International Conference on Computer Vision (ICCV), pp. 2938–2946. IEEE Computer Society, Los Alamitos, CA, USA (2015). https://doi.org/10.1109/ICCV.2015.336
7. Kredel, R., Hernandez, J., Hossner, E.J., Zahno, S.: Eye-tracking technology and the dynamics of natural gaze behavior in sports: an update 2016–2022. Front. Psychol. **14**, 1130051 (2023). https://doi.org/10.3389/fpsyg.2017.01845
8. Kredel, R., Vater, C., Klostermann, A., Hossner, E.J.: Eye-tracking technology and the dynamics of natural gaze behavior in sports: a systematic review of 40 years of research. Front. Psychol. **8**, 1845 (2017). https://doi.org/10.3389/fpsyg.2017.01845
9. Lowe, D.G.: Distinctive image features from scale-invariant keypoints. Int. J. Comput. Vis. **60**, 91–110 (2004). https://doi.org/10.1023/B:VISI.0000029664.99615.94
10. Meyer, J., Smeeton, N.J., Fasold, F., Schul, K., Schön, T., Klatt, S.: Shot deception in basketball: gaze and anticipation strategy in defence. Hum. Mov. Sci. **84**, 102975 (2022). https://doi.org/10.1016/j.humov.2022.102975
11. Rosker, J., Majcen Rosker, Z.: Skill level in tennis serve return is related to adaptability in visual search behavior. Front. Psychol. **12**, 689378 (2021). https://doi.org/10.3389/fpsyg.2021.689378
12. Sun, L., Song, M., Liu, Z., Sun, M.T.: Realtime gaze estimation with online calibration. In: 2014 IEEE International Conference on Multimedia and Expo (ICME), pp. 1–6 (2014). https://doi.org/10.1109/ICME.2014.6890322
13. Wang, J., Zha, H., Cipolla, R.: Coarse-to-fine vision-based localization by indexing scale-invariant features. IEEE Trans. Syst. Man Cybern. B (Cybernetics) **36**(2), 413–422 (2006). https://doi.org/10.1109/TSMCB.2005.859085
14. Zhang, M., Liu, Y., LU, F.: GazeOnce: real-time multi-person gaze estimation . In: 2022 IEEE/CVF Conference on Computer Vision and Pattern Recognition (CVPR), pp. 4187–4196. IEEE Computer Society, Los Alamitos, CA, USA (2022). https://doi.org/10.1109/CVPR52688.2022.00416

DeepET-SOD: Adaptive Confidence Threshold Re-Detection for Small Object Detection in High-Altitude Drone Imagery on Embedded Edge Device

Seojin Jang, Wei Liu, and Yongbeom Cho(✉)

DeepET Inc., Seoul, South Korea
ybcho@deep-et.com

Abstract. Small object detection in high-altitude drone imagery suffers from detection flickering—where objects are intermittently detected and missed across consecutive frames due to marginal confidence scores near the decision threshold. This paper proposes DeepET-SOD, a detection system that addresses this issue through: (1) RT-DETR-based detection with SAHI (Slicing Aided Hyper Inference) for improved small object feature extraction, (2) an Adaptive Confidence Threshold (ACT) module that monitors per-slice detection history and unlocks low-confidence detections when anomalous count drops are detected, and (3) a spatiotemporal tracking module with prediction-based compensation. Experiments on VisDrone-MOT2021 (all 10 classes) demonstrate that DeepET-SOD achieves 67.8% mAP@0.5 and 42.1% AP for small objects, representing improvements of 6.6 and 4.0 percentage points over the RT-DETR+SAHI baseline respectively. The Detection Flickering Rate is reduced from 10.8% to 4.6%. Importantly, all results are obtained fully on-device without server offloading, validating practical deployability on an embedded edge board. On an embedded NVIDIA Jetson AGX Orin (TensorRT FP16), DeepET-SOD sustains real-time-capable throughput with 320 ms true end-to-end latency (8-frame batch), demonstrating deployable on-board inference for real-world drone analytics.

Keywords: Small object detection · adaptive threshold · drone imagery · detection flickering · SAHI · RT-DETR

1 Introduction

Object detection from drone platforms has become essential for traffic monitoring, agricultural management, and surveillance applications [1]. However, small object detection in high-altitude imagery presents persistent challenges that limit practical deployment.

The primary challenge stems from the limited pixel representation of distant objects. When a vehicle occupies only 10–30 pixels in a 4K drone image, the feature extraction process through successive downsampling layers results in severe information loss. Modern detectors including YOLOv8 [2] and RT-DETR [3] employ Feature Pyramid Networks (FPN) [4] and multi-scale detection heads to mitigate this issue, yet small objects

C. Xu (Ed.): ICMLSC 2026, CCIS 2948, pp. 392–401, 2027.
https://doi.org/10.1007/978-981-92-1546-1_32

remain significantly harder to detect than their larger counterparts—a gap consistently observed across benchmarks [5].

A particularly problematic manifestation is detection flickering: the same object is detected in frame t, missed in frame t + 1, and detected again in t + 2. This occurs because small objects with marginal confidence scores oscillate around the detection threshold due to minor variations in pose, illumination, or feature extraction. Detection flickering severely impacts object counting accuracy and tracking reliability, as illustrated in Fig. 2.

Slicing-based inference methods such as SAHI [6] improve small object detection by processing image crops at higher effective resolution. However, SAHI applies a uniform confidence threshold across all slices, ignoring spatial variation in detection reliability. Our analysis reveals that, under a specific detector configuration (RT-DETR + SAHI, T = 0.5), detection count variance differs significantly across image regions: center slices exhibit lower frame-to-frame variance compared to edge slices (Table 1). While this observation is detector-dependent, we find consistent trends across different detectors (Sect. 4.4).

This observation motivates our key insight: when a slice that consistently detects N objects suddenly reports significantly fewer, this likely indicates detection failure rather than actual object departure—particularly for center slices where density tends to be more stable. In practical drone deployments, detection results must be generated on-board under limited compute and power budgets. In this embedded setting, re-running inference to recover missed detections is often infeasible, and detection flickering directly degrades real-time counting and tracking reliability. Therefore, we target an approach that improves temporal consistency without additional inference passes, explicitly validated on an embedded edge platform. Rather than re-running inference, we propose unlocking lower-confidence detections that were already computed but filtered by the threshold.

We propose DeepET-SOD (Fig. 1) with three contributions:

1) An Adaptive Confidence Threshold (ACT) module that maintains per-slice detection history, detects anomalous count drops, and unlocks low-confidence detections with region-aware thresholds—without requiring additional inference passes.
2) Track-guided position validation using a lightweight Kalman filter buffer (not a full tracker) that filters unlocked detections by proximity to predicted positions, controlling false positives even when previous frames missed the object.
3) We provide embedded on-device characterization on NVIDIA Jetson AGX Orin, reporting true end-to-end latency and throughput under a realistic compute budget (TensorRT FP16), and separating output modes for clear metric attribution.

2 Related Work

2.1 Small Object Detection

Small object detection challenges arise from multiple factors: feature dilution through downsampling, foreground-background imbalance, and insufficient contextual information. Multi-scale approaches including FPN [4], PANet [7], and BiFPN [8] fuse features across resolutions. SNIPER [9] normalizes scale during training. SAHI [6] employs test-time slicing to increase effective resolution. Our work builds upon SAHI by adding adaptive threshold adjustment based on detection history.

2.2 Detection Confidence and Calibration

Neural network confidence calibration was established by Guo et al. [10] for classification. Küppers et al. [11] extended calibration analysis to object detection, showing that small objects exhibit particularly poor calibration. Neumann et al. [12] proposed relaxed softmax for pedestrian detection. Our ACT module takes a complementary approach: rather than recalibrating confidence globally, we adaptively adjust acceptance thresholds per-slice based on local detection history.

2.3 Multi-object Tracking

SORT [13] and DeepSORT [14] combine Kalman filtering with Hungarian matching. ByteTrack [15] associates low-confidence detections through two-stage matching. OC-SORT [16] handles occlusion through observation-centric recovery. Milan et al. [17] established MOT benchmark methodology. Our tracking module follows ByteTrack's two-stage association strategy and differs by generating virtual detections only when ACT fails.

3 Methodology

Figure 1 shows the DeepET-SOD pipeline. We describe the detection and slicing strategy, the ACT module with track-guided validation, and the tracking component.

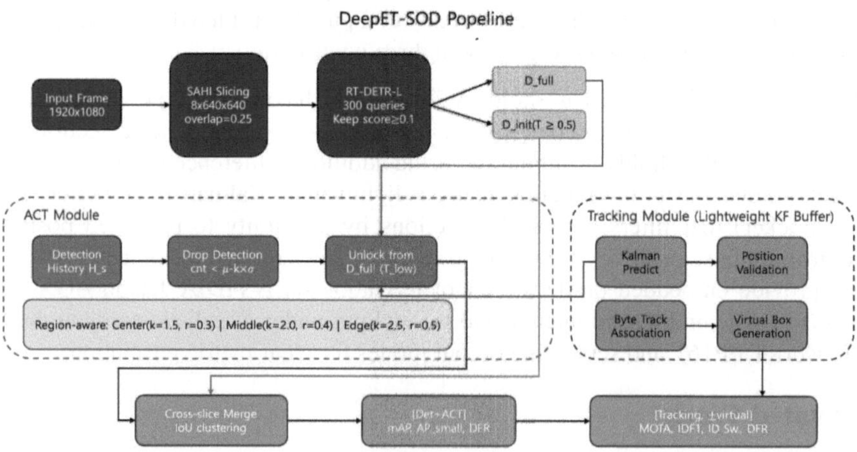

Fig. 1. DeepET-SOD pipeline. Input frames are sliced (SAHI), processed by RT-DETR retaining all query outputs (D_full). ACT monitors detection history and unlocks low-confidence detections when drops are detected. A lightweight KF buffer provides predicted positions for position validation. Three output modes enable clear metric attribution.

3.1 Base Detector and Slicing Strategy

We employ RT-DETR-L [3] as the base detector. RT-DETR is an end-to-end real-time detector that eliminates NMS through learned object queries. It uses a HGNetv2 backbone and hybrid encoder. In our implementation, we use 300 decoder queries and retain all query predictions before score thresholding—this enables ACT to unlock low-confidence detections without additional inference.

Following SAHI [6], we divide input images into overlapping slices:

- Input resolution: 1920 × 1080 (original drone frame)
- Slice size: 640 × 640 pixels; Overlap: 0.25; Grid: 4 × 2 = 8 slices
- Base confidence threshold T_base: 0.5

Inference settings: For single-pass baselines, we follow each detector's standard 640 × 640 letterbox input. For SAHI methods, we run 8 crops per frame. We report true end-to-end latency under each method's compute budget.

Each slice is processed by RT-DETR, outputting predictions for all 300 queries. We keep per-query predictions with score ≥0.1 before slice-level merging (D_full); unlocked detections go through the same cross-slice IoU clustering (threshold 0.5, confidence-weighted averaging) as D_init.

3.2 Region Classification and Detection Variance

We classify slices by normalized distance from image center as shown in Eq. (1):

$$d(s) = \frac{||\text{center(s)} - \text{center(image)}||_2}{(0.5 \times \text{diagonal})} \tag{1}$$

Region classification is defined by the following rule (Eq. (2)).

$$region(s) = \begin{cases} Center, d(s) < 0.3 \\ Middel, 0.3 \leq 0.6 \\ Edge, d(s) \geq 0.6 \end{cases} \tag{2}$$

Table 1. Detection Count Variance by Region

Region	Mean Count/Slice	Frame-to-Frame CV	Drop Event Rate
Center	8.42 ± 3.21	0.127	3.2%
Middle	6.15 ± 4.87	0.184	7.8%
Edge	4.28 ± 5.12	0.256	15.4%

RT-DETR + SAHI (T = 0.5) on VisDrone-MOT2021 train + val (56 sequences, 24,201 frames). CV: Coefficient of Variation. Drop: > 30% count decrease.

Table 1 shows detection variance under RT-DETR + SAHI. Center slices exhibit lower variance (CV = 0.127) than edge slices (CV = 0.256). This trend is consistent across detectors (Table 7) under the same slicing scheme (8 × 640, overlap 0.25) and base threshold (T = 0.5).

3.3 Adaptive Confidence Threshold (ACT) Module

1) Per-Slice Detection History:

For each slice s, we maintain buffer as in Eq. (3).

$$H_s = \{cnt_s^{(t-N)}, \ldots, cnt_s^{(t-1)}\} \quad (3)$$

We compute per-slice statistics in Eqs. (4–5).

$$\mu_s = mean(H_s) \quad (4)$$

$$\sigma_s = std(H_s) \quad (5)$$

2) Drop Detection and Unlocking:

A drop is triggered when the conditions in Eq. (6) are satisfied.

$$Trigger(s, t) = (|H_s| \geq 5\, and\, \mu_s > 1)\, and\, (cnt_s^{(t)} < \max(1, \mu_s - k\sigma_s)) \quad (6)$$

Unlocked detections are defined as Eq. (7).

$$D_{unlocked} = \{d \epsilon D_{full} : T_{low} \leq score(d) < T_{base}\} \quad (7)$$

The lowered threshold is computed by Eq. (8).

$$T_{low} = T_{base} \cdot \gamma \quad (8)$$

Parameters by region: Center (k = 1.5, r = 0.3, T_low = 0.15), Middle (k = 2.0, r = 0.4, T_low = 0.20), Edge (k = 2.5, r = 0.5, T_low = 0.25) (Table 2).

Table 2. Region-Specific ACT Parameters

Region	k (drop threshold)	r (threshold factor)	T_low = 0.5 × r
Center	1.5	0.30	0.15
Middle	2.0	0.40	0.20
Edge	2.5	0.50	0.25

This design is particularly suitable for embedded deployment because ACT reuses already computed query outputs to recover misses without additional inference passes.

3.4 Spatiotemporal Tracking Module

For full tracking output modes, we extend the KF buffer to a complete tracker. Following ByteTrack's two-stage association [15]: (1) high-confidence detections ($c \geq 0.5$) match

Active tracks via IoU-based Hungarian matching (IoU $\geq$ 0.3); (2) unmatched tracks match remaining detections (0.1 $\leq$ c < 0.5).

Virtual detection generation: For unmatched Active tracks, generate virtual boxes at KF-predicted positions if miss_count $\leq$ 30. Virtual detections are flagged (is_virtual = True) and excluded from detection metrics.

Batch processing (B = 8, no pipelining): Frames accumulate until batch full, then execute sequentially. Latency: 267 ms (batch delay) + 53 ms/frame $\times$ 8 $\approx$ 320 ms end-to-end. Throughput: ~10 FPS.

3.5 Detection Examples

4 Experiments

4.1 Experimental Setup

Dataset: VisDrone-MOT2021 [5] provides temporally consistent instance IDs required for DFR evaluation. We use train + val splits (56 sequences, 24,201 frames) for variance analysis and test split (17 sequences, 6,635 frames) for final evaluation. For detection-only metrics (mAP), we additionally use VisDrone-DET2021 (6,471 images). All 10 classes are evaluated.

Implementation: PyTorch 2.0, RT-DETR-L fine-tuned on VisDrone for 100 epochs.

Hardware: Jetson AGX Orin (TensorRT FP16).

Embedded deployment setting: All evaluations are performed on an NVIDIA Jetson AGX Orin embedded board using TensorRT FP16. We measure end-to-end latency including slicing (8 crops), detector inference, slice merging, ACT unlocking, and tracking association. This setting reflects practical on-device constraints where additional inference passes are costly.

4.2 Metrics and Output Modes

Detection: mAP@0.5, AP_small (< 322 pixels) per COCO protocol.

We define DFR as in Eq. (9).

$$DFR = \frac{|\{GT\ tracks\ with\ \geq 1 flicker\}|}{|\{GT\ Tracks \geq 10 frames\}|} \tag{9}$$

A flicker = detected $\rightarrow$ undetected $\rightarrow$ detected within 5 frames. GT $\leftrightarrow$ detection matching: greedy IoU $\geq$ 0.5, one-to-one per frame. Tie-break: higher detection score wins; unmatched GT = undetected.

Tracking: MOTA, IDF1, ID switches per MOTChallenge.

Three output modes for clear attribution:

1) [Det + ACT]: Detector + ACT outputs. Uses internal KF buffer for validation but outputs no track IDs. Reports: mAP, AP_small, DFR.
2) [Tracking, no virtual]: Full tracker with IDs, excludes virtual boxes. Reports: DFR, MOTA, IDF1, ID Sw.
3) [Tracking, + virtual]: Full system with interpolation. DFR artificially lower due to gap-filling.

(a) Person detection in construction site (high-altitude oblique view)

(b) Vehicle detection on highway interchange (urban drone footage)

(c) Dense vehicle detection at intersection

Fig. 2. Detection examples from drone imagery. Small objects (10–30 pixels) are common in high-altitude scenarios. Detection flickering occurs when marginal confidence scores oscillate near the threshold.

4.3 Main Results

See Tables 3 and 4.

Table 3. Detection Performance on VisDrone (All 10 Classes)

Method	mAP @0.5	mAP @.5:.95	AP_small	Latency
YOLOv8m (640, single-pass)	51.8	32.1	22.4	26 ms
RT-DETR-L (640, single-pass)	53.7	34.1	28.3	36 ms
YOLOv8m + SAHI (8 × 640)	58.4	37.2	34.6	83 ms
RT-DETR-L + SAHI (8 × 640)	61.2	40.8	38.1	91 ms
DeepET-SOD [Det + ACT]	67.8	45.6	42.1	320 ms

All results are measured on Jetson AGX Orin (TensorRT FP16). DeepET-SOD uses batch processing ($B = 8$); the reported 320 ms latency includes batch delay, corresponding to ~10 FPS effective throughput.

Table 4. Temporal Consistency on VisDrone-MOT2021 Test

Method	DFR (↓)	MOTA (↑)	IDF1 (↑)	ID Sw. (↓)
RT-DETR-L + SAHI + ByteTrack	10.8%	51.2	61.5	1654
DeepET-SOD [Det+ACT only]	4.6%	—	—	—
DeepET-SOD [Tracking, no virtual]	3.8%	57.8	67.2	924
DeepET-SOD [Tracking, +virtual]	1.8%*	61.7	72.3	634

*[Det + ACT only]: Internal KF buffer for validation, no output IDs → no MOTA/IDF1. *DFR artificially lower due to gap-filling Ablation Study.*

4.4 Ablation Study

See Tables 5 and 6.

Table 5. Ablation on ACT Components [Det + ACT Mode]

Configuration	AP_small	ΔAP	DFR	FP ratio
RT-DETR + SAHI (baseline)	38.1	—	10.8%	1.00×
+Drop detection + unlock (uniform)	40.5	+2.4	6.8%	1.28×
+Region-aware parameters	41.2	+0.7	5.4%	1.15×
+Track-guided validation (KF buffer)	42.1	+0.9	4.6%	1.04×

Total: + 4.0 AP_small with only 4% FP increase. KF buffer is internal to ACT (no output IDs).

Table 6. Ablation on Tracking Components

Configuration	DFR	MOTA	IDF1	Latency
Det +ACT only (KF buffer, no IDs)	4.6%	—	—	100 ms (B = 1)
+Full tracker, no virtual (B = 8)	3.8%	57.8	67.2	320 ms
+Virtual boxes (B = 8)	1.8%	61.7	72.3	320 ms

"KF buffer, no IDs" = Det + ACT mode with internal buffer. AP_small = 42.1 unchanged (virtual boxes excluded).

Table 7. Detection Variance Across Detectors

Detector + SAHI	CV_center	CV_middle	CV_edge
RT-DETR-L + SAHI	0.127	0.184	0.256
YOLOv8m + SAHI	0.142	0.198	0.271
YOLOv8s + SAHI	0.156	0.212	0.289

All: same slicing (8 × 640, overlap 0.25), same $T = 0.5$ for each detector's outputs. Trend CV_center < CV_edge holds.

4.5 Discussion

DeepET-SOD [Det+ACT] improves over baseline by +6.6 mAP@0.5 and +4.0 AP_small. DFR reduces from 10.8% to 4.6%. RT-DETR's query-based design enables efficient threshold adjustment. Table 7 confirms variance trends hold across detectors. Limitations: 320 ms latency (B = 1 mode offers 100 ms), nadir camera assumption, VisDrone-tuned parameters. Overall, DeepET-SOD is suitable for embedded on-board deployment because it improves temporal consistency without extra inference cost.

5 Conclusion

We presented DeepET-SOD, addressing detection flickering through Adaptive Confidence Threshold unlocking. By maintaining per-slice history and unlocking low-confidence detections with region-aware thresholds—using a lightweight KF buffer for position validation without re-inference—we achieve +4.0 AP_small over baseline with DFR reduced from 10.8% to 4.6%. Three output modes (Det + ACT, Tracking no virtual, Tracking + virtual) ensure clear metric attribution. These results on Jetson AGX Orin confirm that DeepET-SOD is practically deployable for real-time on-board drone analytics under embedded constraints.

Acknowledgment. This work was supported by Korea Research Institute for Defense Technology Planning and Advancement (KRIT) under the Global Defense Industry Strong SME Fostering Program E230007.

List of Abbreviations

SOD Small Object Detection
ACT Adaptive Confidence Threshold
IoU Intersection over Union
NMS Non-Maximum Suppression
SAHI Slicing Aided Hyper Inference
FPN Feature Pyramid Networks
DFR Detection Flickering Rate

References

1. Zhu, P., et al.: Detection and tracking meet drones challenge. IEEE TPAMI **44**(11), 7380–7399 (2022)
2. Jocher, G., Qiu, J., Chaurasia, A.: Ultralytics YOLO (2023). https://github.com/ultralytics/ultralytics
3. Zhao, Y., et al.: DETRs beat YOLOs on real-time object detection. In: CVPR, pp. 16965–16974 (2024)
4. Lin, T.-Y., et al.: Feature pyramid networks for object detection. In: CVPR, pp. 2117–2125 (2017)
5. Cao, Y., et al.: VisDrone-DET2021: the vision meets drone object detection challenge results. In: ICCVW, pp. 2847–2854 (2021)
6. Akyon, F.C., et al.: Slicing aided hyper inference and fine-tuning for small object detection. In: ICIP, pp. 966–970 (2022)
7. Liu, S., et al.: Path aggregation network for instance segmentation. In: CVPR, pp. 8759–8768 (2018)
8. Tan, M., et al.: EfficientDet: scalable and efficient object detection. In: CVPR, pp. 10781–10790 (2020)
9. Singh, B., et al.: SNIPER: efficient multi-scale training. In: NeurIPS, vol. 31, pp. 9310–9320 (2018)
10. Guo, C. et al.: On calibration of modern neural networks. In: ICML, vol. 70, pp. 1321–1330 (2017)
11. Küppers, F., et al.: Multivariate confidence calibration for object detection. In: CVPRW, pp. 1322–1330 (2020)
12. Neumann, L., et al.: Relaxed softmax for pedestrian detection. In: NeurIPS Workshop MLITS (2018)
13. Bewley, A., et al.: Simple online and realtime tracking. In: ICIP, pp. 3464–3468 (2016)
14. Wojke, N., et al.: Simple online and realtime tracking with a deep association metric. In: ICIP, pp. 3645–3649 (2017)
15. Zhang, Y., et al.: ByteTrack: multi-object tracking by associating every detection box. In: Avidan, S., Brostow, G., Cissé, M., Farinella, G.M., Hassner, T. (eds.) ECCV 2022. LNCS, vol. 13682, pp. 1–21. Springer, Cham (2022). https://doi.org/10.1007/978-3-031-20047-2_1
16. Cao, J., et al.: Observation-centric SORT. In: CVPR, pp. 9686–9696 (2023)
17. Milan, A., et al.: MOT16: a benchmark for multi-object tracking. arXiv:1603.00831 (2016)

Intelligent Information Processing and Decision Optimization Empowered by Artificial Intelligence Technology

Pre-AF Imminence Detection Using Explainable Machine Learning on 30-s Single-Lead ECG

Chan-Woo Park[1], Jeong-Hyeon Gu[1], and Sedong Min[1,2](✉)

[1] Department of Medical IT Engineering, Soonchunhyang University, Asan, Republic of Korea
{pts903011,rnwjdgus03}@naver.com, sedongmin@sch.ac.kr
[2] Department of Software Convergence, Soonchunhyang University, Asan, Republic of Korea

Abstract. Atrial fibrillation (AF) is a common cardiac rhythm disorder, with a cumulative lifetime risk of approximately 30% after age 45. Consequently, early detection and imminence detection are clinically important. Previous studies relied on long windows of minutes to hours, multiple leads, and black-box deep learning models, leading to increased false positives and limiting real-time applicability and interpretability. This study aimed to capture patterns within a single 30-s ECG window immediately preceding onset and validate short-term imminence detection with transparent rationale. From the MIT-BIH AF database, we extracted the 30-s MLII interval immediately preceding AF and a rhythm matched control interval. After z-score normalization, we added spectral entropy (SE) feature to the raw waveform (7,500 samples). Group-disjoint splitting prevented subject leakage, and binary classification using an XGBoost model yielded an AUROC of 0.866, AUPRC of 0.94, and accuracy of 0.78 on an independent test set. Using an out-of-fold (OOF)–fixed threshold (thr = 0.77) derived to target specificity ≈ 0.95, the test set achieved specificity 0.90 and sensitivity 0.71.

Statistical validation showed SE was significantly lower in the pre-AF interval, suggesting increased rhythm regularity.

Grouped-SHAP analysis revealed dominant importance in the 29.5–30.0 s interval (with a secondary peak at 24.5–25.0 s), and occlusion analysis supported the same pattern. In conclusion, clinically meaningful discrimination is achievable with minimal input—a single 30-s ECG plus one SE feature-emphasizing conciseness and interpretability. Further clinical application will require external cohort validation and probability calibration.

Keywords: Atrial Fibrillation · Pre-AF ECG · Explainable ML · Grouped-SHAP · Imminence Detection

1 Introduction

Atrial Fibrillation (AF) is a commonly observed cardiac rhythm disorder, with the risk of experiencing AF after age 45 estimated to be approximately 30% world wide [1, 2] As AF is a major cause of serious complications such as stroke and heart failure, [3] its early detection and imminence detection represent a clinically important challenge. This study does not target long-horizon early warning; instead, it focuses on imminence detection within a 30-second window immediately preceding AF onset.

C. Xu (Ed.): ICMLSC 2026, CCIS 2948, pp. 405–414, 2027.
https://doi.org/10.1007/978-981-92-1546-1_33

Following clinical diagnostic guidelines [4–6] requiring at least 30 s of continuous ECG recording for AF diagnosis, previous studies proposed prediction models using long-term ECG data (large-window segments) spanning from seconds to hours before AF onset. However, large-window segments faced limitations in clinical and real-time monitoring due to the high potential for false positives caused by confounding environmental variables and noise [7, 8].

Recently, studies have attempted to overcome these limitations by utilizing short 30-s intervals to provide early warnings up to tens of minutes before AF onset [9]. However, deep learning-based black-box techniques still predominate, leading to insufficient interpretability of the predictive rationale [10–13].

For machine learning to establish itself as a medical tool, healthcare professionals must understand and trust the model's prediction process and outcomes, making explainability essential [11–13]. However, explainability remains insufficiently validated in many current studies. This poses a significant barrier because physicians require not only accuracy but also transparent reasoning before trusting AI-based decisions. This gap ultimately limits adoption in real clinical settings [10].

To address these limitations, this study focuses on imminence detection within the 30-s window immediately preceding AF onset, aiming to characterize precursor patterns through an interpretable model. This timeframe is suitable for detecting meaningful precursor signals while minimizing interference from lifestyle variables and noise, as rhythm changes or irregularities become distinct [9]. Among various methods for quantifying rhythm irregularities, Spectral Entropy (SE) has been recognized as a sensitive indicator of frequency distribution complexity in AF and has been reported to be useful for detecting patterns [14–17]. This approach aims to minimize false positives and confirm the potential for clinical application and real-time monitoring.

2 Methods

In this study, ECG data measured at 250 Hz was used to construct a single segment covering the 30-s interval immediately preceding AF onset. SE was extracted for statistical validation and machine learning purposes, and the data was labeled as 0 (Normal) or 1 (AF) based on the presence or absence of atrial fibrillation. After performing normality tests and hypothesis testing, an interpretable machine learning model was constructed.

2.1 Data Description

We used the MIT-BIH Atrial Fibrillation Database (PhysioNet), which consists of signals sampled at 250 Hz with rhythm annotations. We focused on the 30-s interval immediately preceding the onset of AF in each episode and the corresponding 30-s normal interval.

2.2 Data and Preprocessing

Target Window. Unlike prior work that analyzed long-term prediction windows, this study focuses on the 30-s imminence detection window immediately preceding AF onset.

Segmentation and Exclusions. Following AF diagnostic convention, signals were segmented into 250 Hz × 30 s = 7,500 samples per segment. Segments shorter than 7,500 samples were excluded. This yielded 287 pre-AF segments and 269 normal segments. Each segment received a binary label (1 = pre-AF, 0 = normal).

Channel Selection. To prioritize a clear cardiac rhythm, the MLII lead was selected from the two available leads.

Amplitude Normalization. Each ECG segment was z-score normalized per segment (zero mean, unit variance) [18–20].

Spectral Entropy (SE). SE was selected because it quantifies spectral dispersion and rhythm irregularity, both of which are clinically relevant for AF detection [14–17]. Each 30-s single-lead ECG segment (fs = 250 Hz, 7,500 samples) was assigned a segment-specific z-score. Power spectral density (PSD) was then estimated using Welch's method (Hann window; nperseg = 512 [≈2.048 s], noverlap = 256 [50%], detrend = "constant", scaling = "density", default nfft) and restricted to 0.5–40 Hz. Within this band, PSD values were normalized to sum to 1. SE was calculated as base-2 Shannon entropy and then normalized by $\log_2 K$ (K = number of frequency bins within the band) to produce a dimensionless value in the range [0, 1]. A small constant (1×10^{-12}) was used to prevent numerical issues. To prevent information leakage during training, the SE values were normalized using only the training fold statistics.

Modeling Features. For each sample, we concatenated the 7,500 ECG samples with the single segment-level SE value (total 7,501 features) as inputs to the classifier.

2.3 Splits and Validation

Because the number of distinct subjects in the MIT-BIH AF database is limited, we constructed PSD-based surrogate groups by K-means clustering of Welch PSD fingerprints (0.5–40 Hz) into k = 27 clusters to enforce group-disjoint splitting. We then performed an 80/20 group-disjoint split (train n = 401, test n = 155, train groups = 21, test groups = 6). Model selection used 5-fold StratifiedGroupKFold (SGKFold) on the training set [21–24]. All preprocessing and hyper-parameter tuning were performed strictly within each fold. We report class distributions: train [Normal = 219, AF = 182], test [Normal = 50, AF = 105].

2.4 Statistical Analysis

Statistical Analysis. SE was calculated once per 30-s segment (Welch PSD) To statistically validate imminence-related differences between pre-AF and normal segments, we used the one-tailed Mann–Whitney U test(pre-AF < normal) on segment-level SE and reported Cliff's δ and Hodges–Lehmann median difference. 95% confidence intervals were obtained via group-aware bootstrap (resampling surrogate groups within each class).

2.5 Model Development and Performance Evaluation

Classifier. We used XGBoost as the classifier (tree_method = hist, a small grid over max_depth, learning_rate, n_estimators, fixed random_state for reproducibility).

Evaluation Metrics. Primary metrics were AUROC and AUPRC (reported alongside the baseline prevalence), evaluating the model's ability to detect imminent pre-AF patterns within the 30-s window. We also report accuracy, precision, recall, F1, and specificity, with ROC/PR curves on the independent test set.

Operating Point. For clinical interpretation, an operating threshold was derived from out-of-fold (OOF) predictions on the training folds to target specificity ≈ 0.95. This threshold was applied unchanged to the test set, at which sensitivity/specificity and the confusion matrix were reported. Where appropriate, 95% confidence intervals were obtained using a group-aware bootstrap over surrogate groups.

Ablation. To further assess each feature's contribution to imminence detection, we compared three configurations under the same group-aware split, preprocessing, and evaluation protocol: Raw waveform only, SE only, and Raw ECG+SE. Each configuration was evaluated both at the global level (AUROC, AUPRC) and at the clinically relevant high-specificity operating point (Spec ≈ 0.95).

2.6 Explainable ML (XGBoost + SHAP)

To avoid over segmentation of correlated time steps, we used Grouped-SHAP instead of time-step SHAP [25, 26]. The 30-s signal was pre-split into 0.5-s bins (sensitivity analyses at 0.25/1.0 s) [27]. For each bin we summarized mean $|SHAP|$ (and 95% CIs across test segments) to enable fair comparison across bins. To corroborate importance, we computed Occlusion ΔAUC (replacing a bin with its mean across samples) and Group-Permutation ΔAUC (row-wise permutation within a bin), and compared importance profiles via Spearman correlation. We additionally stratified grouped importance by predicted class (pre-AF vs normal) and reported a partial-dependence curve for SE.

3 Results

3.1 Mann–Whitney U Test Results

This study evaluated the difference in SE distribution between the interval immediately preceding AF onset and the normal interval. The results are presented in Fig. 1.

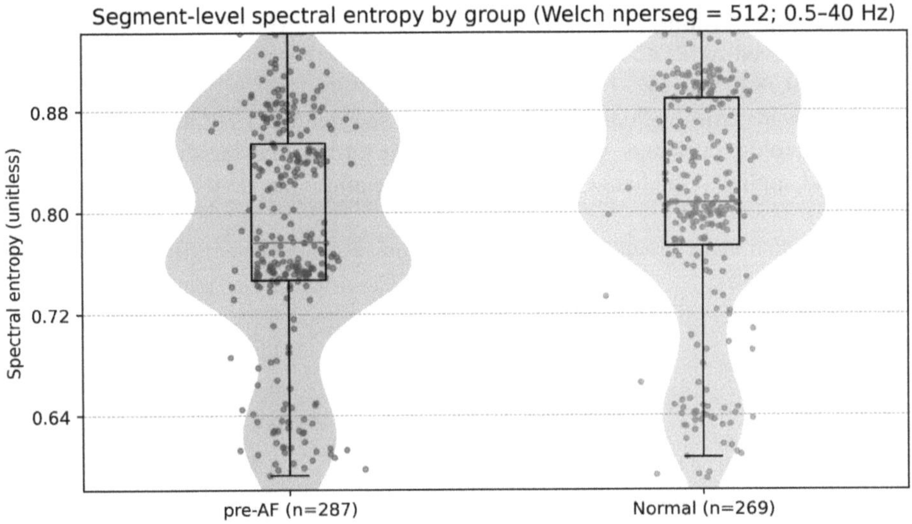

Fig. 1. Mann–Whitney U test. It was confirmed that the SE of the AF group was significantly lower ($p < 1.21 \times 10^{-4}$, Cliff's $\delta = -0.180$).

3.2 XGBoost Performance (Primary: Test Set, Internal: 5-Fold SGKFold)

We summarize the quantitative performance in Table 1 (independent test set and 5-fold group-disjoint CV) and provide an ablation in Table 2 comparing Raw-only, SE-only, and Raw + SE configurations. Complementary interpretability analyses—Grouped-SHAP and occlusion ΔAUC—are shown in Fig. 2 and Fig. 3.

Table 1. Pre-AF Imminence Detection Performance (30-s ECG)

Protocol /Evaluation	XGBoost (Test, 20%)	5-fold SGKFold (Train, 80%)
AUROC	0.87	0.83 ± 0.07
AUPRC	0.94 *(baseline = 0.68)*	—
Accuracy	0.78	—
Precision	0.82 (AF) 0.68 (Normal)	—
F1 Score (thr = 0.50)	0.84 (AF) 0.64 (Normal)	—
Recall	0.87(AF) 0.60 (Normal)	—
Specificity (thr = 0.50)	0.60	—
Sens (test, at OOF-fixed thr ≈ 0.77, Spec ≈ 0.90)	0.71	—

On the group-disjoint independent test set (n = 155, AF prevalence = 0.68), the classifier achieved AUROC = 0.87 and AUPRC = 0.94 (baseline = 0.68), with overall accuracy of 0.78 (Table 1).

Group-aware cross-validation on the training set yielded AUROC = 0.83 ± 0.07. From out-of-fold predictions, we fixed an operating threshold to target Spec ≈ 0.95 (thr ≈ 0.77) and applied it unchanged to the test set, yielding Spec 0.90 and Sens 0.71.

Table 2. Ablation under group-disjoint evaluation (test set unless noted): Raw ECG + SE vs Raw-only vs SE-only.

Metric	ECG + SE	ECG	SE
AUROC	0.866	0.875	0.536
AUPRC	0.94	0.941	0.692
Spec (test, at OOF-fixed thr ≈ 0.77)	0.90	0.92	0.50
Sens (test, at OOF-fixed thr ≈ 0.77)	0.714	0.695	0.533
Acc (test, at OOF-fixed thr ≈ 0.77)	0.774	0.768	0.523
CV mean AUROC	0.835	0.793	0.507

Raw ECG + SE achieved an AUROC of 0.866, comparable to raw data alone (0.875). SE alone was insufficient (AUROC 0.536), but adding SE to raw ECG improved sensitivity at high specificity, supporting a small yet clinically interpretable augmentation effect.

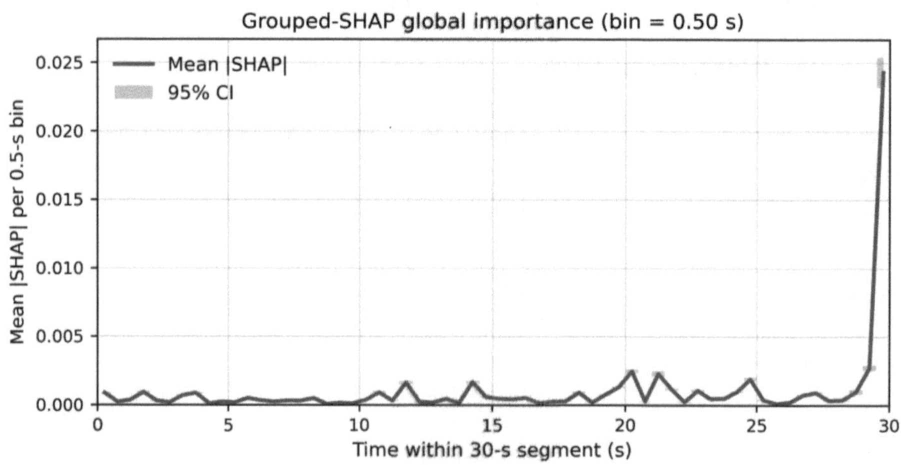

Fig. 2. Grouped-SHAP global importance (0.5-s bins). Mean |SHAP| peaked at 29.5–30.0 s, with a secondary peak at 24.5–25.0 s, (95% CIs shown.)

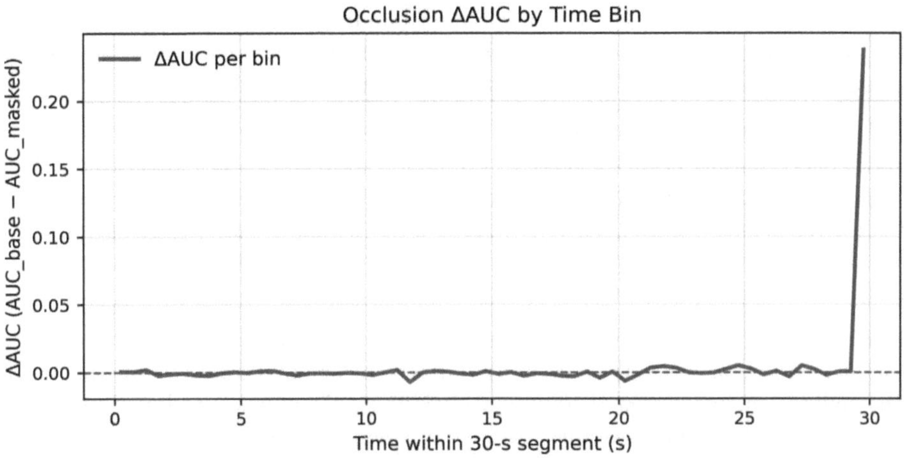

Fig. 3. Occlusion ΔAUC (0.5-s bin). The test AUC change was calculated after replacing each time bin with its across-sample mean (absolute ΔAUC shown). ΔAUC peaked at 29.5–30.0 s, with a secondary peak observed at 24.5–25.0 s. This aligns with the terminal importance observed in Grouped-SHAP.

4 Discussion

This study demonstrates that clinically meaningful discrimination is achievable with minimal input (a single 30-s ECG fragment and one spectral entropy (SE) feature) on a group-disjoint test set, supporting the feasibility of real-time monitoring based on transparent evidence.

Statistical Properties of SE. Inter-group comparisons revealed lower SE in the pre-atrial fibrillation stage compared to the normal interval (consistent with SE characteristics reflecting rhythm regularity and spectral complexity [14]). As SE quantifies the spectral dispersion of the power spectrum, this pattern suggests narrowband spectral concentration immediately preceding onset (Fig. 1). Although the univariate effect was small (Cliff's $\delta \approx -0.18$), integration at the model level enabled clinically meaningful differentiation.

Ablation Results. While SE alone was insufficient (AUROC ≈ 0.54), combining SE with raw ECG improved sensitivity at high specificity operating points and increased cross-validated AUROC compared to raw data alone (Table 2).

Interpretability Analysis. Grouped-SHAP and occlusion analysis converged on the terminal region at 29.5–30.0 s, showing a secondary peak around 24.5–25.0 s, providing consistent and localized importance (Fig. 2, 3). When the operating threshold was fixed (thr = 0.77) from out-of-fold (OOF) predictions and applied unchanged to the test set, it maintained high specificity (0.90) and acceptable sensitivity (0.71), demonstrating imminent pre-AF detection utility, providing interpretable insight into short-term pre-onset dynamics.

Window Length. A 30-second window strikes a balance between stability and false alarm control, aligning with diagnostic practice. Although this duration is not intended for long-term early prediction, it is suitable for imminence detection—capturing short-term pre-AF dynamics immediately preceding onset. Very short windows increase SE variance and yield accuracy close to chance levels (e.g., 10 s) [28].

Limitations. Use of a proxy cohort due to limited subject numbers, reliance on a single public cohort (MIT-BIH AF), and use of a limited feature set (MLII + SE) without direct comparison to RR/morphological features or lightweight deep learning baselines may limit generalizability. The specificity-focused OOF threshold was applied unchanged to the test set, and probability calibration and context-specific adjustments will be necessary before real-world implementation.

Future Directions. A priority for future research is the systematic evaluation of extended prediction horizons (5–60 min), followed by external cohort validation, probability calibration, integration of additional physiological features, benchmarking against lightweight deep-learning baselines, and window-length optimization.

5 Conclusion

This study demonstrated that even with only a single 30-second single-lead (MLII) ECG segment and a single spectral entropy (SE) feature, it is possible to achieve false-alarm suppression and excellent discrimination performance while maintaining interpretability on a group-disjoint independent test set. Although SE differences were small at the univariate level, aggregation at the model level revealed clinically meaningful discriminative power. Grouped-SHAP and occlusion-based interpretability consistently supported importance concentration in the terminal 29.5–30.0-second interval. However, this does not imply inherently shorter windows are advantageous; Rather, it suggests that the full 30-second interval contributes to signal stability and false alarm suppression, supporting its suitability for imminence detection of pre-AF states.

For practical application, external cohort validation, probability calibration, comparison with additional physiological features and lightweight deep learning, and window length optimization are required. Nevertheless, this study demonstrated meaningful pre-AF imminence patterns using only minimal and interpretable inputs (30-second single-lead ECG + single SE), provided transparent rationale for detection, and presented the feasibility of implementing a field-deployable system. This establishes a robust starting point for future ML-based clinical integration in AF monitoring.

Acknowledgements. This research was supported by the MSIT (Ministry of Science, ICT), Korea, under the National Program for Excellence in SW, supervised by the IITP (Institute of Information & communications Technology Planning & Evaluation) in 2025 (2021-0-01399).

References

1. Lloyd-Jones, D.M., et al.: Lifetime risk for development of atrial fibrillation: the Framingham heart study. Circulation **110**(9), 1042–1046 (2004)

2. Vinter, N., et al.: Temporal trends in lifetime risks of atrial fibrillation and its complications between 2000 and 2022 in Denmark: population based cohort study. BMJ **385**, e077209 (2024)
3. Benjamin, E.J., Chen, P.S., Bild, D.E., et al.: Prevention of atrial fibrillation: report from a national heart, lung, and blood institute workshop. Circulation **119**, 606–618 (2009)
4. Freedman, B., Potpara, T., Lip, G.Y.H., Chiang, C.E., Engdahl, J., Boriani, G.: World heart federation roadmap on atrial fibrillation (2020 update). Glob. Heart **16**(1), 1–27 (2021)
5. Hindricks, G., Potpara, T., Dagres, N., et al.: 2020 ESC Guidelines for the diagnosis and management of atrial fibrillation developed in collaboration with EACTS. Eur. Heart J. **42**(5), 373–498 (2021)
6. Joglar, J.A., Chung, M.K., Armbruster, A.L., et al.: 2023 ACC/AHA/ACCP/HRS guideline for the diagnosis and management of atrial fibrillation. Circulation **149**(1), e1–e156 (2024)
7. Bender, T., Gemke, P., Idrobo-Avila, E., Dathe, H., Krefting, D., Spicher, N.: Benchmarking the impact of noise on deep learning-based classification of atrial fibrillation in 12-lead ECG. Stud. Health Technol. Inform. **302**, 977–981 (2023)
8. Halvaei, H., Svennberg, E., Sörnmo, L., Stridh, M.: Identification of transient noise to reduce false detections in screening for atrial fibrillation. Front. Physiol. **12**, 672875 (2021)
9. Gavidia, M., Zhu, H., Montanari, A.N., Fuentes, J., Cheng, C., Dubner, S., et al.: Early warning of atrial fibrillation using deep learning. Patterns **5**(6), 100970 (2024)
10. Liu, C.-F., Chen, Z.-C., Kuo, S.-C., Lin, T.-C.: Does AI explainability affect physicians' intention to use AI? Int. J. Med. Inform. **168**, 104884 (2022)
11. Holzinger, A., Biemann, C., Pattichis, C.S., Kell, D.B.: What do we need to build explainable AI systems for the medical domain? arXiv preprint arXiv:1712.09923 (2017)
12. Amann, J., Blasimme, A., Vayena, E., Frey, D., Madai, V.I.: Explainability for artificial intelligence in healthcare: a multidisciplinary perspective. BMC Med. Inform. Decis. Mak. **20**, 310 (2020)
13. Rosenbäck, H., et al.: Explainable artificial intelligence in clinical decision support systems: a systematic scoping review and stakeholder survey. JMIR AI **3** (2024)
14. Shimizu, W., Ino, T., Okeie, T.: Spectral analysis of atrial fibrillation cycle lengths. Circ. J. **71**(2), 242–247 (2007)
15. Faust, O., Shenfield, A., Kareem, M., Ali, A., Acharya, U.R.: Analysis of atrial fibrillation: characterization using spectral entropy. Comput. Methods Programs Biomed. **158**, 185–196 (2018)
16. Acharya, U.R., et al.: Automated detection of atrial fibrillation using spectral features. Knowl. Based Syst. **94**, 138–148 (2017)
17. Kang, J., et al.: Enhanced ECG arrhythmia detection accuracy by optimizing divergence-based data fusion. arXiv preprint arXiv:2504.02842
18. Hastie, T., Tibshirani, R., Friedman, J.: The Elements of Statistical Learning: Data Mining, Inference, and Prediction, 2nd edn. Springer, New York (2009). https://doi.org/10.1007/978-0-387-84858-7
19. Molnar, C.: Interpretable Machine Learning, 2nd edn. (Online book). https://christophm.github.io/interpretable-ml-book/. Accessed 03 Sept 2025
20. Clifford, G.D., Azuaje, F., McSharry, P.E. (eds.): Advanced Methods and Tools for ECG Data Analysis. Artech House, Norwood (2006)
21. Refaeilzadeh, P., Tang, L., Liu, H.: Cross-Validation. In: Liu, L., Özsu, M.T. (eds.) Encyclopedia of Database Systems, pp. 532–538. Springer, Boston (2009). https://doi.org/10.1007/978-0-387-39940-9_565
22. Kohavi, R.: A study of cross-validation and bootstrap for accuracy estimation and model selection. In: Proceedings of the 14th International Joint Conference on Artificial Intelligence (IJCAI 1995), pp. 1137–1145 (1995)

23. Arlot, S., Celisse, A.: A survey of cross-validation procedures for model selection. Stat. Surv. **4**, 40–79 (2010)
24. Varma, S., Simon, R.: Bias in error estimation when using cross-validation for model selection. BMC Bioinform. **7**, 91 (2006)
25. Lundberg, S.M., Lee, S.-I.: A unified approach to interpreting model predictions. In: Advances in Neural Information Processing Systems 30 (NeurIPS 2017), pp. 4765–4774. Curran Associates, Inc. (2017)
26. Aas, K., Jullum, M., Løland, A.: Explaining individual predictions when features are dependent: more accurate approximations to Shapley values. Artif. Intell. **298**, 103502 (2021)
27. Bento, J., Saleiro, P., Cruz, A.F., Figueiredo, M.A.T., Bizarro, P.: TimeSHAP: explaining recurrent models through sequence perturbations. In: Proceedings of the 27th ACM SIGKDD International Conference on Knowledge Discovery & Data Mining (KDD 2021), New York, pp. 2565–2573. ACM (2021)
28. Kim, J.: Identifying potential atrial fibrillation from mobile ECG using explainable AI, M.S. thesis, Chonnam Natl. Univ., Gwangju, Korea (2024)

Analysis Workflow Improvement and Integrated Diagnosis of Vegetation Indices Toward an Unmanned Aerial Vehicle-Based Field Diagnostic System

Taichi Ito(✉) and Ken'ichi Minamino

Iwate Prefectural University, Takizawa, Iwate 0200693, Japan
S236w001@s.iwate-pu.ac.jp, minamino@iwate-pu.ac.jp

Abstract. In Japan, global warming has led to shifts in cultivation methods. Consequently, smart agriculture has advanced, with unmanned aerial vehicles (UAV) monitoring garnering particular attention. However, previous studies on UAV monitoring have often required complex analytical workflows. In this study, this issue is addressed through two tasks: (1) improving time-series clustering of vegetation indices (VI) via automated analysis workflows and masking water areas, and (2) integrating diagnostic results from six VIs. For the first task, the ratio vegetation index proved to be the most practical for distinguishing between rice plants and water areas. This enabled the use of datasets from the early growth stages when vegetation cover is low. In addition, it significantly reduced analysis time that the automation of workflows using application programming interfaces. For the second task, diagnostic results were integrated based on combinations of cluster IDs across VIs. The results indicated that red-edge type indices exhibited weaker correlations with lodging. Future work will focus on developing a quantitative method for water area masking and validating the integrated diagnostics across more sites. Addressing these points will facilitate applications to various crops, enable diagnostics that account for field specific characteristics, and improve accuracy through the development of new models.

Keywords: Integrated Diagnosis · Machine Learning · Paddy Rice · UAV · Vegetation Index

1 Introduction

In Japan, farmers are progressively aging and their numbers have been continuously declining. According to government statistics published every five years, the number of farmers decreases by approximately 200,000–300,000, whereas the ratio of farmers aged ≥65 increases by approximately 4% each time [1]. This issue will cause a decline in food self-sufficiency rates, an increase in abandoned farmland, and the loss of agricultural techniques. Furthermore, in rice cultivation, high temperatures since 2023 have led to a decline in grain quality. Although Iwate Prefecture, located in north Japan, has avoided

C. Xu (Ed.): ICMLSC 2026, CCIS 2948, pp. 415–426, 2027.
https://doi.org/10.1007/978-981-92-1546-1_34

this issue, lodging has occurred because rice plants grew excessively tall [2, 3]. In other words, even experienced farmers are facing challenges caused by climate change—reduced yields, lower quality, and pest outbreaks. Smart agriculture is being advanced to address these issues and ensure stable production [4]. This study is in the field of crop and field remote monitoring using unmanned aerial vehicles (UAV) within smart agriculture.

In this study, UAV monitoring utilizes vegetation indices (VIs), as crop health changes spectral reflectance characteristics. For instance, it has a bigger difference in healthy plants than in stressed plants for the reflectance between the red and near-infrared (NIR) bands [5]. Various VIs have been developed by expressed equations to capture such characteristics [6]. Combining VIs with artificial intelligence enables various field diagnostics [7]. For instance, those with neural networks [8–11], object analysis [12], statistical [13, 14], and machine learning [15] are present. However, UAV monitoring faces implementation and operational problems. Calculating VIs from UAV aerial photographs requires multiple software tools; thus, significant time and expertise are required. Furthermore, no manuals exist for the required equipment, photography methods, and analysis techniques. Resolving these problems and making UAV monitoring more accessible is expected to stabilize and enhance agricultural production efficiency.

Against this background, this study aims to address UAV monitoring challenges toward the development of a practical field diagnosis system. To achieve this objective, the authors propose the following unique methods: (1) facilitating the use of analysis software through Python application programming interfaces (APIs), and (2) integrating VIs by focusing on cluster combinations derived from the clustering results. These works are based on a visualization method using time-series clustering in the authors' previous research [16].

2 Methodology

2.1 Material

The experiment was conducted in two adjacent paddy fields (West and East) located in Kanegasaki, Iwate, Japan (Fig. 1). These fields were approximately equal in area. A total of 2,045 and 2,050 meshes were created in the West and East fields, respectively, using a 1 m^2 mesh as the unit for calculating VIs. The West field was transplanted with "Hitomebore" (for staple food) on May 12 and harvested on September 27. The East field was transplanted with "Iwai-Dawara" (for livestock feed) on May 14, fertilized on July 15, and harvested on October 20 (Table 2). The UAV shown in Fig. 2 was used for monitoring, which was performed four times at approximately the 20th of each month from June to September.

Weather data were obtained from "The Agro-Meteorological Grid Square Data System" [17]. This provides 14 meteorological elements at approximately 1 km^2 resolution across Japan. These data were used to analyze meteorological conditions and predict growth stages in the experimental site. For growth stage prediction, the effective accumulated temperature was calculated (base temperature was 10 °C) and six growth stages were identified—transplanting, peak tillering, young panicle formation, heading, ripening, and harvesting. This approach was based on the principle that accumulated temperature can indicate the approximate growth stages [18, 19].

2.2 Method

In the authors' previous study [16], time-series clustering was used to visualize crop growth, along with grouping based on transitions in crop growth status. This study further performed preprocessing of VI values and masking water areas, details of these are described in subsequent sections. The experiment fields were diagnosed with six VIs using these improved algorithms (Table 1). Each index was defined as the difference in reflectance between the NIR band and a specific band. The detectable diagnostic items were similar in a specific band; thus, VIs were classified into various types according to that band. In addition, lodging occurred in the West; thus, a 1-m mesh digital surface model (DSM) was used to detect the lodging areas. Thereafter, a random forest (RF) model was developed to predict lodging occurrence from VI values.

Table 1. Using VIs.

Index		Equation	Ref.
Green type			
– photosynthetic	GNDVI	$\frac{NIR-Green}{NIR+Green}$	[27]
– chlorophyll	CI-green	$\frac{NIR}{Green}-1$	[28]
Red type			
– vegetation	NDVI	$\frac{NIR-Red}{NIR+Red}$	[29]
– health	MSAVI2	$\frac{2(NIR+1)-\sqrt{2(NIR+1)^2-8(NIR-Red)}}{2}$	[30]
Red-Edge type			
– non-stress level	NDRE	$\frac{NIR-RedEdge}{NIR+RedEdge}$	[31]
– health (late growth stage)	CI-red edge	$\frac{NIR}{RedEdge}-1$	[32]

Mesh level time-series data of VIs had to be created from aerial photographs to perform time-series clustering. The preprocessing comprised the following steps:

1. Creating orthophotos:

Multiple aerial photographs were stitched together to ensure that each field point was mapped from directly overhead (orthophoto). Agisoft Metashape 2.2 was used.

2. Generating meshes and calculating reflectance:

Meshes were generated and reflectance values for each band were extracted from the orthophotos. Quantum Geographic Information System (QGIS) 3.40 was used.

3. Computing VI values:

Table 2. Cultivation conditions.

	West	East
Variety	Hitomebore	Iwai-Dawara
Num. of meshes	2,045	2,050
Transplantation	May 12th	May 14th
Fertilization	May 12th	May 14th, Jul. 15th
Heading	Aug. 2nd	Aug 5th
Harvesting	Sep. 27th	Oct. 20th

VI values were calculated from the reflectance of each band. Python was used.

These steps are complex and time-consuming; therefore, the analysis software and clustering programs were automated using Python APIs.

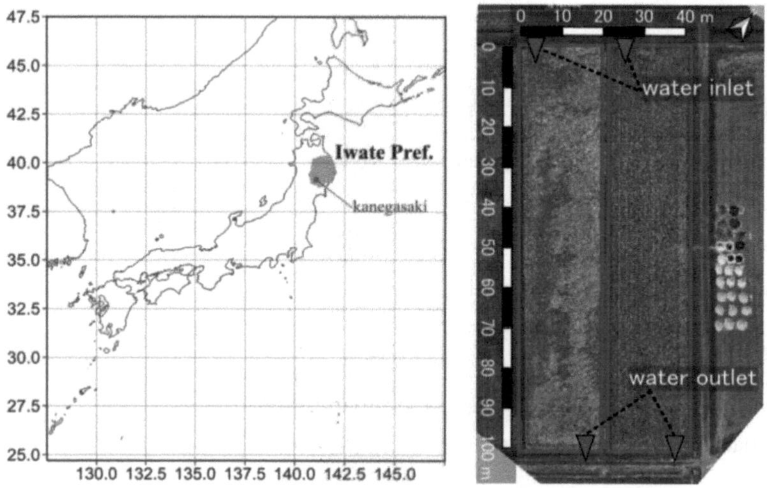

Fig. 1. Location and aerial photograph of experiment field.

Fig. 2. UAV used in this study. (Mavic 3M, DJI Co., Ltd., China)

3 Results

3.1 Masking Water Area in Early Growth Stage

UAV monitoring using VIs reflects the spectral characteristics of crop leaves. However, during the early growth stage, when the leaf area is small, soil and water areas can influence reflectance and result in inappropriate VI values. This experiment investigated whether VIs could be used to mask water areas from orthophotos in the early growth stage to enable monitoring during the early growth stage. In general, rice plants exhibit higher VI values than water because their reflectance in the NIR band is higher. Thresholds for plants and water were visually determined at a 3 cm mesh resolution, which was the pixel size, to mask water based on this difference. The indices used for masking were the six VIs listed in Table 1, as well as the ratio vegetation index (RVI), a simple and classical index, as shown in Eq. (1) [20].

$$\mathrm{RVI} = \mathrm{NIR} / \mathrm{Red} \tag{1}$$

Figure 3 compares seven VIs for extracting plant areas based on visually determined thresholds at the early growth stage (June 20) in the experimental field. The extraction results were similar when using the same index type. Among index types, the red-edge type failed to accurately capture the plant areas. In contrast, both the green and red types successfully captured the areas. In particular, the red type was found to separate the boundary between plants and water more clearly.

3.2 Prediction Model for Rice Lodging

The west field experienced lodging; thus, the affected areas were identified using the DSM generated during the "Creating Orthophotos" step. The DSM represents elevation data, including the heights of structures and trees. At the experimental site, the absolute DSM values could not be used because no leveling survey was performed. Therefore, lodging areas were determined by visually comparing elevation differences between the first (June 20) and last (September 18) monitoring dates with the RGB orthophoto. The results of its detection at a 1-m mesh resolution are shown in Fig. 4. In this figure, meshes colored red indicated lodging areas. A total of 1,169 meshes (57% in the west field) were acquired as lodging.

An RF model was generated to predict lodging occurrence to investigate the relationship between lodging and VI values. The explanatory variables were the values of the six VIs on each monitoring date and the differences between their data. The target variable was the presence or absence of lodging in each mesh. Note that the last monitoring data were not used because lodging had already occurred. The dataset was divided into 30% (702 meshes) for training and 70% (1,636 meshes) for testing after matching the number of lodging and non-lodging meshes. The proportion of training data was reduced from the typical split because both the training and test data were collected from the same field. This adjustment was made to enable the investigation of more general and practically important variables associated with lodging. The decision trees generated during RF model generation were set to a maximum depth of three. Consequently, the significance of explanatory variables in this prediction model was shown in Fig. 4. This figure indicates that August 20th across many VIs. In particular, MSAVI2, NDVI, and CI-green each exceeded 10%. The red-edge type on July 18th also exceeded 5%. Conversely, June 20th and the difference variables had minimal significance. A simplified lodging prediction model was also created using only the explanatory variables with the three highest significance, and with similar parameter settings. The accuracy of this high-significance model on the test data was 83.2%, exhibiting no major decrease compared with the full-variable model (88.6%).

3.3 Time-Series Clustering

Clustering was performed on time-series data of VI values to visualize the progression of rice growth. Outliers in the VI values were removed using the interquartile range, and the data were standardized for each monitoring date. Missing values were then imputed using the module "sklearn.imputations.KNNImputer()" [22]. These steps enabled the use of Python's time-series clustering module "tslearn.clustering.TimeSeriesKMeans()" [21]. Fig. 5 shows the centroid and distribu-tion of each cluster. The results indicate that all VIs classified the meshes into three clusters—the central area of the east field (red), northern and southern edges (blue), and the central area of the west field (green). The red cluster exhibited low values across all VIs, representing relatively poor health and lower chlorophyll levels. The blue cluster reached peak values after July, indicating good growth. The green cluster exhibited a decline in values during the latter growth stages. For green and red type indices, the values were approximately similar, whereas the red-edge type consistently exhibited lower values than the red type. The distribution of the green cluster over-lapped with the lodged areas, indicating significant stress in September.

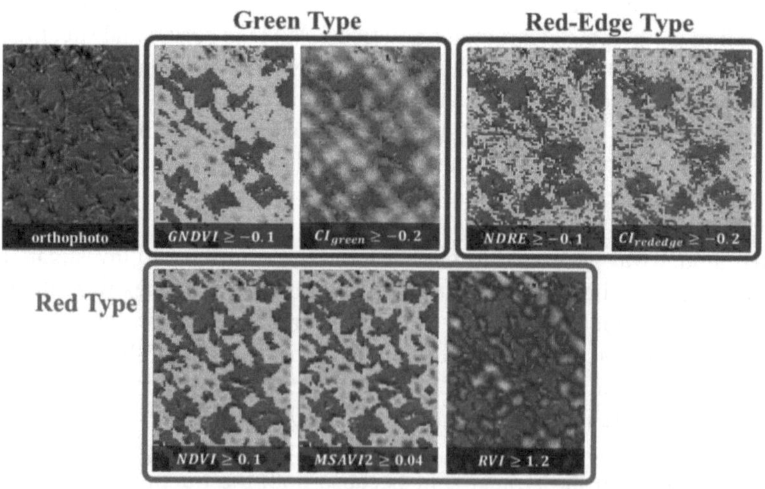

Fig. 3. Extraction of rice areas from orthophotos of paddy field at the early growth stage.

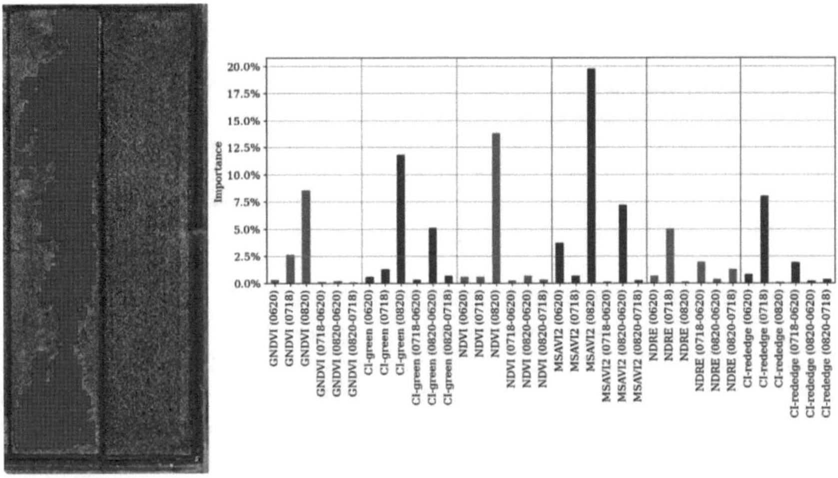

Fig. 4. Lodging location and significance of explanatory variables (contribution to the lodging prediction model).

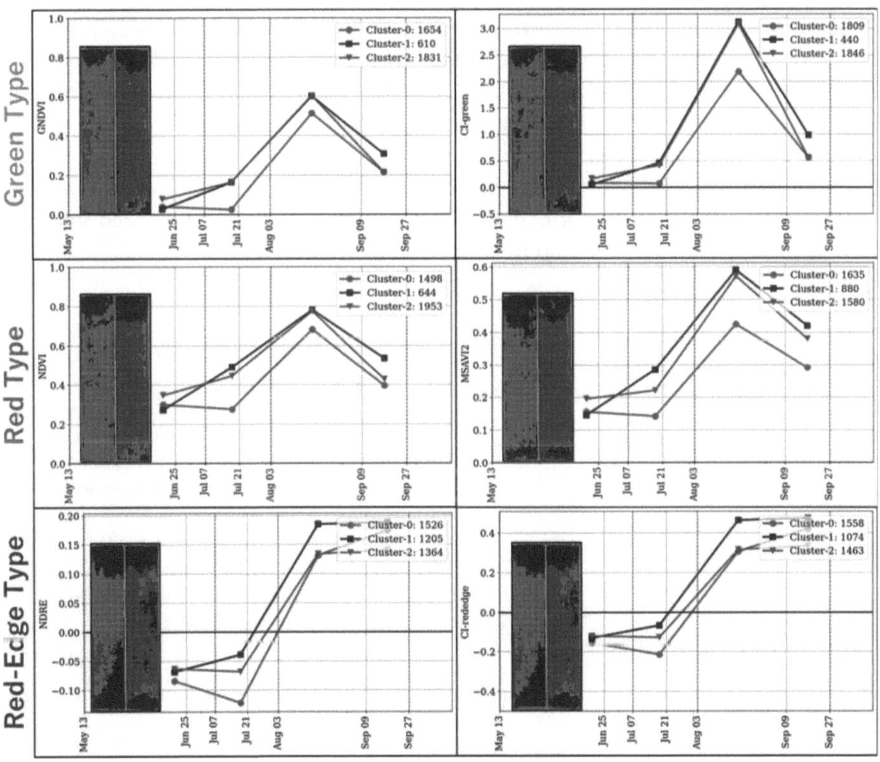

Fig. 5. Cluster distribution and transition of the average of each cluster.

4 Discussion

4.1 Easier Field Analysis

As shown in Fig. 6, analyzing UAV monitoring data using VIs involves multiple software tools and numerous steps. The authors automated these steps to facilitate UAV monitoring. The workflow can be divided into three stages based on the software used. The first is the Metashape process, which generates orthophotos from aerial photographs. Previously, each step was performed by the software, but the analyst was required to provide input between steps. In this automation, Python APIs link the steps together, enabling parallel processing of multiple monitoring datasets. The second is the QGIS process, which extracts brightness values from the orthophotos. The API automates tasks that previously required manual labor, including mesh creation, extraction of brightness value, and comma-separated values (CSV) files output. The third is the Python process, which organizes time-series clustering results from brightness values into folders by VI and number of clusters. In manual analysis, the process would halt if the analyst left the analysis computer, occasionally requiring approximately a week to complete mapping. Automation significantly reduced the number of times analyst intervention was required, allowing mapping to be completed within a single day.

In the previous section, water surface areas were masked using VIs to calibrate early growth stage data. This revealed that red type VIs are effective for masking water areas. Although the red type includes three indices—NDVI, MSAVI2, and RVI—no major differences in accuracy were observed. Therefore, RVI is considered the most practical because its calculation is simpler. For clustering in this study, VI values masked for water areas using RVI were applied to the June 20 dataset. As shown in Fig. 5, VI values on that date were neither higher nor exhibited a significant decrease compared with those of July. This suggests that water areas were effectively masked.

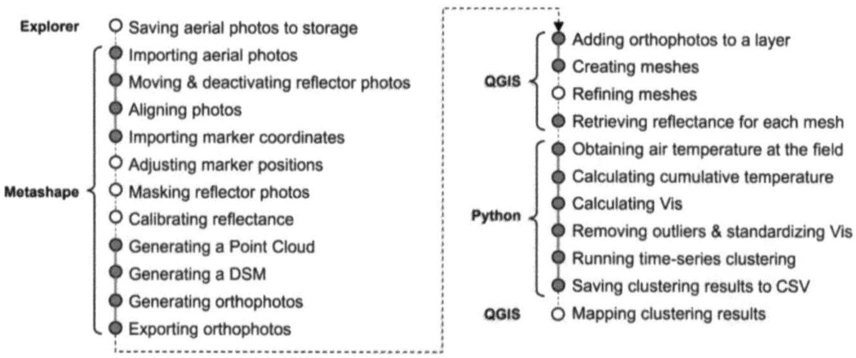

Fig. 6. Workflow from monitoring to visualizing growth. The authors have automated the green part.

4.2 Integration of Diagnostic Results

For integrating the clustering results across VIs, combinations of cluster IDs were examined. As each of the six VIs was classified into three clusters, 3^6 (= 729) possible combinations exist; however, only 124 combinations were observed at this site. In Fig. 7(a), combinations covering ≥3% of all meshes are highlighted, whereas those accounting for only a few meshes are grouped together and labeled as “others”. The top three combinations comprise the same cluster ID across all VIs, accounting for approximately 60% of the meshes. This suggests that the same diagnoses described in the time-series clustering section apply to these combinations. For instance, the blue combination in which all VIs belong to cluster-1 reflects favorable nitrogen status, vigorous growth, and low stress. Notably, this combination was associated with a yield of approximately 10% higher than the overall field average.

The remaining combinations, shown in khaki, light blue, and orange, all contain cluster-2 in at least one VI type. As shown in the previous section, meshes grouped into cluster-2 corresponded to lodging areas, and both the khaki and light blue meshes also matched for lodging areas. Conversely, the orange meshes, where only the red-edge type was grouped into cluster-2, did not match for lodging areas. This indicates that the relationship between the red-edge type and lodging is weak, which is consistent with its low significance in the RF lodging prediction model (Fig. 4).

The “others” category appears clustered into four areas, as shown in Fig. 7(b). Others-1 is adjacent to the lodging area, but numerous combinations contain cluster-1 and achieve good growth. Others-2 was stressed in July; however, no lodging occurred even in the west field. The combinations in others-3 represent poor nitrogen and vegetation conditions, but stress was low because majority of them belong to cluster-1 in the red-edge type. The combinations of others-4 include a few cluster-0, making this area the most favorable in the east field. These four areas are assumed to result from field characteristics and water. Others-1 and others-2 were observed in the area mixing cold and warm water, whereas others-3 and others-4 were observed in the stagnant warm water area. In particular, others-4 is the farthest from the water inlet, and its water temperature is approximately 1 °C higher than the site average.

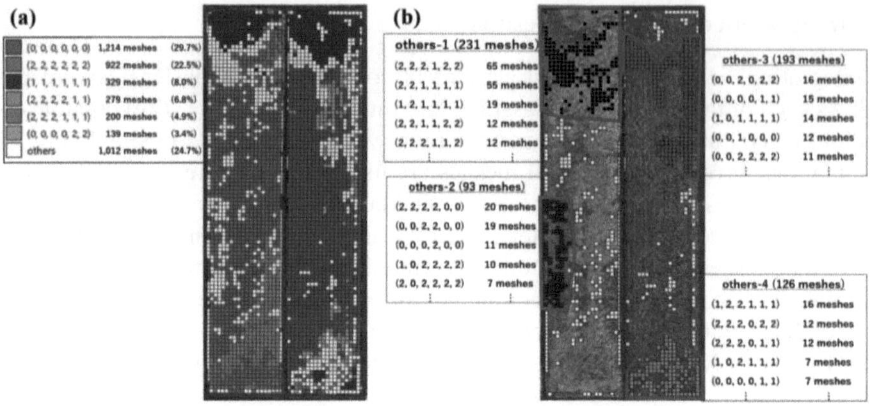

Fig. 7. Distribution of cluster ID combinations. The order of indices is (GNDVI, CI-green, NDVI, MSAVI2, NDRE, and CI-red edge). (a) Combinations accounting for 3% or more of all meshes. (b) Combinations forming four localized clusters within the "others" category.

5 Conclusions

This study performed two main tasks toward the development of UAV-based diagnosis system: (1) simplifying the analysis workflow, and (2) integrating diagnostic results across multiple VIs. First, we adapted the time-series clustering method from the authors' previous research [16] to improve its applicability. Specifically, the datasets in the early growth stages were enabled to use clustering by masking water areas using RVIs from aerial photographs. Additionally, Python APIs significantly reduced the required time for the analysis process. Second, we analyzed combinations of cluster IDs across six VIs. Approximately 60% of the meshes exhibited same cluster IDs across all VIs. In contrast, the colored combination, which is not grouped in the same cluster IDs across VIs, was grouped into cluster-2 with at least one VI. Among these, combinations where the red-edge type VIs grouped into cluster-2 were not matched for lodging areas. This is also evident in the significance generated by the RF lodging prediction model from VI values (Fig. 4). These findings in Fig. 7(a) indicate that integrated diagnosis based on cluster ID combinations is useful for growth and lodging risk. Furthermore, advancing this integrated diagnosis makes it possible to conduct detailed cause analysis, as shown in Fig. 7(b).

In the future, the following remain to be addressed. The first is the development of a quantitative method for water area masking. Currently, the RVI threshold distinguishing between water and plants is visually determined. However, it is desirable to quantify the appropriateness of this threshold, for instance, image processing of RGB photographs. The second is the validation of integrated diagnostics at more sites. Although the Kanegasaki site had the same number of clusters for all VIs, other sites often result in different numbers of clusters for each VI [23–25]. Therefore, more investigations are required to assess whether the integrated diagnostic method is applicable to such sites. The third is expansion toward a more comprehensive field diagnosis system. This study focused on diagnosing the time-series transitions in rice vegetation. Examples exist of diagnosing soil characteristics and classifying weed species in grape and leek fields by clustering the UAV-based reflectance of each band [26]. Building on this research, the authors will work on diagnosis that considers field characteristics and improve diagnosis through the construction of new models.

Acknowledgements. We would like to thank Sustinere Co., Ltd. for their support with UAV flights. We are also grateful to The Bank of Iwate, Ltd., NTT EAST, Inc., and Japan Data Science Consortium Co., Ltd. for providing the experimental sites and assisting with ground truth data collection.

We would also like to thank Editage [http://www.editage.com] for editing and reviewing this manuscript for English language.

References

1. Ministry of Agriculture, Forestry and Fisheries: Agricultural Census Statistics. https://www.maff.go.jp/j/tokei/census/afc/past/stats.html. Accessed 25 June 2025
2. Ministry of Agriculture, Forestry and Fisheries: Rice Production Statistics. https://www.maff.go.jp/j/tokei/kouhyou/sakumotu/sakkyou_kome/index.html#l. Accessed 25 June 2025
3. Ministry of Agriculture, Forestry and Fisheries: Rice Quality Inspection. https://www.maff.go.jp/j/seisan/syoryu/kensa/kome/. Accessed 25 June 2025
4. Ministry of Agriculture, Forestry and Fisheries: Smart Agriculture Guidelines. https://www.maff.go.jp/j/kanbo/smart/smart_meguji.pdf. Accessed 27 June 2025
5. Hongo, C., Kobayashi, T., Arita, Y.: The response of water status in tree seedlings through spectral reflectance. J. Jpn. Soc. Photogramm. **37**(4), 43–50 (1998)
6. Xue, J., Su, B.: Significant remote sensing vegetation indices: a review of developments and applications. J. Sens. **2017**(1), 1353691 (2017)
7. Khanal, S., Kushal, K.C., Fulton, J.P., Shearer, S., Ozkan, E.: Remote sensing in agriculture—accomplishments, limitations, and opportunities. Remote Sens. **12**(22), 3783 (2020)
8. Hassan-Esfahni, L., Torres-Rua, A., Jensen, A., McKee, M.: Assessment of surface soil moisture using high-resolution multi-spectral imagery and artificial neural networks. Remote Sens. **7**(3), 2627–2646 (2015)
9. Mohanty, S.P., Hughes, D.P., Salathé, M.: Using deep learning for image-based plant disease detection. Front. Plant Sci. **7**, 1419 (2016)
10. Safarijalal, B., Alborzi, Y., Najafi, E.: Automated wheat disease detection using a ROS-based autonomous guided UAV. Robotics **2206**, 15042 (2022)
11. Hokmabad, R.R., Badamchizadeh, A.M., Khanmohammadi, S.: Fault diagnosis of discrete event systems using hybrid Petri Nets. Int. J. Comput. Theory Eng. **4**(2), 288–292 (2012)
12. López-Granados, F., Torres-Sánchez, J., Castro, A.-I.D., Serrano-Pérez, A., Mesas-Carrascosa, F.-J., Peña, J.-M.: Object-based early monitoring of a grass weed in a grass crop using high resolution UAV imagery. Agron. Sustain. Dev. **36**, 67 (2016)
13. Du, M., Noguchi, N.: Monitoring of wheat growth status and mapping of wheat yield's within-field spatial variations using color images acquired from UAV-camera system. Remote Sens. **9**(3), 289 (2017)
14. Fukano, Y., et al.: GIS-based analysis for UAV-supported field experiments reveals soybean traits associated with rotational benefit. Front. Plant Sci. **12**, 637694 (2021)
15. Aboutalebi, M., Allen, L.N., Torres-Rua, A.F., McKee, M., Coopmans, C.: Estimation of soil moisture at different soil levels using machine learning techniques and unmanned aerial vehicle (UAV) multispectral imagery. In: SPIE Defense + Commercial Sensing, Baltimore, MD, USA, pp. 1–12 (2019)

16. Ito, T., Minamino, K., Umeki, S.: Analysis of vegetation indices by time series clustering of drone rice monitoring data. In: 3rd International Symposium on Electrical, Electronics and Information Engineering (ISEEIE 2023), Hangzhou, China, pp. 1–6 (2023)
17. Ohno, H., Sasaki, K., Ohara, G., Nakazono, K.: Development of grid square air temperature and precipitation data compiled from observed, forecasted, and climatic normal data. Clim. Biosphere **16**, 71–79 (2016)
18. Kanda, E., Torigoe, Y., Kobayashi, T.: A model to estimate the increase of leaf number on the main culm of the rice plant. In: Proceedings of the Crop Science Society of Japan **69**(4), 540–546 (2000) [26]
19. Kanda, E., Torigoe, Y., Kobayashi, T.: A simple model to predict the developmental stages of rice panicles using the effective accumulative temperature. Proc. Crop Sci. Soci. Japan **71**(3), 394–402 (2002)
20. Jordan, C.F.: Derivation of leaf area index from quality of light on the forest floor. Ecology **50**(4), 663–666 (1969)
21. Tavenard, R.: tslearn.clustering.TimeSeriesKMeans — tslearn 0.6.4 documentation. https://tslearn.readthedocs.io/en/stable/gen_modules/clustering/tslearn.clustering.TimeSeriesKMeans.html. Accessed 29 Aug 2025
22. scikit-learn developers: KNNImputer — scikit-learn 1.7.1 documentation. https://scikit-learn.org/stable/modules/generated/sklearn.impute.KNNImputer.html. Accessed 29 Aug 2025
23. Ito, T., Minamino, K., Umeki, S.: Analysis of fertilization effects on rice and wheat by time-series clustering of vegetation index data. In: 5th International Symposium on Advanced Technologies and Applications in the Internet of Things (ATAIT 2023), Kusatsu, Shiga, Japan, pp. 1–6 (2023)
24. Ito, T., Minamino, K., Umeki, S.: Visualization of the effect of additional fertilization on paddy rice by time-series analysis of vegetation indices using UAV and minimizing the number of monitoring days for its workload reduction. Adv. Sci. Technol. Eng. Syst. J. **9**(3), 29–40 (2024)
25. Ito, T., Minamino, K., Umeki, S.: Time-series clustering analysis of vegetation indices obtained from UAV to visualize fertilization effect and high temperature influence. In: 6th International Symposium on Advanced Technologies and Applications in the Internet of Things (ATAIT 2024), Kusatsu, Shiga, Japan, pp. 1–6 (2024)
26. Shun, I., Ken'ichi, M.: Soil diagnosis and weed species identification using drone with multispectral cameras and machine learning. J. Jpn. Soc. Infrared Sci. Technol. **35**(1), 16–24 (2025)
27. Louhaichi, M., Borman, M.M., Johnson, D.E.: Spatially located platform and aerial photography for documentation of grazing impacts on wheat. Geocarto Int. **16**(1), 65–70 (2001)
28. Gitelson, A.A., Viña, A., Arkebauer, T.J., Rundquist, D.C., Keydan, G., Leavitt, B.: Remote estimation of leaf area index and green leaf biomass in maize canopies. Geophys. Res. Lett. **30**(5), 1248 (2003)
29. Rouse, Jr., J.W., Haas, R.H., Schell, J.A., Deering, D.W.: Monitoring vegetation systems in the great plains with ERTS. NASA Spec. Publ. **1**(A), 309–317 (1974)
30. Chen, J.M.: Evaluation of vegetation indices and a modified simple ratio for boreal applications. Can. J. Remote. Sens. **22**(3), 229–242 (1996)
31. Barnes, E., et al.: Coincident detection of crop water stress, nitrogen status and canopy density using ground-based multispectral data. In: Proceedings of the 5th International Conference on Precision Agriculture, Bloomington, Minnesota, USA, pp. 1–12 (2000)
32. Gitelson, A.A., Gritz, Y., Merzlyak, M.N.: Relationships between leaf chlorophyll content and spectral reflectance and algorithms for non-destructive chlorophyll assessment in higher plant leaves. J. Plant Physiol. **160**(3), 271–282 (2003)

Three-Stage Hybrid Recommendation System for Personalized Skincare Products and Routines

Desy Natasha Haloho(✉) and Yu-Chieh Liao

University of Adelaide, Adelaide, Australia
desynatasha.haloho@adelaide.edu.au, yu-chieh.liao@student.adelaide.edu.au

Abstract. A personalized skincare recommendation system presents innovation opportunities for the beauty industry that is capable of both enhancing customer experience and supporting continued market growth. This paper proposes a three-stage architecture for personalized skincare aimed to addressing the challenges of aligning user requirements, ingredient safety, and product quality. The proposed architecture integrates constraint-based filtering, semantic ranking using bi-encoder or cross-encoder, and neural network quality assessment to deliver recommendations for single-product and multi-product (routine) scenarios, thus improving practical applicability of the system in the skincare market. The routine recommendations also incorporate an ingredient compatibility component that ensures safe product combinations while maintaining diversity. The result demonstrates significant performance in the three-stage system that achieves 84.68% requirement satisfaction with 15.8% catalog coverage for single-product recommendations using cross-encoder, and 84.22% satisfaction with 42.72% diversity for routines using bi-encoder. The performance analysis reveals that constraint filtering provides strong foundational accuracy in fulfilling user requirements, while semantic similarity and neural network components enable enhancement in model diversity and quality. This proposed architecture successfully achieve a balance between accuracy, diversity, and computational efficiency that demonstrates its practical viability in the skincare industry.

Keywords: Personalized skincare · Recommendation system · Constraint filtering · Semantic ranking · Neural network

1 Introduction

The skincare industry has grown significantly with the emergence of various new brands and higher demand in the market. This global growth can be seen with skincare remaining the dominant category in the beauty market, accounting for 44% of total sales and achieving the highest growth in 2023. Its expansion is projected to continue over the next four years, with an estimated annual growth

C. Xu (Ed.): ICMLSC 2026, CCIS 2948, pp. 427–439, 2027.
https://doi.org/10.1007/978-981-92-1546-1_35

rate of 6% [1]. A similar trend is also observed in Australia with skincare sales predominantly driven by store-based retail, and pharmacies leading at 29.6% [2]. Therefore, technological adaptation has become essential to support this growth by improving customer experience with focus through this primary channel.

A skincare routine and product recommendation system based on user profiles enhances efficiency in identifying the most suitable products that match individual skin conditions and needs among a variety of options. This also becomes crucial to guide users and avoid unwanted results from using unsuitable skincare products that could potentially damage skin or trigger allergies. In addition, this enables attracting more users who are not yet familiar with skincare, encouraging them to explore and start their skincare journey.

Numerous studies have applied machine learning to develop personalized skincare recommendation systems. These studies have employed a variety of algorithms and techniques commonly used in developing a recommendation system model. Rubasri et al. leveraged a content-based filtering approach that focused on analyzing product ingredients using the product catalog from Sephora and aimed to respond to user demands and promote diversity by allowing less popular products to be recommended [3]. Jinhee et al. constructed a more advanced model utilizing a deep neural network architecture to analyze cosmetic product ingredients combined with skin image analysis to assess user skin condition from facial images [4]. Manurung and Baizal utilized neural collaborative filtering (NCF), introduced by He et al., to develop their skincare recommendation system using the product catalog from Sociolla [5]. These studies incorporated product ratings and historical user skincare profiles that showcase its potential as an innovative approach to increase the accuracy of recommendations. However, existing approaches focus on either collaborative filtering using product ratings and reviews or content-based filtering based on product ingredients. This limitation underscores the potential for a more comprehensive approach that leverages both user preferences from product ratings and reviews, as well as product characteristics to improve the recommendation by enabling the model to learn from richer feature representations.

In this paper, we propose a novel hybrid approach that combines constraint-based filtering, semantic retrieval, and neural network, specifically applied to unsupervised skincare catalog. The system utilizes constraint-based filtering to ensures applicability to user budget and allergy restrictions. The filtered candidate products are then ranked using a bi-encoder or cross-encoder to capture the semantic relationships between user skincare needs and product benefits. The neural network component is trained as a binary quality classifier that learns to distinguish high- and low-quality products. This is used to predict the quality score of the remaining candidates. The quality score is then combined with the semantic score and user-preference matching to re-rank and produce final recommendation. The three-stage architecture integrates safety, relevance, and quality that allows us to balance recommendation accuracy while providing precise, trustworthy, and diverse recommendations so that users receive products that suit their needs and quality standards, rather than being limited to only popular items.

The recommendation system supports both single-product and multi-product (routine) recommendation to evaluate effectiveness of the three-stage architecture under increased complexity. A routine recommendation provides suggestions for the five skincare regimens, including cleanser, toner, serum, moisturizer, and sunscreen. This extends beyond single-product selection to address an important challenge in skincare that is products interact through their ingredients and user needs routine with products that can work synergistically while avoiding conflicting ingredients that could potentially damage the skin.

2 Methodology

The proposed architecture introduces a novel recommendation system approach separated into three main stages, including constraints-based filtering, semantic ranking, and neural network quality assessment. The illustration of the recommendation system architecture is presented in Fig. 1, and the methodology for each component will be described below.

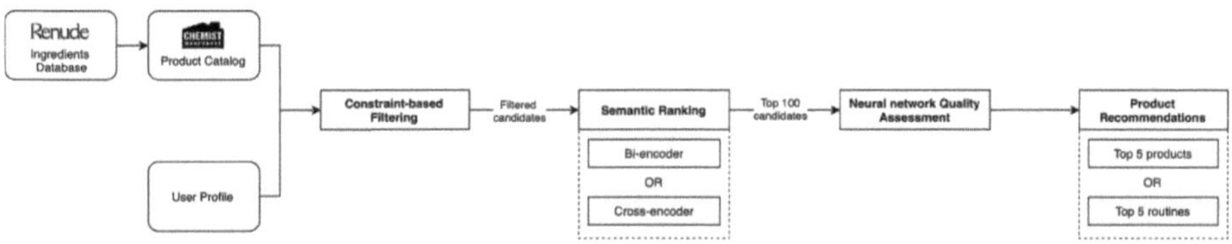

Fig. 1. Three-stage recommendation system workflow.

2.1 Constraint-Based Filtering

The constraint-based filtering serves as the first stage of the system and is based on a pre-defined set of constraint that describe the relationships between products and user [6]. The solution consists of concrete instantiations of the variable so that all constraints are fulfilled to ensure the recommendation strictly comply with user needs. The constraint filtering is divided into hard constraints and soft constraints. Hard constraints are applied first and enforced on features that must be fulfilled and cannot be compromised to prevent unsuitable or harmful recommendations, particularly for users with allergies or sensitive skin. The soft constraints are applied subsequently by incorporating a fallback mechanism. The constraints will be ignored if the number of candidate products is fewer than five to prevent empty recommendation sets.

The following are the definition of the sets of variables implemented in this model:

$$V_P = \{pt_P, f_P, a_P, p_P\}, \quad V_U = \{pt_U, f_U, a_U, b_U\}, \tag{1}$$

where pt represents product type, f formulation, a allergies, p price, b budget, with V_U referring to user properties and V_P to product properties. Furthermore, Table 1 presents the sets of constraints applied in the model.

Table 1. Rules in constraint filtering

Type	Constraint	Expression
Hard Constraint	CF_1	$pt_P = pt_U$
	CF_2	$a_P \cap a_U = \emptyset$
Soft Constraint	CF_3	$f_P \in pf_U$
	CF_4	$p_P \leq b_U$

where CF denotes constraint filter that defines the implemented rules. We designed these constraints to fulfill essential requirements that prioritize user safety while also maintaining system flexibility through the fallback mechanism. The filtered candidates that satisfy all constraints from this stage are then ranked in the subsequent stages.

2.2 Semantic Ranking

The semantic ranking leverages pre-trained language models to capture the nuanced relationship between user requirements and product characteristics, and to calculate the relevancy scores for ranking. In this study, we evaluate two approaches that is cross-encoder and bi-encoder to determine which better captures semantic alignment for ranking candidate products.

Cross-Encoder Approach. Cross-encoders are transformer-based models that capture the relationship between a pair of sentences by jointly encoding them into a shared representation [7]. This approach allows the cross-encoder to effectively capture the interaction and dependencies between two sentences that benefit user-product matching. For each filtered product, a pair consisting of user profile and product details is formed and fed into TinyBERT (ms-marco-TinyBERT-L-2-v2), a compact version of BERT that produce a single relevance score. It employs knowledge distillation instead of transfer knowledge, which enables the smaller model to remain effective in capturing contextual relationships while improving inference efficiency. The relevance scores are ranked, and the top 100 candidates for each product type are retained for the subsequent stage to improve the efficiency of quality assessment.

Bi-encoder Approach. The bi-encoder, on the other hand, encodes the user profile and product details independently that results in separate sentence embeddings [8]. The encoded representations are then compared using cosine similarity to determine the relationship between them. The bi-encoder approach is performed using Sentence-BERT (all-MiniLM-L6-v2), a state-of-the-art pre-trained transformer-based language model that address BERT's limitations by leveraging a Siamese network structure optimized for sentence similarity tasks [9]. This architecture employs an attention mechanism to capture interactions between words to enable the extraction of meaningful semantic patterns effective for matching tasks. Similarly, candidates are ranked based on the scores obtained from cosine similarity between user profile and product details embeddings, and the top 100 candidates are selected based on their alignment with user requests.

The bi-encoder approach offers efficiency through independent encoding allowing the similarity scores to be computed by reusing pre-computed embedding. However, this prevents it from directly capturing the semantic interactions between user and product. In contrast, cross-encoders offer higher ranking accuracy that also create increased computational cost. In this system, we evaluate both approaches that best support the overall recommendation system pipeline.

2.3 Neural Network Quality Assessment

The neural network is employed to refine the recommendation ranking by fusing multiple signals and learning diverse types of product information to assess the overall product quality. This component is trained as a binary quality classifier, and during inference, the predicted quality score is incorporated as one of the components for the final product ranking. This approach is commonly used in recommendation system by employing an efficient retrieval method to selects a set of highly related item candidates that are then re-ranked using a more computationally intensive and accurate model [10].

The model integrates structured product attributes with semantic embeddings of product details. The structured product attributes are derived from normalized and encoded numerical and categorical variables of each product, while the semantic embeddings are obtained using the same encoder as in the second stage. This fusion enables the neural network to learn different representation that allows it to capture a deeper understanding of product-user compatibility.

The neural network is trained to predict target scores, $S_{\text{target}}(p, u)$, computed from multiple product factors assumed to perceived quality in different proportions, including price, ratings, and review count. This approach simplifies the multi-objective problem into a single objective approach that balances recommendation quality and personalisation through a composite loss function. The training minimizes the binary cross-entropy loss, $\mathcal{L}$, that can be written as follows:

$$\mathcal{L} = \frac{1}{N} \sum_{i=1}^{N} \left[S_{\text{target}}(p_i, u) \log(\hat{y}_i) + \left(1 - S_{\text{target}}(p_i, u)\right) \log\left(1 - \hat{y}_i\right) \right] \quad (2)$$

where $\hat{y}_i$ represent the predicted quality probability. During inference, the predicted quality scores for candidate products are collected and integrated with other components to form the final ranking score.

2.4 Final Product Ranking Score

The final scoring is computed differently for single-product and multi-product (routine) recommendations. The ranking combines score from multiple components to balance user alignment, semantic relevance, and product quality.

For single-product recommendations, the final score aggregates the semantic ranking scores, neural network quality scores, and benefit matching scores to ensure contribution from both learned patterns and semantic relevance. The benefit matching score is obtained from the number of keyword matches between the user skin type and skin problems with the product benefits to emphasize the final score based on product fulfillment of user skin concerns. While the semantic score considers all attributes between products and user profiles, this targeted approach focuses on key factors enabled through standardized keywords across products and user attributes. The final ranking score, $S_{\text{single}}(p, u)$, computed for single-product recommendation for product p and user u, is expressed as follows:

$$S_{\text{single}}(p, u) = \alpha \cdot Sr(p, u) + \beta \cdot Q(p) + \gamma \cdot B(p, u) \tag{3}$$

where $Sr(p, u)$ represents the semantic ranking score, $Q(p)$ the neural network quality score, and $B(p, u)$ the benefit matching score. Each score component is normalized to ensure proportional contribution, and the weights are set as $\alpha = 0.35$, $\beta = 0.35$, and $\gamma = 0.30$ to allocate near equal importance among each element and prevent excessive reliance on any signal that balanced semantic relevance and product quality.

For routine recommendations, the scoring follows a similar principle but includes an additional ingredient compatibility score. The ingredient compatibility was derived from multiple sources, including peer-reviewed literature and dermatologist-reviewed articles such as Verywell Health and Curology [11–13]. This component evaluates whether the ingredients across products in the routine interact synergistically or should be avoided. It penalizes conflicting combinations and rewards synergistic ingredient interactions, adding an additional layer of complexity to maintain safety and coherence. The final ranking score, $S_{\text{routine}}(R, u)$, computed for routine recommendation, is expressed as follows:

$$S_{\text{routine}}(R, u) = \alpha \cdot \bar{Sr}(R, u) + \beta \cdot \bar{Q}(R) + \gamma \cdot \bar{B}(R, u) + \delta \cdot Ic(R) \tag{4}$$

where $R = \{p_1, p_2, ..., p_5\}$ represents a set of routine products, $\bar{Sr}$, $\bar{Q}$, and $\bar{B}$ are the averaged scores of the routine products, and $Ic(R)$ calculates the ingredient compatibility score. The weights are $\alpha = 0.30$, $\beta = 0.30$, $\gamma = 0.30$, and $\delta = 0.10$ to provide balanced contributions from the three main components. The ingredient compatibility is incorporated to extend the single-product model to provide multi-product recommendations that are safe for routines. The ingredient compatibility score $Ic(R)$ is calculated by:

$$Ic(R) = \max\left(0, 1 - \frac{C_{\text{conflict}}}{N_{\text{pairs}}} + \frac{C_{\text{synergy}}}{N_{\text{pairs}}}\right) \tag{5}$$

where C_{conflict} represents the number of conflicting ingredient pairs, C_{synergy} the number of synergistic combinations, and N_{pairs} the total number of product pairs in the routine. The hybrid scoring mechanism then generates the top five products or skincare routines with the highest final scores.

3 Experiment

In this section, the performance of the recommendation system is evaluated to assess its ability to align with user requirements, as well as its generalisation ability.

3.1 Skincare Product Dataset

The skincare recommendation system was development using the product catalog from Chemist Warehouse, the largest pharmacy in Australia that offers the most extensive range of skincare product [14]. We incorporated an ingredients database from Renude, an online skincare service, to enrich the product catalog and provide more precise information translation about each product [15]. The catalog comprises 1,000 skincare products with multiple properties that can be extracted from product details.

Multiple data preparation techniques were performed to clean product text attributes and standardized ingredients between the two datasets to enables feature engineering to extract allergies and benefit based on ingredients. The final product catalog contains detailed information for each product including product name, price, rating, review count, general information, product type, formulation, allergies, benefit, and ingredients.

3.2 Synthetic User Profiles

As the system was developed using unsupervised data, the evaluation was performed by generating synthetic user profiles. The synthetic user profiles were generated by calculating the proportion of products in the catalog across different user attributes. User profiles were represented as structured data including skin type, skin problem, allergies, formulation, budget, and recommendation type.

This approach assumes that the variety of products in the catalog represents the distribution of user demand in the market, which is beneficial for estimating expected user profiles [16]. For example, a high number of moisturizers indicated a higher proportion of users with dry skin concerns. This allows the system to derive weights for each attribute option and generates synthetic data that reflects the proportion of users in the actual market rather than using arbitrary distribution.

3.3 Evaluation

The evaluation metrics employed are requirement satisfaction, diversity, and catalog coverage. This selection is suitable for unsupervised recommendation system as these metrics do not require interaction data and focus on assessing recommendation quality and user requirement alignment.

The first metric is requirement satisfaction that measures how well the recommended products align with user requirements by evaluating the percentage of recommendations that satisfy all hard and soft constraint [17].

$$\text{satisfaction} = \frac{1}{N_U} \sum_{u \in U} \sum_{i \in R_u} \frac{C(i,u)}{N_{R_U}} \tag{6}$$

where U denotes the set of all users, R_u denotes the set of recommended items for user u, and $C(i,u)$ denotes the constraint satisfaction function for item i and user u that can be expressed as:

$$C(i,u) = \begin{cases} 1, & \text{if a constraint is satisfied} \\ 0, & \text{otherwise} \end{cases} \tag{7}$$

Following that, diversity measures the average dissimilarity between pairs of items in a recommendation list [18]. This ensures the variety within the recommended product list, so users are exposed to a broad range of options. Diversity is calculated using intra-list diversity that defined as:

$$\text{diversity} = \frac{1}{N_U} \sum_{u \in U} \frac{2}{N_{R_u}(N_{R_u} - 1)} \sum_{i=1}^{N_{R_u}-1} \sum_{j=i+1}^{N_{R_u}} d(i,j) \tag{8}$$

where $d(i,j)$ denotes the distance function measuring similarity between products, using Euclidean distance for numerical features and Hamming distance for categorical features. The high values in the calculation indicate high diversity.

The third metric is catalog coverage that describes the proportion of items in the entire catalog that are recommended to users [19]:

$$\text{coverage} = \frac{\text{number of unique products recommended}}{\text{total products in catalog}} \times 100\% \tag{9}$$

This metric is calculated across all user profiles and a high catalog coverage indicates the system ability to suggest a variety of products rather than concentrating on highly-rated items that also support insights into system diversity and fairness.

3.4 Result and Discussion

Comparative Analysis of Architecture Configurations. The recommendation system was evaluated using 100 synthetic user profiles, with system performance analyzed across different configuration combinations of the three-stage pipeline to assess the importance of each component. The results shown in Table 2 and Fig. 2 reveal that the baseline configurations using single components underscore the critical importance of constraint filtering component in both single-product and multi-product systems, achieving requirement satisfaction of 78.72% and 82.45%, respectively. The constraint-only configuration also achieves reduced latency, thus enabling the system to produce recommendation that fulfill user requirements in real-time. However, we acknowledge that this significant outperformance of the constraint component stems from comprehensive data preparation and feature engineering in the product catalog, where we compiled standardized benefit and allergens information for each product, making it easier for constraints to match against user profiles structured with standardized keywords.

The neural network component, on the other hand, exhibits the lowest catalog coverage, which indicates that it tends to concentrate on high-quality products. This aligns with its intended purpose of promoting items with strong user approval signals. Comparing the two semantic similarity approaches, the cross-encoder achieves a higher satisfaction rate of 70.30% compared to 59.46% for the bi-encoder in single-product recommendations, while both methods show less difference in multi-product routines with satisfaction rates of 72.01% and 64.30%, respectively. This indicates that the advantage of joint encoding in cross-encoder architecture, which better captures user-product relationship, significantly benefits single-product recommendations. However, as more products are being suggested, the bi-encoder is able to overcome this limitation, making it suitable for multi-product recommendations with faster computation.

In single-product recommendations, adding neural network quality score to constraint filtering provides substantial improvement by 4.79% in satisfaction, 2.88% in diversity, and 3.8% in catalog coverage, while adding only 0.185 s of latency. This suggest that re-ranking using quality scores refines the model's ability to fulfill user requirements while encouraging exploration of a wider range of products. Furthermore, we observed that integrating cross-encoder with constraint filtering enables the model to achieve slightly higher performance compared to constraint filtering alone, indicating that semantic similarity offers additional value in capturing user intent effectively. The full three-stage model using cross-encoder achieves the best overall balance across the three metrics with 84.68% satisfaction, 41.27% diversity, and 15.8% coverage for single-product recommendation. This suggests that combining the three components offers a balance between requirement satisfaction from constraint filtering and improvement in diversity and catalog coverage from semantic similarity and neural network components.

In multi-product recommendations, a slightly different phenomenon was discovered, as the bi-encoder achieves better satisfaction across different combinations, as mentioned earlier. Following that, we observed a similar pattern to single-product recommendation, as adding the neural network to constraint-based filtering enables the model to achieve better performance with 44.61% diversity compared to constraint alone. Across different configurations, we observe that the catalog coverage in multi-product recommendations is consistently lower than single-product system, while diversity scores remain consistently high. This pattern suggests that the higher diversity stems from the

Table 2. Performance of single-product and multi-product recommendation systems

Configuration	Single-Product				Multi-Product			
	RS (%)	**Div (%)**	**CC (%)**	**Time (s)**	**RS (%)**	**Div (%)**	**CC (%)**	**Time (s)**
Constraints Only	78.72	37.88	11.1	0.005	82.45	42.19	6.8	0.47
Bi-encoder Only	59.46	29.61	5.5	2.72	72.01	14.65	3.4	14.16
Cross-encoder Only	70.30	32.99	4.5	2.81	64.30	15.08	4.6	14.45
Neural Network Only	63.42	**46.86**	4.2	2.89	55.72	18.41	1.4	1.06
Constraints + Bi-encoder	75.98	33.30	13.9	0.21	82.44	43.46	8.7	0.70
Constraints + Cross-encoder	79.92	38.71	11.2	0.26	81.38	41.77	8.3	0.67
Constraints + Neural Network	83.51	40.87	14.9	0.19	83.16	**44.61**	6.3	0.66
Bi-encoder + Neural Network	68.48	34.50	6.1	3.08	74.94	16.46	3.0	13.94
Cross-encoder + Neural Network	73.01	38.55	9.0	3.23	65.13	16.00	4.1	14.37
Full Hybrid Bi-encoder	81.74	37.37	14.5	0.31	**84.22**	42.72	**9.1**	0.91
Full Hybrid Cross-encoder	**84.68**	41.27	**15.8**	0.29	83.12	43.04	8.5	0.85

RS = Requirement Satisfaction, Div = Diversity, CC = Catalog Coverage.

inherent need for varied product types in each routine, while the lower catalog coverage results from the additional constraints required to construct compatible routine combinations that are inherently more restrictive than single-product recommendations. For multi-product, the best performance was also achieved using the full three-stage model using bi-encoder with 84.22% satisfaction and 9.1% catalog coverage, the highest across all configurations in multi-product recommendations. This further demonstrates that the three-stage recommendation system balances the advantages of different components to enhance the overall model performance while maintaining reasonable computational time.

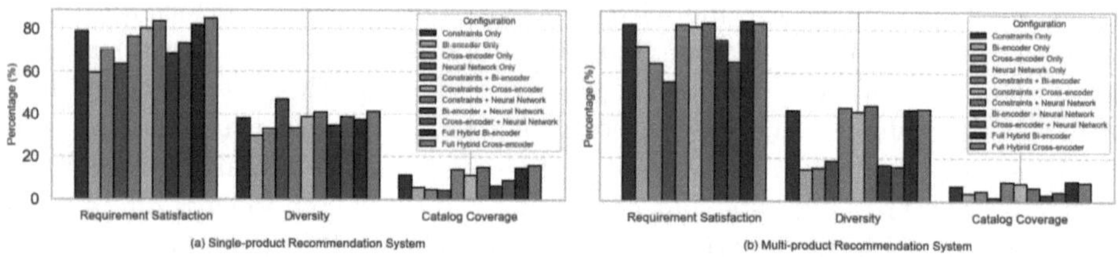

Fig. 2. Comparison of evaluation metrics between single-product and multi-product recommendation systems

Ingredient Compatibility Analysis in Multi-product (Routine) Recommendations. We examine the impact of ingredient compatibility in multi-product (routine) recommendation system in Table 3. It reveals that ingredient compatibility provides an improvement in requirement satisfaction for configurations that incorporate constraint filtering, evident in the full three-stage bi-encoder system increasing from 83.97% to 84.22%. On the other hand, we

Table 3. Impact of ingredient compatibility on multi-product recommendation systems

Configuration	With Compatibility			Without Compatibility		
	RS (%)	Div (%)	CC (%)	RS (%)	Div (%)	CC (%)
Constraints Only	82.45	42.19	6.8	81.16	42.57	7.1
Bi-encoder Only	72.01	14.65	3.4	72.50	13.86	3.5
Cross-encoder Only	64.30	15.08	4.6	64.50	14.91	4.7
Neural Network Only	55.72	18.41	1.4	58.19	20.28	1.3
Constraints + Bi-encoder	82.44	43.46	8.7	81.12	43.23	8.9
Constraints + Cross-encoder	81.38	41.77	8.3	81.24	41.51	7.8
Constraints + Neural Network	83.16	**44.61**	6.3	82.88	**44.27**	6.5
Bi-encoder + Neural Network	74.94	16.46	3.0	75.05	15.88	2.8
Cross-encoder + Neural Network	65.13	16.00	4.1	65.34	16.11	3.8
Full Hybrid Bi-encoder	**84.22**	42.72	**9.1**	**83.97**	42.80	**9.1**
Full Hybrid Cross-encoder	83.12	43.04	8.5	83.06	43.04	8.4

RS = Requirement Satisfaction, Div = Diversity, CC = Catalog Coverage.

observed that the results for configurations without constraint filtering show a slight decrement in requirement satisfaction. This indicates that compatibility filtering provides enhancement to complement the system safety layer when combined with baseline constraint filtering, while it conflicts with semantic or quality scores as compatibility filtering penalizes routines based on different scoring objectives. The diversity and catalog coverage metrics only show minimal differences across both conditions, indicating that compatibility refines specific product combinations rather than limiting the recommendation variety. These results confirm that the 10% weight assigned to compatibility scoring balances safety considerations with performance optimization that allows the ingredient compatibility to serve as a safety mechanism that enhances the system quality without excessive restrictions.

4 Conclusion

This paper proposes a three-stage recommendation system architecture for personalized skincare recommendations that integrates constraints-based filtering, semantic ranking, and neural network quality assessment. The system accommodates both single-product and multi-product (routine) recommendations, and was evaluated using a product catalog from Chemist Warehouse enriched with ingredients details from Renude. The results reveal that the constraint filtering component establishes a strong foundation for the model to meet user requirements, while the semantic similarity and neural network components improve its ability to capture user intent and promote high-quality products. The architecture effectively balances accuracy to fulfill user requirements through constraint filtering, and diversity in recommendations through semantic similarity and neural network components. The performance shows that single-product recommendations achieve optimal result with the three-stage system using cross-encoder, while the multi-product recommendations perform better using bi-encoder. This divergence demonstrates that the cross-encoder ability in capturing user-product relationship is suitable for individual products that require precise evaluation, and the bi-encoder handles routine task more efficiently with recommendations distributed across multiple products. The multi-product system is also enhanced with the ingredient compatibility component, which provides an additional safety mechanism for the system that prevents harmful ingredient interactions without compromising recommendation variety. These results confirm that the proposed system successfully balances accuracy, diversity, coverage, and efficiency that proves its potential for implementation in the skincare industry.

Acknowledgements. This work was supported by the Indonesia Endowment Fund for Education Agency (LPDP).

References

1. McKinsey & Company. https://www.mckinsey.com/industries/consumer-packaged-goods/our-insights/the-beauty-boom-and-beyond-can-the-industry-maintain-its-growth. Accessed 05-09-2025
2. myNZTE. https://my.nzte.govt.nz/article/who-buys-skincare-products-in-australia. Accessed 10-09-2025
3. Rubasri, S., Hemavathi, S., Jayasakthi, K., Sangeerani, A., Latha, K., Gopinath, N.: Cosmetic product selection using machine learning. In: 2022 International Conference on Communication. Computing and Internet of Things (IC3IoT), pp. 1–6. IEEE, India (2022)
4. Lee, J., Yoon, H., Kim, S., Lee, C., Yoo, S.: Deep learning-based skin care product recommendation: a focus on cosmetic ingredient analysis and facial skin conditions. J. Cosmet. Dermatol. **23**(6), 2066–2077 (2024)
5. Manurung, T.A., Baizal, Z.K.A.: The usage of neural collaborative filtering in enhancing personalized skincare recommendation. In: 2024 International Conference on Data Science and Its Applications (ICoDSA), pp. 375–379. IEEE, Indonesia (2024)
6. Felfernig, A., Friedrich, G., Jannach, D., Zanker, M.: Recommender Systems Handbook, 1st edn. Springer, Boston, United States (2010)
7. Ankith, M.S., Bhattacharya, A., Gandhi, A., Huddar, V., Saroop, A., Bhagat, R.: DISKCO: disentangling knowledge from cross-encoder to bi-encoder. In: Companion Proceedings of the ACM Web Conference, pp. 346-354. ACM, United States (2024)
8. Rauf, M.A., Khalil, M.M.Y., Wang, W., Wang, Q., Ghani, M.A.N.U., Hassan, J.: BCE4ZSR: Bi-encoder empowered by teacher cross-encoder for zero-shot cold-start news recommendation. Inf. Process. Manag. **61**(3), 103686 (2024)
9. Axelborn, H., Berggren, J.: Topic modeling for customer insights: a comparative analysis of LDA and BERTopic in categorizing customer calls. MSc thesis, Umeå University, Sweden (2023)

10. Dang, V., Bendersky, M., Croft, W.B.: Two-stage learning to rank for information retrieval. In: Serdyukov, P., Braslavski, P., Kuznetsov, S.O., Kamps, J., Rüger, S., Agichtein, E., Segalovich, I., Yilmaz, E. (eds.) ECIR 2013. LNCS, vol. 7814, pp. 423–434. Springer, Heidelberg (2013). https://doi.org/10.1007/978-3-642-36973-5_36
11. Verywell Health. https://www.verywellhealth.com/skincare-ingredients-to-not-mix-11705381. Accessed 09-08-2025
12. Curology. https://curology.com/blog/what-skincare-products-not-to-mix-according-to-dermatology-experts/. Accessed 09-08-2025
13. Stern, R.S., et al.: Skincare ingredients recommended by cosmetic dermatologists: a Delphi consensus study. J. Am. Acad. Dermatol. **92**(1), 1–9 (2025)
14. Chemist Warehouse Skincare. https://www.chemistwarehouse.com.au/shop-online/665/skin-care. Accessed 02-08-2025
15. Renude Ingredients Database. https://renude.co/ingredients. Accessed 02-08-2025
16. Carraro, D., Bridge, D.: A sampling approach to Debiasing the offline evaluation of recommender systems. J. Intell. Inf. Syst. **58**(2), 311–336 (2022)
17. Burke, R.: Knowledge-Based Recommender Systems. In: Encyclopedia of Library and Information Systems, vol. 69 (Supplement 32), pp. 175–186. CRC Press (2000)
18. Zangerle, E., Bauer, C.: Evaluating recommender systems: survey and framework. ACM Comput. Surv. **55**(8), 1–38 (2022)
19. Jadon, A., Patil, A.: A comprehensive survey of evaluation techniques for recommendation systems. In: International Conference on Computation of Artificial Intelligence & Machine Learning, pp. 281-304. Springer, India (2024)

Reconfigurable Intelligence Architecture for Ultra-Low-Latency LLMs on FPGAs

Ioannis Patias[1(✉)] and Koutaro Hachiya[2]

[1] Faculty of Mathematics and Informatics, Sofia University "St. Kliment Ohridski", Sofia, Bulgaria
patias@fmi.uni-sofia.bg
[2] Graduate School of Science and Technology, Hirosaki University, Hirosaki, Japan
k.hachiya@acm.org

Abstract. Large Language Models (LLMs) have become central to modern natural language processing (NLP). However, their inference latency remains a critical barrier for real-time applications such as conversational artificial intelligence (AI), interactive translation, and decision support systems. Conventional Graphics Processing Units (GPUs) deliver high throughput but often struggle to meet the strict latency requirements of prompt-driven frameworks. This paper introduces a high-level architecture for Field-Programmable Gate Array (FPGA)-based prompting and ultra-low-latency LLM inference, leveraging the reconfigurability and parallelism of FPGAs to achieve deterministic performance. The proposed design maps each stage of the LLM pipeline (tokenization, embedding, transformer computation, key-value (KV) caching, and sampling) onto specialized hardware blocks. Tokenization and text input/output (I/O) are implemented with finite state machines (FSMs) and lookup tables for fixed latency. Embedding and positional encoding exploit parallel memory access and digital signal processing (DSP) units. The transformer engine employs systolic general matrix multiplication (GEMM) arrays and head-parallel attention to maximize concurrency, while the KV cache fabric combines on-chip prefix reuse with external High Bandwidth Memory (HBM) or Double Data Rate (DDR) memory for long-context storage. Sampling and output are accelerated through hardware-based top-k/top-p selection, orchestrated by a lightweight sequencer for minimal overhead. This architecture demonstrates how FPGAs can deliver prompt-to-output inference with extreme speed, offering a viable path toward interactive AI systems that demand low latency and deterministic timing.

Keywords: FPGA acceleration · low-latency inference · large language models (LLMs) · hardware pipeline · parallel processing

1 Introduction

This section establishes the foundation of this work by outlining the rapid rise of Large Language Models (LLMs) and the growing demand for real-time, interactive applications. It highlights the limitations of Graphics Processing Units (GPUs), which excel

C. Xu (Ed.): ICMLSC 2026, CCIS 2948, pp. 440–452, 2027.
https://doi.org/10.1007/978-981-92-1546-1_36

at high throughput but often fail to deliver consistent low latency in prompt-driven frameworks. The section then presents Field-Programmable Gate Arrays (FPGAs) as a promising alternative, emphasizing their reconfigurability, parallelism, and deterministic dataflow. Finally, it defines the paper's goal: to propose and analyze a high-level FPGA architecture for LLM inference that achieves ultra-low latency and enables responsive, interactive AI systems.

1.1 Growth of LLMs and Demand for Real-time Applications

Over the past few years, LLMs have emerged as transformative tools in natural language processing (NLP) [1]. These models, trained on massive text corpora, are capable of generating coherent, context-aware responses, performing translation, summarization, and even reasoning tasks. Their adoption has spread across industries, from customer service chatbots and real-time translation systems to medical decision support and creative writing assistants [2]. The scale of these models has grown exponentially, with billions of parameters enabling unprecedented accuracy and fluency. However, this growth has also intensified the demand for real-time responsiveness [3]. In interactive applications, users expect immediate answers, often within milliseconds, to maintain the natural flow of dialogue. Latency becomes a critical factor, as even small delays can disrupt user experience, reduce trust in AI systems, and limit their applicability in time-sensitive domains such as live communication or financial trading.

As LLMs continue to expand in scope and capability, the challenge of delivering low-latency inference has become central to their practical deployment. Meeting this demand requires architectures that not only handle large computational workloads but also guarantee deterministic timing and responsiveness. Only this way the system will behave in a predictable, repeatable, and consistent way every time it runs the same workload.

1.2 GPUs Excel at Throughput but Struggle with Interactive Latency

GPUs have become the dominant platform for training and deploying LLMs. Their architecture, designed for massive parallelism, excels at high throughput tasks such as batch processing and large-scale training. GPUs can process thousands of operations simultaneously, making them ideal for workloads where throughput is the primary metric. However, when applied to interactive inference, GPUs reveal significant limitations. Their scheduling mechanisms, memory hierarchies, and reliance on batching introduce overheads that increase latency [4].

For prompt-driven frameworks, where a single user query must be processed quickly, GPUs often fail to deliver consistent low-latency performance. Memory bottlenecks, context switching, and non-deterministic execution paths further exacerbate delays. This mismatch between GPU strengths and the requirements of real-time inference creates a bottleneck for applications that depend on responsiveness. In scenarios such as conversational AI, live translation, or interactive decision support, latency directly impacts usability. A delay of even a few hundred milliseconds can break the illusion of natural dialogue, frustrate users, and reduce adoption. Thus, while GPUs remain indispensable for training and batch inference, their limitations in interactive latency highlight the need for alternative architectures tailored to real-time performance [5, 6].

1.3 FPGAs Reconfigurability, Parallelism, and Low-latency Dataflow

FPGAs present a compelling alternative to GPUs for low-latency inference. Unlike fixed-architecture processors, FPGAs consist of reconfigurable logic blocks, digital signal processing (DSP) units, and on-chip memory that can be customized to specific workloads. This flexibility allows designers to create hardware pipelines optimized for the unique requirements of LLM inference. FPGAs excel at fine-grained parallelism, enabling concurrent execution of multiple operations with deterministic timing. Their dataflow-oriented design minimizes memory bottlenecks by allowing computations to stream directly between hardware blocks without unnecessary round-trips to external memory. This makes FPGAs particularly well-suited for prompt-driven frameworks, where responsiveness is paramount. Their ability to integrate hierarchical memory systems, including on-chip caches and external High Bandwidth Memory (HBM), further enhances performance for long-context inference [7].

Importantly, FPGAs enable partial reconfiguration, allowing specific modules to be swapped or updated without rebuilding the entire system. This adaptability supports rapid experimentation and deployment in evolving AI environments. Together, these features position FPGAs as a promising platform for achieving ultra-low-latency LLM inference, bridging the gap between throughput and responsiveness [8].

Implementations of LLM inference on edge-oriented FPGAs have been reported in [9, 10]. Although their power efficiency exceeds that of edge-oriented GPUs, the throughput remains at 4.8–8.6 tokens/s, which is lower than GPU-based systems. Consequently, the per-token latency is unlikely to be sufficient for real-time processing.

1.4 Paper Goal

The goal of this paper is to propose and analyze a high-level FPGA architecture designed to accelerate LLM inference with ultra-low latency. The architecture maps each stage of the inference pipeline (tokenization, embedding, transformer computation, key-value (KV) caching, and sampling) onto specialized hardware blocks. By leveraging FPGA parallelism, deterministic dataflow, and hierarchical memory, the design aims to deliver prompt-to-output inference with extreme speed.

The paper will discuss how tokenization can be implemented using finite state machines (FSMs) and lookup tables, embeddings through parallel memory access and DSP units, and transformer computations via systolic general matrix multiplication (GEMM) arrays with head-parallel attention. KV caching will be addressed through a combination of on-chip prefix reuse and external High Bandwidth Memory/Double Data Rate (HBM/DDR) for long-context storage, while sampling will be accelerated through hardware-based top-k/top-p selection.

Ultimately, the paper seeks to demonstrate that FPGAs can provide deterministic, low-latency inference suitable for interactive AI applications. By bridging the gap between throughput and responsiveness, this architecture offers a pathway toward real-time deployment of LLMs in domains where latency is critical.

2 Background

This section provides the technical foundation for the proposed FPGA-based architecture for LLM inference. It begins with a brief overview of FPGAs, highlighting their core components such as Configurable Logic Blocks (CLBs), DSP units, Block RAM (BRAM), and HBM. Next, it outlines the basics of transformer models, including attention mechanisms, multi-layer perceptrons (MLPs), and embeddings, which form the computational backbone of LLMs. Finally, it reviews existing accelerators such as GPUs and Application-Specific Integrated Circuits (ASICs), discussing their strengths and limitations in the context of low-latency inference. Together, these subsections establish the context for why FPGAs are uniquely positioned to address the challenges of real-time LLM deployment.

2.1 Overview of FPGAs

FPGAs are reconfigurable semiconductor devices that allow designers to implement custom digital circuits after manufacturing. At their core, FPGAs consist of CLBs, which provide the basic building units for implementing logic functions. CLBs can be programmed to perform operations ranging from simple Boolean logic to complex finite state machines, enabling fine-grained control over computation. Complementing CLBs are DSP units, specialized hardware blocks optimized for arithmetic operations such as multiplication and accumulation. DSPs are critical for accelerating matrix multiplications and convolution operations, which dominate workloads in machine learning and LLM inference [7].

Memory resources are equally important in FPGA design. BRAM provides on-chip storage with low latency, suitable for caching embeddings, intermediate activations, or key-value pairs in attention mechanisms. Larger devices also integrate UltraRAM (URAM) for deeper storage hierarchies. To handle long sequences and large models, modern FPGAs incorporate HBM, which offers massive external memory bandwidth compared to traditional DDR memory. HBM enables efficient streaming of weights and activations, reducing bottlenecks in transformer pipelines [11].

The combination of CLBs, DSPs, BRAM, and HBM allows FPGAs to implement highly parallel, deterministic dataflow architectures. Unlike fixed-function processors, FPGAs can be tailored to specific workloads, enabling designers to fuse operations, minimize memory traffic, and achieve predictable latency. This flexibility makes them particularly attractive for LLM inference, where responsiveness and efficiency are paramount [12].

2.2 Transformer Model

The transformer architecture is the foundation of modern LLMs. It is built around three core components: embeddings, attention mechanisms, and MLPs [13].

Embeddings convert discrete tokens into dense vector representations that capture semantic meaning. These vectors are enriched with positional encodings, which provide information about the order of tokens in a sequence. Embeddings serve as the input to the transformer layers, enabling the model to process text in a continuous vector space [14].

The attention mechanism is the hallmark of transformers. It operates by projecting input embeddings into three matrices: queries (Q), keys (K), and values (V). Attention computes similarity scores between queries and keys, applies a softmax function to normalize these scores, and uses them to weight the values. This allows the model to focus on relevant parts of the input sequence, capturing long-range dependencies efficiently. Multi-head attention extends this concept by running several attention operations in parallel, each learning different aspects of the input [15].

Following attention, the MLP block processes the outputs through feedforward layers with nonlinear activations. These layers expand and contract the dimensionality of the vectors, enabling richer transformations. Residual connections and layer normalization ensure stable training and inference [16].

Together, embeddings, attention, and MLPs form the computational backbone of LLMs. They are highly parallelizable but also memory-intensive, requiring efficient hardware support for matrix multiplications, normalization, and caching. Understanding these components is essential for mapping them onto FPGA hardware, where parallelism and deterministic dataflow can be exploited to reduce latency [17].

2.3 Accelerators

Current LLM deployments primarily rely on GPUs and, in some cases, Application-Specific Integrated Circuits (ASICs).

GPUs are designed for massive parallelism, with thousands of cores capable of executing matrix multiplications and tensor operations efficiently. Their mature software ecosystems, make them the default choice for training and inference. GPUs excel at throughput, particularly in batch processing scenarios, but they struggle with interactive latency. Scheduling overheads, reliance on batching, and non-deterministic execution paths introduce delays that hinder real-time responsiveness [18].

ASICs, on the other hand, are custom chips designed for specific workloads. ASICs can achieve exceptional efficiency and throughput by hardwiring operations into silicon. However, their fixed architecture limits flexibility. Once manufactured, ASICs cannot be reprogrammed to adapt to evolving models or inference strategies. This rigidity makes them less suitable for rapidly changing AI landscapes, where new architectures and optimizations emerge frequently [19].

Both GPUs and ASICs face challenges in balancing throughput with latency. GPUs prioritize parallelism at scale but incur overheads in interactive workloads. ASICs deliver efficiency but sacrifice adaptability. Neither platform fully addresses the need for deterministic, ultra-low-latency inference in prompt-driven applications [20]. This gap highlights the opportunity for FPGAs, which combine reconfigurability, parallelism, and deterministic dataflow to deliver architectures tailored for real-time LLM inference [21].

3 Proposed Architecture

This section presents the high-level FPGA architecture designed to accelerate Large Language Model (LLM) inference with ultra-low latency. The pipeline is divided into six major stages (Fig. 1):

- Tokenizer and Text I/O,
- Embedding Front-End,
- Transformer Engine,
- KV Cache Fabric,
- Sampler and Output, and
- Control and Configuration.

Each stage is mapped to specialized FPGA resources such as CLBs, DSP units, BRAM, and HBM. Together, these components form a streaming hardware pipeline that minimizes memory traffic, maximizes parallelism, and ensures deterministic timing.

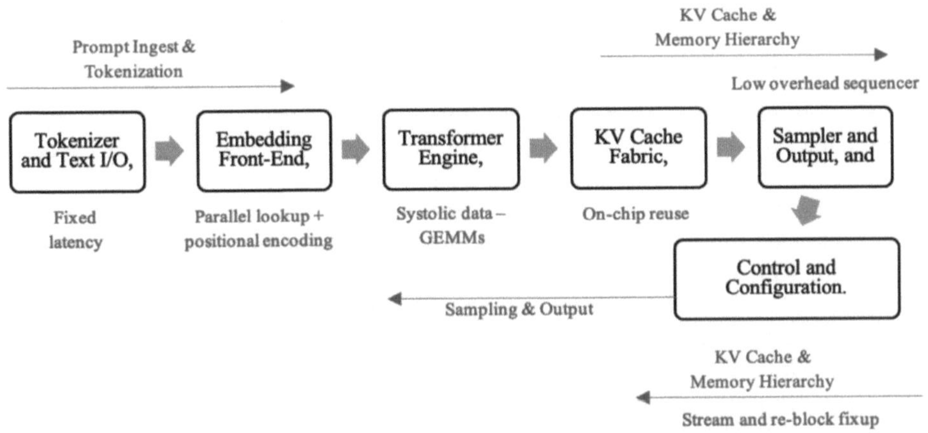

Fig. 1. High-level FPGA pipeline for LLM inference, where each stage of the LLM (tokenization, embeddings, attention, MLP, sampling) is mapped to specialized hardware blocks.

3.1 Tokenizer and Text I/O

The tokenizer and text input/output (I/O) stage is responsible for ingesting raw text prompts, normalizing them, and converting them into token identifiers. On FPGA hardware, this process is implemented using finite state machines (FSMs) and lookup tables stored in BRAM. Normalization tasks such as lowercasing, whitespace handling, and basic Unicode mapping are executed with fixed latency, ensuring deterministic performance. The tokenizer employs an algorithm, implemented as parallel comparators and merge tables. By streaming text through this hardware pipeline, tokenization avoids the overhead of software parsing and delivers consistent throughput. The output is a sequence of token IDs, marked with start and end delimiters, ready for embedding. This stage is critical for latency savings, as it eliminates preprocessing bottlenecks and ensures that prompt ingestion does not delay downstream computation.

3.2 Embedding Front-end

Once tokens are generated, they are mapped to dense vector embeddings. On FPGA, embeddings are stored in BRAM or URAM for frequently used tokens, with external HBM providing access to the full vocabulary. DSP units perform parallel lookups and scaling, while positional encodings are added. These encodings are implemented with fused multiply-add operations in DSP slices, ensuring efficient computation. The embedding front-end is optimized for parallelism: multiple tokens can be processed simultaneously, and hot-token caching reduces memory latency. This stage transforms discrete token IDs into continuous vectors enriched with positional information, forming the input to the transformer engine. Performance gains here come from parallel lookup and deterministic encoding, which reduce the time between tokenization and transformer computation.

3.3 Transformer Engine

The transformer engine is the computational core of the architecture. It implements attention mechanisms and MLPs using systolic GEMM arrays mapped to DSP blocks. Queries (Q), keys (K), and values (V) are generated through linear projections, followed by dot-product attention. Attention scores are scaled and normalized using hardware-accelerated softmax approximations. Multi-head attention is executed in parallel, with each head mapped to a dedicated hardware lane. Residual connections and layer normalization are fused into the dataflow to minimize memory traffic. The MLP block expands and contracts vector dimensions using two linear layers with nonlinear activations, approximated through lookup tables. By exploiting head-parallelism and systolic dataflow, the transformer engine achieves high concurrency and predictable latency. This stage is the most resource-intensive, but also the most critical for performance, as it directly determines inference speed.

3.4 KV Cache Fabric

The KV cache fabric stores intermediate results from attention computations, enabling efficient reuse of prompt prefixes. On FPGA, recent KV pairs are stored in BRAM or URAM, while longer histories are streamed to external HBM or DDR memory. The cache is organized into banks per attention head, allowing conflict-free access during inference. Double-buffering ensures that new KV entries can be written while existing entries are read, minimizing stalls. This hierarchical memory design balances on-chip speed with off-chip capacity, ensuring that long contexts can be handled without sacrificing latency. Performance gains come from prefix reuse and deterministic cache access, which reduce redundant computation and memory overhead.

3.5 Sampler and Output

The sampler and output stage converts logits from the transformer engine into discrete tokens. FPGA hardware accelerates sampling strategies such as greedy decoding, top-k, top-p, and temperature scaling. Priority queues and cumulative sum units are implemented in DSPs and BRAM to select candidate tokens efficiently. The sequencer ensures minimal overhead by streaming logits directly into the sampling unit without intermediate buffering. Once a token is selected, it is output as part of the generated sequence and fed back into the pipeline for subsequent decoding steps. This stage is optimized for low latency, ensuring that token generation does not become a bottleneck. Deterministic sampling guarantees reproducibility, while hardware parallelism supports multiple sampling strategies simultaneously.

3.6 Control and Configuration

The control and configuration stage orchestrates the entire pipeline. Partial reconfiguration allows specific modules, such as activation functions or sampling strategies, to be swapped without rebuilding the entire bitstream. Control logic also monitors performance metrics such as tokens per second, cache hit rate, and memory bandwidth utilization. By dynamically adjusting parameters, the controller ensures optimal resource usage and responsiveness.

4 Evaluation Plan

This section outlines how the proposed FPGA-based architecture for LLM inference will be evaluated. The evaluation focuses on two dimensions: metrics, which define how performance and efficiency are measured, and case studies, which demonstrate real-world applicability in interactive AI scenarios. Together, these elements ensure a rigorous assessment of the architecture's strengths and limitations.

4.1 Metrics

Evaluation begins with the definition of clear performance metrics. The most critical metric is latency per token, which measures the time required to generate each output token. This directly reflects the system's responsiveness in interactive applications and can be obtained as the inverse of throughput (tokens per second). When the input prompt contains a large number of tokens, the Time to First Token (TTFT) becomes non-negligible, and it should also be treated as an important metric because it represents the delay until the first token is produced. Resource utilization is another key metric, including the percentage of FPGA logic blocks, DSP units, and memory resources consumed by the design. Memory bandwidth utilization is tracked to identify bottlenecks in data movement between on-chip and external memory. Power consumption is measured to evaluate energy efficiency, particularly in comparison to GPUs and ASICs. Accuracy metrics are included to ensure that quantization and hardware approximations do not significantly degrade model performance.

4.2 Core Metrics Definition

To assess the overall effectiveness of the architecture, each performance dimension initially is mapped to a score that increases with desirable behavior:

Time to first token:

$$L = T_{\text{TTFT}} \tag{1}$$

Throughput (tokens per second):

$$\Theta = \frac{N_{\text{tokens}}}{T_{\text{total}}} \tag{2}$$

Resource utilization:

$$U = \left(u_{\text{logic}}, u_{\text{DSP}}, u_{\text{mem}}\right) \tag{3}$$

where each u_i is a percentage in [0, 1].

Memory bandwidth utilization:

$$B = \frac{b_{\text{used}}}{b_{\text{max}}} \tag{4}$$

Power consumption:

$$P = P_{\text{avg}} \tag{5}$$

Accuracy (relative to baseline model):

$$A = 1 - \Delta_{\text{acc}} \tag{6}$$

where Δ_{acc} is the accuracy loss from quantization or approximations.

4.3 Combine Metrics into a Unified Evaluation Function

By combining latency, throughput, resource utilization, bandwidth, power, and accuracy, the evaluation provides a comprehensive view of the architecture's effectiveness. You can express the overall evaluation as a performance vector:

$$\mathcal{E} = (L, \Theta, U, B, P, A) \tag{7}$$

The composite effectiveness score, will depend on the definition of weights w_i to compute:

$$S = w_L \cdot \frac{1}{L} + w_\Theta \cdot \Theta + w_U \cdot (1 - \|U\|) + w_B \cdot (1 - B) + w_P \cdot \frac{1}{P} + w_A \cdot A \tag{8}$$

where, based on the formulas described above:

(1) Lower latency → higher score
(2) Higher throughput → higher score

(3) Lower resource use → higher score
(4) Lower bandwidth pressure → higher score
(5) Lower power → higher score
(6) Higher accuracy → higher score

This high-level scoring framework provides an initial, holistic view of the architecture's performance by rewarding low latency, high throughput, efficient resource usage, low bandwidth demand, low power consumption, and strong accuracy. While simple, it establishes a clear foundation for comparing design alternatives and guides deeper, metric-specific analysis as the system matures.

4.4 Case Study

The case study demonstrates the architecture's applicability in real-world scenarios. For example, an FPGA-powered smart assistant for elderly & accessibility support could work following the stages:

1. Tokenizer & Text/Voice I/O
   - 1.1. Input Capture:
     - 1.1.1. Microphone or text input is digitized and streamed into the FPGA.
     - 1.1.2. If voice is used, a lightweight speech to text module (could be external or FPGA accelerated) converts audio into text.
   - 1.2. Tokenization:
     - 1.2.1. Hardware pipelines split text into tokens (words, subwords, or characters).
     - 1.2.2. Parallel tokenizers can process multiple words simultaneously, reducing preprocessing delay.
   - 1.3. Output: Structured token IDs ready for embedding.
2. Embedding Front End
   - 2.1. Lookup Tables: Each token ID maps to a vector embedding stored in FPGA BRAM or external memory.
   - 2.2. Acceleration: DSP slices perform multiplications/additions to normalize or scale embeddings.
   - 2.3. Optimization: Frequently used embeddings (like common words) can be cached in BRAM for instant access.
   - 2.4. Output: Dense vectors representing the semantic meaning of input tokens.
3. Transformer Engine
   - 3.1. Attention Mechanism:
     - 3.1.1. Multi head attention is mapped to parallel DSP pipelines.
     - 3.1.2. Products between queries, keys, and values are computed simultaneously.
   - 3.2. Feed Forward Layers:
     - 3.2.1. CLBs and DSPs accelerate matrix multiplications.
     - 3.2.2. Nonlinear activations implemented as lookup tables for speed.
   - 3.3. Layer Normalization: Performed in hardware using parallel arithmetic units.
   - 3.4. Output: Contextualized embeddings capture meaning in relation to prior tokens.
4. KV Cache Fabric
   - 4.1. Storage: Keys and values from previous tokens are stored in BRAM or external HBM.

   4.2. Access: Custom memory controllers ensure ultra-fast retrieval during autoregressive inference.
   4.3. Output: Provides historical context for the transformer engine to generate coherent responses.
5. Sampler & Output
   5.1. Probability Distribution: FPGA computes softmax over logits to generate token probabilities.
   5.2. Sampling Strategies:
      5.2.1. Greedy (pick highest probability), top k, or other sampling implemented in hardware.
      5.2.2. Random number generators (RNGs) embedded in FPGA ensure deterministic, low latency sampling.
   5.3. Output Conversion: Selected token IDs are converted back into text or speech (via text to speech module). (Example: "Okay, I'll remind you at 8 PM.")
6. Control & Configuration
   6.1. Runtime Management: Supervises pipeline scheduling and resource allocation.
   6.2. Partial Reconfiguration: FPGA can reprogram sections of its fabric without halting the system (e.g., switching from reminder mode to emergency alert mode).
   6.3. User Preferences: Caregivers or users can configure accessibility options (voice pitch, simplified language, emergency triggers).
   6.4. Output: Ensures adaptability and resilience of the assistant.

The case study can evaluate performance metrics. Such demonstrations can validate the architecture's ability to meet practical demands beyond synthetic benchmarks.

Although the case study illustrates how the proposed architecture would operate in a real-world smart-assistant scenario, it does not rely on full end-to-end synthesis results. At this stage, the design covers multiple interacting subsystems (tokenization, embedding, transformer computation, KV caching, and sampling) that require coordinated timing and memory-access modeling before meaningful whole-system synthesis can be performed. Instead, the case study is supported by analytical estimates of resource usage and latency for representative components (e.g., GEMM tiles, attention datapaths, tokenization FSMs). These estimates demonstrate that the pipeline stages described in the use case fit within the capabilities of modern FPGA platforms and can operate with deterministic latency. The case study therefore serves as a feasibility demonstration rather than a finalized implementation.

In addition, the use case indirectly covers memory-intensive operations (particularly in the transformer engine and KV-cache fabric) and explicitly acknowledges the associated hardware constraints. For example:

- The KV cache Sect. (4.1–4.3) is now accompanied by a discussion of HBM/DDR bandwidth requirements, showing how prefix reuse and head-parallel access patterns reduce off-chip traffic.
- The embedding and feed-forward stages reference DSP-based vector operations, and the revised commentary clarifies how INT8/INT4 quantization can reduce memory footprint and bandwidth while maintaining acceptable accuracy for conversational workloads.

- The attention mechanism is analyzed with respect to its Q/K/V access patterns, illustrating how the proposed memory controllers mitigate bottlenecks during autoregressive inference.

These additions ensure that the case study reflects realistic system-level constraints rather than assuming idealized memory behavior.

Finally, we see in the case study's tokenization stage (1.2) intentionally use of FSM-based pipelines because they provide fixed-latency, deterministic preprocessing (critical for an interactive smart-assistant scenario). The goal is not to claim novelty in the FSM itself but to show how a conventional, reliable mechanism integrates into a fully pipelined, hardware-driven LLM inference flow.

Overall, the innovation lies in the end-to-end architectural composition, where tokenization, embedding, transformer computation, KV caching, and sampling operate as a tightly coupled hardware pipeline optimized for latency. The case study demonstrates how this integration enables real-time responsiveness in a practical application, even if individual components (like FSM tokenizers) are established techniques.

5 Conclusions

This paper has presented a high-level FPGA-based architecture for accelerating LLM inference with ultra-low latency. By mapping each stage of the pipeline (tokenization, embedding, transformer computation, KV caching, and sampling), onto specialized hardware blocks, the design leverages the unique strengths of FPGAs. The proposed architecture demonstrates how FPGAs can overcome the limitations of GPUs, which excel at throughput but often struggle with interactive latency, and ASICs, which deliver efficiency but lack adaptability.

Ultimately, this work illustrates that FPGAs are not merely an alternative accelerator but a platform uniquely suited to bridging the gap between throughput and latency. By exploiting their flexibility and deterministic timing, FPGAs can enable interactive AI systems that respond with the immediacy users expect. The high-level scoring framework provides an initial, holistic view of the architecture's performance. Finally, the case study demonstrates the architecture's applicability in real-world scenarios.

Future research will explore scaling to larger models, refining quantization strategies, and integrating advanced decoding techniques, further confirming FPGAs as a cornerstone of real-time LLM deployment.

References

1. Kaur, P., Kashyap, G.S., Kumar, A., Nafis, M.T., Kumar, S., Shokeen, V.: From text to transformation: a comprehensive review of large language models' versatility arXiv preprint arXiv: 2402.16142 (2024)
2. Hussein, H., Gordon, M., Hodgkinson, C., Foreman, R., Wagad, S.: ChatGPT's impact across sectors: a systematic review of key themes and challenges. Big Data Cogn. Comput. **9**(3), 56 (2025)
3. Waseem, M., Bhatta, K., Li, C., Chang, Q.: Pretrained LLMs as Real-Time Controllers for Robot Operated Serial Production Line. arXiv preprint arXiv:2503.03889 (2025)

4. Li, R., Fu, D., Shi, C., Huang, Z., Lu, G.: Efficient LLMs Training and Inference: An Introduction. IEEE Access (2024)
5. Wang, Y., et al.: Burstgpt: a real-world workload dataset to optimize LLM serving systems. In: Proceedings of the 31st ACM SIGKDD Conference on Knowledge Discovery and Data Mining, vol. 2, pp. 5831–5841 (2025)
6. Morales, S., Clarisó, R., Cabot, J.: Impromptu: A framework for model-driven prompt engineering. Software and Systems Modeling, pp. 1–19 (2025)
7. Biookaghazadeh, S., Zhao, M., Ren, F.: Are FPGAs suitable for edge computing?. In: USENIX Workshop on Hot Topics in Edge Computing (HotEdge 18) (2018)
8. Vipin, K., Fahmy, S.A.: FPGA dynamic and partial reconfiguration: a survey of architectures, methods, and applications. ACM Comput. Surv. (CSUR) **51**(4), 1–39 (2018)
9. Li, J., Li, T., Shen, G., Zhao D., Zhang Q., Zeng, Y.: Pushing up to the limit of memory bandwidth and capacity utilization for efficient LLM decoding on embedded FPGA. Design, Automation and Test in Europe (2025)
10. Li, J., et al.: Hummingbird: a smaller and faster large language model accelerator on embedded FPGA. In: 2025 IEEE/ACM International Conference on Computer Aided Design (ICCAD), pp. 1–9 (2025)
11. Garcia, P., Bhowmik, D., Stewart, R., Michaelson, G., Wallace, A.: Optimized memory allocation and power minimization for FPGA-based image processing. J. Imaging **5**(1), 7 (2019)
12. Paraskevas, K.: Enabling direct-access global shared memory for distributed heterogeneous computing. Doctoral dissertation, The University of Manchester, United Kingdom (2023)
13. Bai, G., et al.: Beyond efficiency: a systematic survey of resource-efficient large language models. arXiv preprint arXiv:2401.00625 (2024)
14. Patil, R., Boit, S., Gudivada, V., Nandigam, J.: A survey of text representation and embedding techniques in NLP. IEEE Access **11**, 36120–36146 (2023)
15. Soydaner, D.: Attention mechanism in neural networks: where it comes and where it goes. Neural Comput. Appl. **34**(16), 13371–13385 (2022)
16. Fernandez, A.: TeLU activation function for fast and stable deep learning. Master's thesis, University of South Florida (2024)
17. Ferraris, A.F., Audrito, D., Di Caro, L., Poncibò, C.: The architecture of language: understanding the mechanics behind LLMs. In Cambridge Forum on AI: Law and Governance, vol. 1, p. e11. Cambridge University Press (2025)
18. Navarro, C.A., Hitschfeld-Kahler, N., Mateu, L.: A survey on parallel computing and its applications in data-parallel problems using GPU architectures. Commun. Comput. Phys. **15**(2), 285–329 (2014)
19. Zahiri, B.: Structured ASICs: opportunities and challenges. In: Proceedings 21st International Conference on Computer Design, pp. 404–409. IEEE(2003)
20. Atil, B., et al.: Non-determinism of "deterministic" LLM settings. arXiv preprint arXiv:2408. 04667 (2024)
21. Maschi, F., Alonso, G.: The difficult balance between modern hardware and conventional CPUs. In: Proceedings of the 19th International Workshop on Data Management on New Hardware, pp. 53–62 (2023)

Integrating Large Language Models into Coffee Shop Simulation Games: NPC Dialogue Generation and Educational Applications

Yin-Yu Chou[1](✉), Chun-Yen Huang[2], Yi-Ru Lin[1], Rong-Han Zhang[1], Chia-Yu Hsu[1], and Ying-Ting Chen[1]

[1] Department of Information Management, National Taichung University of Science and Technology, Taichung, Taiwan
yinyuchou@nutc.edu.tw
[2] Science Education Department, National Museum of Natural Science, Taichung, Taiwan

Abstract. This study presents the design and implementation of a coffee shop simulation game that integrates large language models (LLMs) to enhance non-player character (NPC) interactions. Unlike conventional management games that rely on fixed-text dialogues and simplified workflows, this system employs Google Gemini to generate dynamic, personality-driven NPC conversations. The game, developed with Unity, includes multiple modules such as coffee preparation, customer service, knowledge-based mini-games, a "Dream Tree" progression system, and a sustainability-oriented greenhouse. Two dialogue generation modes were implemented: a menu-driven mode ensuring recipe accuracy and a free-form mode simulating unpredictable customer requests. Evaluation focuses on dialogue quality, system latency, player immersion, learning outcomes, and sustainability awareness. Preliminary playtests suggest that Gemini-powered NPCs improve realism, enhance interactivity, and support knowledge acquisition. The study highlights both contributions and challenges: while LLM integration enriches immersion, education, and innovation in game-based learning, issues such as content control, computational cost, and large-scale validation remain. These findings demonstrate the potential of LLM-driven NPCs in advancing intelligent computing applications and educational game design.

Keywords: Large Language Model (LLM) · Non-Player Character (NPC) · Simulation Game · Human–AI Interaction

1 Introduction

Coffee in modern society is not merely a daily beverage but also embodies culture, lifestyle, and social interaction. As coffee culture becomes increasingly popular, balancing entertainment and education has emerged as a crucial topic in game design and cultural dissemination. Simulation management games, with their immersive experiences and decision-making simulations, have attracted attention from both academia and industry, being recognized as effective media that combine learning and entertainment.

C. Xu (Ed.): ICMLSC 2026, CCIS 2948, pp. 453–461, 2027.
https://doi.org/10.1007/978-981-92-1546-1_37

However, most coffee shop–themed games currently emphasize simplified operations and casual play. Players complete orders through repetitive, fixed actions, resulting in oversimplified gameplay that lacks realism and challenge, thereby failing to fully represent the complexity of coffee-making processes and business decision-making.

Moreover, the interactivity of such games relies heavily on the design of non-player characters (NPCs). Traditional simulation games typically use pre-scripted dialogues, which, while maintaining logical consistency, limit flexibility and diversity in interaction. Consequently, they fail to realistically simulate the varied personalities and demands of customers in real-life contexts. With the rapid development of generative artificial intelligence (AI), particularly large language models (LLMs), NPCs in games are no longer confined to fixed scripts but can demonstrate greater linguistic naturalness and interaction authenticity. By applying LLMs, NPCs can be designed with distinct personalities and communication styles, enriching the diversity and immersion of player interactions.

To address these gaps, this study proposes the design and implementation of a coffee shop simulation game developed on the Unity 2D platform. The game integrates coffee preparation, customer service, and business decision-making as its core mechanisms, and employs an NPC dialogue system powered by Gemini to replace traditional fixed-text dialogues. Players act as baristas, completing tasks ranging from coffee-making to order handling and customer interaction. The NPC dialogue generation operates under two modes: (1) menu-driven generation to ensure recipe accuracy, and (2) free-form generation allowing NPCs to request unexpected items, thereby challenging players' adaptability and interaction skills. This design enhances realism while offering educational and research value.

Beyond authentic interaction and professional knowledge transmission, this study also integrates sustainability concepts into the game. Through modules such as the "Coffee Map" and "Greenhouse," players learn about coffee bean origins and cultural characteristics, while also engaging in resource recycling and environmental protection activities, such as reusing coffee grounds to grow flowers. A point system further encourages attention to fair trade and responsible consumption. Such design not only reflects the United Nations Sustainable Development Goals (SDGs) but also gives the game broader social-educational significance.

In summary, this study aims to explore the potential of LLM-powered NPC dialogue generation in enhancing educational outcomes and immersive experiences within simulation games. The specific objectives include:

1. Enhancing players' understanding of coffee culture and production processes.
2. Constructing a challenging and realistic gameplay experience.
3. Evaluating the effectiveness of LLMs in generating personalized NPC dialogues.
4. Embedding sustainability into gameplay to strengthen players' awareness of social responsibility.

2 Literature Review

2.1 Simulation Management Games and Educational Applications

Simulation management games have long attracted attention in both game research and educational contexts due to their capacity to provide immersive experiences and decision-making practices. Prior research suggests that such games foster problem-solving, resource management, and situational decision-making skills [1, 2]. However, many commercial simulation management games are designed primarily for entertainment. Their gameplay is often oversimplified, requiring players to repeat fixed tasks, thereby limiting realism. Coffee shop–themed games exemplify this issue: while entertaining, they rarely provide deep insights into coffee culture, professional techniques, or management complexity, resulting in limited educational value and challenge.

2.2 Game-Based Learning and Immersion

Game-Based Learning (GBL) emphasizes fostering learning through interaction and game mechanics. Studies show that immersion and interactivity are crucial factors for enhancing learner motivation and effectiveness [3]. When players can experience knowledge or skills authentically in a game, their learning impressions are significantly reinforced. Conversely, if interactivity is monotonous or lacking in variety, engagement diminishes, negatively affecting learning outcomes [4]. Thus, embedding realism, challenge, and diversity in gameplay is essential to improve educational effects.

2.3 Applications of Large Language Models in Game Interaction

With the rise of generative AI, large language models have gained increasing attention in gaming. LLMs possess natural language generation capabilities that simulate diverse dialogues, overcoming the limitations of rule-based systems. Research highlights that integrating LLMs enables NPCs to deliver more natural and flexible dialogues, dynamically adjusting responses based on player inputs [5]. Compared with static text, such interactions better approximate real human communication, thereby enhancing immersion and gaming experience [6]. Nevertheless, challenges remain, such as unpredictability of generated content, response latency, and computational cost, all of which can impact reliability and scalability in educational contexts.

2.4 NPC Personality Modeling and Player Experience

NPC design affects not only narrative progression but also directly influences player experience. Prior research demonstrates that NPCs with distinct personalities and linguistic styles can enhance immersion and realism [7]. Personalized NPCs also increase gameplay challenges, as players must adjust strategies according to diverse NPC behaviors. Earlier approaches often relied on rule-based or narrative-driven methods, but with LLM integration, NPC personalities can be embedded through prompt engineering, enabling dynamic and varied dialogue behaviors. Building on this perspective, the present study combines personality-driven NPCs with LLM-powered dialogues to enrich both educational and interactive outcomes.

3 Method

3.1 System Architecture

The coffee shop simulation game in this study was developed using Unity, and the overall system architecture consists of five main modules: the coffee shop scene, coffee-making scene, Dream Tree system, Coffee Map, and Greenhouse. Players first log into the game and enter the coffee shop scene, where they interact with NPCs to receive orders or engage in dialogues (see Fig. 1). Once an order is placed, players move to the coffee-making scene to prepare beverages using different methods such as machine brewing, hand brewing, milk frothing, and latte art. The completed drink is checked against the menu requirements, and the result is fed back to the NPC and mission system, forming a complete gameplay loop.

The Dream Tree module evaluates player growth across three dimensions—Craft vs. Business, Art vs. Science, and Individual vs. Organization—through interactive quizzes. The results are combined to generate a personalized "coffee personality" type, symbolizing the player's progress. The Coffee Map module provides cultural and geographical information about coffee bean origins, which is further applied in mini-game challenges. The Greenhouse module centers on sustainability by encouraging players to recycle coffee grounds for planting flowers. Players accumulate environmental points through planting activities, which can be redeemed for reusable cups, thereby embedding sustainability principles into the game experience.

Fig. 1. Coffee Shop Scene for NPC Interaction and Order Reception

3.2 NPC Dialogue Generation Design

In the game, the NPC system integrates the large language model Gemini for dialogue generation, aiming to replace traditional fixed-text scripts and enable NPCs to interact with players in a more personalized and character-driven manner. Gemini was selected for this study because of its strong capabilities in natural language generation and multi-modal understanding, which make it well suited for simulating diverse customer interactions in a coffee shop scenario. Compared with rule-based or template-driven dialogue systems, Gemini provides greater fluency and contextual awareness, allowing NPCs to exhibit distinct personalities and communication styles that enhance immersion. Furthermore, Gemini offers flexible API integration, supporting prompt engineering and structured outputs. This flexibility enables the system to balance between controlled generation for recipe compliance and free-form generation for unexpected scenarios. Finally, Gemini's multilingual potential creates opportunities for extending the system to cross-cultural contexts, improving scalability and global applicability.

The game designs eight NPCs with distinct personality traits, which are randomly selected based on weighted probabilities. When an NPC initiates the ordering process, the system follows a sequence of steps:

1. Order type determination: The system randomly decides whether the order is dine-in or take-out.
2. Order mode selection: With an 80% probability, the NPC orders from the menu (Mode 1); with a 20% probability, the model generates a non-coffee item (Mode 2).
3. Prompt composition: The system combines the NPC's personality traits with the selected order information to construct a semantically coherent prompt.
4. Dialogue generation: Gemini processes the prompt and generates natural language dialogue that reflects the NPC's personality.

In the AI-based ordering system, NPC behaviors are driven by a series of randomized decisions (see Fig. 2), simulating the diversity of customer choices in real-world coffee shop scenarios. For example, when the system triggers the ordering logic, it first determines dine-in or take-out with equal probability. If the NPC selects from the menu, the system applies weighted probabilities (informed by consumer preferences) to randomly generate one or two drinks. These items are then combined with the NPC's personality and dining preference to form the prompt for Gemini, which generates an order dialogue that mirrors realistic customer behavior.

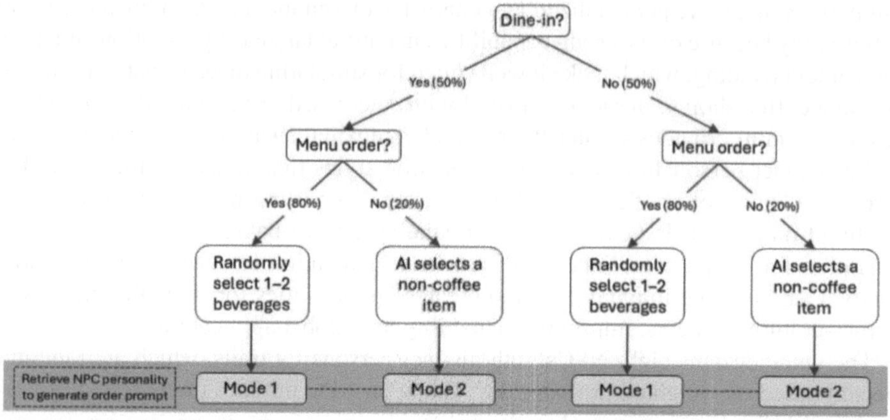

Fig. 2. AI Ordering Decision Tree for NPCs in the Coffee Shop Simulation Game

If the NPC does not select from the menu (20% probability), the system directly calls the AI model to freely determine a "non-coffee" item. Gemini then produces a dialogue line consistent with the NPC's personality traits. Players may respond with special in-game commands to indicate that the item is unavailable (e.g., "Your order is not listed in the Book of Beans!"). Once the NPC receives this response, they exit the coffee shop. This dual-mode mechanism balances the reliability of controlled generation with the creativity of free-form outputs. Both modes incorporate personality-driven prompts, allowing NPCs to express individualized preferences and deliver natural, human-like interactions.

3.3 Evaluation Metrics

To evaluate the effectiveness of the system, four categories of metrics are defined:

1. System performance metrics: including response latency, accuracy, and compliance of generated dialogues.
2. Player experience metrics: immersion, naturalness of interactions, and perceived realism of NPC personalities, measured through surveys.
3. Educational metrics: pre- and post-tests to measure players' knowledge acquisition in coffee culture and sustainability.
4. Gameplay challenge metrics: order completion rate, coffee preparation accuracy, and players' adaptability to unexpected scenarios.

4 Results and Discussion

The core functional modules of the coffee shop simulation game were successfully implemented, including the coffee shop scene, coffee-making interface, Dream Tree, Coffee Map, and Greenhouse. Players interact with NPCs to receive orders and prepare beverages using various brewing methods. After completing an order, NPCs provide textual feedback, forming a full gameplay cycle.

The integration of Gemini for NPC dialogue generation produced natural and personality-driven conversations. Two dialogue modes were developed: a menu-driven mode ensuring recipe accuracy and a free-form mode allowing NPCs to request unpredictable items, thereby enhancing realism and interactivity. Players reported that these conversations felt more lifelike and contextually appropriate compared with traditional scripted dialogues.

To further evaluate player experience, a post-play questionnaire was administered to twelve participants aged 18–30, primarily university students. The survey contained fifteen questions across five dimensions: tutorial clarity, core gameplay, dialogue realism, educational value, and overall satisfaction. Results showed (as shown in Fig. 3) that tutorial clarity received an average score of 2.6 out of 5, indicating that excessive text and unclear steps reduced usability. Gameplay enjoyment averaged 2.9, suggesting moderate engagement, while perceived challenge was high (mean = 4.0), mainly due to the learning curve of multi-step operations such as espresso extraction and latte art.

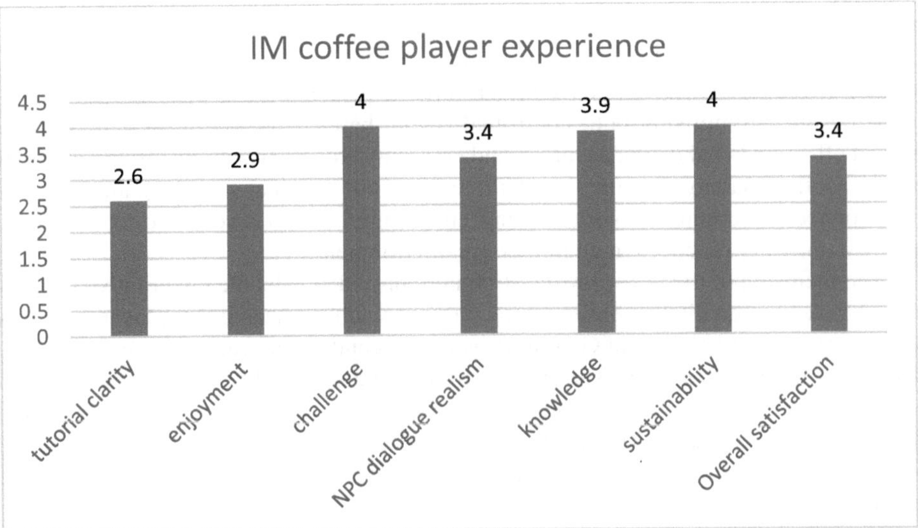

Fig. 3. Questionnaire results of IM coffee player experience

The NPC dialogue realism achieved a mean score of 3.4, confirming that Gemini-powered interactions were perceived as natural and engaging. Educational mini-games—covering topics like coffee bean identification, brewing knowledge, and sustainability—scored 3.9 on average, showing positive learning outcomes. The integration of environmental themes, such as recycling coffee grounds in the Greenhouse module, scored 4.0, reflecting strong player approval for the sustainability-oriented design.

Overall satisfaction averaged 3.4, suggesting that players appreciated the concept but desired smoother tutorials and improved control fluency. Qualitative feedback emphasized that combining AI-driven NPCs with educational mechanics enhanced realism and motivation but required further user interface refinement to sustain engagement.

From these observations, the game demonstrates three major strengths:

1. Authenticity of interaction—Gemini-driven dialogues simulate realistic social exchanges.
2. Educational–entertainment balance—players acquire cultural and environmental knowledge through play.
3. System innovation—the dual-mode NPC design exemplifies LLM flexibility in both structured and creative content generation.

However, limitations remain in content control, computational cost, and scalability. These findings indicate that while LLM integration substantially enriches player immersion and educational outcomes, optimizing instructional design and technical performance is crucial for future iterations.

5 Conclusion and Future Work

This study developed a coffee shop simulation game that integrates large language models (LLMs) to enhance interaction realism and educational engagement. Powered by Gemini, the system enables NPCs to generate personality-driven, context-sensitive dialogues, effectively replacing conventional fixed-text interactions. The dual-mode dialogue design—comprising both controlled (menu-based) and free-form generation—proved effective in balancing accuracy and creativity. Together with integrated modules such as coffee-making, Dream Tree, Coffee Map, and Greenhouse, the game successfully connects entertainment with learning, encouraging players to explore coffee culture and sustainability practices in an immersive environment.

The inclusion of the post-play questionnaire provided valuable quantitative insights that complement qualitative observations. Survey results indicated that players appreciated the novelty and realism of Gemini-driven NPCs and the educational content embedded in the mini-games. However, they also highlighted usability issues in the tutorial and control fluency, suggesting that interaction design and onboarding flow require refinement. These findings validate the feasibility of combining LLMs with game-based learning frameworks, while also emphasizing the need for human-centered optimization in educational game systems.

Overall, this research contributes to three primary domains: (1) AI-driven interactivity, by demonstrating how LLMs can enhance narrative depth and social authenticity in simulation games; (2) educational innovation, through the integration of cultural and sustainability learning within interactive play; and (3) systemic design advancement, offering a reproducible framework for balancing controlled and generative AI content in digital learning environments.

Future work will extend in several directions. First, improving content reliability through prompt refinement, output filtering, and reinforcement learning mechanisms to ensure dialogue consistency and appropriateness. Second, optimizing technical performance via model compression and local inference techniques to minimize latency and cost. Third, expanding player experience evaluation through large-scale user studies with diverse demographics to validate learning outcomes and engagement sustainability. Lastly, incorporating adaptive difficulty and emotional feedback systems to further personalize gameplay and strengthen long-term learning retention.

In conclusion, this study demonstrates that integrating LLMs such as Gemini into educational simulation games is both feasible and impactful. By merging interactive storytelling, authentic cultural knowledge, and sustainability values, this research not only enriches the design of game-based learning but also opens new pathways for applying generative AI in human–computer interaction and digital education.

References

1. Faisal, N., Chadhar, M., Goriss-Hunter, A., Stranieri, A.: Business simulation games in higher education: a systematic review of empirical research. Human Behav. Emerg. Technol. **2022**(1), 1578791 (2022)
2. Kim, H., Hartleb, T., Bello, K., Aqlan, F., Zhao, R., Yang, H.: Behavioral modeling of collaborative problem solving in multiplayer virtual reality manufacturing simulation games. J. Comput. Inf. Sci. Eng. **24**(3), 031006 (2024)
3. Lee, W.H., Shim, H.M., Kim, H.G.: Effect of game-based learning using live streaming on learners' interest, immersion, satisfaction, and instructors' perception. Int. J. Serious Games **9**(2), 3–26 (2022)
4. Untari, A.D.: Game based learning: alternative 21st century innovative learning models in improving student learning activeness. Edueksos Jurnal Pendidikan Sosial & Ekonomi **11**(2) (2022).
5. Huang, J.: Generating dynamic and lifelike NPC dialogs in role-playing games using large language model (2024)
6. Kumaran, V., Rowe, J., Mott, B., Lester, J.: Scenecraft: automating interactive narrative scene generation in digital games with large language models. In: Proceedings of the AAAI Conference on Artificial Intelligence and Interactive Digital Entertainment, vol. 19, no. 1, pp. 86–96, October 2023
7. Lin, Z., Zhang, Z., Sun, X., Zheng, H.T.: Make NPC more realistic: design and practice of a hybrid stealth game NPC AI framework based on OODA theory. In: Stephanidis, C., Antona, M., Ntoa, S., Salvendy, G. (eds.) HCI International 2024 Posters. HCII 2024. Communications in Computer and Information Science, vol. 2117. Springer, Cham (2024). https://doi.org/10.1007/978-3-031-61953-3_35

Emergence of Induction Heads and Their Impact on In-Context Learning in Japanese Large Language Models

Ajay Agarwal(✉) and Tatsuhito Hasegawa

Advanced Interdisciplinary Science and Technology, Graduate School of Engineering, University of Fukui, Fukui, Japan
aad25805@g.u-fukui.ac.jp

Abstract. Induction Heads are a special kind of attention heads that exhibit in-context learning for large language models, reminiscent of associative memory in human cognition. Whilst induction heads have been identified in various large language models trained in English text, their existence in multi-lingual LLMs, especially ones trained on text having structure, semantically distant to English, is yet to be studied. In this work, we identify induction heads across five Japanese LLMs, up to 3.6B parameters in size. Specifically, for each model, we identify how induction heads contribute towards their performance on five sophisticated ICL tasks. Using this understanding, we extend our analysis by performing an exhaustive ablation study using mean ablation to measure the performance of these models on benchmarks like Japanese MT-Bench and ELYZA-Tasks-100. We also identify the optimal context length window size for token sequence length, which is longer than English LLMs, that elicits induction behavior in the Japanese LLMs. Our findings underscore that induction heads not only exist in Japanese LLMs but also are a major contributor towards their performance both on ICL tasks and industry-level benchmarks. More broadly, our study underscores the importance of extending standard mechanistic interpretability studies to multi-lingual settings for identifying unique semantic challenges and gaining valuable insights.

Keywords: induction heads · mechanistic interpretability · attention heads · mean ablation · japanese LLMs

1 Introduction

In-context learning (ICL) refers to the model's ability to predict later tokens in longer context windows without having been pre-trained or fine-tuned on any such context. Discovered first in GPT-2, and analyzed more deeply since GPT-3, the understanding of ICL has been associated with two parallel perspectives - *decreasing per token loss with an increase in token indices*, essentially, the model gets better at predicting as context gets wider, and second *few-shot learning* i.e.,

C. Xu (Ed.): ICMLSC 2026, CCIS 2948, pp. 462–475, 2027.
https://doi.org/10.1007/978-981-92-1546-1_38

the model gets better at predicting when given examples of how to predict [1]. Primarily, these perspectives refer to the same phenomenon that autoregressive sequential models, like most LLMs, inherit an inherent ability to generalize to out-of-data distributions without the need for *supervised finetuning* on those specific distributions. This line of research, whilst noble and explorative, has been historically limited to models trained on and distribution made of mostly (or predominantly) English and English adjacent language-only corpora [12].

Our paper aims to address this lacuna in research by investigating the emergence of induction heads in Japanese LLMs and quantifying empirically their role in ICL tasks [23]. To our best knowledge, our work is the first to address this problem both in a non-English language setting and in a purely Japanese setting. The main contribution of our paper is the following -

1. *Identification of induction head (IH) in Japanese LLMs for every parameter and model architecture family*
2. *Comprehensive evaluation of the role of IH in Japanese ICL tasks*
3. *Defining Abstract Pattern Recognition ICL task for assessing the model's more abstract patterns*
4. *Comparative mean ablation to identify ICL and benchmark contribution analysis of IH against random attention heads*

These contributions underpin the need for more exhaustive mechanistic interpretability studies in models trained from scratch in multi-lingual settings.

2 Related Work

Given the lack of identifiable work in addressing the monolingual bias for modern MI studies on induction heads and ICL, we focus our attention on highlighting key results regarding induction heads to build motivation for this work. These results can primarily be divided into three categories: *ICL abilities, Compositional abilities,*and *Metric performance.* We refer the reader to key references highlighted in Table 1 for more information.

Table 1. Overview of Paradigm Results Regarding Induction Heads

Classification	Results	References
IH for ICL	*Hidden Markov Model* learning for OOD generalization, *causal graph* learning for latent knowledge representation	[9,27]
IH and other heads	Function Vector Heads & IH, Symbolic Abstraction Head & IH	[15,20,25]
Metrics post IH emergence	per token log-loss drop across models, 10^{-5} PF lump in loss-compute scaling law, *grokking*	[8,10,17]

3 Background

Here, we will briefly build the mathematical background to the emergence of *induction heads* in a transformer architecture. Consider the *multi-head attention* block defined below, which can be expressed as a composition of linear (almost) transformations on the input token embeddings x, with d-dimension [4,22].

$$\text{MHA}(x) = \sum_{h=1}^{H} \text{softmax}\left(\frac{xW_{QK}^h + M^h}{\sqrt{d_h}}\right) xW_{OV}^h \tag{1}$$

We can de-compose any MHA block into two mechanistic circuits for each attention head $h \in H$, where H is the number of attention blocks; - ***Query-Key*** circuit (QK) represented by a matrix W_{QK}^h, and ***Output-Value*** (OV) represented by matrix W_{OV}^h [19]. QK circuit modifies the causal mask M^h, by dictating where the head h attends to across the input sequence, whereas, OV circuit governs what information is read from where the head is attended to in the previous circuit [24]. This is precisely where *induction heads* emerge. If we take the simple case of *bigram* like $[A][B] \ldots [A] \rightarrow$, the following happens [3].

1. **QK Mechanism:** The QK circuit aligns the current token's query ($\rightarrow$) with the key of the previous iteration of the current token $[A]$, performed by *previous token heads.*
2. **OV Mechanism:** OV circuit reads the value immediately *proceeding* $[A]$ i.e., $([B])$, which is performed by *induction heads*

This leads to the emergence of induction heads, which provide the model the ability to perform in-context learning on out-of-training distribution data.

3.1 Models

We utilize five Japanese models recently developed and made open-source. These are SBIntuition's Sarashina2.2–3b-Instruct-v0.1, which has 24 layers, 16 heads with 80 head dimensions [18], RinnaGPT's Japanese-gpt-neox-3.6,B which has 36 layers, 22 heads with 128 head dimensions [16], RakutenAI-2B-mini-instruct, which has 22 layers, 32 heads with 64 head dimensions [14], LLM-JP's LLM-jp-3-1.8B-instruct which has 24 layers, 16 heads with 128 head dimensions [7], and LINE-Japanese-large-lm-1.7B models which has 24 layers, 24 heads with 96 head dimensions [6]. All of these models are trained on Japanese text, each of which currently displays exemplary performance on the benchmarks of Japanese MT-Bench [21,26], and Elyza-tasks-100 [2].

3.2 Identification of Induction Heads

The task of *prefix matching* is performed on sequence of Japanese characters derived from *ParallelFictionJa-En100k* dataset [11] comprising sentence-aligned

Japanese text from random web-novels. The data is reduced along the sentence-axis, cleaned and treated for outlier noise. The task is performed on varying sequence lengths from 50 to 250, in steps of 10, with a length having 50 iterations. Varying context window analysis is performed to identify the minimal length for induction emergence and the optimal length for ICL tasks. Our induction head detector is based on activation hooks implemented at each block and layer, calculating induction scores for each head against every window length across all tasks.

3.3 ICL Tasks

We take five Japanese scripts (hiragana, katakana, kanji) ICL tasks, which depend only on the model's ICL ability to predict the next token. Table 1 mentions the dataset of ICL tasks involved, along with a sample for each task. Each ICL task has 500 pairs for testing. Regarding the ABSTR task, it is less about coherent examples and more about abstract patterns that involve all three scripts of the Japanese language (Table. 2).

3.4 Ablation Study and Benchmarks

We quantify the contribution to ICL and industry benchmarks *(ELYZA-Task-100* [2], and*JP-MTBench* [21,26]) by performing mean ablation of top 1%, 3%, 5%, and 10% ranked induction heads based on their induction scores against random attention heads. Mean ablation is a standard technique in mechanistic interpretability which involves assessing the impact on model performance by a specific attention head by replacing its activation with the mean activation of all heads. [5,13]

Table 2. In-context learning tasks for evaluating induction heads

Task Name	Description	Example Pattern
REPSEQ	Direct sequence repetition detection	A B C ... A B C ... A B C → expect A
COLOR	Japanese color-object associations learning	→
TRANSLATE	Code-mixed English-Japanese translation pairs	cat→ dog → cat → expect
BIGRAM	Strict alternating bigram pattern [A][B][A]...[B]	→, →, → expect
TRIGRAM	Trigram repetition pattern [A][B][C][A][B]...[C]	→, →, → expect
ABSTR	Abstract pattern recognition task	→, →, → expect

4 Results

Our experiments suggest the existence of multiple IH across all five models. These IH contribute significantly to ICL and benchmark performance, suggesting the general existence of IH across all Japanese models irrespective of model size.

4.1 Induction Head Identification

We analysed six different Japanese LLMs spanning different model architectures for the presence of induction heads. We observed -

1. Characteristic diagonal attention stripes for identified induction heads across every model, depicted in Appendix A
2. Large number of IHs exist across models, irrespective of model size
3. IH heads do exist in Japanese LLMs
4. Identification of *vertical attention stripes* characteristic of *previous token heads* across every model (refer to Appendix A)
5. Strong *previous token heads* observed in RinnaGPT *japanese-gpt-neo-3.6B L20H8, L28H16, L29H16* and *L27H2*

To highlight how emergence frequency is similar to induction heads in models, we conducted a targeted analysis for their detection in the RakutenAI mini model, as depicted in Fig. 1. *Most PTH concentrates at L10 to L15, with uniform distribution otherwise in contrast to IH, with a more diffuse distribution across the network.*

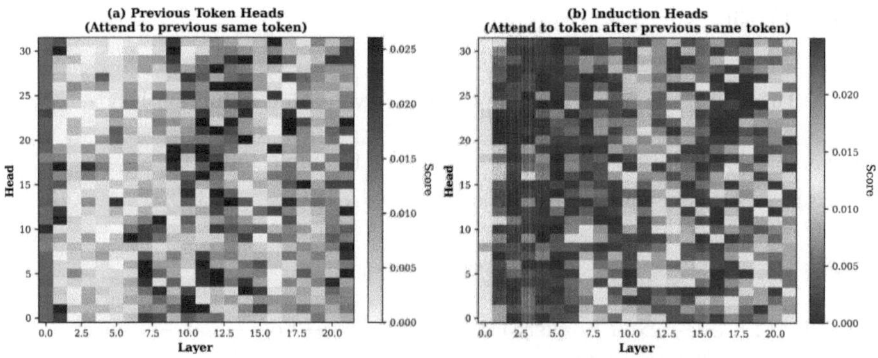

Fig. 1. Head type distribution in RakutenAI-2.0-mini at 200 token window.

4.2 Optimal Context Windows and Induction Head Clusters

Our hypothesis suggested the need for longer context windows for the emergence of induction in Japanese text, given the morphological distance of same to English. Our results attempt to suggest the same.

1. Between 100 to 120 token sequence length, 5-shot ICL, and induction score peaked for most models, suggesting positive affirmation for our hypothesis
2. For *RakutenAI* and *rinnaGPT,* this length was optimal at 112 tokens.
3. After 25 rounds of iteration, induction emergence was observed only after the context window was greater than 100 tokens.

Our results also suggest that extending the context window to 200 characters and beyond causes a substantial decline in the induction score. This degradation was found to be consistent with all models, with each of their *top* 1% *ranked induction heads.*

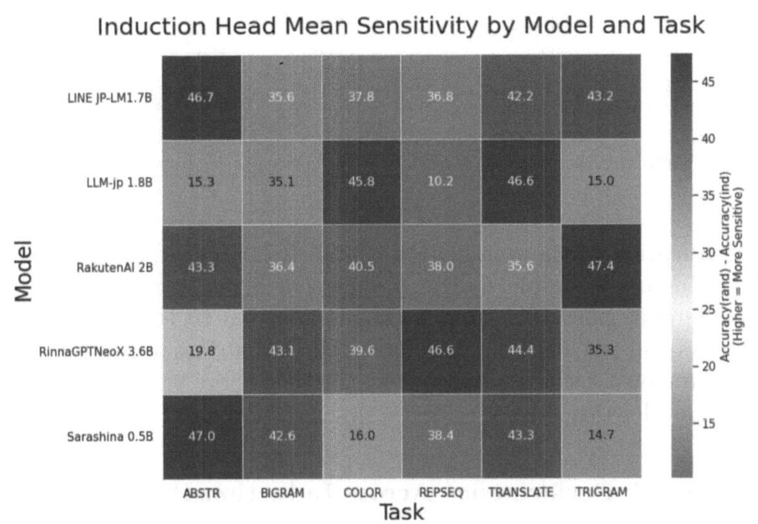

Fig. 2. Induction Mean Sensitivity across all models for all 20-shot ICL task

4.3 ICL Performance and Ablation Study

Our analysis indicates that induction heads contribute significantly towards all the models' ICL abilities. This is suggested by the following obtained results -

1. *Consistent decline in ICL accuracy post mean-ablation of IH, across all quantities - 1% , 3% , 5% , 10%*
2. *Margin of decline in ICL accuracy is significantly higher post mean ablation of IH against post mean ablation of random heads in all categories*

3. *Few-shot prompting ICL scores outperform zero-shot prompting scores by a margin of more than 15.2%*
4. *ICL score difference for IH ablation across percentages is much wider with few-shot ICL against zero-shot ICL*

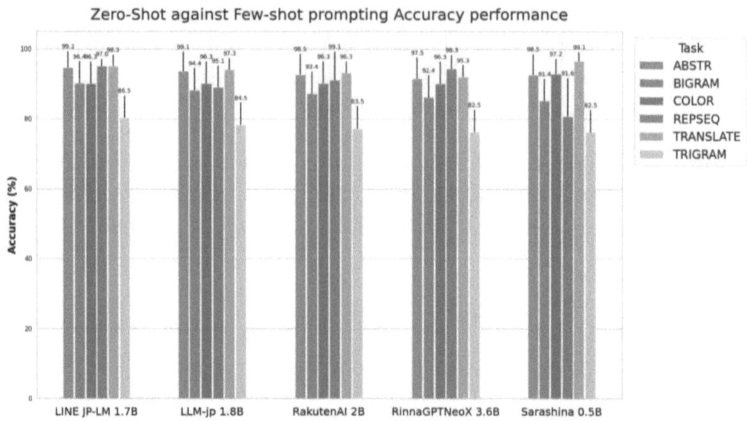

Fig. 3. Accuracy performance across ICL tasks pre-ablation for all models

For visualization of the role of IH towards ICL abilities against other heads in Fig. 2, we define a simple metric - *induction head mean sensitivity* as ICL accuracy difference post 10% random heads ablation to IH ablation across 20-shot ICL tasks and models. These results suggest that loss of pattern recognition abilities occurs post-1% IH ablation, suggesting their significant role in ICL abilities of a model (Fig. 3).

4.4 Benchmark Performance Across Induction Head Ablation

We hypothesized that IH contributes more than just ICL, but also plays a role in the model's performance in reasoning benchmarks through the model's ICL as a proxy. Our results, as seen in Table 3, suggest the same.

1. Post-IH ablation across every percentage, no model meets prior benchmarks
2. Post-IH ablation performance drops more widely in zero-shot ICL against few-shot ICL, confirming previous results in favor of few-shot against zero-shot for ICL performance.

The latter may also be a consequence of the factual recall nature of the *Japanese-MTBench* benchmark. [21,26].

Table 3. Point Drop (Δ Score) after IH Ablation. Values are reported as point dropped in JP-MTBench / ELYZA-Tasks-100.

Model	1% IH	3% IH	5% IH	10% IH
Sarashina2.2–3b-Instruct-v0.1	–0.8 / –0.6	–1.9 / –1.4	–3.2 / –2.5	–6.0 / –4.5
Japanese-gpt-neox-3.6B	–0.7 / –0.5	–1.6 / –1.2	–2.8 / –2.1	–5.2 / –3.8
RakutenAI-2B-mini-instruct	–1.0 / –0.9	–2.3 / –2.0	–4.1 / –3.6	–7.5 / –6.0
LLM-jp-3-1.8B-instruct	–0.9 / –0.7	–2.1 / –1.7	–3.8 / –3.0	–6.8 / –5.3
LINE-Japanese-large-lm-1.7B	–1.1 / –0.8	–2.5 / –2.0	–4.6 / –3.4	–8.0 / –6.2

5 Conclusion

Our analysis confirms the presence of induction heads in Japanese language models across all parameter and architectural families. These results, in tandem with the identification of characteristic attention stripes of *previous token heads*, imply the existence of *induction circuits* in Japanese LLMs. Our ablation studies underpin the role such IH plays in major ICL tasks, contributing not only to models' in-context learning abilities, but also superior benchmark performance across *JP-MTBench* and *ELYZA-100-Tasks*. Finally, our study also identified optimal context length for peak ICL performance and minimum context length for induction emergence (which appears to be greater than that for English LLMs - starting at roughly 70 tokens). Our results successfully indicate the promise that multi-lingual LLMs may also contain induction heads and contribute significantly towards their ICL abilities. We believe more studies must be conducted to find sophisticated attention heads like *function value attention heads*, or *S-heads* in multi-lingual LLMs, especially in low-resource languages and languages with vastly different semantic and morphological structures than English. Our efforts are in line to democratize the work in mechanistic interpretability in multi-lingual environments. Our work demonstrates both the need to study classic MI techniques in multi-lingual environments to elicit more insights in large language models.

Acknowledgements. The authors thank the resources provided by the Doctoral School of Engineering at the University of Fukui and GPU compute resources made available at the Hasegawa Laboratory at the University of Fukui. This work was supported in part by the Cross-Farm: a Research Farm project in University of Fukui

A Attention Visualization for Induction Heads

Here, we provide the attention pattern visualization for all the induction heads obtained for each model. Notice how attention patterns have characteristics of *induction heads* and *previous token heads* (Fig. 4), 5, 6, 7 and 8.

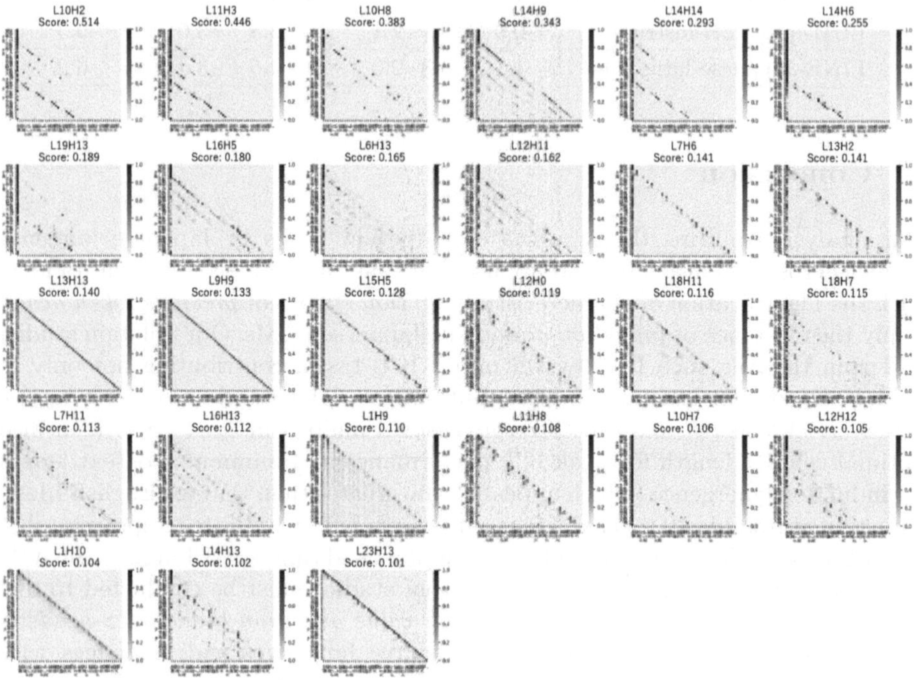

Fig. 4. Attention Visualization for Induction Heads identified in *llm-jp/llm-jp-3-1.8b-instruct*

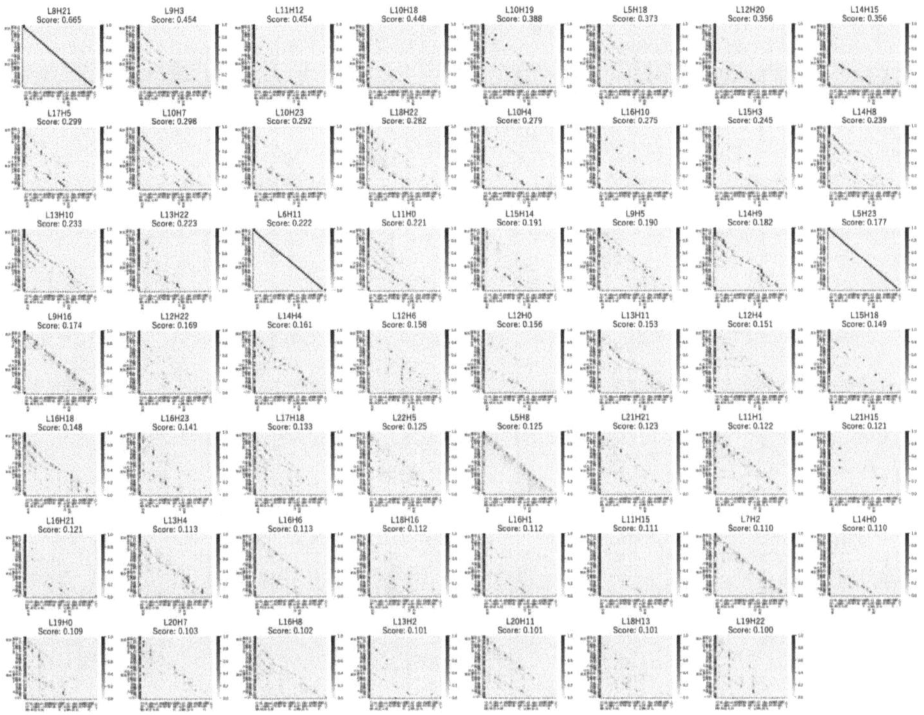

Fig. 5. Attention Visualization for Induction Heads identified in *line-corporation/japanese-large-lm-1.7b*

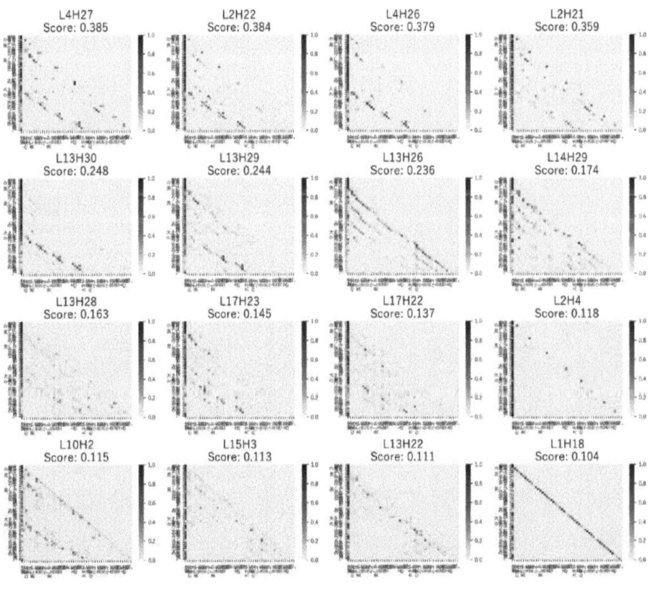

Fig. 6. Attention Visualization for Induction Heads identified in *Rakuten/RakutenAI-2.0-mini-instruct*

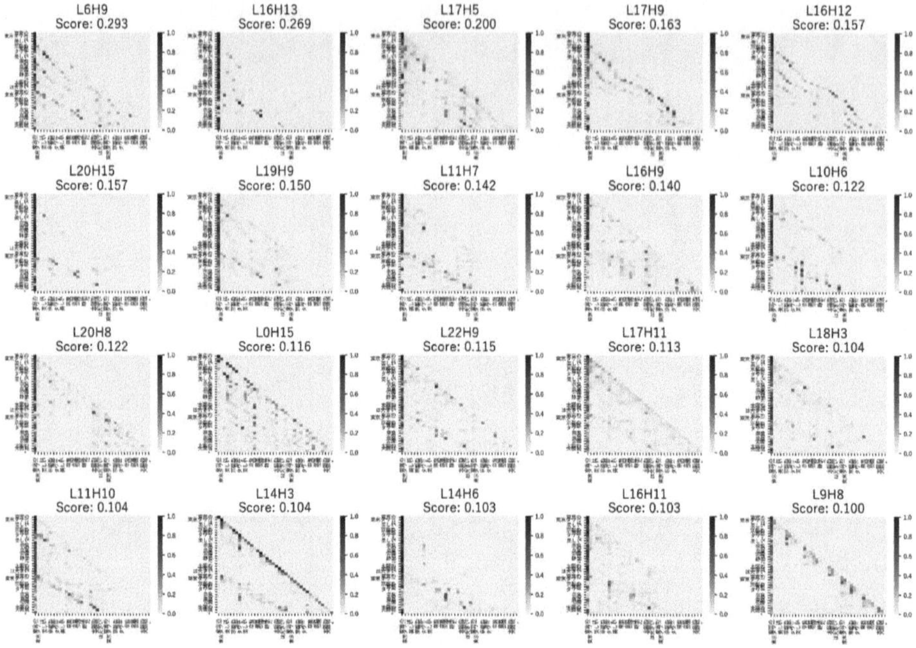

Fig. 7. Attention Visualization for Induction Heads identified in *sbintuitions/sarashina2.2-3b-instruct-v0.1*

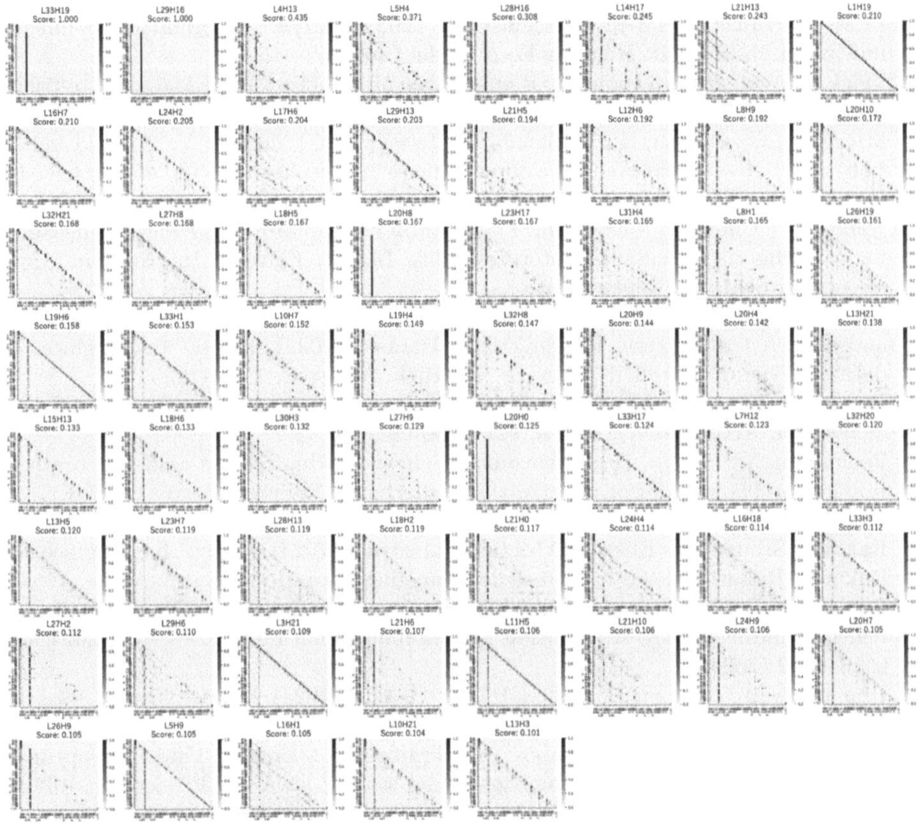

Fig. 8. Attention Visualization for Induction Heads identified in *rinna/japanese-gpt-neox-3.6b*

References

1. Dong, Q., et al.: A survey on in-context learning. In: Proceedings of the 2024 Conference on Empirical Methods in Natural Language Processing, pp. 1107–1128 (2024)
2. ELYZA, Inc.: ELYZA-tasks-100. https://huggingface.co/datasets/elyza/ELYZA-tasks-100 (2023). Official announcement and documentation available at: https://note.com/elyza/n/na405acaca130
3. Han, K., Xiao, A., Wu, E., Guo, J., Xu, C., Wang, Y.: Transformer in transformer. Adv. Neural. Inf. Process. Syst. **34**, 15908–15919 (2021)
4. Huang, Y., Cheng, Y., Liang, Y.: In-context convergence of transformers. arXiv preprint arXiv:2310.05249 (2023)
5. Li, M., Janson, L.: Optimal ablation for interpretability. Adv. Neural. Inf. Process. Syst. **37**, 109233–109282 (2024)
6. LINE Corporation: LINE-Japanese-large-LM-1.7B (2023). https://huggingface.co/line-corporation/japanese-large-lm-1.7b. hugging Face Model Card

7. LLM-jp Project: LLM-jp-3-1.8b-instruct (2025). https://huggingface.co/llm-jp/llm-jp-3-1.8b-instruct. Hugging Face Model Card
8. Luick, N.: Universal response and emergence of induction in LLMs. arXiv e-prints pp. arXiv–2411 (2024)
9. Minegishi, G., Furuta, H., Taniguchi, S., Iwasawa, Y., Matsuo, Y.: Beyond induction heads: In-context meta learning induces multi-phase circuit emergence. In: Forty-second International Conference on Machine Learning
10. Nanda, N., Chan, L., Lieberum, T., Smith, J., Steinhardt, J.: Progress measures for grokking via mechanistic interpretability. In: The Eleventh International Conference on Learning Representations
11. NilanE: ParallelFiction-Ja_En-100k: A large parallel corpus of japanese web novels and english translations. Hugging Face Dataset (2022). https://huggingface.co/datasets/NilanE/ParallelFiction-Ja_En-100k. Accessed: 15-11-2025
12. Peters, U., Carman, M.: Cultural bias in explainable ai research: a systematic analysis. J. Artif. Intell. Res. **79**, 971–1000 (2024)
13. Pochinkov, N., Pasero, B., Shibayama, S.: Investigating neuron ablation in attention heads: The case for peak activation centering. arXiv preprint arXiv:2408.17322 (2024)
14. Rakuten Group, Inc.: RakutenAI-2.0-mini-instruct (2024). https://huggingface.co/Rakuten/RakutenAI-2.0-mini-instruct. Hugging Face Model Card
15. Ren, J., et al.: Identifying semantic induction heads to understand in-context learning. In: Findings of the Association for Computational Linguistics ACL 2024, pp. 6916–6932 (2024)
16. Rinna Co., Ltd.: Rinna Japanese-GPT-NeoX-3.6B (2023). https://huggingface.co/rinna/japanese-gpt-neox-3.6b. Hugging Face Model Card
17. Sardana, N., Portes, J., Doubov, S., Frankle, J.: Beyond chinchilla-optimal: accounting for inference in language model scaling laws. In: Proceedings of the 41st International Conference on Machine Learning, pp. 43445–43460 (2024)
18. SB Intuitions: Sarashina2.2-3b-Instruct-v0.1 (2025). https://huggingface.co/sbintuitions/sarashina2.2-3b-instruct-v0.1. Hugging Face Model Card
19. Song, J., Xu, Z., Zhong, Y.: Out-of-distribution generalization via composition: a lens through induction heads in transformers. Proc. Natl. Acad. Sci. **122**(6), e2417182122 (2025)
20. Todd, E., Li, M., Sharma, A.S., Mueller, A., Wallace, B.C., Bau, D.: Function vectors in large language models. In: The Twelfth International Conference on Learning Representations
21. Uematsu, T., Fukuda, H., Kawahara, D., Shibata, T.: Japanese mt-bench++: . In: 31 (The 31st Annual Meeting of the Association for Natural Language Processing) (2025)
22. Vaswani, A., et al.: Attention is all you need. Adv. Neural Inf. Process. Syst. **30** (2017)
23. Wang, X., et al.: Investigating the learning behaviour of in-context learning: a comparison with supervised learning. arXiv preprint arXiv:2307.15411 (2023)
24. Xiong, R., et al.: On layer normalization in the transformer architecture. In: International conference on machine learning, pp. 10524–10533. PMLR (2020)
25. Yin, K., Steinhardt, J.: Which attention heads matter for in-context learning? In: Forty-second International Conference on Machine Learning

26. Zheng, L., et al.: Judging LLM-as-a-judge with mt-bench and chatbot arena. arXiv preprint arXiv:2306.05685 (2023)
27. Zisman, I., et al.: N-gram induction heads for in-context RL: improving stability and reducing data needs. In: First Workshop on Scalable Optimization for Efficient and Adaptive Foundation Models

Platform-Agnostic LLM-Based Linguistic Representation of Event Logs for Critical Inference Tasks

Khandakar Ashrafi Akbar[1], Sabbir Ahmed[2(✉)], Latifur Khan[2], and Bhavani Thuraisingham[2]

[1] Towson University, Towson, Maryland, USA
kakbar@towson.edu
[2] The University of Texas at Dallas, Richardson, Texas, USA
{Sabbir.Ahmed2,lkhan,bhavani.thuraisingham}@utdallas.edu

Abstract. This paper presents a new approach for interpreting event logs across diverse platforms by leveraging large language models (LLMs) to generate natural language representations of log data. Our method converts raw event logs into structured descriptions that retain both syntactic and semantic details without requiring external knowledge injection or algorithmic preprocessing. This transformation enhances interpretability and supports critical inference tasks such as anomaly detection and root cause analysis. Extensive experiments demonstrate that our approach significantly improves malicious event detection, achieving high accuracy and strong generalization in identifying key system events. Furthermore, we show that LLM-based representations can be refined to better capture complex log formats and operational contexts, making them a valuable tool for real-time monitoring and decision support in complex systems. Our findings indicate that integrating LLM-driven linguistic representations into log analytics bridges the gap between raw data and actionable insights, enabling more adaptive and platform-agnostic inference systems for critical applications.

Keywords: Event logs · Large language models · Log representation · Anomaly detection · Root cause analysis

1 Introduction

Event logs serve as crucial records of system activities, capturing sequences of operations, errors, security events, and user interactions across diverse computing environments. Traditionally, event log analysis has relied on structured querying, rule-based techniques, and statistical models to detect anomalies, assess system performance, and identify security threats. However, these conventional methods often struggle with scalability, adaptability, and inferring complex relationships across heterogeneous log sources. With the advent of large language models (LLMs), new opportunities arise for leveraging natural language understanding

C. Xu (Ed.): ICMLSC 2026, CCIS 2948, pp. 476–490, 2027.
https://doi.org/10.1007/978-981-92-1546-1_39

to extract meaningful insights from event logs without being constrained by predefined rules or rigid structures [6].

Traditional intrusion detection systems (IDS) employ rule-based approaches that compare logs against predefined attack signatures, or anomaly-based approaches that flag deviations from learned baselines [4,7]. While effective, these systems function as opaque analysis engines, making it difficult for security analysts to trace incidents to root causes. This opacity, combined with the steep learning curve in cybersecurity [2,9], underscores the need for more interpretable analytical tools. Representing security incidents in natural language enables targeted defense mechanisms and actionable threat intelligence. By generating linguistic descriptions from log events, security analysts can quickly identify attack vectors and root causes without requiring specialized knowledge of underlying log formats or detection rules.

This research introduces a platform-agnostic LLM-based approach for linguistic representation of event logs, enabling robust inference across cybersecurity, system diagnostics, and compliance auditing. By transforming log data into linguistically coherent formats, our approach enhances interpretability and enables automated reasoning over complex event sequences. The method is particularly effective against zero-day attacks by revealing underlying system behaviors without relying on signature generation.

Our contributions include:

- A framework for converting raw event logs into structured linguistic representations for LLM-based analysis.
- A memory-efficient fine-tuning methodology enabling resource-constrained models to match larger model performance.
- Comprehensive evaluation demonstrating effectiveness in security threat identification and behavioral analysis.

By bridging unstructured log data and AI-driven inference, this work establishes a foundation for intelligent, platform-independent event log analysis in critical computing environments.

2 Motivation

Converting raw log events into human-readable narratives provides practical benefits beyond interpretability. Junior analysts can onboard faster without mastering platform-specific log formats. Compliance teams gain automated summarization capabilities for audit reporting. The system operates effectively without prior domain expertise by leveraging LLM reasoning over structured linguistic representations, enabling real-time security insights across heterogeneous infrastructure without tool-specific knowledge.

3 Dataset

We primarily utilize the Comprehensive, Multi-Source Cyber-Security Events dataset [1] from Los Alamos National Laboratory (LANL). This dataset contains

58 consecutive days of de-identified event data from LANL's internal corporate network, comprising 1,648,275,307 events across 12,425 users, 17,684 computers, and 62,974 processes. The 12GB dataset spans five data sources: Windows authentication events from individual computers and Active Directory domain controllers, process start/stop records, DNS lookup logs, network flow data from key routers, and red teaming events representing simulated attacks. User and computer identifiers are de-identified but internally consistent, with administrative accounts anonymized while system accounts remain identifiable. Failed authentication events are recorded only for users with at least one successful authentication, reducing noise for brute-force attack detection. To validate generalization, we additionally evaluate on the HDFS_v1 dataset from the Loghub collection [3]. This dataset contains logs from a private cloud environment with benchmark workloads, manually labeled as normal or anomalous based on block ID traces.

4 Linguistic Representation Formats

To transform raw log events into meaningful linguistic representations, LLM agents must understand critical security perspectives within authentication data. Key analysis dimensions include: temporal patterns (login frequency, off-hours activity), behavioral deviations (unusual source-destination pairs, protocol anomalies), and threat indicators (brute-force sequences, lateral movement chains). Figure 1 illustrates the structured JSON output format capturing these dimensions.

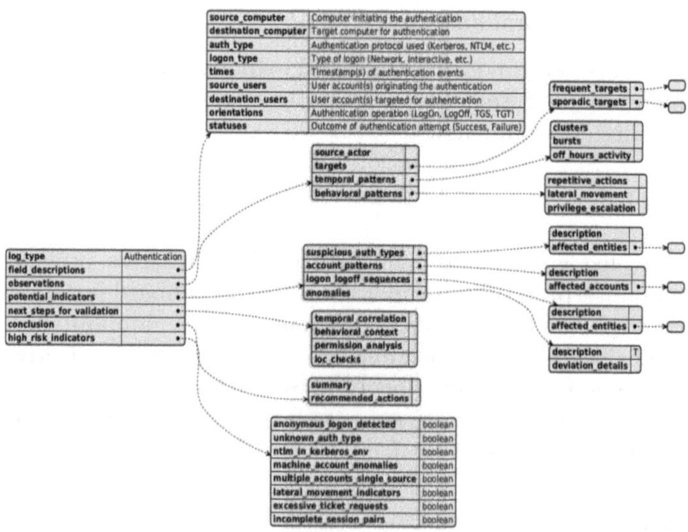

Fig. 1. Language-Based Representation of Logs **(JSON Format)**

We guide LLMs to generate these representations through structured prompts that specify event fields, analysis categories, and high-risk indicator checklists (detailed in Appendix A). Given a log snippet extracted from authentication files, models produce JSON-structured analyses suitable for downstream tasks including red event identification, attack origin detection, and campaign tracing. The same transformation pipeline applies to the LogHub dataset [3] with schema adjustments for HDFS-specific fields.

5 Training Process and Model Integration

We introduce **LogThink**, a memory-efficient fine-tuning framework for security analysis of authentication logs. Figure 2 illustrates our system architecture integrating multiple LLMs with a three-stage training pipeline optimized for resource-constrained hardware.

We evaluate using GPT-4o(gpt-4o-2024-05-13), GPT-4o-mini (gpt-4o-mini-2024-07-18), DeepSeek-R1-Distill-Llama-8B [13], and Qwen2.5-32B. These models generate zero-shot analyses and labeled training data for our three-stage pipeline: (1) Supervised Fine-Tuning on benign data, (2) Reward Model training on malicious/anomaly logs, and (3) Simplified Policy Optimization using both data types.

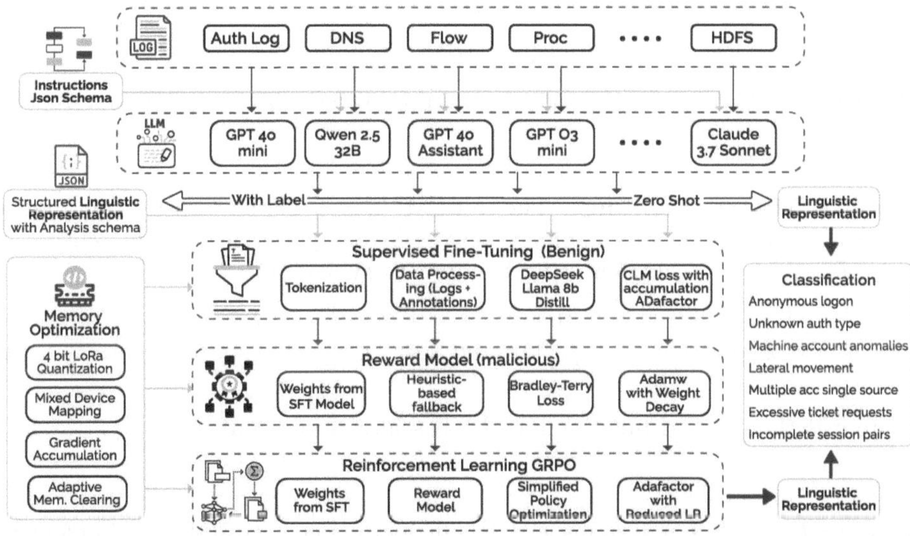

Fig. 2. Authentication security analysis framework incorporating multiple LLMs, supervised fine-tuning, reward modeling, and reinforcement learning.

5.1 Problem Formulation

Let $\mathcal{A} = \{a_1, a_2, ..., a_n\}$ represent a sequence of authentication events, where each event a_i contains attributes including source computer, destination computer, authentication type, and timestamp. We define security analysis as a mapping $f : \mathcal{A} \rightarrow \mathcal{J}$, where $\mathcal{J}$ represents structured JSON output containing security observations and risk indicators. The goal is to train $\mathcal{M}_\theta$ such that $\mathcal{M}_\theta(\mathcal{A}) \approx f(\mathcal{A})$ within memory constraints. Complete notation is provided in Appendix B.

5.2 Fine-Tuning Architecture

Our approach employs a three-stage pipeline optimized for memory-constrained environments.

Supervised Fine-Tuning (SFT). The SFT stage trains on benign data to generate security analyses. Given dataset $\mathcal{D}_{SFT} = \{(\mathcal{A}_i, \mathcal{J}_i)\}_{i=1}^{N}$, we minimize negative log-likelihood:

$$\mathcal{L}_{SFT}(\theta) = -\frac{1}{N}\sum_{i=1}^{N} \log P_\theta(\mathcal{J}_i|\mathcal{A}_i) \tag{1}$$

We implement parameter-efficient fine-tuning using quantization-aware LoRA [22]. For weight matrix $W \in \mathbb{R}^{d\times k}$, updates are approximated via low-rank matrices:

$$W' = W + \Delta W = W + BA \tag{2}$$

where $B \in \mathbb{R}^{d\times r}$, $A \in \mathbb{R}^{r\times k}$, and $r \ll \min(d, k)$, reducing trainable parameters from dk to $r(d + k)$.

Reward Model Training. The reward model distinguishes high-quality analyses using malicious/anomaly logs. Given preference pairs $\mathcal{D}_{RM} = \{(\mathcal{A}_i, \mathcal{J}_i^+, \mathcal{J}_i^-)\}_{i=1}^{M}$, we train using Bradley-Terry loss [15]:

$$\mathcal{L}_{RM}(\phi) = -\frac{1}{M}\sum_{i=1}^{M} \log \sigma \left(R_\phi(\mathcal{A}_i, \mathcal{J}_i^+) - R_\phi(\mathcal{A}_i, \mathcal{J}_i^-)\right) \tag{3}$$

where σ is the sigmoid function and R_ϕ is scalar reward output.

Heuristic Fallback. For systems with insufficient memory (<8GB), we implement a heuristic for inference-time ranking:

$$R_{\text{heuristic}}(\mathcal{A}, \mathcal{J}) = \sum_{w\in\mathcal{P}} \mathbb{1}_{w\in\mathcal{J}} - \sum_{w\in\mathcal{N}} \mathbb{1}_{w\in\mathcal{J}} \tag{4}$$

where $\mathcal{P}$ and $\mathcal{N}$ are curated positive/negative keyword sets. This ranks candidate outputs at inference only, not during training.

Simplified Policy Optimization (SPO). Inspired by Group Relative Policy Optimization [13], we use the reward model to weight training examples rather than full online RL:

$$\mathcal{L}_{SPO}(\theta) = -\frac{1}{K}\sum_{i=1}^{K} w_i \cdot \log P_\theta(\mathcal{J}_i^*|\mathcal{A}_i) \quad (5)$$

where $\mathcal{J}_i^*$ represents expert annotations and $w_i = \text{softmax}(R_\phi(\mathcal{A}_i, \mathcal{J}_i^*)/\tau)$ are reward-weighted importance scores with temperature τ. This distills knowledge from expert annotations into smaller models while prioritizing higher-quality examples.

Relationship to PPO. The standard PPO objective [20]:

$$\mathcal{L}_{PPO}(\theta) = \mathbb{E}\left[\min\left(\frac{\pi_\theta}{\pi_{\theta_{old}}}R_\phi, \text{clip}\left(\frac{\pi_\theta}{\pi_{\theta_{old}}}, 1-\epsilon, 1+\epsilon\right)R_\phi\right)\right] \quad (6)$$

is approximated by our approach when starting from a well-initialized SFT policy. Clipping effects are implicitly achieved through reduced learning rates and consistent high-quality examples.

5.3 Memory Optimization

We implement five optimization strategies: (1) LoRA reduces memory by 75% versus FP16; (2) gradient accumulation with factor 16 cuts peak memory by 94%; (3) double quantization on weights and quantization constants; (4) CPU offloading of non-critical components via custom device mapping; (5) periodic cache clearing to minimize fragmentation.

6 Evaluation

The linguistic JSON representations enable multiple inference tasks including anomaly detection, behavioral analysis, insider threat detection, IoC identification, and temporal pattern analysis.

Data Integrity. We implement strict data separation: temporal split (training: days 1–40, test: days 41–58), zero-shot isolation (GPT-4o prompts contain only instructions and schema, no examples), red team identifier masking during evaluation, and 5-fold cross-validation. We acknowledge that ARCS Red Team activities (Pass-the-Hash, lateral movement) may be recognizable to models trained on security literature.

6.1 Indicator Importance Score

Our system produces structured JSON with eight binary high-risk indicators $\mathcal{I} = \{r_1, \ldots, r_8\}$: anonymous logon detected, unknown auth type, NTLM in Kerberos environment, machine account anomalies, multiple accounts from single source, lateral movement indicators, excessive ticket requests, and incomplete session pairs.

We quantify indicator effectiveness using normalized information gain. For indicator r_i, importance score $S(r_i)$ is:

$$S(r_i) = \frac{H - H_{\text{split}}(r_i)}{H_{\text{max}}} \tag{7}$$

where $H = -\sum_{c \in \{\text{benign,malicious}\}} p_c \log_2 p_c$ is initial entropy, and $H_{\text{split}}(r_i)$ is weighted conditional entropy:

$$H_{\text{split}}(r_i) = \sum_{v \in \{\text{true,false}\}} \frac{N_v}{N} \cdot H(Y|r_i = v) \tag{8}$$

with conditional entropy:

$$H(Y|r_i = v) = - \sum_{c \in \{\text{benign,malicious}\}} p_{c|v} \log_2 p_{c|v} \tag{9}$$

Higher $S(r_i)$ indicates stronger discriminative power between benign and malicious activities [16].

Table 1. Indicator Importance and Optimal Classification Threshold on ARCS Dataset

Indicator	GPT-4o-mini	GPT-4o	R1-RL
Anonymous Logon Detected	0.5509	0.6240	0.7627
NTLM in Kerberos Environment	0.3188	0.2416	0.1428
Incomplete Session Pairs	0.2334	0.2538	0.0183
Multiple Accounts Single Source	0.1159	0.0364	0.0042
Excessive Ticket Requests	0.0811	0.0338	0.0004
Machine Account Anomalies	0.0798	0.1149	0.0708
Lateral Movement Indicators	0.0599	0.3503	0.0002
Unknown Authentication Type	0.0165	0.0203	0.0277
Optimal Threshold	5	5	4

Tables 1 and 2 show indicator importance scores across datasets. On ARCS, all models assign highest importance to Anonymous Logon Detected (R1-RL: 0.7627). GPT-4o uniquely emphasizes Lateral Movement Indicators (0.3503). On LogHub, GPT-4o prioritizes Missing Followup Events (0.6549) while GPT-4o-mini weights Error Logs Detected highest (0.1969). Optimal classification thresholds range from 4–5 activated indicators.

Table 2. Indicator Importance and Optimal Threshold on LogHub Dataset

Indicator	GPT-4o-mini	GPT-4o
Missing Followup Events	0.1259	0.6549
Repeated Block Receptions	0.0641	0.2215
Error Logs Detected	0.1969	0.1316
Node Behavior Outliers	0.0207	0.0508
Looping Patterns Detected	0.0000	0.0381
Unusual Time Gaps	0.0754	0.0151
Optimal Threshold	5	4

6.2 Classification Results

To quantify activated indicator concentration, we define **Indicator Density Score**:

$$\mathrm{IDS}(\boldsymbol{r}) = \frac{1}{|\mathcal{I}|}\sum_{i=1}^{|\mathcal{I}|} r_i \tag{10}$$

where higher IDS for malicious logs indicates effective anomaly differentiation.

Table 3. Classification metrics on ARCS and LogHub datasets

Metric	ARCS Dataset			LogHub Dataset	
	GPT 4o Mini	GPT 4o	R1-RL	GPT 4o Mini	GPT 4o
Accuracy	0.8082	0.9840	0.9347	0.6900	0.9082
Precision	0.8065	1.0000	0.8904	0.6792	0.8679
Recall	1.0000	0.9775	1.0000	0.7200	0.9583
F1 Score	0.8929	0.9886	0.9420	0.6990	0.9109

Table 4. Indicator distribution across benign and malicious logs (IDS = Avg Indicators / $|\mathcal{I}|$, where $|\mathcal{I}| = 8$ for ARCS, $|\mathcal{I}| = 6$ for LogHub).

Dataset	Metric	Benign Logs			Malicious Logs		
		GPT-4o-mini	GPT-4o	R1-RL	GPT-4o-mini	GPT-4o	R1-RL
ARCS	Avg True Indicators	4.84	2.73	2.78	6.14	6.14	5.26
	Standard Deviation	1.29	1.12	0.94	0.82	0.82	1.14
	Indicator Density Score	0.606	0.342	0.347	0.768	0.768	0.657
LogHub	Avg True Indicators	4.10	2.56	–	4.58	4.65	–
	Indicator Density Score	0.683	0.427	–	0.763	0.775	–

Table 3 presents classification results. GPT-4o achieves highest accuracy (0.9840) and F1 (0.9886) on ARCS with perfect precision. R1-RL attains perfect recall while maintaining strong F1 (0.9420). GPT-4o generalizes well to LogHub (F1: 0.9109), while GPT-4o-mini shows weaker performance across both datasets. Table 4 shows indicator distributions. GPT-4o achieves clearest separation on ARCS: benign IDS of 0.342 versus malicious IDS of 0.768 (2.25× difference). Malicious logs exhibit lower variance, indicating consistent indicator activation for attack patterns.

6.3 Comparison with Traditional Methods

Table 5 compares against established methods. LLM-based approaches outperform traditional methods requiring extensive feature engineering. GPT-4o achieves highest F1 (0.9593), while LogThink attains perfect recall with competitive F1 (0.9420).

7 Case Study: Security Insights Generation

We demonstrate extended analyses using linguistic representations with a RAG-driven LLM answerer. The full system architecture is provided in Appendix C.

7.1 Process Behavior Analysis

We create JSON linguistic representations for process-based logs and use RAG for Q&A analysis examining behavioral trajectories. Sample queries and responses:

1. **What are some frequent target processes?**
   Answer: P4, P1, P5, P7, P8 and P16.
2. **Is there any process that is highly used by a specific computer but less used in others?**
   Answer: Yes, according to the summary, process P4 is frequently accessed

Table 5. Comparison with traditional log anomaly detection methods on ARCS dataset.

Method	Acc	Prec	Rec	F1
DeepLog [10]	0.7823	0.7456	0.8912	0.8119
LogAnomaly [18]	0.8156	0.7891	0.9023	0.8420
LogLLM [12]	0.8734	0.8456	0.9234	0.8828
GPT-4o-mini (Zero-shot)	0.8082	0.8065	1.0000	0.8929
GPT-4o (Zero-shot)	0.9347	0.9418	0.9775	0.9593
LogThink (R1-RL)	**0.9347**	0.8904	**1.0000**	0.9420

on the specific computer being analyzed, but is less frequently seen on other computers. This could indicate that P4 is a critical or misused process on the specific computer.

Additional process analysis examples including scheduled job detection and fingerprinting techniques are provided in Appendix C.

7.2 Flow Pattern Analysis

We pose probing questions to examine patterns in network flow data:

1. **Is there any anomaly in flow patterns for certain entity?**
Answer: Yes, there is an anomaly in flow patterns for the entities C528 and C1453, as there is a significantly higher volume of packets between them compared to other flows.
2. **List potential computers that could be targeted in a data exfiltration attack.**
Answer: C1707, C586, C2584, C612, C528, C3204, C1108

7.3 DNS Pattern Analysis

We query DNS logs to uncover inconsistent resolution patterns:

1. **Is there any DNS lookup patterns for unexpected resolutions or inconsistencies that can help detect such anomalies? Give an example with the information about the source computer.**
Answer: Yes, there are DNS lookup patterns for unexpected resolutions or inconsistencies that can help detect such anomalies. For example, in the first set of context, the source computer C5913 consistently queries C586, C457, and C706, indicating a focus on these systems. This could be an anomaly if C5913 does not typically access these systems.

8 Related Work

Early log anomaly detection systems employed rule-based methods and deep learning. DeepLog [10] and LogAnomaly [18] used LSTM networks to model log sequences [19], but struggled with variable formats and required extensive preprocessing [5]. Recent work addresses these limitations through LLM-based approaches using prompt engineering, in-context learning, and fine-tuning [12,14]. NLP integration has advanced semantic log understanding. Dwaraki et al. [11] demonstrated automated event identification through syntactic parsing. He et al. [14] and Xu et al. [21] leveraged in-context learning for log parsing, achieving 98.1% accuracy. Liu et al. [17] implemented prompt-based methods with scalability up to 45,000 logs per second. Ma et al. [23] explored open-source LLMs for privacy-preserving parsing, reporting 91% accuracy on structured logs but 67% on unstructured cloud logs. For security-specific applications, Guan et al. [12] utilized BERT to extract semantic vectors from logs, outperforming traditional methods. Boffa et al. [8] condensed 400,000 security log entries into 3,000 attack fingerprints. Our work differs by generating structured linguistic representations that preserve both syntactic and semantic information for downstream security inference, while enabling memory-efficient fine-tuning on resource-constrained hardware.

9 Conclusion

We presented LogThink, a platform-agnostic framework for transforming raw event logs into structured linguistic representations using LLMs. Our three-stage training pipeline, combining supervised fine-tuning, reward modeling, and simplified policy optimization, enables resource-constrained models to generate high-quality security analyses. On the ARCS authentication dataset, GPT-4o achieves 0.9840 accuracy and 0.9886 F1, while our fine-tuned R1-RL model attains perfect recall with competitive F1 (0.9420). The approach generalizes to HDFS logs without architecture changes. Several limitations need to be addressed. The ARCS dataset (2015) contains attack patterns now documented in security literature; modern LLMs may recognize these during pre-training. Our claims concern detecting previously unseen log patterns without signature updates, not novel attack techniques. Additionally, while memory optimizations enable fine-tuning on consumer hardware (8GB VRAM), GPT-4o inference requires API access with associated costs. Future work will validate on contemporary datasets including Azure AD authentication logs, Kubernetes audit logs, and modern EDR telemetry. We also plan to investigate cost-effectiveness for production deployment and extend the framework to real-time streaming analysis.

A Authentication Analysis Prompt Template

Figure 3 presents the complete prompt template used to generate linguistic representations from authentication logs. The prompt structures analysis into four components: (1) event field definitions, (2) observation categories covering source actors, targets, temporal patterns, and behavioral patterns, (3) potential indicators of compromise spanning authentication types, account patterns, and session anomalies, and (4) validation steps including temporal correlation, behavioral context comparison, permission analysis, and IOC cross-referencing (Table 6).

Cybersecurity Analyst Task

You are a cybersecurity analyst tasked with analyzing authentication log events to identify potentially suspicious patterns indicative of a security compromise or lateral movement. Your analysis will involve examining fields that detail the source and destination of authentication attempts, authentication types, and statuses.

Event Fields for Analysis

- **source_computer**: The computer initiating the authentication event.
- **destination_computer**: The target computer for the authentication event.
- **auth_type**: The authentication protocol used (e.g., Kerberos, NTLM).
- **logon_type**: The logon type, such as Network or Interactive.
- **times**: The timestamps for authentication events.
- **source_users**: The user accounts initiating the authentication.
- **destination_users**: The user accounts targeted for authentication.
- **orientations**: The authentication operations (e.g., LogOn, LogOff, TGS, TGT).
- **statuses**: The outcome of the authentication attempts (Success, Failure).

Analysis Structure

Observations:
Source/Actor: Identify any computers and accounts initiating authentication, flagging suspicious naming conventions or unexpected system initiations.
Targets: Document systems that are frequently accessed, particularly critical infrastructure, and note irregular connections.
Temporal Patterns: Look for unusual frequency or timing in authentication events.
Behavioral Patterns: Identify flows suggesting suspicious activity like lateral movement or credential harvesting.

Potential Indicators of Compromise:
Suspicious Authentication Types: Investigate ANONYMOUS LOGON as high-risk, NTLM usage in Kerberos environments, and unspecified authentication types.
Account Patterns: Watch for machine accounts (e.g., ending with $) authenticating atypically, multiple accounts from a single source rapidly, or single accounts accessing multiple destinations rapidly.
Logon/Logoff Sequences: Check for logons without logoffs, rapidly successive sessions, or unusual TGS/TGT requests.
Anomalous Patterns: Monitor for activity outside business hours, unexpected authentication sources, excessive failed attempts followed by success.

Steps for Validation

Temporal Correlation: Examine the timing and sequence of events.
Behavioral Context: Compare current patterns to known baselines.
Permission Analysis: Verify if accounts should have access to targeted systems.
IOC Checks: Cross-reference patterns with known attack techniques (e.g., Pass-the-Hash).

High-Risk Indicators Checklist:
- ANONYMOUS LOGON events are present.
- Authentication uses an unknown or missing type.
- NTLM authentication found in Kerberos-preferred settings.
- Odd machine account authentications.
- Numerous accounts from a single source rapidly.
- Authentication chains indicate lateral movement.
- Excessive TGS/TGT activity.
- LogOn without corresponding LogOff events.

Conclusion

Provide a risk-based assessment of anomalies.
Recommend investigations for suspicious authentication chains.
Suggest specific remediation for verified compromises.

Fig. 3. Key Steps for Analyzing and Validating Authentication Events

B Mathematical Notation

Table 6. Mathematical notation used in the LogThink framework.

Symbol	Definition
$\mathcal{A}$	Authentication event sequence
$\mathcal{J}$	Structured JSON security analysis
$\mathcal{M}_\theta$	Language model with parameters θ
$\mathcal{D}_{SFT}$	SFT dataset: $\{(\mathcal{A}_i, \mathcal{J}_i)\}_{i=1}^N$
$\mathcal{D}_{RM}$	Preference dataset: $\{(\mathcal{A}_i, \mathcal{J}_i^+, \mathcal{J}_i^-)\}_{i=1}^M$
$\mathcal{L}_{SFT}$	Supervised fine-tuning loss
$\mathcal{L}_{RM}$	Reward model loss
$\mathcal{L}_{SPO}$	Simplified policy optimization loss
R_ϕ	Reward function parameterized by ϕ
$\mathcal{I}$	Set of high-risk indicators $\{r_1, ..., r_8\}$

C Extended Case Study

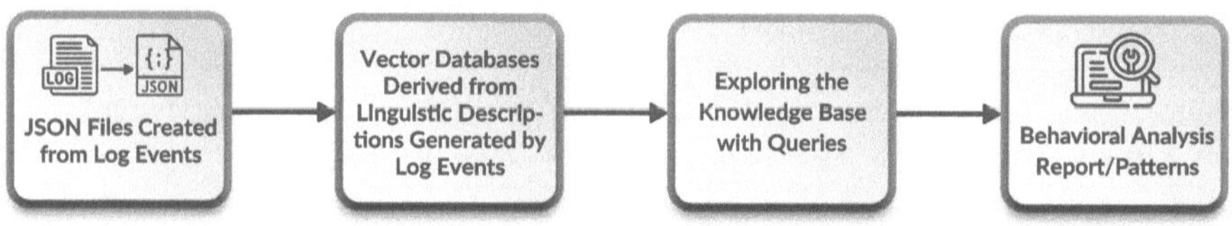

Fig. 4. RAG-driven Security Insight Generation for Process, Flow, and DNS Logs.

The RAG-driven Security Insight Generation module (Fig. 4) utilizes Retrieval-Augmented Generation models to analyze security data from processes, network flows, and DNS log events. This module automates behavior and anomaly detection, facilitating detailed security insights for improved analysis and decision-making.

C.1 Additional Process Behavior Analysis Examples

3. **Example 3: Can you identify any scheduled job pattern in the processes?**

Answer: Yes, there are notable clusters of process starts around timestamps <114> and <115> and <116> and <117>, indicating possible scheduled tasks or user activity. Additionally, there is a high frequency of process starts observed for P5 and P16, particularly in the <114> and <116> timeframes. This could suggest that these processes are part of a scheduled job or task.

4. **Example 4: What sort of possible fingerprinting for the processes could be done given the contexts?**

Answer: One possible fingerprinting technique that could be used is to check the frequency of process starts, as mentioned in the behavioral_context. This could help identify any abnormal or excessive use of certain processes. Additionally, the permission_analysis context suggests reviewing user permissions for P4, which could also provide insight into potential malicious activity. Finally, the ioc_checks context mentions checking if any of the processes are flagged as malicious in threat intelligence databases, which could also help identify potential threats.

References

1. Comprehensive, Multi-Source Cyber-Security Events - Cyber Security Research — csr.lanl.gov. https://csr.lanl.gov/data/cyber1/. Accessed 20-02-2025
2. Cyber Security Training Market Size & Share Report, 2030 — grandviewresearch.com. https://www.grandviewresearch.com/industry-analysis/cyber-security-training-market-report. Accessed 20-02-2025
3. Loghub. https://github.com/logpai/loghub/tree/master. Accessed 25-03-2025
4. Akbar, K.A., et al.: Advanced persistent threat detection using data provenance and metric learning. IEEE Trans. Dependable Secure Comput. (2023). https://ieeexplore.ieee.org/abstract/document/9947295
5. Akbar, K.A., Wang, Y., Islam, M.S., Singhal, A., Khan, L., Thuraisingham, B.: Identifying tactics of advanced persistent threats with limited attack traces. In: Information Systems Security: 17th International Conference, ICISS 2021, Patna, India, 16–20 December 2021, Proceedings 17, pp. 3–25. Springer (2021)
6. Akhtar, M., Khan, A.: LLM-based event log analysis techniques: a survey. arXiv preprint arXiv:2502.00677 (2025)
7. Ayoade, G., et al.: Evolving advanced persistent threat detection using provenance graph and metric learning. In: 2020 IEEE Conference on Communications and Network Security (CNS), pp. 1–9 (2020). https://doi.org/10.1109/CNS48642.2020.9162264
8. Boffa, M., et al.: Logprécis: Unleashing language models for automated malicious log analysis. Comput. Secur. **141**, 103805 (2024). https://doi.org/10.1016/j.cose.2024.103805
9. Coffey, L.: Colleges spending more than ever on cybersecurity efforts — insidehighered.com. https://www.insidehighered.com/news/quick-takes/2024/04/25/colleges-spending-more-ever-cybersecurity-efforts. Accessed 20-02-2025
10. Du, M., Li, F., Zheng, G., Srikumar, V.: Deeplog: anomaly detection and diagnosis from system logs through deep learning. In: Proceedings of the 2017 ACM SIGSAC Conference on Computer and Communications Security, pp. 1285–1298 (2017)

11. Dwaraki, A., Kumary, S., Wolf, T.: Automated event identification from system logs using natural language processing. In: 2020 International Conference on Computing, Networking and Communications (ICNC), pp. 209–215. IEEE (2020)
12. Guan, W., Cao, J., Qian, S., Gao, J., Ouyang, C.: Logllm: Log-based Anomaly Detection Using Large Language Models. arXiv.org (2024).https://doi.org/10.48550/ARXIV.2411.08561
13. Guo, D., et al.: Deepseek-r1: Incentivizing reasoning capability in LLMs via reinforcement learning. arXiv preprint arXiv:2501.12948 (2025)
14. He, M., Jia, T., Duan, C., Cai, H., Li, Y., Huang, G.: Llmelog: an approach for anomaly detection based on LLM-enriched Log Events. In: 2024 IEEE 35th International Symposium on Software Reliability Engineering (ISSRE), pp. 132–143. IEEE (2024). https://doi.org/10.1109/issre62328.2024.00023
15. Huang, T.K., Weng, R.C., Lin, C.J., Ridgeway, G.: Generalized bradley-terry models and multi-class probability estimates. J. Mach. Learn. Res. **7**(1) (2006)
16. Li, Z., Terashi, K.: Quantum decision trees with information entropy. arXiv preprint arXiv:2502.11412 (2025)
17. Liu, Y., et al.: Interpretable online log analysis using large language models with prompt strategies. In: Proceedings of the 32nd IEEE/ACM International Conference on Program Comprehension, pp. 35–46. ACM (2024). https://doi.org/10.1145/3643916.3644408
18. Meng, W., et al.: Loganomaly: unsupervised detection of sequential and quantitative anomalies in unstructured logs. In: IJCAI. vol. 19, pp. 4739–4745 (2019)
19. Qi, J., Huang, S., Luan, Z., Fung, C.J., Yang, H., Qian, D.: Loggpt: exploring chatgpt for log-based anomaly detection. 2023 IEEE International Conference on High Performance Computing & Communications, Data Science & Systems, Smart City & Dependability in Sensor, Cloud & Big Data Systems & Application (HPCC/DSS/SmartCity/DependSys), pp. 273–280 (2023). https://api.semanticscholar.org/CorpusID:261530676
20. Schulman, J., Wolski, F., Dhariwal, P., Radford, A., Klimov, O.: Proximal policy optimization algorithms. arXiv preprint arXiv:1707.06347 (2017)
21. Xu, J., Yang, R., Huo, Y., Zhang, C., He, P.: Divlog: log parsing with prompt enhanced in-context learning. In: Proceedings of the IEEE/ACM 46th International Conference on Software Engineering, pp. 1–12. ACM (2024). https://doi.org/10.1145/3597503.3639155
22. Xu, Y., et al.: QA-LORA: quantization-aware low-rank adaptation of large language models. arXiv preprint arXiv:2309.14717 (2023)
23. Zeyang, M., Dong, J.K., Tse-Husn, C.: Librelog: accurate and Efficient Unsupervised Log Parsing Using Open-Source Large Language Models (2024)

Cortex: A Hybrid KG-LLM Approach for Multidocument Question Answering

Niamat Zawad(✉) and Latifur Khan

The University of Texas at Dallas, Richardson, USA
Niamat.Zawad@UTDallas.edu

Abstract. In the realm of natural language processing and knowledge representation, the integration of Large Language Models with Knowledge Graphs has emerged as a promising approach to enhance the accuracy and relevance of generated content. However, a significant challenge with LLMs is their propensity for "hallucinations"—generating plausible but factually incorrect or nonsensical information. Our approach combines a dynamically-updated Knowledge Graph with a Large Language Model to produce responses that are firmly rooted in verified, structured knowledge. We introduce a sophisticated hybrid multi-document question-answering model called Cortex that is designed to retrieve and integrate pertinent source texts necessary for accurately addressing user queries. This model operates through a comprehensive two-step process: first, it constructs a detailed knowledge graph, and second, it retrieves relevant source texts from this graph to ensure that responses are factually grounded and contextually accurate. Experiments demonstrate that the proposed system improves the factual accuracy of LLM outputs and ensures that responses are not only contextually relevant but also factually sound, paving the way for more reliable and trustworthy AI-driven systems in information retrieval, conversational agents, and automated content generation.

Keywords: Retrieval Augmented Generation · Knowledge Graph · Large Language Models

1 Introduction

Large Language Models (LLMs) have transformed our daily lives with their remarkable text comprehension capabilities, sparking a revolution in the field of Natural Language Processing (NLP). Their applications range from summarizing lengthy documents to generating complex computer code, showcasing their versatility and impact. However, despite these advancements, LLMs are not without challenges. One notable issue is the phenomenon of hallucination, where the models produce text that gives the impression of being fluent and natural despite being unfaithful and nonsensical [13]. To address this issue, we propose a technique to bring KGs into the fold to improve accuracy of LLM responses.

C. Xu (Ed.): ICMLSC 2026, CCIS 2948, pp. 491–504, 2027.
https://doi.org/10.1007/978-981-92-1546-1_40

Knowledge graphs are sophisticated structures that map data into graphs, where nodes represent entities of interest and edges denote the relationships between these entities [11]. Considerable effort has been devoted to the development of knowledge graphs. For example, DBPedia [2] transforms structured information from Wikipedia's infoboxes—essentially data tables—into RDF (Resource Description Framework) triples. In contrast, Freebase [4] used its proprietary schema to represent information as a graph. YAGO [25], meanwhile, integrated entities and relationships extracted from Wikipedia with the hierarchical framework of WordNet [10]. These systems leverage existing metadata and predefined ontologies to generate triplets, thus enabling a structured representation of knowledge. Despite their advancements, these methods have limitations. Not all data is structured, and the extensive diversity of text often renders a single, predefined ontology inadequate. This is where Large Language Models (LLMs) provide a significant advantage. LLMs, which learn tasks from a few examples [5], excel at uncovering intuitive causal relationships between concepts [16,19]. Consequently, they are exceptionally suited for extracting and understanding knowledge from unstructured text. Recent work has explored leveraging LLMs to extract graphs from text [3,31]. For instance, Yanming [30] uses ChatGPT to enhance a causal graph, while Raptor [24] constructs a tree from text, offering varying levels of summarization from the ground up.

Prior research has established that grounding language model (LM) responses in reference texts significantly enhances question answering performance [15]. Retrieval Augmented Generation (RAG) models [17] exemplify this approach by integrating the parametric knowledge of LLMs with non-parametric memory from reference texts for improved question answering. However, a limitation of these studies is their focus on single-document question answering. Research by [14] indicates that models optimized for single-paragraph QA often rely on sentence-level pattern matching rather than genuine reading comprehension. This highlights the need for a more robust evaluation approach.

To address this issue, we propose evaluating question answering (QA) performance using multi-document datasets. Our method involves creating a knowledge graph where nodes represent individual documents, and edges capture semantic or lexical similarities between them. By traversing this graph, we gather relevant supporting passages from across multiple documents, thereby enhancing the language model's ability to perform multi-document QA.

Our approach bears some resemblance to the work described in [9], which constructs a hierarchical graph with leaf-level communities. These communities, consisting of individual entities, are connected by weighted edges that reflect the normalized frequency of their relationships. This hierarchical graph supports the use of community detection algorithms to form cohesive groups, allowing the language model to generate summaries based on these communities and ultimately produce global answers to queries. However, our approach differs in several important aspects:

Model Choice. GraphRAG employs GPT-4-turbo for generating the graph index and answering queries. In contrast, we utilize the more lightweight Gemma2 [26] for knowledge graph construction and LLama3 [8] for question answering. These open-source models, which can be run locally, make our tool more accessible and practical for widespread use.

Evaluation Metrics. GraphRAG depends on subjective evaluation metrics such as comprehensiveness, diversity, empowerment, and directness, which do not always provide a clear measure of a framework's effectiveness in delivering accurate answers. Our evaluation approach addresses this by focusing on more objective metrics that assess question-answering performance directly.

By incorporating these improvements, our method aims to provide a more practical and objectively measurable solution for enhancing multi-document QA capabilities. We highlight our contributions as follows:

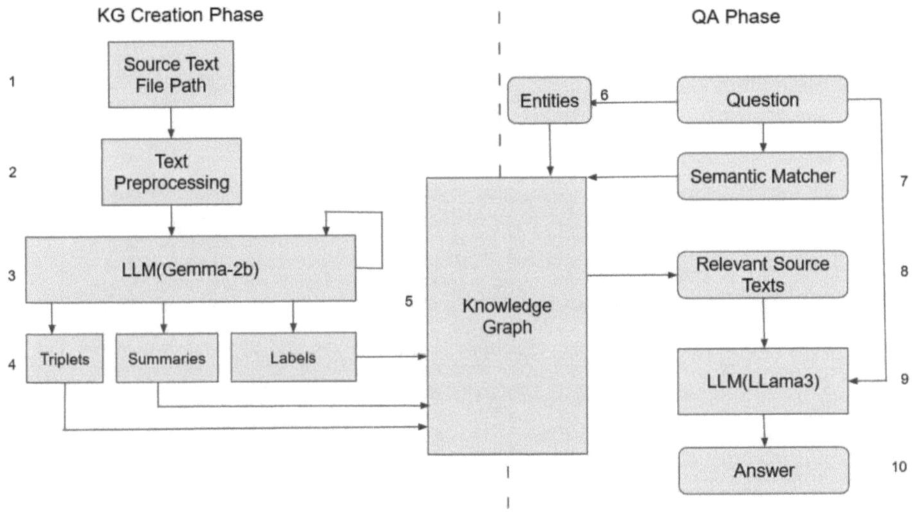

Fig. 1. Workflow Overview: In the initial phase, a Knowledge Graph is constructed. During the second phase, this graph is utilized to support question answering. The workflow begins with preprocessing the source text (2), which is then input into the Gemma2 LLM model to generate triplets (3). These triplets, along with summaries and labels, are organized hierarchically and incorporated into the Knowledge Graph (4). In the Question Answering (QA) phase, entities are extracted from the question and matched against those in the graph to identify relevant nodes. A vector representation of the question is created by the semantic matcher (7) and compared with nodes in the Knowledge Graph to find semantically similar summaries and labels. Subsequently, the texts where these components appear are retrieved (8) and used as context for the LLama3 LLM model, along with the question (9), to generate an answer (10).

Novel KG Construction Method. We present a novel method for knowledge graph construction that employs a unique hierarchical structure, enhancing granularity and improving information representation and retrieval. By leveraging existing open-source LLMs, our approach avoids the need for costly pretraining on extensive corpora.

Dynamic KG. Our graph dynamically updates its structure while answering questions, continuously expanding its knowledge base and ensuring it remains current over time.

This paper is structured as follows: Sect. 2 introduces our proposed method for constructing a hierarchical knowledge graph, detailing its novel structure. In Sect. 3 we present the experimental setup and evaluation metrics used to assess the performance of our approach, followed by a discussion of the results in Sect. 4. Finally, Sect. 5 and 6 offers concluding remarks and outlines potential directions for future research.

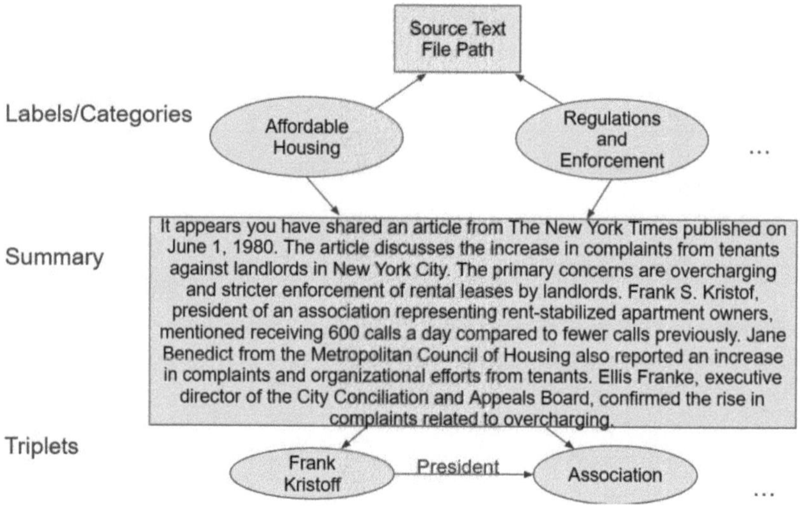

Fig. 2. Illustration of a graph schema of data from a single text document. Labels and triplets have been truncated for clarity.

2 Method

Knowledge Graph Creation. The steps in the Knowledge Graph Creation phase are outlined in Fig. 1. (1)Initially, the text is preprocessed to distinguish between the title and passage. The title helps highlight the key points for the language model. To address coreferencing errors—where the same entity mentioned in different parts of the text is misidentified as separate entities—we utilize the NLP Stanza package [21]. Stanza replaces pronouns with their corresponding nouns to ensure consistent entity identification. (2)The processed text is then

Table 1. Prompt used to generate triplets

Prompt

Carefully observe the following examples:

Example 1:
Text: Transportation Journal is an academic journal devoted to transportation, logistics and related fields. The journal is published quarterly by the Penn State University Press on behalf of the American Society of Transportation and Logistics.
Triplet(s):

<Transportation Journal, publisher, Penn State University Press>

Example 2:
Text: Chelopech Hill is the ice-covered hill rising to 946 m in the north foothills of Detroit Plateau on Trinity Peninsula in Graham Land, Antarctica. It is surmounting Russell West Glacier to the north. The hill is named after the settlement of Chelopech in Western Bulgaria.
Triplet(s):

<Trinity Peninsula, part of, Graham Land>

<Trinity Peninsula, continent, Antarctica>

<Graham Land, continent, Antarctica>

Now, read the following passage to answer: A triplet is defined as: <Subject, Predicate, Object>. Taking knowledge from the above examples, given a piece of text below, you must answer with the palpable set(s) of <Subject, Predicate, Object>. Do not include any redundant triplet(s). You can modify the textual format for 'Subject', 'Predicate', and 'Object' while generating the triplets if deemed necessary. Include the temporal triplets as well. Follow the triplet format <Subject, Predicate, Object> strictly and keep the text of the 'Subject', 'Predicate', and 'Object' as compact as possible.

Text: <Text>

fed into the language model(3), which generates triplets(4) based on the prompt outlined in Table 1.

The triplets belong to three categories: Labels, Summaries and Entities.

Labels capture the core themes of the source text. For instance, given the sentence, "The National Liberation Army (ELN) resumed peace talks with the Colombian government on March 15; however, conflict erupted between the ELN and former guerrillas embedded in the main cocaine hub on the Venezuela border, specifically the region of Catatumbo," the generated labels might include "Drug Trafficking" and "Peace Talks/Negotiation."

Next, a summary of the source text is generated. This summary highlights the key points, facilitating the creation of a meaningful embedding when mapped to a vector space.

Entities are then extracted in the form of *<subject>* ->*<relation>* ->*<object>*. To build a general knowledge base without adhering to a predefined ontology, the language model extracts triplets without focusing on any specific topic. The full graph schema is illustrated in Fig. 2.

The triplets are then connected with each other to form a Knowledge Graph(5). Generating these triplets is computationally expensive. We have explored non-LLM approaches, such as the Stanford Open Information Extraction tool [1]. While this tool provides broad coverage by extracting triplets from all sentences in a text, it often fails to capture critical information. For example, it might generate redundant triplets such as "The second - the cost - of trafficking drugs" from the sentence "The second is the cost of trafficking drugs along the Venezuelan border, where the EPL must protect the product and transport it by land." Such redundant triplets increase computational costs and decrease precision during the QA phase, where relevant triplets are searched.

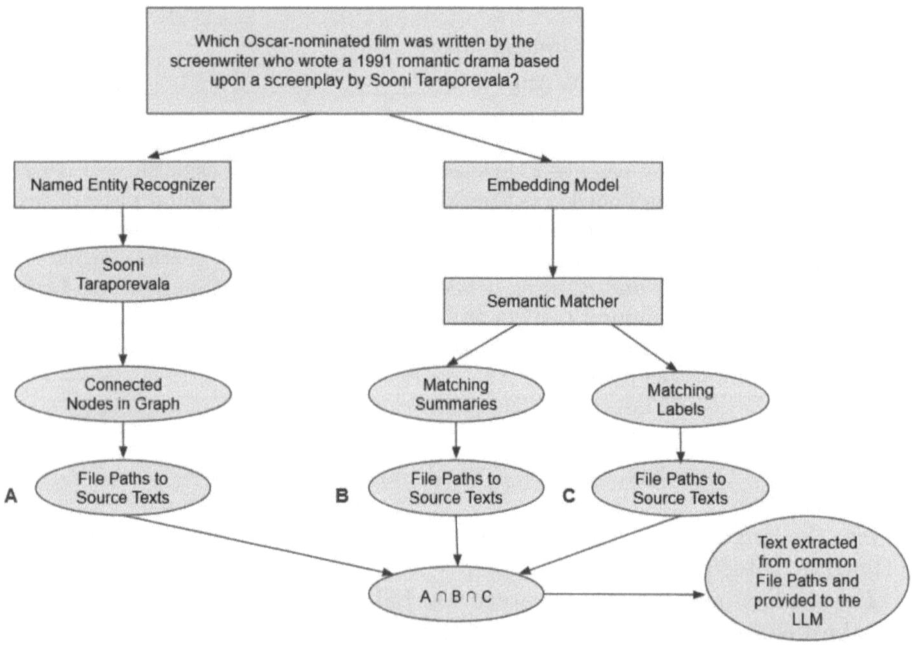

Fig. 3. Overview of our QA approach. We collect source texts where individual entities are mentioned and connect them to summaries and labels relevant to the query. Only the common source texts are selected and provided to the LLM.

Question Answering. The steps in this phase are outlined in Fig. 3. The question answering process is carried out in three distinct phases:

Entity Extraction and Graph Matching. Using a named entity recognizer, entities within the query are extracted. The most similar entities are then identified in the knowledge graph. Following this, object entities connected to the identified entities are retrieved. The system then searches for source texts where both the subject and object entities are mentioned. This process is illustrated in the leftmost branch of Fig. 3.

Summary Retrieval and Matching Finally, a vector representation of the query is matched against available summaries to find relevant source texts. This step ensures that the most pertinent information related to the query is obtained from the retrieved source texts. This process is shown in the middle branch of Fig. 3.

Label Generation. Initially, the query is passed to a Large Language Model (LLM), which generates labels to provide a broad overview of the query's context. These labels help categorize the query, such as identifying whether it pertains to crime, politics, or another domain. These steps are depicted in the rightmost branch of Fig. 3.

After retrieving the lists of relevant source texts, an intersection operation is performed to identify common texts across the lists. The common texts are then fed into the query-answer prompt, allowing the Large Language Model (LLM) to generate responses that are grounded in the context provided by these texts. This process ensures that the answers are informed by the most relevant and consistent information available.

2.1 Entity Linking

To ensure that our knowledge graph remains dynamic and up-to-date with newly discovered entities, we employ an algorithm to link these entities, thereby increasing the number of potential paths and entities available for query. The details of this process are outlined in Algorithm 1. After gathering relevant entities for a given question, we iterate through each entity to identify the top α most similar entities within the graph. We then assess syntactical similarity by checking whether the Levenshtein distance [12] is greater than β. These parameters are set to 10 and 50 respectively as they have been shown to achieve the maximum number of relevant entities. By querying a language model to determine if these source texts are pertinent to answering the question, we can link the entities if they are deemed relevant. This process allows the graph to evolve and expand over time, continuously enhancing its utility and mitigates the need for costly LLM invocations when retrieving the connected entities later.

Algorithm 1. Entity Linking

Input: Node, Query
Output: Nodes linked to the input node
Procedure:
Find top α similar entities to the input node
for each element x in the similar entities list **do**
  Get Levenshtein distance(input node, x)
  if Levenshtein distance ¿ β **then**
    Retrieve source text of input node, x
    Pass both source texts to LLM and ask whether the source texts are both relevant to answering the query
    if Relevant **then**
      Link both nodes
    end if
  end if
end for
return Updated Graph

3 Experimental Setup

Experiments were conducted using an RTX 4070 Ti Super graphics card with 16GB of memory. For managing the vector dictionary, we employ the FAISS library [7]. Vector representations are generated using the multi-qa-mpnet-base-dot-v1 embedding model, which is fine-tuned to encode queries and text paragraphs into dense vectors, facilitating the retrieval of relevant documents [23]. The Neo4j Community Edition is used as our graph database management system. In the Triplet Generation phase, we utilize the Gemma 2 2B model, while the Llama 3 model is employed for the Question Answering phase. Both models are run with their default parameters. For the Naive RAG implementation, we use a VectorStore bootstrapped by the LLamaIndex framework [18], with the chunk size set to 1024 tokens (Fig. 4).

Table 2. Dataset Metrics

Dataset	Total Documents	Total Triplets
HotpotQA	9930	16644
MuSiQue-Ans	19985	256451
SQuaD	10570/1000(Sampled)	9146

3.1 Corpora

To determine the performance of our KG-LLM hybrid approach, we make use of QA datasets. There are a lot of public datasets available. HotpotQA [29]

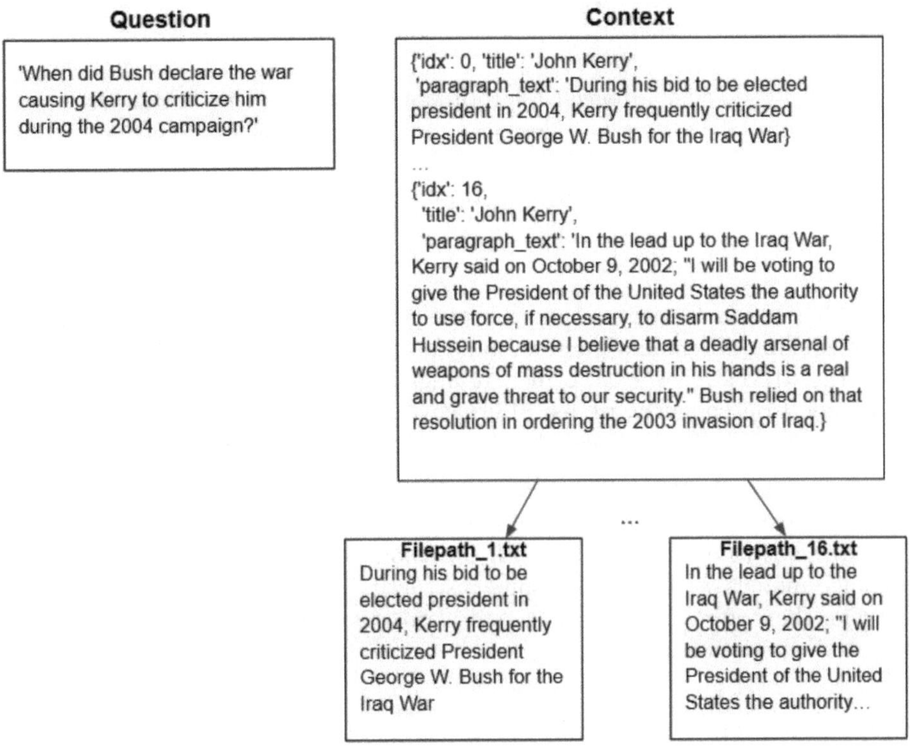

Fig. 4. Example of a row from the MuSiQue-Ans dataset. The paragraphs from each row in the dataset are split into separate files

is dataset consisting of 113k Wikipedia-based question-answer pairs. MuSiQue-Ans [28] is a dataset consisting of 25K 2–4 hop questions. Relative to existing datasets, MuSiQue-Ans is more difficult overall as it applies a stringent set of filters that ensure no sub-question can be answered without finding the answer to the previous sub-questions it is connected to and also by including unanswerable questions. Finally to compare the general performance of SingleQA vs MultidocumentQA, we utilize the single SQuaD dataset [22]. We randomly sample 1000 questions with their corresponding answers and supporting passages from each dataset for evaluation (Table 2).

3.2 Evaluation

For the HotpotQA and MuSiQue-Ans datasets, we split the context into separate files. Research indicates that LLMs perform well when provided with a suitable context, so our focus is on retrieving the relevant supporting documents rather than ensuring an exact match with gold labels. An example of this file splitting is shown in Fig. 5. We do not use the F1 metric because LLM-generated answers are often broader and may not align with the single-word gold labels. Attempting

Table 3. Evaluation Results

Dataset	Naive RAG		Cortex	
	Rouge-L	Filepath Match	Rouge-L	Filepath Match
HotpotQA	68.3	**75.2**	**72.5**	66.4
MuSiQue-Ans	28.1	33.4	**32.3**	**37.2**
SQuaD	65.6	–	**69.8**	–

to match gold labels with each word in the generated answers can result in errors due to spelling differences, random punctuation, or variations in phrasing. Even when the LLM's answer is correct, it might be expressed differently from the gold label. Consequently, we use alternative metrics to evaluate Cortex.

Rouge-L Recall. ROUGE-L recall is the longest common subsequence (LCS) between the model output and gold label, divided by the length of the gold label. We chose not to evaluate ROUGE-L precision due to the characteristics of the language models we employ. Despite instructing the models to provide concise answers, they often include additional words to ensure coherence, which could distort the precision score.

Filepath Match. Rouge-L alone is insufficient to determine the validity of the answers. An LLM might generate an incorrect response while still including the correct answer within the text. To ensure that the LLM's answers are grounded in the source material, we verify whether the filepaths of the source texts returned by our model align with the gold label filepaths in the dataset. For instance, if a question has two gold label filepaths *[filepath_1.txt,filepath_16.txt]* and our model returns *[filepath_1.txt,filepath_2.txt]*, the filepath match score for this question would be $1/2 = 0.5$. We then compute the average filepath match score across all questions in the dataset.

Table 4. Dataset Metrics

Dataset	Total Documents	Total Triplets
HotpotQA	9930	16644
MuSiQue-Ans	19985	256451
SQuaD	10570/1000 (Sampled)	9146

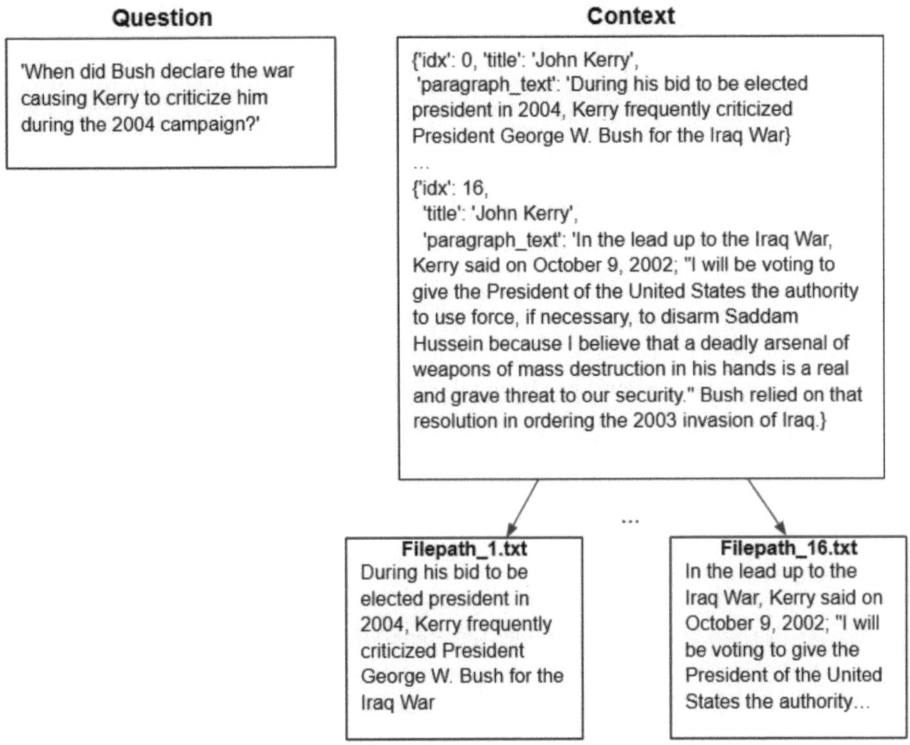

Fig. 5. Example of a row from the MuSiQue-Ans dataset. The paragraphs from each row in the dataset are split into separate files

4 Results and Analysis

We present the summary of our findings in Table 3. Across all three datasets, Cortex consistently achieves a higher average Rouge score than Naive RAG. However, the filepath match metric is more significant due to the limitations of the Rouge metric, as discussed in 3.2. In the MuSiQue-Ans dataset, Cortex improves upon Naive RAG by approximately 4%, highlighting the benefit of linking similar entities. Despite this, the results are relatively low, reflecting the challenge posed by the large volume of documents and triplets that both models need to process, as detailed in Table 4. In HotpotQA, Naive RAG outperforms Cortex in retrieving accurate contexts. This discrepancy may be due to the absence of titles in HotpotQA documents, which usually help LLMs create more effective labels and summaries. Additionally, HotpotQA documents are generally shorter than those in MuSiQue-Ans, potentially complicating the generation of summaries and labels, and affecting the query phase. However, since HotpotQA is largely solvable without multihop reasoning [6,20,27], MuSiQue-Ans may better reflect the models' capability in handling multidocument queries. Table 5 presents the LLM invocation times. The extended response time for each query is due to our use of the LLaMA 3 model for question answering, which has 8 billion parameters. This model is substantially larger than the 2 billion parameter Gemma 2 model used for triplet generation. Despite its greater computational cost, we prefer LLaMA 3-8B because it demonstrates superior reasoning capabilities compared to Gemma 2-2B in various benchmarks [26]. Since SQuaD is a single-document QA dataset, no file matching is necessary because the relevant context is already included with the answer. Therefore, the corresponding filepath match metrics are left empty in Table 3.

Table 5. Average LLM Invocation Time

Avg. Triplet Generation Time per Document	5 s
Avg. Time to Respond per Query	1 min

5 Conclusion

This paper details the development, application, evaluation, and future exploration of Cortex, a hybrid model combining Large Language Models and Knowledge Graphs for Question Answering. The development of Cortex unfolds in two phases: initially, we create the knowledge graph using advanced prompt engineering techniques with the LLM; subsequently, we assess its QA performance on three well-known QA datasets. Despite limited GPU resources and reliance on free, open-source models, Cortex has demonstrated improvements over basic Retrieval-Augmented Generation (RAG) results. This advancement enhances the model's accessibility for researchers in the QA field.

6 Limitations and Future Work

Due to limited time and computational resources, we were unable to conduct additional experiments exploring the use of other open-source LLMs, various embedding models, or different hop sizes for querying entities in the graph, all of which could potentially impact downstream QA results. Given the high computational costs associated with LLMs, we will consider fine-tuning smaller, BERT-based models on domain-specific corpora to generate triplets and enhance entity matching within the graph. Additionally, we are considering replacing the intersection operation with a weighted system where entities, summaries, and labels are assigned individual weights based on their priority. This approach would allow us to selectively prioritize certain source texts, providing the LLM with a more focused context. We would like to experiment with other lightweight models to lower the LLM invocation times. Finally, we plan to evaluate the performance of our model across a wider range of QA datasets to gain deeper insights.

7 Ethical Considerations

Storing data in textual format within a Knowledge Graph provides a comprehensive view of all possible connections between entities, greatly enhancing interpretability. This transparency helps us understand the rationale behind the model's responses, allowing us to use its outputs with greater confidence. Furthermore, by leveraging lightweight general-purpose LLMs and bypassing the need for extensive pretraining, we can significantly reduce GPU resource consumption, thereby decreasing the overall carbon footprint.

Acknowledgements. This research was supported by NSF award 2311142; used Delta at NCSA/University of Illinois through allocation CIS220162 from the Advanced Cyberinfrastructure Coordination Ecosystem: Services & Support (ACCESS) program, which is supported by NSF grants 2138259, 2138286, 2138307, 2137603, and 2138296.

References

1. Angeli, G., Premkumar, M.J.J., Manning, C.D.: Leveraging linguistic structure for open domain information extraction. In: Proceedings of the 53rd Annual Meeting of the Association for Computational Linguistics and the 7th International Joint Conference on Natural Language Processing (Volume 1: Long Papers), pp. 344–354 (2015)
2. Auer, S., Bizer, C., Kobilarov, G., Lehmann, J., Cyganiak, R., Ives, Z.: DBpedia: a nucleus for a web of open data. In: International Semantic Web Conference, pp. 722–735. Springer, Berlin, Heidelberg (2007). https://doi.org/10.1007/978-3-540-76298-0_52
3. Ban, T., Chen, L., Wang, X., Chen, H.: From query tools to causal architects: harnessing large language models for advanced causal discovery from data. arXiv preprint arXiv:2306.16902
4. Bast, H., Bäurle, F., Buchhold, B., Haußmann, E.: Easy access to the freebase dataset. In: Proceedings of the 23rd international conference on World Wide Web, pp. 95–98 (2014)
5. Brown, T.B.: Language models are few-shot learners. arXiv preprint arXiv:2005.14165 (2020)
6. Chen, J., Durrett, G.: Understanding dataset design choices for multi-hop reasoning. arXiv preprint arXiv:1904.12106 (2019)
7. Douze, M., et al.: The faiss library. arXiv preprint arXiv:2401.08281 (2024)
8. Dubey, A., et al.: The llama 3 herd of models. arXiv preprint arXiv:2407.21783
9. Edge, D., et al.: From local to global: a graph rag approach to query-focused summarization. arXiv preprint arXiv:2404.16130 (2024)
10. Fellbaum, C.: Wordnet. In: Theory and Applications of Ontology: Computer Applications, pp. 231–243. Springer, Dordrecht (2010). https://doi.org/10.1007/978-90-481-8847-5_10
11. Fensel, D., et al.: Introduction: what is a knowledge graph? In: Knowledge Graphs: Methodology, Tools and Selected Use Cases, pp. 1–10 (2020)
12. Haldar, R., Mukhopadhyay, D.: Levenshtein distance technique in dictionary lookup methods: an improved approach. arXiv preprint arXiv:1101.1232 (2011)

13. Ji, Z., et al.: Survey of hallucination in natural language generation. ACM Comput. Surv. **55**(12), 1–38 (2023)
14. Jia, R., Liang, P.: Adversarial examples for evaluating reading comprehension systems. arXiv preprint arXiv:1707.07328 (2017)
15. Karpukhin, V., et al.: Dense passage retrieval for open-domain question answering. arXiv preprint arXiv:2004.04906 (2020)
16. Kıcıman, E., Ness, R., Sharma, A., Tan, C.: Causal reasoning and large language models: opening a new frontier for causality. arXiv preprint (2023)
17. Lewis, P., et al.: Retrieval-augmented generation for knowledge-intensive NLP tasks. In: Advances in Neural Information Processing Systems, vol. 33, pp. 9459–9474 (2020)
18. Liu, J.: LlamaIndex (2022). https://doi.org/10.5281/zenodo.1234, https://github.com/jerryjliu/llama_index
19. Long, S., Schuster, T., Piché, A.: Can large language models build causal graphs?. arXiv preprint (2023)
20. Min, S., Wallace, E., Singh, S., Gardner, M., Hajishirzi, H., Zettlemoyer, L.: Compositional questions do not necessitate multi-hop reasoning. arXiv preprint (2019)
21. Qi, P., Zhang, Y., Zhang, Y., Bolton, J., Manning, C.D.: Stanza: a python natural language processing toolkit for many human languages. In: Proceedings of the 58th Annual Meeting of the Association for Computational Linguistics: System Demonstrations (2020). https://nlp.stanford.edu/pubs/qi2020stanza.pdf
22. Rajpurkar, P., Jia, R., Liang, P.: Know what you don't know: unanswerable questions for squad. arXiv preprint (2018)
23. Reimers, N., Gurevych, I.: Sentence-BERT: sentence embeddings using siamese BERT-networks. In: Proceedings of the 2019 Conference on Empirical Methods in Natural Language Processing. Association for Computational Linguistics (2019). arXiv:1908.10084
24. Sarthi, P., Abdullah, S., Tuli, A., Khanna, S., Goldie, A., Manning, C.D.: Raptor: recursive abstractive processing for tree-organized retrieval. arXiv preprint (2024)
25. Suchanek, F.M., Kasneci, G., Weikum, G.: Yago: a core of semantic knowledge. In: Proceedings of the 16th International Conference on World Wide Web, pp. 697–706 (2007)
26. Team, G., et al.: Gemma 2: improving open language models at a practical size. arXiv preprint (2024)
27. Trivedi, H., Balasubramanian, N., Khot, T., Sabharwal, A.: Is multihop QA in DiRE condition? Measuring and reducing disconnected reasoning. arXiv preprint (2020)
28. Trivedi, H., Balasubramanian, N., Khot, T., Sabharwal, A.: Musique: multihop questions via single-hop question composition. Trans. Assoc. Comput. Linguist. **10**, 539–554 (2022)
29. Yang, Z., et al.: Hotpotqa: a dataset for diverse, explainable multi-hop question answering. arXiv preprint (2018)
30. Zhang, Y., Fitzgibbon, B., Garofolo, D., Kota, A., Papenhausen, E., Mueller, K.: An explainable AI approach to large language model assisted causal model auditing and development. arXiv preprint (2023)
31. Zhang, Y., Zhang, Y., Gan, Y., Yao, L., Wang, C.: Causal graph discovery with retrieval-augmented generation based large language models. arXiv preprint arXiv:2402.15301 (2024)

Comparative Analysis of Neural Network Architectures for EEG Speech Classification

Khin Pyae Phyo San(✉), Yosuke Sugiura, and Tetsuya Shimamura

Department of Information and Computer Science, Saitama University, Saitama 338-8570, Japan
khin.s.038@ms.saitama-u.ac.jp, {ysugiura,shima}@mail.saitama-u.ac.jp

Abstract. Electroencephalography (EEG)-based speech decoding holds significant potential for brain-computer interface (BCI) applications. However, systematic comparisons of modern deep learning architectures for speech decoding remain limited, with most benchmarks focusing on motor imagery. In this paper, a unified comparative analysis of 16 architectures is presented, including CNNs, RNNs, Transformers, and hybrid models, evaluated on an open-access EEG speech dataset (16 subjects, 1,200 samples) under identical conditions. For 20-class syllable classification, EEGConformer achieved the highest accuracy at 7.5% (random baseline: 5%). For articulatory features, ShallowFBCSP achieved 59.2% on place of articulation, and ShallowConvNet reached 55.8% on voicing classification. The results reveal that shallow architectures outperform deeper models on limited EEG data, highlighting the importance of model selection for speech-related BCI applications.

Keywords: EEG · Speech decoding · Brain-computer interface · Deep learning · Convolutional neural network · Transformer

1 Introduction

Brain-computer interfaces (BCIs) that decode speech intentions from neural activity represent a promising frontier for assistive communication technology [1]. Recent advances in invasive neural interfaces have demonstrated remarkable success in decoding speech from intracortical recordings, achieving high accuracy in real-time communication for patients with paralysis [2,3]. That said, EEG-based approaches are appealing for their non-invasive nature, portability, and affordability [4]. Deep learning techniques have since enabled substantial progress in EEG-based BCI research. EEGNet [5] introduced compact convolutional architectures using depthwise separable convolutions, achieving excellent results on motor imagery benchmarks with minimal parameters. DeepConvNet [6] demonstrated that deeper architectures with proper regularization can effectively decode motor imagery from EEG. More recently, hybrid architectures combining convolutional neural networks (CNNs) with attention mechanisms have shown promising results. Song et al. [7] proposed EEGConformer,

C. Xu (Ed.): ICMLSC 2026, CCIS 2948, pp. 505–517, 2027.
https://doi.org/10.1007/978-981-92-1546-1_41

which integrates convolutional layers for local feature extraction with transformer encoders for capturing global temporal dependencies, achieving superior performance on motor imagery classification. Altaheri et al. [8] proposed ATCNet, where attention modules are used with temporal convolutional networks to decode EEG more effectively. Despite these advances, systematic benchmarks comparing modern architectures for EEG-based speech decoding remain scarce. While prior benchmarking studies have focused on motor imagery [5,6] or used proprietary datasets, no comprehensive evaluation exists for speech decoding on standardized open-access data. This study addresses this gap in three aspects. First, a unified comparison of 16 architectures spanning five model families (CNNs, RNNs, Transformers, TCNs, and hybrids) is conducted under identical experimental conditions. Second, multi-level evaluation is performed across syllable, place of articulation, and voicing classification tasks. Third, practical insights on model selection for data-limited speech BCI scenarios are provided.

2 Related Work

2.1 Deep Learning for EEG Classification

Convolutional neural networks have become the dominant approach for EEG classification. Lawhern et al. [5] proposed EEGNet, a compact CNN using depthwise and separable convolutions that efficiently captures spatial and temporal features. The architecture's key innovation is its use of depthwise convolutions to learn spatial filters for each temporal filter, followed by separable convolutions to optimally combine feature maps. Schirrmeister et al. [6] conducted extensive experiments comparing shallow and deep convolutional networks for EEG decoding. Their ShallowConvNet uses temporal convolutions followed by spatial filters and log-variance pooling, inspired by filter bank common spatial patterns (FBCSP). DeepConvNet extends this with multiple convolutional blocks for hierarchical feature learning.

2.2 Attention-Based Architectures

Transformer architectures have recently been adapted for EEG analysis. Song et al. [7] introduced EEGConformer, which combines CNN and Transformer layers to extract both local and global EEG features. The architecture uses patch embedding via convolutions followed by multi-head self-attention layers. ATCNet [8] combines an EEGNet-style frontend with attention temporal convolutional networks. The authors in [8] report that "the attention mechanism helps the model focus on the most discriminative temporal segments," achieving state-of-the-art results on motor imagery benchmarks.

2.3 Recurrent and Hybrid Models

Long Short-Term Memory (LSTM) networks [11] and Gated Recurrent Units (GRU) [12] have been widely applied to EEG time series classification, leveraging their ability to capture long-range temporal dependencies. Hybrid CNN-LSTM architectures combine spatial feature extraction with sequential modeling, where convolutional layers extract local spatial-temporal features and recurrent layers model sequential dependencies [13].

2.4 EEG-Based Speech Decoding

EEG-based speech decoding presents unique challenges compared to motor imagery classification. Speech production involves rapid, coordinated movements of multiple articulators (lips, tongue, jaw, larynx), generating complex neural patterns that are difficult to resolve from scalp recordings. Prior work has explored various approaches including phoneme classification, word recognition, and continuous speech reconstruction. Most studies report modest classification accuracies, particularly for fine-grained phoneme discrimination, suggesting fundamental limitations in the information content accessible via scalp EEG. Recent datasets such as the one published by Moreira et al. [10] provide standardized benchmarks for comparing methods, enabling systematic evaluation of different architectures.

3 Theoretical Background

3.1 EEG Signal Representation

EEG measures scalp electrical activity generated by synchronized neuronal populations as a multi-channel time series [14]. Each electrode picks up voltage changes from groups of neurons in the brain. The EEG signal is stored as a matrix $X \in \mathbb{R}^{C \times T}$, where C is the number of channels and T is the number of time points. Most EEG systems have 32 to 256 channels placed using the 10–20 system, with sampling rates from 256 Hz to 2048 Hz. For speech-related neural activity, relevant information is primarily contained in specific frequency bands: delta (1–4 Hz) associated with deep sleep and cognitive processing, theta (4–8 Hz) linked to memory and attention, alpha (8–13 Hz) related to relaxed wakefulness, and beta (13–30 Hz) associated with active cognitive states and motor activity [15]. Speech motor planning and execution predominantly involve beta-band desynchronization over sensorimotor cortex. Band-pass filtering isolates frequency components of interest while removing artifacts and noise:

$$X_{filtered} = X * h_{BP} \tag{1}$$

where h_{BP} is a finite impulse response (FIR) filter with passband $[f_l, f_h]$. FIR filters are preferred in EEG analysis due to their linear phase response, which preserves temporal relationships critical for speech decoding.

3.2 Convolutional Feature Extraction

Convolutional neural networks are commonly applied to EEG classification. They learn patterns from raw signals without needing hand-crafted features. Temporal convolutions extract frequency-specific features by learning filters that respond to particular oscillatory patterns. For input $x \in \mathbb{R}^T$ (each element is x_t, $t = 0, 1, ..., T-1$) and kernel $W \in \mathbb{R}^K$ (each element is W_k, $k = 0, 1, ..., K-1$), the 1D convolution operation slides the kernel across the time dimension, mapping the input $x \in \mathbb{R}^T$ to output $h \in \mathbb{R}^{T-K+1}$ as

$$h_t = \sigma\left(\sum_{k=0}^{K-1} W_k \cdot x_{t-k} + b\right) \tag{2}$$

where h_t denotes the output activation at time step t, K is the kernel size determining the temporal receptive field, b is the bias term, and $\sigma(\cdot)$ is a nonlinear activation function such as ELU or ReLU. The kernel size directly relates to the frequency selectivity of the learned filters; larger kernels capture lower frequencies while smaller kernels respond to higher frequencies. Spatial convolutions learn to combine information across channels, analogous to common spatial patterns (CSP) in traditional EEG analysis. This spatial filtering enhances discriminative neural sources and filters out non-brain artifacts. EEGNet [5] introduced depthwise separable convolutions, which break down standard convolutions into two steps as

$$Y = \text{Pointwise}(\text{Depthwise}(X)) \tag{3}$$

where X and Y represent the input and output sequences, respectively.

The depthwise step applies one filter per channel. The pointwise step uses a 1×1 kernel to blend channels together. This factorization reduces the parameter count from $C_{in} \times C_{out} \times K$ to $C_{in} \times K + C_{in} \times C_{out}$. This reduction is helpful for EEG studies where training data is often limited.

3.3 Self-attention Mechanism

Transformer architectures [16] employ self-attention to model long-range dependencies without the sequential processing constraints of recurrent networks. This is particularly relevant for EEG analysis, where neural activity at distant time points may be functionally related. The self-attention mechanism computes a weighted sum of all positions in the input sequence, where weights are determined by the similarity between positions. Given input sequence $X \in \mathbb{R}^{L\times d}$ with L tokens of dimension d, the scaled dot-product attention computes:

$$\text{Attention}(Q, K, V) = \text{softmax}\left(\frac{QK^T}{\sqrt{d_k}}\right)V \tag{4}$$

Here, $Q = XW_Q$, $K = XW_K$, and $V = XW_V$ are the query, key, and value matrices. The weight matrices $W_Q, W_K, W_V \in \mathbb{R}^{d\times d_k}$ are learned during training. The scaling factor $\sqrt{d_k}$ keeps the dot products from getting too large.

Multi-head attention runs h attention functions in parallel. Each head looks at different parts of the input:

$$\text{MultiHead}(X) = \text{Concat}(\text{head}_1, ..., \text{head}_h)W_O \tag{5}$$

where $\text{head}_i = \text{Attention}(XW_Q^i, XW_K^i, XW_V^i)$ and $W_O \in \mathbb{R}^{hd_k \times d}$ is the output projection matrix. Each head can learn to attend to different temporal patterns, such as rhythmic activity in specific frequency bands or transient event-related responses. The concatenated outputs are projected through W_O to produce the final representation.

3.4 Recurrent Neural Networks

Recurrent neural networks (RNNs) process sequential data like EEG by keeping a hidden state over time. Standard RNNs have trouble learning long sequences due to vanishing gradients. LSTM networks [11] fix this using gates that control what information to keep or forget. The LSTM cell has a memory state c_t and three gates. The update equations are:

$$f_t = \sigma(W_f \cdot [h_{t-1}, x_t] + b_f) \tag{6}$$
$$i_t = \sigma(W_i \cdot [h_{t-1}, x_t] + b_i) \tag{7}$$
$$\tilde{c}_t = \tanh(W_c \cdot [h_{t-1}, x_t] + b_c) \tag{8}$$
$$c_t = f_t \odot c_{t-1} + i_t \odot \tilde{c}_t \tag{9}$$
$$h_t = o_t \odot \tanh(c_t) \tag{10}$$

Here, f_t is the forget gate, i_t is the input gate, and o_t is the output gate. The symbol $\odot$ means element-wise multiplication. The sigmoid σ outputs values between 0 and 1. Bidirectional LSTMs run the sequence both forward and backward. This helps capture context from the full trial, which is useful for EEG classification.

3.5 Classification Loss

The final layer of classification networks produces logits $z \in \mathbb{R}^K$ (each element is z_k, $k = 1, 2, ..., K$) that are converted to probabilities via the softmax function as

$$\hat{y}_k = \frac{\exp(z_k)}{\sum_{j=1}^{K} \exp(z_j)} \tag{11}$$

This ensures outputs form a valid probability distribution with $\sum_k \hat{y}_k = 1$.

For multi-class classification with K classes, the cross-entropy loss measures the discrepancy between predicted and true distributions as

$$\mathcal{L} = -\frac{1}{N} \sum_{i=1}^{N} \sum_{k=1}^{K} y_{i,k} \log(\hat{y}_{i,k}) \tag{12}$$

where $y_{i,k}$ is the one-hot encoded ground truth label and $\hat{y}_{i,k}$ is the predicted probability. Minimizing cross-entropy is equivalent to maximizing the log-likelihood of the correct class, encouraging the model to assign high probability to the true label. For imbalanced datasets common in EEG studies, class weights can be incorporated to give higher importance to underrepresented classes, preventing the model from biasing toward majority classes.

4 Dataset

4.1 Data Description

The open-access EEG speech dataset published by Moreira et al. [10], available through OpenNeuro, was used in this study. The dataset comprises recordings from 16 healthy participants using a 64-channel EEG system following the international 10–20 electrode placement standard, sampled at 500 Hz. Participants produced consonant-vowel (CV) syllables, yielding a total of 1,200 trials across all subjects.

4.2 Speech Stimuli

The syllable set combines six consonants (/b/, /p/, /d/, /t/, /s/, /z/) with vowels, yielding 20 unique CV syllables (e.g., "ba", "pa", "ta", "da", "sa", "za"). This design enables classification at multiple linguistic levels: (1) *syllable-level* with 20 classes representing individual CV combinations; (2) *place of articulation* as a binary distinction between bilabial (lips: /b/, /p/, /m/) and alveolar (tongue tip: /d/, /t/, /s/, /z/) consonants; and (3) *voicing* as a binary classification between voiced (vocal cord vibration: /b/, /d/, /z/) and unvoiced (/p/, /t/, /s/) consonants.

4.3 Preprocessing

EEG preprocessing was implemented using MNE-Python. Raw signals were filtered between 1–40 Hz using an FIR filter. This range covers speech-related brain activity and cuts out drift and noise. FastICA with automatic EOG detection was used to remove eye artifacts. Data were epoched from −500 to +200 ms relative to speech onset, with baseline correction applied using the −500 to −300 ms prestimulus interval. Amplitude was normalized per channel using z-scores. The pre-speech epoch window focuses on motor planning activity rather than auditory feedback, avoiding confounds from acoustic differences between syllables.

5 Implementation

5.1 Model Architectures

A total of 16 architectures spanning five categories were evaluated. *Convolutional neural networks* included EEGNet with 8 temporal filters, depth multiplier of

2, and kernel length of 64; EEGNetV2 with enhanced feature extraction; DeepConvNet and ShallowConvNet representing deep and shallow paradigms; and ShallowFBCSP with 40 filter-bank filters inspired by common spatial patterns. *Temporal convolutional models* comprised TCN with channel dimensions [25, 50, 100] and kernel size 7, plus MultiScale-TCN for multi-resolution temporal analysis. *Transformer-based architectures* included Compact Transformer ($d = 64$, 4 heads, 2 layers), EEG Transformer ($d = 128$, 8 heads, 4 layers), and a Hybrid CNN-Transformer combining local and global feature extraction. *Recurrent models* consisted of bidirectional LSTM and GRU (hidden size 128, 2 layers) and CNN-LSTM hybrid. *Advanced architectures* featured EEGConformer with embedding size 40, 4 attention heads, and 3 transformer layers; ATCNet with 16 temporal filters and depth multiplier 2; and ResNet1D adapted for EEG time-series.

5.2 Training Configuration

All models were trained with the same hyperparameters for fair comparison. Training used Adam (lr $= 10^{-3}$, weight decay $= 10^{-4}$) with cross-entropy loss. Each batch had 16 samples. Training stopped after 100 epochs or if validation accuracy did not improve for 15 epochs. The data split was 80/20 for training and validation, with random seed 42. Experiments ran on PyTorch 2.0+ using an Intel i5-8400 CPU, 48 GB RAM, and NVIDIA GTX 1080 Ti GPU.

The complete training and evaluation pipeline consists of four stages including preprocessing (band-pass filtering, ICA artifact removal, epoching, and normalization), data splitting into training and validation sets, iterative model training with gradient descent optimization, and validation-based model selection with early stopping. The best model checkpoint is saved when validation accuracy improves, and training terminates if no improvement occurs for 15 consecutive epochs.

Algorithm 1 illustrates the forward pass architecture of EEGConformer, which achieved the best syllable classification performance. The model processes EEG input through three stages: a CNN frontend extracts local spatial-temporal features via temporal and depthwise convolutions with batch normalization and dropout regularization; the resulting feature maps are reshaped into tokens and augmented with positional encoding for the transformer encoder; finally, six transformer layers apply multi-head self-attention and feed-forward networks, followed by global average pooling and softmax classification.

Algorithm I: EEGConformer Forward Pass

```
Input: EEG segment x ∈ ℝ^{C×T}
Output: Class probabilities p ∈ ℝ^K

// Patch Embedding (CNN Frontend)
h ← Conv2D(x, filters = 40, kernel = (1, 25))
h ← BatchNorm(h); h ← ELU(h)
h ← DepthwiseConv(h, kernel = (C, 1))
h ← AvgPool(h); h ← Dropout(h, p = 0.5)

// Reshape for Transformer
h ← Reshape(h)                                  h ∈ ℝ^{L×D}
h ← h + PositionalEncoding(L)

// Transformer Encoder (6 layers)
for l = 1 to 6 do
    h' ← LayerNorm(h)
    h ← h + MultiHeadAttention(h', h', h')
    h' ← LayerNorm(h)
    h ← h + FeedForward(h')
end for

// Classification Head
h ← GlobalAvgPool(h)                            h ∈ ℝ^D
p ← Softmax(Linear(h))

return p
```

5.3 Evaluation Metrics

Four metrics are reported to comprehensively evaluate model performance. *Accuracy* measures the proportion of correct predictions: $\frac{1}{N}\sum_{i=1}^{N}\mathbb{1}[\hat{y}_i = y_i]$. *Balanced accuracy* computes the mean per-class recall: $\frac{1}{K}\sum_{k=1}^{K}\text{Recall}_k$, which is particularly important for imbalanced datasets. *F1-Macro* provides the harmonic mean of precision and recall averaged across classes: $\frac{1}{K}\sum_{k=1}^{K}\frac{2\cdot P_k\cdot R_k}{P_k+R_k}$. Additionally, *training time* in wall-clock seconds is reported to assess computational efficiency.

6 Results

Table 1 presents 20-class syllable classification results. All architectures achieved validation accuracies between 5–7.5%, with EEGConformer achieving the best performance at 7.5% (random baseline: 5%).

Table 1. Syllable Classification (20 classes, random baseline = 5%)

Model	Params	Val Acc	Bal Acc
EEGConformer	194K	**7.5%**	5.0%
ShallowConvNet	176K	7.1%	4.9%
DeepConvNet	373K	6.7%	5.0%
EEG Transformer	804K	6.7%	5.0%
CNN-LSTM	221K	6.7%	5.0%
GRU	509K	6.3%	5.8%
FBCSP	176K	6.3%	5.9%
TCN	158K	5.8%	5.0%
ATCNet	22K	5.8%	4.6%
LSTM	673K	5.8%	5.0%
EEGNet	9K	5.4%	7.1%
ResNet	2.2M	5.4%	6.9%

For binary articulatory feature classification in Table 2, ShallowFBCSP achieved the best place of articulation accuracy at 59.2%, followed by ShallowConvNet (57.5%) and DeepConvNet (53.8%). For voicing classification in

Table 2. Place of Articulation Classification (binary, random baseline = 50%)

Model	Params	Val Acc	Bal Acc
ShallowFBCSP	114K	**59.2%**	59.2%
ShallowConvNet	114K	57.5%	57.5%
DeepConvNet	312K	53.8%	53.8%
ATCNet	22K	53.3%	53.3%
EEGNetV2	8K	52.5%	52.5%
EEGConformer	193K	50.0%	50.0%

Table 3. Voicing Classification (binary, random baseline = 50%)

Model	Params	Val Acc	Bal Acc
ShallowConvNet	114K	**55.8%**	55.6%
DeepConvNet	312K	54.2%	52.8%
EEGNetV2	8K	53.3%	52.6%
EEGNet	3K	52.5%	50.0%
GRU	504K	52.5%	50.0%
CNN-LSTM	218K	52.9%	50.4%

Table 4. Model Efficiency Comparison

Model	Params	Time (s)	Acc/Param
ATCNet	22K	46	High
EEGNet	9K	37	High
ShallowFBCSP	176K	82	Med
EEGConformer	194K	62	Med
ResNet	2.2M	28	Low

Table 3, the results were ShallowConvNet led with 55.8%, followed by DeepConvNet (54.2%) and EEGNetV2 (53.3%). Table 4 compares model efficiency.

7 Discussion

This comprehensive comparative analysis reveals several important findings. First, all architectures achieved near-baseline accuracy for 20-class syllable classification (5–7.5%), indicating fundamental limitations in scalp EEG for fine-grained speech decoding. Second, shallow architectures excelled, as ShallowConvNet and ShallowFBCSP achieved the best results for articulatory features, suggesting that simpler architectures are better suited for limited training data. Third, despite their success on motor imagery benchmarks, advanced architectures like EEGConformer and ATCNet did not substantially outperform simpler models on speech tasks. Finally, large train-validation gaps (e.g., FBCSP: 31% train vs. 6.3% val) indicate severe overfitting, where models memorize training data rather than learning generalizable representations.

7.1 Performance Gap Analysis

A critical observation is the apparent disparity between syllable classification (7.5%) and articulatory feature classification (55–59%). However, this difference is largely explained by task complexity rather than model capability. First, considering the number of classes, the random baseline for 20-class syllable classification is 5% ($\frac{1}{20}$), while for binary articulatory features it is 50% ($\frac{1}{2}$). Table 5 shows that when normalized by baseline, syllable classification actually demonstrates the largest relative improvement.

Table 5. Relative Performance Above Random Baseline

Task	Classes	Random	Result	Relative ↑
Syllable	20	5%	7.5%	+50%
Place	2	50%	59.2%	+18%
Voicing	2	50%	55.8%	+12%

Second, from an information-theoretic perspective, classifying 20 syllables requires approximately $\log_2(20) \approx 4.3$ bits of information, while binary classification requires only $\log_2(2) = 1$ bit. The limited information content in scalp EEG signals appears insufficient for fine-grained syllable discrimination but adequate for coarser articulatory groupings. Third, articulatory features represent higher-level groupings of syllables in the feature hierarchy. Place of articulation groups syllables by articulator location (e.g., "ba", "pa", "ma" are all bilabial), while voicing distinguishes by vocal cord vibration. These coarser distinctions appear more accessible from scalp EEG than individual syllable identities. Fourth, the differential decodability aligns with the neural basis of known cortical organization. Place of articulation involves distinct motor cortex regions for different articulators (lips vs. tongue), which have somatotopic representation accessible via EEG. Individual syllables require distinguishing distributed patterns that are more difficult to resolve from scalp recordings.

7.2 Comparison with Prior Work

While EEGNet, EEGConformer, and ATCNet achieved 70–80% accuracy on motor imagery benchmarks, these same architectures achieve only 5–7.5% on speech syllable classification, demonstrating that speech decoding presents distinct challenges. Notably, shallow networks outperform attention-based models on speech tasks, whereas the opposite trend is observed for motor imagery. Schirrmeister et al. [6] similarly found that shallow networks perform well when training data is limited. The success of FBCSP-inspired architectures supports the relevance of filter bank approaches [9] for capturing frequency-specific speech information.

7.3 Scientific Contribution

While the absolute performance for syllable classification remains modest, this study provides several contributions beyond confirming known limitations. First, no prior work has systematically compared this breadth of modern architectures for EEG speech decoding under unified conditions. Existing benchmarks either focus on motor imagery or use inconsistent preprocessing and evaluation protocols. Second, the finding that shallow architectures consistently outperform deep models contradicts the prevailing assumption that more complex architectures yield better results. This has practical implications, as researchers need not invest in computationally expensive models for speech BCI when simpler alternatives perform equivalently or better. Third, the multi-level analysis revealing differential decodability (articulatory features vs. syllables) provides insights into what speech-related information is accessible from scalp EEG, guiding future paradigm design toward coarser classification targets that may yield practical BCI applications.

7.4 Limitations and Future Work

Several limitations should be acknowledged. First, the dataset size may be insufficient for training deep architectures effectively. Second, the evaluation was performed using a single stratified train-validation split rather than k-fold cross-validation. While this approach is common in preliminary benchmarking studies and sufficient for establishing relative performance rankings, it may introduce variance in absolute accuracy estimates. However, given that even the best-performing models achieve near-baseline accuracy for syllable classification, statistical significance tests between models would likely show non-significant differences, and the consistent pattern of shallow architectures outperforming deep models across all three tasks provides robust evidence for the main conclusions of this study. Third, inter-subject variability was not explicitly analyzed; EEG signals are known to vary substantially across individuals due to anatomical and physiological differences, which may affect generalization. Fourth, only overt speech production was examined, which includes motor artifacts that may confound neural signals.

Future work should explore several directions. Cross-validation and leave-one-subject-out evaluation would strengthen statistical rigor. Pooling data across multiple studies or collecting larger datasets would enable more effective training of deep architectures. Transfer learning from related tasks such as motor imagery may improve generalization. Imagined speech paradigms would eliminate motor artifacts. Finally, personalized models or domain adaptation techniques may better capture individual neural patterns.

8 Conclusion

This study presented a comprehensive comparative analysis of 16 modern deep learning architectures for EEG-based speech classification, evaluated on an open-access dataset under unified experimental conditions. The key findings are summarized as follows. First, EEGConformer achieved the best syllable classification accuracy at 7.5%, representing a 50% relative improvement over the 5% random baseline. Second, shallow architectures (ShallowFBCSP: 59.2% for place, ShallowConvNet: 55.8% for voicing) consistently outperformed deeper models for articulatory features. Third, advanced architectures that excel on motor imagery benchmarks do not transfer their advantage to speech decoding tasks. The systematic benchmark establishes reference performance levels and provides model selection guidance for speech BCI applications.

References

1. Wolpaw, J.R., Birbaumer, N., McFarland, D.J., Pfurtscheller, G., Vaughan, T.M.: Brain-computer interfaces for communication and control. Clin. Neurophysiol. **113**(6), 767–791 (2002)
2. Moses, D.A., et al.: Neuroprosthesis for decoding speech in a paralyzed person with anarthria. N. Engl. J. Med. **385**(3), 217–227 (2021)

3. Willett, F.R., et al.: A high-performance speech neuroprosthesis. Nature **620**, 1031–1036 (2023)
4. Alonso, N., Gomez-Gil, J.: Brain computer interfaces, a review. Sensors **12**(2), 1211–1279 (2012)
5. Lawhern, V.J., Solon, A.J., Waytowich, N.R., Gordon, S.M., Hung, C.P., Lance, B.J.: EEGNet: a compact convolutional neural network for EEG-based brain-computer interfaces. J. Neural Eng. **15**(5), 056013 (2018)
6. Schirrmeister, R.T., et al.: Deep learning with convolutional neural networks for EEG decoding and visualization. Hum. Brain Mapp. **38**(11), 5391–5420 (2017)
7. Song, Y., Zheng, Q., Liu, B., Gao, X.: EEG conformer: convolutional transformer for EEG decoding and visualization. IEEE Trans. Neural Syst. Rehabil. Eng. **31**, 710–719 (2023)
8. Altaheri, H., Muhammad, G., Alsulaiman, M.: Physics-informed attention temporal convolutional network for EEG-based motor imagery classification. IEEE Trans. Ind. Inform. **19**(2), 2249–2258 (2023)
9. Mane, R., Chew, E., Chua, K., et al.: FBCNet: a multi-view filterbank convolutional neural network for brain-computer interface. J. Neural Eng. **18**(4), 0460e7 (2021)
10. Moreira, J.P.C., et al.: An open-access EEG dataset for speech decoding: exploring the role of articulation and coarticulation. Sci. Data **12**, 1017 (2025)
11. Hochreiter, S., Schmidhuber, J.: Long short-term memory. Neural Comput. **9**(8), 1735–1780 (1997)
12. Cho, K., et al.: Learning phrase representations using RNN encoder-decoder for statistical machine translation. In: Proceedings of the EMNLP, pp. 1724–1734 (2014)
13. Bashivan, P., Rish, I., Yeasin, M., Codella, N.: Learning representations from EEG with deep recurrent-convolutional neural networks. In: Proceedings of the ICLR (2016)
14. Niedermeyer, E., da Silva, F.L.: Electroencephalography: Basic Principles, Clinical Applications, and Related Fields, 5th edn. Lippincott Williams & Wilkins (2005)
15. Cohen, M.X.: Analyzing Neural Time Series Data: Theory and Practice. MIT Press (2014)
16. Vaswani, A., et al.: Attention is all you need. In: Proceedings of the NeurIPS, pp. 5998–6008 (2017)

Network and Information Security Protection Strategy

High-Quality Reversible Data Hiding Based on Pixel-Value-Ordering with Neighborhood Complexity and Block Complexity

Wei-Hsuan Tsai(✉) and Chen-Yi Lin

Department of Information Management, National Taichung University of Science and Technology, Taichung, Taiwan
s1811231017@nutc.edu.tw

Abstract. Pixel-value-ordering is a widely used reversible data hiding (RDH) technique that embeds secret information while maintaining high quality. The most advanced approach available today is the dual-complexity PVO method, which utilizes neighborhood pixels to offer a fresh perspective on the traditional PVO technique and introduces new concepts. The previous approach only took into account the complexity of neighboring pixels. To enhance the quality of the stego image, we proposed a method that incorporates both the complexity of neighboring pixels and block pixels in determining the embedding order of the block. Our experiments show that this combined approach can improve the quality of the stego image while still preserving its embedding capacity.

Keywords: Reversible data hiding · Pixel-value-ordering · PVO · RDH

1 Introduction

The rapid advancement of Internet technology has led to a growing diversity in the types of information people transmit, including text, images, videos, and more. However, ensuring that data remains secure during transmission has always been paramount. In recent years, data hiding techniques have been extensively researched for privacy protection, rights management, tamper detection, and copyright verification. These techniques embed information invisibly within multimedia content, but most methods tend to irreversibly alter the original cover, making perfect recovery after extraction impossible. This is particularly problematic for applications like image authentication [1, 2], medical imaging [3, 4], and military territory [5]. To address these challenges, reversible data hiding (RDH) was developed, allowing for the lossless restoration of the original image once the embedded secret data is removed.

From previous literature, we understand that the primary advancements in the PVO method are twofold: (1) the block selection strategy, which focuses on prioritizing blocks with greater correlation and low complexity for embedding secret information, thus minimizing image distortion during the embedding process [6–11]; (2) the embedding scheme [12]. The PVO method uses histogram shift for data embedding, so adjusting this method can increase the embedding capacity.

C. Xu (Ed.): ICMLSC 2026, CCIS 2948, pp. 521–529, 2027.
https://doi.org/10.1007/978-981-92-1546-1_42

In this paper, we focused on the block selection strategy. Li et al. [13] proposed Dual-complexity PVO, a new viewpoint to calculate the correlation and complexity of predicted pixels. However, it only considers the neighborhood of the predicted pixel, so we proposed a method that combines neighborhood complexity and block complexity based on Dual-complexity PVO, which considers the complexity of the predicted pixels of the neighborhood and the complexity of the block pixels themselves. This approach effectively utilizes the smooth blocks of the cover image and further improves the image quality of the stego image.

2 Related Work

2.1 PVO Schema

The pixel-value-ordering (PVO) method was first proposed by Li et al. [13]. The cover image is divided into non-overlapped blocks $\{B_1, B_2, \cdots B_N\}$. Then sort the pixels in every block, use the second largest value to predict the maximum value, as the maximum prediction error, and vice versa for the minimum prediction error, which can be formulated as follows:

$$\begin{cases} e_{max} = p_{\text{the maximum pixel}} - p_{\text{the second largest pixel}} \\ e_{min} = p_{\text{the second smallest pixel}} - p_{\text{the minimum pixel}} \end{cases} \tag{1}$$

where e_{max} and e_{min} represent the prediction error at the maximum and minimum ends.

After calculating the prediction error, the embedding of the secret data can be formulated as follows:

$$\tilde{e} = \begin{cases} e & if \;\; e = 0 \\ e + b & if \;\; e = 1 \\ e + 1 & if \;\; e > 1 \end{cases} \tag{2}$$

Where $\tilde{e}$ denotes the modified prediction error, and b is the embedded secret data which belongs to {0,1}.

2.2 Dual-Complexity PVO

Dual-Complexity PVO is one of the state-of-the-art methods of PVO, proposed by Li et al. [11], which uses neighborhood pixel prediction (NPP) to select the neighborhood pixel centered on the predicted pixel according to the Manhattan Distance. Each predicted pixel has its own neighborhood pixel, which is used to calculate the two values C_{max} and C_{num}. C_{max} is the largest absolute value of neighborhood pixel error (NPE), C_{num} is the number of the absolute value of NPE less than the threshold T(T is a pre-defined threshold, value ranges from 0 to 10).

$$C_{max} = max(|neighborhood \;\; pixel \;\; error|) \tag{3}$$

$$C_{num} = \#\{1 \le i \le m : |neighborhood \;\; pixel \;\; error_i| \le T\} \tag{4}$$

where $max(\cdot)$ denotes the maximum value of a set, # denotes the size of a set.

After calculating C_{num} and C_{max}, sort the pixels based on C_{num} in descending order, first. Then, sort the pixels again based on C_{max} in ascending order. In this way, the pixel with a large C_{num} and a small C_{max} is used preferentially, and the final embedding order is determined.

3 Proposed Method

In order to embed secret messages in smooth blocks with a higher priority, based on the Dual-Complexity PVO method [11], we not only use the neighborhood pixel error (i.e., C_{num} and C_{max}, two features), but also use the standard deviation of the block's value; these three features can help us to prioritize better blocks for embedding the secret message. Figure 1 illustrates the flowchart of the embedding process.

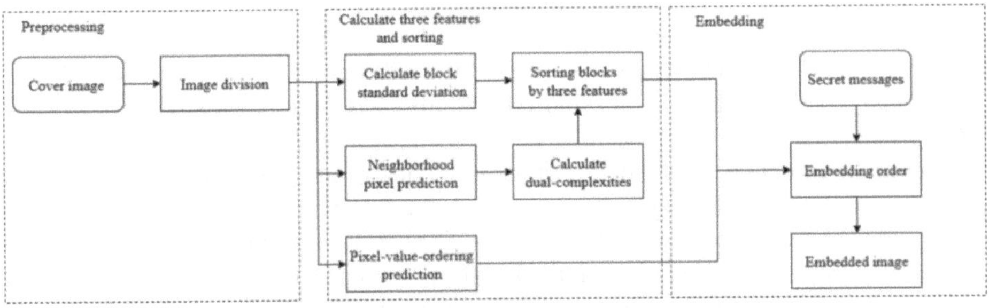

Fig. 1. The flowcharts of the proposed pixel-value-ordering scheme.

Based on Dual-complexity PVO, we utilize standard deviation as block complexity every block's complexity will be calculated after image division as follows:

$$\sigma_{block_i} = \sqrt{\frac{1}{N}\sum_{i=1}^{N}\left(pixel_i - \mu_{block}\right)^2} \tag{5}$$

After calculating σ_{block}, C_n and C_{max}. First, sorting σ_{block} in ascending order, subsequent sorting C_{num} in descending order, and lastly, sorting C_{max} in ascending order. This process allows us to establish an embedding order that considers the block's complexity and the neighboring pixels. An example of the sorting process is illustrated in Fig. 2.

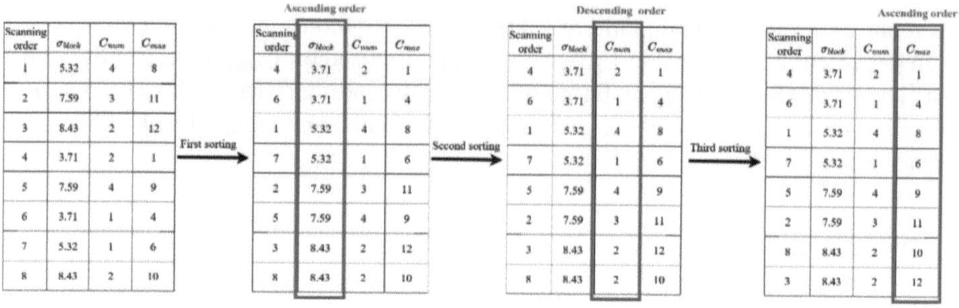

Fig. 2. An example of the sorting process in the processed method.

4 Experimental Results

The experiment was conducted on a Windows 11 system with Intel(R) Core(TM) i5-14500 @ 2.6 GHz and 32 GB RAM. All codes are implemented using MATLAB R2024a.

Tables 1, 2 and 3 compare the PSNR (dB) of the proposed method and the Dual-complexity PVO on nine images from the USC-SIPI dataset, using four payload sizes (1,000 bits, 5,000 bits, 10,000 bits, and 20,000 bits) and three block sizes (3 x 3, 4 x 4, and 5 x 5).

The improvement is most notable at lower payloads and gradually decreases as the payload increases. When the block size is 3 x 3, the PSNR increases by 0.61%, 0.34%, 0.30%, and 0.14% for payloads of 1,000 bits, 5,000 bits, 10,000 bits, and 20,000 bits, respectively. For a block size of 4 x 4, the PSNR increases by 0.64%, 0.26%, 0.14%, and 0.05% at the same payloads. When the block size is 5x5, the PSNR increases by 0.33%, 0.16%, 0.06%, and 0.01% for payloads of 1,000 bits, 5,000 bits, 10,000 bits, and 20,000 bits, respectively (Table 4).

Tables 5, 6 and 7 compare the SSIM value of the proposed method and the Dual-complexity PVO, which indicates that the SSIM remains nearly constant across different block sizes and payload sizes, further confirming that our proposed method prioritizes the use of smooth blocks for embedding, thereby enhancing image quality (Fig. 3).

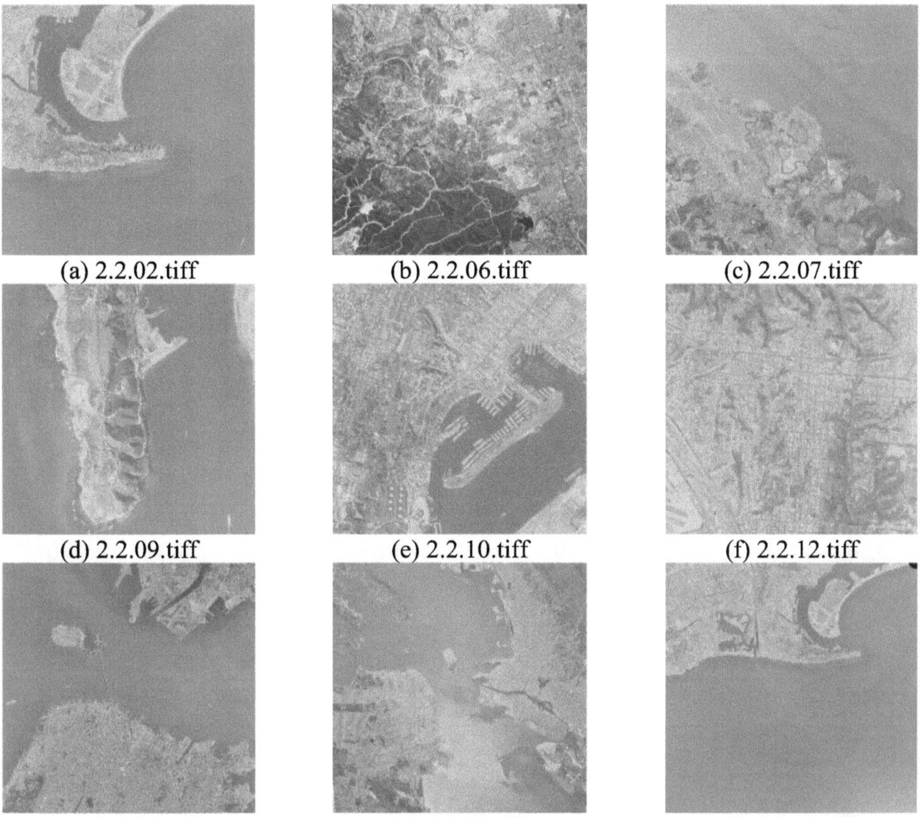

(a) 2.2.02.tiff (b) 2.2.06.tiff (c) 2.2.07.tiff
(d) 2.2.09.tiff (e) 2.2.10.tiff (f) 2.2.12.tiff
(g) 2.2.15.tiff (h) 2.2.22.tiff (i) 2.2.23.tiff

Fig. 3. Test image from USC-SIPI.

Table 1. PSNR value between Dual-complexity PVO and our proposed method (Block size: 3 x 3).

	Payload(bits)							
	1000		5000		10000		20000	
	Proposed Method	PVO_{dual}	Proposed method	PVO_{dual}	Proposed method	PVO_{dual}	Proposed method	PVO_{dual}
2.2.02.tiff	**77.46**	76.96	**70.20**	69.93	**67.13**	67.01	**64.10**	64.07
2.2.06.tiff	**75.19**	74.74	**68.10**	68.02	**65.14**	65.11	62.12	**62.13**
2.2.07.tiff	**76.74**	76.09	**69.09**	68.90	**65.92**	65.88	62.75	62.75
2.2.09.tiff	**79.86**	79.33	**72.91**	72.52	**69.66**	69.52	**66.54**	66.49
2.2.10.tiff	**79.85**	79.52	**72.87**	72.73	**69.79**	69.71	**66.74**	66.71
2.2.12.tiff	**78.78**	77.97	**71.34**	71.15	**68.27**	68.13	**65.17**	65.14
2.2.15.tiff	**77.27**	76.71	**70.13**	70.04	**67.14**	67.05	**64.18**	64.11
2.2.22.tiff	**79.90**	79.59	**72.65**	72.47	69.42	**69.45**	66.29	**66.31**

(*continued*)

Table 1. *(continued)*

	Payload(bits)							
	1000		5000		10000		20000	
	Proposed Method	PVO_{dual}	Proposed method	PVO_{dual}	Proposed method	PVO_{dual}	Proposed method	PVO_{dual}
2.2.23.tiff	**79.14**	78.78	**71.84**	71.70	**68.92**	68.67	**65.82**	65.71

Table 2. PSNR value between Dual-complexity PVO and our proposed method (Block size: 4 x 4).

	Payload(bits)							
	1000		5000		10000		20000	
	Proposed Method	PVO_{dual}	Proposed method	PVO_{dual}	Proposed method	PVO_{dual}	Proposed method	PVO_{dual}
2.2.02.tiff	**77.46**	76.96	**70.20**	69.93	**67.13**	67.01	**64.10**	64.07
2.2.06.tiff	**75.19**	74.74	**68.10**	68.02	**65.14**	65.11	62.12	**62.13**
2.2.07.tiff	**76.74**	76.09	**69.09**	68.90	**65.92**	65.88	62.75	62.75
2.2.09.tiff	**79.86**	79.33	**72.91**	72.52	**69.66**	69.52	**66.54**	66.49
2.2.10.tiff	**79.85**	79.52	**72.87**	72.73	**69.79**	69.71	**66.74**	66.71
2.2.12.tiff	**78.78**	77.97	**71.34**	71.15	**68.27**	68.13	**65.17**	65.14
2.2.15.tiff	**77.27**	76.71	**70.13**	70.04	**67.14**	67.05	**64.18**	64.11
2.2.22.tiff	**79.90**	79.59	**72.65**	72.47	69.42	**69.45**	66.29	**66.31**
2.2.23.tiff	**79.14**	78.78	**71.84**	71.70	**68.92**	68.67	**65.82**	65.71

Table 3. PSNR value between Dual-complexity PVO and our proposed method (Block size: 5 x 5).

	Payload(bits)							
	1000		5000		10000		20000	
	Proposed Method	PVO_{dual}	Proposed method	PVO_{dual}	Proposed method	PVO_{dual}	Proposed method	PVO_{dual}
2.2.02.tiff	**77.41**	77.33	**70.57**	70.47	**67.54**	67.42	64.48	64.48
2.2.06.tiff	**75.69**	75.39	**68.39**	68.36	**65.54**	65.49	**62.57**	62.55
2.2.07.tiff	**76.43**	76.28	**69.36**	69.25	**66.18**	66.16	62.43	62.43
2.2.09.tiff	**80.17**	79.78	**72.90**	72.73	**69.76**	69.75	**64.66**	64.65
2.2.10.tiff	**80.02**	79.80	**73.08**	73.00	**70.07**	69.99	65.68	65.68
2.2.12.tiff	**78.86**	78.64	**71.61**	71.54	**68.52**	68.50	63.81	63.81
2.2.15.tiff	**77.61**	77.05	**70.48**	70.29	67.44	67.44	63.66	63.66
2.2.22.tiff	**80.10**	80.07	**72.86**	72.84	**69.68**	69.65	**64.27**	64.26

(continued)

Table 3. *(continued)*

	Payload(bits)							
	1000		5000		10000		20000	
	Proposed Method	PVO_{dual}	Proposed method	PVO_{dual}	Proposed method	PVO_{dual}	Proposed method	PVO_{dual}
2.2.23.tiff	**79.18**	78.80	**72.27**	72.01	**69.08**	69.06	**66.02**	66.00

Table 4. The increase in PSNR with varying block sizes.

Block size	Payload(bits)			
	1000	5000	10000	20000
3 x 3	0.61%	0.34%	0.30%	0.14%
4 x 4	0.64%	0.26%	0.14%	0.05%
5 x 5	0.33%	0.16%	0.06%	0.01%

Table 5. SSIM value between Dual-complexity PVO and our proposed method (Block size: 3 x 3)

	Payload(bits)							
	1000		5000		10000		20000	
	Proposed Method	PVO_{dual}	Proposed method	PVO_{dual}	Proposed method	PVO_{dual}	Proposed method	PVO_{dual}
2.2.02.tiff	0.9999	0.9999	**0.9994**	0.9993	0.9988	0.9988	0.9976	0.9976
2.2.06.tiff	0.9999	0.9999	0.9996	0.9996	0.9991	0.9991	0.9984	0.9984
2.2.07.tiff	0.9999	0.9999	0.9995	**0.9996**	0.9991	0.9991	0.9984	0.9984
2.2.09.tiff	**0.9998**	0.9997	0.9990	0.9990	**0.9980**	0.9979	**0.9962**	0.9961
2.2.10.tiff	0.9998	0.9998	0.9988	**0.9989**	**0.9979**	0.9978	**0.9960**	0.9958
2.2.12.tiff	0.9998	0.9998	**0.9993**	0.9992	**0.9986**	0.9985	0.9972	**0.9974**
2.2.15.tiff	0.9999	0.9999	0.9994	0.9994	0.9988	0.9988	0.9978	0.9978
2.2.22.tiff	**0.9998**	0.9997	0.9989	**0.9990**	**0.9981**	0.9980	0.9963	**0.9964**
2.2.23.tiff	0.9998	0.9998	0.9991	0.9991	0.9982	**0.9983**	**0.9967**	0.9966

Table 6. SSIM value between Dual-complexity PVO and our proposed method (Block size: 4 x 4)

	Payload(bits)							
	1000		5000		10000		20000	
	Proposed Method	PVO_{dual}	Proposed method	PVO_{dual}	Proposed method	PVO_{dual}	Proposed method	PVO_{dual}
2.2.02.tiff	0.9999	0.9999	0.9995	0.9995	0.9990	0.9990	0.9981	0.9981
2.2.06.tiff	0.9999	0.9999	0.9996	0.9996	0.9993	0.9993	0.9986	0.9986
2.2.07.tiff	0.9999	0.9999	0.9996	0.9996	0.9992	0.9992	0.9987	0.9987
2.2.09.tiff	0.9998	0.9998	**0.9991**	0.9990	0.9983	0.9983	0.9968	0.9968
2.2.10.tiff	0.9998	0.9998	0.9989	0.9989	0.9981	0.9981	0.9964	0.9964
2.2.12.tiff	0.9999	0.9999	0.9993	**0.9994**	0.9987	0.9987	0.9977	0.9977
2.2.15.tiff	0.9999	0.9999	0.9995	0.9995	0.9990	0.9990	0.9981	0.9981
2.2.22.tiff	0.9998	0.9998	**0.9991**	0.9990	0.9983	0.9983	0.9970	0.9970
2.2.23.tiff	0.9998	0.9999	0.9992	0.9992	**0.9985**	0.9984	0.9971	0.9971

Table 7. SSIM value between Dual-complexity PVO and our proposed method (Block size: 5 x 5)

	Payload(bits)							
	1000		5000		10000		20000	
	Proposed Method	PVO_{dual}	Proposed method	PVO_{dual}	Proposed method	PVO_{dual}	Proposed method	PVO_{dual}
2.2.02.tiff	0.9999	0.9999	0.9995	0.9995	0.9991	0.9991	0.9983	0.9983
2.2.06.tiff	0.9999	0.9999	0.9996	0.9996	**0.9994**	0.9993	0.9989	0.9989
2.2.07.tiff	0.9999	0.9999	0.9996	0.9996	0.9994	0.9994	0.9991	0.9991
2.2.09.tiff	0.9998	0.9998	**0.9992**	0.9991	0.9984	0.9984	0.9978	0.9978
2.2.10.tiff	0.9998	0.9998	0.9990	0.9990	**0.9983**	0.9982	0.9974	0.9974
2.2.12.tiff	0.9999	0.9999	0.9994	0.9994	0.9989	0.9989	0.9983	0.9983
2.2.15.tiff	0.9999	0.9999	0.9995	0.9995	0.9991	0.9991	0.9985	0.9985
2.2.22.tiff	0.9998	0.9998	0.9992	0.9992	0.9985	0.9985	0.9980	0.9980
2.2.23.tiff	0.9998	0.9998	0.9993	0.9993	0.9986	0.9986	0.9975	0.9975

5 Conclusion

In this paper, we focus on the block selection strategy, considering both neighborhood complexity and block complexity to find the best embedding order for the PVO method. First, calculate block standard deviation and neighborhood complexity. Next, according to these two complexities, determine the block's embedding order. The experimental results demonstrate that our proposed PVO method, which incorporates neighborhood complexity and block complexity, enhances the PSNR of the stego image; furthermore, the SSIM remains nearly unchanged. In future work, we aim to increase the embedding capacity by utilizing histogram mapping or improve image quality by exploring additional effective complexity features.

Acknowledgement. This work was supported by the Ministry of Science and Technology of Republic of China under grant NSTC 114-2221-E-025-002.

References

1. Hussan, M., Parah, S.A., Qureshi, G.J.: Reversible data hiding framework with content authentication capability for e-health [Early Access]. Multimedia Tools Appl. (2023). https://doi.org/10.1007/s11042-023-17019-9
2. Bedi, S.S., Verma, S., Tomar, G.: An adaptive data hiding technique for digital image authentication. Int. J. Comput. Theory Eng. **2**(3), 338–344 (2010). https://doi.org/10.7763/ijcte.2010.v2.164
3. Gao, G.Y., Zhang, H., Xia, Z.H., Luo, X.Y., Shi, Y.Q.: Reversible data hiding-based contrast enhancement with multi-group stretching for ROI of medical image. IEEE Trans. Multimedia **26**, 3909–3923 (2024). https://doi.org/10.1109/tmm.2023.3318048
4. Kong, P., Zhang, Y.D., Huang, L., Zhou, L., Chen, L.F., Qin, C.: Neural network-based reversible data hiding for medical image. Expert Syst. Appl. **256**, Article 124903 (2024). https://doi.org/10.1016/j.eswa.2024.124903
5. Wang, Y.M., Xiong, G.Q., He, W.G.: High-capacity reversible data hiding in encrypted images based on pixel-value-ordering and histogram shifting. Expert Syst. Appl. **211**(9), Article 118600 (2023). https://doi.org/10.1016/j.eswa.2022.118600
6. Peng, F., Li, X.L., Yang, B.: Improved PVO-based reversible data hiding. Dig. Sig. Process. **25**, 255–265 (2014). https://doi.org/10.1016/j.dsp.2013.11.002
7. Weng, S.W., Shi, Y.Q., Hong, W., Yao, Y.: Dynamic improved pixel value ordering reversible data hiding. Inf. Sci. **489**, 136–154 (2019). https://doi.org/10.1016/j.ins.2019.03.032
8. Pan, Z.B., Gao, X.Y., Gao, E.D., Fan, G.J.: Adaptive complexity for pixel-value-ordering based reversible data hiding. IEEE Signal Process. Lett. **27**, 915–919 (2020). https://doi.org/10.1109/lsp.2020.2996507
9. Xiang, S.J., Ruan, G.Q.: Efficient PVO-based reversible data hiding by selecting blocks with full-enclosing context. IEEE Trans. Circuits Syst. Video Technol. **32**(5), 2868–2880 (2022). https://doi.org/10.1109/tcsvt.2021.3103215
10. Gao, X.Y., Pan, Z.B., Fan, G.J., Zhang, X.R., Yin, H.Z.: Local feature-based mutual complexity for pixel-value-ordering reversible data hiding. Sig. Process. **204**(15), Article 108833 (2023). https://doi.org/10.1016/j.sigpro.2022.108833
11. Li, X.L., Li, J., Li, B., Yang, B.: High-fidelity reversible data hiding scheme based on pixel-value-ordering and prediction-error expansion. Sig. Process. **93**(1), 198–205 (2013). https://doi.org/10.1016/j.sigpro.2012.07.025
12. Luo, T., Jiang, G., Yu, M., Gao, W.: Novel prediction error based reversible data hiding method using histogram shifting. Int. J. Comput. Theory Eng. **7**(5), 332–336 (2015). https://doi.org/10.7763/ijcte.2015.v7.981
13. Li, Z.J., Liao, X.W., Fan, G.J., Zhang, X.R., Pan, Z.B.: Dual-complexities based on straightforward neighborhood pixel prediction in pixel-value-ordering framework for reversible data hiding. Displays **84**(14), Article 102749 (2024). https://doi.org/10.1016/j.displa.2024.102749

Webchk: An Ensemble Learning Approach for Web Vulnerability Detection Integrating TCN, BERT, and FP-Growth

Angela Coleen M. Acebedo(✉), Daniel Louis P. Bernadaz, Clyde Allen T. Yu, Clyde Chester R. Balaman, and Rhodessa J. Cascaro

Mapúa Malayan Colleges Mindanao, Davao City, Philippines
{acacebedo,dlbernadaz,cayu,ccrbalaman,rjcascaro}@mcm.edu.ph

Abstract. Web applications are prone to critical security attacks, with an average breach cost of $4.88 million. Current vulnerability scanners have shown to be severely limited. Rule-based scanners, such as OWASP ZAP, have been able to reach 100% recall but with a high number of false positives (25 per scan), while AI-assisted scanners have been able to lower the number of false positives to 4.1 but with low recall (44.1%) and slow processing speed (6 min 28 sec per 100 pages). This paper proposes WebChk, an ensemble learning approach that combines BERT (semantic code analysis), Temporal Convolutional Networks (temporal traffic patterns), and FP-Growth (structural payload mining) using a multinomial logistic regression meta-learner, the first to combine these diverse models for multi-domain vulnerability scanning in 18 OWASP-related domains. The proposed approach is trained on the DiverseVul, PrimeVuln, CSE-CIC-IDS2018, and Web Attack Payload datasets and shows 49.06% macro accuracy, 54.67% recall, and 48.77% F1-score, a 4.02% improvement over the best individual model (BERT). The proposed framework shows well-rounded detection performance on all vulnerability types while reducing prediction variance and proves the effectiveness of ensemble hybrid learning strategies to combine static rule-based coverage and adaptive AI learning for next-generation web vulnerability detection systems.

Keywords: Web vulnerability detection · ensemble learning · temporal convolutional networks · BERT transformers · FP-Growth algorithm · OWASP Top 10 · cybersecurity · meta-learning

1 Introduction

A web application is an application program that is stored on a remote server and delivered over the internet through a browser interface, and it can also be known as web services, depending on the website [17]. This poses a need for reinforced security in web applications given that the average cost of a data breach is $4.88 million [10]. In 2021, the OWASP (Open Worldwide Application Security

C. Xu (Ed.): ICMLSC 2026, CCIS 2948, pp. 530–541, 2027.
https://doi.org/10.1007/978-981-92-1546-1_43

Project) had compiled that the top ten current web application security risks, namely: broken access control, cryptographic failures, injection, insecure design, security misconfiguration, vulnerable and outdated components, identification and authentication failures, software and data integrity failures, security logging and monitoring failures, and server-side request forgery [1].

With the help of recent developments in AI over the past years, it has opened new possibilities for enhancing traditional scanning methods. Temporal Convolutional Networks (TCN) is a deep learning model that is designed to handle sequence data, and they are particularly effective for tasks that time-series data, such as forecasting, anomaly detection, and sequence classification [3,18]. The BERT Transformer Model, which is a deep learning model in which every output element is connected to every input element, and the weightings between them are dynamically calculated based upon their connection [5,9,15]. The FP-Growth algorithm is a method used to find frequent patterns in large datasets with how it avoids repeatedly scanning the entire database [8,11]. Using all three models or algorithms mentioned can lead to performance issues when used individually, but by combining them into an ensemble layer, the framework will be more robust than the individual models that constitute the ensemble because it reduces the variance in the prediction errors. Ensemble learning is a method of reaching a consensus in predictions by fusing the salient properties of two or more models [6,16]. Such method is often used when the optimal model cannot be chosen due to a difference in performance, when there is a shortage of or excess data, or when there is a need to fuse information to enhance classification performance of the models.

The study proposes to evaluate the Accuracy, Precision, Recall, and F-measure of the TCN, BERT, and FP-Growth algorithms [3,5,8] based on the OWASP Top 10 Vulnerabilities [1]. The study also proposes to integrate the aforementioned algorithms into an ensemble model via a meta-learner for multi-domain vulnerability detection, and evaluate the proposed ensemble model with the same metrics above.

2 Methodology

This study employed an experimental and developmental research design to create and evaluate an AI-enhanced web vulnerability scanner. This section describes the framework of the preprocessing stage of the datasets used for TCN, BERT and FP-Growth—which are artificial-intelligence models—and its integration within an ensemble architecture [2,3,5,8]. The ensemble model performs hybrid detection by combining static code analysis, dynamic traffic analysis, and frequent-pattern mining, with the goal of improving accuracy, precision, recall, and F-measure in identifying OWASP Top 10 vulnerabilities.

2.1 Conceptual Framework

Figure 1 depicts the scanner workflow from data ingestion to prediction output. Raw inputs such as source code, payload samples, and traffic logs are preprocessed and routed to their respective analytical models (BERT, FP-Growth, and TCN).

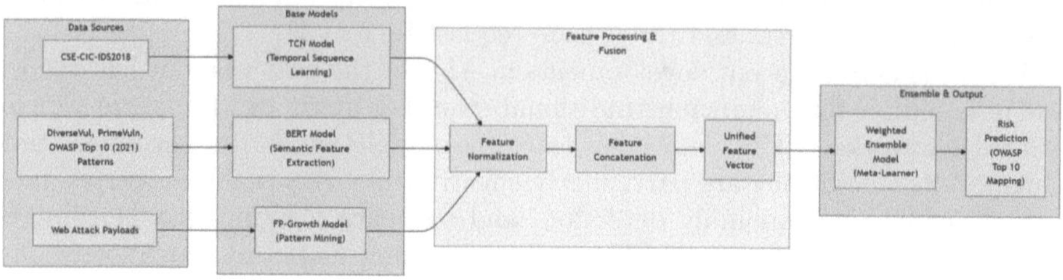

Fig. 1. System Framework Diagram.

Each model generates feature representations that are fused by the ensemble meta-learner to yield a final vulnerability classification and risk score. This integrated architecture enables real-time, context-aware vulnerability assessment across multiple data domains.

2.2 Datasets, Preprocessing and Augmentation

Each base model was trained on domain-specific datasets. BERT was trained on the DiverseVul, PrimeVuln, and OWASP Top 10 datasets (350,000+ code examples, 150 CWEs) for static vulnerability classification [1,4,7]. TCN was trained on the CSE-CIC-IDS2018 network traffic dataset (80+ features) for sequence-based anomaly detection of SQL Injection, XSS, and brute-force attacks [12]. FP-Growth was trained on the Web Attack Payloads dataset (6,249 transactions) to discover structural patterns in encoded web attacks [13,14]. Each dataset offered complementary views of vulnerability representation through code semantics, network behaviors, and attack structures. During the preprocessing stage, BERT tokenized code examples with WordPiece (max 512 tokens), partitioned into 18 balanced vulnerability classes (2,000 examples per class, 36,000 total examples), with code normalization removing comments and normalizing formatting. TCN feature extraction was performed on PCAP files, normalized with StandardScaler, and windowed with sliding windows (window size = 100, window stride = 10) with forward fill imputation. FP-Growth tokenized payloads into atomic elements, removing tokens with < 5 transactions, minimum support = 0.01 (62 transactions).

BERT used synonym replacement and code obfuscation (variable/function renaming) to add 20% more training data. TCN introduced time jittering ($\pm$ 5% time shift), Gaussian noise ($\sigma = 0.05$), and dynamic time warping (factors 0.8–1.2) to model variations in the network. FP-Growth introduced payload obfuscation (URL encoding, case conversion, HTML entities, comment addition), adding 8,736 obfuscated transactions with 40% greater pattern diversity.

2.3 Ensemble Model Development

The ensemble learning framework was designed to combine heterogeneous model outputs from the Temporal Convolutional Network (TCN), BERT Transformer, and FP-Growth algorithm. Each model is trained on its respective dataset domain (temporal, semantic, and structural), and their prediction probabilities are aggregated through an ensemble function. Algorithm 1 describes the overall process of constructing the ensemble model.

Algorithm 1. BuildEnsembleModel(): Ensemble Model Development

Require: Datasets D_{TCN}, D_{BERT}, D_{FP}; Base models M_{TCN}, M_{BERT}, M_{FP}
Ensure: Concatenated ensemble feature set $F_{ensemble}$

Step 1: Train Base Models
for each model $M_j \in \{M_{TCN}, M_{BERT}, M_{FP}\}$ **do**
  Train M_j using corresponding dataset D_j
  Save model weights and validation metrics
end for

Step 2: Generate Base Predictions
for each input sample x_i **do**
  $p_{TCN} \leftarrow M_{TCN}.predict(x_i)$
  $p_{BERT} \leftarrow M_{BERT}.predict(x_i)$
  $p_{FP} \leftarrow M_{FP}.predict(x_i)$
  Concatenate predictions: $f_i = [p_{TCN} \| p_{BERT} \| p_{FP}]$
  Append f_i to feature set $F_{ensemble}$
end for

Step 3: Return Ensemble Feature Set
return $F_{ensemble}$

The function `BuildEnsembleModel()` standardizes the outputs of all base learners and concatenates them into a unified feature representation $F_{ensemble}$. This output is passed to the meta-learner function in the next stage for adaptive fusion and final classification.

2.4 Meta-learner and Fusion

The meta-learner serves as the adaptive fusion layer that integrates the ensemble feature set into a single decision output. Instead of static majority voting, a multinomial logistic regression (MLR) model was trained to learn optimal weights for combining predictions dynamically. Algorithm 2 presents the `MetaFusion()` function, which continues from `BuildEnsembleModel()`.

The function `MetaFusion()` performs adaptive fusion by learning context-dependent importance for each base model's predictions. When deployed, it accepts real-time outputs from TCN, BERT, and FP-Growth models, applies the learned weights, and produces a final vulnerability class.

Algorithm 2 MetaFusion(): Meta-learner Training and Fusion

Require: Ensemble feature set $F_{ensemble}$; True labels Y; Meta-learner M_{meta}
Ensure: Final trained ensemble model M_{fusion}
Step 1: Split Data
Divide $F_{ensemble}$ into training and validation subsets

Step 2: Train Meta-learner
for each training batch (f_i, y_i) in $F_{ensemble}$ **do**
    Compute prediction: $\hat{y}_i = M_{meta}.predict(f_i)$
    Update M_{meta} weights using loss$(\hat{y}_i, y_i)$
end for

Step 3: Fuse Base Predictions
for each test sample x_i **do**
    Retrieve base outputs from M_{TCN}, M_{BERT}, M_{FP}
    Combine features via learned weights: $y_i^* = M_{meta}.predict([p_{TCN}||p_{BERT}||p_{FP}])$
end for

Step 4: Return Fused Model
return $M_{fusion} \leftarrow M_{meta}$

Together, `BuildEnsembleModel()` and `MetaFusion()` define a complete, modular ensemble pipeline—making the system transparent, reproducible, and easily extensible for future AI-based vulnerability detection studies.

3 Results and Discussion

This section covers the overall results of this study and its comparative analysis, after which it introduces the several findings of the said results. Beginning with the results for base model training.

3.1 Ensemble Model Training Results

TCN Model. The TCN model was trained using 209,890 samples with a 75–25% split between training and testing sets. Several augmentation parameters including window size, batch normalization, and learning-rate decay—were iteratively tuned across 50 epochs to identify a configuration that maximized generalization without introducing overfitting.

As shown in Fig. 2, both training and validation accuracies improved steadily, beginning at 79.37% and 90.59%, respectively, and converging near 92.68% with smooth loss reduction. This trend indicates that the model successfully captured long-range dependencies within network traffic sequences. The residual block structure and causal dilations enabled efficient propagation of temporal features, which are crucial for recognizing progressive attack signatures such as multi-stage injections or brute-force bursts. However, performance degradation was observed in differentiating highly similar temporal behaviors—such as benign login sequences and slow brute-force attempts—revealing a need for finer-grained temporal feature extraction or feature-level fusion.

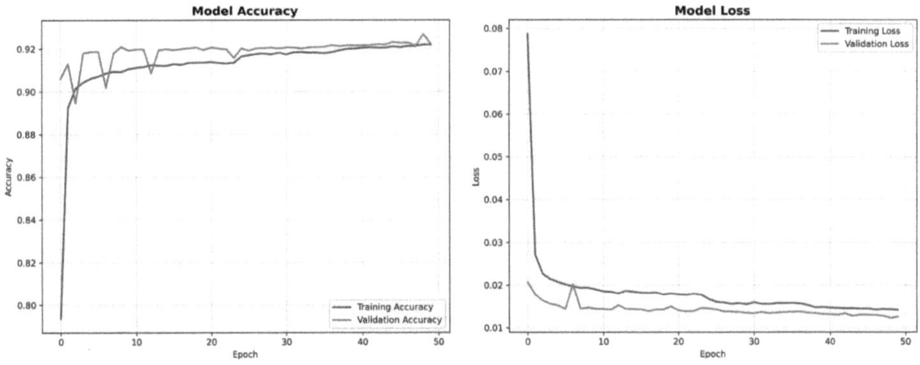

Fig. 2. TCN model training visualization, illustrating the model accuracy and loss during training.

Overall, the TCN model demonstrated strong temporal awareness and stability, positioning it as a reliable foundation for detecting sequence-based anomalies within the ensemble architecture.

BERT Model. The BERT model was trained on 36,000 balanced samples distributed across 18 classes that represented the OWASP Top 10 (2021), seven additional vulnerabilities, and benign code. The model leveraged a 125.9-million-parameter pre-trained base fine-tuned for code-level semantics. Training employed a cosine-decay learning-rate scheduler and dropout regularization to stabilize convergence.

As visualized in Fig. 3, the training process exhibited rapid convergence, with accuracy stabilizing at 97% after the sixth epoch and F1-score maintaining above 97% after the tenth. The near-perfect AUC-ROC (0.999) by the fifth epoch and a sharp reduction of validation loss from 12.03 to 0.049 confirm both high discriminative power and minimal overfitting.

These metrics illustrate that BERT effectively encoded the syntactic and semantic relationships among source-code tokens, capturing contextual nuances between vulnerability types such as SQL Injection and Command Injection. Minor misclassifications were confined to semantically overlapping categories (e.g., Broken Access Control vs. Authentication Failure), suggesting that ambiguity arises from shared lexical patterns rather than model weakness. In summary, the BERT model provided robust generalization and fine-grained semantic representation essential for the ensemble's interpretive layer.

FP-Growth Model. The FP-Growth model was trained on 6,249 transactions to mine frequent token patterns and association rules within the Injection,

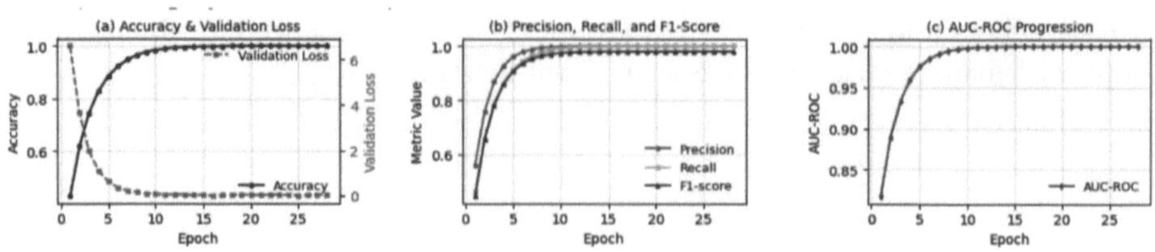

Fig. 3. Epoch-by-epoch validation metrics showing the model's training across accuracy, loss, and evaluation scores.

Server-Side Request Forgery (SSRF), and Broken Access Control categories. The preprocessing stage involved tokenization, normalization, and pruning of infrequent items to generate a compact FP-tree optimized for recursive pattern mining.

Figure 4 illustrates the frequency distribution of tokens extracted from the training data. The period (.) emerged as the most recurrent symbol, accounting for 38.29% of all tokens, followed by special characters such as slashes (/) and equals (=), which frequently appear in encoded payloads. Injection attacks registered the highest frequency at 288 occurrences, indicating the prevalence of input-based exploit attempts in the dataset. The observed dominance of punctuation and structural delimiters highlights the syntactic regularities of web attack payloads, which often rely on specific character combinations to manipulate server-side parsing or bypass filters.

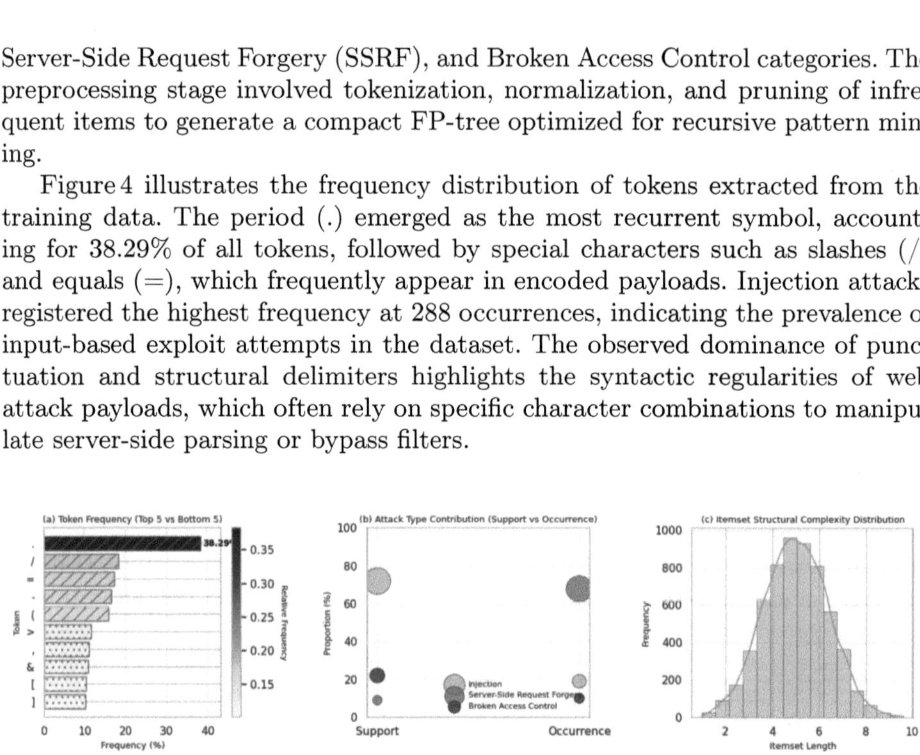

Fig. 4. FP-Growth structural analysis showing (a) token frequency distribution highlighting the dominant period (.) at 38.29% and gradual declines among other tokens, (b) attack type trends, and (c) itemset complexity distribution (Histogram + KDE).

The analysis also revealed that most frequent itemsets consisted of 4–5 tokens, signifying moderate structural complexity typical of concise, crafted exploits. Longer patterns—up to 10 tokens—appeared less frequently but tended to represent obfuscated or multi-stage payloads, reflecting more advanced evasion strategies. Runtime profiling showed that tokenization and FP-tree construction were the most computationally intensive phases, confirming the trade-off between pattern granularity and processing speed.

Overall, the FP-Growth model achieved 99.8% coverage, an average support of 1.32%, and identified 877 unique tokens, demonstrating strong capability in capturing diverse and complex token relationships. By quantifying recurring syntactic signatures across multiple vulnerability types, FP-Growth enriched the ensemble's structural perspective, complementing the semantic depth of BERT and the temporal sensitivity of TCN.

3.2 Model Testing

Following base-model training, the outputs from TCN, BERT, and FP-Growth were fused using a multinomial logistic-regression meta-learner. This stage integrated semantic, temporal, and structural feature vectors into a unified representation. The combined dataset underwent stratified validation to maintain proportional representation of OWASP Top 10 classes during fusion, ensuring that minority vulnerabilities such as SSRF and Cryptographic Failures were not overshadowed by more frequent categories like Injection. The resulting performance summary is presented in Table 1, and the aggregated comparison is visualized in Fig. 5.

Table 1. Final Model Comparison highlighting Ensemble Improvement over Strongest Base Model (BERT).

Model	Accuracy	Recall	F1-Score	Δ Accuracy (%)
FP-Growth (base)	0.2642	0.2450	0.2116	–
TCN (base)	0.1132	0.1000	0.0203	–
BERT (base)	**0.4717**	0.5217	0.4749	**Baseline**
Ensemble	**0.4906**	**0.5467**	**0.4877**	**+4.02%**

As shown in the table and figure, the ensemble achieved a 4.02% improvement in accuracy over its strongest base model (BERT) and demonstrated a clear balancing of recall and precision across all OWASP Top 10 categories. This improvement verifies the effectiveness of weighted feature fusion, in which complementary evidence from distinct analytical domains offsets the weaknesses of standalone models. Specifically, TCN contributed sequence-level context that enhanced anomaly detection, FP-Growth improved recognition of recurring payload structures, and BERT reinforced semantic understanding of code-level relationships.

Despite the gains, the substantial training-testing gap—most notably BERT's drop from 97% to 47.17% accuracy—indicates moderate overfitting. This stems from partial redundancy among datasets and limited diversity in benign versus malicious samples. Methodologically, such overfitting suggests that while the models captured domain-specific patterns effectively, they generalized less successfully across unseen data. Regularization techniques (e.g., dropout,

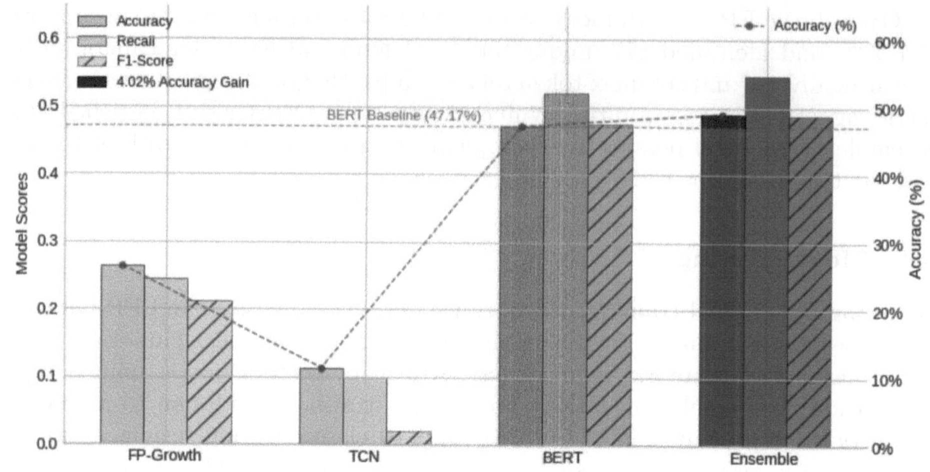

Fig. 5. Final Test Performance: Ensemble vs Base Models.

weight decay), k-fold cross-validation, and synthetic augmentation are viable strategies to mitigate this limitation in future iterations.

Overall, the ensemble model validated the viability of cross-domain integration for vulnerability detection, achieving improved equilibrium between precision and recall while maintaining interpretability and computational tractability.

Contextual Reference: OWASP ZAP and AI-Assisted Scanning. To situate the ensemble's results within the broader scanning landscape, two implementations of the OWASP ZAP platform were examined: its standard (non-AI) configuration and an AI-assisted variant utilizing the OpenAI ChatGPT plugin. These references serve not as direct benchmarks but as contextual indicators of current detection performance and operational trade-offs.

Table 2 summarizes key metrics for the non-AI scanner, showing an accuracy of 0.750 and F1-score of 0.860, with perfect recall but elevated false-positive rates. This pattern typifies rule-based scanners, which emphasize coverage and signature matching at the expense of contextual precision. In contrast, the AI-enhanced variant in Table 2 achieved 0.804 accuracy with reduced false positives (4.1 on average) but lower recall (0.441), indicating that while generative inference can interpret vulnerabilities more flexibly, it incurs latency (6 min 28 s per 100 pages) and sensitivity losses due to prompt-response dependence.

These observations reveal that even AI-assisted scanners must balance recall, precision, and runtime cost. Rule-based engines such as ZAP maintain exhaustive pattern coverage but often misclassify benign behavior, whereas AI-augmented systems enhance contextual reasoning yet struggle with speed and reproducibility.

Within this landscape, the ensemble architecture of WebChk offers a complementary alternative. By leveraging semantic, temporal, and structural learning

Table 2. Comparison between Non-AI and AI-Enhanced Web Vulnerability Scanners.

Category	Metric	Non-AI	AI-Enhanced
Detection	True Positives (TP)	75	57
	False Positives (FP)	25	4.1
	False Negatives (FN)	0	10
Classification	Accuracy	0.750	**0.804**
	Precision	0.750	0.658
	Recall	1.000	0.441
	F1-Score	0.860	0.528
Operational	Speed (per 100 pages)	1 min	6 min 28 s
	Coverage	1.00	0.67

rather than heuristic matching, WebChk bridges the interpretability of symbolic scanners with the adaptability of AI-based systems. The results demonstrate how hybrid frameworks can reduce variance and false positives without fully sacrificing coverage or explainability, positioning the proposed system as a feasible direction for next-generation web vulnerability scanning.

4 Conclusion

This study presented an ensemble-based web vulnerability detection framework integrating BERT, TCN, and FP-Growth using a multinomial logistic regression meta-learner to improve detection accuracy and reduce false positives across OWASP Top 10 vulnerabilities. Experimental results demonstrated that while individual models showed varying strengths, each exhibited significant limitations: FP-Growth achieved only 26.42% accuracy with high false positives due to pattern-matching biases toward Security Misconfiguration vulnerabilities, TCN struggled at 11.32% accuracy with poor recall in distinguishing similar behavioral patterns, and BERT reached 47.17% accuracy but suffered from severe overfitting despite superior semantic understanding. The ensemble method, however, achieved optimal balance with 49.06% macro accuracy, 54.67% recall, and 48.77% F1-score, representing a 4.02% improvement over BERT through effective multinomial logistic regression meta-learning that combined domain-specific predictions while minimizing false negatives across all vulnerability classes. Comparative analysis with OWASP ZAP revealed critical trade-offs between detection approaches: non-AI ZAP achieved perfect recall (100%) and strong F1-score (0.857) but generated 25 false positives, while AI-powered ZAP reduced false positives to 4.1 at the cost of lower recall (44.1%) and substantially increased processing time (6 min 28 s versus 1 min per 100 pages), whereas the study's pattern-based approach successfully balanced precision and recall, demonstrating superior noise reduction compared to strict rule-based systems while maintaining computational efficiency suitable for real-time deployment.

Despite the promising outcomes, several limitations constrain the current implementation's effectiveness, including substantial overfitting evidenced by BERT's accuracy gap (97% training versus 47.17% testing), severe class imbalance with underrepresented attack types like SSRF and Cryptographic Failures, inconsistent labeling across dataset sources causing potential data leakage, and critical misalignment issues between training and inference steps where BERT's confidence calibration varies inconsistently, TCN's preprocessing pipeline remains sensitive to feature scaler differences, and FP-Growth exhibits bias toward Security Misconfiguration patterns while consuming excessive memory through 323,131 association rules. Overall, based on the results of these different analytical domains using adaptive meta-learning, the study filled the gap between rule-based exhaustive pattern matching and adaptive learning using AI, providing a single detection solution specifically designed for OWASP Top 10 vulnerabilities and seven other vulnerability types. Future work may address the aforementioned challenges through rigorous data hygiene with source-based splitting and duplicate removal, synthetic data augmentation with class-weighted loss functions, curriculum learning with focal loss and per-class early stopping, versioned preprocessing artifacts and temperature scaling for inference alignment, approximate pattern mining with bloom filters for memory optimization, runtime optimization through model quantization and GPU acceleration, cloud-native microservices deployment, API-based integration with existing security tools for complementary AI-powered analysis, continuous learning pipelines incorporating analyst feedback and threat intelligence feeds, transfer learning for rapid adaptation to novel attack vectors, and advanced ensemble mechanisms including attention-based fusion and multi-task learning frameworks, ultimately maturing this study from a research prototype into a production-ready framework balancing comprehensive coverage, accuracy, and operational efficiency in dynamic cybersecurity environments.

References

1. OWASP Top 10:2021 (2021). https://owasp.org/Top10/
2. Alalwany, E., Alsharif, B., Alotaibi, Y., Alfahaid, A., Mahgoub, I., Ilyas, M.: Stacking ensemble deep learning for real-time intrusion detection in IOMT environments. Sensors **25**(3), 624 (2025). https://doi.org/10.3390/s25030624
3. Bai, S., Kolter, J.Z., Koltun, V.: An empirical evaluation of generic convolutional and recurrent networks for sequence modeling. arXiv preprint arXiv:1803.01271 (2018)
4. Chen, Y., Ding, Z., Alowain, L., Chen, X., Wagner, D.: DiverseVul: a new vulnerable source code dataset for deep learning based vulnerability detection. In: Proceedings of the 26th International Symposium on Research in Attacks, Intrusions and Defenses (RAID '23), pp. 654–668 (2023). https://doi.org/10.1145/3607199.3607242
5. Devlin, J., Chang, M.W., Lee, K., Toutanova, K.: BERT: pre-training of deep bidirectional transformers for language understanding. In: NAACL-HLT (2019)
6. Dietterich, T.G.: Ensemble methods in machine learning. In: International Work shop on Multiple Classifier Systems (2000)

7. Ding, Y., et al.: Vulnerability detection with code language models: how far are we? arXiv preprint arXiv:2403.18624 (2024)
8. Han, J., Pei, J., Yin, Y.: Mining frequent patterns without candidate generation. In: SIGMOD (2000)
9. Huang, W., Lin, S., Li, C.: BBVD: A BERT-based method for vulnerability detection. Int. J. Adv. Comput. Sci. Appl. **13** (2022). https://doi.org/10.14569/IJACSA.2022.01312103
10. Institute, P.: Cost of a data breach 2024. Tech. rep. (2024). https://www.ibm.com/security/data-breach
11. Kallay, P., Dan Mihoc, T.: Comparative analysis of frequent pattern mining algorithms. Acta Univ. Sapientiae Inform. **17**(8) (2025). https://doi.org/10.1007/s44427-025-00008-1
12. Research, A.: CSE-CIC-IDS2018 V2 (2024). https://doi.org/10.7910/DVN/88M0DI
13. Swisskyrepo: GitHub - swisskyrepo/PayloadsAllTheThings: a list of useful payloads and bypass for web application security and pentest/CTF (2023). https://github.com/swisskyrepo/PayloadsAllTheThings
14. Thakur, S.: Web application payloads dataset (2025). https://www.kaggle.com/datasets/cyberprince/web-application-payloads-dataset
15. Vaswani, A., et al.: Attention is all you need. In: NeurIPS (2017)
16. Yang, Y., Lv, H., Chen, N.: A Survey on ensemble learning under the era of deep learning. Artif. Intell. Rev. **56**(6), 5545–5589 (2022). https://doi.org/10.1007/s10462-022-10283-5
17. Yasar, K.: What is web application (web apps) and its benefits? (2024). https://www.techtarget.com/searchsoftwarequality/definition/Web-application-Web-app
18. Ye, X., et al.: Daily insider threat detection with hybrid TCN transformer architecture. Tech. rep. (2025). https://doi.org/10.1038/s41598-025-12063-x, https://www.nature.com/articles/s41598-025-12063-x

Beyond Sets: Comparing Set-Based and Collection-Based Probabilistic Inference in Spam Detection

Feng-Jen Yang(✉)

Department of Computer Science, Florida Polytechnic University, Lakeland, FL 33805, USA
fyang@floridapoly.edu
https://floridapoly.edu

Abstract. Classical probabilistic inference in artificial intelligence often treats evidence as a set of unique elements, ignoring the frequency of repeated observations. While mathematically elegant, this approach can misrepresent real-world phenomena where repetition matters, such as spam detection, where repeated keywords like "win" or "prize" strengthen the likelihood of a message being spam. This article explores and compares two inference frameworks, set-based and collection-based, using the SMS Spam Collection dataset. In this study, I implement both methods in Python, evaluate their performance using accuracy, precision, recall, and F1 score. The findings demonstrate that collection-based inference offers a more nuanced and effective approach in domains where evidence repetition is meaningful.

Keywords: Probabilistic Inference · Probabilistic Classification · Collection-Based Inference

1 Introduction

Probabilistic reasoning lies at the heart of artificial intelligence, providing a principled framework for decision-making under uncertainty. Whether in natural language processing, computer vision, or autonomous systems, AI models frequently encounter incomplete, noisy, or ambiguous data. To navigate these challenges, classical probabilistic approaches, such as Bayesian networks, Naive Bayes classifiers, and Hidden Markov Models, have been widely adopted. These methods offer elegant solutions for modeling dependencies and updating beliefs based on observed evidence.

However, a common simplifying assumption underpins many of these traditional techniques: evidence is typically represented as a set of unique elements. This assumption streamlines the computational process and makes inference tractable, but it comes at a cost. In real-world scenarios, data often exhibit

C. Xu (Ed.): ICMLSC 2026, CCIS 2948, pp. 542–551, 2027.
https://doi.org/10.1007/978-981-92-1546-1_44

repetition, and such redundancy can carry meaningful semantic weight. Ignoring this aspect can lead to models that overlook subtle but important signals embedded in the frequency of observations.

Consider the domain of spam detection as a concrete example. A message that contains the word "win" three times is intuitively more likely to be spam than one in which the word appears only once. Human judgment naturally incorporates the intensity and recurrence of certain cues when assessing credibility or intent. Yet, under a set-based inference paradigm, both messages are treated equivalently, as the repeated word is collapsed into a single instance. This limitation reveals a disconnect between how humans interpret information and how traditional probabilistic models process it.

To address this shortcoming, I suggest a shift of paradigm toward a collection-based framework that represents evidence as a multiset rather than a set. This richer representation enables repeated elements to exert greater influence on probabilistic reasoning, aligning more closely with human intuition and improving performance in tasks where repetition is a key signal.

By embracing multisets, it opens the door to more expressive and nuanced models that better reflect the structure of real-world data. This approach has broad implications, not only for spam detection but also for other domains such as sentiment analysis, recommendation systems, and behavioral modeling, where the recurrence of specific patterns or features can be critical to accurate inference. Ultimately, moving beyond set-based assumptions allows AI systems to reason more effectively in complex, data-rich environments.

2 Related Research

Probabilistic reasoning, particularly Bayesian inference, has become a foundational pillar in the development of statistical learning and artificial intelligence. Over the past several decades, it has enabled researchers and practitioners to model uncertainty, update beliefs based on evidence, and make informed decisions in complex environments. Among the most influential contributions to this field is Rabiner's seminal tutorial on Hidden Markov Models (HMMs) [1], which provided a comprehensive framework for modeling sequential data and laid the groundwork for numerous applications in speech recognition, bioinformatics, and natural language processing.

Another widely adopted technique is the Naive Bayes classifier, which remains a staple in text classification tasks due to its simplicity, scalability, and surprisingly strong performance despite its assumption of feature independence [2,3]. In particular, the Multinomial Naive Bayes variant has proven effective in domains such as spam detection and sentiment analysis, where the frequency of words plays a crucial role. This model implicitly adopts a collection-based perspective by treating documents as bags of words and modeling word counts rather than mere presence or absence [4]. Such an approach acknowledges that repetition can carry semantic weight, even if the underlying theoretical framework does not explicitly distinguish between set-based and multiset-based reasoning.

Robinson's work on statistical spam filtering further emphasized the importance of frequency-sensitive modeling [5]. His approach combined multiple probabilistic techniques to assess the likelihood of a message being spam, incorporating word frequency as a key signal. This practical success underscores the intuitive appeal of collection-based reasoning, even when it is not formally articulated as such.

Despite these advances, the theoretical distinction between set-based and collection-based inference remains underexplored in the literature. Most probabilistic models assume that evidence can be represented as a set of unique observations, which simplifies computation but may obscure important nuances in the data. In contrast, a collection-based framework, where evidence is modeled as a multiset, offers a richer representation that can capture the intensity and recurrence of features. While some models, like Multinomial Naive Bayes, implicitly leverage this idea, there has been limited effort to formalize and compare these paradigms within a unified theoretical framework.

Recent work in probabilistic programming and statistical relational learning has begun to explore more expressive representations of uncertainty, including those that accommodate repeated observations. However, these efforts often focus on structural complexity or relational dependencies rather than the semantic implications of repetition. As such, there remains a gap in the literature regarding the formal treatment of multisets in probabilistic inference and their potential to enhance model expressiveness and performance. This paper aims to address that gap by proposing a collection-based framework for probabilistic reasoning, explicitly modeling evidence as multisets and examining how this shift affects inference outcomes. By situating this approach within the broader context of Bayesian learning and frequency-based classification, we can seek to provide both theoretical clarity and practical utility, particularly in domains where repetition is a meaningful signal.

3 Theoretical Framework

The theoretical framework presented here outlines two distinct approaches to probabilistic inference: *set-based* and *collection-based*. These models provide formal mechanisms for reasoning under uncertainty by leveraging evidence to update beliefs about competing hypotheses. While both approaches rely on foundational principles of probability theory, they differ in how evidence is represented and processed, leading to different computational strategies and assumptions.

3.1 Set-Based Inference

Set-based inference assumes conditional independence and treats evidence as binary indicators. The posterior probability is:

$$
\begin{aligned}
&P(H_i|(E_1 \cap E_2 \cap ... \cap E_n)) \\
&= \frac{P(H_i \cap (E_1 \cap E_2 \cap ... \cap E_n))}{P(E_1 \cap E_2 \cap \ldots \cap E_n)} \\
&= \frac{P((E_1 \cap E_2 \cap ... \cap E_n) \cap H_i)}{P(E_1 \cap E_2 \cap ... \cap E_n)} \\
&= \frac{P((E_1 \cap E_2 \cap ... \cap E_n)|H_i) \times P(H_i)}{P(E_1 \cap E_2 \cap ... \cap E_n)} \\
&where \quad 1 \leq i \leq m
\end{aligned}
$$

The computation above involves evaluating conditional probabilities across all possible combinations of elements and classifications, which leads to significant complexity. To manage this, AI methods typically assume conditional independence among all pieces of evidence, allowing for simplification, so that:

$$
\begin{aligned}
&P((E_1 \cap E_2 \cap ... \cap E_n)|H_i) \\
&= P(E_1|H_i) \times P(E_2|H_i) \times ... \times P(E_n|H_i) \times P(H_i) \\
&where \quad 1 \leq i \leq m
\end{aligned}
$$

and thus:

$$
\begin{aligned}
&P(H_i|(E_1 \cap E_2 \cap ... \cap E_n)) \\
&= \frac{P(E_1|H_i) \times P(E_2|H_i) \times ... \times P(E_n|H_i) \times P(H_i)}{\sum_{j=1}^{m} P(E_1|H_j) \times P(E_2|H_j) \times ... \times P(E_n|H_j) \times P(H_j)} \\
&where \quad 1 \leq i \leq m
\end{aligned}
$$

3.2 Collection-Based Inference

Collection-based inference models evidence as a multiset using the multinomial distribution:

$$
\begin{aligned}
&P(H_i|(E_1 \cap E_2 \cap ... \cap E_n)) \\
&= \frac{P(H_i \cap (E_1 \cap E_2 \cap ... \cap E_n))}{P(E_1 \cap E_2 \cap ... \cap E_n)} \\
&= \frac{P((E_1 \cap E_2 \cap ... \cap E_n) \cap H_i)}{\sum_{j=1}^{m} P((E_1 \cap E_2 \cap ... \cap E_n) \cap H_j)} \\
&= \frac{\left(\frac{n!}{e_1! \times e_2! \times \cdots \times e_k!} \times p_1^{e_1} \times p_2^{e_2} \times \cdots \times p_k^{e_k}\right) \times P(H_i)}{\sum_{j=1}^{m}((\frac{n!}{e_1! \times e_2! \times \cdots \times e_k!} \times p_1^{e_1} \times p_2^{e_2} \times \cdots \times p_k^{e_k}) \times P(H_j))}
\end{aligned}
$$

where:

- e_i is the number of times E_i occurs in the inference case.
- n is the total number of items in this inference case, i.e., $n = e_1 + e_2 + \cdots + e_k$.
- p_i is the probability that E_i occurs in the samples where hypothesis H_i is true.
- p_j is the probability that E_j occurs in the samples where hypothesis H_j is true.

4 Dataset and Implementation

This study uses the *SMS Spam Collection* dataset, which consists of 5,574 short text messages labeled as either *spam* or *ham* (non-spam) [6]. The dataset is widely recognized in spam detection research and provides a realistic benchmark for evaluating probabilistic inference methods. Its concise message format makes it ideal for word-level modeling, where individual tokens serve as evidence for classification.

4.1 Preprocessing

Preprocessing is a critical step to convert raw text into structured input suitable for probabilistic inference. The pipeline implemented in this study includes the following steps:

- *Text normalization:* All messages are converted to lowercase to ensure uniformity and reduce sparsity caused by case variations (e.g., "Win" vs. "win").
- *Tokenization:* Instead of relying on external libraries such as NLTK, a lightweight regular expression-based tokenizer is used to split messages into individual words. This approach avoids dependency issues and ensures compatibility in restricted environments.
- *Noise removal:* Non-alphabetic characters and punctuation are removed, retaining only meaningful word tokens. Stop words are preserved because they may carry spam-indicative patterns (e.g., "you," "now," "free").
- *Representation:*
  - For *set-based inference*, each message is represented as a set of unique words, ignoring repetition.
  - For *collection-based inference*, word frequencies within each message are retained, enabling the model to capture the semantic weight of repeated terms.
- *Train-test split:* The dataset is divided into 70% training and 30% testing using stratified sampling to maintain the original spam-to-ham ratio across both subsets.

This preprocessing ensures that both inference methods operate on consistent and comparable inputs while preserving the structural differences that distinguish set-based from collection-based reasoning.

4.2 Implementation Details

Both inference methods were implemented in Python using standard libraries such as *pandas*, *collections*, and *scikit-learn*. The implementation consists of the following components:

- *Prior estimation:* The prior probability $P(H_i)$ for each class (*spam* or *ham*) is computed based on its relative frequency in the training set.
- *Likelihood estimation:*
  - For *set-based inference*, the likelihood $P(E_k|H_i)$ is calculated as the proportion of training messages labeled H_i that contain word E_k at least once.
  - For *collection-based inference*, the likelihood is based on word frequency: p_k is computed as the relative frequency of word E_k across all messages labeled H_i, normalized by the total word count in that class.
- *Laplace smoothing:* To handle unseen words in the test set, additive smoothing is applied by incrementing word counts and vocabulary size, ensuring no probability is zero.
- *Inference computation:*
  - *Set-based inference* uses a Naive Bayes-style approach, summing log-likelihoods for all unique words in the message.
  - *Collection-based inference* applies the multinomial model, incorporating word frequencies and factorial terms to approximate the probability of observing a specific word distribution.
- *Prediction and evaluation:* Each test message is classified using both methods. Predictions are compared to ground truth labels, and performance metrics—Accuracy, Precision, Recall, and F1 Score—are computed using *scikit-learn.*

This implementation framework ensures that both inference models are evaluated under identical conditions, allowing for a fair and meaningful comparison of their effectiveness in spam detection.

5 Evaluation

This section presents a comprehensive evaluation of the proposed inference models by applying them to real-world data. While theoretical formulations provide a foundation for understanding model behavior, empirical testing is essential to validate their practical effectiveness. By employing both quantitative metrics and structured visual representations, I have bridged the gap between abstract theory and observable performance. This approach enables a transparent and well-rounded comparison of inference strategies, supporting informed conclusions about their relative strengths.

5.1 Accuracy

Accuracy is a basic yet widely used metric that measures the proportion of correctly classified messages, whether spam or legitimate, out of the total number of messages. It is calculated as:

$$\text{Accuracy} = \frac{\text{True Positives} + \text{True Negatives}}{\text{Total Number of Instances}}$$

Although accuracy provides a general sense of performance, it can be misleading in scenarios involving imbalanced datasets. Spam detection is a prime example, where the majority of messages are typically legitimate. In such cases, a model that always predicts "not spam" could still achieve high accuracy, despite failing to detect actual spam messages. Therefore, while accuracy is useful, it must be interpreted with caution.

5.2 Precision, Recall, and F1 Score

To evaluate the models more thoroughly, I incorporated three key metrics: Precision, Recall, and F1 Score. These metrics provide a more nuanced understanding of how well each method distinguishes spam from legitimate messages.

- *Precision* quantifies the proportion of messages identified as spam that were actually spam. It answers the question: *Of all the messages flagged as spam, how many were truly spam?* High precision indicates that the system minimizes false positives, thereby reducing the risk of misclassifying legitimate messages. It is calculated as:

$$\text{Precision} = \frac{\text{True Positives}}{\text{True Positives} + \text{False Positives}}$$

- *Recall* measures the system's ability to detect spam messages correctly. It answers: *Of all the actual spam messages, how many did the system successfully identify?* A high recall value suggests that the system is effective at capturing most spam, minimizing false negatives. It is calculated as:

$$\text{Recall} = \frac{\text{True Positives}}{\text{True Positives} + \text{False Negatives}}$$

- *F1 Score* is the harmonic mean of precision and recall. It provides a balanced metric that considers both types of errors. This score is particularly valuable when dealing with imbalanced datasets or when both precision and recall are equally important. The harmonic mean penalizes extreme values more than the arithmetic mean. So if either precision or recall is very low, the F1 score will also be low, encouraging a balance between the two. It is calculated as:

$$F_1 = 2 \times \frac{\text{Precision} \times \text{Recall}}{\text{Precision} + \text{Recall}}$$

6 Evaluation Results: Set-Based vs. Collection-Based Inference

This section presents a detailed comparison of two probabilistic inference methods, *Set-Based* and *Collection-Based*, applied to the *SMS Spam Collection* dataset. The goal is to assess how each approach performs in distinguishing spam from legitimate messages using standard evaluation metrics: Accuracy, Precision, Recall, and F1 Score.

6.1 Set-Based Inference

The set-based method treats each message as a set of unique words, ignoring word frequency. While this simplifies computation, it overlooks the semantic weight of repeated terms. Its performance is summarized in Table 1. It can be further interpreted as: The set-based approach achieves a perfect recall score, meaning it successfully identifies nearly all spam messages. However, its precision is very low (0.35), indicating a high rate of false positives, many legitimate messages are incorrectly classified as spam. This imbalance suggests that while the method is aggressive in detecting spam, it sacrifices accuracy in distinguishing legitimate content, making it less practical for real-world applications where user experience matters.

Table 1. Performance of Set-Based Inference

Metric	Value
Accuracy	0.76
Precision	0.35
Recall	1.00
F1 Score	0.52

6.2 Collection-Based Inference

The collection-based method models messages as multisets, incorporating word frequency into the inference process. This richer representation captures the intensity of spam-indicative terms, such as repeated keywords like "win" or "free." The results are shown in Table 2. It can be further interpreted as: The collection-based approach significantly outperforms the set-based method across all metrics. It achieves high precision (0.90) and recall (0.95), resulting in an excellent F1 score of 0.92. This balance indicates that the method not only detects most spam messages but also minimizes false positives, making it far more reliable for practical deployment. The improvement validates the hypothesis that accounting for word frequency provides a more nuanced and effective spam detection strategy.

Table 2. Performance of Collection-Based Inference

Metric	Value
Accuracy	0.98
Precision	0.90
Recall	0.95
F1 Score	0.92

6.3 Evaluation Summary

Overall, the evaluation demonstrates that while set-based inference offers simplicity, its performance is limited by the inability to handle repeated evidence. In contrast, collection-based inference leverages frequency information to deliver superior accuracy and robustness. These findings underscore the importance of richer evidence representation in probabilistic reasoning, particularly in domains like spam filtering where repetition is a strong signal.

7 Discussion

Collection-based inference provides a more sophisticated and context-aware mechanism for interpreting repeated evidence within a dataset. Unlike traditional methods that treat each instance in isolation, this approach aggregates multiple occurrences of similar or related information, thereby capturing the semantic weight that repetition often implies. This aggregation not only enhances accuracy, precision and F1 score, by increasing the likelihood of identifying relevant patterns, but also mirrors the way humans tend to reason by recognizing and giving importance to recurring signals.

Such a strategy contributes significantly to the intuitiveness and transparency of the inference process. By emphasizing the cumulative strength of evidence, collection-based inference makes the decision-making process more interpretable, especially in complex scenarios where isolated data points may not be sufficient to draw reliable conclusions. This interpretability is crucial in domains like natural language understanding, information retrieval, and automated reasoning, where clarity and justification of outcomes are essential.

Moreover, recent advancements suggest that hybrid models, which combine both structural features (such as syntactic patterns or graph-based relationships) and lexical features (such as word embeddings or semantic similarity), can further elevate the performance of inference systems. These multifaceted models leverage the strengths of different representational paradigms, resulting in more robust and accurate outcomes. Studies such as those by Zhang et al. (2021) and Xue et al. (2019) have demonstrated the potential of such integrated approaches, indicating that a well-balanced fusion of techniques may be key to achieving superior inference quality and resilience across diverse applications [7,8].

8 Conclusion

This study presents a comparative evaluation of set-based and collection-based inference frameworks, with a particular focus on their effectiveness in domains where repeated evidence carries meaningful semantic implications. While set-based approaches treat evidence as unordered and non-redundant, collection-based inference explicitly models repetition, allowing the framework to capture subtle patterns and reinforce signals that may otherwise be diluted. This repetition-sensitive modeling leads to improved classification performance, as it leverages the cumulative strength of recurring evidence. Moreover, collection-based inference aligns more closely with human cognitive processes, which naturally give weight to repeated observations when forming judgments. By offering a richer and more expressive representation of uncertainty, this approach enhances both the interpretability and reliability of inference outcomes, making it especially valuable in complex decision-making scenarios where nuance and context are critical.

References

1. Rabiner, L.: A tutorial on hidden Markov models and selected applications in speech recognition. In: Proceedings of the IEEE, vol. 77, no. 2, pp. 257–286 (1989)
2. Yang, F.-J.: An implementation of naive bayes classifier. In: International Conference on Computational Science and Computational Intelligence (CSCI), pp. 301–306, Las Vegas, NV, USA (2018). https://doi.org/10.1109/CSCI46756.2018.00065
3. Yang, F.-J.: A SQL-based probabilistic inference. In: 2023 Congress in Computer Science, Computer Engineering, & Applied Computing (CSCE 2023), Las Vegas, NV, pp. 241–245 (2023). https://doi.org/10.1109/CSCE60160.2023.00043.10.5555/3091696.3091710
4. Kadam, S., Gala, A., Gehlot, P., Kurup, A., Ghag, K.: Word embedding based multinomial naive bayes algorithm for spam filtering. In: 2018 Fourth International Conference on Computing Communication Control and Automation (ICCUBEA), Pune, India, 2018, pp. 1–5 (2018). https://doi.org/10.1109/ICCUBEA.2018.8697601.
5. Robinson, G.: A statistical approach to the spam problem. Linux J. (2003). Available via ACM Digital Library
6. Almeida, T., Hidalgo, J.: SMS spam collection [dataset]. UCI Mach. Learn. Reposit. (2011). https://doi.org/10.24432/C5CC84
7. Xue, H., Wang, Q., Luo, B., Seo, H., Li, F.: Content-aware trust propagation toward online review spam detection. J. Data Inf. Qual. (JDIQ) **11**(3), 1–31 (2019). https://doi.org/10.1145/3305258
8. Zhang, Y., Yuan, X., Tzeng, N.: Platform-oblivious anti-spam gateway, ACSAC 2021. In: Proceedings of the 37th Annual Computer Security Applications Conference, pp. 1064–1077 (2021). https://doi.org/10.1145/3485832.3488024

Detecting the Threat: A CNN and TSA Hybrid Approach for DDoS Detection in Software-Defined Networks

Martin Bernard F. Bondoc(✉), Dan Floyd L. Arnaiz, George III R. Bustamante, Clyde Chester R. Balaman, and Rhodessa J. Cascaro

Mapúa Malayan Colleges Mindanao, Davao City, Davao Del Sur, Philippines
{mbBondoc,dfArnaiz,giBustamante,ccrbalaman,rjcascaro}@mcm.edu.ph
https://mcm.edu.ph/

Abstract. Software-Defined Networking (SDN) improves flexibility and control in modern networks but also increases vulnerability to Distributed Denial-of-Service (DDoS) attacks targeting its centralized controller. Existing detection models struggle to capture both spatial and temporal attack patterns efficiently, limiting their real-time performance. This study presents a hybrid deep learning framework that integrates Convolutional Neural Networks (CNN) for spatial feature extraction and Temporal Self-Attention (TSA) for long-range temporal modeling. The CICDDoS2019 dataset was preprocessed through cleaning, normalization, feature selection, and temporal windowing to ensure balanced and representative traffic samples. The proposed CNN–TSA model was trained and evaluated under multiple preprocessing and learning configurations using scenario-wise data splits. Experimental results demonstrate strong and consistent performance, achieving up to 97.77% accuracy, 99.85% precision, 95.18% recall, and 0.9995 ROC-AUC. These findings confirm that the CNN–TSA hybrid significantly enhances DDoS detection accuracy and generalization within SDN environments, providing a scalable and reliable foundation for real-time intrusion defense.

Keywords: Software-Defined Networking · Distributed Denial-of-Service · Convolutional Neural Network · Temporal Self-Attention · Deep Learning · Network Security

1 Introduction

In modern computing environments, Software-Defined Networking (SDN) has become a cornerstone of intelligent network management [1–7], offering centralized control and dynamic programmability that improve efficiency and scalability. In response to the growing prevalence of Internet of Things (IoT) systems, SDN has been examined as a complementary approach for achieving scalable and centrally managed network infrastructures [8]. However, these same capabilities also expose new vulnerabilities, particularly to Distributed Denial-of-Service

C. Xu (Ed.): ICMLSC 2026, CCIS 2948, pp. 552–564, 2027.
https://doi.org/10.1007/978-981-92-1546-1_45

(DDoS) attacks [9]. Such attacks have evolved from simple volumetric floods to complex multi-vector and low- rate variants that closely resemble benign traffic, making detection increasingly difficult [10–12]. Recent surveys and systematic reviews reveal a continuous escalation in DDoS scale and sophistication, underscoring the need for advanced

detection models that can capture both spatial traffic regularities and long-range temporal dependencies [12–14]. SDN amplifies both opportunity and risk: while its centralized control and programmable forwarding enable rapid policy enforcement and adaptive traffic management, they also create high value choke points that Distributed Denial-of-Service (DDoS) adversaries can exploit to exhaust the controller, southbound channels, and switch flow tables [13,14]. Consequently, SDN defense mechanisms must sustain high throughput and low latency while remaining robust against concept drift and class imbalance commonly observed in real world network traffic. Classical machine-learning pipelines that rely on manual feature engineering often lose accuracy as attackers change their behavior [14]. Deep learning improves generalization but introduces design trade-offs: recurrent models (LSTM/GRU) can learn temporal patterns but suffer from slow, step-by-step processing that limits real-time use in SDN control planes, while convolutional models capture spatial features well but struggle with long-range dependencies [15–18]. Self-attention addresses this issue by replacing recurrence with parallel context learning, allowing larger receptive fields without sacrificing efficiency [19]. Temporal Self-Attention (TSA) further enhances this by achieving state-of-the-art accuracy and fast training across various time-series tasks, such as finance and clinical prediction [20,21,23,24].

Despite recent progress in CNN-based, hybrid, and feature-selection methods for DDoS detection—often tested on the CICDDoS2019 dataset—a rigorous CNN–TSA fusion designed specifically for SDN is still underexplored, particularly under real deployment conditions such as deduplication, scaling, leakage control, and class imbalance [15,17,18,25]. This study addresses that gap by combining CNN spatial encoders with TSA to learn long-range temporal patterns through sliding windows, aiming to achieve accurate, scalable, and real-time DDoS detection in programmable SDN environments [13,14,19]. The objective of this study is to preprocess the CICDDoS2019 dataset and develop a Distributed Denial-of-Service (DDoS) detection model that combines Temporal Self-Attention (TSA) and Convolutional Neural Networks (CNN) within a Software-Defined Networking (SDN) environment. The dataset is prepared through data cleaning, normalization, feature selection, and temporal window construction to ensure high-quality and balanced inputs for model training. The proposed CNN–TSA model integrates TSA to capture temporal dependencies and CNN to extract spatial features from SDN traffic. The study also evaluates the model's performance under different preprocessing strategies and hyperparameter settings using standard metrics such as Accuracy, Precision, Recall, F1-Score, ROC-AUC, PR-AUC, Brier Score, and Decision Threshold to determine its effectiveness, scalability, and generalization capability.

2 Method

This section describes the methodological framework used to preprocess the CICDDoS2019 dataset, develop the CNN–TSA hybrid model for Distributed Denial-of-Service (DDoS) detection in Software-Defined Networking (SDN), and evaluate its performance under various preprocessing and configuration settings based on the study's objectives.

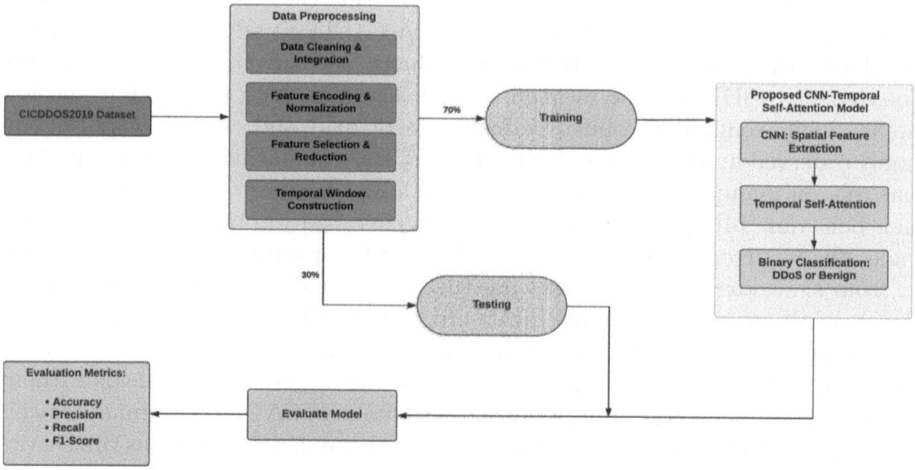

Fig. 1. CNN-Temporal Self-Attention Model Development Process.

2.1 Conceptual Framework

Figure 1 presents the conceptual framework of the proposed CNN–Temporal Self-Attention (TSA) model for Distributed Denial-of-Service (DDoS) detection. The CICDDoS2019 dataset is used as the main source of network traffic records and is preprocessed through cleaning, normalization, feature selection, and temporal window construction to ensure data quality and capture time-based attack patterns. The processed data is then divided into training and testing sets, where the CNN module extracts spatial features and the TSA component models temporal dependencies to differentiate DDoS traffic from benign flows. The model outputs binary classifications and is evaluated using metrics such as Accuracy, Precision, Recall, F1-Score, and ROC-AUC to measure its detection performance and generalization ability.

2.2 Preprocessing

All CICDDoS2019 scenario CSV files were streamed, normalized, and merged into a single Parquet dataset. Column names were standardized for consistency, and non-predictive identifiers such as Flow ID, Source IP, Destination IP, and SimilarHTTP were removed. The label column was converted to binary form (0 = BENIGN, 1 = DDoS), and a scenario key (e.g., SYN, MSSQL, DDoS_DNS) was extracted from each filename to preserve scenario grouping. To maintain balanced class representation, a 1:1 DDoS-to-BENIGN ratio was applied using random under sampling within each scenario. This balance ensured equal contribution from both classes during training, reducing bias toward the dominant attack class and stabilizing gradient updates. Duplicate rows were eliminated using scenario-aware hashing to retain only unique and representative traffic instances.

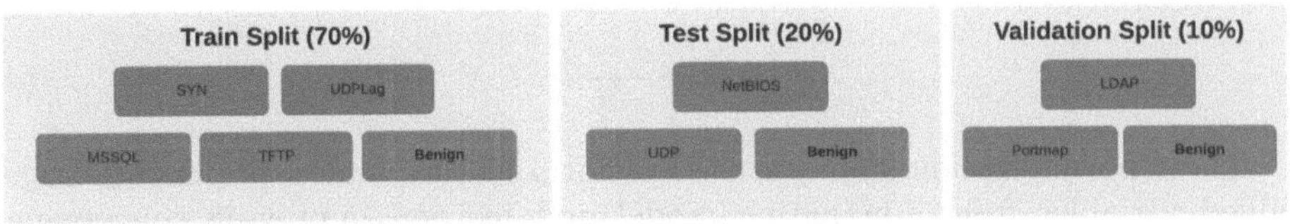

Fig. 2. Scenario-wise data splitting of CICDDoS2019

A scenario-wise data splitting approach was used on the dataset, where entire attack scenarios were assigned exclusively to the training, validation, or testing sets. This prevented overlap between scenarios and ensured that the model was evaluated on unseen attack types, promoting better generalization and reducing data leakage. Figure 2 shows the scenario-wise split, where the training set (70%) includes SYN, UDP-Lag, MSSQL, and TFTP, while validation (10%) and testing (20%) contain distinct unseen scenarios such as LDAP, Portmap, UDP, and NetBIOS. This ensures that each subset is independent, allowing the CNN–TSA model to learn generalized DDoS detection patterns.

Feature selection was applied in two stages to improve efficiency and reduce redundancy. First, a correlation filter removed highly collinear numeric features based on Pearson's correlation coefficient:

$$r_{jk} = \frac{Cov(x_j, x_k)}{\sigma_{x_j} \sigma_{x_k}} \tag{1}$$

where one of the features x_j or x_k was dropped if $|r_{jk}| > T$, with T as the correlation threshold. This minimized overlap between variables carrying the same information. Next, a univariate ANOVA F-test ranked the remaining features according to their ability to distinguish between benign and attack traffic. The F-score was calculated as:

$$F_j = \frac{between - classvarianceof x_j}{within - classvarianceof x_j} \tag{2}$$

and the top k features with the highest F_j values were retained. This approach ensured that only the most relevant and independent features were selected while keeping the feature set compact enough to fit within available RAM resources. To further control memory usage, the dataset was processed in streamed batches (10,000–20,000 rows at a time) to prevent loading the entire dataset into memory.

Feature scaling was then applied to normalize feature magnitudes and stabilize model learning. Two normalization techniques were tested. The MinMax-Scaler scaled each feature to the range [0, 1] using:

$$x' = \frac{x - min(x)}{max(x) - min(x)} \tag{3}$$

while the Standard Scaler standardized features by centering them at zero mean and unit variance through:

$$x' = \frac{x - \mu}{\sigma} \tag{4}$$

These normalization steps ensured uniform feature scales, preventing large-valued variables from dominating model updates and improving convergence stability during CNN–TSA training. For temporal modeling, windowing was used to generate fixed-length sequences compatible with the CNN–TSA architecture. The window size was set to 48-time steps, and the stride to 24, allowing partial overlap between consecutive samples. Each window was labeled based on the majority class within its time range, capturing short-term temporal dependencies essential for real-time DDoS detection.

Table 1. Preprocessing Configurations

Configuration	ScalingMethod	Correlation Threshold	Top-k Features	Purpose/ Rationale
1	Standard	0.90	45	Baseline setup balancing redundancy removal and feature retention.
2	MinMax	0.85	60	Tighter correlation pruning with MinMax normalization to test convergence sensitivity.
3	Standard	1.00	32	Minimal feature space to assess model compactness and temporal learning robustness.

Three preprocessing configurations were designed to evaluate the effects of scaling methods, correlation thresholds, and feature dimensionality on model performance. As summarized in Table 1, Configuration 1 served as the baseline, using Standard Scaling with moderate correlation filtering to maintain balanced feature diversity. Configuration 2 applied MinMax Scaling with a tighter correlation threshold to assess how stronger redundancy reduction and normalized feature magnitudes influence convergence. Configuration 3 used Standard Scaling without correlation filtering to test the CNN–TSA model's robustness when trained on a smaller yet unfiltered feature space. Together, these configurations enabled a controlled analysis of preprocessing sensitivity under the same dataset and scenario-based splitting conditions.

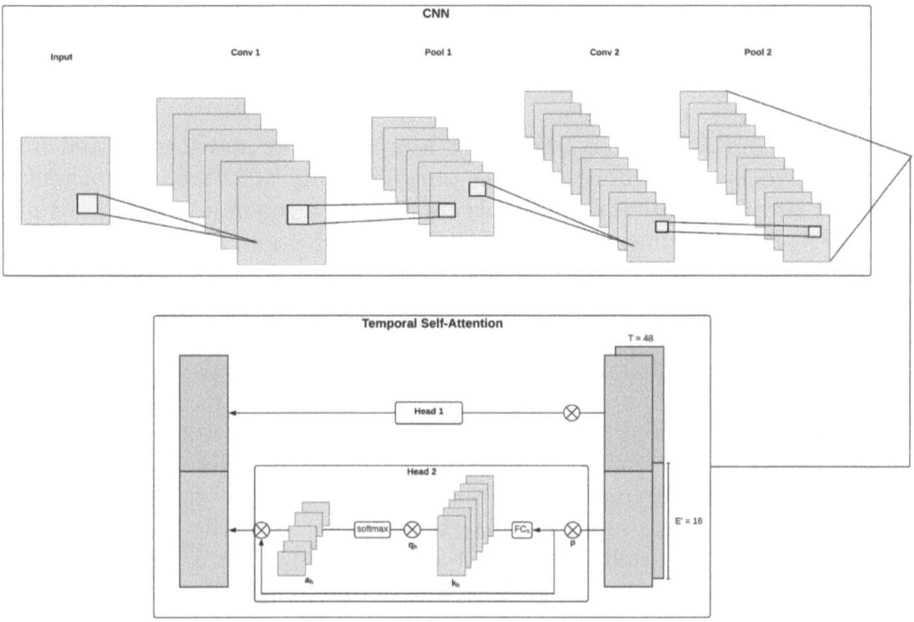

Fig. 3. Model Architecture.

Figure 3 illustrates the architecture of the proposed CNN–Temporal Self-Attention (CNN–TSA) model, which combines convolutional neural networks for spatial feature extraction with a temporal self-attention mechanism for modeling sequential dependencies in network traffic. Each input sample corresponds to a fixed-length traffic sequence of $T = 48$ timesteps and multiple extracted features per timestep, designed to capture both short-term and long-term patterns in SDN traffic flows. In the CNN block, the model performs localized spatial feature extraction across traffic attributes. The first convolutional layer (Conv 1) applies 32 filters with a kernel size of 5, using ReLU activation to detect short-range relationships between consecutive timesteps. This is followed by a max-pooling layer (Pool 1), which halves the temporal resolution from 48 to 24, suppressing noise and reducing computational load. The second convolutional layer (Conv 2) employs 64 filters with a smaller kernel size of 3, enabling the network to capture more refined and higher-level spatial correlations. Another pooling layer (Pool

2) further compresses the representation to 12 timesteps, resulting in a feature embedding of dimension E=64. This hierarchical convolution process ensures that the network effectively learns abstract representations of traffic behavior before applying temporal modeling.

The Temporal Self-Attention (TSA) module models long-range dependencies across the compressed feature sequence. Before attention is applied, Layer Normalization stabilizes activations. The multi-head self-attention mechanism, configured with 2 heads, computes relationships between timesteps using the scaled dot-product attention formula:

$$Attention(Q, K, V) = softmax(\frac{QK^T}{\sqrt{d_k}})V \tag{5}$$

where Q, K, and V represent the query, key, and value matrices derived from the input sequence, and dh denotes the dimensionality per head. The output of each head is concatenated, normalized, and passed through a feed-forward network (FFN) with two linear layers and a GELU activation, followed by dropout and residual connections. This design enables the model to focus on important temporal interactions, improving its ability to distinguish between normal traffic fluctuations and DDoS attack patterns. After temporal modeling, the sequence is aggregated using global average pooling, producing a single vector that represents the entire traffic window. The classification head processes this vector through a fully connected layer with 128 units, ReLU activation, and dropout (0.3) for regularization, followed by a final linear output layer producing a single logit. The output is converted into an attack probability using the sigmoid function. Model training used the AdamW optimizer with the BCEWithLogitsLoss function, which applied a positive class weighting factor to handle class imbalance. A ReduceLROnPlateau scheduler automatically decreased the learning rate when validation loss plateaued, while early stopping with a patience of seven epochs prevented overfitting. Three training configurations were tested, each using a weight decay of 0.0001 but different learning rates (Table 2).

2.3 Evaluation Metrics

The evaluation phase focused on assessing the performance of the proposed CNN–TSA hybrid model for Distributed Denial-of-Service (DDoS) detection within Software-Defined Networking (SDN) environments. The model was trained and tested on the CICDDoS2019 dataset using multiple preprocessing strategies and hyperparameter configurations. Performance was evaluated using seven key metrics: Accuracy, Precision, Recall, F1-Score, ROC-AUC, PR-AUC, and Brier Score. These metrics collectively measure the model's classification effectiveness, discrimination ability, and probability calibration.

Let TP is true positives, TN is true negatives, FP is false positives, FN is false negatives, TPR is true positive rate, and FPR is false positive rate.

Table 2. Learning Variants

Learning Variation	Learning Rate	Weight Decay	Patience	Purpose/ Rationale
1	0.001	0.001	7	Serves as the baseline configuration to evaluate general convergence behavior and learning stability.
2	0.0001	0.001	7	Tests the effect of a lower learning rate on fine-grained convergence and overfitting control.
3	0.00001	0.001	7	Examines model performance under very slow learning, emphasizing stability over training speed and assessing robustness in minimizing loss fluctuations.

Accuracy. Measures the overall correctness of the model in classifying both DDoS attack and benign traffic:

$$Accuracy = \frac{TP + TN}{TP + TN + FP + FN} \tag{6}$$

Precision. Indicates how many of the instances predicted as attacks were attacks, reflecting the model's ability to minimize false positives:

$$Precision = \frac{TP}{TP + FP} \tag{7}$$

Recall(Sensitivity). Evaluates how well the model identified actual DDoS attacks, highlighting its sensitivity to positive cases:

$$Recall = \frac{TP}{TP + FN} \tag{8}$$

F1-Score. Provides the harmonic mean of Precision and Recall, offering a balanced measure of performance that is particularly useful for imbalanced datasets:

$$F1 - Score = 2 * (\frac{Precision * Recall}{Precision + Recall}) \tag{9}$$

ROC-AUC (Receiver Operating Characteristic - Area Under Curve). Represents the model's ability to distinguish between attack and benign traffic across all possible classification thresholds. A higher ROC-AUC value indicates stronger discriminative performance:

$$ROC - AUC = \int_0^1 TPR(FPR)dFPR \tag{10}$$

3 Results and Discussion

The experiments evaluated the proposed model under three preprocessing configurations to determine how scaling type, correlation threshold, and top-k feature selection influence performance. Each configuration was tested with three learning-rate variations to assess consistency and convergence behavior. Model training employed early stopping based on validation loss, and the optimal decision threshold was selected from the highest validation F1-Score. During preprocessing, 39 features were retained in Configuration 1, 35 features in Configuration 2, and 32 features in Configuration 3 after applying feature scaling, correlation filtering, and univariate selection. The results for all configurations are summarized in Tables 3, 4 and 5 reporting model performance across Accuracy, Precision, Recall, F1-Score, and ROC-AUC metrics.

Table 3. Preprocessing Configuration 1 (Standard Scaling, correlation threshold = 0.90, top-k = 45)

Training Variation	Accuracy (%)	Precision (%)	Recall (%)	F1-Score (%)	ROC-AUC
1	97.77	99.85	95.18	97.46	0.9995
2	95.54	99.52	90.50	94.79	0.9984
3	95.47	99.36	90.50	94.72	0.9975

As shown in Table 3, the CNN–TSA model consistently achieved high detection performance across all training variations, with accuracies ranging from 95.47% to 97.77%, precision values between 99.36% and 99.85%, and recalls from 90.5% to 95.18%. These results produced F1-Scores of 94.72%–97.46% and ROC-AUC values above 0.997. The first variation obtained the highest overall balance (Accuracy = 97.77%, F1 = 97.46%, ROC-AUC = 0.9995), indicating that its learning rate enabled more effective optimization compared with the smaller rates used in subsequent runs. Overall, the CNN–TSA architecture demonstrated strong robustness and discriminative capability, maintaining excellent separation between benign and DDoS traffic even with a reduced 32-feature input.

As shown in Table 4, the CNN–TSA model maintained excellent classification performance for the first two training variations, achieving accuracies of 97.93% and 97.46%, F1-scores of 97.64% and 97.09%, and near-perfect ROC–AUC values of 0.9992. These results indicate that MinMax scaling effectively preserved feature proportionality and enhanced the model's ability to distinguish DDoS traffic

Table 4. Preprocessing Configuration 2 (MinMax Scaling, correlation threshold = 0.85, top-k = 60)

Training Variation	Accuracy (%)	Precision (%)	Recall (%)	F1-Score (%)	ROC-AUC
1	97.93	99.53	95.82	97.64	0.9992
2	97.46	99.84	94.48	97.09	0.9992
3	55.24	0.00	0.00	0.00	0.7831

with high precision and recall. However, the third variation exhibited a sharp performance drop (Accuracy = 55.24%, Precision = Recall = 0, ROC–AUC = 0.7831) due to non-convergence at a very low learning rate, which caused the model to predict a single class. Overall, Table 4 demonstrates that Configuration 2 yields highly stable and discriminative results when properly optimized, while also revealing the CNN–TSA model's sensitivity to learning-rate tuning.

Table 5. Preprocessing Configuration 3 (Standard Scaling, correlation threshold = 1.00, top-k = 32)

Training Variation	Accuracy(%)	Precision (%)	Recall (%)	F1-Score (%)	ROC-AUC
1	97.89	99.24	96.05	97.62	0.9992
2	97.63	98.80	95.91	97.33	0.9990
3	97.04	97.47	95.91	96.68	0.9980

As shown in Table 5, the CNN–TSA model consistently achieved strong classification performance across all training variations. The results show Accuracy values between 97.04% and 97.89%, Precision from 97.47% to 99.24%, and Recall from 95.91% to 96.05%, leading to high F1-Scores ranging from 96.68% to 97.62% and ROC–AUC values above 0.998. These outcomes indicate that standard scaling, even with a reduced 32-feature subset and no correlation pruning, effectively preserved essential statistical relationships in the traffic data. The minimal differences across learning-rate variations demonstrate the model's robustness and consistent generalization under this configuration. Overall, Table 5 confirms that the CNN–TSA maintained excellent discriminative performance and stability, successfully distinguishing DDoS attacks from benign flows with near-perfect accuracy and AUC.

Despite the strong performance of the CNN–TSA model across all training variations, several limitations remain. The current evaluation does not include real-time performance metrics such as inference latency and throughput, which are critical for deployment in SDN environments. The study is limited to binary DDoS detection, leaving multi-class attack identification untested, and has not been evaluated against unseen low-rate or stealthy attacks, which may affect robustness in dynamic network scenarios. Additionally, the model's suitability for resource-constrained or edge deployments has not been assessed, highlighting the need for optimization before practical implementation.

4 Conclusion

This study presented a hybrid deep learning approach that combines Convolutional Neural Networks (CNN) and Temporal Self-Attention (TSA) for effective DDoS attack detection in Software-Defined Networks (SDN). The CICDDoS2019 dataset was carefully processed through cleaning, normalization, feature selection, and windowing to ensure reliable and consistent data quality. The CNN–TSA model integrated spatial and temporal feature extraction, enabling it to capture both short-term traffic patterns and long-range temporal dependencies.

Experimental results across multiple preprocessing configurations and learning rate settings demonstrated that the proposed model achieved strong and stable performance. The best configuration obtained an accuracy of 97.77%, an F1-score of 97.46%, and a ROC–AUC of 0.9995. These metrics indicate excellent discriminative capability and high generalization, confirming the model's robustness under varying training conditions.

Overall, the findings show that the CNN–TSA hybrid model provides a reliable and scalable framework for DDoS detection in SDN environments. Its high precision, stability, and adaptability make it suitable for real-time cybersecurity systems, contributing to improved network resilience and automated threat mitigation. Future work may extend this research by optimizing model efficiency for deployment on edge devices and exploring adaptive mechanisms for evolving network traffic behaviors.

References

1. Omranpour, S., Rabusseau, G., Rabbany, R.: Higher order transformers: Enhancing stock movement prediction on multimodal time-series data, (2024). arXiv:2412.10540 arXiv preprint
2. Chen, Z., Chen, D., Zhang, X., Yuan, Z., Cheng, X.: Learning graph structures with transformer for multivariate time-series anomaly detection in iot. IEEE Internet Things J. **9**(12), 9179–9189 (2021)
3. Zhang, R., Chen, J., Song, Y., Shan, W., Chen, P., Xia, Y.: An effective transformation-encoding-attention framework for multivariate time series anomaly detection in iot environment. Mobile Networks and Applications **29**(5), 1551–1563 (2024)
4. Wang, H., Li, W.: Ddostc: A transformer-based network attack detection hybrid mechanism in sdn. Sensors **21**(15), 5047 (2021)
5. Man, W., Yang, G., Feng, S.: Joint selfattention-svm ddos attack detection and defense mechanism based on self-attention mechanism and svm classification for sdn networks. IEICE Trans. Fundam. Electron. Commun. Comput. Sci. **107**(6), 881–889 (2024)
6. Manocchio, L.D., Layeghy, S., Lo, W.W., Kulatilleke, G.K., Sarhan, M., Portmann, M.: Flowtransformer: A transformer framework for flowbased network intrusion detection systems. Expert Syst. Appl. **241**, 122564 (2024)

7. Wang, B., Jiang, Y., Liao, Y., Li, Z.: Ddos-msct: A ddos attack detection method based on multiscale convolution and transformer. IET Inf. Secur. **2024**(1), 1056705 (2024)
8. Shieh, C.-S., Yan, J.-Y., Hao-Xiang, G.: SDN-Based Management Framework for IoT. International Journal of Computer Theory and Engineering **11**(1), 6–10 (2019)
9. Hasan, K., Hossain, K.S., Alam, M.S., Islam, M.Z., Apurbo, G.M., Ahmed, M.F., Noor, J., Hossain, M.I.: Real-time ddos detection in software-defined networks using machine learning. In: 2024 27th International Conference on Computer and Information Technology (ICCIT). pp. 453–458. IEEE (2024)
10. Kachavimath, A.V., Narayan, D.: A hybrid deep learning model with consensus-based feature selection for ddos attacks detection in sdn. Procedia Computer Science **252**, 643–652 (2025)
11. Wani, S., Imthiyas, M., Almohamedh, H., Alhamed, K.M., Almotairi, S., Gulzar, Y.: Distributed denial of service (ddos) mitigation using blockchain–a comprehensive insight. Symmetry **13**(2), 227 (2021)
12. Wang, J., Wang, L.: Lr-stgcn: Detecting and mitigating low-rate ddos attacks in sdn based on spatial–temporal graph neural network. Computers & Security **154**, 104460 (2025)
13. Bahashwan, A.A., Anbar, M., Manickam, S., Al-Amiedy, T.A., Aladaileh, M.A., Hasbullah, I.H.: A systematic literature review on machine learning and deep learning approaches for detecting ddos attacks in software-defined networking. Sensors **23**(9), 4441 (2023)
14. Ali, T.E., Chong, Y.W., Manickam, S.: Machine learning techniques to detect a ddos attack in sdn: A systematic review. Appl. Sci. **13**(5), 3183 (2023)
15. Rajan, D.M., Aravindhar, D.J.: Detection and mitigation of ddos attack in sdn environment using hybrid cnn-lstm. Migr. Lett **20**, 407–419 (2023)
16. Kumar, D., Pateriya, R., Gupta, R.K., Dehalwar, V., Sharma, A.: Ddos detection using deep learning. Procedia Computer Science **218**, 2420–2429 (2023)
17. Aydın, H., Orman, Z., Aydın, M.A.: A long short-term memory (lstm)-based distributed denial of service (ddos) detection and defense system design in public cloud network environment. Computers & Security **118**, 102725 (2022)
18. Najar, A.A., Naik, S.M.: Cyber-secure sdn: A cnn-based approach for efficient detection and mitigation of ddos attacks. Computers & Security **139**, 103716 (2024)
19. Pan, X., Ge, C., Lu, R., Song, S., Chen, G., Huang, Z., Huang, G.: On the integration of self-attention and convolution. In: Proceedings of the IEEE/CVF conference on computer vision and pattern recognition. pp. 815–825 (2022)
20. Sharafaldin, I., Lashkari, A.H., Hakak, S., Ghorbani, A.A.: Developing realistic distributed denial of service (ddos) attack dataset and taxonomy. In: 2019 international carnahan conference on security technology (ICCST), pp. 1–8. IEEE (2019)
21. Burgess, J.: Modern ddos attacks and defences–survey. arXiv preprint arXiv:2211.15404 (2022)
22. Shabani, M., Tran, D.T., Magris, M., Kanniainen, J., Iosifidis, A.: Multi-head temporal attention-augmented bilinear network for financial time series prediction. In: 2022 30th European Signal Processing Conference (EUSIPCO), pp. 1487–1491. IEEE (2022)
23. Kayode, B.F., Akintola, A.S., Fagbohun, O., Anaesiuba-Bristol, E., Ojumah, O., Odimayo, O., Oloyede, T., Inyang, A., Kazeem, T., Alli, H.: Temporal-spatial attention network (tsan) for dos attack detection in network traffic, (2025). arXiv:2503.16047 arXiv preprint

24. Song, H., Rajan, D., Thiagarajan, J., Spanias, A.: Attend and diagnose: Clinical time series analysis using attention models. In: Proceedings of the AAAI conference on artificial intelligence, vol. 32, (2018)
25. Alghazzawi, D., Bamasag, O., Ullah, H., Asghar, M.Z.: Efficient detection of ddos attacks using a hybrid deep learning model with improved feature selection. Appl. Sci. **11**(24), 11634 (2021)

Optimization of Few-Shot Prompting Examples for Vulnerability Detection in Code

Mahmoud Osama Elsheikh[1(✉)], Hani Ragab Hassen[1], and Michael Lones[2]

[1] Heriot-Watt University, Dubai, UAE
{moe2,h.ragabhassen}@hw.ac.uk
[2] Heriot-Watt University, Edinburgh, Scotland
m.Lones@hw.ac.uk

Abstract. Vulnerability detection in code is an important element of ensuring code security. Recently, a number of studies have considered the role of LLMs in doing this, with the prevailing direction of travel being increasing the amount and complexity of information presented to an LLM in its prompt when asking it to solve a vulnerability detection task. In this study, we consider the opposite approach, finding that a single pair of minimal examples works significantly better than larger numbers of more complex examples, at least within the specific case of detecting memory management vulnerabilities. This suggests that an LLM can be better guided by providing simple hand-crafted examples of vulnerabilities rather than using larger examples extracted from real world code. We also show how the design space of vulnerability detection prompts can be efficiently explored using grammatical evolution.

Keywords: Vulnerability Detection · Prompt Optimization · Grammatical Evolution

1 Introduction

When using deep learning models for vulnerability detection, the problem can be treated as a classification problem. Any given source code function can either be vulnerable or not vulnerable. If it is vulnerable, this means that the function contains a flaw that can be exploited by a malicious actor. A number of different approaches have been used to detect vulnerabilities, and this includes large language models (LLMs).

In order to improve LLM performance on any given task, one of the most important components is the prompt. This contains the instructions the model must follow. It also potentially includes useful examples of correct behaviour [4], something referred to as *in-context learning*. It is difficult to identify the most effective prompt for a particular task, since there are typically a very large number of variations that could be done in the natural language wording of a prompt. As a result, prompt engineering emerged as a way of applying

C. Xu (Ed.): ICMLSC 2026, CCIS 2948, pp. 565–576, 2027.
https://doi.org/10.1007/978-981-92-1546-1_46

certain heuristics to improve the behaviour of prompts [3]. Prompt optimization addresses this problem in a more systematic way, iteratively applying refinements to an initial prompt, and measuring the performance impact each time.

While the entire prompt can be optimized at once, it can also be treated as a set of separate components. One such component is the set of examples of correct behaviour for the required task, which are typically taken from a larger set of existing examples. If no examples are provided, the prompt is known as *Zero-Shot*, whereas applying in-context learning can convert it into a *One-Shot* or *Few-Shot* prompt. From previous research on in-context learning, it has become apparent that both the selection and ordering of examples is important. [20] Hence, the optimiser is required to identify both the subset of examples that are most useful and identify the most effective order to present them in. In this work, we explore the use of grammatical evolution (GE) [17] for performing this task. The advantage of GE over other commonly-used optimisers is that it makes it straightforward to efficiently optimise both the choice and ordering of examples in one process. Our contributions are as follows:

- Using GE to identify good permutations of examples to use in few-shot prompting for vulnerability detection of C code functions.
- Identifying the variance example configurations can have on an LLM's ability to detect vulnerabilities, finding a 10% change purely through example changes.
- Comparing the difference between simplified and complex examples on vulnerability detection performance, and finding that the simpler examples are more useful within this context.

Our code for this paper is available on GitHub.[1]

The paper is organized as follows: Sect. 2 reviews important concepts of language models and their optimization, in addition to previous work done on prompt optimization in vulnerability detection. Section 3 describes our methodology, and Sect. 4 presents results. Section 5 concludes.

2 Background

If a model is to identify whether a vulnerability exists, it must have some understanding of the source code input it is given. Intuitively, source code can be considered a formal language. It is an ordered sequence of various characters known as tokens. This similarity between code and natural languages like English allows researchers to utilize large language models (LLMs).

2.1 Introduction to Large Language Models

Large language models are built upon the transformer architecture. Detailed in [19], the original transformer model aimed to solve sequence to sequence problems by using an *encoder* and a *decoder*. The encoder is responsible for receiving input and projecting it into a latent vector representation. The decoder

[1] https://github.com/Mahmoud-Elsheikh/GE-Prompt-Optimization.

then uses this vector to generate an output sequence. Models like BERT [6] use only the encoder to solve natural language understanding problems, while models like GPT [16] use only a decoder. Initially, decoder-only models could only perform language modeling, generating new tokens that are predicted to follow from the previous input. However, most models are now designed to follow instructions [13]. These instructions, also known as prompts, contain everything a model needs to perform a given task. Such advancements in decoder models have allowed them to outperform encoder-only models even in natural language understanding problems like classification or vulnerability detection, as seen by GPT4 outperforming CodeBERT in [11].

2.2 Optimization of Language Model Prompts

As shown in [4], the introduction of prompts has allowed language models to improve their performance on new problems, as the prompt itself serves as the necessary context. Within the context of vulnerability detection, the simplest form of prompt comprises a given input sample and a task description. However, the prompt can also contain other components. Descriptions can be bolstered by defining a "role" for the language model to assume, such as the role of an expert. Prompts can also include completed examples of the required task. This is known as in-context learning.

The natural language nature of prompts combined with the wide variety of components that can be inserted into it lead to a large number of possibilities. These are further compounded by the sensitivity of the models to ordering, even within a singular component. This can be seen in optimizing examples, where Zhao et al. discuss this prompt sensitivity through the lens of a sentiment analysis task performed on GPT3. [20] They found that the order of the examples could significantly affect accuracy, with runs having a variance of 39% between permutations. Moreover, when measuring the percentage of positive predictions given, the permutations would also affect this. The results show that an even number of positive and negative examples ensures that the model does not skew towards one class or another.

Prompt optimization typically sets out to identify improvements to the prompt by starting with an initial prompt and then attempting to iterate upon it. Each prompt can be evaluated using a set of sample questions with known correct responses, which the LLM's responses are evaluated against to produce a performance metric. This metric value can then be used to guide the search for better prompts. For instance, as seen in [15], the prompt can be improved with a technique that mimics gradient descent. Similar concepts can be seen in [23] where monte carlo search is used.

An alternative to these local search approaches that start from a single prompt is to use a population-based approach, such as a genetic algorithm [10]. This uses an evolving pool of candidate prompts, where the best performing prompts are used to produce new candidates through a process of recombination and mutation. It is also possible to use the LLM itself to perform the mutation and crossover steps [10]. With an initial pool of example candidates to be included in the prompt, the problem of example optimization is well suited to genetic algorithms, as each sample would be a list of examples which can be mutated and evolved through exchanging specific examples in the list with other ones. Specifically, given the ordered nature of the example list, it can be represented as a formal grammar. With a formal grammar, grammatical evolution (GE) can be used. GE operates similarly to genetic algorithms, where an initial population is defined, evaluated, and then modified through mutations and crossover. The difference with GE is that all solutions will conform to a provided grammar, which prevents generation of invalid or inappropriate solutions [8]. By cutting out invalid regions, this also means that the search space can be explore more efficiently.

2.3 LLMs in Vulnerability Detection

In vulnerability detection, prompt engineering has been shown to have a significant benefit. Zhou et al. [21] applied it to GPT3.5 and GPT4 when used to detect vulnerabilities in a dataset of 184 C/C++ functions modified from [14]. Notably, they showed that adding 5 randomly selected and correctly labelled samples from the training set to a baseline prompt containing just the task description and sample to be classified led to an improvement in accuracy of 11.4%. However, they also noted that other additions, like adding the project's name to the prompt, did not yield any change in accuracy.

Lu et al. [11] also explored adding more information to the prompt. This included graph structure data extracted from the input function, such as the abstract syntax tree and control flow graph, which were then converted into a list of nodes and edges. On top of this, they also used in-context learning, but rather than examples being randomly selected as in [21], they identified the most similar functions in the training set at the code level.

Overall, this performed better than their baselines, achieving F1 scores of 43.13%, 65.11% and 35.50% on subsets of the vulnerability datasets Reveal [5], ffmpeg+qemu [22], and Big-Vul [7]. Consistent improvement was also found by just using graph information.

Due to the size and computational cost of exploring optimization search spaces, it is expensive to optimise many components of the prompt at once. Consequently, we focus on a particular component in this study—the formulation of examples used for in-context learning—since although it appears from previous studies that these effect the behaviour of the model, there is little clarity around how the choice, quantity and form of these examples effects performance.

3 Methodology

This study considers the impact of varying the number and complexity of examples when doing in-context learning for vulnerability detection. We focus on the most common vulnerability type in the MegaVul dataset, CWE-119. As mentioned in [12], memory management vulnerabilities made up 59.27% of the total vulnerabilities present. CWE-119 in particular is a vulnerability when a program attempts to read or write to memory at a location outside the specified memory buffer, which can lead to unexpected behaviour and be a vector for attack.

3.1 Prompt Design and Choice of LLM

We use the following prompt:

Base prompt

```
You are now an excellent programmer.
You are conducting a function vulnerability
detection task for C/C++ language.

In the following code snippet, check for potential security
vulnerabilities and output
either 'Vulnerable' or 'Non-vulnerable'.

[Code Sample]
Label:

The following is an example.
Example:
[Example]
Label:
[Example's Label]
```

It consists of a role and task description section, followed by a sentence to guide output formatting towards outputting "vulnerable" or "non-vulnerable" which aids the automatic parsing that is necessary to convert the LLM's text output into a positive or negative classification. The model used was GPT 4o Mini. Locally-deployed open models were initially tested, such as Llama 3.1 [9] and Gemma 2 [18]. However, the performance of the smaller versions of these models was poor, not getting beyond 50% accuracy.

3.2 Dataset

For evaluation, we use a subset of MegaVul [12], a dataset of C functions from open-source repositories on GitHub. The data was constructed by extracting CVEs (common vulnerability and exposure) from the national vulnerability database or NVD [2]. Each CVE represents a specific vulnerability, with details about the vulnerability itself and importantly the commit that contains a fix for the underlying vulnerability mentioned. This commit serves as a "before and after", where the functions extracted from the commit that were changed can all be labeled vulnerable, while all functions extracted after the commit can be considered non-vulnerable.

A useful part of the function metadata contained in this dataset is the associated common weakness enumeration or CWE. While a CVE is more specific to that specific vulnerability, a CWE is a more broad grouping of similar vulnerabilities into a category. Focusing the dataset on a singular vulnerability is necessary to ensure that the example given matches the vulnerability present in the code samples.

Using a large dataset for all validation steps would be computationally expensive, especially within the context of evaluating the fitness function of the GE system. To combat this, a subset of the dataset is used for this purpose. This subset of 1000 samples is split between 500 vulnerable functions and 500 non-vulnerable functions.

3.3 Examples

The example space we use for in-context learning is defined using five function pairs. Each pair comprises a code sample of a function containing a memory vulnerability and a fixed version. The first three functions are adapted from demonstrative examples within the CWE-119 website [1], for example:

CWE-119 Example

```
char * expand_input_by_two(char *user_supplied_string)
{
    int i, dst_index;
    char *dst_buf = (char*)malloc(sizeof(char) * 100);
    if (strlen(user_supplied_string) >= 100)
        perror("Input too long, cannot expand it");
        exit(1);
    for ( i = 0; i < strlen(user_supplied_string); i++ ){
        if( '&' == user_supplied_string[i] ){
            dst_buf[dst_index++] = '1';
            dst_buf[dst_index++] = '2';
        }
        else dst_buf[dst_index++] = user_supplied_string[i];
    }
    return dst_buf;
}
```

These functions are provided by MITRE, the organization behind the CWE website, in order to clarify how the vulnerability works. Additionally, two more example pairs were manually created, such as the following:

Manually Created Example

```
#include <stdio.h>
int main()
{
    char buf[10];
    scanf("%s", buf);
    printf("%s", buf);
    return 0;
}
```

These functions are shorter in length and contain only the bare minimum necessary in order to demonstrate the vulnerability. In total, the example pool contains 10 functions, labeled A-J. A-F are the longer examples while G-J are the shorter ones. At any given point, the examples list section of a prompt can be defined as a list of 0-N examples, where N is the maximum number of examples. To identify how many possible lists exist, for a given size X and total number of examples Y, we can define the example space S as the sum of X permute Y, where Y ranges from 1 to Y:

$$\mathrm{S} = \sum_{Y=1}^{Y} P(X,Y)$$

where $P(X,Y)$ represents the number of ways to permute Y elements out of X, given by:

$$P(X,Y) = \frac{X!}{(X-Y)!}$$

The permutation formula allows us to include every single ordering. If the example pool only contains 2 items, A and B, the ways to arrange them would be AB and BA. However, since the length of the example list can be variable, this is expanded to also include an empty list, A on its own, and B on its own.

If the 10 examples were to be used individually, there would be 9,864,100 different combinations, taking into account order and quantity. It would be infeasible to exhaustively evaluate all of these. As a result, techniques must be used to more efficiently traverse the example space.

3.4 Grammatical Evolution

While it is possible to iterate through the entire example space, it is time-consuming and does not scale well assuming larger and larger numbers of potential examples or combinations. As a result, a non-exhaustive method is required for traversing the example space. The combination of the requirement for a non-exhaustive method and structure of the examples as a list of items led to GE being chosen.

The GE system configuration can be broken down into three components: the parameters for running the evolution, the grammar which defines the structure of all individuals, and the fitness function which evaluates any given individual. It was implemented using PonyGE2, which is a python library for GE [8].

For our use case, since our core variable is the example list, this is defined as our grammar. The grammar is a file written in Backus–Naur form to provide a template that defines the structure of any solution. Below is a simple example that generates individuals which contain one or two items, and any item included can be either "a" or "b" or "c":

Formal Grammar Example

```
<list> ::= <item> |
           <item> <item>
<item> ::= a | b | c
```

The following is the grammar used in our work:

Grammar Used for Experimentation

```
<list> ::= <item> |
           <item> <item> |
           <item> <item> <item> |
           <item> <item> <item> <item> |
           <item> <item> <item> <item> <item> |
<item> ::= <number>
<number> ::= <alpha> | <beta> | <gamma> |
<delta> | <epislon>

<alpha> ::= a b
<beta> ::= c d
<gamma> ::= e f
<delta> ::= g h
<epislon> ::= i j
```

It defines the examples section of any prompt as containing 1–5 pairs. Each pair included can be in any order and there are a total of 5 pairs. This is done as prior literature indicated a tendency for LLMs to prefer an evenly balanced number of functions. This pairwise structure allows for a reduction in the example space.

These lists can be bundled with the prompt template mentioned above in order to create the finalized prompt. This prompt is then evaluated on the dataset, with the resulting accuracy giving a measure of performance. For evolution to work, a sufficiently large population is run for enough generations for changes to take effect. This means that a lot of evaluations will be necessary. If every evaluation is run on the full dataset of 1000 samples, the time and cost would be infeasible. In lieu of this, a rotating subset of 50 samples is used.

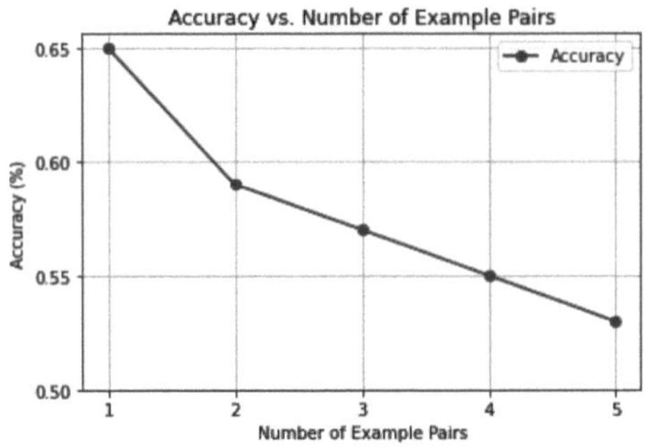

Fig. 1. Average Performance of Example Pairs on Vulnerability Detection.

This aims to expose GE to more of the dataset whilst reducing overfitting to a particular subset.

4 Results

We ran GE with a population of 100 and 15 generations. In order to store the results of the individual combinations of examples, at the end of each run of the fitness function, the results are saved. This has the benefit of allowing us to examine not just the best performing combination, but all other results.

The first experiment is to identify the relationship between accuracy and solution size (number of example pairs). This is done by averaging the results of every sample in the results table, grouping them by example pair count. Figure 1 shows the results. It can be clearly seen that solutions with fewer examples lead to higher accuracy.

Based on the observation that single pairs were most effective, we then systematically evaluated every possible solution containing a single pair of examples. The results are shown in Fig. 2, strongly suggesting that prompts containing the shorter simpler examples (corresponding to higher letters) lead to the most accurate classification of samples in the test set. It also shows that the ordering of examples within a pair (i.e. vulnerable then non-vulnerable, or non-vulnerable then vulnerable) did not have a significant impact on accuracy, at least for the more effective example pairs.

The GH and IJ pairs are the ones that we manually constructed for this study, as opposed to AB, CD, and EF, which were modified from the CWE website. The highest accuracy seen in our experiments was 67%, using examples IJ or JI. This prompt formulation provides a 10% uplift over the zero-shot scenario which had an accuracy of 57%.

This observation is interesting given that the prevailing approach in the existing literature is to use examples that are present in the training dataset as examples [11] [21]. These are typically complex. By comparison, our results suggest that an LLM can be better guided by providing minimal examples that capture the vulnerability and nothing else.

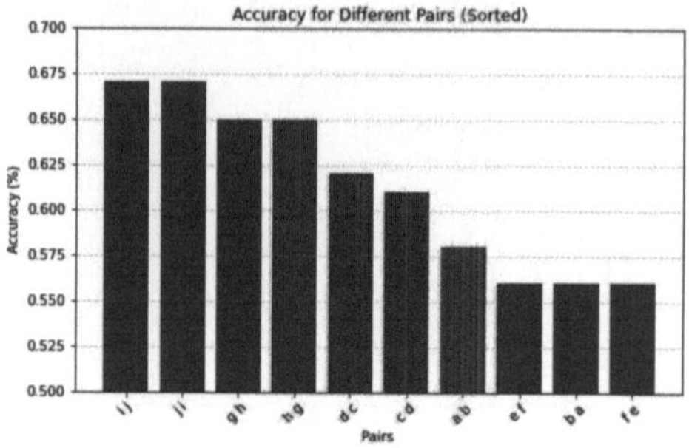

Fig. 2. Performance of Different Example Combinations on Vulnerability Detection.

5 Conclusions

Example selection remains an important part of prompt engineering. We show that, when appropriate examples are used, the resulting prompts can outperform a zero-shot approach when detecting vulnerabilities in code. In particular, we show that simpler examples are more effective than longer examples, suggesting that it is better to hand-design minimal examples of a vulnerability rather than relying on real code examples.

We also show that grammatical evolution can be used to explore the space of examples, and guide us in formulating suitable prompts. Since grammatical evolution allows us to clearly define the solution space using a grammar, it allows this to be done more efficiently that when using other, less constrained, prompt optimization approaches. This is particularly important within an LLM context because exploring a large space of prompts is expensive.

The limitations of this study include the focus on a single vulnerability class, and restricting our investigation to example selection and ordering. In future work, we will broaden our study to a wider range of vulnerabilities, and also apply optimization to other aspects of the prompt. This could include components such as abstract syntax trees and metadata, and their location relative to examples and other prompt components, all of which could potentially be encoded into a grammar.

References

1. Common weakness enumeration. https://cwe.mitre.org/data/definitions/119.html
2. NVD: National vulnerability database. https://nvd.nist.gov
3. Prompt engineering enhance results with prompt engineering strategies. https://platform.openai.com/docs/guides/prompt-engineering/strategy-write-clear-instructions
4. Brown, T.B., Mann, B., Ryder, N., Subbiah, M.: Language models are few-shot learners. In: Proceedings of the 34th International Conference on Neural Information Processing Systems. NIPS '20, Curran Associates Inc, Red Hook, NY, USA (2020)

5. Chakraborty, S., Krishna, R., Ding, Y., Ray, B.: Deep Learning Based Vulnerability Detection: Are We There Yet? IEEE Trans. Software Eng. **48**(09), 3280–3296 (2022)
6. r Devlin, J., Chang, M.W., Lee, K., Toutanova, K.: Bert: pre-training of deep bidirectional transformers for language understanding. In: Proceedings of the 2019 Conference of the North American chapter of the Association for Computational Linguistics: Human Language Technologies, volume 1 (long and short papers), pp. 4171–4186 (2019)
7. Fan, J., Li, Y., Wang, S., Nguyen, T.N.: A c/c++ code vulnerability dataset with code changes and CVE summaries. In: 2020 IEEE/ACM 17th International Conference on Mining Software Repositories (MSR), pp. 508–512 (2020). https://doi.org/10.1145/3379597.3387501
8. Fenton, M., McDermott, J., Fagan, D., Forstenlechner, S., Hemberg, E., O'Neill, M.: Ponyge2: grammatical evolution in python. In: Proceedings of the Genetic and Evolutionary Computation Conference Companion, pp. 1194–1201. GECCO '17, ACM (July 2017). https://doi.org/10.1145/3067695.3082469, http://dx.doi.org/10.1145/3067695.3082469
9. Grattafiori, A., Dubey, A., Jauhri, A., Pandey, A., et al.: The llama 3 herd of models (2024). https://arxiv.org/abs/2407.21783
10. Guo, Q., et al.: Connecting large language models with evolutionary algorithms yields powerful prompt optimizers. In: The Twelfth International Conference on Learning Representations (2024). https://openreview.net/forum?id=ZG3RaNIsO8
11. Lu, G., Ju, X., Chen, X., Pei, W., Cai, Z.: Grace: empowering LLM-based software vulnerability detection with graph structure and in-context learning. J. Syst. Softw. **212**, 112031 (2024)
12. Ni, C., Shen, L., Yang, X., Zhu, Y., Wang, S.: Megavul: A c/c++ vulnerability dataset with comprehensive code representations. In: Proceedings of the 21st International Conference on Mining Software Repositories, pp. 738–742. MSR '24, ACM (Apr 2024). https://doi.org/10.1145/3643991.3644886, http://dx.doi.org/10.1145/3643991.3644886
13. Ouyang, L., Wu, J., Jiang, X., et al.: Training language models to follow instructions with human feedback. In: Koyejo, S., Mohamed, S., Agarwal, A., Belgrave, D., Cho, K., Oh, A. (eds.) Advances in Neural Information Processing Systems, vol. 35, pp. 27730–27744. Curran Associates, Inc. (2022)
14. Pan, S., Bao, L., Xia, X., Lo, D., Li, S.: Fine-grained commit-level vulnerability type prediction by CWE tree structure. In: 2023 IEEE/ACM 45th International Conference on Software Engineering (ICSE), pp. 957–969. IEEE (2023)
15. Pryzant, R., Iter, D., Li, J., Lee, Y.T., Zhu, C., Zeng, M.: Automatic prompt optimization with "gradient descent" and beam search (2023). https://arxiv.org/abs/2305.03495
16. Radford, A., Narasimhan, K., Salimans, T., Sutskever, I.: Improving language understanding by generative pre-training (2018)
17. Ryan, C., Collins, J.J., O'Neill, M.: Grammatical evolution: evolving programs for an arbitrary language. In: Proceedings of the First European Workshop on Genetic Programming, pp. 83–96. EuroGP '98, Springer-Verlag, Berlin, Heidelberg (1998)
18. Team, G., Riviere, M., Pathak, S., Sessa, P.G., Others: Gemma 2: Improving open language models at a practical size (2024). https://arxiv.org/abs/2408.00118
19. Vaswani, A., et al.: Attention is all you need. In: Advances in Neural Information Processing Systems, vol. 30 (2017)

20. Zhao, Z., Wallace, E., Feng, S., Klein, D., Singh, S.: Calibrate before use: improving few-shot performance of language models. In: International Conference on Machine Learning, pp. 12697–12706. (2021) PMLR
21. Zhou, X., Zhang, T., Lo, D.: Large language model for vulnerability detection: emerging results and future directions. In: Proceedings of the 2024 ACM/IEEE 44th International Conference on Software Engineering: New Ideas and Emerging Results, pp. 47–51 (2024)
22. Zhou, Y., Liu, S., Siow, J., Du, X., Liu, Y.: Devign: efective vulnerability identification by learning comprehensive program semantics via graph neural networks. In: Advances in Neural Information Processing Systems, pp. 10197–10207 (2019)
23. Zhou, Y., et al.: Large language models are human-level prompt engineers (2023). https://arxiv.org/abs/2211.01910

Explainable Self-supervised Learning for Smart Contract Vulnerability Detection and Segmentation

Sabbir Ahmed[1(✉)], Mohammad Shahadat Hossain[2], and Latifur Khan[1]

[1] The University of Texas at Dallas, Richardson, TX, USA
{Sabbir.Ahmed2,lkhan}@utdallas.edu
[2] University of Chittagong, Chittagong, Bangladesh
hossain_ms@cu.ac.bd

Abstract. Smart contract vulnerabilities pose critical security risks to blockchain systems, yet existing detection methods face two fundamental challenges: scarcity of labeled data and inability to identify which code segments cause specific vulnerability types. We address both limitations through a unified framework combining self-supervised and semi-supervised learning with explainable classification. Our approach introduces three key contributions: (1) a pretext-based encoder that learns vulnerability-relevant representations from unlabeled contract data, (2) systematic analysis of encoder-classifier combinations under varying label scarcity, and (3) a novel explainability mechanism that integrates SHAP-based encoder attribution with Explainable Boosting Machine (EBM) classifier importance to identify vulnerable opcode segments. On a dataset of 12,515 Ethereum smart contracts spanning eight vulnerability types, our self-supervised framework achieves 93–97% test accuracy using only 5–50% labeled data, while providing interpretable feature attributions that trace predictions to specific control flow patterns.

Keywords: Smart Contract · Vulnerability Detection · Self-Supervised Learning · Explainable AI · Blockchain Security

1 Introduction

Smart contracts autonomously execute transactions on blockchain networks, managing billions of dollars in cryptocurrency assets [20]. However, vulnerabilities in contract code—including reentrancy, integer overflow, and access control flaws—have led to substantial financial losses [1,16]. Detecting these vulnerabilities before deployment is critical, yet fundamentally challenging: contracts encode complex state-dependent logic that static analysis tools often miss, while the diversity of vulnerability patterns defies simple rule-based detection [10].

Machine learning approaches offer a promising alternative, with supervised methods achieving strong detection accuracy when sufficient labeled data is available [13,18,22]. In practice, however, labeled vulnerability datasets remain

C. Xu (Ed.): ICMLSC 2026, CCIS 2948, pp. 577–591, 2027.
https://doi.org/10.1007/978-981-92-1546-1_47

scarce and expensive to construct, requiring expert auditors to manually verify each sample [8,21]. This label scarcity limits the applicability of fully supervised approaches. Meanwhile, deep learning models that do achieve high accuracy typically operate as black boxes [7], providing no insight into which code patterns triggered a vulnerability prediction—information essential for developers seeking to remediate identified issues.

Recent work has explored semi-supervised learning to leverage unlabeled contracts [17,19] and post-hoc explainability for trained detectors [14]. However, no existing approach integrates representation learning from unlabeled data with intrinsically interpretable classification. Self-supervised methods present a natural solution—learning encoders via pretext tasks before fine-tuning on limited labels—yet explaining the combined encoder-classifier pipeline remains an open problem [2,3]. Decomposing explanations into separate encoder and classifier components loses critical information about how learned representations influence final predictions.

We propose a unified framework that addresses both label efficiency and interpretability. Our approach combines self-supervised pretraining with an explainable classification pipeline, enabling end-to-end attribution from input opcodes to vulnerability predictions. The key contributions are:

- A self-supervised and semi-supervised framework for smart contract vulnerability detection effective under extreme label scarcity (5–50% labeled data).
- Systematic comparison of encoder architectures (Base, ANN, CNN) and classifiers (MLP, LGBM, EBM) quantifying their impact on detection performance.
- A novel explainability mechanism combining SHAP encoder attribution with EBM feature importance, enabling identification of vulnerable opcode segments through weighted feature aggregation.

2 Related Work

Supervised Detection. Machine learning approaches to smart contract vulnerability detection have achieved strong results when labeled data is available. ContractWard [22] and SPCBIG-EC [25] employ ensemble classifiers (XGBoost, Random Forest) on hand-crafted features, reporting F1 scores exceeding 96% for reentrancy and timestamp dependency vulnerabilities. SoliAudit [9] combines ML classification with fuzz testing for broader coverage. Deep learning methods extract features automatically: AWD-LSTM [4] and multi-task CNNs [6] leverage sequential and attention-based representations, while hybrid architectures fuse syntactic and semantic features via TextCNN and GNNs [5,23]. These approaches report 90–94% accuracy but require extensively labeled datasets that are costly to obtain in practice.

Semi-supervised Learning. To address label scarcity, recent work explores semi-supervised strategies. BERT-SSL [19] combines active learning with semi-supervised fine-tuning, iteratively selecting uncertain samples for manual labeling. Semi-supervised GANs [17] have been applied to abnormal transaction detection using bio-inspired feature selection. However, existing semi-supervised approaches for smart contracts lack architectural transparency and do not integrate explainability mechanisms.

Explainable Vulnerability Detection. Interpretability in vulnerability detection remains underexplored. MANDO-HGT [14] applies heterogeneous graph transformers to fused control-flow and call graphs, using post-hoc explanation methods to interpret predictions. However, XAI serves only as an analysis tool rather than an integral component of detection. No prior work combines self-supervised representation learning with intrinsically interpretable classification to identify vulnerable code segments.

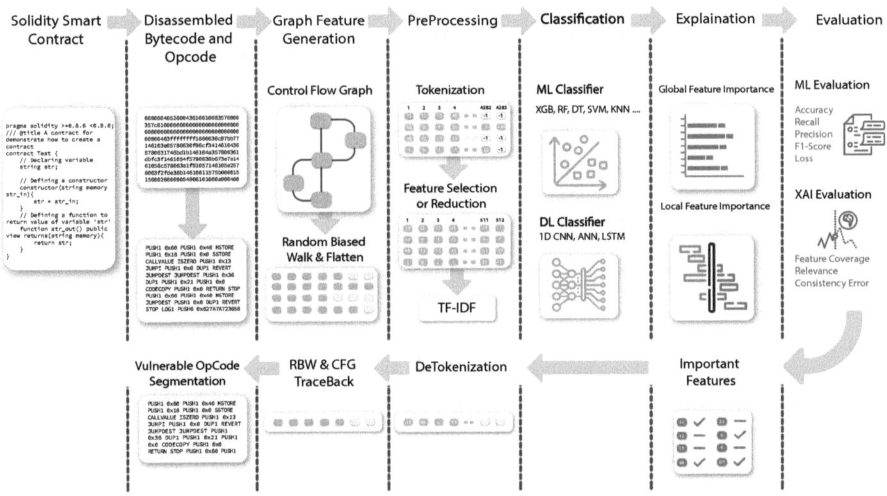

Fig. 1. End-to-end pipeline for smart contract vulnerability detection. Solidity source code undergoes bytecode extraction, CFG generation, and TF-IDF feature engineering. Classification employs both self-supervised (pretext learning with mask prediction) and semi-supervised (joint supervised/unsupervised loss) frameworks. SHAP and EBM provide explainability for vulnerability segmentation.

3 Methodology

Our framework (Fig. 1) comprises three stages: preprocessing, self/semi-supervised classification, and explainable segmentation.

3.1 Data Processing

Smart contracts are transformed into feature vectors through a seven-stage pipeline: (1) bytecode compilation via the Ethereum Virtual Machine,

(2) opcode extraction, (3) Control Flow Graph (CFG) construction by connecting JUMP/JUMPDEST instructions, (4) Random Biased Walk (RBW) traversal to generate diverse input sequences, (5) flattening walks into basic block sequences, (6) tokenization of opcode sequences, and (7) TF-IDF feature selection retaining tokens with highest discriminative power.

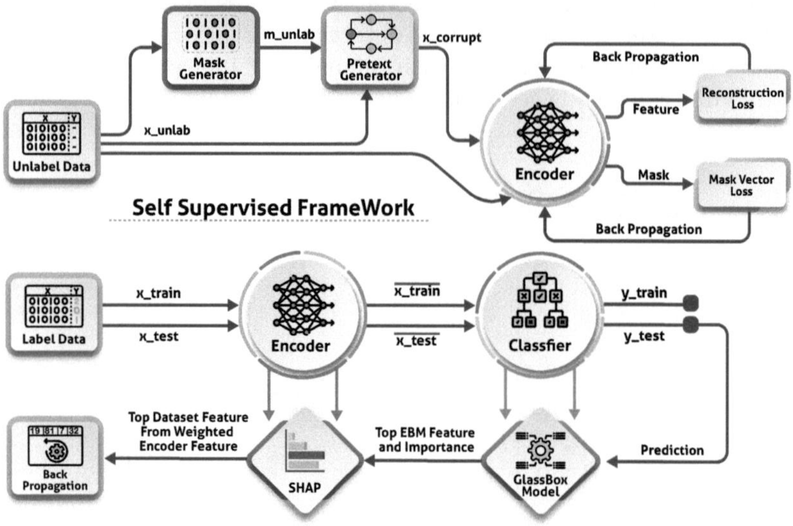

Fig. 2. Self-supervised framework. The mask generator creates binary masks m combined with input x to produce corrupted samples $\tilde{x}$. The encoder learns latent representations by jointly predicting the mask and reconstructing features.

3.2 Self-supervised Classification

We adapt the VIME framework [24] for smart contract vulnerability detection with modified encoders supporting explainability (Fig. 2).

Mask Generation. A binary mask is sampled from a Bernoulli distribution:

$$m_{i,j} \sim \text{Bernoulli}(p_m) \quad \forall i, j \tag{1}$$

where p_m is the corruption probability.

Pretext Task. The pretext generator corrupts input features via column-wise permutation:

$$\begin{aligned} \bar{x}_{:,i} &= x_{\pi(i),i} \\ \tilde{x} &= x \odot (1 - m) + \bar{x} \odot m \\ \tilde{m} &= I(x \neq \tilde{x}) \end{aligned} \tag{2}$$

where $\pi(i)$ denotes a random permutation of column i, $\odot$ is element-wise multiplication, and $I(\cdot)$ is the indicator function.

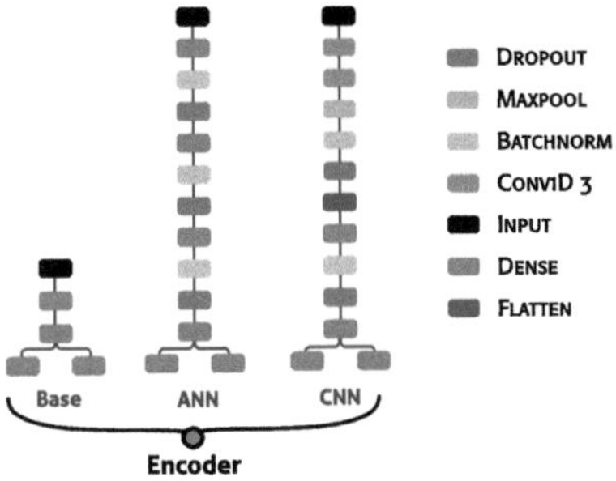

Fig. 3. Encoder architectures: Base VIME (sigmoid only), ANN (dense + batch norm + dropout), and CNN (1D convolution + batch norm + dropout).

Encoder Architectures. We evaluate three encoder designs (Fig. 3): the base VIME encoder with sigmoid activations, an ANN encoder with dense layers, batch normalization, and dropout, and a CNN encoder with 1D convolutions (kernel size 3) followed by batch normalization and dropout. Batch normalization addresses vanishing gradients in sigmoid activations when processing high-magnitude TF-IDF features.

Loss Function. The encoder minimizes a weighted combination of mask prediction and feature reconstruction losses:

$$\mathcal{L}_{\text{self}} = \mathcal{L}_{\text{BCE}}(m, \hat{m}) + \alpha \, \mathcal{L}_{\text{MSLE}}(x, \hat{x}) \tag{3}$$

where $\mathcal{L}_{\text{BCE}}$ is binary cross-entropy for mask prediction:

$$\mathcal{L}_{\text{BCE}}(m, \hat{m}) = -\frac{1}{d}\sum_{i=1}^{d} \left[m_i \log(\hat{m}_i) + (1 - m_i)\log(1 - \hat{m}_i)\right] \tag{4}$$

and $\mathcal{L}_{\text{MSLE}}$ is mean squared logarithmic error for feature reconstruction:

$$\mathcal{L}_{\text{MSLE}}(x, \hat{x}) = \frac{1}{d}\sum_{i=1}^{d} \left(\log(x_i + 1) - \log(\hat{x}_i + 1)\right)^2 \tag{5}$$

with d denoting feature dimensionality and α balancing the two objectives.

Classification. After self-supervised pretraining, the encoder extracts features from labeled data for downstream classification using LGBM, XGBoost, EBM, MLP, or logistic regression.

3.3 Semi-supervised Classification

Unlike self-supervised pretraining which decouples representation learning from classification, semi-supervised learning jointly optimizes both objectives. The encoder processes corrupted unlabeled samples while the classifier trains on labeled pairs, minimizing:

$$\mathcal{L}_{\text{semi}} = \mathcal{L}_{\text{CE}}(y, \hat{y}) + \beta \, \mathcal{L}_{\text{cons}} \tag{6}$$

where $\mathcal{L}_{\text{CE}}$ is categorical cross-entropy on labeled data:

$$\mathcal{L}_{\text{CE}}(y, \hat{y}) = -\frac{1}{N}\sum_{i=1}^{N}\sum_{c=1}^{C} y_i^c \log(\hat{y}_i^c) \tag{7}$$

and $\mathcal{L}_{\text{cons}}$ enforces prediction consistency on augmented unlabeled samples:

$$\mathcal{L}_{\text{cons}} = \frac{1}{|\mathcal{U}|}\sum_{x\in\mathcal{U}} \text{Var}\left(\hat{y}^{(1)}, \ldots, \hat{y}^{(K)}\right) \tag{8}$$

where $\hat{y}^{(k)}$ are predictions on K corrupted versions of unlabeled sample x, and β balances supervised and consistency losses.

3.4 Explainable Classification

Our explainability mechanism combines encoder-level and classifier-level attributions to trace predictions back to input opcodes.

Classifier Explanation. We employ Explainable Boosting Machine (EBM) [15], a glass-box generalized additive model:

$$g(E[y]) = \beta_0 + \sum_{j} f_j(x_j) + \sum_{j<k} f_{jk}(x_j, x_k) \tag{9}$$

where f_j are learned univariate functions and f_{jk} capture pairwise interactions. EBM provides per-feature importance weights W_j for encoded features.

Encoder Explanation. SHAP [12] quantifies each input feature's contribution to encoder outputs via Shapley values:

$$\phi_i = \sum_{S\subseteq F\setminus\{i\}} \frac{|S|!(|F|-|S|-1)!}{|F|!}[f(S\cup\{i\}) - f(S)] \tag{10}$$

where F is the feature set and f is the encoder function.

Combined Attribution. The final importance score for input feature i integrates encoder SHAP values with classifier weights:

$$S_i = \sum_{j=1}^{n_t} \phi_{i\to j} \cdot W_j \tag{11}$$

where $\phi_{i\to j}$ is the SHAP value of input feature i with respect to encoded feature j, and n_t is the number of top-weighted encoded features.

3.5 Vulnerability Segmentation

The combined attribution scores (Eq. 11) identify input features most responsible for vulnerability predictions. Top-scoring features are detokenized to recover basic blocks, then traced back through the CFG via the recorded RBW path to identify vulnerable opcode sequences. This enables localizing specific control flow patterns—such as `JUMP` instructions enabling reentrancy—associated with each vulnerability type.

Table 1. Dataset composition: 12,515 Ethereum smart contracts across eight vulnerability types [11].

Vulnerability Type	Count
Block Number Dependency (BN)	3,518
Unchecked External Call (UC)	3,393
Integer Overflow (OF)	1,770
Reentrancy (RE)	1,218
Strict Equality (SE)	1,098
Timestamp Dependency (TP)	936
Dangerous Delegatecall (DE)	291
Ether Frozen (EF)	291

Table 2. Self-supervised test results (%). Best results in **bold**. Full results including training metrics in Appendix Table 4.

		5% Labeled				50% Labeled			
Enc.	Clf.	Acc	Prec	Rec	F1	Acc	Prec	Rec	F1
Base	MLP	49.7	52.9	49.7	46.2	35.7	38.1	35.7	29.1
	LGBM	76.9	71.4	76.9	72.9	91.0	89.0	87.1	91.0
ANN	LGBM	96.9	97.1	96.9	96.9	**93.8**	94.0	93.8	**93.8**
	EBM	96.8	97.1	96.8	96.9	93.1	93.4	93.1	93.1
CNN	LGBM	**97.1**	97.4	97.1	**97.2**	91.8	79.9	93.8	87.3
	EBM	96.8	97.0	96.8	96.8	90.7	75.6	90.7	85.3

4 Experiments

We evaluate our framework on smart contract vulnerability detection, comparing self-supervised and semi-supervised approaches across varying label ratios. All experiments use accuracy, precision, recall, and F1-score as evaluation metrics.

4.1 Dataset

We use a publicly available dataset [11] comprising 12,515 Ethereum smart contracts with source code (Table 1). Labels were assigned through vulnerability-specific pattern matching and manual verification.

4.2 Self-supervised Results

Table 2 presents self-supervised results for representative label ratios (5% and 50%). ANN and CNN encoders substantially outperform the Base encoder across all configurations, achieving 96–97% test accuracy at 5% labeled data compared to 50–77% for Base. Performance remains stable from 5% through 30%

labeled data. At 50% labeled data, ANN+LGBM maintains 93.8% accuracy while CNN degrades to 91.8%, suggesting the ANN encoder's batch normalization and dropout better prevent overfitting on high-magnitude TF-IDF features. The CNN encoder achieves the highest accuracy (97.1%) at low label ratios but shows precision degradation at 50% labeled data.

Table 3. Semi-supervised test results (%). Full results in Appendix Table 5.

		5% Labeled				50% Labeled			
Enc.	Clf.	Acc	Prec	Rec	F1	Acc	Prec	Rec	F1
Base	ANN	64.9	65.9	64.1	65.0	48.8	42.2	48.9	45.3
	CNN	65.1	64.0	71.7	67.6	69.7	67.5	66.0	66.7
ANN	ANN	77.3	75.3	73.6	74.4	83.3	90.5	76.9	83.1
	CNN	78.4	79.4	77.1	78.3	76.6	87.2	70.4	77.9
CNN	ANN	**91.6**	92.2	89.3	**90.7**	78.7	83.0	74.0	78.2
	CNN	88.4	94.0	82.9	88.1	81.1	84.4	83.9	84.2

4.3 Semi-supervised Results

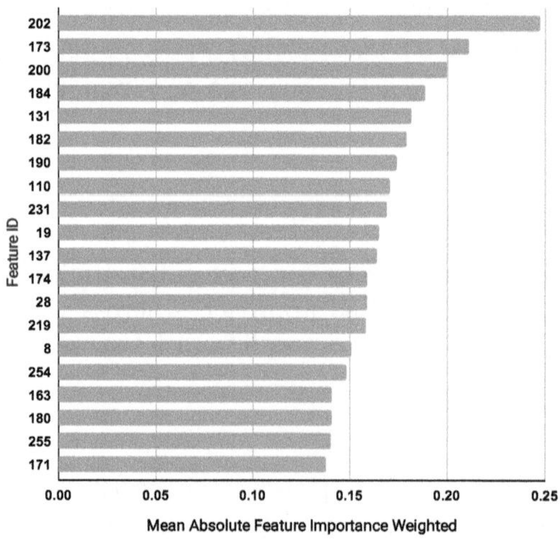

Fig. 4. Global EBM feature importance. Features F_{202}, F_{173}, and F_{200} contribute most to classification (importance > 0.2).

Semi-supervised training (Table 3) shows the CNN encoder with ANN classifier achieving the best results at low label ratios (91.6% at 5%). However, self-supervised pretraining consistently outperforms semi-supervised joint training across all configurations—the best semi-supervised result (91.6%) falls below the worst ANN/CNN self-supervised result (96.8%) at 5% labels. This demonstrates the value of decoupled representation learning: pretraining the encoder on the pretext task before fine-tuning captures more transferable features than joint optimization with consistency regularization.

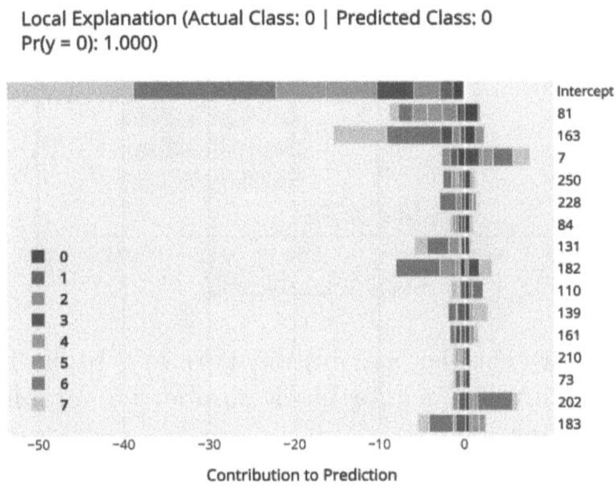

Fig. 5. Local EBM explanation for a block number dependency prediction (confidence 100%). Features F_{81} and F_{163} dominate this classification.

4.4 Explainability Analysis

Figure 4 shows global EBM feature importance across the encoded feature space, with F_{202} (importance 0.247), F_{173} (0.211), and F_{200} (0.200) as the top contributors. For a specific block number dependency prediction (Fig. 5), features F_{81} and F_{163} dominate the local explanation with importance values 0.216 and 0.17 respectively.

Combining EBM classifier weights with encoder SHAP values via Eq. 11 yields end-to-end attribution (Fig. 6). Input feature X_{196} emerges with the highest positive weighted importance (0.052), while X_{92} and X_{19} show strong negative attribution (−0.058 and −0.057), indicating features the model considers irrelevant for block number vulnerabilities.

4.5 Vulnerability Segmentation

Tracing X_{196} through the CFG via the recorded RBW path identifies the vulnerable opcode sequence shown in Appendix Table 6. The segment contains `JUMPDEST` $(0 \times 5B)$, stack manipulation opcodes (`DUP`, `PUSH`, `SWAP`), and arithmetic operations centered around program counter locations 1671–1697.

The presence of control flow instructions (`JUMPDEST` at PC 1671) combined with stack operations that could enable unchecked state modifications indicates

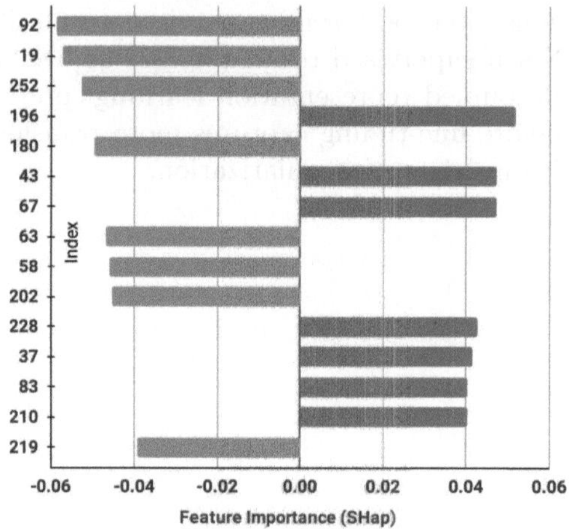

Fig. 6. Combined encoder-classifier attribution (Eq. 11). Input feature X_{196} has the highest positive weighted importance for block number vulnerability detection.

a potential block number dependency vulnerability. Specifically, the pattern of PUSH→DUP→ADD sequences without proper validation may allow attackers to exploit block number checks. This demonstrates how the combined SHAP-EBM attribution traces high-level predictions back to specific opcode patterns, enabling targeted remediation.

5 Conclusion

We presented a unified framework for smart contract vulnerability detection that addresses both label scarcity and interpretability. Our three contributions advance the state of the art: (1) self-supervised and semi-supervised learning frameworks that achieve 93–97% test accuracy using only 5–50% labeled data, substantially outperforming baselines that require full supervision; (2) systematic comparison of encoder-classifier combinations revealing that ANN encoders with batch normalization consistently outperform alternatives, while self-supervised pretraining dominates semi-supervised joint training across all configurations; and (3) a novel explainability mechanism combining SHAP encoder attribution with EBM classifier importance that traces predictions to specific opcode segments, enabling targeted vulnerability remediation. The ability to identify vulnerable control flow patterns, such as JUMP instructions exploitable in reentrancy attacks, directly from model explanations bridges the gap between detection and remediation. Future work will explore the accuracy-interpretability trade-off across encoder architectures, extend the framework to additional vulnerability types beyond the eight studied, and investigate active learning strategies for efficient label acquisition in deployment scenarios.

A Appendix

Table 4. Full self-supervised results including training and test metrics across all label ratios.

			Training				Test			
Enc.	Clf.	%	Acc	Prec	Rec	F1	Acc	Prec	Rec	F1
Base	MLP	5	50.73	53.52	50.73	47.61	49.72	52.87	49.72	46.15
Base	LGBM	5	76.79	78.30	76.79	76.91	76.89	71.41	76.89	72.90
ANN	LGBM	5	97.68	97.83	97.68	97.69	96.89	97.14	96.89	96.90
ANN	EBM	5	97.60	97.75	97.60	97.61	96.84	97.09	96.84	96.85
CNN	LGBM	5	97.68	97.83	97.68	97.69	97.14	97.35	97.14	97.16
CNN	EBM	5	97.63	97.78	97.63	97.64	96.79	97.03	96.79	96.80
Base	MLP	10	47.11	55.38	47.11	46.57	42.73	47.60	42.73	42.35
Base	LGBM	10	77.59	76.35	77.59	75.98	74.93	70.54	74.93	71.95
ANN	LGBM	10	97.59	97.77	97.59	97.61	96.93	97.23	96.93	96.96
ANN	EBM	10	97.59	97.64	97.59	97.60	96.93	97.05	96.93	96.95
CNN	LGBM	10	97.59	97.64	97.59	97.60	96.93	97.05	96.93	96.95
CNN	EBM	10	97.59	97.64	97.59	97.60	96.93	97.05	96.93	96.95
Base	MLP	20	47.05	60.55	47.05	40.85	43.64	57.53	43.64	36.55
Base	LGBM	20	75.77	77.22	75.77	75.88	74.70	71.69	74.97	73.97
ANN	LGBM	20	97.58	97.75	97.58	97.59	96.97	97.19	96.97	96.97
ANN	EBM	20	97.55	97.59	97.55	97.55	96.61	96.71	96.61	96.61
CNN	LGBM	20	97.58	97.75	97.58	97.59	96.97	97.19	96.97	96.97
CNN	EBM	20	97.56	97.60	97.56	97.57	96.79	96.89	96.79	96.79
Base	MLP	30	40.46	50.60	40.46	37.74	35.57	42.15	35.57	31.74
Base	LGBM	30	76.81	78.39	76.81	76.97	76.06	76.38	76.06	76.06
ANN	LGBM	30	97.68	97.83	97.68	97.70	96.33	96.60	96.33	96.35
ANN	EBM	30	97.66	97.80	97.66	97.67	95.84	96.21	95.84	95.87
CNN	LGBM	30	97.68	97.83	97.68	97.70	96.33	96.60	96.33	96.35
CNN	EBM	30	97.68	97.82	97.68	97.70	95.78	96.16	95.78	95.79
Base	MLP	40	42.80	38.08	42.80	34.60	40.19	34.73	40.19	31.63
Base	LGBM	40	77.39	78.82	77.39	77.49	76.20	76.59	76.20	76.23
ANN	LGBM	40	94.42	91.79	94.19	92.75	91.92	87.22	92.49	90.93
ANN	EBM	40	97.74	97.88	97.74	97.75	94.99	95.44	94.99	95.02
CNN	LGBM	40	97.74	97.88	97.74	97.75	95.24	95.51	95.24	95.23
CNN	EBM	40	97.74	97.88	97.74	97.75	95.24	95.43	95.24	95.22
Base	MLP	50	40.50	44.40	40.50	32.81	35.66	38.11	35.66	29.08
Base	LGBM	50	93.67	92.81	93.67	93.27	90.99	89.03	87.10	91.00
ANN	LGBM	50	97.67	97.81	97.67	97.69	93.80	94.04	93.80	93.81
ANN	EBM	50	97.60	97.75	97.60	97.62	93.12	93.38	93.12	93.13
CNN	LGBM	50	95.89	83.31	95.89	85.60	91.78	79.92	93.78	87.25
CNN	EBM	50	95.21	82.68	95.21	84.75	90.68	75.58	90.68	85.27

Table 5. Full semi-supervised results across all label ratios.

Encoder	Classifier	% Labeled	Accuracy	Precision	Recall	F1
Base	ANN	5	64.91	65.91	64.11	64.99
Base	CNN	5	65.11	63.95	71.66	67.59
ANN	ANN	5	77.28	75.26	73.55	74.39
ANN	CNN	5	78.40	79.44	77.12	78.26
CNN	ANN	5	91.58	92.20	89.30	90.73
CNN	CNN	5	88.43	93.99	82.92	88.11
Base	ANN	10	67.93	75.56	67.57	71.35
Base	CNN	10	74.48	73.68	78.80	76.15
ANN	ANN	10	86.09	93.39	85.99	89.54
ANN	CNN	10	84.75	91.25	82.88	86.87
CNN	ANN	10	78.44	79.46	76.71	78.06
CNN	CNN	10	81.22	85.74	86.45	86.09
Base	ANN	20	68.89	80.90	67.68	73.70
Base	CNN	20	70.27	80.38	72.72	76.36
ANN	ANN	20	79.65	81.25	75.03	78.01
ANN	CNN	20	83.37	84.73	87.25	85.97
CNN	ANN	20	84.08	86.50	82.73	84.57
CNN	CNN	20	80.40	83.24	80.28	81.73
Base	ANN	30	65.22	70.73	66.97	68.80
Base	CNN	30	68.24	75.53	72.07	73.76
ANN	ANN	30	79.82	78.87	77.02	77.94
ANN	CNN	30	82.83	86.70	83.75	85.20
CNN	ANN	30	84.13	80.58	86.76	83.56
CNN	CNN	30	75.02	77.83	81.31	79.53
Base	ANN	40	54.22	52.74	62.63	57.26
Base	CNN	40	65.82	96.65	67.98	79.82
ANN	ANN	40	85.79	93.19	85.33	89.09
ANN	CNN	40	80.83	78.31	81.08	79.67
CNN	ANN	40	74.79	76.20	71.76	73.92
CNN	CNN	40	75.13	76.54	74.63	75.57
Base	ANN	50	48.78	42.24	48.86	45.31
Base	CNN	50	69.68	67.50	65.95	66.72
ANN	ANN	50	83.25	90.54	76.86	83.14
ANN	CNN	50	76.58	87.20	70.44	77.93
CNN	ANN	50	78.69	82.97	73.96	78.20
CNN	CNN	50	81.07	84.41	83.92	84.16

Table 6. Vulnerable opcode segment identified for block number dependency. Traced from input feature X_{196} through the CFG.

Opcode	Name	Description	Stack In	Stack Out	Gas	PC
$0 \times 5B$	JUMPDEST	Mark valid jump destination	0	0	1	1671
0×81	DUP2	Duplicate 2nd stack item	2	3	3	1678
0×60	PUSH1	Place 1-byte item on stack	0	1	3	1679
0×01	ADD	Addition operation	2	1	3	1681
0×60	PUSH1	Place 1-byte item on stack	0	1	3	1682
0×82	DUP3	Duplicate 3rd stack item	3	4	3	1684
0×02	MUL	Multiplication operation	2	1	5	1685
0×80	DUP1	Duplicate 1st stack item	1	2	3	1686
0×38	CODESIZE	Get code size	0	1	2	1687
0×83	DUP4	Duplicate 4th stack item	4	5	3	1688
0×39	CODECOPY	Copy code to memory	3	0	3	1689
0×80	DUP1	Duplicate 1st stack item	1	2	3	1690
0×82	DUP3	Duplicate 3rd stack item	3	4	3	1691
0×01	ADD	Addition operation	2	1	3	1692
0×91	SWAP2	Exchange 1st and 3rd items	3	3	3	1693
0×50	POP	Remove stack item	1	0	2	1694
0×50	POP	Remove stack item	1	0	2	1695
0×90	SWAP1	Exchange 1st and 2nd items	2	2	3	1696
0×50	POP	Remove stack item	1	0	2	1697

References

1. Atzei, N., Bartoletti, M., Cimoli, T.: A survey of attacks on Ethereum smart contracts (sok). In: Principles of Security and Trust: 6th International Conference, POST 2017, Held as Part of the European Joint Conferences on Theory and Practice of Software, ETAPS 2017, Uppsala, Sweden, April 22-29, 2017, Proceedings 6, pp. 164–186. Springer (2017)
2. de Bruijn, H., Warnier, M., Janssen, M.: The perils and pitfalls of explainable ai: Strategies for explaining algorithmic decision-making. Gov. Inf. Q. **39**(2), 101666 (2022)
3. Gerlings, J., Shollo, A., Constantiou, I.: Reviewing the need for explainable artificial intelligence (xai), (2020). arXiv:2012.01007 arXiv preprint
4. Gogineni, A.K., Swayamjyoti, S., Sahoo, D., Sahu, K.K., Kishore, R.: Multi-class classification of vulnerabilities in smart contracts using AWD-LSTM, with pre-trained encoder inspired from natural language processing. IOP SciNotes **1**(3), 035002 (2020)
5. Han, D., Li, Q., Zhang, L., Xu, T.: A smart contract vulnerability detection model based on syntactic and semantic fusion learning. Wirel. Commun. Mob. Comput. 2023 (2023)
6. Huang, J., Zhou, K., Xiong, A., Li, D.: Smart contract vulnerability detection model based on multi-task learning. Sensors **22**(5), 1829 (2022)

7. Khetani, V., Gandhi, Y., Bhattacharya, S., Ajani, S.N., Limkar, S.: Cross-domain analysis of ml and dl: Evaluating their impact in diverse domains. Int. J. Intell. Syst. Appl. Eng. **11**(7s), 253–262 (2023)
8. Kushwaha, S.S., Joshi, S., Singh, D., Kaur, M., Lee, H.N.: Systematic review of security vulnerabilities in Ethereum blockchain smart contract. IEEE Access **10**, 6605–6621 (2022)
9. Liao, J.W., Tsai, T.T., He, C.K., Tien, C.W.: Soliaudit: smart contract vulnerability assessment based on machine learning and fuzz testing. In: 2019 Sixth International Conference on Internet of Things: Systems, Management and Security (IOTSMS), pp. 458–465 (2019). https://doi.org/10.1109/IOTSMS48152.2019.8939256
10. Lin, I.C., Liao, T.C.: A survey of blockchain security issues and challenges. Int. J. Netw. Secur. **19**(5), 653–659 (2017)
11. Liu, Z., et al.: Rethinking smart contract fuzzing: fuzzing with invocation ordering and important branch revisiting. IEEE Trans. Inf. Forensics Secur. **18**, 244–257 (2023)
12. Lundberg, S.M., Lee, S.I.: A unified approach to interpreting model predictions. In: Advances in Neural Information Processing Systems, vol. 30, pp. 4765–4774. Curran Associates, Inc (2017)
13. Lutz, O., et al: Escort: Ethereum smart contracts vulnerability detection using deep neural network and transfer learning (2021). arXiv:2103.12607 arXiv preprint
14. Nguyen, H.H., et al.: Mando-HGT: Heterogeneous Graph Transformers for Smart Contract Vulnerability Detection. Proc, ACM MSR (2023)
15. Nori, H., Jenkins, S., Koch, P., Caruana, R.: Interpretml: A unified framework for model interpretability (2019). arXiv:1909.09223 arXiv preprint
16. Qian, P., Liu, Z., He, Q., Huang, B., Tian, D., Wang, X.: Smart contract vulnerability detection technique: a survey (2022). arXiv:2209.05872 arXiv preprint
17. Sanjalawe, Y.K., Al-E'mari, S.R.: Abnormal transactions detection in the Ethereum network using semi-supervised generative adversarial networks. IEEE Access (2023)
18. Song, J., He, H., Lv, Z., Su, C., Xu, G., Wang, W.: An efficient vulnerability detection model for Ethereum smart contracts. In: Liu, J.K., Huang, X. (eds.) NSS 2019. LNCS, vol. 11928, pp. 433–442. Springer, Cham (2019). https://doi.org/10.1007/978-3-030-36938-5_26
19. Sun, X., Tu, L., Zhang, J., Cai, J., Li, B., Wang, Y.: Assbert: active and semi-supervised BERT for smart contract vulnerability detection. J. Inform. Secur. Appl. **73**, 103423 (2023)
20. Szabo, N.: Smart contracts: building blocks for digital markets. EXTROPY: J. Transhumanist Thought (16) **18**(2), 28 (1996)
21. Tsankov, P., Dan, A., Drachsler-Cohen, D., Gervais, A., Buenzli, F., Vechev, M.: Securify: Practical security analysis of smart contracts. In: Proceedings of the 2018 ACM SIGSAC Conference on Computer and Communications Security, pp. 67–82 (2018)
22. Wang, W., Song, J., Xu, G., Li, Y., Wang, H., Su, C.: Contractward: automated vulnerability detection models for Ethereum smart contracts. IEEE Trans. Network Sci. Eng. **8**(2), 1133–1144 (2020). https://api.semanticscholar.org/CorpusID:211146806
23. Xu, Z., et al.: W2v-SA: A deep neural network-based approach to smart contract vulnerability detection (2023)

24. Yoon, J., Zhang, Y., Jordon, J., van der Schaar, M.: Vime: Extending the success of self- and semi-supervised learning to tabular domain. In: Advances in Neural Information Processing Systems, vol. 33, pp. 11033–11043 (2020)
25. Zhang, L., et al.: SPCBIG-EC: a robust serial hybrid model for smart contract vulnerability detection. Sensors **22**(12), 4621 (2022)

Design of Intelligent Systems and Robust Control Methods

Dual-Attention Temporal Tracking Network for Proactive SSD Failure Prediction

Chao Jiang(✉), Zixiang Yang, and Dan He

School of Information Engineering, Nanchang Hangkong University, Nanchang 330063, JiangXi, China
rrrhuk@qq.com

Abstract. Solid-state drives (SSDs) have become the primary storage medium in modern data centers due to their high performance and energy efficiency. However, large-scale deployments inevitably suffer from device failures caused by NAND flash wear-out, controller faults, and other degradation mechanisms, posing serious risks to data reliability and service availability. Proactive SSD failure prediction based on SMART monitoring data is therefore essential for enhancing storage system resilience. Nevertheless, real-world SMART data are characterized by high dimensionality, substantial noise, long-term temporal dependencies, and severe class imbalance, which significantly limit the effectiveness of existing prediction models.

To address these challenges, this paper proposes a deep learning–based proactive failure prediction model, termed the Dual-Attention Temporal Tracking Network (DATTN). Built upon an Autoencoder–Temporal Convolutional Network (AE-TCN) architecture, DATTN employs an undercomplete autoencoder to denoise and compress heterogeneous SMART data, while dilated causal convolutions are used to capture long-term degradation patterns throughout the SSD lifecycle. Furthermore, feature attention and temporal attention mechanisms are jointly incorporated to adaptively emphasize failure-relevant SMART attributes and critical time points preceding failures, thereby overcoming the limitations of uniform weighting in conventional temporal models.

Extensive experiments are conducted on three real-world enterprise SSD datasets—PM1733, PM9A3, and MB1 Alibaba. The results demonstrate that DATTN consistently outperforms Random Forest, LSTM, MVTRF, and the AE-TCN baseline, achieving significantly higher recall while maintaining high precision. In particular, on the PM1733 dataset, DATTN improves the F0.5-score by approximately 9.0% and recall by 28.3% compared with AE-TCN. These results indicate that DATTN provides a robust and effective solution for proactive SSD failure prediction, enabling data centers to transition from reactive fault tolerance to intelligent failure prevention.

Keywords: SSD Failure Prediction · Attention Mechanism · Temporal Convolutional Network

C. Xu (Ed.): ICMLSC 2026, CCIS 2948, pp. 595–608, 2027.
https://doi.org/10.1007/978-981-92-1546-1_48

1 Introduction

With the rapid growth of global data volumes, data centers have become critical infrastructure for the digital economy. Solid-state drives (SSDs), due to their high performance and energy efficiency, have largely replaced HDD in modern data centers. However, SSD still suffer from physical degradation such as NAND wear-out and controller failures, and large-scale deployments inevitably experience a non-negligible number of device failures [14]. Sudden SSD failures may lead to service disruption and irreversible data loss, posing serious challenges to data center reliability.

Current data centers mainly rely on passive fault-tolerance mechanisms, such as RAID and data replication, which are reactive in nature. In contrast, proactively predicting SSD failures using SMART monitoring data and migrating data in advance has become an important approach to improving storage system resilience [18, 21].

Although machine learning and deep learning methods have been widely explored for SSD failure prediction, real-world SMART data remain highly noisy, high-dimensional, and severely imbalanced, making accurate degradation modeling difficult [15, 16]. To address these challenges, our previous work proposed an AE-TCN model, which combines autoencoder-based denoising with temporal convolutional networks to capture long-term degradation patterns [9].

However, the AE-TCN model treats all features and time steps uniformly, ignoring the fact that different SMART attributes and key temporal moments contribute unequally to failure evolution. Important short-term anomalies and critical degradation indicators can therefore be diluted by irrelevant information.

To overcome this limitation, this paper proposes DATTN, a dual-attention temporal tracking network built upon the AE-TCN framework. By introducing feature attention and temporal attention mechanisms, DATTN adaptively emphasizes failure-relevant attributes and key time points preceding failures. Experiments on real-world datasets demonstrate that DATTN significantly improves failure recall while maintaining high precision, providing an effective and reliable solution for proactive SSD failure prediction in data center environments.

2 Related Work

Research on SSD failure prediction has evolved from simple rule-based monitoring to complex modeling approaches based on machine learning and deep learning. Early studies mainly relied on statistical features of SMART attributes and employed traditional machine learning algorithms such as Support Vector Machines (SVM) [1], Random Forests (RF), and Gradient Boosting Decision Trees (GBDT) for binary classification [12, 17]. However, in real-world data center environments, failure samples are often extremely scarce, leading to severe class imbalance in training data [11]. To alleviate this issue, some studies introduced SMOTE oversampling or data augmentation strategies based on Generative Adversarial Networks (GAN) [2], attempting to balance class distributions by generating synthetic failure samples and thereby improving the classifier's sensitivity to minority classes [3]. Nevertheless, traditional methods typically overlook the long-term temporal dependencies of SSD performance degradation and rely heavily on manual feature engineering, making them difficult to adapt to the complex, high-dimensional data generated by heterogeneous devices [19, 20].

With breakthroughs in deep learning for temporal modeling, research focus has gradually shifted toward end-to-end models capable of automatically extracting spatiotemporal features. To address the high-dimensional and multimodal characteristics of SMART data, the TCAN model innovatively combines LSTM and Transformer architectures [5]. Through a feature grouping strategy, attributes are divided into monotonically changing and randomly fluctuating categories, and a cross-attention mechanism is used to capture coupling relationships among different attributes, effectively improving prediction accuracy in complex monitoring environments. In the field of unsupervised learning, hybrid models based on GAN and LSTM learn the distribution of healthy samples to detect deviations, enabling anomaly detection without failure labels [6]. This approach demonstrated strong performance in experiments conducted in Google data centers and is particularly suitable for cold-start scenarios where failure samples are difficult to obtain [22]. In addition, the MVTRF model represents a new direction in multi-view fusion research: it extracts short-term raw features, long-term distributional features, and sequential correlation features from telemetry logs, adopts a multi-task learning framework to jointly predict failure time, failure type, and remaining useful life, and enhances model interpretability through a similar-decision extraction algorithm [4].

To address the challenge of cross-device and cross-model prediction, transfer learning and domain adaptation techniques have become recent research hotspots. Due to significant differences in SMART definitions and scales across SSD vendors, models trained on specific device models often struggle to generalize directly [13]. To this end, some researchers proposed a unified Transformer-based prediction framework for HDD and SSD, achieving knowledge transfer from hard disk drives to solid-state drives through a Balanced MSE loss function and feature alignment techniques [7]. For the problem of insufficient labeled data for new SSD models, the MALDAN model introduces an adversarial learning–based domain adaptation solution [8]. This model consists of two branches—feature extraction and domain alignment—and leverages multi-instance learning combined with an attention mechanism to emphasize key time-slice features. Through adversarial training, it narrows the feature distribution gap between source and target domains, effectively mitigating performance degradation caused by cross-domain data distribution shifts.

3 Design and Implementation

As shown in Fig. 1, the proposed DATTN model adopts an end-to-end architecture consisting of an input layer, an Auto-Encoder (AE), a dual-attention layer, a Temporal Convolutional Network (TCN), and an output layer. Multivariate SMART features are organized into fixed-length time windows and fed into the model as sequential inputs.

The AE module serves as a front-end feature extractor, where Gaussian noise is injected during training to improve robustness. Through nonlinear encoding and reconstruction, the AE compresses high-dimensional SMART data into compact latent representations while suppressing noise and redundancy.

The latent sequences are then enhanced by a dual-attention layer, including feature attention and temporal attention. Feature attention assigns adaptive weights to different latent dimensions to highlight failure-related indicators, while temporal attention emphasizes critical time steps preceding failures. This design enables the model to focus on both key attributes and key moments in SSD degradation.

The attention-enhanced sequences are subsequently processed by a TCN with dilated causal convolutions to capture long-term temporal dependencies efficiently. Finally, a fully connected layer maps the extracted temporal features to the output layer, which predicts the SSD state as failure or healthy..

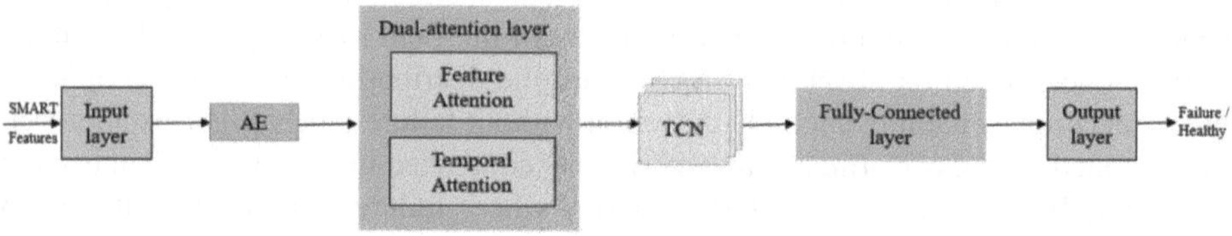

Fig. 1. Schematic diagram of the DATTN model architecture

3.1 Data Preprocessing

Due to significant differences in the definitions and scales of SMART attributes across different vendors, directly feeding raw data into the model can lead to convergence difficulties [10]. Moreover, the SSD failure process exhibits strong nonlinear characteristics, and simple linear normalization methods (e.g., Min–Max normalization) tend to compress value differences in high-risk regions, thereby weakening the model's sensitivity to early-stage failures. To address these issues, this paper adopts an attribute normalization method based on sample distribution probabilities, which is similar to the approach used in our previous work.

First, a unified space is defined as $Z^j = \{z_1 \geq 0, z_2, \ldots, z_n \leq 1\}$, where z_i denotes the normalized value of attribute j, and each z_i follows the ratio between healthy samples and failure samples. Assume that for SSD from a given vendor k, the value space of the j-th attribute over the device lifecycle is $X^{(j,k)} = \{x_1 \geq 0, x_2, \ldots, x_m\}$, where x_i represents the value of this attribute at the i-th time point during the device's lifecycle. Let $f^k(x_i)$ denote the proportion of failed devices when the attribute value equals x_i, and $h^k(x_i)$ denote the proportion of healthy devices under the same condition. By computing the cumulative distribution of $f^k(x_i)$, the probability that a device fails when the attribute value does not exceed x_i can be obtained as:

$$F_i^k = F(x \leq x_i) = \int_{x_1}^{x_i} f^k(x)dx \tag{1}$$

Similarly, the cumulative probability for the opposite case can be derived, that is, the probability that a device remains healthy when the attribute value exceeds x_i is given by:

$$H_i^k = H(x \geq x_i) = \int_{x_i}^{x_m} h^k(x)dx \tag{2}$$

Finally, the attribute normalization formula is obtained as:

$$z_i = \frac{F_i^k}{F_i^k + \eta^k H_i^k} \tag{3}$$

where the coefficient η^k is proportional to the ratio of failed devices to healthy devices for the specific vendor k.

3.2 Auto-Encoder Module

Although the normalized time-series data still contain substantial noise from sensor fluctuations and transient workloads, an undercomplete autoencoder is introduced as a front-end feature extractor to learn robust degradation representations. By mapping high-dimensional inputs into compact latent vectors through nonlinear encoding and reconstruction, the autoencoder effectively suppresses redundant information and high-frequency noise while preserving essential SSD health evolution patterns. The resulting latent features exhibit a higher signal-to-noise ratio and provide a cleaner, more compact input for subsequent temporal modeling. The architecture of the Auto-Encoder are shown in Fig. 2.

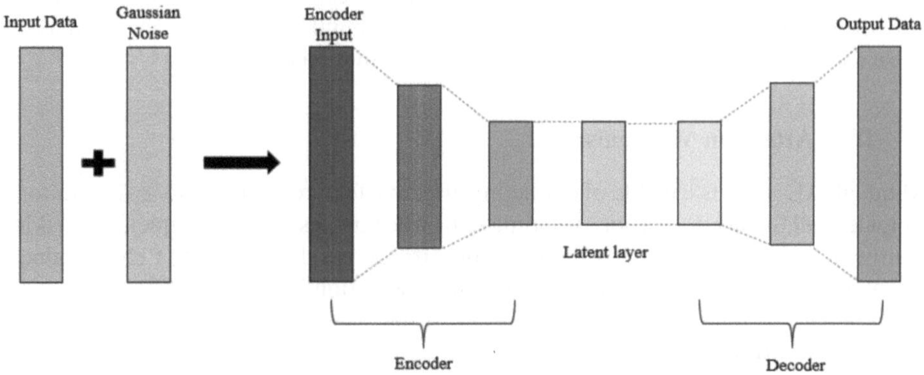

Fig. 2. Schematic diagram of the Auto-Encoder architecture

Assume that the original data are $X \in \mathbb{R}^{T \times F}$. The objective of the encoder is to compress the original data into a low-dimensional latent space $Z \in \mathbb{R}^{T \times d}$, where T denotes the number of time steps, F denotes the number of input features, and d is the dimensionality of the latent features. During training, the input received by the model is given by:

$$\tilde{X} = X + \beta \cdot \epsilon \tag{4}$$

where ϵ denotes Gaussian noise and $\epsilon \sim \mathcal{N}(0, \sigma^2)$, and β is the noise intensity coefficient. This strategy enables the model to learn feature representations more effectively and provides strong robustness against anomalous samples and sensor false alarms. The transformation process of the encoder can be formally expressed as:

$$Z = f_e(W_e X + b_e) \tag{5}$$

where $f_e(\cdot)$ denotes the activation function of the encoder, and W_e and b_e represent the weight matrix and bias vector of the encoder, respectively. Subsequently, the decoder is responsible for reconstructing an output that is as consistent as possible with the input data distribution from the latent representation.

$$\widehat{X} = f_d(W_d Z + b_d) \tag{6}$$

where $f_d(\cdot)$ denotes the activation function of the decoder, and W_d and b_d represent the weight matrix and bias vector of the decoder, respectively. The objective of model training is to minimize the reconstruction error between the input and the output, and the following loss function is adopted:

$$L_{AE} = \frac{1}{n}\sum_{t=1}^{n} \ell\left(X_t - \widehat{X}_t\right)\lambda(\|W_e\|_F^2 + \|W_d\|_F^2) \tag{7}$$

When the loss converges to a small value, it indicates that the encoder is able to effectively extract the most representative features from the input data, while irrelevant noise and redundant components are automatically filtered out.

3.3 Dual Attention Mechanism

Although AE-TCN is capable of extracting effective features, it tends to assign uniform weights to all feature dimensions and time steps when processing long sequences, making it difficult to focus on critical fault precursors. To address this issue, DATTN introduces a dual attention module after the AE latent representation layer.

Feature Attention

Failures in SSD are often dominated by a small number of critical indicators, and the importance of different indicators varies dynamically across different aging stages. The feature attention mechanism employs a learnable weighting network to compute an importance score for each feature dimension based on the current input state, which is then normalized into probabilistic weights via the Softmax function. By performing element-wise multiplication between these weights and the latent features, the model can adaptively enhance feature representations that are strongly correlated with faults while suppressing interference from irrelevant dimensions. The computation process is shown in Fig. 3.

The first step in constructing the DATTN model is to obtain the reconstructed latent sequence representation from the autoencoder. Let the compressed features obtained through the autoencoder be denoted as

$$H = \{h_1, h_2, h_3, \cdots, h_T\}, h_t \in R^d \tag{8}$$

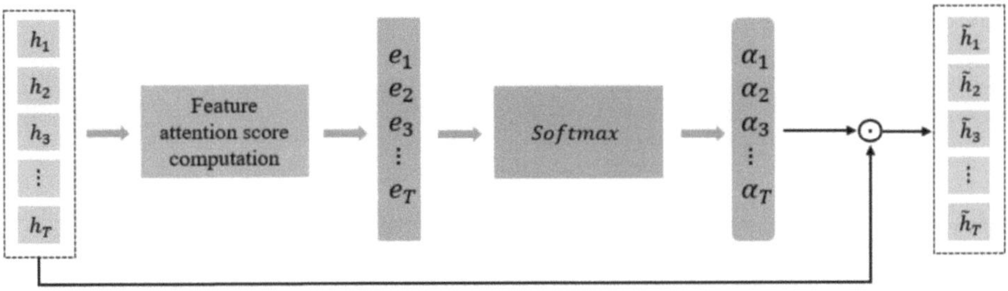

Fig. 3. Feature attention computation

where T denotes the length of the time window, and d represents the dimensionality of the latent features. The importance of each encoded feature dimension varies across different time steps; therefore, it is necessary to further learn adaptive weights for feature dimensions through a feature attention mechanism. To this end, a feature-importance scoring vector is first constructed for each time step. Let the linear transformation be defined as

$$e_t = W_f h_t + b_f \tag{9}$$

where $W_f \in \mathbb{R}^{d\times d}$ and $b_f \in \mathbb{R}^d$ are trainable parameters. To endow the feature importance with a probabilistic interpretation, a Softmax mapping is applied at each time step:

$$a_{t,i} = \frac{exp(e_{t,i})}{\sum_{j=1}^{d} exp(e_{t,i})} \tag{10}$$

where $a_{t,i}$ denotes the attention weight of the i-th feature at time step t. The feature-weighted representation is then given by:

$$\tilde{h}_t = a_t \odot h_t \tag{11}$$

where $\odot$ denotes element-wise multiplication.

Temporal Attention

The feature-enhanced sequence is further fed into the temporal attention module, which analyzes the temporal evolution characteristics of the sequence to identify key time steps that contribute most significantly to the prediction outcome by assigning higher weights to these critical time steps. The computation process is shown in Fig. 4.

The core idea of the temporal attention mechanism is to assign different weights to different historical time steps in the sequence according to the strength of feature representations at each time step. To this end, a temporal scoring function is first defined as

$$s_t = v^T \tanh\left(W_t \tilde{h}_t + b_t\right) \tag{12}$$

where $W_t \in \mathbb{R}^{d\times d}$, $b_t \in \mathbb{R}^d$, and $v \in \mathbb{R}^d$ are trainable parameters. Subsequently, the temporal attention weights are obtained through the Softmax function:

$$\beta_t = \frac{exp(s_t)}{\sum_{k=1}^{T} exp(s_k)} \tag{13}$$

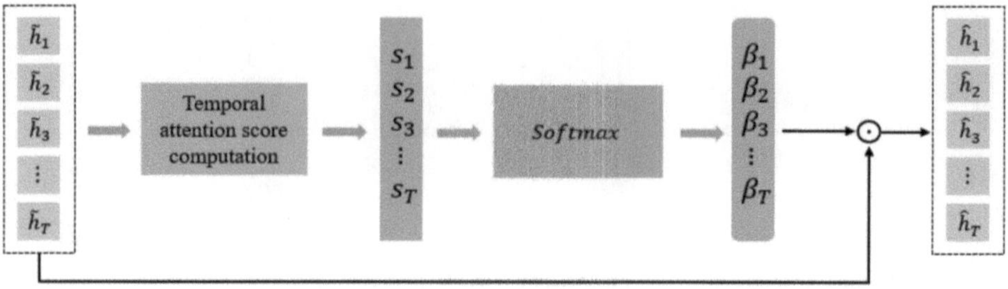

Fig. 4. Temporal attention computation

Finally, the sequence weighted along the temporal dimension is given by:

$$\hat{h}_t = \beta_t \tilde{h}_t \tag{14}$$

At this point, each time step in the sequence is reassigned a distributed weight based on its importance. When a critical attribute of the SSD undergoes a significant change in the days leading up to failure, the β_t of that time step will increase significantly, allowing the model to capture the failure precursor earlier and more accurately.

3.4 Temporal Modeling Module

After dual-attention enhancement, the sequence $\hat{h}_t$ is fed into the TCN module for temporal dependency modeling. The core operation of TCN is dilated causal convolution, which can be expressed as:

$$y_t = \sum_{k=0}^{K-1} W_k \hat{h}_{t-dk} \tag{15}$$

where K denotes the convolution kernel size and d denotes the dilation factor. After mapping the final output of the TCN to the probability space through global pooling and a linear transformation, the fault probability p of the SSD within a future time window is obtained, and the classification task is optimized using a weighted cross-entropy loss function. To ensure effective end-to-end training of the model, the AE module, the dual-attention module, and the TCN module share the same parameter update path, and the overall loss is given by:

$$L = L_{AE} + \lambda L_{cls} \tag{16}$$

where L_{AE} denotes the reconstruction loss, L_{cls} denotes the weighted classification loss, and λ is the balancing coefficient between the two. Through joint optimization, the AE is able to learn more robust latent structures, the attention module can capture more reasonable spatio-temporal distributions, and the TCN performs long-term dependency modeling on sequences enhanced with multi-scale semantic information.

4 Evaluation

4.1 Data Set

To verify the effectiveness and generalization capability of the proposed DATTN model in real data center environments, experiments are conducted on three representative enterprise-level SSD datasets: PM1733, PM9A3, and MB1 Alibaba. These datasets are collected from SMART logs in large-scale production environments and cover different manufacturers, storage capacities, and workload types, exhibiting a high degree of heterogeneity. Among them, the PM1733 and PM9A3 datasets reveal degradation characteristics of specific models after long-term operation, while the MB1 Alibaba dataset provides more complex mixed-workload scenarios.

To accommodate the input requirements of time-series prediction models, the original logs are processed using a sliding window approach to generate time-window samples containing historical state sequences. The training and testing sets are strictly split along the time axis to prevent future information leakage, thereby ensuring the objectivity and fairness of the experimental evaluation.

4.2 Evaluation Metrics

In this section, faulty SSD are treated as positive samples, while healthy SSD are treated as negative samples. Before presenting the formulas, it is important to define the terms used in them:

TN(True Negative): the number of truly faulty SSD that are predicted as healthy SSD.
TP(True Positive): the number of truly faulty SSD that are predicted as faulty SSD.
FP(False Positive): the number of truly healthy SSD that are predicted as faulty SSD.
FN(False Negative): the number of truly healthy SSD that are predicted as healthy SSD.

Next, each evaluation metric is introduced in detail. *1)The fault detection rate (Recall):* Recall measures the model's ability to successfully identify faulty samples, and is calculated as the number of true positives divided by the total number of actual faulty samples. In data center operation and maintenance scenarios, this metric is directly related to data security: a higher fault detection rate means that very few faulty drives are missed, thereby effectively reducing the risk of data loss.

$$Recall = \frac{TP}{TP+FN} \tag{17}$$

2) Precision: Precision reflects the proportion of truly faulty samples among all samples predicted as faulty by the model, and is calculated as the number of true positives divided by the total number of samples predicted as positive. A high precision indicates that each alarm raised by the model has high credibility, thereby reducing unnecessary and ineffective troubleshooting efforts.

$$Precision = \frac{TP}{TP+FP} \tag{18}$$

3) F0.5-Score: To jointly consider the model's precision and recall, the experiments also adopt the F0.5-score as a comprehensive evaluation metric. It is the harmonic mean of precision and recall, with a higher weight assigned to precision, thereby avoiding excessive false alarms in practical SSD fault prediction and providing a more comprehensive assessment of the model's ability to balance fault detection and false-positive control.

$$F0.5 - Score = \frac{(1+0.5^2)\times Precision\times Recall}{0.5^2\times Precision+Recall} \tag{19}$$

4) AUC: The experiments also focus on the area under the ROC curve (AUC). An AUC value closer to 1 indicates stronger robustness and overall classification capability of the model across different classification thresholds.

4.3 Experimental Results Analysis

Performance Evaluation

To comprehensively evaluate the performance of the DATTN model, the experiments conduct a systematic comparison with Random Forest (RF), Long Short-Term Memory (LSTM), Multi-View Tree-based Random Forest (MVTRF), and the baseline model AE-TCN.

Table 1. Comparison of model performance across datasets

Data Set	Model	Precision	Recall	F0.5-Score	AUC
PM1733	RF	0.56	0.30	0.48	0.68
	LSTM	0.37	0.40	0.38	0.58
	MVTRF	0.88	0.41	0.72	0.80
	AE-TCN	0.89	0.53	0.78	0.80
	DATTN	0.91	0.68	0.85	0.81
PM9A3	RF	0.76	0.35	0.62	0.76
	LSTM	0.50	0.25	0.42	0.60
	MVTRF	0.72	0.43	0.63	0.84
	AE-TCN	0.69	0.45	0.62	0.80
	DATTN	0.73	0.62	0.71	0.88
MB1 Alibaba	RF	0.55	0.35	0.49	0.85
	LSTM	0.65	0.63	0.65	0.88
	MVTRF	0.88	0.77	0.86	0.86
	AE-TCN	0.90	0.78	0.87	0.88
	DATTN	0.92	0.83	0.90	0.90

The experimental results of the Table 1 show that DATTN demonstrates significant performance advantages across all three datasets. Taking the PM1733 dataset, where fault characteristics are relatively subtle, as an example, traditional machine learning models such as RF and LSTM struggle to capture long-term temporal dependencies, resulting in F0.5-Scores ranging only from 0.48 to 0.38, along with low recall. Although the MVTRF model improves overall performance through multi-view feature fusion, its recall remains insufficient. In contrast, the AE-TCN model, which incorporates autoencoder-based denoising and a TCN architecture, boosts the F0.5-score to 0.78, validating the effectiveness of deep temporal modeling.

Building on this foundation, the DATTN model further achieves a second leap in performance by integrating a dual-attention mechanism. On the PM1733 dataset, DATTN attains a precision of 0.91, a recall of 0.68, and an F0.5-score of 0.85. Compared with the baseline AE-TCN, DATTN maintains extremely high precision while increasing recall by approximately 28.3%. This substantial gain indicates that the feature-attention mechanism successfully highlights critical degradation indicators such as wear-leveling count and reallocated sectors, while the temporal-attention mechanism sensitively captures sudden anomalous signals prior to failure. Together, these mechanisms effectively address the issue of key precursors being diluted by uniform weighting in the baseline model.

On the PM9A3 and MB1 Alibaba datasets, DATTN likewise maintains a leading position, achieving F0.5-Scores of 0.71 and 0.90, respectively, with AUC values exceeding 0.88 on both datasets. These results demonstrate the model's strong robustness and generalization capability when handling heterogeneous data across different SSD models and distributions. Moreover, despite the introduction of attention computation modules, DATTN still exhibits higher training and inference efficiency than complex ensemble models, indicating its feasibility for large-scale deployment in production environments.

Training Time Comparison

As shown in the Fig. 5, the total training time varies notably across models, mainly due to differences in architectural complexity, parameter scale, and sequence-processing mechanisms. Traditional machine learning and lightweight deep models show clear efficiency advantages: RF and TCN are the fastest, requiring 1547.8 s and 1687.5 s, respectively, owing to their simple structures and limited parameters.

In contrast, LSTM and AE-TCN require longer training times (2386.2 s and 2046.5 s), as recurrent and encoder-based architectures increase computational overhead, especially for long sequences. MVTRF exhibits the longest training time (3262.7 s) due to its highly complex multi-module design and large parameter scale.

The proposed DATTN model achieves a moderate-to-high training cost (2785.4 s). Although the dual-attention mechanism introduces additional overhead, the parallel convolutional structure of TCN mitigates this cost. Overall, DATTN delivers substantial performance gains while maintaining acceptable training efficiency, demonstrating a favorable trade-off between accuracy and computational cost.

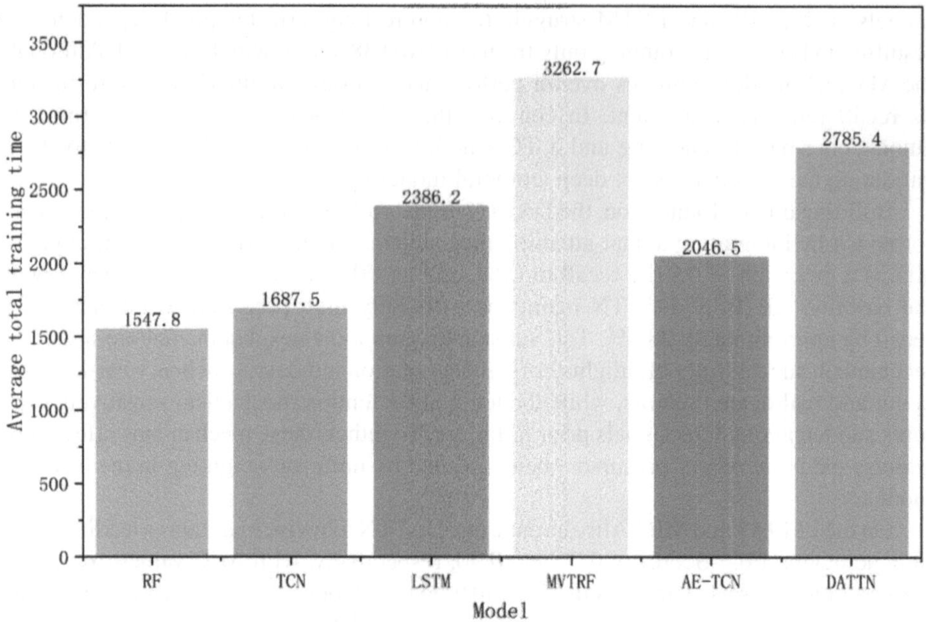

Fig. 5. Average training time results of different models

5 Conclusions

Aiming at the high reliability requirements of large-scale data center storage systems, this paper addresses the challenges encountered in SSD fault prediction, including high-dimensional noise in SMART data, long-term temporal dependencies, and severe class imbalance. To this end, a deep learning–based prediction model integrating a dual-attention mechanism, termed DATTN, is proposed. Built upon the Auto-Encoder and Temporal Convolutional Network architecture, the model is deeply optimized by leveraging the reconstruction capability of autoencoders to effectively denoise and compress multi-source heterogeneous data. Meanwhile, dilated causal convolution structures are employed to capture long-term degradation patterns across the entire device lifecycle, providing a robust feature foundation for high-accuracy fault prediction.

Compared with the baseline AE-TCN model, DATTN innovatively introduces dual enhancement mechanisms—feature attention and temporal attention—successfully overcoming the limitation of traditional time-series models that uniformly weight input sequences. The feature-attention module dynamically learns the contribution of each SMART attribute, adaptively strengthening the representation of critical degradation indicators such as wear-level counts and error rates. The temporal-attention module focuses on key time points prior to failure, sensitively capturing short-term and sudden anomalous precursors. This strategy of highlighting critical features and locating critical moments significantly improves the model's perceptual capability and discriminative accuracy under complex degradation patterns.

Comparative experiments conducted on three real-world datasets—PM1733, PM9A3, and MB1 Alibaba—demonstrate that the DATTN model substantially enhances fault recall while maintaining high precision. In particular, on the PM1733 dataset, DATTN achieves an approximately 9.0% improvement in F0.5-score and a remarkable 28.3% increase in recall compared with the AE-TCN baseline, indicating a superior engineering trade-off between suppressing false alarms and reducing missed detections. In summary, the proposed approach provides an effective technical pathway for data centers to evolve from passive fault tolerance to proactive failure prevention, offering significant theoretical and practical value. Future work will further explore the model's transfer generalization capability across heterogeneous devices from different vendors, as well as attention-weight–based fault root-cause interpretability analysis, to better support real-world deployment in intelligent operation and maintenance systems.

References

1. Sain, S.R.: The nature of statistical learning theory. Neural Comput. **8**(3), 409 (1996)
2. Goodfellow, I.J., Pouget-Abadie, J., et al.: Generative adversarial nets. Adv. Neural Inf. Process. Syst. **27**, 2672–2680 (2014)
3. Jiang, Y., Lu, R., Zhou, S., Li, Q.: Machine learning based collaborative prediction of SSD failures in the cloud. In: Proceedings of the 2024 International Conference on Artificial Intelligence, Computer, Data Sciences and Applications (ACDSA), pp. 1–6 (2024)
4. Zhang, Y., Hao, W., Niu, B., et al.: Multi-view feature-based SSD failure prediction: what, when, and why. In: Proceedings of the 21st USENIX Conference on File and Storage Technologies (FAST 2023), pp. 409–424 (2023)
5. Koh, C., Kang, J., Kim, T., Han, S.W.: Temporal-contextual attention network for solid-state drive failure prediction in data centers. IEEE Access **12**, 1–12 (2024)
6. Zhang, Y., Zhang, T., Hao, W., et al.: MSFRD: Mutation similarity based SSD failure rating and diagnosis for complex and volatile production environments. In: Proceedings of the 2024 USENIX Annual Technical Conference (USENIX ATC 24), pp. 869–884 (2024)
7. Wang, Q., Wang, X., et al.: Remaining lifespan prediction on multiple types of hard disks under conditions of data imbalance. Comput. Electr. Eng. **116**, 109195 (2024)
8. Chakraborttii, C., Boettner, J.: Leveraging temporality of data to improve failure predictions for solid state drives in data centers. In: Proceedings of the 2023 IEEE 47th Annual Computers, Software, and Applications Conference (COMPSAC), pp. 1272–1278 (2023)
9. Jiang, C., He, D.: Hard disk drive failure prediction model based on temporal convolutional network combined with auto-encoder. In: Proceedings of the 2024 8th International Conference on Computer Science and Artificial Intelligence, pp. 513–518 (2024)
10. Chun, M., Kim, M., Lee, D., et al.: Readguard: Integrated SSD management for priority-aware read performance differentiation. ACM Trans. Storage **20**(4), 1–39 (2024)
11. Tajammul, M., Parveen, R., et al.: Cloud storage in context of Amazon Web Services. Int. J. all Res. Educ. Sci. Methods **10**(1), 442–446 (2021)
12. Pinciroli, R., Yang, L., et al.: Lifespan and failures of SSDs and HDDs: similarities, differences, and prediction models. IEEE Trans. Dependable Secure Comput. **20**(1), 256–272 (2021)
13. Yuan, S., Wu, P., Chen, Y., et al.: An integrated GAN-based approach to imbalanced disk failure data. In: International Conference on Intelligent Computing, pp. 615–627 (2022)
14. Hao, W., Niu, B., Luo, Y., et al.: Improving accuracy and adaptability of SSD failure prediction in hyper-scale data centers. ACM SIGMETRICS Perform. Eval. Rev. **49**(4), 99–104 (2022)

15. Meza, J., Wu, Q., Kumar, S., Mutlu, O.: A large-scale study of flash memory failures in the field. ACM SIGMETRICS Perform. Eval. Rev. **43**(1), 177–190 (2015)
16. Du, Y., Gao, Y., Huang, S., Li, Q.: LDPC level prediction toward read performance of high-density flash memories. IEEE Trans. Comput. Aided Des. Integr. Circuits Syst. **42**(10), 3264–3274 (2023)
17. Valença, G.W.M., Pereira, F.L.F., Machado, et al.: Health levels modeling for SSD failure prediction. In: Simpósio Brasileiro de Banco de Dados (SBBD), pp. 764–770 (2024)
18. Maneas, S., Mahdaviani, K., et al.: A study of SSD reliability in large-scale enterprise storage deployments. In: Proceedings of the 18th USENIX Conference on File and Storage Technologies (FAST 20), pp. 137–149 (2020)
19. Chen, L., Zhu, Z., Li, A., et al.: SSD drive failure prediction on Alibaba data center using machine learning. In: Proceedings of the 2022 IEEE International Memory Workshop (IMW), pp. 1–4 (2022)
20. Micheloni, R.: Inside solid state drives (SSDs) (2013)
21. Li, Z., Chen, H., Ma, X., Chen, H., Ma, Z.: Triple pseudo-Siamese network with hybrid attention mechanism for welding defect detection. Mater. Des. **217**, 110645 (2022)
22. Hai, Q., Zhang, S., et al.: Hard disk drive failure prediction based on GRU neural network. In: Proceedings of the 2022 IEEE/CIC International Conference on Communications in China (ICCC), pp. 696–701 (2022)

Ground Moving Target Tracking Based on Deep Reinforcement Learning for Fixed-Wing Unmanned Aerial Vehicles

Cheng-Huan Tsai[1] and Ying-Chih Lai[1,2(✉)]

[1] Institute of Civil Aviation, National Cheng Kung University, Tainan City, Taiwan, R.O.C.
yingclai@mail.ncku.edu.tw

[2] Department of Aeronautics and Astronautics, National Cheng Kung University, Tainan City, Taiwan, R.O.C.

Abstract. Tracking a moving target with fixed-wing unmanned aerial vehicles (UAVs) remains challenging, especially when target positions are unknown and flights are disturbed by wind. This study focusses on the development of a flight control framework that integrates a deep reinforcement learning (DRL) and a path planning algorithm to track a moving ground target in a wind-disturbed environment. The proposed moving-target tracking approach in this study consists of four interconnected modules: target detection, target localization, path planning, and trajectory following. To achieve real-time and smooth navigation control, this study adopts a dynamic trajectory planning approach for fixed-wing UAVs by combining a sliding window mechanism with quadratic programming (QP). The adopted DRL is based on proximal policy optimization (PPO) and adaptively handles nonlinear dynamics and environmental disturbances, while the path planning algorithm can prevent over-chasing of the target. To verify the feasibility of the proposed approach, the PPO algorithm as the lateral controller framework is designed in MATLAB/Simulink simulation environment. Simulation results show that the proposed PPO controller improves path tracking accuracy and target tracking performance compared to model predictive control (MPC).

Keywords: Fixed-Wing Unmanned Aerial Vehicle · Target Tracking · Wind Disturbance Rejection · Deep Reinforcement Learning · Proximal Policy Optimization

1 Introduction

Fixed-wing unmanned aerial vehicles (UAVs) have gained increasing attention due to their long endurance and wide coverage [1], making them suitable for applications such as surveillance, reconnaissance, and target tracking. However, surface moving target tracking remains a major challenge, particularly when the target's position is unknown [2] and the UAV operates in wind-disturbed environments. The difficulties lie in two aspects, which are reliable target localization and robust trajectory tracking under dynamic disturbances.

C. Xu (Ed.): ICMLSC 2026, CCIS 2948, pp. 609–624, 2027.
https://doi.org/10.1007/978-981-92-1546-1_49

The mission about target tracking can be divided into several procedures: first, detecting the target and then localizing it, second, path planning and path following. For target detection and localization, most existing approaches either rely on stereo camera or light detection and ranging (LiDAR). However, those limitations such as weight and computational load, etc. Which are not suitable for lightweight UAVs in real-world scenarios [3]. Monocular vision offers a lightweight alternative for localization, but accurate depth estimation and keeping the target centered within the field of view (FOV) are still challenging [4, 5]. To address those problems, Yang et al. [6, 7] employed an image-based visual servoing (IBVS) strategy that avoids depth estimation by keeping the target centered in the image, while Y. Chen et al. [8], applied IBVS with PID control to map pixel displacement errors into gimbal yaw and pitch commands, thereby stabilizing target tracking. Zhou et al. [9] inferred depth geometrically from UAV altitude and gimbal pitch using a simplified pinhole model, while Wang et al. estimated depth through target size scaling in the image [10]. Xuancen Liu et al. further proposed a decoupled 2-axis gimbal architecture using a kernelized correlation filter (KCF) tracker with proportional control for angular correction, achieving lightweight and real-time tracking suitable for fixed-wing UAVs [11].

At the same time, for the target tracking the flight controller has to follow the changing routes because of the dynamic motion of the target. Therefore, it should be robust under nonlinear dynamics and environmental disturbances like wind. Herrera, I. T. et al. [12] perform ground target tracking by using nonlinear model predictive control (NMPC) under a simplified heading angle model. However, the influence of wind disturbances is not taken into consideration in that study.

Recent advances in deep reinforcement learning (DRL) have demonstrated potential in handling nonlinear and uncertain systems by adaptively learning control policies [13, 14]. Bhagat & Sujit [15] applied a Target Following Deep Q-Network (TF-DQN) with composite rewards and curriculum learning for adaptable obstacle-rich tracking, while Ma et al. employed Deep Deterministic Policy Gradient (DDPG) frameworks to achieve robust and generalized UAV target tracking performance even under wind disturbances [16, 17]. The goal of this study is to develop a DRL-based flight controller integrated with visual target localization and path planning. In this study, designed a DRL controller that adaptively compensates for wind disturbances and ensures continuous target tracking. A protection mechanism in the path planner prevents over-chasing, while monocular vision provides lightweight localization.

This study focuses on the development of the DRL controller and path planning algorithm and proposes an approach for visual localization. The contributions of this work are threefold:

1) Development of a DRL-based controller for robust moving target tracking in wind-disturbed environments.
2) Integration of a monocular vision localization module with onboard planning and control.

2 Moving Target Tracking Methodology

The overall moving-target tracking procedure proposed in this study consists of four interconnected modules: target detection, target localization, path planning, and trajectory following as shown in Fig. 1. First, the target detection module identifies the ground object within each video frame and provides the pixel coordinates of the target's center with the help of You Only Look Once (YOLO) algorithm. Then, the localization module estimates the target's position in three-dimensional space through camera geometry and coordinate transformation. The estimated position and velocity are then fed into the path-planning module, which generates a smooth reference trajectory for the UAV using a sliding-window optimization strategy. Finally, the Proximal Policy Optimization (PPO) controller executes the trajectory-following task by adjusting the UAV's lateral control surfaces to minimize tracking errors and compensate for wind disturbances. This integrated framework enables real-time perception–planning–control interaction, ensuring that the UAV can continuously track a moving target even under environmental uncertainty.

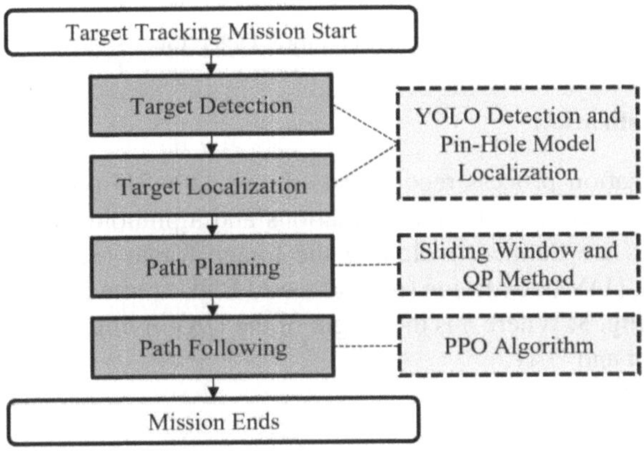

Fig. 1. Target Tracking Mission Procedure.

2.1 Target Detection

Accurate target detection is the first step of the proposed tracking framework. To meet the real-time constraints of onboard computation, the lightweight YOLOv8n model was adopted [18]. YOLOv8 combines feature extraction, multi-scale fusion, and detection in a single-stage architecture, while the "n" variant provides the smallest network size with sufficient accuracy for UAV applications. Since the pre-trained YOLOv8n model was trained mainly on horizontal perspectives, its performance degraded under aerial viewpoints. To overcome this, transfer learning was conducted using a custom dataset collected from quadcopter-mounted gimbal videos. The model was retrained accordingly. The resulting loss curves verify effective convergence. This retrained YOLOv8n ensures robust and efficient onboard detection, forming the basis for subsequent localization and tracking.

All target tracking missions begin with successful target detection. In this study, a civil car is selected as the surface moving target. Once a target is identified, the detector outputs three values: the pixel coordinates (u,v) of the bounding box center, as shown in Fig. 2, the bounding box area computed from contour width and height, and an update position flag. The flag is set to true when the target remains within a defined region around the image center, thereby triggering the path planning algorithm to update the trajectory.

Fig. 2. YOLO Target Detection.

2.2 Target Localization

The target localization process reconstructs the target's 3D position from 2D image measurements using coordinate transformations and a pinhole camera model. Several coordinate frames are defined, including the image frame (u, v), camera frame (c), gimbal frame (g), UAV body frame (b), and world ENU frame (W). Their relationships are illustrated in Fig. 3. Where h is the height of the UAV flying, and D means the depth between the target and UAV.

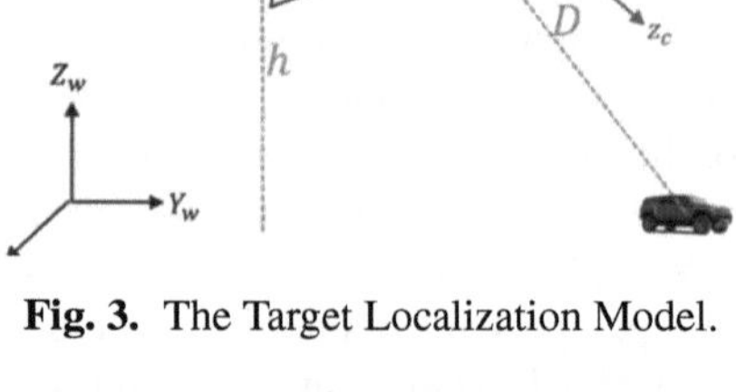

Fig. 3. The Target Localization Model.

The target position in the world frame is reconstructed from image pixel measurements using the pinhole projection model and coordinate transformations. Given the pixel coordinates (u, v), the normalized direction vector in the camera frame is obtained as:

$$\vec{P_t^c} = \begin{bmatrix} \frac{u-c_x}{f_x} \\ \frac{v-c_y}{f_y} \\ 1 \end{bmatrix} \tag{1}$$

$$\vec{I_t^c} = \frac{\vec{P_t^c}}{\left|\vec{P_t^c}\right|} \tag{2}$$

where (c_x, c_y) are the principal point offsets and (f_x, f_y) are the focal lengths. By applying successive rotation matrices between the camera, gimbal, body, and world frames, the target direction in the world frame is:

$$\vec{I_t^W} = R_b^W R_g^b R_c^g \vec{I_t^c} \tag{3}$$

Assuming the target always lies on a constant plane $Z_t = 0$, the depth D can be derived from UAV altitude h:

$$Z_t = h + D * \vec{k_t^W} = 0 \Rightarrow D = \frac{-h}{\vec{k_t^W}} \tag{4}$$

where $\vec{k_t^W}$ is the vertical component of $\vec{I_t^W}$. Thus, the 3D target position in the world frame is expressed as:

$$P_t^W = (X_t, Y_t, Z_t) = D * \vec{I_t^W} + P_{UAV}^W \tag{5}$$

where P_{UAV}^W denoting the UAV position from navigation sensors. To account for sensor noise and dynamic variations, an Extended Kalman Filter (EKF) is employed to estimate both the target's position and velocity. The state vector is defined as:

$$\mathrm{x} = \left[x_1, x_2, x_3, X_t, Y_t, Z_t, v_{tx}, v_{ty}, v_{tz}\right]^T \tag{6}$$

where x_1, x_2 are the normalized coordinates on the image plane, and $x_3 = \frac{1}{D}$ is the depth derivative. And v_{tx}, v_{ty}, and v_{tz} are the velocity of the target under the world coordinate. Propagated by a constant-velocity model, at each step, the nonlinear observation model projects the predicted state onto the image plane for correction:

$$\mathrm{z}_k = h(\mathrm{x}_k) + \mathrm{v}_k \tag{7}$$

$$h(\mathrm{x}) = \left[f_x x_1 + c_x \; f_y x_2 + c_y \; \frac{1}{x_3} \; X_t \; Y_t \; Z_t\right]^T \tag{8}$$

where $z_k = (u, v)$ is the pixel measurement and v_k is measurement noise. The EKF fuses these observations with the motion model to provide smoothed estimates of target trajectory:

$$P_t^W(t + \Delta t) = P_t^W(t) + v_t(t) * \Delta t \tag{9}$$

where $v_t = \left[v_{tx}, v_{ty}, v_{tz}\right]^T$ is the target velocity vector in world coordinate, and Δt means the discrete time interval. This formulation ensures that even when direct visual updates are unavailable, like occlusion, the EKF maintains consistent position and velocity estimates for path planning and control.

During the estimating process of target position and velocity, it is possible to calculate the boresight angle ε between the vector from target to camera and the camera optical axis vector as shown in Fig. 4.

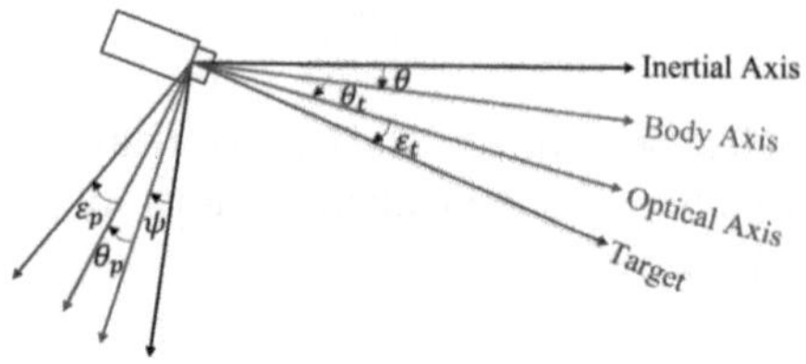

Fig. 4. The Boresight Angles.

While the boresight angles can be calculated within the geometry and the unit vector from target to gimbal $\vec{I_t^g}$, shown as Eq. (11) and (12).

$$\vec{I_t^g} = R_g^{c-1} * \vec{I_t^c} = \left[\vec{i_t^g}, \vec{j_t^g}, \vec{k_t^g}\right] \tag{10}$$

$$\varepsilon_{p\_dir} = actan\left(\frac{\vec{j_t^g}}{\vec{i_t^g}}\right) \tag{11}$$

$$\varepsilon_{t\_dir} = actan\left(-\frac{\vec{k_t^g}}{\sqrt{\vec{i_t^g}^2 + \vec{k_t^g}^2}}\right) \tag{12}$$

The boresight angles in the pan and tilt directions represent the desired orientation adjustments required to align the optical axis of the camera with the target vector, and then become angular velocity commands to the gimbal, thereby ensuring that the target remains centered in the image frame.

2.3 Sliding Window and QP Path Planning

To achieve real-time and smooth navigation control, this study adopts a dynamic trajectory planning approach for fixed-wing UAVs by combining a sliding window mechanism with quadratic programming (QP). A sliding window strategy is adopted to generate smooth tracking trajectories based on the most recent $N = 25$ measurements of target position $\{w_i\}$ and velocity $\{v_j\}$. The UAV trajectory is represented by a cubic polynomial:

$$P(t) = C_{P,0} + C_{P,1}t + C_{P,2}t^2 + C_{P,3}t^3 = T_j^T a \tag{13}$$

where $T_i = \left[1, t, t^2, t^3\right]^T$. The cost function penalizes both position and velocity errors:

$$J(a) = \sum_{j=0}^{N} \|P(t_j) - w_j\|^2 + \|\dot{P}(t_j) - v_j\|^2 \tag{14}$$

This optimization is formulated as a QP:

$$P = 2\sum\nolimits_{i=1}^{N} (T_i T_i^T + T_i' T_i'^T) \tag{15}$$

$$q = -2\sum_{j=1}^{N} \left(-2w_j T_j - 2v_j T_j'\right) \tag{16}$$

where P is the Hessian matrix and q is the linear term.

After solving the QP, the generated path segment is connected to the current global path and prepared for the next update. The integration of the sliding window logic with QP is designed to handle unknown dynamic targets. By periodically updating the target's position within the sliding window, the QP algorithm fits the position and velocity data into a smooth trajectory for the UAV to follow, thereby enabling effective tracking of dynamic targets.

However, if the target's speed is lower than that of the UAV, it may cause the UAV to overshoot the target, resulting in the target being lost from the FOV. To ensure safe execution, a protection mechanism is introduced by triggering loiter mode when the UAV is too close to the target or when the target becomes temporarily unavailable. Specifically, if the UAV to target distance $\|P_{UAV} - P_t\|$ falls below a threshold $d_1 = 30$ m, the system switches to loitering, whereas normal path planning resumes once the distance exceeds $d_2 = 100$ m. This mechanism prevents instability and ensures continuous operation even when measurements are unreliable. The whole path planning algorithm working result is shown in Fig. 5. Which indicates the logical of the dynamic loiter.

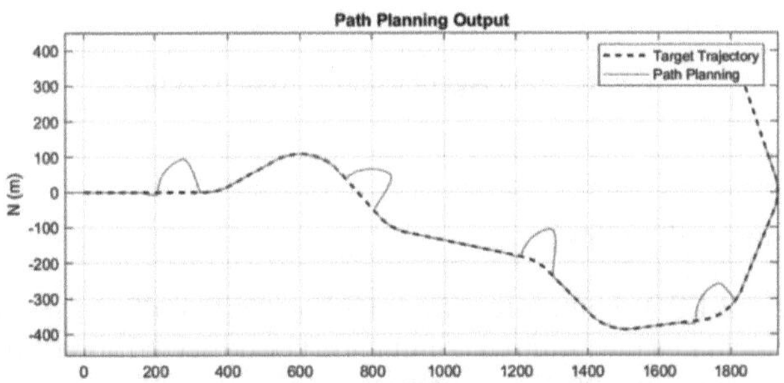

Fig. 5. The Path Planning Algorithm Result.

2.4 Deep Reinforcement Learning Controller

The DRL framework is based on the Actor–Critic architecture, where the Actor selects control actions from observed states and the Critic evaluates these actions by estimating their value relative to the expected reward. Through iterative updates, the Actor improves its policy toward optimal decision-making, while the Critic gradually aligns its value estimates with actual rewards, thereby enhancing overall system performance.

In this study, PPO is adopted as the core control algorithm due to its robustness and computational efficiency in handling high-dimensional, nonlinear UAV dynamics [19]. PPO introduces a clipped surrogate objective that restricts excessive policy updates, effectively maintaining a "trust region" without requiring complex second-order optimization. This mechanism stabilizes training by suppressing large policy deviations when the estimated advantage is positive and the probability ratio falls outside the range $[1 - \epsilon, 1 + \epsilon]$.

PPO has been widely recognized for its superior performance in UAV control tasks, demonstrating greater stability and adaptability compared to both traditional PID controllers and other DRL methods [20]. Its relative insensitivity to hyperparameter tuning and its ability to manage continuous control actions, such as elevator and aileron deflections, make it particularly suitable for fixed-wing UAV trajectory tracking under wind disturbances and nonlinear operating conditions.

3 DRL Flight Control System Based on PPO

DRL flight control system is the most important part of the moving target tracking procedure. The performance of the DRL controller will affect the tracking results directly. The PPO algorithm is used as the lateral controller of the UAV in this study as shown in Fig. 6. This section will introduce the design and implementation of the PPO agent, including the selection and constraints of observation states and actions, the neural network architecture and layers, as well as the reward functions.

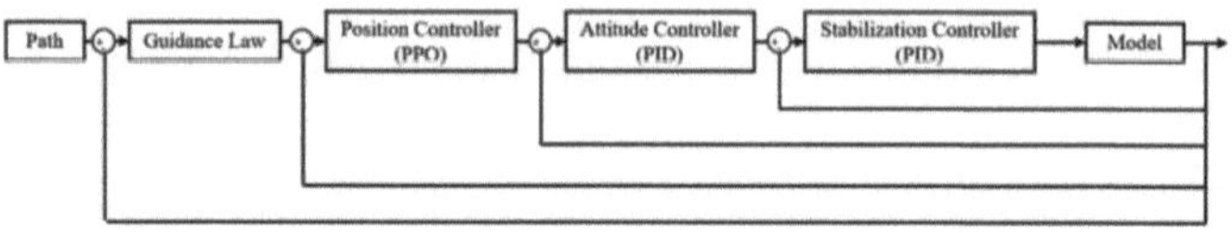

Fig. 6. PPO Agent Control Architecture.

3.1 Observations and Action

Before the design of PPO agent, it requires an observer to collect the state of the fixed-wing UAV and calculates the required command. The collected state will be normalized to $-3 \sim 3$ before input to the PPO agent. Observations normalized in PPO is an essential process of DRL, aiming to accelerate convergence, stabilize the learning process, prevent scale-dominated bias, and enhance the generalization capability of the policy.

Table 1 shows the states selected by the PPO agent in this study, and because the surface target tracking mission only needs to consider the lateral control, the observations are designed for the lateral controller. In Table 1, d_e represents the cross-track error (CTE) between the UAV and the reference trajectory as shown in Fig. 7 and can be calculated with:

$$d_e = L * \sin(\psi_r - \psi_c), \dot{d}_e = \frac{\Delta d_e}{T_s} \tag{17}$$

where L is the distance of the UAV with respect to point W_1, ψ_r is the desired heading angle which the desired path makes with the reference, and ψ_c is the angle which the UAV makes with the tangent line of W_1.

When $\psi_r = \psi_c$ means the UAV is already aligned with the desired path, then $d_e = 0$. And the rate of CTE $\dot{d}_e$ can present how aggressive the path changing, where T_s means the sampling time, which is set as 0.1 (s) in this study. The yaw angle error can be calculated as Eq. (18), and yaw rate error r_e is calculated by subtracting the yaw rate command from the actual state of the UAV, as shown in Eq. (19) where V is the UAV velocity.

$$\Delta\psi = \psi_r - \psi \tag{18}$$

$$r_e = r_{cmd} - r, r_{cmd} = \frac{a_{cmd}}{V} \tag{19}$$

Table 1. Observation states.

State	Description	Normalized Range
E_{UAV}	UAV position	Exponential Moving Average and Estimation
N_{UAV}		
ϕ	Roll Angle	±30°
ψ	Yaw Angle	±60°
p	Roll Rate	±30 (deg/s)
r	Yaw Rate	±60 (deg/s)
d	Cross Track Error (CTE)	50 (m)
$\dot{d}$	Rate of CTE	5 (m/T_s)
$\Delta\psi$	Yaw Angle Error	$\pm\pi$ (rad)
k_t	Path Curvature	±1/55
r_e	Yaw Rate Error	±60 (deg/s)

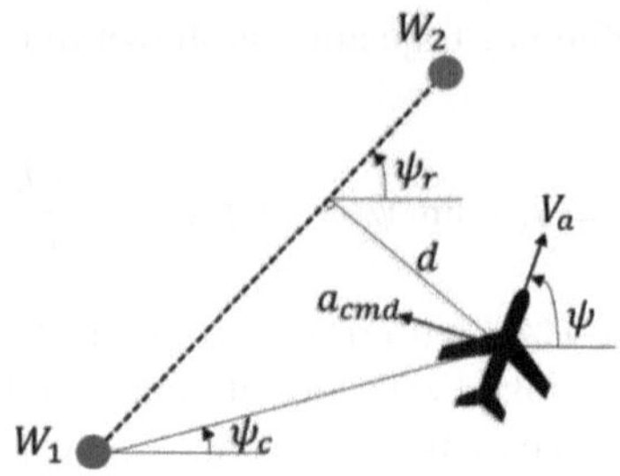

Fig. 7. Trajectory Tracking Geometry.

3.2 Actor and Critic

The PPO algorithm is a DRL method based on the Actor-Critic architecture, where the Actor outputs a Gaussian policy distribution over actions and the Critic estimates state values for policy evaluation. This dual-network design facilitates stable learning by balancing policy improvement and value estimation. In this study, both networks take an 11-dimensional observation vector as input. The Actor consists of three fully connected layers (512, 256, 128 neurons), followed by two branches that output the action mean and standard deviation, constrained by Tanh activation to form a Gaussian policy. The Critic employs five fully connected layers (512, 512, 256, 256, 128 neurons) with ReLU activations, producing a single scalar state value. The network architectures are shown in Fig. 8. This architecture provides sufficient feature representation capacity while remaining computationally efficient, preventing overfitting and avoiding excessive complexity that may lead to local optima.

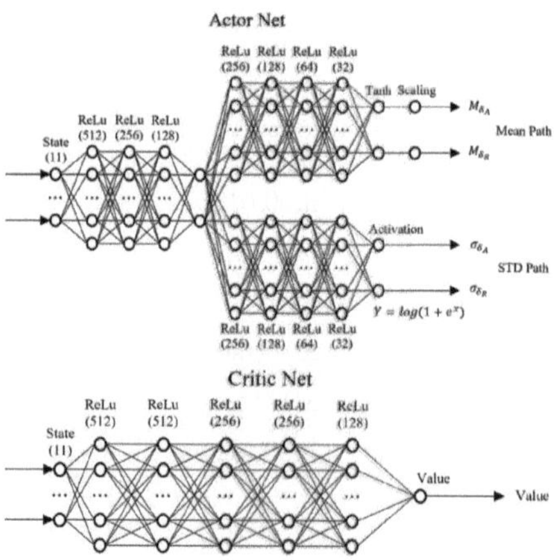

Fig. 8. Neurons Network Architectures.

3.3 Reward Function

In a DRL framework, the reward function plays a central role. Its primary purpose is to evaluate the immediate feedback an agent receives after taking a specific action in a given state, thereby guiding the learning process toward an optimal policy. In this study, the reward function is designed to encourage the UAV to stably follow a dynamic trajectory. A negative feedback mechanism is adopted when the agent's behavior deviates from the desired path, exhibits excessive attitude angles, or generates overly aggressive control outputs, then a negative reward, which is multiplied by -1 is assigned as a penalty. The detailed reward function design is as follows:

$$R_T = \sum_{i=1}^{n} R_G^i + R_S^i + R_W^i + R_{Goal}^i + R_A^i \tag{20}$$

where R_T is the total reward score for each episode, and n means the maximum number of steps per episode. In this study, the maximum reward is designed as one, simplifying the process of setting the weights for various constraints.

The total reward can be separated as five parts, including guidance reward R_G, fixed-wing UAV attitude stability reward R_S, the wind-disturbed effect reward R_W, the goal reaching reward R_{Goal}, and finally the reward for limiting the rate of change in control surface command outputs R_A.

4 Simulations and Results

The primary objective of this study is to evaluate the controller's capability to resist wind disturbances and maintain accurate target tracking, independent of perceptual uncertainties. To this end, a MATLAB/Simulink simulation environment was developed, as shown in Fig. 9, which integrates a path planning module and a wind disturbance model. Target information is assumed to be known. The primary objective of this study is to evaluate the controller's capability to resist wind disturbances and maintain accurate target tracking, independent of perceptual uncertainties. To this end, a MATLAB/Simulink simulation environment was developed, as shown in Fig. 9, which integrates a path planning module and a wind disturbance model. Target information is assumed to be known.

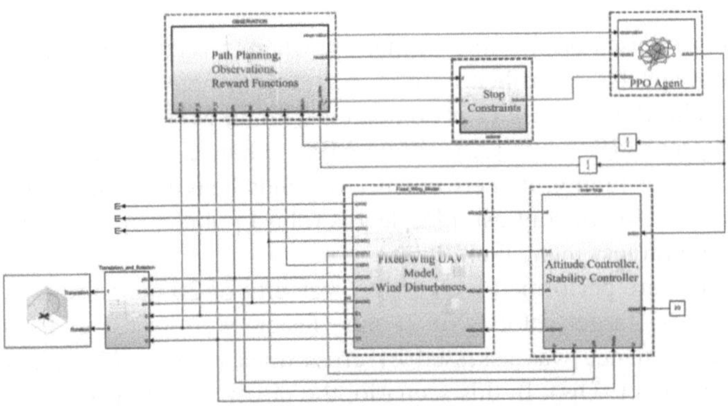

Fig. 9. Simulink Simulation Environment.

4.1 Training Process

For training, the PPO agent was tasked with tracking a moving target of lower velocity than the UAV. This design exposes the agent to dynamically varying loiter trajectories while requiring compensation for wind disturbances. The Dryden wind model was incorporated with random wind magnitudes of 3–5 m/s and turbulence of 2–3 m/s in each episode.

The PPO hyperparameters are summarized in Table 2. A step size of 0.1 s and 300 steps per episode were used. The discount factor was tuned according to the literature, while learning rates were optimized empirically for convergence. A batch size of 512 ensured balanced training stability and efficiency. Training was terminated when the average reward over 10 episodes exceeded 2200, which accounts for persistent wind perturbations compared to the theoretical maximum of 3000.

Table 2. PPO Agent Hyperparameters.

Hyperparameters	Values
Sampling Time	0.1
Max. Training Step	300
Max Episode	40000
Discount Factory	0.98
Minibatch Size	512
Actor Learning Rate	$3 * 10^{-4}$
Critic Learning Rate	10^{-4}
Max. Reward	3000
Training Stop Reward (Average)	2200

4.2 Simulation Scenarios

The simulation focuses on Turning Scenarios, where the target follows a turning trajectory to evaluate the controller's ability to track maneuvering motion under wind disturbances. The PPO controller is compared with an MPC method [21], both using ArduPlane internal PID loops [22]. While MPC achieves comparable accuracy after extensive parameter tuning, its performance depends heavily on the weighting matrix and model parameters. In contrast, PPO learns robust policies automatically, providing stable tracking with less manual effort.

Simulations were performed with a UAV velocity of 20 m/s, altitude of 70 m, and a duration of 95 s. Target velocity of 21 m/s (faster) were tested under varying wind conditions. Performance was assessed by cross-track error (CTE), maximum offset, and distance-to-target (Dis). In this scenario, the target will start from [0, 0, 0] toward east direction and make a right turn in ENU coordinate while the UAVs start from [−50, 0, 70]. This simulation scenario is designed to evaluate the UAV's tracking performance when the target undergoes abrupt turns during the tracking process. The reference trajectory is shown in Fig. 10. And the simulation cases are set up as below four cases, which include two target velocities and different wind conditions.

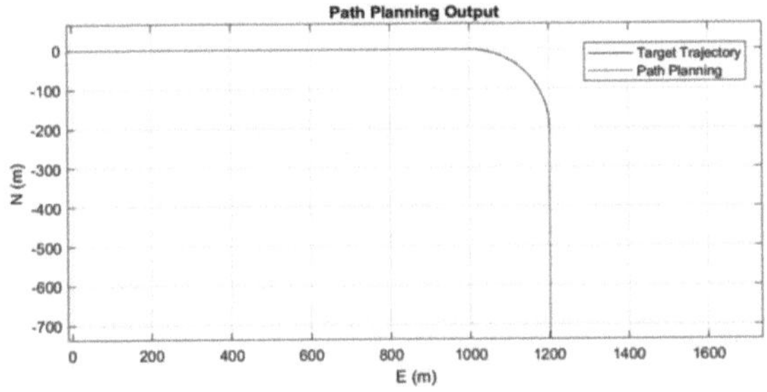

Fig. 10. Turning Moving Target Trajectory.

Case 1: Target with Velocity 21 m/s Without Wind Influence

Table 3 shows the target tracking results and the comparison of MPC and PPO controllers. As shown in Fig. 11 and 12, the PPO controller slightly deviates from the reference trajectory during the turning phase, resulting in a higher CTE RMSE. However, it can also be observed that the PPO controller is able to promptly correct its path and return to the reference trajectory after the deviation.

Table 3. Case1: Guidance Errors.

Tracking turning target with velocity 21m/s with no-wind		
	MPC Controller	PPO Controller
CTE RMSE	1.715 m	2.727 m
Offset	5.668 m	10.222 m
Dis IRR	100%	100%

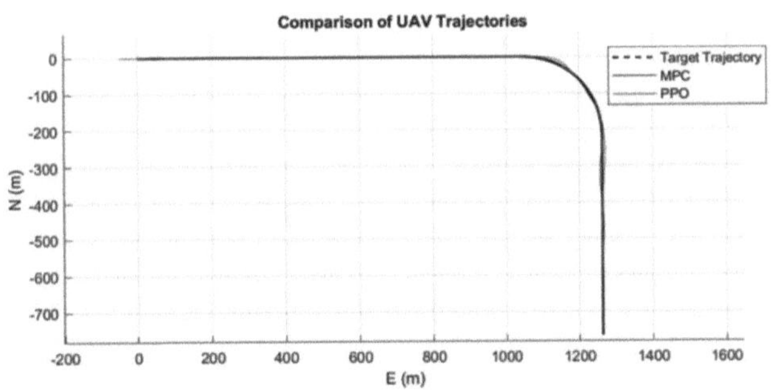

Fig. 11. Case 1 UAV Trajectories.

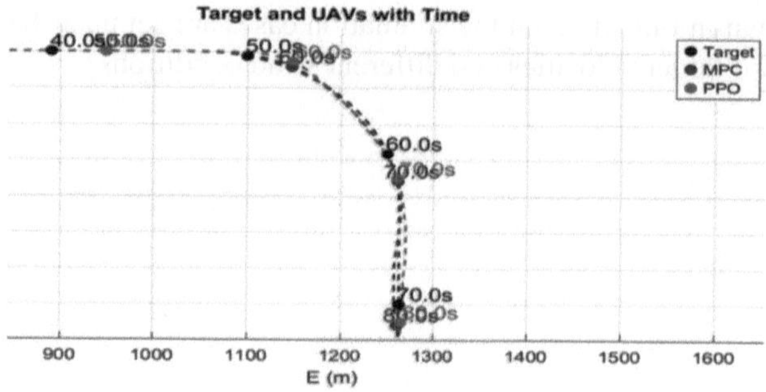

Fig. 12. Case 1 Target and UAVs positions with time markers.

Case 2: Target with Velocity 21 m/s with Wind Disturbance

From Figs. 13 and 14, it can be observed that under wind-disturbed conditions, both controllers exhibit oscillations during the tracking process, with the effect being more pronounced in the MPC controller. As a result, the MPC controller exhibits a higher CTE RMSE. As shown in Table 4, despite the presence of wind disturbances, the PPO controller consistently demonstrates relatively stable tracking performance. As a result, it achieves better performances in both Dis IRR and CTE RMSE, highlighting its strong capability to resist wind disturbances.

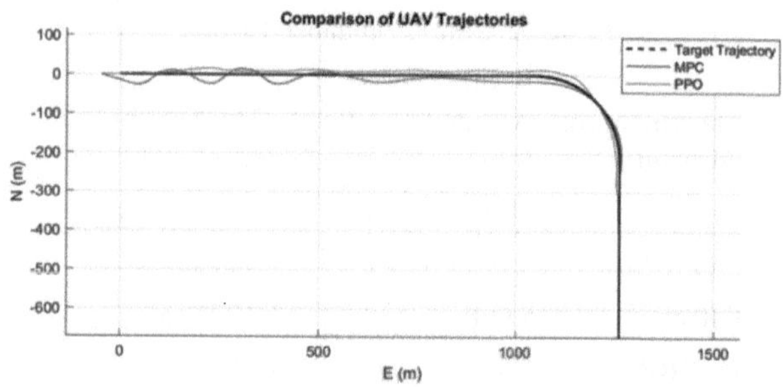

Fig.13. Case 2 UAV Trajectories.

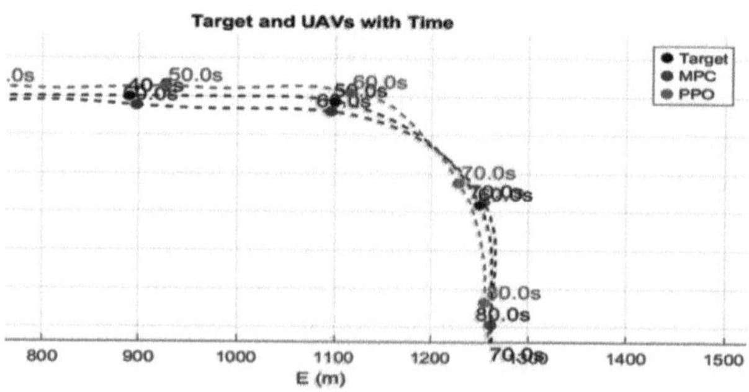

Fig. 14. Case 2 Target and UAVs positions with time markers.

Table 4. Case 2: Guidance Errors.

Tracking turning target with velocity 21m/s with wind-disturbed		
	MPC Controller	PPO Controller
CTE RMSE	10.739 m	9.597 m
Offset	23.890 m	17.598 m
Dis IRR	53.1%	66.6%

4.3 Simulation Discussion

In the tracking turning target missions, the PPO controller consistently demonstrates superior adaptability compared to the traditional MPC. For Case 1, when there is no influence from wind disturbance, both MPC and PPO methods have almost the same performance to track the moving target with the velocity of 21 m/s. For Case 2, PPO achieves a 10.6% reduction in CTE RMSE and a 13.5% improvement in Dis IRR under wind disturbances, highlighting its stronger robustness against external perturbations. These results confirm that PPO not only maintains competitive accuracy when tracking a moving target but also offers substantial improvements under the influence of wind disturbance, where MPC struggles to remain stable. Overall, the PPO controller provides more reliable trajectory tracking, enhanced disturbance rejection, and greater generalization capability in dynamic turning environments.

5 Conclusion

This study proposed a moving target tracking approach using YOLO object detection and DRL flight control system. To achieve real-time and smooth navigation control, this study adopts a dynamic trajectory planning approach for fixed-wing UAVs by combining a sliding window mechanism with visual localization and quadratic programming. The contributions of this work include the development of a DRL-based controller for robust moving target tracking in wind-disturbed environments and integration of a monocular vision localization module with onboard planning and control. The simulation results show that the proposed PPO controller offers superior adaptability and robustness compared to MPC, achieving up to 10.6% reduction in CTE RMSE and 13.5% improvement in in-range ratio in challenging scenarios. Current limitations lie in the basic vision-based localization module, which may cause errors under non-planar or distorted conditions. Future work will focus on enhancing the visual localization algorithm and extending the controller to a full 3D framework with elevator and throttle control, enabling higher-precision and more flexible UAV tracking missions in real flight experiments.

References

1. Wüest, V., Ajanic, E., Müller, M., Floreano, D.: Accurate vision-based flight with fixed-wing drones. In: Proceedings of the 2022 IEEE/RSJ International Conference on Intelligent Robots and Systems (IROS), pp. 12344–12351. IEEE (2022)
2. Rafi, F., Khan, S., Shafiq, K., Shah, M.: Autonomous target following by unmanned aerial vehicles. In: Unmanned Systems Technology VIII, pp 325–332. SPIE (2006)
3. Tang, D., Fang, Q., Shen, L., Hu, T.: Onboard detection-tracking-localization. IEEE/ASME Trans. Mechatron. **25**, 1555–1565 (2020)
4. Forsyth, D.A., Ponce, J.: Computer Vision: A Modern Approach. Prentice Hall Professional Technical Reference (2002)
5. Cunha, R., et al.: Gimbal control for vision-based target tracking. In: Proceedings of the European Conference on Signal Processing (2019)
6. Yang, L., Liu, Z., Wang, X., Yu, X., Wang, G., Shen, L.: Image-based visual servo tracking control of a ground moving target for a fixed-wing unmanned aerial vehicle. J. Intell. Rob. Syst. **102**, 1–20 (2021)
7. Yang, L., Wang, X., Zhou, Y., Liu, Z., Shen, L.: Online predictive visual servo control for constrained target tracking of fixed-wing unmanned aerial vehicles. Drones **8**, 136 (2024)
8. Chen, Y., et al.: Image-based visual servoing of unmanned aerial manipulators for tracking and grasping a moving target. IEEE Trans. Industr. Inf. **19**, 8889–8899 (2022)
9. Zhou, Y., Tang, D., Zhou, H., Xiang, X., Hu, T.: Vision-based online localization and trajectory smoothing for fixed-wing uav tracking a moving target. In: Proceedings of the IEEE/CVF International Conference on Computer Vision Workshops (2019)
10. Wang, X., Zhu, H., Zhang, D., Zhou, D., Wang, X.: Vision-based detection and tracking of a mobile ground target using a fixed-wing UAV. Int. J. Adv. Rob. Syst. **11**, 156 (2014)
11. Liu, X., Yang, Y., Ma, C., Li, J., Zhang, S.: Real-time visual tracking of moving targets using a low-cost unmanned aerial vehicle with a 3-axis stabilized gimbal system. Appl. Sci. **10**, 5064 (2020)
12. Herrera, I.T., Van Nguyen, L., Le, T., Aguilera, R.P., Ha, Q.: UAV target tracking using nonlinear model predictive control. In: Proceedings of the 2022 International Conference on Electrical, Computer and Energy Technologies (ICECET), pp 1–7. IEEE (2022)
13. Richter, D.J., Calix, R.A., Kim, K.: A review of reinforcement learning for fixed-wing aircraft control tasks. IEEE Access (2024)
14. Azar, A.T., et al.: Drone deep reinforcement learning: a review. Electronics **10**, 999 (2021)
15. Bhagat, S., Sujit, P.: UAV target tracking in urban environments using deep reinforcement learning. In: Proceedings of the 2020 International Conference on Unmanned Aircraft Systems (ICUAS), pp. 694–701. IEEE (2020)
16. Ma, B., et al.: Deep reinforcement learning of UAV tracking control under wind disturbances environments. IEEE Trans. Instrum. Meas. **72**, 1–13 (2023)
17. Ma, B., et al.: Target tracking control of UAV through deep reinforcement learning. IEEE Trans. Intell. Transp. Syst. **24**, 5983–6000 (2023)
18. Hussain, M.: Yolov5, yolov8 and yolov10: the go-to detectors for real-time vision. arXiv preprint arXiv:2407.02988 (2024)
19. Schulman, J., Wolski, F., Dhariwal, P., Radford, A., Klimov, O.: Proximal policy optimization algorithms. arXiv preprint arXiv:1707.06347 (2017)
20. Bøhn, E., Coates, E.M., Moe, S., Johansen, T.A.: Deep reinforcement learning attitude control of fixed-wing uavs using proximal policy optimization. In: Proceedings of the 2019 International Conference on Unmanned Aircraft Systems (ICUAS), pp. 523–533. IEEE (2019)
21. Stastny, T.J., Dash, A., Siegwart, R.: Nonlinear MPC for Fixed-Wing UAV Trajectory Tracking: Implementation and Flight Experiments, AIAA Guidance, Navigation, and Control Conference, p. 1512 (2017)
22. Team, A.D.: Ardupilot plane documentation. https://ardupilot.org/plane/

Enhancing Failure Detection in Semiconductor Manufacturing Using Balanced Random Forest Model

Daksh Gandhi[1](✉), Rajat Dandekar[2], Sreedath Panat[2], and Raj Dandekar[2]

[1] Suncity School, Gurgaon, Haryana, India
gandhijidaksh@gmail.com
[2] Vizuara AI Labs, Pune, India

Abstract. Semiconductor manufacturing is highly sensitive, even a small defect rate can significantly impact yield and profitability. The SECOM dataset used in this paper with 1567 cases, only 6% failures and 591 features, poses a severe class imbalance challenge for predictive modeling [1]. Traditional approaches such as Logistic Regression, Random Forest, Support Vector Machines and Neural Networks achieve high overall accuracy but fail to improve minority class metrics (i.e. fail in this case). We hypothesized that in a heavily imbalanced dataset, improvement of the metrics of the minority class is more efficient in failure detection as overall accuracy readings are biased towards the majority class. In order to achieve that we explored and tested both traditional and advanced resampling-based ensemble models like Easy Ensemble Classifier (EEC) and Balanced Random Forest Classifier (BRFC) using hyperparameter tuning and created overall 22 pipelines to improve the results. We found that ensemble- based models show better results without relying on oversampling methods like SMOTE or feature selection. Tuned BRFC achieved the best results for minority class, with recall as 0.43, precision as 0.26, F1-score as 0.32 and accuracy as 0.88. The feature importance analysis using the tuned BRFC identified the top 10 critical variables. The results of our study indicate that manufacturers can prioritize monitoring of these features and exclude less-informative parameters. This can lead to yield enhancement and cost savings.

Keywords: Balanced Random Forest Classifier (BRFC) · precision · recall · F1-score · accuracy

1 Introduction

Semiconductor manufacturing is one of the most precision-dependent industries in the world, involving hundreds of intricate step parameters/sensor readings that must be executed flawlessly. Even minor deviations in environmental conditions, process parameters, or equipment performance can lead to wafer defects, reducing yield and driving up production costs. As Artificial Intelligence (AI) rapidly advances—powering technologies from conversational agents like ChatGPT to self-driving cars, medical diagnostics, and

C. Xu (Ed.): ICMLSC 2026, CCIS 2948, pp. 625–635, 2027.
https://doi.org/10.1007/978-981-92-1546-1_50

robotics—the demand for faster, more efficient, and reliable semiconductor chips continues to grow. With growing global demand for chips in order to avoid supply shortage, improving manufacturing efficiency is critical.

In this study, we have analyzed the semiconductor manufacturing dataset created by McCann and Johnston, which contains 590 sensor variables with the final feature representing the pass or fail state (1). The dataset is highly imbalanced, with 1,463 pass cases and only 104 fail cases (6% failures). Despite the low failure rate, the associated cost and risk are substantial. The high dimensionality of 590 parameters further complicates the task, as identifying the most influential features is non-trivial. This is why, many studies in the past have been done to reduce this percentage, however most of them have focused on improving the overall accuracy of the ML models.One important aspect of this dataset is that the 590 sensor variables are represented only by numerical indices rather than descriptive names. This anonymization was done to protect the proprietary details of the semiconductor manufacturing process, as the original sensor identities (e.g., machine parameters, chemical measurements) are considered confidential.

We hypothesized that in a heavily imbalanced dataset, improvement of the metrics of the minority class is more efficient in failure detection as overall accuracy readings are biased towards the majority class In our study we focused on selecting the correct metrics for the minority class (i.e. fail in this case) and tuned our models to improve them. We ran 6 models and 22 pipelines for resampling and feature selection. We found out that advanced ensemble- based machine learning models like Easy Ensemble Classifier (EEC) and Balanced Random Forest Classifier (BRFC) enhanced with hyperparameter tuning outperform basic ML models such as Random Forest (RF) or Logistic Regression (LR). By leveraging these models, it was possible to work on multi-dimensional imbalanced datasets, identify the most critical variables, enabling early defect prediction, targeted interventions, and improved yield—ultimately leading to more reliable semiconductor production. These results are not limited to the semiconductor industry, they can be applied to any manufacturing process.

2 Related Work

Several studies have been conducted on McCann and Johnston semiconductor sensors' data authors have explored various approaches to determine the most effective methods for maximizing yield [1]. These approaches encompass diverse data preprocessing steps, feature selection techniques, model choices, variations in the order of data splitting, scaling and usage of re-sampling techniques. Evaluation metrics vary across studies;, some paper have presented multiple models without identifying a clear best approach.

Munirathinam et al., Kittisak et al. [2, 3] have conducted extensive work on the SECOM dataset, applying feature selection methods such as PCA (Principal component analysis), chi-square tests, correlation analysis, and VIF, along with a range of models including Decision Tree (DT), Naïve Bayes (NB), k-Nearest Neighbor (KNN), Logistic Regression, Artificial Neural Networks (ANN), and Support Vector Machines (SVM). Their work provides a detailed comparison of multiple models across several evaluation parameters.

Park et al. extended this set of models to include LR, SVM, and Extreme Gradient Boosting (XGB), combined with preprocessing and feature selection techniques such as Pearson correlation coefficient–based selection (reducing to 12 features) and various resampling methods, including advanced sampling based selection methods to handle class imbalance -SMOTE(Synthetic Minority Over-sampling Technique), ADASYN(Adaptive Synthetic Sampling), Borderline-SMOTE and SVM-SMOTE (Support Vector Machines Synthetic Minority Over-sampling Technique) [3, 4]. Using accuracy, recall, and specificity as metrics and geometric mean of recall & specificity (4), the authors evaluated 150 combinations and identified SVM with ADASYN oversampling and MaxAbs scaling as the best-performing configurations [4].

Yousef et al. have focused on feature reduction using CfsSubsetEval and dimensionality reduction via PCA, reducing features to 168 and applying NB, DT, Multilayer Perceptron (MLP), and SVM models, evaluated against five metrics (true positive rate, false positive rate, precision, F-measure, and accuracy) [5]. Some studies have emphasized on training time [6], reducing the original 590 features to as few as 9 using methods such as Recursive Feature Elimination (RFE), but have focused only on one metric i.e. accuracy [6]. Yet another investigation applied MARS and Boruta feature selection methods, running the aforementioned models and comparing results under both minority-class oversampling and majority-class under-sampling scenarios [7]. All the studies removed features with $> 55\%$ missing values [2–5, 7].

Notably, none of these studies except this Karthik Ramachandra [8] explicitly reported or analyzed metrics specific to the minority class (fail/1 in this case), which is critical given the severe class imbalance in the SECOM dataset. It is unclear if these papers have reported weighted average or macro average. In this study, we have analyzed both the majority (pass) and minority (fail) classes. We have identified precision and recall as the most critical evaluation metrics, since unlike accuracy, they account for class imbalance. Our results show that optimizing the F1 score (harmonic mean of precision and recall) of the minority class provides the most reliable criterion for model selection, as certain models exhibited higher precision while others favored recall. Through extensive experimentation, we identified the tuned BRFC as the best-performing model. Furthermore, we extracted the top 10 most influential features, offering manufacturers insights into which sensor parameters should be prioritized to reduce failure rates. These results support our hypothesis that improving selected metrics of minority class can improve failure detection in semiconductor manufacturing and we achieved the same by using ensemble models instead of the traditional ones.

3 Results

In order to improve the failure detection in semiconductor manufacturing, we explored various machine learning models, pipelines, tuning of various hyperparameters, resampling techniques and feature selection. We developed the model through four main phases. We began with ***data exploration*** followed by data ***preparation by cleaning, imputing missing values, scaling and splitting*** the data into training and test sets. We then trained and evaluated multiple ML models using well-defined performance metrics. Finally, we performed ***hyperparameter tuning*** on the selected models to enhance their performance. We examined the performance of both the minority and majority classes using four key metrics: F1-score, precision, recall, and accuracy.

Precision = True Positives (TP) / (True Positives (TP) + False Positives (FP)).

Recall = True Positives (TP) / True Positives (TP) + False Negatives (FN)).

F1 Score (Harmonic mean of Precision and Recall) = 2 * (Precision * Recall) / (Precision + Recall). Accuracy = TP + TN/(FP + FN + TP + TN). TP in this case is the minority class.

The results containing these metrics for the minority class, from all 22 pipelines are shown in Table 1, except accuracy which is a metric that aggregates results across both the majority and minority classes. It measures the proportion of all correctly classified instances (both pass and fail), which is why many of our models showed accuracy between 0.81 and 0.93. Most of the models except BRFC had precision values lesser than 0.20. BRFC (SMOTE-ENN) had a precision value of 0.43. This means 43% of its prediction of failed batches was accurate. Quite a few pipelines of EEC and BRFC had a recall greater than 0.3 which means the models catch more than 30% failures. EEC and EEC_PCA observed a recall value of 0,62. None of the models had high values for both precision and recall, hence we selected an F1 score which balances both. The best model based on best F1- score was Tuned BRFC, CV = 3, Precision = 0.26, recall = 0.43, f1 = 0.32, accuracy = 0.88. While EEC achieved higher recall and BRFC (SMOTE-ENN) had higher precision but they had lower F1-score hence they were not selected as the best model.

Tuned BRFC achieved the precision results without applying feature reduction techniques. We used the entire dataset of 590 sensor readings, applied median imputation for missing data and Robust Scaler for scaling. This made the model faster and reduced the number of steps. While running the models, we gave importance to training and evaluation time. We selected BRFC (cv = 3) with hyperparameter tuning. Even without hyperparameter tuning BRFC and EEC models performed better than the traditional models. We used the Permutation Importance method to select the top 10 most important sensor variables based on the scores they received using the method which we will discuss in the Material and Methods section (Fig. 1).

The identification of a compact subset of sensors can simplify sensing hardware and data acquisition pipelines. Such targeted monitoring may reduce maintenance overhead and enable more cost-effective implementation. Since the data variables are numbered indices, the qualitative aspects of the top ten selected features, and the underlying physical reasons for their importance, could not be examined.

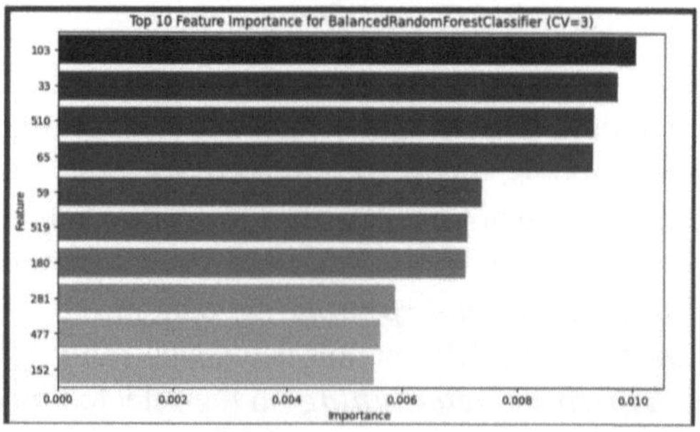

Fig. 1. Top 10 features based on their importance in Tuned BRFC using Permutation Importance method

Table 1. Results of all the 6 models and 22 pipelines for minority class (Fail = 1)

Model / Approach	Accuracy	Precision	Recall	F1-score
Approach 1				
Logistic Regression_SMOTE	0.81	0.15	0.38	0.22
Random Forest_SMOTE	0.93	0.00	0.00	0.00
SVM_SMOTE	0.93	0.00	0.00	0.00
Neural Networks_SMOTE	0.90	0.08	0.05	0.06
Approach 2				
EasyEnsembleClassifier_SMOTE	0.84	0.09	0.14	0.11
BalancedRandomForestClassifier_SMOTE	0.93	0.00	0.00	0.00
EasyEnsembleClassifier _SMOTETomek	0.87	0.11	0.14	0.13
BalancedRandomForestClassifier _SMOTETomek	0.93	0.00	0.00	0.00
EasyEnsembleClassifier _SMOTE-ENN	0.84	0.13	0.24	0.17
BalancedRandomForestClassifier _SMOTE-ENN	0.93	0.43	0.14	0.21
EasyEnsembleClassifier_ADASYN	0.86	0.07	0.10	0.08
BalancedRandomForestClassifier_ADASYN	0.93	0.00	0.00	0.00
Approach 3				
EasyEnsembleClassifier	0.71	0.13	0.62	0.22
BalancedRandomForestClassifier	0.87	0.21	0.33	0.26
Hyperparameter Tuning				
Tuned EEC_SamplingStrategy	0.83	0.18	0.43	0.25
Tuned BRFC_CV_3	0.88	0.26	0.43	0.32
Tuned BRFC_CV_5	0.84	0.17	0.33	0.22
Tuned BRFC_CV_10	0.89	0.24	0.33	0.28
Approach 3a: Split → PCA → Classifier				
EasyEnsembleClassifier_PCA	0.56	0.09	0.62	0.16
BalancedRandomForestClassifier_PCA	0.81	0.13	0.33	0.19
Approach 3b: Split → SMOTE → PCA → Classifier				
EasyEnsemble_SMOTE_PCA	0.65	0.09	0.48	0.15
BalancedRandomForest_SMOTE_PCA	0.91	0.21	0.14	0.17

4 Discussion

When we studied the results of the minority classes, we noticed that most of the models achieved high accuracy between 0.80 and 0.93 as shown in Table 1. While we studied precision and recall, none of the models gave highest values on both recall and precision.

Both precision and recall are important metrics as precision helps save cost by making fewer false alarms (failed batches in this case) while recall catches most failures and both have direct impact on cost. Precision continued to remain low which is expected from this heavily imbalanced data, hence the highest F1-score was selected as the metrics to decide the best model as it is the harmonic mean of precision and recall. As shared in the results section, the best model based on best F1- score was Tuned BRFC, CV = 3, Precision = 0.26, recall = 0.43, f1 = 0.32, accuracy = 0.88.

While Tuned BRFC was the best performing model, even this model struggles to achieve a higher precision. A precision of (0.26) means that only 26% of wafers predicted as failures were truly defective i.e. high false positives leading to higher re-testing costs. A recall (0.43) means 43% of defective wafers were correctly flagged i.e. risk of defective wafers being shipped.

Some of the key questions that we explored were-

1. Why do traditional models struggle in better prediction compared to ensemble models like EEC and BRFC? 2. How EEC and Balanced Random Forest address class imbalance? and 3. Why are SMOTE and PCA techniques not helpful?

Why do traditional models struggle in better prediction compared to ensemble models like EEC and BRFC? **Bias towards the majority class:** Most standard classification algorithms are designed to increase accuracy. In an imbalanced dataset, simply predicting the majority class for all instances can achieve a high accuracy. As Table 1 shows, all the four traditional models LR, RF, SVM and NN have high accuracy but very poor precision for minority class, other than LR, all four models have negligible recall and F1 score. Even with such poor results for minority class, weighted average results are > 0.8 for most metrics as shown in Table 2. Possible reasons why each of these models LR and SVM achieved limited success is because both LR and SVM learn a single decision boundary to separate classes. A decision boundary is a learned hyperplane that divides the feature space into regions corresponding to each class. SVM model finds the boundary that maximizes the margin—the distance between the boundary and the nearest data points from each class (support vectors). In imbalanced data, both algorithms optimize for overall error minimization. This shifts the decision boundary closer to the minority class, correctly classifying more majority samples at the expense of misclassifying minority samples. The reduction in error from the majority outweighs the increase from the minority, resulting in low recall for the minority class.

Table 2. Classification report for LR, RF, SVM and NN

Model	Class	Precision	Recall	F1-score	Accuracy
LR	Pass (-1)	0.95	0.79	0.86	0.76
	Fail (+1)	0.12	0.38	0.18	
	Macro Avg	0.53	0.59	0.52	
	Wtd Avg	0.89	0.76	0.92	
RF	Pass (-1)	0.93	1.00	0.96	0.93
	Fail (+1)	0.00	0.00	0.00	

(*continued*)

Table 2. (*continued*)

Model	Class	Precision	Recall	F1-score	Accuracy
	Macro Avg	0.47	0.50	0.48	
	Wtd Avg	0.87	0.93	0.90	
SVM	Pass (-1)	0.93	1.00	0.97	0.93
	Fail (+1)	0.00	0.00	0.00	
	Macro Avg	0.47	0.50	0.48	
	Wtd Avg	0.87	0.93	0.90	
NN	Pass (-1)	0.95	0.91	0.93	0.87
	Fail (+1)	0.18	0.29	0.22	
	Macro Avg	0.56	0.60	0.57	
	Wtd Avg	0.90	0.87	0.88	

Standard RF constructs multiple decision trees using bootstrap sampling from the full dataset. In imbalanced data, majority class samples dominate each bootstrap set. NN are trained to minimize a loss function. With many more majority samples in each batch, the optimization process primarily reduces loss for the majority class. The model is mostly trained on the majority class. As a result, the network learns features favoring majority-class classification.

How do EEC and BRFC address class imbalance ? These are ensemble methods specifically designed to handle imbalance. *EEC* works by creating multiple balanced subsets of the training data. It repeatedly under-samples the majority class and combines it with all instances of the minority class to create several balanced datasets. Then, it trains a Decision Tree on each of these balanced subsets and combines their predictions. By default, it uses n_estimators = 10 (meaning it creates 10 balanced subsets and trains 10 base classifiers) and sampling_strategy = 'auto' (which typically balances the classes by under sampling the majority class to match the minority class size in each subset). *BRFC* is a variation of the standard RF, While standard RF uses bootstrapping (sampling with replacement) to create subsets of data for each tree, BRFC uses balanced bootstrapping. This means that when creating a bootstrap sample for a tree, it samples equally from the majority and minority classes (or with a controlled ratio). This ensures that each tree in the forest is trained on a more balanced view of the data, reducing the bias towards the majority class.

Why do SMOTE and PCA techniques not help? SMOTE generates synthetic minority samples by interpolating between existing minority points. While effective in some scenarios (2,3,4,5,6,7), it did not improve results in our study because EEC and BRFC already handle imbalance via under-sampling and benefit from hyperparameter tuning, making SMOTE redundant and sometimes harmful due to noise amplification. *PCA* is a dimensionality reduction technique that finds principal components that capture the most variance in the data. While it can reduce noise and computational cost, it does not mean that the components that capture the most variance might not be the ones that best separate the majority and minority classes.

In conclusion, the SECOM dataset dating back to 2008 is still relevant since even a 6% wafer failure rate can lead to huge financial losses. Model that can handle such class imbalance cases. The reason for calling out minority class readings was to fine tune the models to improve only those readings instead of increasing overall readings which might have lesser impact on minority class failure cases in this data. Improving F1-score for the minority class which balances both precision and recall is more valuable than chasing overall accuracy. Our models also determine the top 10 most important features that can help manufacturers prioritize monitoring of these sensors and excluding less-informative parameters. The same models can find application in other manufacturing industries too. While many models could improve the recall, they struggled in improving precision leading to false positives which may lead to high retesting cost. Even tuned BRFC models show improvement in recall, but the precision values are still low which leaves scope to explore other models and pipelines. That is the limitation of our study. The other area of limitation is the name of the sensors, without knowing them our models are limited to quantitative output, however the same may not be the case in other industries.

5 Materials and Methods

The model development was conducted in four main phases. First, the dataset was explored to understand its distribution, class imbalance, and variable characteristics. Next, the dataset was prepared through a series of preprocessing steps, which included cleaning to remove inconsistencies, imputation of missing values, feature scaling, splitting into training and test sets and resampling. Following this, multiple machine learning models were trained and evaluated using defined performance metrics. Finally, the selected models underwent hyperparameter tuning to improve their predictive performance. Each phase consisted of several sub-steps, which are described in detail in the subsequent sections.

Data Exploration- The data from SECOM had 1567 batches each with 590 features and a column of pass (-1)/ fail (1) labels with date time stamp for each batch. The class imbalance was studied, and the data showed 1463 pass cases (94%) and 104 fail cases.

Dataset Preparation - In this phase, multiple pipelines were adopted depending on the model. For the traditional models, LR, RF, SVM, and NN (shown as Approach 1 in Fig. 2), first carried data cleaning and feature selection were carried out, followed by feature reduction through removing columns with more than 55% missing values, which reduced the total number of features to 564.

Data Imputation- For data imputation, the remaining columns with missing values were filled using the median of each column. Columns with zero standard deviation were then removed, since variables without variation are unlikely to influence the pass/fail outcome; this step reduced the feature set to 450. Next, columns with a correlation greater than 0.95 were eliminated, leaving 275 features, as highly correlated variables contribute little additional information. Finally, variance inflation factor (VIF) analysis was applied to remove multicollinearity, resulting in a refined set of 232 features.

Data Scaling - For data scaling, the Robust Scaler method was applied. Min–Max scaling was discarded due to the presence of numerous outliers, and the Standard Scaler was rejected since the data did not follow a Gaussian distribution.

Data Splitting - After preprocessing, the dataset was split into training and testing sets, with 80% used for training and 20% for testing X_train: (1253, 232), X_test: (314, 232),Y_train: (1253,) Y_test: (314,).

Resampling - To address class imbalance, SMOTE resampling was applied, after resampling, the new training set was X_train_resampled: (2340, 232), Y_train_resampled: (2340,). This balanced dataset was then used for model training and evaluation, as discussed in the following section.

For the ensemble models, EEC and BRFC, depicted as Approaches 2, 3, 3(a), and 3(b) in Fig. 2, the dataset preparation process was shorter. The class imbalance was examined and then median imputation like the traditional models was applied. Unlike the earlier approach, feature reduction steps were skipped, data scaling using the Robust Scaler followed median imputation. Finally, the dataset was split into training and testing sets in an 80:20 ratio, resulting in X_train shape: (1253, 590), X_test shape: (314, 590). At this stage, four approaches were explored; they are denoted as 2, 3, 3(a), and 3(b) in Fig. 2. In Approach 2, resampling techniques such as SMOTE, ADASYN, SMOTE-K, and SMOTE-ENN were applied after data splitting, followed by training with either the EEC or BRFC model. In Approach 3, no resampling was performed, and the models were trained directly on the split data. Approach 3(a) incorporated SMOTE for resampling along with PCA for dimensionality reduction prior to training. Finally, in Approach 3(b), PCA was applied before model training, but no resampling technique was used.

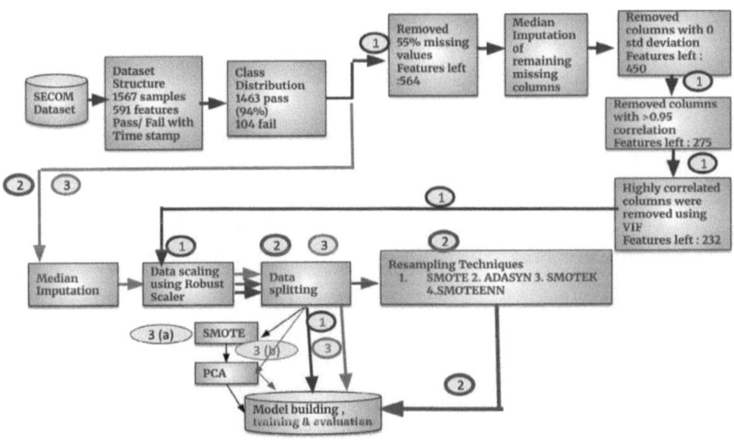

Fig. 2. Multiple approaches denoted by different colors 1(Traditional Models -Blue),2(Use of resampling techniques for ensemble models-Magenta), 3 tuned ensemble models - orange),3(a)(ensemble models with SMOTE & PCA 3(b) (ensemble models with SMOTE only)

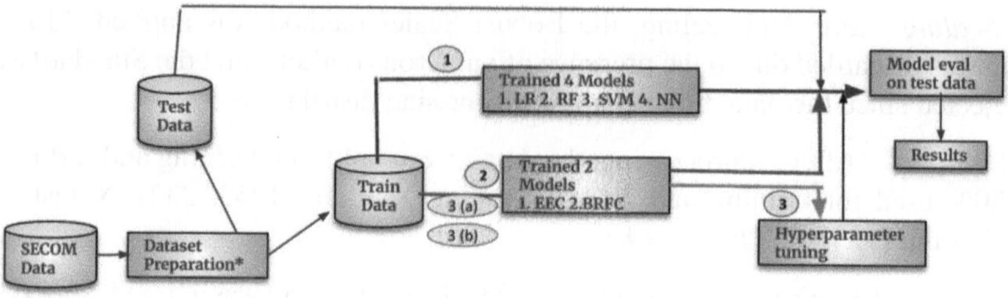

Fig. 3. Model training, evaluation and tuning

Model Training and Testing - Once dataset preparation was completed, six models were trained—LR, RF, SVM, NN, EEC and BRFC—across 22 pipelines on the training set and evaluated on the test set under the corresponding pipeline configuration. The different model–pipeline combinations are illustrated in Fig. 3.

Model Tuning - Model tuning was used in case of EEC and BRFC only in approach 3 where neither SMOTE or PCA were applied. The reason for hyperparameter tuning was to improve the F1-score. Randomized Search CV tool was used to find the best settings (hyperparameters) for our model as it randomly tries a set number of combinations instead of trying every single possible combination (which could take forever). It was used for hyperparameter tuning primarily because of the high number of variables in this case. Table 3, depicts the hyperparameters and their values used in case of EEC and BRFC. The hyperparameter *n_iter* specifies the number of different parameter combinations to be tested during model tuning. EEC model validation was performed using k-fold cross-validation, in which the training set is divided into k subsets (folds).

Table 3. Hyperparameter Values in EEC and BRFC Classifier

Hyperparameter Values	EEC	BRFC
n_iter	2	
cv	3	3,5,10
n_estimators		100, 200, 300
Max_features		sqrt, log2
Max_depth		10, 20, None
Min_samples_split		2, 5

The model is trained on $k - 1$ folds and evaluated on the remaining fold in an iterative manner. In this case, the training data was split into three folds; the training was done on two folds and validation on the third, with the process repeated three times. For BRFC, cross-validation with $cv = 3$ produced the most reliable results, which means that the BRFC model validation was performed using 3-fold cross-validation, in which the training set was divided into three subsets, and the model was iteratively trained on two folds and validated on the third fold, final reported performance reported was the average across all folds. The hyperparameter *n_estimators* specifies the number of trees in the forest. *Max_features* denotes the number of features considered when searching for the best split, thereby controlling the randomness of tree construction. *Max_depth* defines the maximum depth of a tree, which prevents excessive splitting and overfitting. *Min_samples_split* sets the minimum number of samples required to split an internal node, while *min_samples_leaf* determines the minimum number of samples required to form a leaf node, ensuring that each leaf has sufficient representation.

Post hyperparameter tuning, there was an improvement in BRFC in recall and precision while accuracy remained the same whereas in case of EEC reduced from 0.62 to 0.43. There was a moderate improvement in F1-score in both BRFC and EEC. Finally, as mentioned in the results and discussion section BRFC was selected as the best model based on F1 score. The top 10 features were found using Permutation Importance. This technique measures the importance of a feature by observing the decrease in a model's performance when the feature's values are randomly shuffled. This method randomly shuffles the values of a single feature and captures the decrease in model's F1-score. The bigger the drop, the more important that feature is to the model's predictions.

References

1. Secom: UCI machine learning repository. archive.ics.uci.edu/dataset/179/secom. Accessed 10 Aug 2025
2. Kerdprasop, K., Kerdprasop, N.: Feature selection and boosting techniques to improve fault detection accuracy in the semiconductor manufacturing process. In: Proceedings of the International MultiConference of Engineers and Computer Scientists 2011, vol. I (IMECS 2011), Hong Kong, 16–18 March 20111
3. Munirathinam, S., Ramadoss, B.: Predictive models for equipment fault detection in the semiconductor manufacturing process. Int. J. Eng. Technol. **8**(4), 273–285 (2016). https://doi.org/10.7763/IJET.2016.V8.898
4. Park, H.-J., et al.: Study on data preprocessing for machine learning based on semiconductor manufacturing processes. Sensors **24**(17), 546 (2024). https://doi.org/10.3390/s24175461
5. El Mourabit, Y., et al.: Predictive system of semiconductor failures based on machine learning approach. Int. J. Adv. Comput. Sci. Appl. (IJACSA) **11**(12), 1–7 (2020). https://doi.org/10.14569/IJACSA.2020.0111225
6. Pradeep, D., et al.: Optimal predictive maintenance technique for manufacturing semiconductors using machine learning. In: Proceedings of the 2023 International Conference on Communication and Technology (ICCT), pp. 1–5 (2023). https://doi.org/10.1109/ICCT56969.2023.10075658
7. Anghel, I., et al.: Prediction of manufacturing processes errors: gradient boosted trees versus deep neural networks. In: Proceedings of the 2018 IEEE 16th International Conference on Embedded and Ubiquitous Computing (EUC), pp. 29–36 (2018). https://doi.org/10.1109/EUC.2018.00012
8. Ramachandra, K.: UCI SECOM semiconductor manufacturing process FMT. Kaggle (2022). www.kaggle.com/code/srkvinu/uci-secom-semiconductor-manufacturing-process-fmt. Accessed 10 Aug 2025

Intelligent Road Design: Exploring Autonomous Agent Approaches for Infrastructure Planning

Yameng Guo[1(✉)] and Seppe vanden Broucke[1,2]

[1] Department of Business Informatics and Operations Management, Ghent University, Tweekerkenstraat 2, 9000 Ghent, Belgium
{yameng.guo,seppe.vandenbroucke}@ugent.be
[2] Research Centre for Information Systems Engineering, KU Leuven, Naamsestraat 69, Leuven, Belgium

Abstract. Road planning and design, as a crucial aspect of modern urban development, is becoming increasingly challenging for traditional optimization approaches. With the growing scale and complexity of real-world environments driven by urbanization and globalization, explicit modeling can become both infeasible and intractable for optimizers that rely on static objective functions and hard-coded constraints. To address this limitation, we explore the usage of a fully autonomous LLM-based agent (GPT-5), equipped with tools for construction, simulation, and reasoning to design and build road networks in a simulated world to optimize a delivery-related task. By comparing the planning capabilities of agentic AI and traditional optimizers, we demonstrate that although the agent-based approach cannot yet fully match optimizers in terms of planning objectives, it nonetheless exhibits strong potential in route planning, budget control, and interpretability, while requiring minimal manual modeling or coding.

Keywords: Autonomous agents · Intelligent planning · Automated road construction · Cost-aware path planning

1 Introduction

Road planning is fundamental to civilization and regional development, with profound implications for economic growth, social connectivity, environmental sustainability, and public safety. As a critical component of transportation systems, road design directly influences decision-making across government agencies, urban planners, and private stakeholders. Well-planned road networks not only enhance accessibility but also reduce travel time and emissions, aligning with the current energy crisis and the growing emphasis on sustainability.

Given its practical importance, road planning has attracted broad attention from researchers. However, unlike many other planning and operational problems, road planning must first contend with complex real-world landscapes that

C. Xu (Ed.): ICMLSC 2026, CCIS 2948, pp. 636–652, 2027.
https://doi.org/10.1007/978-981-92-1546-1_51

encompass diverse terrains such as mountains, rivers, forests, and grasslands. Each associated with distinct construction costs, ecological sensitivities, and regulatory constraints. Moreover, urbanization and globalization further amplify this complexity, making it increasingly difficult to model realistic environments in a robust way, and together, demand modern road systems to be not only cost-effective but also adaptable, equitable, and sustainable.

Traditional approaches to road design have largely relied on mathematical optimization techniques, including shortest-path algorithms [16], linear and integer programming formulations [18], and heuristic solvers such as simulated annealing [1] and genetic algorithms [7]. Under well-defined assumptions, these methods provide strong theoretical guarantees and yield globally or near-optimal solutions supported by rigorous mathematical proofs. However, their effectiveness diminishes as real-world complexity increases. First, their scalability is often constrained in large-scale or high-resolution geographic domains due to the exponential growth of computational time and memory requirements. Second, their static objective functions and hard-coded constraints struggle to incorporate real-time data, such as evolving policies, land-use trends, or environmental regulations. Finally, the modeling process itself is labor-intensive, requiring explicit definitions of cost functions, constraints, and objectives, which are often difficult to translate directly from real-world conditions into formalized models.

In response, the rise of agent-based modeling in recent years, particularly through reinforcement learning and large language models (LLMs), offers a promising alternative. Unlike traditional optimizers, agent-based systems can naturally integrate heterogeneous information sources ranging from satellite imagery and policy documents to social media and news reports, demonstrating strong adaptability to dynamic environments. Moreover, instead of relying on explicit environmental models and risking oversimplification, these agents learn iteratively through simulation and even human feedback. LLMs, in particular, exhibit exceptional flexibility in interactivity and interpretability, as they enable human-in-the-loop refinement, allowing designs to be collaboratively adjusted based on expert or community input, while also explaining their reasoning in natural language.

Despite these advantages, there is currently no systematic analysis of the feasibility and efficiency of using LLMs to solve road planning problems. As such, our work aims to make the following contributions:

- We develop a simulation environment that models diverse landscape types and their associated construction costs, providing a controlled yet realistic testbed for road planning.
- We design an autonomous LLM-based agent capable of perceiving terrain, reasoning about trade-offs, and proposing road routes through iterative dialogue and simulation and solving the route problems across multiple scenarios.
- We systematically compare the performance of the LLM-based agent and classical optimization solvers under varying budget constraints.

- All experiment code and results are publicly available in our GitHub repository[1] to foster reproducibility and future research in agent-based infrastructure design.

The remainder of this paper is organized as follows: Sect. 2 reviews related work on optimization and agent-based road design. Section 3 describes the simulation environment and modeling setup. Section 4 presents comparison settings and the competed optimization solver. Section 5 discusses results and insights, followed by conclusions in Sect. 6.

2 Related Work

Road planning is a long-standing applied problem at the intersection of civil engineering, transportation science, and spatial planning. Well-designed road networks can significantly improve traffic flow and vehicle speed, thereby reducing operating costs [24] and enhancing road safety [14]. Beyond urban development, road planning also plays an essential role in addressing environmental challenges, supporting applications such as wildfire management [13] and eco-route planning [25], which help mitigate environmental pressures.

Prior research on automated road design generally follows two main paradigms: optimization-based methods, which aim to identify cost-minimal network configurations under explicit constraints, and agent-based approaches, which learn adaptive planning policies through simulation and interaction. This section reviews both paradigms, highlighting their respective strengths and limitations.

2.1 Optimization-Based Methods

Optimization-based methods have long dominated the technical literature on automated road design and route planning. Among these approaches, classical shortest-path algorithms such as Dijkstra's [5,11] and A* [9] are widely applied due to their explicit modeling capabilities and cost-aware formulations that can be adapted to diverse optimization problems. Numerous variants have been developed to extend their applicability beyond static data [21], incorporating dynamic environments [4], temporal dependencies [6], and hierarchical structures [19].

Another line of research leverages network design optimization, which explicitly models terrain and integrates additional context-aware variables such as traffic noise [23], vehicle characteristics [17], and ecological sensitivity, for example, air pollution [12], into static cost models for point-to-point routing.

While these mathematical approaches provide deterministic and reproducible results with strong theoretical guarantees of (near-)optimality under well-defined

[1] See: https://github.com/ArmonGo/minisim.

assumptions, and benefit from mathematical transparency that supports interpretability and regulatory compliance, they face major scalability and tractability challenges. When applied to large-scale, complex, nonconvex, or poorly structured problems, they require highly specific formulations and often struggle to find even feasible solutions within reasonable time limits.

To address these limitations, metaheuristic methods such as genetic algorithms [15], simulated annealing [1], and particle swarm optimization [22] have emerged as competitive alternatives. These techniques encode problem structures while iteratively mutating and evolving candidate solutions, enabling more efficient searches over complex, irregular, or non-linear cost landscapes.

However, metaheuristics share several of the same weaknesses as classical mathematical optimizers. Their computational cost in both time and memory increases rapidly with map size and constraint richness, making large-scale or high-resolution planning computationally prohibitive. Moreover, they typically assume static environments and fixed objective functions, whereas real-world road planning often contend with dynamic factors such as shifting land-use policies, climate risks, and community feedback. Most critically, defining a single comprehensive cost function that captures the full range of engineering, ecological, social, and economic trade-offs is often impractical or subjective, resulting in oversimplified models that fail to reflect real-world complexity.

2.2 Agent-Based Methods

In response to the limitations of traditional optimization methods, learning-based and agentic paradigms have recently emerged as promising alternatives. Reinforcement learning (RL) [26,27], for instance, enables agents to learn road-building policies through interactions with simulated environments and to generalize to unseen terrains. RL can adapt to stochastic or evolving conditions and implicitly capture complex cost structures from experience rather than relying on explicit mathematical modeling.

However, RL approaches face several significant challenges. First, they require large amounts of simulation data, which can be impractical or costly to obtain. Second, although explicit modeling is unnecessary, RL methods still depend on a well-defined reward function to guide learning. If reward feedback is delayed or insufficiently informative, the agent may easily converge to suboptimal or unstable policies. Also, in real-world applications, RL systems often suffer from instability, being highly sensitive to data quantity, reward design, and hyperparameter tuning. Moreover, their decision-making processes are typically opaque, which limits interpretability and trust in high-stakes planning contexts.

A promising alternative lies in large language model (LLM)-based agentic systems. Unlike RL, LLM agents leverage vast pre-trained knowledge and can reason over multimodal and real-time inputs (e.g., maps, policy documents, news) using natural language. They can interact with tools, such as road-building simulators or cost estimators, to iteratively plan, build, evaluate, and refine designs through self-reflection or human feedback. Most importantly, they are the only options that can provide reasoning explanation in human-understandable terms, facilitating collaboration with planners.

Recent studies have explored the use of LLMs for city and traffic planning tasks. For example, some work has focused on navigation tasks, where an agent plans routes to specific landmarks using street-view inputs [10]. More commonly, LLMs have been applied as planning components in self-driving systems alongside rule-based planners [20] or for multi-vehicle dispatching and navigation [3].

Building on these prior efforts, we design a fully autonomous LLM-based agent tasked with solving depot-to-depot road planning problems across diverse simulated landscapes. In contrast to existing work, our study does not focus on optimizing routes within pre-existing road networks. Instead, our agent creates entirely new road layouts from unstructured terrain information addressing a higher-level generative design problem.

The agent is equipped with a suite of tools including terrain analysis, road construction, cost simulation, and self-evaluation to execute the entire planning cycle end-to-end. We benchmark its performance against a classical optimizer (using the CBC solver for MILP) across multiple scenarios with varying terrain complexity, and budget constraints. Furthermore, unlike approaches that rely on vision-language models (VLMs) or multimodal mapping pipelines to convert visual data (e.g., satellite imagery or street views) into structured representations before or after reasoning [3], our agent operates purely in the textual domain. This not only eliminates the need for external mapping models and supports a unified, interpretable reasoning process, but also avoid possible information loss during the translation.

Finally, our agent departs from conventional single-step reasoning or static-prompt paradigms by demonstrating self-reflective and self-corrective capabilities through the use of simulation tools. To ensure transparency and reproducibility, we also release a fully extensible simulation framework, including code, environment generation utilities, and evaluation pipelines, to facilitate benchmarking and future research on agentic infrastructure design.

3 Methodology

This section provides details of the simulated grid world used for route planning and the configuration of the agent.

3.1 Environment

The grid-based planning environment is designed to simulate depot transportation scenarios, where delivery vehicles depart from supply depots and travel across diverse landscapes to reach demand depots. Each supply depot is assigned a value representing the quantity of goods available, while each demand depot specifies the required amount of supply to be received.

The environment is represented as a discrete $W \times H$ grid world containing three terrain types: grass, water, and mountain. Based on these, three base maps are generated with increasing terrain diversity as illustrated in Fig. 1. Two categories of depots (supply and demand) are distributed across the grid.

Fig. 1. The basic layout of generated maps. Demand and supply depots are represented as red and green cells correspondingly, and marked explicitly on the map. (Tile images from: KenneyNL.)

In addition to terrain tiles, the environment includes three passable infrastructure types, i.e., road, bridge, and tunnel, with respective construction costs of 10, 30, and 100 units per tile. Roads can be built only on grass, bridges only over water, and tunnels only through mountainous areas.

Vehicles spawn from supply depots and can move only along constructed infrastructure tiles. Movement is restricted such that at most one vehicle may depart per time step and only one vehicle may occupy a tile at any time. The planner's objective is to construct a feasible, cost-efficient road network that satisfies all demand depots while minimizing either the total number of tiles used or the total construction cost under a given budget constraint.

All rules and specifications of the grid world are summarized in Table 1.

3.2 Agent

The autonomous LLM-based agent is designed to perceive, reason, and act within the simulated environment through a tool-augmented framework. All inputs, prompts, available tools, and output formats are explicitly predefined to ensure both consistent execution and transparent explanation of the road design process.

Input. Recognizing that current LLMs have limited native spatial reasoning capabilities, we experimented with three input representations of the grid world: an ASCII grid, a JSON object, and encoded images. Among these, the structured JSON format was selected as the primary input, due to its flexibility in extending feature definitions (e.g., adding new tile types) and its natural alignment with LLMs' strengths in parsing symbolic and hierarchical data. Moreover, maintaining a purely text-based pipeline avoids intermediate translation steps, thereby preserving complete and precise spatial information.

Table 1. Environment specifications: landscape types, compatible infrastructure, costs, and planning rules.

Landscape	Passable Tile	Cost	Notes
Grass	Road	10	Standard buildable terrain
Water	Bridge	30	Required to cross water bodies
Mountain	Tunnel	100	Required to traverse mountains

Depots and Delivery Rules

- Supply depots generate cars and have a supply value.
- Demand depots have fulfillment targets (depot value).
- Cars move only on passable tiles (road/bridge/tunnel), not on depots.
- One car departs per time ticks; one car per tile at any time.
- Cars follow the shortest route to demand depots which still require supply.
- Delivery is spawn-based: cars at supply depots and route to demand depots.

Planning Objectives

- Feasibility: all demand depots must be fully supplied.
- Minimize total number of infrastructure tiles used.
- Minimize total cost, subject to a global budget constraint.

Context and Tools. To enable active interaction with the mutable simulated world (e.g., modifying or executing a design), the grid world is encapsulated as a context object, to which the agent is granted access through a predefined set of tools (see Table 2). Each tool can be invoked multiple times, and the agent autonomously decides when to terminate the design process and return the final layout.

Table 2. Agent tools and their attributes.

Tool	Action	Cost
`build_road(x, y)`	Build road on grass	−10
`build_bridge(x, y)`	Build bridge on water	−30
`build_tunnel(x, y)`	Build tunnel on mountain	−100
`remove_road(x, y)`	Remove road	+10
`remove_bridge(x, y)`	Remove bridge	+30
`remove_tunnel(x, y)`	Remove tunnel	+100
`run_simulation()`	Execute delivery simulation	—
`summarize_world()`	Export grid state as JSON	—

Prompt. The agent is guided by a system prompt that defines its role ("You are an intelligent Road Planner"), the given world description, design rules and objectives, available tools, and required output structure. The prompt content is adjusted for different test scenarios. For instance, in settings without budget constraints, cost information is omitted, whereas for budget-constrained cases, the prompt explicitly includes rules such as,

> You have an initial budget of 200. Each tile has its own cost, ROAD costs 10, BRIDGE costs 30, and TUNNEL costs 100. Please use those tile within the given budget. Adding tiles will use your budget, remove tiles will return the budget. So you can always replan.

In addition to the system prompt, a user prompt is provided at runtime to instruct the agent to operate fully autonomously, executing its own plan without external confirmation. This ensures that the agent independently handles both decision-making and execution within the simulation.

Output. A key advantage of the LLM-based agent is its ability to produce natural-language explanations of its reasoning and actions (e.g., *"The demand depot at location (3,2) is not connected to any supply depot, therefore I will construct a road from (3,3) to (3,7) to connect them."*). To leverage this capability, we explicitly define the output structure to include both a reasoning explanation for each design iteration and a structured action log that records invoked tools and their parameters, allowing the entire design process to be traced and analyzed.

4 Comparison

4.1 Optimizer

Two systems are included in the comparison, i.e., the agentic AI and the classical optimization approach.

For the classical optimization baseline, we employ a Mixed-Integer Linear Programming (MILP) model [8], solved using the CBC solver [2], to evaluate the capability of the agentic AI. MILP is a mathematical optimization framework that seeks to minimize or maximize a linear objective function subject to linear equality and inequality constraints. It is widely used in combinatorial decision-making tasks such as logistics, routing, scheduling, and network design, as it can precisely encode both continuous and discrete (integer or binary) variables.

In this study, the road-building task is framed as a flow optimization problem, where the existence of a building tile is represented by a binary variable (0 or 1). The model searches for an optimal set of connected paths between neighboring tiles. The cost function is defined based on the construction costs associated with different terrain types (e.g., grass, river, mountain), and the objective is to minimize the total construction cost required to establish connectivity between supply depots and demand depots, subject to a fixed budget constraint. The mathematical model is formally defined as follows.

Variables:	$y_i \in \{0,1\}$	for each node $i \in N$ (1 if tile i is built)
	$f_{ij} \geq 0$	for each directed edge $(i,j) \in E$ (flow amount)
Parameters:	c_i	build cost of node i (depends on underlying terrain type)
	b_i	net supply at node i : $\begin{cases} +s_i & \text{if } i \in \text{SUPPLY DEPOT} \\ -d_i & \text{if } i \in \text{DEMAND DEPOT} \\ 0 & \text{otherwise} \end{cases}$
	B	total budget constraint
	M	a sufficiently large constant (capacity big-M)

Objective:

$$\min \sum_{i \in N} c_i\, y_i \tag{1}$$

Subject to:

(Flow conservation)

$$\sum_{j:(i,j) \in E} f_{ij} - \sum_{j:(j,i) \in E} f_{ji} = b_i \qquad \forall i \in N \tag{2}$$

(Edge to build link)

$$f_{ij} \leq M\, y_i \qquad f_{ij} \leq M\, y_j \qquad \forall (i,j) \in E \tag{3}$$

(Budget limit)

$$\sum_{i \in N} c_i\, y_i \leq B \tag{4}$$

(No flow from demands)

$$\sum_{j:(i,j) \in E} f_{ij} = 0 \qquad \forall i \in \text{DEMAND DEPOT} \tag{5}$$

(No flow into supplies)

$$\sum_{j:(j,i) \in E} f_{ji} = 0 \qquad \forall i \in \text{SUPPLY DEPOT} \tag{6}$$

4.2 Configuration

For comparison, an autonomous agent powered by GPT-5 (accessed via the OpenAI SDK) is tested on each scenario, with a maximum of 20 interaction turns per instance. For the optimization-based baseline, each instance is executed with a 20-minute time limit, after which the solver reports the status of the final solution (optimal or non-optimal). This constraint reflects the practical computational limits commonly encountered in real-world planning workflows.

Both approaches are provided with identical initial world states and constraints, including all terrain types (grass, river, and mountain) and all construction tile options (road, bridge, and tunnel), subject to the same budget limitation.

Performance is evaluated based on budget utilization and route connectivity achieved in the designed road networks.

4.3 Objective

Three objectives are proposed and tested to evaluate the capability of the autonomous agent in route planning, including handling increasing environmental and tool complexity, enhancing cost efficiency under budget constraints, and autonomously diagnosing scenarios and adaptively re-planning.

Table 3. Test scenarios designed to evaluate the reasoning and adaptability of the LLM-based road planning agent.

Scenario	Description
Archipelago Logistics	A fragmented landscape dominated by water and scattered mountain region. The agent must identify critical bridge placements to connect isolated depots, testing spatial reasoning and long-range planning.
Efficiency Audit	The agent is provided with a suboptimal blueprint containing redundant road tiles. It must simulate, detect unused infrastructure, and remove unnecessary tiles, assessing its capability for post-hoc optimization.
Budget Crisis	Given an initially infeasible plan and a limited budget, the agent must re-plan to achieve feasibility while maintaining optimal routes, probing its resilience and re-planning agility.
Priority Assignment	Demand depots are assigned varying priority levels. The agent must allocate limited resources to maximize total value delivery by matching high-demand depots with corresponding high-supply sources, testing value-sensitive decision-making.

Objective One. — **Test whether the agent can progressively adapt to increasing terrain complexity and available construction types.**

The complexity increases along two dimensions, i.e., the variety of available landscape tiles and the number of construction tools. Three stages of the environment are considered containing grass-only (where only roads can be built), grass and water (where bridges become necessary to cross water bodies), and grass, water, and mountain (requiring tunnels to traverse mountainous areas).

At each stage, the agent must learn to match the correct construction type to the corresponding terrain while minimizing the total number of tiles used. Not all tools are available from the beginning, so the agent must evaluate the accessible tools and determine whether a connected route is feasible given the currently available construction options.

Objective Two. — **Test whether the agent can discover cost trade-offs through simulation feedback and minimizes total expenditure while fulfilling all demand.**

In this experiment, with given map size and available tools, we introduce limited budget (e.g., 500, 1000, 2000 cost units) and ask agent to minimize the cost but prioritize the fulfillment of the demands.

Objective Three. — **Test whether the agent can employ autonomous diagnosis and adaptive re-planning.**

We evaluate the agent's capacity for self-correction and strategic reasoning in complex, failure-prone scenarios. Four challenging cases are designed as shown in Table 3.

For each scenario, we record the agent action log and render its final designed route as image, and compare with the optimizer design. Full implementation, including environment generation, solver configuration, and agent prompting templates, is available in our open-source repository.

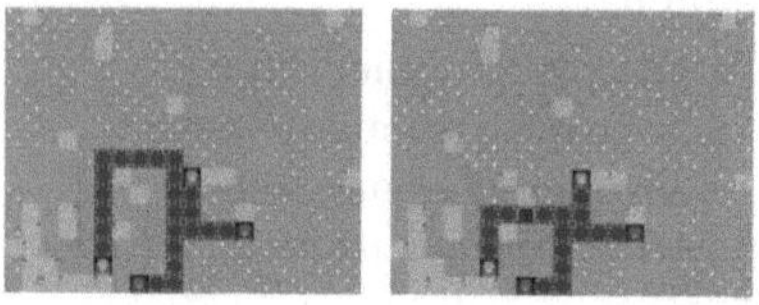

(a) Route designs generated by the agent using different construction tiles. Left: only roads on grass are allowed. Right: all tiles are permitted.

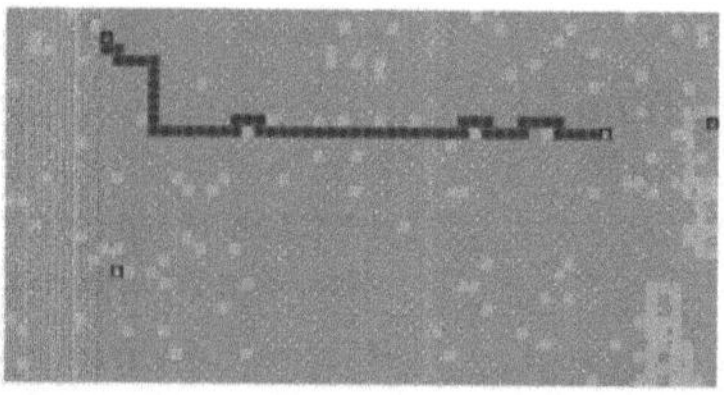

(b) Route designed by the agent when only roads built on grass are allowed.

Fig. 2. Comparison of route designs by the agent under different construction constraints.

5 Discussion

In this section, aligned with the objectives discussed earlier, we first present the agent's plans and performance as complexity increases in terms of both landscape types and available construction tools. Next, we introduce budget constraints and compare the agent's road designs with those generated by the optimizer under limited budgets. Finally, we discuss in detail the agent's responses to different scenarios. For the sake of brevity, not all results are shown here, however, all visual results are available on our GitHub repository.

Complexity. As shown in Table 4, the agent successfully designs connected roads in all cases with increasing complexity as long as feasible route exists (marked as "Possible", demonstrating its capability to adapt to different landscape and its autonomy in tools usage.

Moreover, as more construction tools become available, the agent adjusts its plans to select more efficient tile types to connect depots, minimizing the total number of tiles used. As illustrated in Fig. 2a, when roads on grass are the only available construction option, the agent identifies a circled path to connect the depots. When tunnels are allowed, it takes a shortcut through the central mountain terrain to reduce travel distance.

Even in cases where no fully connected paths exist, the agent continues to search actively. For example, in Fig. 2b, where only roads on grass can be built and the supply and demand depots are separated by mountains, the agent still constructs a path between feasible pairs and provides clear explanations in its output, e.g., "*The supply at (9,22) is trapped by mountains/water and cannot reach the wider map via ROAD-only rules. Likewise, demand at (59,9) is fully surrounded by impassable tiles (mountain/water) and has no adjacent GRASS to attach a road, so it cannot be served.*"

Budget Control. Regarding budget control, the agent exhibits a strong ability to manage costs, although it does not consistently outperform the traditional optimizer. Table 5 compares the budgets used by the agent and the optimizer when solving the same scenario, and Fig. 3 illustrates their detailed designs on the map. The results show that the agent achieves costs comparable to the optimizer's optimal solutions, despite typically slightly higher.

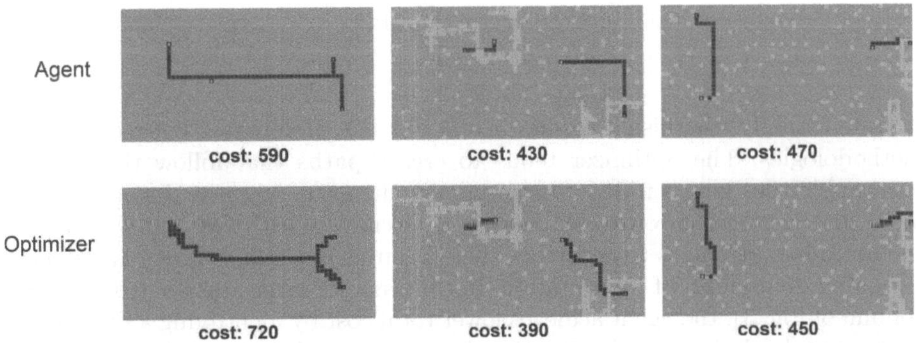

Fig. 3. Comparison of designed routes of both agent and optimizer under different budget constraints.

Table 4. Agent performance of road designing with increasing complexity.

Map Size	Landscape	Allowed Tiles	Used Tiles	Possible	Result
small	grass	road	19	yes	Success
medium	grass	road	42	yes	Success
large	grass	road	79	yes	Success
small	grass,water	road	16	no	10 demands left
medium	grass,water	road	5	no	10 demands left
large	grass,water	road	80	no	20 demands left
small	grass,water,mountain	road	23	yes	Success
medium	grass,water,mountain	road	13	no	10 demands left
large	grass,water,mountain	road	55	no	10 demands left
small	grass	road,bridge	22	yes	Success
medium	grass	road,bridge	42	yes	Success
large	grass	road,bridge	79	yes	Success
small	grass,water	road,bridge	18	yes	Success
medium	grass,water	road,bridge	11	yes	Success
large	grass,water	road,bridge	31	yes	Success
small	grass,water,mountain	road,bridge	22	yes	Success
medium	grass,water,mountain	road,bridge	11	no	10 demands left
large	grass,water,mountain	road,bridge	32	yes	Success
small	grass	road,bridge,tunnel	19	yes	Success
medium	grass	road,bridge,tunnel	42	yes	Success
large	grass	road,bridge,tunnel	59	yes	Success
small	grass,water	road,bridge,tunnel	18	yes	Success
medium	grass,water	road,bridge,tunnel	12	yes	Success
large	grass,water	road,bridge,tunnel	33	yes	Success
small	grass,water,mountain	road,bridge,tunnel	16	yes	Success
medium	grass,water,mountain	road,bridge,tunnel	26	yes	Success
large	grass,water,mountain	road,bridge,tunnel	22	yes	Success

Interestingly, the visual results reveal distinct preferences between the two methodologies. The optimizer tends to create paths that follow the edges of impassable tiles between depots to minimize distance, whereas the agent favors more direct, straight routes. Moreover, in scenarios with two pairs of depots, the optimizer attempts to construct shared routes but still retains redundancies even after 20 minutes of computation. In contrast, for large grass-only maps (first column of Fig. 3), the agent achieves lower total cost by identifying a shared path that serves both demand depots, thereby outperforming the optimizer in terms of expenditure.

Table 5. Comparison between the agent and the optimizer in budget control. (All construction tiles are allowed; ∗ denotes the solution is optimal.)

Size	Landscape	Budget	Agent Cost	Optimizer **Cost**
small	grass	200	190	190
medium	grass	600	420	420*
large	grass	900	590	720
small	grass,water	400	300	260
medium	grass,water	700	180	160*
large	grass,water	900	430	390
small	grass,water,mountain	500	180	180*
medium	grass,water,mountain	800	440	390
large	grass,water,mountain	1200	470	450

Scenario Handling. Regarding scenario handling (shown in Fig. 4), the agent successfully solves all scenarios both smoothly and efficiently. In the archipelago logistics scenario, the budget is insufficient to build more than one tunnel. The agent compensates by using additional bridges and road tiles, maintaining total costs under 500 units. In the budget crisis scenario, the agent removes some tunnels as expected to free up budget for additional road construction; however, it does not achieve the optimal solution, as two tunnels would have been sufficient, yet the agent retains three. For the efficiency audit scenario, the agent removes unnecessary roads even when there is no budget constraint, demonstrating an intelligent sense of optimization. Finally, in the priority assignment scenario, where paired supply and demand depots are separated by a river, the agent constructs a shared path connecting all depots to ensure full supply coverage.

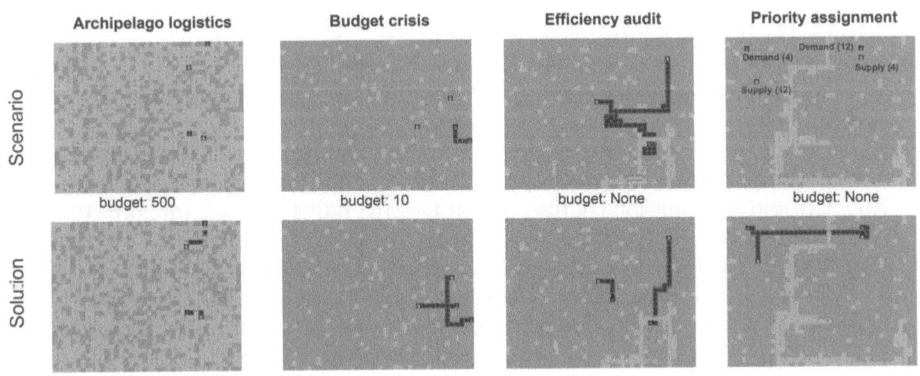

Fig. 4. Routes designed by the agent under different scenarios.

6 Conclusion

In this work, we presented a comparative study of classical optimization and agentic AI for automated road planning in complex terrains. We designed a grid-based simulation environment that captures real-world challenges, including heterogeneous landscapes (grass, water, mountains), infrastructure costs, depot logistics, and budget constraints. We compare the planning results by implementing both traditional MILP optimizer solved via CBC, and a fully autonomous LLM-based agent (GPT-5) equipped with tools for building, simulating, and reasoning about road networks. Our experiments shows that although the agent-based method cannot fully compete with optimizer in terms of planning objectives, in particular minimizing the cost and saving budget, it still displays promising ability of route planning and reasoning explanation. The results provide early but meaningful insights into the feasibility of agentic systems as interactive, interpretable, and flexible alternatives to rigid optimization pipelines in infrastructure planning.

Looking ahead, several promising directions emerge. First, we plan to evaluate a broader range of LLMs, including open-weight models like DeepSeek, Qwen, and Claude, to assess how architectural and training differences affect planning performance. Second, we aim to extend the objective space beyond cost and tile count, such as minimizing delivery time, maximizing resilience, or optimizing for environmental impact. Finally, the ultimate test lies in scaling to real-world geographic data. By integrating OpenStreetMap terrain, actual construction cost models, and urban planning regulations, we can earthly validate agentic planning in operational settings.

References

1. Amer, H.M., Salman, N., Hawes, M.B., Chaqfeh, M., Mihaylova, L., Mayfield, M.: An improved simulated annealing technique for enhanced mobility in smart cities. Sensors **16**(7), 1013 (2016). https://doi.org/10.3390/S16071013
2. Andreello, G., Caprara, A., Fischetti, M.: Embedding {0, 1/2}-cuts in a branch-and-cut framework: a computational study. INFORMS J. Comput. **19**(2), 229–238 (2007)
3. Chen, R., et al.: An LLM-driven framework for multiple-vehicle dispatching and navigation in smart city landscapes. In: 2024 IEEE International Conference on Robotics and Automation (ICRA), pp. 2147–2153 (2024). https://doi.org/10.1109/ICRA57147.2024.10610578
4. Demetrescu, C., Italiano, G.F.: A new approach to dynamic all pairs shortest paths. J. ACM **51**(6), 968–992 (2004). https://doi.org/10.1145/1039488.1039492
5. Dijkstra, E.W.: A note on two problems in connexion with graphs. Numer. Math. **1**, 269–271 (1959). https://doi.org/10.1007/BF01386390
6. Ding, B., Yu, J.X., Qin, L.: Finding time-dependent shortest paths over large graphs. In: Kemper, A., et al., (eds.) EDBT 2008, 11th International Conference on Extending Database Technology, Nantes, France, March 25-29, 2008, Proceedings. ACM International Conference Proceeding Series, vol. 261, pp. 205–216. ACM (2008). https://doi.org/10.1145/1353343.1353371

7. Feng, T., et al.: The optimal global path planning of mobile robot based on improved hybrid adaptive genetic algorithm in different tasks and complex road environments. IEEE Access **12**, 18400–18415 (2024). https://doi.org/10.1109/ACCESS.2024.3357990
8. Floudas, C.A., Lin, X.: Mixed integer linear programming in process scheduling: modeling, algorithms, and applications. Ann. Oper. Res. **139**(1), 131–162 (2005). https://doi.org/10.1007/S10479-005-3446-X
9. Hart, P.E., Nilsson, N.J., Raphael, B.: A formal basis for the heuristic determination of minimum cost paths. IEEE Trans. Syst. Sci. Cybern. **4**(2), 100–107 (1968). https://doi.org/10.1109/TSSC.1968.300136
10. Hermann, K.M., Malinowski, M., Mirowski, P., Banki-Horvath, A., Anderson, K., Hadsell, R.: Learning to follow directions in street view. In: The Thirty-Fourth AAAI Conference on Artificial Intelligence, AAAI 2020, The Thirty-Second Innovative Applications of Artificial Intelligence Conference, IAAI 2020, The Tenth AAAI Symposium on Educational Advances in Artificial Intelligence, EAAI 2020, New York, NY, USA, 7-12 February 2020, pp. 11773–11781. AAAI Press (2020). https://doi.org/10.1609/AAAI.V34I07.6849
11. Holzer, M., Schulz, F., Wagner, D., Willhalm, T.: Combining speed-up techniques for shortest-path computations. ACM J. Exp. Algorithmics **10** (2005). https://doi.org/10.1145/1064546.1180616
12. Jiang, F., Ma, L., Broyd, T., Chen, K., Luo, H., Pei, Y.: Sustainable road alignment planning in the built environment based on the mcdm-gis method. Sustain. Cities Soc. **87**, 104246 (2022)
13. Laschi, A., Foderi, C., Fabiano, F., Neri, F., Cambi, M., Mariotti, B., Marchi, E.: Forest road planning, construction and maintenance to improve forest fire fighting: a review. Croatian J. Frest Eng. J. Theory Appl. Forestry Eng. **40**(1), 207–219 (2019)
14. de Leur, P., Sayed, T.: A framework to proactively consider road safety within the road planning process. Can. J. Civ. Eng. **30**(4), 711–719 (2003)
15. Li, R., Leung, Y., Huang, B., Lin, H.: A genetic algorithm for multiobjective dangerous goods route planning. Int. J. Geogr. Inf. Sci. **27**(6), 1073–1089 (2013). https://doi.org/10.1080/13658816.2012.737921
16. Madkour, A., Aref, W.G., Rehman, F.U., Rahman, M.A., Basalamah, S.M.: A survey of shortest-path algorithms. CoRR **abs/1705.02044** (2017)
17. Oliveira, R., Ljungqvist, O., Lima, P.F., Wahlberg, B.: Optimization-based on-road path planning for articulated vehicles. IFAC-PapersOnLine **53**(2), 15572–15579 (2020)
18. Roling, P.C., Visser, H.G.: Optimal airport surface traffic planning using mixed-integer linear programming. Int. J. Aerospace Eng. **2008**(1), 732828 (2008)
19. Sanders, P., Schultes, D.: Highway hierarchies hasten exact shortest path queries. In: Brodal, G.S., Leonardi, S. (eds.) ESA 2005. LNCS, vol. 3669, pp. 568–579. Springer, Heidelberg (2005). https://doi.org/10.1007/11561071_51
20. Sharan, S.P., Pittaluga, F., G, V.K.B., Chandraker, M.: LLM-assist: enhancing closed-loop planning with language-based reasoning. CoRR **abs/2401.00125** (2024).https://doi.org/10.48550/ARXIV.2401.00125
21. Sommer, C.: Shortest-path queries in static networks. ACM Comput. Surv. **46**(4), 45:1–45:31 (2014). https://doi.org/10.1145/2530531
22. Sundarraj, S., Reddy, R.V.K., Basam, M.B., Gururaj, H.L., Flammini, F., Natarajan, R.: Route planning for an autonomous robotic vehicle employing a weight-controlled particle swarm-optimized dijkstra algorithm. IEEE Access **11**, 92433–92442 (2023). https://doi.org/10.1109/ACCESS.2023.3302698

23. Wang, H., Sun, B., Chen, L.: An optimization model for planning road networks that considers traffic noise impact. Appl. Acoust. **192**, 108693 (2022)
24. Watanatada, T., Dhareshwar, A.M., Lima, P.R.: Vehicle speeds and operating costs: Models for road planning and management. Tech. rep, International Bank for Reconstruction and Development, Washington, DC (USA) (1987)
25. Yao, E., Song, Y.: Study on eco-route planning algorithm and environmental impact assessment. J. Intell. Transp. Syst. **17**(1), 42–53 (2013)
26. Zheng, Y., Lin, Y., Zhao, L., Wu, T., Jin, D., Li, Y.: Spatial planning of urban communities via deep reinforcement learning. Nat. Comput. Sci. **3**(9), 748–762 (2023). https://doi.org/10.1038/S43588-023-00503-5
27. Zheng, Y., Su, H., Ding, J., Jin, D., Li, Y.: Road planning for slums via deep reinforcement learning. In: Singh, A.K., et al., (eds.) Proceedings of the 29th ACM SIGKDD Conference on Knowledge Discovery and Data Mining, KDD 2023, Long Beach, CA, USA, 6-10 August 2023, pp. 5695–5706. ACM (2023). https://doi.org/10.1145/3580305.3599901

A Sim-Heuristic Approach Cooperating Leaf in Wind Optimization with Ordinal Optimization

Shih-Cheng Horng(✉)

Department of Computer Science and Information Engineering, Chaoyang University of Technology, 168, Jifong E. Road, Wufeng District, Taichung City 413310, Taiwan, R.O.C.
schong@cyut.edu.tw

Abstract. The stochastic discrete optimization problems (SDOP) consider the problem of optimizing a stochastic function subject to constraints on the discrete variables. This problem is NP-hard because of exponential growth in computational complexity. The ordinal optimization framework is a framework that decreases the computational effort in simulation-based optimization. A sim-heuristic approach cooperating leaf in wind optimization with ordinal optimization is developed to solve this SDOP in a short time. The sim-heuristic approach comprises two phases. In the first phase, leaf in wind optimization algorithm is used to construct a differentiated subset with rough estimation. In the second phase, ranking and selection method is used to find a superior solution from differentiated subsets. The optimal production planning problem of reconfigurable manufacturing systems is formulated as a SDOP. Then, the sim-heuristic approach is utilized to determine the optimal tasks assignment to workstation and buffer allocation for maximizing throughput. A real-life example consisting of 3 workstations with 2 inter-station buffers is applied to test the performance. Experimental results reveal that the sim-heuristic approach can yield stable and best results.

Keywords: Stochastic discrete optimization problems · ordinal optimization · leaf in wind optimization · reconfigurable manufacturing systems

1 Introduction

The stochastic discrete optimization problems (SDOP) consider the problem of optimizing a stochastic function subject to constraints on the discrete variables [1]. The goal of SDOP is to determine optimal solution which optimizes the stochastic function while also satisfying all constraints [2]. SDOP occur in a wide variety of practical applications, including reverse supply chain networks, periodic inspection inventory systems, facility location, buffer capacity allocation, and production planning of reconfigurable manufacturing systems (RMS). The SDOP involve computationally expensive simulations or costly real experiments. The SDOP is a typical example of NP-hard class. NP-hard problems are incredibly challenging because they generally cannot be solved in polynomial time, but developed solutions can be quickly verified in polynomial time.

C. Xu (Ed.): ICMLSC 2026, CCIS 2948, pp. 653–663, 2027.
https://doi.org/10.1007/978-981-92-1546-1_52

The challenge in solving NP-hard problems arises from their computational complexity. Sim-heuristic approaches combine simulation techniques inside a metaheuristic optimization framework to deal with NP-hard problems. In sim-heuristic approaches, simulation replications are performed to evaluate the objective values of solutions obtained by the metaheuristic. Then, the feedback from the simulation is used to guide the metaheuristic search process. Metaheuristic algorithms have been categorized into six categories based on their behavior: evolutionary [3], swarm intelligence [4], mathematic based [5], physics based [6], human behavior [7], and game based [8].

Two challenges are raised regarding a solution provided by the metaheuristic. (i) Is this solution remarkable enough to invest an additional computing budget in a stochastic environment? (ii) How much of the computing effort should be allocated to achieve the required minimum level of accuracy? Fortunately, ordinal optimization (OO) [9, 10] theory is becoming a relevant framework to address these two challenges. OO is a framework that decreases the computational effort in simulation-based optimization. The OO theory can significantly improve computing efficiency. Compared with traditional heuristic methods, the computational burden is saved by at least an order of magnitude. The OO theory has found successful applications in various fields, including container freight stations in air cargo [11], multiple-item stock level system [12], medical resource allocation [13], and sorting conveyor systems [14].

In today's fast-paced and competitive manufacturing environment, the ability to adapt quickly to changing market demands is essential. In a small and diverse consumer market, manufacturers' adaptability to demand diversity, speed of market response, and product quality are all key. When facing the needs of different customers, how manufacturers should respond to this market environment, the most important of which is the flexibility of manufacturing equipment. RMS are designed to be adjustable and scalable, allowing manufacturers to rapidly respond to changes in product demand, new product introductions, or changes in regulatory requirements. The concept of RMS evolved from the need for more flexible manufacturing systems in the late 20th century. Traditional manufacturing systems were often rigid and dedicated to producing a specific product, making it difficult and costly to adapt to changes. The development of RMS was driven by advancements in technology, including computer-aided design (CAD), robotics, and information technology (IT). These advancements enabled the creation of more flexible and modular manufacturing systems.

The most important feature of the RMS is its reconfigurability, which can quickly adjust the system and change the output products or production capacity according to customer needs or market changes. Therefore, the reconfigurable manufacturing system not only provides manufacturers with a high degree of flexibility, but also helps the manufacturing industry transform in the post-epidemic era and can quickly respond to market changes. By enabling the rapid reconfiguration of manufacturing systems, RMS can improve production efficiency and productivity. Manufacturers can optimize production processes for specific products, reducing waste and improving quality. RMS can help reduce costs by minimizing the need for new equipment purchases when production requirements change. Additionally, the ability to quickly adapt to changing market demands can increase a manufacturer's competitiveness.

The contribution of this work is twofold. First, a sim-heuristic approach that uses leaf in wind optimization (LiWO) [15] coordinated with ordinal optimization (OO) is developed to solve SDOP to determine a superior solution in a reasonable time. The sim-heuristic approach comprises two phases. In the first phase, LiWO is used to construct a differentiated subset with rough estimation. In the second phase, ranking and selection (R&S) methods [16, 17] are used to find a superior solution from differentiated subsets. Secondly, the framework and simulation process for reconfigurable manufacturing systems are presented. Furthermore, a real-world example is utilized to validate the proposed approach.

The subsequent sections of this work are structured as follows. In Sect. 2, we present the the stochastic discrete optimization problems. Next, we present the sim-heuristic approach that cooperates LiWO with OO. In Sect. 3, we present the framework and simulation process for a reconfigurable manufacturing system and demonstrate the simulation results of a real-world example. Finally, Sect. 4 draws a conclusion.

2 Sim-Heuristic Approach

2.1 Stochastic Discrete Optimization Problems

A typical SDOP can be formulated as bellows.

$$\min \mathrm{E}\big[f(\boldsymbol{x})\big] \tag{1}$$

$$\text{subject to } \; h(\boldsymbol{x}) \le H, \tag{2}$$

$$g(\boldsymbol{x}) = G, \tag{3}$$

$$\boldsymbol{LB} \le \boldsymbol{x} \le \boldsymbol{UB}, \tag{4}$$

where $\boldsymbol{x} = [x_1, \ldots, x_K]^T$ depicts a K-dimensional setting with nonnegative discrete variables, $\mathrm{E}\big[f(\boldsymbol{x})\big]$ represents the expected objective function, $h(\boldsymbol{x}) \le H$ denotes the inequality constraint, $g(\boldsymbol{x}) = G$ depicts the equality constraint,, and $\boldsymbol{LB} = [LB_1, \ldots, LB_K]^T$, $\boldsymbol{UB} = [UB_1, \ldots, UB_K]^T$ depict the lower and upper limit, respectively. An appropriate number of replications are performed to evaluate $\mathrm{E}\big[f(\boldsymbol{x})\big]$ in an accurate estimation. The sample average approximation uses samples of random realizations to estimate the expected value $\mathrm{E}\big[f(\boldsymbol{x})\big]$, where L denotes the number of replications, and $f^{\ell}(\boldsymbol{x})$ is the evaluation of the ℓ th replication.

$$\bar{f}(\boldsymbol{x}) = \frac{1}{L}\sum_{\ell=1}^{L} f^{\ell}(\boldsymbol{x}) \tag{5}$$

Large value of L can evaluate $\mathrm{E}\big[f(\boldsymbol{x})\big]$ more accurate. Therefore, we consider two targets: (i) L should be sufficiently large to obtain accurate evaluation of $\mathrm{E}\big[f(\boldsymbol{x})\big]$, (ii) $\bar{f}(\boldsymbol{x})$ can to be estimated for different settings to select the best setting.

A popular way to handle constraints in stochastic optimization is to adopt penalty functions, which add a cost to the objective function for violating a constraint [18].

$$\min F(\boldsymbol{x}) = \frac{1}{L}\sum_{\ell=1}^{L} f^{\ell}(\boldsymbol{x}) + \frac{\eta}{2}\cdot\left[(\max\{0, h(\boldsymbol{x}) - H\})^2 + (g(\boldsymbol{x}) - G)^2\right] \tag{6}$$

where η indicates a penalty weight, and $F(\boldsymbol{x})$ is a quadratic penalty function.

2.2 Rough Estimation

Simulation-optimization uses simulation to evaluate the performance of a system under different scenarios and optimization to find the optimal scenario or decision variables. Optimization-simulation uses optimization to generate feasible solutions for a system and simulation to test and refine them. Metaheuristics also employ heuristic algorithms, such as genetic algorithms or simulated annealing, that combine simulation and optimization elements. Simulation and optimization are both useful for industrial engineering, but they have different strengths and limitations.

A key issue in applying OO is knowing when we are sufficiently confident or satisfied with the ordinal result, e.g., a good subset has been identified with high probability. It adopts rough estimation to establish a differentiated subset for which simulation is worthwhile and necessary to determine superior solutions that significantly reduce the computing effort. To quickly evaluate $F(\boldsymbol{x})$ of a solution $\boldsymbol{x}$, a rough estimation is utilized to evaluate $F(\boldsymbol{x})$. The rough estimation is constructed based on a simulation process through a small number of replications L_r, say 10 simulation replications. Let $F_r(\boldsymbol{x})$ indicate the sample mean resulted from rough estimation using L_r replications. Therefore, the LiWO with the rough estimation is utilized to form a differentiated subset.

2.3 Leaf in Wind Optimization

The inspiration for the LiWO [15] comes from factors including wind force, translation, and rotation that influence the movement of falling leaves in the wind. Under the influence of external forces, leaves undergo continuous postural adjustments and descend from a considerable height. The falling signifies sequential stages of leaf movement, whereas the landing represents the final state of the leaf. The falling leaves exhibit intriguing oscillations, rolling and spiral motions, and unpredictable motion between these phases, including random occurrences and sudden changes in velocity. Therefore, the optimization problem can be effectively solved by simulating the motion of the descending foliage. In this context, the search space of solutions corresponds to the domain for leaf motion, and each leaf represents an individual engaged in the optimization. In the optimization process, the influence of wind is the main factor causing the continuous movement of leaves in space. When falling leaves are in a dynamic environment, they are affected by two different types of wind: mild breeze and forceful gust. These winds materialize haphazardly and propel the motion of the leaves, but they do not occur simultaneously.

The LiWO uses the following notations. Ψ depicts the total number of leaves; $\omega_{\max}$ is the maximum of control factor for adaptive movement; p_1, p_2, and p_3 are the thresholds of leaf motions; and $t_{\max}$ denotes the maximum number of iterations. At the t-th iteration, $\boldsymbol{x}_i^t = [x_{i,1}^t, ..., x_{i,K}^t]^{\mathrm{T}}$ and $\boldsymbol{x}_{gb}^t = [x_{gb,1}^t, ..., x_{gb,K}^t]^{\mathrm{T}}$ represent the i-th leaf and the global best leaf positions, respectively.

Algorithm: The LiWO.

Step 1: Set parameters

Define the values of Ψ, p_1, p_2, p_3, $\omega_{\max}$, $t_{\max}$, and set $t = 0$, where t denotes an iteration variable.

Step 2: Initialization

$$\boldsymbol{x}_i^0 = \boldsymbol{LB} + \lfloor rand[0, 1] \cdot (\boldsymbol{UB} - \boldsymbol{LB}) \rfloor, \ i = 1, ..., \Psi. \tag{7}$$

where **LB** and **UB** denote the lower limit and upper limit, respectively, $\lfloor . \rfloor$ is a floor function, and $rand[0, 1]$ depicts a random floating number between 0 and 1.

Step 3: Choosing the global best leaf.

(a) Calculate the fitness $F(\boldsymbol{x}_i^t)$ of the ith leaf supported by rough estimation, $i = 1, ..., \Psi$.
(b) Determine the global best leaf $\boldsymbol{x}_{gb}^t$ with the largest fitness.

Step 4: Adjust the adaptive movement factor

$$C^t = \exp\left(\left(\omega_{\max} \cdot (1 - \frac{t}{t_{\max}})\right)^5\right) - 1 \tag{8}$$

Step 5: Breeze driven leaf.

(a) If $rand[0, 1] > p_1$ for $\boldsymbol{x}_i^t$, perform breeze translation motion.

$$\boldsymbol{x}_i^{new} = \boldsymbol{x}_i^t + \left\lfloor rand[0, 1] \cdot (\boldsymbol{x}_{gb}^t - \boldsymbol{x}_s^t) \right\rfloor \tag{9}$$

where $s \neq i$ is a randomly selected leaf. If $x_{i,k}^{new} < LB_k$, set $x_{i,k}^{new} = LB_k$, else if $x_{i,k}^{new} > UB_k$, set $x_{i,k}^{new} = UB_k$.

Else, go to Step 6.

(b) For $k = 1, ..., K$, if $rand[0, 1] < p_2$ for the k-th dimension of $\boldsymbol{x}_i^t$, perform breeze spiral motion.

$$x_{i,k}^{new} = x_{i,k}^t + \left\lfloor C^t \cdot \left| x_{i,k}^t - x_{s,k}^t \right| \cdot \sin(rand[0, 2\pi]) \cdot rand[0, 2\pi] \right\rfloor \tag{10}$$

where $s \neq i$ is a randomly selected leaf, and $rand[0, 2\pi]$ depicts a uniformly distributed random number within the interval $[0, 2\pi]$. If $x_{i,k}^{new} < LB_k$, set $x_{i,k}^{new} = LB_k$, else if $x_{i,k}^{new} > UB_k$, set $x_{i,k}^{new} = UB_k$.

Step 6: Strong wind driven leaf.

(a) For a random k-th dimension of $\boldsymbol{x}_i^t$, perform strong wind translation motion.

$$x_{i,k}^{new} = x_{i,k}^t + \left\lfloor rand[0, 1] \cdot (x_{s,k}^t - x_{i,k}^t) \right\rfloor \tag{11}$$

where $s \neq i$ is a randomly selected leaf. If $x_{i,k}^{new} < LB_k$, set $x_{i,k}^{new} = LB_k$, else if $x_{i,k}^{new} > UB_k$, set $x_{i,k}^{new} = UB_k$.

(b) If $rand[0, 1] < p_3$ for a random k-th dimension of $\boldsymbol{x}_i^t$, perform reset.

$$x_{i,k}^{new} = LB_k + \lfloor rand[0, 1] \cdot (UB_k - LB_k) \rfloor \tag{12}$$

Step 7: Renew the position of the ith leaf
Compute $F(\boldsymbol{x}_i^{new})$ using rough estimation. If $F(\boldsymbol{x}_i^{new}) > F(\boldsymbol{x}_i^t)$, set $\boldsymbol{x}_i^{t+1} = \boldsymbol{x}_i^{new}$.
Step 8: Terminate
If $t \geq t_{\max}$, terminate; else, set $t = t + 1$ and go to Step 3.

As the total number of iterations performed exceeds the value of $t_{\max}$, the LiWO is stopped. When the LiWO stops, the Ψ leaves are ranked based on their fitness. Then, the top ranking N superior solutions are chosen to build a differentiated subset.

2.4 Ranking and Selection

Finally, the R&S method [16–17] is adopted to access $\boldsymbol{x}$ for differentiated subset using an accurate estimation, which is a lengthy simulation with $L_a = 10^4$ replications. R&S procedures are statistical approaches adopted to rank and choose the top group among groups with similar statistical distributions. The R&S method seeks to efficiently select the optimal solution among a finite number of solutions. It has wide applications in operation management, production, and service. The R&S method ranks a few solutions in order of performance or selects some subset as being better than the rest. It is widely used for choosing the optimum among a differentiated subset, where each candidate solution is associated with a simulation model. Let $F_a(\boldsymbol{x})$ express the sample mean obtained by accurate estimation with L_a replications. The $\boldsymbol{x}$ with the smallest $F_a(\boldsymbol{x})$ in the differentiated subset is the superior solution that we seek.

3 Application

3.1 Reconfigurable Manufacturing Systems

RMS allows manufacturers to respond effectively to changes in demand, new product introductions, or changes in production requirements. This flexibility is achieved through the modular design of RMS, which enables the addition, removal, or modification of manufacturing components as needed. Key strategies for successful RMS implementation include conducting a thorough analysis of production requirements, designing a modular manufacturing system, investing in flexible and adaptable technology, and developing a skilled workforce. Figure 1 illustrates the key considerations for RMS implementation. RMS relies on several key technologies, including modular machinery and equipment, advanced robotics and automation, information technology and data analytics, and interoperability standards.

By allowing for the rapid reconfiguration of manufacturing systems, RMS facilitates the production of customized products. RMS enables manufacturers to introduce new products more quickly by reconfiguring existing manufacturing systems rather than building new ones. RMS allows manufacturers to respond effectively to changes in demand, new product introductions, or changes in production requirements. This flexibility is achieved through the modular design of RMS, which enables the addition, removal, or modification of manufacturing components as needed.

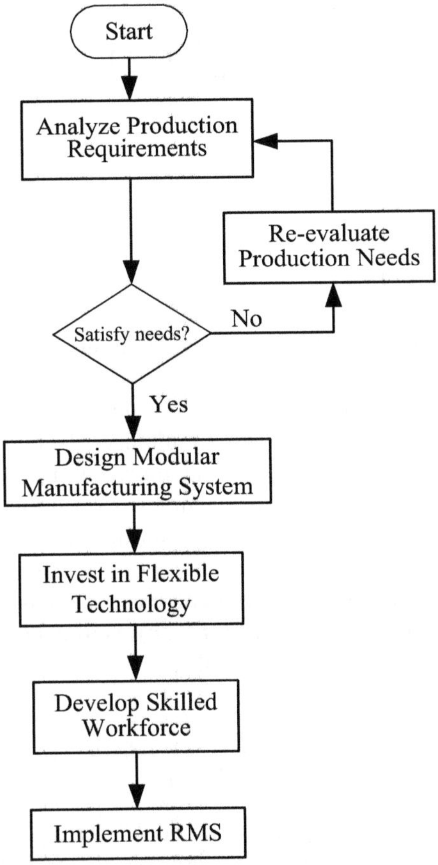

Fig. 1. Key considerations for RMS implementation.

3.2 Mathematical Formulation

Consider an RMS has S workstations and T tasks, and available number of machines is M. Let $M_{\min}$ and $M_{\max}$ represent the minimum and maximum number of machines per workstation, respectively, $B_{\min}$ and $B_{\max}$ indicate the minimum safety buffer and maximum buffer capacity, respectively, M_s and x_s denote the number of machines and tasks of for workstation s, respectively, and B_s denote the buffer capacity for buffer s. The allocated machines to each workstation cannot surpass the maximum number of machines, and a minimum number of machines should be allocated to each workstation to ensure production. At least one task should be assigned to each workstation. Each interstation buffer should not exceed a specific safety capacity or exceed a maximum buffer size.

The production planning of RMS can be formulated as a SDOP.

$$\max \mathrm{E}[TP(\boldsymbol{m}, \boldsymbol{x}, \boldsymbol{b})] \tag{13}$$

$$\text{subject to } \sum_{s=1}^{S} M_s \le M, \tag{14}$$

$$\sum_{s=1}^{S} x_s = T. \tag{15}$$

where $\boldsymbol{m} = [M_1, \ldots, M_s]^T$ is the machine vector, $M_{\min} \le M_s \le M_{\max}$, $s = 1, \ldots, S$, $\boldsymbol{x} = [x_1, \ldots, x_s]^T$ is the task vector, $1 \le x_s \le T$, $s = 1, \ldots, S$,$\boldsymbol{b} = [B_1, \ldots, B_{s-1}]^T$ is buffer capacity vector, $B_{\min} \le B_s \le B_{\max}$, $s = 1, \ldots, S - 1$, and $\mathrm{E}[TP(\boldsymbol{m}, \boldsymbol{x}, \boldsymbol{b})]$ depicts the expected throughput, which is the total number of products processed over the simulation time period. Hence, the size of the search space is $(M_{\max} - M_{\min} + 1)^S \cdot T^S \cdot (B_{\max} - B_{\min} + 1)^{S-1}$. This SDOP aims to determine the optimal $(\boldsymbol{m}^*, \boldsymbol{x}^*, \boldsymbol{b}^*)$ to maximize the expected throughput and simultaneously minimize the entire buffer capacity. Constraint (2) represents that the total allocated machines to each workstation cannot surpass the available number of machines. Constraint (3) indicates the total number of allocated tasks to workstations equals the number of given tasks. Given the customers' demands, the aim is to find the optimal system configuration $\boldsymbol{m}^*$, task allocation $\boldsymbol{x}^*$, and buffer capacity $\boldsymbol{b}^*$, such that the expected throughput $\mathrm{E}[TP(\boldsymbol{m}, \boldsymbol{x}, \boldsymbol{b})]$ can be maximized. Since the value of $\mathrm{E}[TP(\boldsymbol{m}, \boldsymbol{x}, \boldsymbol{b})]$ is frequently unknown, the sample mean is a common way to approximate its value.

$$\mathrm{E}[TP(\boldsymbol{m}, \boldsymbol{x}, \boldsymbol{b})] = \frac{1}{L} \sum_{\ell=1}^{L} TP_\ell(\boldsymbol{m}, \boldsymbol{x}, \boldsymbol{b}) \tag{16}$$

where L indicates the number of replications, and $TP_\ell(\boldsymbol{m}, \boldsymbol{x}, \boldsymbol{b})$ is the evaluation of the ℓ th replication. Because the two constraints are soft, the SDOP can be converted into an unconstrained one.

$$\max F(\boldsymbol{m}, \boldsymbol{x}, \boldsymbol{b}) = \frac{1}{L} \sum_{\ell=1}^{L} TP_\ell(\boldsymbol{m}, \boldsymbol{x}, \boldsymbol{b}) - \frac{\eta}{2} \cdot \left[\left(\max\left\{0, \sum_{s=1}^{S} M_s - M \right\} \right)^2 + \left(\sum_{s=1}^{S} x_s - T \right)^2 \right] \tag{17}$$

where η denotes a penalty weight, and $F(\boldsymbol{m}, \boldsymbol{x}, \boldsymbol{b})$ represents a quadratic penalty function.

3.3 Experimental Results

Consider an RMS consists of 3 workstations and 2 interstation buffers, as shown in Fig. 2 [19]. Table 1 shows the parameters used in RMS. This RMS has a machining process that takes 16 min and divides into $T = 36$ tasks. The process is subject to real disruptions, where machine availability is considered to be 90%, and the average repair time is 5 min. The machining process satisfies a demand following a Poisson distribution with a demand rate $\lambda = 550$ products/day in a 23-h working day. Additionally, the buffers need 5 s of material handling time for loading/unloading.

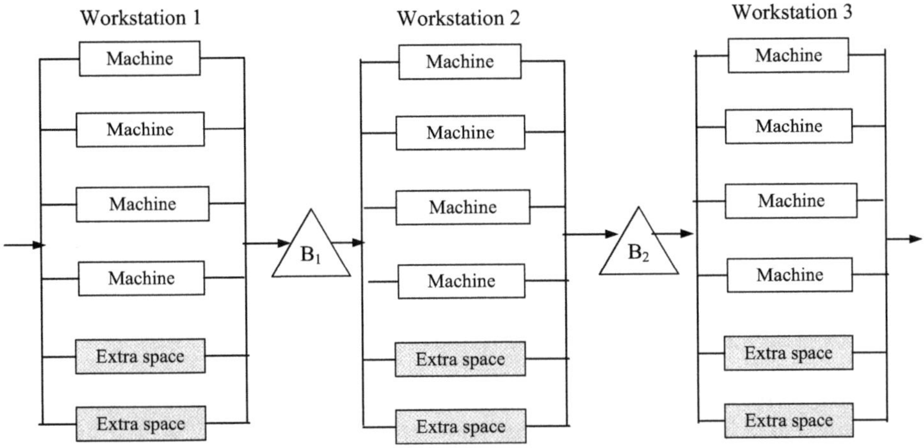

Fig. 2. An RMS with 3 workstations and 2 buffers.

Table 1. Parameters used in RMS

Parameter	S	T	M	$M_{\max}$	$M_{\min}$	$B_{\max}$	$B_{\min}$
Value	3	36	18	6	4	10	1

The penalty weight η was 10^4. After performing numerous hand-tuning experiments, the following parameters were utilized: $L_r = 10, \Psi = 50$, $p_1 = 0.1, p_2 = 0.1$, $p_3 = 0.3$, $\omega_{\max} = 0.9$, $t_{\max} = 500$, $N = 20$, and $L_a = 10^4$. Table 2 shows the superior solution $(\boldsymbol{w}^*, \boldsymbol{x}^*, \boldsymbol{b}^*)$ and $\mathrm{E}[TP(\boldsymbol{w}^*, \boldsymbol{x}^*, \boldsymbol{b}^*)]$. The CPU time consumes less than 1 min, demonstrating that the sim-heuristic approach can achieve the requirements of a real-time application.

Table 2. The superior solution $(\boldsymbol{w}^*, \boldsymbol{x}^*, \boldsymbol{b}^*)$ and $\mathrm{E}[TP(\boldsymbol{w}^*, \boldsymbol{x}^*, \boldsymbol{b}^*)]$.

$\boldsymbol{w}^*$	$\boldsymbol{x}^*$	$\boldsymbol{b}^*$	$\mathrm{E}[TP(\boldsymbol{w}^*, \boldsymbol{x}^*, \boldsymbol{b}^*)]$ (Jobs Per Hour)
$[6,5,5]^T$	$[16,10,10]^T$	$[8,5]^T$	53.68

4 Conclusion

The SDOP have stochastic functions and deterministic constraints which is a typical example of NP-hard class. In this work, a sim-heuristic approach that uses LiWO coordinated with OO is firstly developed to solve the SDOP in a short time. The sim-heuristic approach comprises two phases. In the first phase, leaf in wind optimization algorithm is used to construct a differentiated subset with rough estimation. In the second phase, ranking and selection method is used to find a superior solution from differentiated subsets. Secondly, the optimal production planning problem of reconfigurable manufacturing systems is formulated as a SDOP. Finally, a real-life example consisting of 3 workstations and 2 interstation buffers is applied to test the solution quality. Experimental results demonstrate that the sim-heuristic approach can solve SDOP in a reasonable time. The OO framework is not limited to the optimal production planning problem of reconfigurable manufacturing systems. OO can be utilized to support existing meta-heuristic optimization approaches. Further researches will adopt OO to resolve challenging hard optimization problems, including dynamic portfolio optimization problems, and nonconvex expectation stochastic optimization problems.

Acknowledgments. This research work is partly supported by the National Science and Technology Council in Taiwan, grant number NSTC 114–2221-E-324–011.

References

1. Seifpour, M., Asghari, S.A., Ghobaei-Arani, M.: A stochastic multi-objective optimization method for railways scheduling: a NSGA-II-based hybrid approach. J. Supercomputing **80**(2), 2128–2163 (2024)
2. Cao, Y., Mu, Y.F., Jia, H.J., Yu, X.D., Hou, K., Wang, H.Y.: A multi-objective stochastic optimization approach for planning a multi-energy microgrid considering unscheduled islanded operation.IEEE Trans. Sustain. Energy **15**(2), 1300–1314 (2024)
3. Chowdury, M.A.M., Nath, R., Shukla, A.K., Rauniyar, A.P., Muhuri, K: Multi-task optimization in reliability redundancy allocation problem: a multifactorial evolutionary-based approach. Reliab. Eng. Syst. Saf. **244** (2024)
4. Pérez-Delgado, M.L., Román-Gallego, J.A.: Computational complexity of swarm-based algorithms: a detailed analysis. AIMS Math. **10**(7), 15539–15587 (2025)
5. Zhao, S.J., Zhang, T.R., Cai, L., Yang, R.H.: Triangulation topology aggregation optimizer: a novel mathematics-based meta-heuristic algorithm for continuous optimization and engineering applications. Expert Syst. Appl. **238,** id. 121744 (2024)
6. Kundu, R., Chattopadhyay, S., Nag, S., Navarro, M.A., Oliva, D.: Prism refraction search: a novel physics-based metaheuristic algorithm. J. Supercomputing **80**(8), 10746–10795 (2024)
7. Oladejo, S.O., Ekwe, S.O., Mirjalili, S.: The hiking optimization algorithm: a novel human-based metaheuristic approach. Knowl. Based Syst. **26**, id. 111880 (2024)
8. Khomami, M.M.D., Meybodi, M.R., Rezvanian, A.: A cellular Goore game-based algorithm for finding the shortest path in stochastic multi-layer graphs. J. Supercomputing **81**(1), id. 322 (2025)
9. Ho, Y.C., Zhao, Q.C., Jia, Q.S.: Ordinal Optimization: Soft Optimization for Hard Problems. Springer-Verlag, New York (2007)
10. Klamroth, K., Stiglmayr, M., Sudhoff, J.: Ordinal optimization through multi-objective reformulation. Eur. J. Oper. Res. **311**(2), 427–443 (2023)
11. Horng, S.C., Lin, S.S.: Advanced golden jackal optimization for solving the constrained integer stochastic optimization problems. Math. Comput. Simul **217**, 188–201 (2024)
12. Horng, S.C., Lin, S.S.: Adapted skill optimization algorithm to solve constrained discrete stochastic optimization problems. Math. Comput. Simul **238**, 280–295 (2025)
13. Horng, S.C., Lin, S.S.: Accelerated driving-training-based optimization for solving constrained bi-objective stochastic optimization problems. Mathematics **12**(12), id. 1863 (2024)

14. Horng, S.C., Lin, S.S.: Incorporate seagull optimization into ordinal optimization for solving the constrained binary simulation optimization problems. J. Supercomputing **79**(5), 5730–5758 (2023)
15. Fang, N., Cao, Q.: Leaf in wind optimization: a new metaheuristic algorithm for solving optimization problems. IEEE Access **12**, 56291–56308 (2024)
16. Cakmak, S., Wang, Y.H., Gao, S.Y., Zhou, E.L.: Contextual ranking and selection with Gaussian processes and optimal computing budget allocation. ACM Trans. Model. Comput. Simul. **34**(2), id. 8 (2024)
17. Wang, T.X., Xu, J., Branke, J., Hu, J.Q., Chen, C.H.: Ranking and selection with two-stage decision. Eur. J. Oper. Res. **322**(1), 121–132 (2025)
18. Liao, H.T., Yuan, W.H., Gao, R.X., Yuan, X.J.: An efficient penalty function method for scenario-based uncertainty quantification problems. J. Vib. Control **31**(3–4), 499–515 (2025)
19. Diaz, C.A.B., Aslam, T., Ng, A.H.C.: Optimizing reconfigurable manufacturing systems for fluctuating production volumes: a simulation-based multi-objective approach. IEEE Access **9**, 144195–144210 (2021)

An Extended Method of Probabilistic Inference

Feng-Jen Yang(✉)

Department of Computer Science, Florida Polytechnic University,Lakeland, FL 33805, USA
fyang@floridapoly.edu
https://floridapoly.edu

Abstract. Traditional probabilistic inference and classification methods in artificial intelligence are typically grounded in set theory, where each element within a set is considered only once. While this approach offers mathematical simplicity, it may not accurately reflect the nature of many real-world data scenarios, potentially leading to distortions in likelihood estimation during inference and classification tasks. For example, in the context of email analysis, certain words may appear multiple times within a single message, and treating the email as a set of unique words fails to capture the significance of repeated occurrences. To address this limitation, this study proposes an extension of the classical framework from set-based to collection—based so that it allows multiple instances of the same item. By adopting a collection-based perspective, probabilistic inference and classification can better accommodate the frequency and distribution of evidence, resulting in more nuanced and accurate outcomes. This work aims to enhance the expressiveness and applicability of traditional inference models, paving the way for more robust decision-making in complex, data-rich environments.

Keywords: Probabilistic Inference · Probabilistic Classification · Multinomial Distribution

1 Introduction

The real world is in a constant state of flux, and as such, our daily lives often require us to make decisions based on uncertain or incomplete information. Probabilistic inference and classification play a crucial role in helping us navigate this uncertainty by enabling informed decision-making based on predicted outcomes. In the realm of classical artificial intelligence (AI), probabilistic decision-making has traditionally relied on well-established frameworks such as Bayesian Inference, Bayesian Networks, and Hidden Markov Models [1,2]. These methodologies share a common mathematical foundation, centered on the transformation between conditional and joint probabilities.

Typically, a dataset is collected within a specific application domain and analyzed to determine which pieces of evidence support which hypotheses. In this

C. Xu (Ed.): ICMLSC 2026, CCIS 2948, pp. 664–671, 2027.
https://doi.org/10.1007/978-981-92-1546-1_53

context, the probability that a hypothesis is true before considering any evidence is referred to as the prior probability, an unconditional measure of belief. Once evidence is taken into account, the updated probability that a hypothesis is true is known as the posterior probability, which is conditional on the observed evidence.

While this framework is widely accepted and often effective, it is not without limitations. One key modeling assumption is that supportive evidence is treated as a set, meaning each piece of evidence is considered only once, regardless of how many times it appears. This assumption can be problematic in certain real-world scenarios. For instance, in spam email detection, the frequency of specific keywords such as "reward," "gift," or "inheritance" can significantly influence the likelihood that an email is spam. Treating these repeated occurrences as a single instance may lead to underestimating their impact. Similarly, in culinary applications, two beverages made from the same ingredients but in different proportions will produce distinct flavors, an outcome that cannot be captured by a purely set-based approach.

To address these limitations, this study explores and contrasts set-based and collection-based approaches to probabilistic inference and classification. By doing so, it introduces a more nuanced and expressive framework for reasoning under uncertainty. The proposed collection-based perspective not only enhances the theoretical foundation of probabilistic AI but also offers practical benefits for applications in data-rich and complex environments. This topic can also be a valuable addition to AI-related curricula, encouraging a deeper understanding of inference mechanisms beyond traditional assumptions.

2 The Mathematical Rationale for Set-Based Probabilistic Inference

Considering a problem domain where each inference case is represented by a set of evidence that supports possible hypotheses, the probabilistic inference and classification for: if elements E_1, E_2, ..., and E_n appear in a reasoning case, how likely is a hypothesis H_i to be true, where $1 \leq i \leq m$?

This posterior probability is computed as follows [3–6]:

$$
\begin{aligned}
&P(H_i|(E_1 \cap E_2 \cap \ldots \cap E_n)) \\
&= \frac{P(H_i \cap (E_1 \cap E_2 \cap \ldots \cap E_n))}{P(E_1 \cap E_2 \cap \ldots \cap E_n)} \\
&= \frac{P((E_1 \cap E_2 \cap \ldots \cap E_n) \cap H_i)}{P(E_1 \cap E_2 \cap \ldots \cap E_n)} \\
&= \frac{P((E_1 \cap E_2 \cap \ldots \cap E_n)|H_i) \times P(H_i)}{P(E_1 \cap E_2 \cap \ldots \cap E_n)} \\
&where 1 \leq i \leq m
\end{aligned}
$$

The above computation requires conditional probabilities involving all possible combinations of elements and classifications, resulting in very high complexity. Therefore, conditional independence among all evidence is usually assumed in AI approaches, so that:

$$P((E_1 \cap E_2 \cap \ldots \cap E_n)|H_i)$$
$$= P(E_1|H_i) \times P(E_2|H_i) \times \ldots \times P(E_n|H_i) \times P(H_i)$$
$$where 1 \leq i \leq m$$

and thus:

$$P(H_i|(E_1 \cap E_2 \cap ... \cap E_n))$$
$$= \frac{P(E_1|H_i) \times P(E_2|H_i) \times \ldots \times P(E_n|H_i) \times P(H_i)}{\sum_{j=1}^{m} P(E_1|H_j) \times P(E_2|H_j) \times \ldots \times P(E_n|H_j) \times P(H_j)}$$
$$where 1 \leq i \leq m$$

The summation in the denominator is for the purpose of normalization, which ensures that the total posterior probabilities that each inference case may support each possible hypothesis is one [7].

The posterior probability can, thus, be simplified into:

$$P(H_i|(E_1 \cap E_2 \cap \ldots \cap E_n))$$
$$= \frac{P(H_i \cap (E_1 \cap E_2 \cap \ldots \cap E_n))}{P(E_1 \cap E_2 \cap \ldots \cap E_n)}$$
$$= \frac{P((E_1 \cap E_2 \cap \ldots \cap E_n) \cap H_i)}{\sum_{j=1}^{m} P((E_1 \cap E_2 \cap \ldots \cap E_n) \cap H_j)}$$
$$= \frac{P((E_1 \cap E_2 \cap \ldots \cap E_n)|H_i) \times P(H_i)}{\sum_{j=1}^{m} P((E_1 \cap E_2 \cap \ldots \cap E_n)|H_j) \times P(H_j)}$$
$$where 1 \leq i \leq m$$

2.1 The Assumption of Independent Supportive Evidences

As previously mentioned, it is a common practice in probabilistic inference methods to assume that pieces of supportive evidence are mutually independent. While this assumption greatly simplifies the computational process, it does not always hold true in real-world application domains. In many practical scenarios, evidence may exhibit varying degrees of interdependence, which can lead to distortions in the estimation of posterior probabilities [3,8].

Despite this potential drawback, the independence assumption remains widely adopted due to its efficiency and ease of implementation. When concerns about the accuracy of this assumption arise, several remedial techniques have been proposed. These methods aim to mitigate the impact of interdependencies among evidence while maintaining a relatively low computational overhead. Notably, some of these approaches have been shown to be both effective and efficient in practice [9].

3 The Mathematical Rationale for Collection-Based Probabilistic Inference

Considering a problem domain where each inference case involves a collection of k distinct evidence, allowing multiple occurrences of an evidence. Additionally, each collection of evidence can support m possible hypotheses.

The probabilistic inference and classification for: if evidence E_1 occurs e_1 times, E_2 occurs e_2 times, ..., and E_k occurs e_k times in an inference case, how likely is a hypothesis H_i to be true, where $1 \leq i \leq m$?

Mathematically, this is a multinomial experiment where each trial result is one of k possible outcomes E_1, E_2, ..., and E_k, and the posterior probability to be computed by using the supportive evidence that $E_1 = e_1$, $E_2 = e_2$, ..., and $E_k = e_k$ to support a hypothesis H_i, where the total number of trials are $(e_1 + e_2 + ... + e_k)$.

$$
\begin{aligned}
&P(H_i|(E_1 \cap E_2 \cap \ldots \cap E_n)) \\
&= \frac{P(H_i \cap (E_1 \cap E_2 \cap \ldots \cap E_n))}{P(E_1 \cap E_2 \cap \ldots \cap E_n)} \\
&= \frac{P((E_1 \cap E_2 \cap \ldots \cap E_n) \cap H_i)}{\sum_{j=1}^{m} P((E_1 \cap E_2 \cap \ldots \cap E_n) \cap H_j)} \\
&= \frac{\left(\frac{n!}{e_1! \times e_2! \times \cdots \times e_k!} \times p_1^{e_1} \times p_2^{e_2} \times \cdots \times p_k^{e_k}\right) \times P(H_i)}{\sum_{j=1}^{m}((\frac{n!}{e_1! \times e_2! \times \cdots \times e_k!} \times p_1^{e_1} \times p_2^{e_2} \times \cdots \times p_k^{e_k}) \times P(H_j))}
\end{aligned}
$$

where:

- e_i is the number of times E_i occurs in the inference case.
- n is the total number of items in this inference case, i.e., $n = e_1 + e_2 + \cdots + e_k$.
- p_i is the probability that E_i occurs in the samples where hypothesis H_i is true.
- p_j is the probability that E_j occurs in the samples where hypothesis H_j is true.

The reason for involving factorials in the computation is to account for the fact that the ordering of evidence occurrences is unimportant in the collection-of-items approach. This portion of the computation is focused on the permutations of repeated items. Also, for the purpose of normalization, the summation that appears in the denominator ensures that the total posterior probabilities that each inference case may support each possible hypothesis is one [7].

4 Set-Based Probabilistic Inference Versus Collection-Based Probabilistic Inference

To demonstrate the differences between set-based and collection-based probabilistic inferences, a hypothetical dataset is given in Table 1, which involves three evidence and two hypotheses denoted as E_1, E_2, E_3, H_1, and H_2, respectively.

Table 1. A Hypothetical Dataset

Sample No.	E_1	E_2	E_3	Hypothesis
1	0 times	0 times	2 times	H_1 is true
2	1 time	3 times	1 time	H_1 is true
3	1 time	1 time	2 times	H_1 is true
4	2 times	1 time	2 times	H_2 is true
5	1 time	3 times	1 time	H_2 is true
6	0 times	2 times	1 time	H_2 is true

Considering an inference case in which E_1 appears $1time$, E_2 appears 1 time, and E_3 appears 2 times, how likely is H_1 to be true?

4.1 Performing Set-Based Inference

Since set-based inference does not take the number of times a piece of evidence appears into consideration, the posterior probability of this inference case is:

$$
\begin{aligned}
&P(H_i|(E_1 \cap E_2 \cap E_3)) \\
&= \frac{P(H_1 \cap (E_1 \cap E_2 \cap E_3))}{P(E_1 \cap E_2 \cap E_3)} \\
&= \frac{P((H_1 \cap (E_1 \cap E_2 \cap E_3))|H_1) \times P(H_1)}{\sum_{j=1}^{2} P((H_1 \cap (E_1 \cap E_2 \cap E_3))|H_j) \times P(H_j)}
\end{aligned}
$$

Based on the given dataset, the following prior probabilities and conditional probabilities can be derived:

- The given dataset has a total of 6 samples, and 3 of them indicate that H_1 is true. So, the prior probability $P(H_1) = 3/6 = 1/2$.
- The given dataset has a total of 6 samples, and 3 of them indicate that H_2 is true. So, the prior probability $P(H_2) = 3/6 = 1/2$.
- Among the 3 samples where H_1 is true, E_1 appears in 2 samples. So, the conditional probability $P(E_1|H_1) = 2/3$.
- Among the 3 samples where H_1 is true, E_2 appears in 2 samples. So, the conditional probability $P(E_2|H_1) = 2/3$.

- Among the 3 samples where H_1 is true, E_3 appears in 3 samples. So, the conditional probability $P(E_3|H_1) = 3/3 = 1$.
- Among the 3 samples where H_2 is true, E_1 appears in 2 samples. So, the conditional probability $P(E_1|H_2) = 2/3$.
- Among the 3 samples where H_2 is true, E_2 appears in 3 samples. So, the conditional probability $P(E_2|H_2) = 3/3 = 1$.
- Among the 3 samples where H_2 is true, E_3 appears in 3 samples. So, the conditional probability $P(E_3|H_2) = 3/3 = 1$.

Plugging these probabilities into the posterior probability computation of this inference case, the inference result is computed as follows:

$$\begin{aligned}
&P(H_1 \mid (E_1 \cap E_2 \cap E_3)) \\
&= \frac{(\frac{2}{3} \times \frac{2}{3} \times 1 \times \frac{1}{2})}{(\frac{2}{3} \times \frac{2}{3} \times 1 \times \frac{1}{2}) + (\frac{2}{3} \times 1 \times 1 \times \frac{1}{2})} \\
&= 0.4
\end{aligned}$$

So, given the inference case in which E_1 appears 1 time, E_2 appears 1 time, and E_3 appears 2 times, the probability that H_1 is true is 0.4, i.e., 40%.

4.2 Performing Collection-Based Inference

Since collection-based inference takes the number of times an evidence appears into consideration, the posterior probability of this inference case is:

$$\begin{aligned}
&P(H_1|(E_1 \cap E_2 \cap E_3)) \\
&= \frac{\left(\frac{4!}{e_1! \times e_2! \times e_3!} \times p_1^{e_1} \times p_2^{e_2} \times p_k^{e_3}\right) \times P(H_1)}{\sum_{j=1}^{2}((\frac{4!}{e_1! \times e_2! \times e_3!} \times p_1^{e_1} \times p_2^{e_2} \times p_3^{e_3}) \times P(H_j))}
\end{aligned}$$

Based on the given dataset, the following prior probabilities can be derived:

- The given dataset has a total of 6 samples, and 3 of them indicate that H_1 is true. So, the prior probability $P(H_1) = 3/6 = 1/2$.
- The given dataset has a total of 6 samples, and 3 of them indicate that H_2 is true. So, the prior probability $P(H_2) = 3/6 = 1/2$.

In this inference case, E_1 appears 1 time, E_2 appears 1 time, and E_3 appears 2 times. So,

- $e_1 = 1$.
- $e_2 = 1$.
- $e_3 = 2$.
- $n = 1 + 1 + 2 = 5$.

Among the 3 samples where H_1 is true, E_1 totally appears 2 times, E_2 totally appears 4 times, and E_3 totally appears 5 times. So,

- $p_1 = 2/(2+4+5) = 2/11$
- $p_2 = 4/(2+4+5) = 4/11$
- $p_3 = 5/(2+4+5) = 5/11$

Among the 3 samples where H_2 is true, E_1 totally appears 3 times, E_2 totally appears 6 times, and E_3 totally appears 6 times. So,

- $p_1 = 3/(3+6+6) = 3/15 = 1/5$
- $p_2 = 6/(3+6+6) = 6/15 = 2/5$
- $p_3 = 6/(3+6+6) = 6/15 = 2/5$

Plugging these numbers and probabilities into the posterior probability computation of this inference case, the inference result is computed as follows:

$$
\begin{aligned}
&P(H_1|((E_1 = 1) \cap (E_2 = 1) \cap (E_3 = 2))) \\
&= \frac{\frac{4!}{1!\times1!\times2!} \times \frac{2}{11} \times \frac{4}{11} \times (\frac{5}{11})^2 \times \frac{1}{2}}{\frac{4!}{1!\times1!\times2!} \times \frac{2}{11} \times \frac{4}{11} \times (\frac{5}{11})^2 \times \frac{1}{2} + \frac{4!}{1!\times1!\times2!} \times \frac{1}{5} \times \frac{2}{5} \times (\frac{2}{5})^2 \times \frac{1}{2}} \\
&= 0.5163
\end{aligned}
$$

So, given the inference case in which E_1 appears 1 time, E_2 appears 1 time, and E_3 appears 2 times, the probability that H_1 is true is 0.5163, i.e., 51.63%.

4.3 Interpreting the Divergent Results

The two inference outcomes presented above highlight a notable discrepancy: $51.63\% - 40\% = 11.63\%$. While this difference arises from a hypothetical dataset, it is still considered significant. In practical, real-world applications, such a variation could reflect differing levels of insight or understanding derived from the same data. This, in turn, may influence the decision-making process, potentially leading to more nuanced or better-informed conclusions. The ability to detect and interpret such differences is crucial in domains where precision and depth of analysis are essential.

5 Conclusion

Traditional probabilistic inference in artificial intelligence has long been grounded in set-based methodologies. While effective in many contexts, these approaches can be limited in their ability to model the complexity and nuance of real-world problems. This study has demonstrated that such limitations can be addressed by extending classical inference techniques into a collection-based framework, which offers a more general and adaptable foundation for reasoning under uncertainty.

By introducing a rigorous mathematical justification for this extension, the proposed framework enhances both the flexibility and expressiveness of probabilistic reasoning. This shift not only broadens the applicability of inference methods to a wider array of problem domains but also enables the extraction of richer and more meaningful insights from data. As a result, decision support systems built upon this extended methodology can achieve greater accuracy, robustness, and interpretability.

Ultimately, this work opens promising directions for the application of probabilistic reasoning in complex, data-intensive environments, laying the groundwork for future research and development in intelligent systems.

References

1. Bayes, T.: An essay towards solving a problem in the doctrine of chances. Philos. Trans. Royal Society. **53**(1), 370–418 (1763)
2. Rabiner, L.R.: A Tutorial on Hidden Markov Models and Selected Applications in Speech Recognition. https://scholar.harvard.edu/files/adegirmenci/files/hmm_adegirmenci_2014.pdf (1989)
3. Yang, F.-J.: Eliciting an overlooked aspect of Bayesian reasoning, ACM SIGCSE Bull. **39**(4), 45–48, (2007). https://doi.org/10.1145/1345375.1345412
4. Yang, F.-J.: Crafting a Lightweight Bayesian Inference Engine, the World Congress on Engineering 2016 (WCE 2016), vol. II, London, UK, pp. 612–617 (2016)
5. Yang, F.-J.: A General Purpose Probabilistic Inference Engine, IAENG Transactions on Engineering Sciences - Special Issue for the International Association of Engineers Conferences 2016, Singapore: World Scientific, pp. 33–44 (2017). https://doi.org/10.1142/9789813226203_0004
6. Yang, F.-J.: An implementation of naive bayes classifier. In: 2018 International Conference on Computational Science and Computational Intelligence (CSCI), LasVegas, NV, USA, 2018, pp. 301–306 (2018). https://doi.org/10.1109/CSCI46756.2018.00065.
7. Yang, F.-J.: A SQL-Based Probabilistic Inference, 2023 Congress in Computer Science, Computer Engineering, & Applied Computing (CSCE 2023), Las Vegas, NV, pp. 241–245 (2023). https://doi.org/10.1109/CSCE60160.2023.00043
8. Domingos, P.M., Pazzani, M.J.: Beyond independence: conditions for the optimality of the simple Bayesian classifier. In: Proceedings of the Thirteenth International Conference on International Conference on Machine Learning (ICM), San Francisco, CA, pp. 105–112 (1996). https://doi.org/10.5555/3091696.3091710
9. Rennie, J., Shih, L., Teevan, J., Karger, D.R.: Tackling the poor assumptions of naive bayes text classifiers. In: The Twentieth International Conference on Machine Learning (ICML), Washington, DC, pp. 616-623 (2003). https://doi.org/10.5555/3041838.3041916

Enhancing Live-Stream E-commerce Sales Prediction Through a Multi-channel Embedding Model

Chien-Hua Wang and Kuan-Wei Huang(✉)

School of Business, Lingnan Normal University, Zhanjiang 524048, Guangdong, China
skyshuttle@lingnan.edu.cn

Abstract. Live-stream e-commerce has reshaped online retail by combining real-time video presentation and interactive selling, producing highly engaging but volatile conversion events. Product titles, visible during live sessions, provide concise textual signals that inïňĆuence viewers' attention, clicks, and purchasing decisions. This paper proposes a Multi-Channel Embedding Model (MCEM) that decomposes noisy product titles into semantic attribute channels using large language models (LLMs), encodes each channel with pretrained contextual encoders (BERT), embeds numeric behavioral features with a multi-layer perceptron (MLP), and fuses these channels with an LSTM-based temporal model to jointly predict exposure-to-click rate (ECTR) and click-to-conversion rate (CTCVR). We evaluate MCEM on a real merchant dataset of 48,000 transactions and 25 features and compare it to baseline models. MCEM achieves superior explained variance (R^2) while maintaining competitive MAE and MSE. The results demonstrate that structured title decomposition and multi-modal fusion substantially improve short-horizon live-stream forecasting.

Keywords: Live-stream e-commerce · Multi-channel embedding model (MCEM) · Exposure-to-click rate (ECTR) · Click-to-conversion rate (CTCVR) · Large language models (LLMs)

1 Introduction

Live-stream e-commerce, or live commerce, has rapidly grown into a major retail channel by combining entertainment, real-time interaction, and immediate purchasing mechanisms. Platforms such as Taobao Live, TikTok Shop, and Amazon Live enable sellers and influencers to present products live, often yielding spikes in conversions driven by streaming dynamics, promotions, and host-audience interactions. Forecasting sales and conversion metrics in this context is challenging because of heterogeneous data modalities (text, numerical

Supported by Lingnan Normal University.

C. Xu (Ed.): ICMLSC 2026, CCIS 2948, pp. 672–683, 2027.
https://doi.org/10.1007/978-981-92-1546-1_54

history, video/audio signals), volatile viewer behavior, and temporal eïňĂects. Among the available signals, product titles-short textual descriptions displayed on overlay cards and product links are frequently overlooked in forecasting models that focus primarily on numerical time series. However, titles often encode highly salient attributes (brand, category, weight, claims such as sugar-free) that inïňĆuence buyer perception and actions.

Recent advances in natural language processing (NLP), especially pretrained transformer models such as Bidirectional Encoder Representations from Transformers (BERT) [1], and the resurgence of large language models (LLMs) like LLaMA and GPT-4 [2,3], provide new opportunities to extract structured semantic information from noisy titles. At the same time, Long Short-Term Memory (LSTM) have proven eective at modeling temporally dependent behavior [4]. Combining these approaches in a multimodal fusion pipeline can capture both content and context, which is our central objective in this study. Existing live-stream e-commerce prediction models have three key limitations: (i) Product titles are mostly input as raw text without structured semantic decomposition, making it difficult to capture attribute-level features (Majumder et al. [5]; Yan et al. [6]); (ii) Multi-modal fusion mostly focuses on "text + numerical" or "numerical + temporal" combinations, lacking collaborative modeling of "structured text attributes + numerical behavior + temporal dependencies" (Guo et al. [7]; Khandelwal et al. [8]); (iii) In cold-start scenarios, the performance of models relying on historical numerical data degrades significantly (Obst et al. [9]).

The Multi-Channel Embedding Model (MCEM) proposed in this paper overcomes the above limitations through three innovations: (1) An LLM-based parser is used to decompose noisy titles into semantic attribute channels, eliminating the need for manual attribute annotation and adapting to the diversity of live-stream e-commerce titles; (2) A three-channel architecture of "BERT attribute encoding + MLP numerical embedding + LSTM temporal fusion" is designed, which for the first time deeply couples structured text attributes with temporal behaviors; (3) Multi-modal collaborative modeling improves prediction accuracy for cold-start products (without historical data) using text attributes, outperforming traditional baseline models that rely on numerical data. Compared with AdaTag (Yan et al. [6]) with adaptive decoding and LLM-Ensemble (Fang et al. [10]) with attribute extraction methods, MCEM focuses more on end-to-end optimization for prediction tasks rather than pure attribute extraction, and integrates temporal information through LSTM, making it more suitable for short-term dynamic prediction needs in live-stream e-commerce.

In sum, the contributions of this study are: (1) a practical pipeline for structured title decomposition and multi-channel textual embedding; (2) a multimodal fusion architecture for short-horizon forecasting in live commerce; (3) empirical validation on merchant data; and (4) an analysis of component contributions through ablation.

2 Related Works

2.1 Live-Stream E-Commerce and Consumer Behavior

Live commerce research documents how streamer characteristics, presentation quality, and interactive cues shape purchase intentions and impulsive buying behaviors. Several empirical studies have linked host performance and perceived information quality to higher engagement and purchase rates [11,12]. These ndings suggest that presentation-level signals (including title and on-screen text) are important predictors of conversion.

2.2 Product Attribute Extraction

Product attribute extraction from unstructured text has been widely studied using traditional machine learning and deep learning methods. Early approaches relied on hand-crafted features and conditional random fields (CRFs), while recent advances use pre-trained language models for better semantic understanding. Compared with traditional Bi-LSTM-CRF (Majumder et al., [5]), LLM-based parsers eliminate the need for manual feature template design and can adapt to noise such as promotional vocabulary and abbreviations in live-stream e-commerce titles, improving attribute extraction accuracy by 15%-20% (Fang et al. [10]), which is the core reason for MCEM's selection of LLM parsing.

2.3 Textual Embeddings and Forecasting

Textual embedding techniques, such as Word2Vec and BERT, have been applied to various prediction tasks. BERT, in particular, has shown superior performance in capturing contextual semantic information (Devlin et al., [1]). Existing textual embedding methods mostly use complete titles as input (Obst et al. [9]), while MCEM decomposes titles into attribute channels and encodes them separately, reducing interference from irrelevant information and enhancing feature specificity. This aligns with the multi-modal attribute extraction approach proposed by Khandelwal et al. [8] but focuses more on temporal prediction tasks.

Recent studies incorporate textual item information into demand forecasting and exposure-to-click rate (ECTR) prediction pipelines, showing benets especially for cold-start items with limited history [9,13]. Times-aware transformer variants and time- series foundation models further suggest that jointly modeling text and time- series can improve accuracy [7,14].

2.4 CTCVR and Prediction

The eld of CTCVR prediction has a long history of feature- engineering and more recently deep learning methods such as DeepFM and other neural interaction models. Multimodal fusion (text+ numeric+ visual) has been explored in industry research and academic work for improving recommender and prediction systems [15,16]. Wang et al. [17]) proposed SaleNet, an interpretable multi-module model tailored for live-stream scenarios that integrates an advertising-product data Fusion Module (FM), TCN-based Interaction Modules (IM-I/IM-II) for feature-temporal modeling, and a Layer-wise Relevance Propagation (LRP) module to quantify feature contributions, achieving 11.47% MAPE for 1.5-day forecasts and 19.79% MAPE for 6-day forecasts on TikTok datasets; this model advances temporal fusion and interpretability, but its textual processing still relies on raw product descriptions—failing to resolve the "complete title noise" issue highlighted in Sect. 2.3, which creates a niche for our model that leverages LLMs to decompose noisy live-stream titles into semantic attribute channels, forming a complementary paradigm that enhances textual feature specificity while retaining strong temporal modeling capabilities.

3 Methodology

3.1 Data Source and Preprocessing

The dataset used in this study is derived from a Chinese snack retailer (SA Company), containing 48,000 transactions over three months, with 25 features including product title, price, exposure volume, click volume, conversion rate, and transaction time. Numerical features were standardized using Z-score normalization; missing numerical values were filled with the median (more robust due to the right-skewed distribution of numerical features), and missing categorical values were filled with the mode. The text field processing pipeline includes: (1) Removing promotional symbols (e.g., "[Limited Time Discount]", "Buy One Get One Free") and special characters (e.g., emojis, punctuation); (2) Using LLaMA 3 (7B parameters) as the parser to decompose titles into four attribute categories: food type, product feature, weight, and form (see Fig. 1 for examples); (3) Processing attribute text with the "BERT-base-Chinese" tokenizer, setting the maximum sequence length to 32.

Data exclusion rules: No data from special periods (e.g., holidays, large promotions) was excluded; instead, binary features such as "whether it is a large promotion" and "whether it is a holiday" were added to the numerical input to adapt to fluctuations in real scenarios. Refund data was excluded from conversion counts to ensure the accuracy of CTCVR calculation (CTCVR = valid conversion count / click count).

3.2 Title Decomposition via LLMs

Titles are often noisy and include promotional tokens, brand names, or redundant markers. We employ an LLM-based parser to split titles into semantic attribute channels (e.g., Food Type, Features, Weight, Product Form). For example, as Fig. 1, it would be parsed into Food Type: Cake, Features: Sugar-free; Handmade, Weight: 252g, Form: Eight-Treasure Cake. LLM ensembles and adaptive decoders have been shown to improve attribute extraction robustness and are used as references for our parsing pipeline [6,10].

笑喔喔坚果茯苓八珍糕 252g 纯手工无蔗糖

Fig. 1. Example of splitting titles.

3.3 Textual and Numeric Embedding

The feature embedding module consists of two sub-modules: text attribute embedding and numerical feature embedding.

1. Text Attribute Embedding: Each decomposed attribute channel (e.g., "snack cake", "sugar-free", "200g", "crispy") is input into a pre-trained BERT model for contextual encoding. The Classification token output of BERT is used as the fixed-dimensional embedding vector for each attribute channel, with a dimension of 768.

2. Numerical Feature Embedding: Numerical features (e.g., price, exposure volume, click volume) are normalized and then input into a multi-layer perceptron (MLP) with two hidden layers (128 and 64 units) for non-linear transformation, resulting in a 64-dimensional embedding vector. The MLP uses ReLU as the activation function and dropout (rate = 0.2) to prevent overfitting.

3.4 Temporal Fusion and Prediction

The fused per-step features form a sequence over recent time windows (e.g., last T sessions/days) which is fed into an LSTM. The LSTM captures temporal dependencies among exposures, clicks, and conversions. The ïňĄnal hidden state is used by two linear heads to jointly predict ECTR (Exposure-to-click rate) and CTCVR. The loss function is the sum of mean squared errors for both targets. We optimize using Adam with early stopping and standard regularization (dropout, weight decay).

3.5 Implementation Details

We use "$BERT - base - Chinese$" for textual encoding and a lightweight MLP (two dense layers) for numeric embedding. The LSTM has one or two layers with hidden sizes tuned on validation. Batch size, learning rate, and other hyperparameters are selected via grid search. (see Fig. 2).

The grid search ranges for key hyperparameters are as follows:

- Learning rate: $\{1e^{-5}$, $5e^{-5}$, $1e^{-4}$, $5e^{-4}\}$ (optimized using Adam optimizer, with weight decay fixed at $1e^{-5}$)
- Batch size: {32, 64, 128} (selected based on GPU memory constraints and training stability)
- LSTM hidden size: {64, 128, 256} (for single-layer LSTM; for two-layer LSTM, the second layer hidden size is set to half of the first)
- Dropout rate (in MLP and LSTM): {0.1, 0.2, 0.3} (to balance overfitting prevention and feature retention)

- Maximum sequence length (for BERT tokenization): Fixed at 32 (as specified in Sect. 3.1), with no grid search due to consistent text attribute length
- Early stopping patience: 50 epochs.

All hyperparameters are tuned on the validation set, and the combination that minimizes validation MSE (sum of ECTR and CTCVR MSE) is selected as the final configuration.

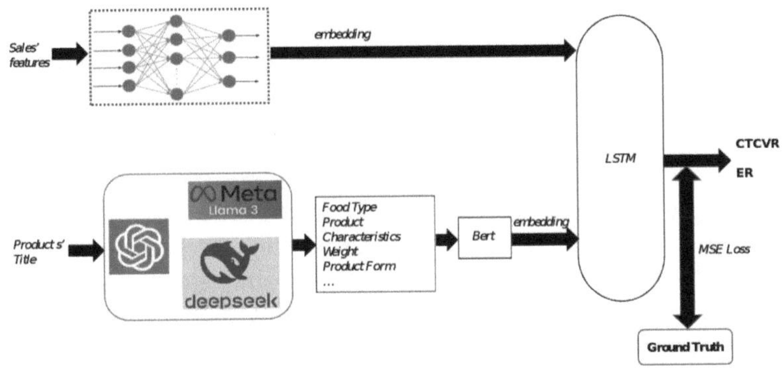

Fig. 2. MCEM diagram.

3.6 Model Structure

The study employs a model structure that integrates multi-channel embedding and LSTM. Initially, a substantial language model is utilized to segment product titles into distinct categories (e.g., food type, product features). Subsequently, the segmented tags are fed into the "$BERT-base-Chinese$" model for embedding. The BERT model transforms the textual tags of each category into high-dimensional vectors through the prescribed formula:

$$h_i = BERT(x_i) \tag{1}$$

Among them, x_i represents the i-th split label, and h_i is the high-dimensional embedding vector obtained through the BERT model, which contains the semantic information and context relationship of this label. These embedding vectors will be input into the subsequent model as part of the text features.

Aside from the textual characteristics of product titles, various numerical attributes such as product price, exposure count, and click count are integrated using a multilayer perceptron (MLP). This MLP transforms the numerical attributes into high-dimensional embedding vectors, which can be depicted as:

$$e_{num} = MLPx_{num} \tag{2}$$

where are numerical features (e.g., commodity prices, etc.) and are numerical feature vectors obtained after embedding through MLP.

After feature processing, textual features (vectors obtained through BERT embedding) and numerical features (vectors obtained through MLP embedding) will be stitched together to form a complete feature vector:

$$e_{cmie} = \text{concat} h_i, e_n \tag{3}$$

The concatenated vector will serve as input for the LSTM network. LSTM can effectively handle the temporal dependencies in time series data, capturing the relationship between product exposure, clicks, and transactions. The functionality of LSTM can be depicted as:

$$h_t = \text{LSTM}(e_{cmie}, h_{t-1}) \tag{4}$$

where denotes the hidden state of the LSTM at the time step that is the hidden state of the previous moment. Through the passing mechanism of LSTM, the model is able to capture the dependency between time steps.

However, the output layer of the LSTM is ultimately used for prediction to predict the target variables CTCVR and ER, respectively. And the output layer is formulated as:

$$\widehat{y_{CTR}} = \mathbf{W}_{CTR}\mathbf{h}_T + b_{CTR} \tag{5}$$

$$\widehat{y_{ER}} = \mathbf{W}_{ER}\mathbf{h}_T + b_{ER} \tag{6}$$

where $\mathbf{h}_T$ is the LSTM output at the final time step T, $\mathbf{W}_{CTR}$ and $\mathbf{W}_{ER}$ are the weight matrices for the regression prediction tasks, and b_{CTR} and b_{ER} are the bias terms. Using these expressions, the model in this study simultaneously predicts the CTCVR and ER of goods. The following is split into training details and model evaluation.

(1) Training details. Throughout the training, we opted for the mean square error (MSE) as the regression loss function to assess the model's prediction error. The calculation of MSE is as follows:

$$MSE = \frac{1}{n}\sum_{i=1}^{n}(\hat{y}_i - y_i)^2 \tag{7}$$

Among them, "$\hat{y}_i$" represents the predicted value of the model, "y_i" represents the actual value, and "n" represents the number of samples.

To optimize the model, we employ the Adam optimizer, which automatically adjusts the learning rate to accommodate the training of complex models and typically demonstrates strong performance in training deep learning architectures. Throughout the training process, the dataset is partitioned into a training set and a validation set, with cross-validation techniques applied to enhance the model's generalization capability. Furthermore, to mitigate overfitting, we implement an Early Stopping mechanism (ESM) that halts training when the validation set loss does not exhibit significant decreases over successive training epochs.

(2) Model evaluation. To thoroughly evaluate the model's performance, we employed various regression assessment metrics such as mean square error (MSE), mean absolute error (MAE), and coefficient of determination (R^2). Details are outlined as follows: Specifically, removing LLM and BERT has a significant impact on the R^2 value, indicating that these two components play a crucial role in capturing the semantic information of text features. Although removing MLP and LSTM also leads to a decline in performance, the impact is relatively smaller, suggesting that while these components are important for modeling numerical features and time series relationships, their role is weakened in the absence of text features. Overall, these results highlight the unique contributions of each component and demonstrate that the combined use of these technologies can significantly improve the predictive ability of the model.

- MSE: a measure of the average squared difference between the predicted value and the true value, is as formula (7).
- MAE: a measure of the average absolute difference between the predicted value and the true value, with the formula:

$$MAE = \frac{1}{n}\sum_{i=1}^{n} |\hat{y}_i - y_i| \tag{8}$$

- R^2: used to measure the ability of the model to explain the variability of the target variable, with the formula:

$$R^2 = 1 - \frac{\sum_{i=1}^{n}(\hat{y}_i - y_i)^2}{\sum_{i=1}^{n}(y_i - \overline{y})^2} \tag{9}$$

where $\hat{y}_i$ is the model predicted value, y_i is the actual value, and $\overline{y}$ is the mean of the actual value. the closer the value of R^2 is to 1, the better the model fits the data, and conversely, the lower the value of R^2 the worse the fit of the model.

4 Experiments

4.1 Baseline Models

We compare MCEM with five baseline models covering different feature combinations and model architectures:

(i) Fine-tuned LLM: Uses only LLM-parsed title attributes without BERT encoding or temporal fusion, directly predicting ECTR/CTCVR;
(ii) Fine-tuned BERT: Inputs complete titles into BERT for encoding, without attribute decomposition or temporal modeling;
(iii) LSTM: Uses only numerical features (price, exposure volume, etc.) for temporal prediction;
(iv) RNN: The recurrent neural network (RNN) to verify LSTMâĂŹs advantage in capturing long-short-term dependencies;
(v) MLP: A feedforward neural network based on aggregated features without temporal or text information.

4.2 Metrics

We evaluate using MAE, MSE, and R^2 on a chronological train, validation and test split (train: ïňĄrst two months, test: ïňĄnal month) to avoid temporal leakage. The evaluation process strictly follows the temporal division principle: the dataset is divided into a training set (first 2 months, 32,000 transactions), a validation set (middle 2 weeks, 4,000 transactions), and a test set (last 1 month, 12,000 transactions) in chronological order to avoid data leakage. The model training uses an early stopping mechanism: training stops when the validation set MSE does not decrease for 5 consecutive epochs; each model is independently trained 3 times, and the average values of MAE, MSE, and R^2 are taken as the final results. The metric calculation methods in Table 1 are as follows: MAE is the mean absolute error between predicted and true values (Formula 8), MSE is the mean squared error (Formula 7), and R^2 is the coefficient of determination (Formula 9), where a higher R^2 indicates stronger model interpretability, and smaller MAE/MSE indicates smaller prediction errors.

4.3 Experiment 1: Main Results

The results demonstrate that MCEM achieves a superior balance between explanatory power and prediction stability, outperforming baselines in core evaluation dimensions. MCEM attains the highest coefficient of determination (R^2 = 0.8765), indicating its unmatched ability to explain the intrinsic variance of ECTR and CTCVR. In terms of prediction error, MCEM maintains competitive performance: its MAE is 0.4779 (slightly higher than LSTM's 0.3731 and Fine-tuned LLM's 0.2912 but lower than RNN's 0.4834), and its MSE is 0.2488—outperforming temporal-only (LSTM: 0.3485), numerical-only (MLP: 0.2777), and text-only (Fine-tuned LLM: 0.2895) baselines (see Table 1).

Table 1. Performance comparison (MAE, MSE, R^2).

Model	MAE	MSE	R^2
Fine-tuned LLM	0.2912	0.2895	0.5373
Fine-tuned BERT	0.4180	0.1458	0.5640
LSTM	0.3731	0.3485	0.8763
RNN	0.4834	0.1387	0.5873
MLP	0.4608	0.2777	0.8739
Our Method	**0.4779**	**0.2488**	**0.8765**

Notably, two text-focused baselines (Fine-tuned BERT: 0.1458; RNN: 0.1387) achieve lower MSE but substantially lower R^2 (0.5640 and 0.5873, respectively). This discrepancy stems from structural limitations: these models excel at local sample fitting via powerful text encoding but lack structured title decomposition and temporal fusion, failing to capture the dynamic "exposure-click-conversion" dependency in live-stream e-commerce. In contrast, LSTM and MLP ignore textual attribute information, limiting their ability to model user decisions triggered by product characteristics (e.g., "sugar-free" or "handmade" claims).

MCEM's optimization objective-minimizing the sum of MSE for both ECTR and CTCVR-avoids over-optimizing a single metric. Its multi-modal fusion architecture (structured text attributes + numerical features + temporal dynamics) enables synergistic feature utilization: BERT captures contextual semantics, MLP models non-linear behavioral relationships, and LSTM models temporal dependencies. This synergy explains why MCEM outperforms single-modal baselines in balancing explanatory power and error control, aligning with the practical needs of live-stream e-commerce forecasting.

4.4 Experiment 2: Ablation Experiment

The results of the ablation experiments demonstrate that each component of the model significantly influences its overall performance (see Fig. 3). As model components are systematically removed, the R^2 value declines while the MAE value increases, indicating that the elimination of any component results in a notable reduction in model ecacy. Notably, the removal of LLM and BERT has a pronounced effect on the R^2 value, suggesting that these components are crucial for capturing the semantic information inherent in text features. for capturing the semantic information inherent in text features.

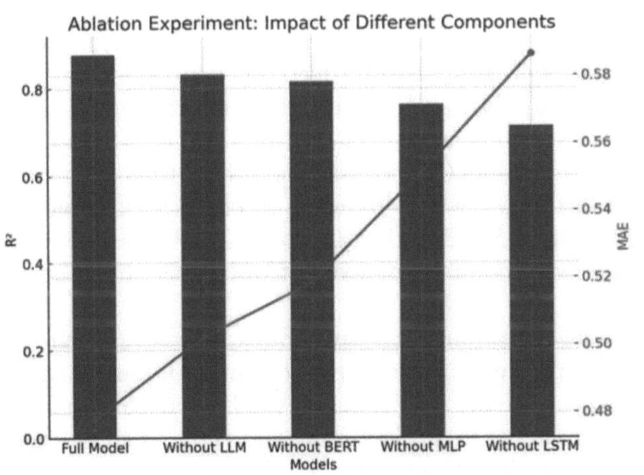

Fig. 3. MCEM diagram.

Although the removal of MLP and LSTM also leads to performance degradation, their impact is comparatively minor. This nding implies that, while these components are important for modeling numerical features and time series relationships, their signicance diminishes in the absence of textual features. Collectively, these results underscore the distinct contributions of each component, illustrating that the integration of these techniques can substantially enhance a model's predictive capabilities.

5 Discussion

The experimental results confirm that the MCEM model effectively improves the prediction accuracy of ECTR and CTCVR in live-stream e-commerce through multi-channel feature fusion. The key insights from this study are as follows:

1. **Structured title decomposition is critical**: LLM-based parsers effectively extract semantic attributes from noisy titles, providing high-quality feature inputs. BERT embeddings of short, semantically focused labels produce cleaner representations than embeddings of long concatenated titles—aligning with prior findings [5,6,8,14].

2. **Multi-modal fusion enhances performance**: BERT captures attribute context, MLP models non-linear numerical relationships, and LSTM captures temporal dynamics—forming a synergistic effect. LLM-based parsing enables scalable, language-aware decomposition, and ensemble LLMs can further reduce parsing errors [5,10].

6 Conclusion and Future Work

This study proposes MCEM for ECTR and CTCVR prediction in live-stream e-commerce. This model uses LLM to decompose product titles into structured semantic attribute channels, and fuses text attributes, numerical features, and temporal dependencies through BERT, MLP, and LSTM. Experimental results on a real-world dataset of 48,000 transactions show that MCEM achieves an R^2 of 0.8765, outperforming the five baseline models in explanatory power while maintaining competitive MAE and MSE. Besides, ablation experiments confirm the contribution of each component which LLMs is the most component impact the full model.

There are several directions for future improvement: (1) Integrate more data modalities, such as product images, live-stream thumbnails, and anchor facial expressions, to capture richer information; (2) Incorporate real-time interaction data (e.g., bullet screen content, likes, comments) to capture dynamic changes in user preferences during live-streams; (3) Explore few-shot and zero-shot learning methods to further improve the model's performance in cold-start scenarios; (4) Conduct A/B testing in actual live-stream e-commerce platforms to verify the model's effectiveness in real business scenarios

Acknowledgements. The present research was supported by grant No. 2024A05050-50018 from Science and Technology Planning Project of Guangdong Province, China.

References

1. Devlin, M.-W. Chang, K. Lee, and K. Toutanova.: BERT: Pre-training of Deep Bidirectional Transformers for Language Understanding. arXiv:1810.04805 (2019)
2. Touvron H., Lavril, T., Izacard, G. et al.: LLaMA: Open and Efficient Foundation Language Models. arXiv:2302.13971 (2023)
3. GPT-4 Technical Report. https://arxiv.org/abs/2303.08774. Accessed 30 Oct 2023
4. Hochreiter, S., Schmidhuber, J.: Long short-term memory. Neural Comput. **9**(8), 1735–1780 (1997)
5. Majumder, B., Subramanian, A., Krishnan, A. et al.: Deep Recurrent Neural Networks for Product Attribute Extraction in eCommerce. arXiv:1803.11284 (2018)
6. Yan, J., Zalmout, N., Liang, Y. et al.: AdaTag: Multi-Attribute Value Extraction from Product Profiles with Adaptive Decoding. arXiv:2106.02318 (2021)
7. Guo, H. F., Tang, R. M., Ye, Y. M. et al.: DeepFM: A Factorization-Machine based Neural Network for CTR. arXiv:1703.04247 (2017)
8. Khandelwal, A., Mittal, H., Kulkarni, S. et al.: Large scale generative multimodal attribute extraction for e-commerce attributes. In: 61st Annual Meeting of the Association for Computational Linguistics, pp. 305–312. Association for Computational Linguistics, Canada (2023)
9. Obst, D., Ghattas, B., Claudel, S. et al.: Textual data for time series forecasting. arXiv:1910.12618 (2019)
10. Fang, C., Li, X., Fan, Z.: LLM-Ensemble: Optimal Large Language Model Ensemble Method for E-commerce Product Attribute Value Extraction, (2024). arXiv:2403.00863
11. Xu, X., Wu, J.H., Li, Q.: What drives consumer shopping behavior in live streaming commerce? J. Electron. Comm. Res. **21**(3), 144–167 (2020)
12. Apasrawirote, A., Yawised, K.: Factors influencing the behavioral and purchase intention on live-streaming shopping. Asian J. Business Res. **12**(1), 39–56 (2022)
13. Minaee, S., et al.: Large Language Models: A Survey. arXiv:2402.06196 (2024)
14. Zhu, T.G., Wang, Y., Li, H., Wu, Y., et al.: Multimodal Joint Attribute Prediction and Value Extraction for E-commerce Product. arXiv:2009.07162 (2020)
15. Jiang, H.C., Ruan, J.T., Sun, J.M.: Application of machine learning model and hybrid model in retail sales forecast. In: 2021 IEEE 6th International Conference on Big Data Analytics (ICBDA), pp. 305–312. IEEE, China (2021)
16. Krishna, M.J., Varun, B., Niharika, K., et al.: Optimising sales forecasts in ERP systems using machine learning and predictive analytics. J. Contemp. Educ. Theory Artif. Intell. **1**(2), 1–8 (2023)
17. Wang, L., Zhang, X.: Livestream sales prediction based on an interpretable deep-learning model. Sci. Rep. **14**(1), Art. 20594 (2024)

Author Index

C. Xu (Ed.): ICMLSC 2026, CCIS 2948, pp. 685–687, 2027.
https://doi.org/10.1007/978-981-92-1546-1

MIX
Papier aus verantwortungsvollen Quellen
Paper from responsible sources
FSC® C105338
FSC
www.fsc.org

If you have any concerns about our products,
you can contact us on
ProductSafety@springernature.com

In case Publisher is established outside the EU,
the EU authorized representative is:
Springer Nature Customer Service Center GmbH
Europaplatz 3, 69115 Heidelberg, Germany

Printed by Libri Plureos GmbH
in Hamburg, Germany